# Priests, Tongues, and Rites

The London-Leiden Magical Manuscripts and Translation in Egyptian Ritual (100–300 CE)

*by*

Jacco Dieleman

BRILL
LEIDEN · BOSTON
2005

This book is printed on acid-free paper.

*This series Religions in the Graeco-Roman World presents a forum for studies in the social and cultural function of religions in the Greek and the Roman world, dealing with pagan religions both in their own right and in their interaction with and influence on Christianity and Judaism during a lengthy period of fundamental change. Special attention will be given to the religious history of regions and cities which illustrate the practical workings of these processes. Enquiries regarding the submission of works for publication in the series may be directed to Professor H.S. Versnel, Herenweg 88, 2361 EV Warmond, The Netherlands, h.s.versnel@hetnet.nl.*

### Library of Congress Cataloging-in-Publication Data

Dieleman, Jacco
    Priests, Tongues and Rites : The London-Leiden Magical Manuscripts and Translation in Egyptian Ritual (100–300 CE) / by Jacco Dieleman
    p. cm. — (Religions in the Graeco-Roman world, ISSN 0927-7633 ; v. 153)
    Originally presented as the author's thesis (doctoral – Leiden University, 2003).
    Includes bibliographical references and indexes.
    ISBN 90-04-14185-5 (hardback : alk. paper)
    1. Egypt—Civilization—332 B.C. - 638 A.D. 2. Magic—Egypt. 3. Rites and ceremonies—Egypt. 4. Bilingualism—Egypt—History–To 1500. 5. Egyptian language—Papyri, Demotic. 6. Manuscripts, Greek (Papyri)—Egypt. I. Title. II. Series.

DT61.D54 2004
133.4'3'0932–dc22

2004058147

ISSN 0927-7633
ISBN 90 04 14185 5

**© Copyright 2005 by Koninklijke Brill NV, Leiden, The Netherlands.
Koninklijke Brill NV incorporates the imprints Brill Academic Publishers,
Martinus Nijhoff Publishers and VSP.**

All rights reserved. No part of this publication may be reproduced, translated, stored in a retrieval system, or transmitted in any form or by any means, electronic, mechanical, photocopying, recording or otherwise, without prior written permission from the publisher.

Authorization to photocopy items for internal or personal
use is granted by Brill provided that
the appropriate fees are paid directly to The Copyright
Clearance Center, 222 Rosewood Drive, Suite 910
Danvers, MA 01923, USA.
Fees are subject to change.

PRINTED IN THE NETHERLANDS

CONTENTS

Preface .................................................................... ix
List of Figures ........................................................... xiii

Chapter One. Introduction ............................................ 1
   1.1. The Paradox of Translation—posing the problem ........ 1
   1.2. Research on the Theban Magical Library ................. 11
   1.3. Aims and methods of the investigation: reading magic ... 21

Chapter Two. Presentation of the Sources P. Leiden I 384 and
P. London-Leiden ....................................................... 25
   2.1. Two bilingual manuscripts from the Anastasi collection .. 25
   2.2. A subgroup within the Theban Magical Library .......... 26
   2.3. Description of the manuscripts and their textual
       contents ...................................................... 29
       2.3.1. P. Leiden I 384 ........................................ 29
       2.3.2. P. London-Leiden .................................... 35
   2.4. Provenance .................................................. 40
   2.5. Date .......................................................... 41
   2.6. Facsimiles and photos ...................................... 44

Chapter Three. The Use of Script ................................... 47
   3.1. Introduction ................................................. 47
   3.2. Native scripts mixed-up ..................................... 48
   3.3. Greek language inscribed ................................... 63
       3.3.1. Greek script and language ........................... 63
       3.3.2. Greek alphabetic devices in Egyptian guise ......... 64
       3.3.3. Alphabetic Demotic and Old-Coptic:
            transcription at work ................................ 69
   3.4. Considering secrecy ......................................... 80
       3.4.1. 'Cipher' script ........................................ 87
       3.4.2. Mystery signs or charaktêres ........................ 96

Chapter Four. The Form and Function of Bilingualism ............ 103
 4.1. Introduction ................................................... 103
 4.2. Language change and language attitude in Roman
      Egypt ......................................................... 104
 4.3. The process of insertion: Greek loanwords in the
      Demotic spells................................................. 110
      4.3.1. Materials of medicine and magic..................... 111
      4.3.2. Medical terminology................................. 117
      4.3.3. House utensils ...................................... 118
      4.3.4. Mixed compounds ..................................... 118
      4.3.5. Conclusions......................................... 119
 4.4. The process of alternation: the ritual power of foreign
      languages ..................................................... 121
      4.4.1. The ritual power of Greek ........................... 123
      4.4.2. Translating from Greek into Demotic................. 127
      4.4.3. Invoking Seth—Typhon ............................... 130
      4.4.4. Fear of Nubia....................................... 138
      4.4.5. The pragmatics of language alternation in the
             Demotic spells ...................................... 143

Chapter Five. Diversity in Rhetoric ................................. 145
 5.1. Alternation of writing traditions in the Greek spells ...... 145
 5.2.1. Consecration of the ring (PGM XII.201–216) ............. 147
 5.2.2. Close reading of the prayer (PGM XII.216–269).......... 149
 5.3. Appropriation of a ritual: 'Opening the Mouth' .......... 170
 5.4. Once again the 'Paradox of Translation' .................. 182

Chapter Six. Of Priests and Prestige. The Need for an
Authoritative Tradition ............................................ 185
 6.1. Introduction ................................................. 185
 6.2. Compound plant names and ancient botany .............. 189
 6.3. Temple scribes, prophets and the like ..................... 203
      6.3.1. Egyptian priestly titles as social classes ............. 205
      6.3.2. Egyptian priests as actors in cult and community .. 211
      6.3.3. Egyptian priests as characters in the literary
             imagination.......................................... 221
             6.3.3.1. Egyptian priests in Egyptian literary texts.. 222
             6.3.3.2. Egyptian priests in Greek and Latin texts
                      of the Roman period ........................ 239

|      |                                                                                      |     |
|------|--------------------------------------------------------------------------------------|-----|
| 6.4. | Packaging the text: rhetorical strategies in the introductions to the recipes        | 254 |
|      | 6.4.1. Advertising introductions to the actual magical recipes                       | 256 |
|      | 6.4.2. Analysis of the mystifying motifs                                             | 261 |
|      | 6.4.3. Combination of separate cultural traditions                                   | 276 |
| 6.5. | What about priests and prestige?                                                     | 280 |

Chapter Seven. Towards a Model of Textual Transmission ........ 285

Appendices ...................................................................... 295

Bibliography .................................................................... 317
Index of Passages ............................................................. 331
Index of Subjects .............................................................. 337

# PREFACE

This book is a study of the social and cultural contexts of two magical handbooks, written partly in Egyptian and in Greek, that once belonged to a larger collection of occult texts, nowadays generally known as the 'Theban Magical Library'. It is an attempt to throw light on the social and cultural identity of the producers and users of the manuscripts by investigating the form, contents and layout of the Demotic and Greek spells that are found on the manuscripts Papyrus Leiden I 384 verso (PGM XII and PDM xii) and Papyrus London-Leiden (consisting of P. BM 10070 and P. Leiden I 383; PDM xiv and PGM XIV). The manuscripts can be dated by palaeography to the second or third century CE. The discovery of the 'Theban Magical Library' is attributed to a group of anonymous Egyptian farmers, who are supposed to have found the cache somewhere in the hills surrounding modern Luxor sometime before 1828. Due to the fact that the hoard of papyrus scrolls and codices was not found during a regular excavation, nothing is known about the archaeological context of the library. This is very unfortunate since the bilingual character of the library poses some haunting questions about the identity of the original owner or owners of this collection of magical books. Who was able to make sense of the variety of scripts and languages and why were Demotic and Greek spells combined on a single manuscript? Information concerning the exact location of the find would have given a first indication of the identity of the owner or owners. Was the collection of texts found in a tomb, a temple or a private house? Were the manuscripts found together with other artefacts? If so, how did these relate to the manuscripts? Were they buried with a corpse as funerary gifts or hidden from the Roman authorities out of fear for prosecutions? These questions can no longer be answered, so that, today, only the texts themselves remain as witnesses of what must once have been a lively interest in the occult in Roman-period Thebes.

The book is a slightly reworked version of my dissertation, which I defended at Leiden University, the Netherlands, in 2003. The research project came about as the result of my interest in the production and function of texts in relation to the society and its members from which these texts originate. When, as a student of Egyptology, I took classes in Comparative Literature and became familiar with interpretative models to study the relationship between text and society in more detail, I reflected upon the possibilities to apply these new insights to ancient Egyptian texts. It was Günter Vittmann, one of my teachers at Würzburg University, who helped me out unintentionally, by directing my attention to the *Demotic Magical Papyri*. This corpus of magical rites and incantations dating from the Roman period not only continues a long tradition of Egyptian magic and ritual, but also forms part of the more international, and in a way innovative, currents of magical thought of the Greco-Roman period. As the spells are relatively well-preserved, the corpus is suitable to pose questions about the author's relationship to the multi-cultural society of Greco-Roman Egypt, and about concepts of tradition and authority in a country where the social and cultural order was changing under the influence of a foreign elite, to wit: Greek and Roman settlers, soldiers, bureaucrats and rulers.

The Research School of Asian, African, and Amerindian Studies (CNWS) of Leiden University provided me, from September 1999 until August 2003, with an inspiring environment and the necessary financial and material means to conduct my research, for which I thank its staff and members heartily. I am highly indebted to my two supervisors, J.F. Borghouts and Mineke Schipper, for their time and confidence in my abilities to complete this project. Maarten J. Raven, the curator of the Egyptian department of the Rijksmuseum van Oudheden te Leiden, was always willing to give me access to the original manuscripts. I thank him for his friendliness and help and for giving me permission to publish the photos of the 'cipher' alphabet and the papyrus scraps pasted to the verso of the Leiden part of P. London-Leiden. I also thank Richard Parkinson and Carol Andrews, curators of the British Museum, for allowing me access to the London part of P. London-Leiden in December 1999. In July 2000 Heinz-J. Thissen invited me to give a paper on my research project at the *Seminar für Ägyptologie* of the University of Cologne. I cannot thank him enough for his hospitality over the weekend and for challenging me to formulate clearly my by then still rather crude and preliminary ideas on the subject during our long informal discussions. In retrospect I realize that the foundations for the present book were laid out during this weekend. In the winter quarter of 2002, I participated in a seminar on the *Greek Magical Papyri* at the University of Chicago. I am indebted to Christopher A. Faraone and Hans Dieter Betz for their invitation and all participants for their insightful remarks on an early draft of chapter 5. The analysis of the *Ouphôr* rite in the second part of chapter 5 has profited greatly from the many discussions with Ian Moyer, who happened to be working on this spell at the same time. During my Chicago stay I spent long and pleasant days in the research library of the Oriental Institute, where Janet H. Johnson took great care that I could do my research in all tranquillity of mind. I thank her for having been such a good host to me and for discussing with me parts of the project. The research stay in Chicago was made possible by a grant from the Netherlands Organisation for Scientific Research (NWO). Now that the research has been done and its results have been written down, I am grateful to Brill Academic Publishers and its editors H.S. Versnel and David Frankfurter for accepting this book as a volume in the series *Religions of the Graeco-Roman World*. I thank David Frankfurter in particular for his insightful comments on the dissertation version.

The pages that follow are the fruit of spending many lonely hours in libraries and, at the same time, of spending time with a number of wonderful people. Throughout the four-year period of my research, my closest friends Jan, Joost, Maarten and Stefan never got tired of putting this project into perspective with their irony. I thank them warmly for their wit and friendship and for making me laugh about my project ever so often. Jackie Murray has also been a good friend and constant source of encouragement and help during these years. I thank her in the first place for her humour, but also for the discussions we had on the subject and for her critical readings of drafts of papers and chapters of the dissertation. Last but not least, this is an opportune place to say a big thank you to my parents, Els den Hamer and Adri Dieleman, who have always supported me during my years of study and never lost interest in my dealings with the ancient world. This book could not have been written without their support.

Los Angeles, April 2004

## LIST OF FIGURES

Martin Henze made the overview drawings of the manuscripts. The reader is warned that the images of textual passages in P. London-Leiden are not facsimiles, but taken from Thompson's hand-copy.

2.1   Two 'cipher' alphabets (photo RMO, Leiden)
2.2   Scrap of papyrus pasted on the verso, under column 19, to London-Leiden manuscript; Leemans nr. 1 (photo RMO, Leiden)
2.3   Scrap of papyrus pasted on the verso, under column 13, to London-Leiden manuscript, Leemans nr. 6 (photo RMO, Leiden)
2.4   Overview P. Leiden I 384 verso: PDM xii & PGM XII
2.5   Figure sitting on stool (after *GMPT*)
2.6   Seth holding two spears (after *GMPT*)
2.7   Anubis standing at the mummy bier (after *GMPT*)
2.8   Figure (Osiris?) standing on basket (after Leemans 1856)
2.9   Facsimile of two 'cipher' alphabets, Leemans nr. 3 (after Leemans 1839)
2.10  Facsimile of scrap of papyrus pasted on the verso to London-Leiden manuscript, Leemans nr. 1 (after Leemans 1839)
2.11  Facsimile of scrap of papyrus pasted on the verso to London-Leiden manuscript, Leemans nr. 6 (after Leemans 1839)
3.1   P. London-Leiden 23/24–26 (after Griffith and Thompson 1921)
3.2   P. London-Leiden 27/1–9 (after Griffith and Thompson 1921)
3.3   P. London-Leiden 28/1–4 (after Griffith and Thompson 1921)
3.4   P. London-Leiden 23/24–26 (after Griffith and Thompson 1921)
3.5   P. London-Leiden 24/6–14 (after Griffith and Thompson 1921)
3.6   P. London-Leiden verso 17/1–8 (after Griffith and Thompson 1921)
3.7   Pseudo-hieroglyphs, P. London-Leiden 5/8–10 (after Griffith and Thompson 1921)
4.1   P. London-Leiden verso 1–3 (after Leemans 1839)
4.2   P. London-Leiden 4/1–22 (after Griffith and Thompson 1921)

4.3   P. London-Leiden 15/24–31 (after Leemans 1839)
4.4   P. London-Leiden 23/1–20 (after Griffith and Thompson 1921)
4.5   P. London-Leiden verso 20/1–7 (after Griffith and Thompson 1921)

CHAPTER ONE

# INTRODUCTION

1.1. *The Paradox of Translation—posing the problem*

A telling theoretical problem regarding the relationship between Egyptian and Greek language presents itself in the introduction of treatise XVI of the *Corpus Hermeticum*. The ancient text articulates a number of clear-cut value judgements on Egyptian and Greek that are thought provoking and that throw an intriguing light on the coexistence of Egyptian and Greek language and script in the two Demotic-Greek magical handbooks that form the topic of this book, P. Leiden I 384 verso and P. London-Leiden, which belong to the corpus of the so-called *Demotic* and *Greek Magical Papyri*. Since the *Corpus Hermeticum* and the two magical handbooks derive from the same native Egyptian priestly circles, treatise XVI begs to serve as a steppingstone for the following chapters on the use of script, language, idiom and imagery in these magical handbooks. The *Corpus Hermeticum* is a loose collection of seventeen treatises, written in Greek, dealing with theosophical issues related to the salvation of man by means of knowledge (*gnôsis*) of the cosmos.[1] The texts formed part of a widespread current of esoteric thought that flourished during the first centuries CE and sought its inspiration in traditional Egyptian and Jewish religion combined with neo-platonic philosophy.[2] As such, the Hermetic treatises were as international in contents and influence as the *Greek Magical Papyri*, which were written around the same time and contain references to this move-

---

[1] The standard edition is A.D. Nock and A.J. Festugière, *Corpus Hermeticum* 4 vols. (Paris 1946–1954) vols. 1–2; still useful in some respects, though based on a corrupt text, is Walter Scott, *Hermetica. The Ancient Greek and Latin Writings Which Contain Religious or Philosophic Teachings Ascribed to Hermes Trismegistus* 4 vols. (Oxford 1924–1936) vols. 1–2. For an English translation with updated philological commentary, see, Brian P. Copenhaver, *Hermetica. The Greek 'Corpus Hermeticum' and the Latin 'Asclepius' in a new English translation, with notes and introduction* (Cambridge 1992).

[2] For introductions to this corpus of texts, see, Garth Fowden, *The Egyptian Hermes. A Historical Approach to the Late Pagan Mind* (Cambridge 1986); A.J. Festugière, *Hermétisme et mystique païenne* (Paris 1967) 28–87, reprint of 'L'Hermétisme' *BSRLL* (1948) 1–58.

ment.[3] Like the *Greek Magical Papyri* the *Corpus Hermeticum* has long been seen by classical scholars as originating from a Greek cultural milieu, while Egyptian and Jewish elements were explained as ornaments for the sole purpose of giving the whole a mystifying flavour. However, scholars are now becoming aware that the basic concepts of the Hermetic doctrines are in fact deeply rooted in ancient Egyptian religious thought, which was still alive among Egyptian priests in the Roman period.[4]

Treatise XVI is presented as a teaching of Asclepius to king Ammon about the constitution of the cosmos.[5] As an introduction to his lessons, Asclepius wants to clarify some misunderstandings with regard to the lucidity of his doctrines.

> [1] I have sent you a long discourse, O king, as a sort of précis or reminder of all the others; it is not composed as to agree with vulgar

---

[3] For an introduction to the *Greek Magical Papyri* as a corpus of ancient magical texts and a field of scholarship, see, chapter 2.2. As for the intertextual relationships, an illustrative example, although not unproblematic, is the 'Prayer of Thanksgiving', which is preserved in three sources. The Latin *Asclepius* gives the prayer as its conclusion and codex VI of the Nag Hammadi Library contains a Coptic version of the prayer among its Hermetic texts (NHC VI, 7: 63,33–65,7). Yet, the prayer also recurs in PGM III.494–611; 591–609. For discussion, see, Copenhaver, *Hermetica*, 92 and 259; James M. Robinson, *The Nag Hammadi Library in English* (rev. ed.; New York 1990) 328–329; P. Dirkse and J. Brashler, 'The Prayer of Thanksgiving' *NHSt* 11 (Leiden 1979) 375–387. See for a synoptic edition of the texts: Jean-Pierre Mahé, *Hermès en Haute-Égypte. Les textes hermétiques de Nag Hammadi et leurs parallèles grecs et latins*. (Bibliothèque Copte de Nag Hammadi, Section: Textes 3; Leuven 1978) 137–167.

[4] The issue of the relationship between the Hermetica and the Egyptian priesthood is still a matter of fervent debate. An important and highly original defence of the Egyptian origin of the Hermetica is Fowden, *The Egyptian Hermes*. A Hermetic treatise in Demotic of which the earliest manuscript derives from the Ptolemaic period has recently been discovered, proving that the Egyptian priesthood was already working with these ideas at least a century before the Greek *Corpus Hermeticum* is generally dated: R. Jasnow and K.-Th. Zauzich, 'A Book of Thoth?', in: C.J. Eyre ed., *Proceedings of the Seventh International Congress of Egyptologists. Cambridge, 3–9 September 1995* (OLA 82; Leuven 1998) 607–618; Jean-Pierre Mahé, 'Preliminary Remarks on the Demotic *Book of Thoth* and the Greek *Hermetica*' *Vigiliae Christianae* 50 (1996) 353–363. See also: B.H. Stricker, *De Brief van Aristeas. De Hellenistische Codificaties der Praehelleense Godsdiensten* (VKNAW, Letterkunde, Nieuwe Reeks, 62/4; Amsterdam 1956) 99, 113; Ph. Derchain, 'L'authenticité de l'inspiration égyptienne dans le "Corpus Hermeticum"' *Revue de l'Histoire des Religions* 161 (1962) 175–198 and Erik Iversen, *Egyptian and Hermetic Doctrine* (Opuscula Graecolatina 27; Copenhagen 1984). Cf. Nock and Festugière, *Corpus Hermeticum*, vol. 1, v.

[5] For its possible relations with Egyptian religion, see, J.P. Sørensen, 'Ancient Egyptian Religious Thought and the XVIth Hermetic Tractate', in: G. Englund ed., *The Religion of the Ancient Egyptians: Cognitive Structures and Popular Expressions* (Uppsala 1987) 41–57.

opinion but contains much to refute it. That it contradicts even some of my own discourses will be apparent to you. My teacher, Hermes—often conversing with me in private, sometimes in the presence of Tat—used to say that those reading my books would find their organization very simple and clear when, on the contrary, it is unclear and keeps the meaning of its words concealed; furthermore, it will be entirely unclear (he said) when the Greeks eventually desire to translate our language to their own and thus produce the greatest distortion and unclarity in what was written. [2] But this discourse, expressed in our paternal language, keeps clear the meaning of its words. The very quality of the sound and the ⟨intonation?⟩ of the Egyptian words contain in themselves the energy of the objects they speak of.

Therefore, in so far as you have the power, (my) king—for sure, you are capable of all things—, keep the discourse untranslated, lest mysteries of such greatness come to the Greeks, lest the extravagant, flaccid and, as it were, dandified Greek idiom extinguish something stately and concise, the energetic idiom of the (Egyptian) words. For the Greeks, O king, have empty speeches capable only of logical demonstration, and this is just what the philosophy of the Greeks is: noise of speeches. We, by contrast, use not speeches but sounds that are full of action.

[*Corpus Hermeticum* XVI 1–2][6]

These two paragraphs present a rather negative language attitude towards Greek, which is considered to be 'extravagant, flaccid and (as it were) dandified', while 'our paternal language', i.e. Egyptian, is highly esteemed as a language full of divine power and energy.[7] By using the phrase '*our* paternal language', an amiable bond based on ethnicity is created between the narrator and the addressee and, at the same time, Egyptians are posited as the in-group opposed to the Greeks as the outsiders. According to the narrator, the hierarchy is not only linguistic but also cultural, because the Egyptians have great mysteries, whereas the Greeks only have philosophy, which is presented as a mere play of vain words. Because of this cultural inequality, Greeks are represented as being eager to obtain Egyptian knowledge. Unfortunately, since Greek is such a poor language, it is impossible to translate the energetic Egyptian sounds without losing their inherent power and without producing obscure texts. The message is clear: divine knowledge originates from Egypt and it cannot be handed over to other cultural groups in general, and to the Greeks in particular. This essentialistic point of view

---

[6] Tr. modified from Brian P. Copenhaver.
[7] See also Heinz J. Thissen, '"…..αἰγυπτιάζων τῇ φωνῇ ….." Zum Umgang mit der ägyptischen Sprache in der griechisch-römischen Antike' *ZPE* 97 (1993) 239–252.

reveals an Egyptian nationalistic discourse that brings the concept of ethnicity into the religious domain. Secrecy and secret knowledge had always been components of Egyptian religion, but were always defined in terms of initiation and cultic purity instead of ethnicity and cultural exclusivity.[8] In the text concerned, the narrator presents mysteries as an Egyptian monopoly that has to be defended against the curiosity of the Greeks. The most productive strategy to exclude Greeks from the Egyptian divine knowledge is to leave the Egyptian language uninterpreted. The loss of inherent power of the Egyptian sounds sensibly motivates the impossibility of translation, but the implicit reason is a conscious attempt to exclude. In such a case, the pretended impossibility to translate becomes an effective inhibition to translate.

However, the argument of the introduction of treatise XVI seems to be contradicted by an ironic detail: the text itself has come down to us in Greek. The fervently argued inhibition to translate is trespassed by the text itself. Moreover, there is no reason whatsoever to assume that the extant text is a translation of an Egyptian original. In all likelihood, the text was directly composed in Greek for a mixed audience of different ethnic groups, Egyptians and Greeks among others. This, then, constitutes a 'paradox of translation': in spite of a religiously motivated inhibition to translate the Egyptian language into a foreign idiom, translations or linguistic transgressions do occur.

The idea that translations are apt to fail because of the inherent powerful qualities of a given language's sounds was a common issue in the debate on magic and divination in intellectual circles during the Roman period.[9] For example, Origen, a Christian apologetic writer of the third century CE, defends the Christian refusal to call their God by any other name, as for example Zeus or Jupiter, by referring to the impossibility of translation:

---

[8] Jan Assmann, 'Unio Liturgica. Die kultische Einstimmung in Götterweltlichen Lobpreis als Grundmotiv "esoterischer" Überlieferung im alten Ägypten', in: Hans G. Kippenberg and Guy G. Stroumsa, *Secrecy and Concealment. Studies in the History of Mediterranean and Near Eastern Religions* (Leiden 1995) 37–60. For a discussion of the origin and development of the Hellenistic representation of Egypt as the origin of all secret and divine knowledge, see, Idem, *Weisheit und Mysterium. Das Bild der Griechen von Ägypten* (Munich 2000) esp. 35–38.

[9] Claire Préaux, 'De la Grèce classique à l'Égypte hellénistique; traduire ou ne pas traduire' *CdE* 42 (1967) 369–383; John Dillon 'The Magical Power of names in Origen and Later Platonism' in: Richard Hanson and Henri Crouzel (eds.), *Origeniana Tertia* (Rome 1985) 203–216; Gillian Clark, 'Translate into Greek; Porphyry of Tyre on the New Barbarians', in: Richard Miles (ed.), *Constructing Identities in Late Antiquity* (London 1999) 112–132.

> On the subject of names I have to say further that experts in the use of charms relate that a man who pronounces a given spell in its native language can bring about the effect that the spell is claimed to do. But if the same spell is translated into any other language whatever, it can be seen to be weak and ineffective. Thus it is not the significance of the things which the words describe that has a certain power to do this or that, but it is the qualities and characteristics of the sounds. By consideration of this kind we would in this way defend the fact that Christians strive to the point of death to avoid calling Zeus God or naming him in any other language. [Origen, *Against Celsus* I, 25][10]

Iamblichus, a Neo-Platonic philosopher of the late third, early fourth century CE and a fervent defender of divination as a means of obtaining knowledge about the nature of things, explains, in the guise of the Egyptian priest Abammon,[11] to Porphyry of Tyre why the use of barbaric names instead of Greek ones is to be preferred in magic:

> Since the gods have shown that the whole language of the sacred nations, such as Assyrians and Egyptians, is appropriate for sacred rites, therefore, we deem it necessary to communicate with the gods in a language akin to them. Moreover, because this mode of speech is the first and most ancient and, in particular, because those who learned the first names concerning the gods passed them on to us after having mingled them with their own language, considered proper and suitable for these (names), we preserve hitherto the law of the tradition unaltered. For if anything befits the gods, clearly the perpetual and unchangeable are natural to them. [Iamblichus, *On the Mysteries of Egypt* VII, 4, 256]

In this passage, Iamblichus not only uses the motif of the impossibility of translation, but also asserts that Egyptian is the most suitable language for divine communication. He expresses a similar idea in a following paragraph in which he retorts Porphyry, who had claimed that the mere meaning of words instead of their sounds is significant:

> From this then it becomes evident how reasonable it is that the language of the sacred nations is to be preferred to that of other men. Because words, when translated, do not preserve entirely the same meaning; there are certain idioms for every nation, which are impossible to convey in language to another nation. What is more, even if it were possible to translate them, they would no longer preserve the same power. Foreign

---

[10] Tr. Henry Chadwick.

[11] As the treatise displays in many instances a remarkably high level of understanding of ancient Egyptian religious concepts and practices, Philippe Derchain has argued to take the opening line at face value and to regard the priest Abammon as the true author of the book: 'Pseudo-Jamblique ou Abammôn? Quelques observations sur l'égyptianisme du *De Mysteriis*' *CdE* 38 (1963) 220–226.

names have both much power of expression and much conciseness, while they lack ambiguity, variety and multiplicity of expression. For all these reasons, these (words) are appropriate for the Higher Powers.

Thus do away with the conjectures which fail in obtaining the truth: 'either the god invoked is Egyptian or speaking Egyptian'. Instead, it is better to understand that, as the Egyptians were the first being allotted the participation of the gods, the gods rejoice when invoked according to the rites of the Egyptians.
[Iamblichus, *On the Mysteries of Egypt* VII, 5, 257–258]

Greco-Roman authors in general not only afforded innate ritual potency to the Egyptian language but also to the hieroglyphic writing system.[12] Hieroglyphs were understood as a pictorial sign system that was not made up of phonemes but of symbols directly referring to concepts. By virtue of divine inspiration, the symbolic character of the signs would enable a profound understanding of the fundamental nature of things. Or, as Plotinus, a third century Neo-Platonic philosopher, wrote:

Each carved image is knowledge and wisdom grasped all at once, not discursive reasoning nor deliberation. [Plotinus, *Enneads* V, 8, 6]

As a result, the semiotic rules of the hieroglyphic writing system raised great interest and several authors, like Plutarch and Clement of Alexandria, described some hieroglyphs together with an explanation of their supposed meaning.[13] They derived their defective knowledge undoubtedly from the *Hieroglyphica*, a now lost list of hieroglyphs with their supposed meaning compiled by Chaeremon, an Egyptian priest of the first century CE, if not from firsthand statements by Egyptian priests.[14] Horapollo, an Egyptian intellectual of the fifth century CE, came up with a similar list of hieroglyphs, also called *Hieroglyphica*, the discovery of which in the Renaissance played an important role in the European intellectual construction of pharaonic Egypt.[15] A conspicuous trait of

---

[12] For an overview, see, Erik Iversen, *The Myth of Egypt and its Hieroglyphs in European Tradition* (Princeton 1993), chapter 2. See also: Assmann, *Weisheit und Mysterium*, 64–71. The relevant Greek and Latin sources are collected in Pierre Marestaing, *Les écritures égyptiennes et l'antiquité classique* (Paris 1913).

[13] Plutarch, *On Isis and Osiris*, 10, 354F; 11, 355B; 32, 363F; 51, 371E. Clement of Alexandria, *Stromateis* V, chapter 4, §20.4–21.3; chapter 7, §41.2–42.3.

[14] Clement was an inhabitant of Alexandria and could therefore very well have based his ideas on personal communication with Egyptian priests. Plutarch was from Chaeroneia, Greece, but visited Egypt once (Moralia 678 C). On the subject of cultural exchange between Egypt and Greece, see also, chapter 6.3.3.2.

[15] Jan Assmann, *Moses der Ägypter. Entzifferung einer Gedächtnisspur* (Frankfurt am Main 2000) esp. 37–41. The most recent edition of Horapollo's 'Hieroglyphica' is Heinz Josef

these lists is the mingling of true hieroglyphs with ordinary religious representations that were visible on temple walls, which proves that the classificatory systems were not grounded in a correct definition of the hieroglyphic sign.

An important element of the Greco-Roman discourse on hieroglyphs was secrecy. According to Clement of Alexandria, a Christian apologetic author of the second century CE, the hieroglyphic script constituted the final stage of the priestly curriculum, after students had first learned Demotic and, after that, the hieratic script.[16] Learning these mysterious signs was only given to the privileged, as only kings and priests of outstanding character were deemed worthy of hieroglyphic education:

> For that reason the Egyptians did not reveal the mysteries that they have to passers-by nor did they transmit knowledge about the divine to profane men; only to those who are to take up kingship and among the priests to those who are deemed to be most fit according to upbringing, education and birth.
>
> [Clement of Alexandria, *Stromateis* V, chapter 7, §41.1–2]

It becomes thus clear that Greco-Roman authors projected a feeling of awe upon the Egyptian priesthood, which they presented as a closed-off community and as the possessor of sacred—and desired—knowledge by virtue of its ancient language and script.[17]

The Greco-Roman authors were hence convinced of the esoteric qualities of the Egyptian priesthood and its script and language. It is however open to discussion whether their conviction was based on a sincere interest in, and profound understanding of, Egyptian culture and religion. Their desire to find esoteric doctrines undoubtedly influenced their perception as much as their superficial knowledge of Egyptian culture. Among their sources were certainly early works like those of the Egyptian priests Manetho and Chaeremon, who wrote histories on Egyptian culture in Greek for a Hellenised audience in, respectively, the Ptolemaic and early Roman period.[18] It is however uncertain to what extent their accounts were truly objective descriptions. Manetho, author of the *Aegyptiaca*, 'History of Egypt', worked at the court of kings

---

Thissen, *Des Niloten Horapollon Hieroglyphenbuch. Band I: Text und Übersetzung* (München 2001).

[16] Clement of Alexandria, *Stromateis* V, chapter 4, §20. 3.

[17] For a more detailed discussion of the Greco-Roman representation of Egypt, see, chapter 6.3.3.2.

[18] Fowden, *The Egyptian Hermes*, 52–57. See also chapter 6.3.3.2.

Ptolemy I and II (306–246 BCE), two kings who were actively interested in the histories and manners of the different ethnic groups that lived in their newly established Ptolemaic empire.[19] Manetho's position at the court was therefore rather ambivalent. He not only had to secure and to position Egyptian culture among the different ethnic groups, he had first of all to deal with, and defend the interests of the Egyptian priesthood among the Macedonian ruling elite that acted as his patron. One way of gaining sympathy for the Egyptian priesthood would certainly have been to live up to the expectations of the Hellenic world to a certain extent and translate Egyptian notions into a 'distorting' Hellenic idiom that emphasised elements as secrecy, divine revelations, etc. Since the original work is for the most part lost, these remarks can only be tentative.[20] However, Plutarch relates that Manetho was consciously involved with the conceptualisation and acceptance of the syncretistic Greco-Egyptian god Sarapis at the Ptolemaic court, which reveals Manetho's politico-cultural intentions.[21] This is even truer for Chaeremon who served as a tutor to the young Nero at the court of emperor Claudius (41–54 CE).[22] Unfortunately, solely his description of the Egyptian priestly way of life is preserved in substantial fragments.[23] These excerpts describe the Egyptian priesthood in terms quite similar to those used in Stoic philosophy, valuing concepts of seclusion, reflection and mental stability. Such an edifying picture of Egyptian priesthood and of the contemplation of the hidden essence of the divine is certainly aimed at raising sympathy for the interests of the Egyptian priesthood. Manetho, Chaeremon and their likes may therefore consciously have taken up the process of setting the Egyptian priesthood apart for the benefit of securing their own position within the Greco-

---

[19] For a collection of testimonies and fragments of the works of Manetho, see, W.G. Waddell, *Manetho* (Loeb Classical Library 350; Cambridge, Mass. and London 1940) and Gerald P. Verbrugge and John M. Wickersham, *Berossos and Manetho. Native Traditions in Ancient Mesopotamia and Egypt* (Michigan 1996).

[20] A work titled *Against Herodotus*, which is not preserved, was attributed to Manetho in antiquity. The title suggests that Manetho was at least concerned with correcting Herodotus' flaws in understanding Egyptian culture or with presenting a more nuanced description.

[21] Plutarch, *On Isis and Osiris*, 28, 361F–362A. For a similar viewpoint on Manetho's intentions, see, John Dillery, 'The First Egyptian Narrative History: Manetho and Greek Historiography' *ZPE* 127 (1999) 93–116.

[22] Chaeremon's involvement in Nero's education is referred to in the Suda, see, test. 3 in P.W. van der Horst, *Chaeremon: Egyptian Priest and Stoic Philosopher* (EPRO 101; 2nd ed.; Leiden 1987) 2–3.

[23] Van der Horst, *Chaeremon*.

Roman ruling ideology. Their audience then fervently acknowledged the image of the exotic Egyptian priest, so much so that, from the Roman period onward, Egyptian religion and priesthood became the chief topic of interest among other things Egyptian.

This Roman-period discourse on Egypt was clearly at work in texts that were produced and read within Hellenised circles, but it is well conceivable that the native priesthood itself may have had no such mystifying ideas about its social and ritual functioning. Moreover, it is highly unlikely that the Egyptian priesthood acted as a single unanimous intellectual body without a social and intellectual stratification. However that may be, treatise XVI of the *Corpus Hermeticum* plays with the Greco-Roman fascination for the inherent power of the Egyptian language and the secrecy of Egyptian traditional knowledge, in spite of the fact that the text originated in Egyptian priestly circles. This willed identity of the alienated Egyptian priest being opposed to Greek outsiders functions also in the Greek sections of the magical handbooks of the Theban Magical Library, the subject of the present book, and the *Greek Magical Papyri* in general.[24] David Frankfurter has introduced the term 'stereotype appropriation' to explain the apparent paradoxical situation.[25] According to Frankfurter, Egyptian priests, who had lost their state subsidies with the introduction of Roman rule, had to look for new sources of income and found those in a Greco-Roman clientele willing to pay for divine illumination like, for example, a character such as Thessalos of Tralles.[26] As a result, Egyptian priests acted to the expectations of their customers and, so, took on the role of the exoticised Egyptian ritual specialist in daily reality as well as in the texts they wrote.

The concept of 'stereotype appropriation' is a useful heuristic device to explain the image of an alienated Egyptian priesthood in Egyptian texts, but its applicability could well prove to be restricted to texts written by Egyptian priests in Greek. Indeed, it has to be taken into account

---

[24] This topic is treated in more detail in chapter 6.

[25] David Frankfurter, *Religion in Roman Egypt. Assimilation and Resistance* (Princeton 1998) 224–237; Idem, 'The Consequences of Hellenism in Late Antique Egypt: Religious Worlds and Actors' *ARG* 2 (2000) 162–194, esp.168–183.

[26] For an insightful analysis of the complex social strategies involved in Thessalos' encounter with Egyptian priests, see, Ian Moyer, 'Thessalos of Tralles and Cultural Exchange', in: Scott Noegel, Joel Walker, and Brannon Wheeler (eds.), *Prayer, Magic, and the Stars in the Ancient and Late Antique World* (University Park, PA 2003) 39–56. See also A.-J. Festugière, 'L'expérience religieuse du médecin Thessalos' *RevBibl* 48 (1939) 45–77.

that several of the *Greek Magical Papyri* are accompanied by extensive Demotic spells that could not be read or understood by a presumed Greco-Roman clientele and therefore must have circulated in a different social context, possibly also a different geographical area. Who read the Demotic sections? And for what readership was the combination of Greek and Demotic spells considered meaningful? As a consequence, these Demotic spells invite us to analyse to what extent the Egyptian priesthood of the Greco-Roman period indeed acted as the Greco-Roman authors imagined. The bilingual manuscripts circulated undoubtedly among Egyptian priests, as the native priesthood formed the only social stratum in society that was still able to read and write Demotic in the Roman period. However, their relationship with Greco-Roman culture was different from that of the ancient authors discussed above. Instead of forming part of, and constituting, the dominant cultural discourse, the native priesthood was subject to economic, political and cultural dominance of that same Greco-Roman ruling elite. Such a contact situation of unequal power relations must inevitably have led to social changes within the dominated group, to renegotiations of social roles and identities within the local priestly community and the Roman world at large. The outcome of this process will have been varied, depending on the particularities of the local context and the specific interests of individual priests and their immediate colleagues, but certainly it will have been determined by a combination of resistance against certain views and practices of the dominant culture and assimilation to other aspects of the dominant culture's ideology. Stereotype appropriation is a clear example of the latter and forms an aspect of the more general term 'mimicry': the dominated subject is invited by the dominant ideology to participate but only on the dominant culture's terms, of which writing in Greek is but one aspect. The Demotic spells preserved on the bilingual manuscripts of the Theban Magical Library offer us then an opportunity to study from a different perspective the beliefs and cultural phenomena articulated in the texts quoted above. Before embarking on this project, the relevant sources and the methodology applied have to be introduced in the remainder of this chapter.

## 1.2. *Research on the Theban Magical Library*

The Theban Magical Library offers a unique opportunity to study aspects of religion, language and acculturation in Roman-period Thebes because of its exceptionally good state of preservation, its coherent make-up, its detailed magical recipes, its elaborate hymns and invocations to deities and demons of Egyptian, Greek, Semitic and Persian origin and, what is truly extraordinary, because of its bilingual character. The majority of manuscripts has been written in Greek, whereas one magical handbook has almost entirely been composed in Demotic. Several other handbooks contain parts, either short or extensive, in Demotic and Old-Coptic next to Greek sections. In certain cases these languages interfere to the extent that a Greek invocation is inserted into a Demotic recipe[27] or that a spell written in Old-Coptic is accompanied by instructions for use in Greek.[28] The multicultural and bilingual character of the magical spells suggests that the corpus is the result of a desire to collect and combine ritual texts of different origins. The spells in their present state testify clearly to several phases of editing, thereby demonstrating that the ancient redactors were highly skilful philologists and proficient in both Egyptian and Greek. Given this complex language situation, modern students looking for the cultural dynamics of the spells within this corpus must include, almost by necessity, both the Egyptian and Greek spells in their research. However, until today, such a line of research has hardly been undertaken. The dominant paradigm in the study of the manuscripts of the Theban Magical Library is determined by a traditional disciplinary division of the material on ethnic and linguistic grounds. This means for example that classicists tend to focus on the Greek spells without taking the Demotic texts into account, irrespective of the fact that these occur alongside Greek spells on a single manuscript. This situation is shaped as much by the preferences and academic training of earlier scholars as by the fact that the different manuscripts of the Theban Magical Library became dispersed over Europe and were rapidly relegated to the margins of both Egyptology and Classics. To understand more fully the developments that led to the currently still prevailing paradigm, the

---

[27] See chapter 4.4.
[28] For example, see, PGM III.633–731; IV.1–25; 52–85; 88–93 and 94–153.

following pages will describe the fate of the Theban Magical Library after its discovery and provide a sketch of the most important stages in the study of its manuscripts.

During the first half of the nineteenth century, Egyptian antiquities were in great demand in Europe, where newly established nation states like France, Prussia and the Netherlands felt a need to confirm their independence and grandeur by appropriating pharaonic symbolism and acquiring Egyptian monuments for their recently founded museums. This development provided opportunities to make large sums of money for people such as Bernadino Drovetti, Henri Salt and Giovanni Anastasi, who have become particularly well known for their rather unscrupulous conduct in amassing Egyptian antiquities.[29] Giovanni Anastasi, a rich merchant from Alexandria, who served as Swedish-Norwegian Consul-General in Egypt from 1828 until his death in 1857,[30] acquired a huge and varied collection of Egyptian antiquities through local antiquity dealers. Through his agents in Luxor, he purchased in the course of time a collection of occult texts currently known as the Theban Magical Library.[31] Nothing is known about the archaeological context of the texts,[32] the identity of the vendors or the circumstances of the sales.

To complicate matters further, Anastasi sold the manuscripts to different European museums and institutions on different occasions. In 1828 Anastasi put the first part of his collection up for sale through

---

[29] An insightful introduction to the early period of collecting antiquities is given in Peter France, *The Rape of Egypt. How the Europeans Stripped Egypt of its Heritage* (London 1991) 27–57. See also Leslie Greener, *The Discovery of Egypt* (New York 1966) 103–139 and Brian M. Fagan, *The Rape of the Nile. Tomb Robbers, Tourists and Archaeologists in Egypt* (New York 1975).

[30] Warren R. Dawson, 'Anastasi, Sallier, and Harris and their Papyri', *JEA* 35 (1949) 158–166, esp. 158–160. Cf. M.J. Bierbrier, *Who was Who in Egyptology* (3rd ed.; London 1995) 15, according to whom Anastasi died on 6 aug. 1860. I assume this is a typo. Giovanni Anastasi also used the name Giovanni d'Athanasi.

[31] More detailed descriptions of the find and its subsequent fate can be found in: Karl Preisendanz, *Papyrusfunde und Papyrusforschung* (Leipzig 1933) 91–95; Garth Fowden. *The Egyptian Hermes. A Historical Approach to the Late Pagan Mind* (Cambridge 1986) 168–172; William M. Brashear, 'The Greek Magical Papyri: An Introduction and Survey; Annotated Bibliography (1928–1994)' *ANRW* II 18. 5 (1995) 3380–684, 3401 ff.

[32] There exists a certain scholarly consensus that the library was found in one of the many tombs situated in the Theban hills, although no circumstantial evidence whatsoever is available to support this hypothesis; see: Preisendanz, *Papyrusfunde und Papyrusforschung*, 94; Fowden, *The Egyptian Hermes*, 170 and Brashear, 'The Greek Magical Papyri', 3402.

three agents in Livorno and found a buyer in the Dutch government, who acquired the entire lot consisting of 5675 items for the recently founded National Museum of Antiquities in Leiden.[33] As a result of this sale, the National Museum of Antiquities in Leiden obtained 126 papyrus manuscripts of which four once belonged to the Theban Magical Library (P. Leiden I 383, 384, 395 and 397[34]). On August 27, 1832, the Swedish Academy of Antiquities in Stockholm sent Anastasi a letter of gratitude for his gift of a papyrus codex with alchemical recipes in Greek.[35] Within the pages of the manuscript (P. Holmiensis), a papyrus sheet with a short Greek magical spell (PGM Va) was found. Although nothing is known about the provenance of the two texts, their attribution to the Theban Magical Library is almost certain, because the hand of the alchemical book is nearly identical with the hand of the P. Leiden I 397, which is also a Greek codex with alchemical recipes.[36] A second public auction was held in London in 1839 on which occasion the British Museum acquired a small magical codex in Greek (PGM V) that is likely to have originally been part of the Theban Magical Library given its hand, contents, and measurements.[37]

After Anastasi's death in 1857, his entire collection was sold at a public auction in Paris, where the British Museum, the Berlin Museum, the Louvre and the Bibliothèque Nationale acquired magical handbooks that are attributed with varying degrees of certitude to the Theban Magical Library.[38] The British Museum obtained a Demotic papyrus

---

[33] See for a detailed reconstruction of the events and problems related to the negotiations about the price Ruurd Binnert Halbertsma, *Le Solitaire des Ruines. De archeologische reizen van Jean Emile Humbert (1771–1839) in dienst van het Koninkrijk der Nederlanden* (unpublished Phd thesis, Leiden 1995) 91–108. Note that this was the first of Anastasi's public auctions, not the second as stated by Dawson, 'Anastasi, Sallier, and Harris and their Papyri', 159; see Adolf Klasens, 'An Amuletic Papyrus of the 25th Dynasty' *OMRO* 56 (1975) 20–28, 20 note 2.

[34] These manuscripts were numbered in the Anastasi catalogue as A(nastasi) 65, 75, 76, 66. The last three manuscripts were given the numbering V, W, X in the Leemans facsimile editions.

[35] Otto Lagercrantz, *Papyrus Graecus Holmiensis (P. Holm.): Recepte für Silber, Steine und Purpur* (Arbeten utgifna med understöd af Vilhelm Ekmans Universitetsfond 13; Uppsala and Leipzig 1913) 45.

[36] Lagercrantz, *Papyrus Graecus Holmiensis (P. Holm.)*, 50, 53; Robert Halleux, *Les alchimistes grecs 1: Papyrus de Leyde, Papyrus de Stockholm* (Paris 1981) 5–6, 9–12.

[37] Dawson, 'Anastasi, Sallier, and Harris and their Papyri', 159. Note that this was actually the second, not the third shipment as Dawson writes.

[38] The magical handbooks bought by the Berlin Museum (PGM I and II) and the

that, years later, was found to fit exactly to P. Leiden I 383, forming thus a magical manuscript of more than 60 Demotic columns (PDM xiv).[39] The Bibliothèque Nationale bought a codex of 66 pages of magical recipes in Greek (PGM IV), being the largest magical handbook of antiquity extant. According to François Lenormant, who supervised the auction and wrote the catalogue, the codex came from Thebes and belonged originally to the library.[40]

The manuscripts that can be assigned in all probability to the Theban Magical Library can now be listed as follows:[41]

| | | |
|---|---|---|
| P. Bibl.Nat.Suppl. 574 | magical handbook | PGM IV |
| P. London 46 | magical handbook | PGM V |
| P. Holmiensis p. 42 | magical spell | PGM Va |
| P. Leiden I 384 | magical handbook | PGM XII/PDM xii |
| P. Leiden I 395 | magical handbook | PGM XIII |
| P. Leiden I 383 & P. BM 10070 | magical handbook | PDM xiv/PGM XIV |
| P. Leiden I 397 | alchemical handbook | |
| P. Holmiensis | alchemical handbook | |

The following manuscripts formed possibly part of the Theban Magical Library, although no decisive arguments can be given:

| | | |
|---|---|---|
| P. Berlin 5025 | magical handbook | PGM I |
| P. Berlin 5026 | magical handbook | PGM II |
| P. Louvre 2391 | magical handbook | PGM III |

---

manuscripts that are nowadays stored in the Louvre (PGM III and PDM Suppl.) are of unknown provenance and cannot be linked directly to any of the handbooks securely assigned to the Theban Magical Library. Preisendanz and Fowden include the Berlin papyri in their reconstruction of the library, whereas Brashear expresses serious doubts; see Brashear, 'The Greek Magical Papyri', 3403f.

[39] The join was discovered by Willem Pleyte and published by J.-J. Hess in 1892: J.-J. Hess, *Der gnostische Papyrus von London* (Freiburg 1892).

[40] A citation from the auction catalogue is given in Karl Preisendanz, *Papyri Graecae Magicae. Die griechischen Zauberpapyri* 2 vols. (2$^{nd}$ ed., ed. by Albert Henrichs; Stuttgart 1973–1974) vol. 1, 65. The catalogue to the auction is: *Catalogue d'une Collection d'Antiquités Egyptiennes par M. François Lenormant. Cette Collection Rassemblée par M.D. Anastasi Consul Générale de Suède a Alexandrie* (Paris 1857) [non vidi]. The Paris Magical Book (PGM IV) contains an interesting (intertextual) link with P. London-Leiden, which manuscript definitely belongs to the Theban Magical Library, in the form of an Old-Coptic spell (PGM IV.1–25) that includes a rather faithful translation of a passage in a Demotic spell preserved on P. London-Leiden (21/ 1–9 = PDM xiv.627–635). The corresponding passages are: PGM IV. 11–14 and P. London-Leiden 21/ 2–3 = PDM xiv.627–629.

[41] This and the following table are based on Brashear, 'The Greek Magical Papyri', 3402–3404 and Fowden, *The Egyptian Hermes*, 169ff.

P. London 121     magical handbook     PGM VII
P. BM 10588      magical handbook     PGM LXI/PDM lxi
P. Louvre 3229   magical handbook     PDM Suppl.

Upon their arrival in Europe the magical handbooks did not produce general enthusiasm among scholars of the day. C.J.C. Reuvens, the first director of the National Museum of Antiquities in Leiden, recognized immediately the importance of the Greek and Old-Coptic glosses in the bilingual magical handbooks for the decipherment of the Demotic script.[12] Most scholars, however, were not impressed by the find, since they regarded the texts to be the barbaric products of superstition and of a bastardised society in which not much was left of the standards and ideals of either classical Greek or pharaonic culture. The scientific paradigm of those days defined syncretism and hybridity, racial as well as cultural, as pollution and degeneration, with the effect that scholars were reluctant to include the highly syncretistic corpus into their discipline.[13] It was only at the end of the nineteenth century that the discipline of Classics drew fuller attention to these handbooks, initiated by the studies of the classicist Albrecht Dieterich.[14] The underlying assumption which provoked this rise in interest, was that the hymns and ritual procedures contained in the handbooks were relics of texts once used by practitioners in the mystery religions of the Greek Classical period. Therefore, much stress was placed on reconstructing the original texts.[15] Consequently, the magical texts were not studied for

---

[12] C.J.C. Reuvens, *Lettres à M. Letronne sur les papyrus bilingues et grecs, et sur quelques autres monumens gréco-égyptiens du Musée d'Antiquités de l'Université de Leide* (Leiden 1830) 4.

[13] For a critical analysis of the concept of hybridity, see, Robert Young, *Colonial Desire: Hybridity in Theory, Culture and Race* (London 1995). An insightful assessment of the general negative judgement of Greco-Roman Egypt on the part of early classicists and Egyptologists is given in Heinz Heinen, 'L'Egypte dans l'historiographie moderne du monde hellénistique', in: L. Criscuolo and G. Geraci (eds.), *Egitto e storia antica dell' ellenismo all' età araba* (Bologna 1989) 105–135, esp. 115–133.

[14] Brashear, 'The Greek Magical Papyri', 3408–3411. That Dieterich won a student prize for his edition and analysis of PGM XII is probably not without importance and demonstrates a shift in the perception of the magical papyri. The dissertation was published as *Papyrus magica musei Lugdunensis Batavi*, Jahrbücher für klassische Philologie, Suppl. 16, 749–830; the prolegomena are reprinted in Albrecht Dieterich, *Kleine Schriften* (Leipzig and Berlin 1911) 1–47. Important contributions to the study of the magical papyri are also his *Abraxas. Studien zur Religionsgeschichte des späten Altertums* (Leipzig 1891) and *Eine Mithrasliturgie* (Leipzig 1903).

[15] Fritz Graf, *Magic in the Ancient World* (Cambridge 1997) 12. Illustrative examples are Dieterich's reconstruction of the Mithras Liturgy (PGM IV.475–829) and Preisendanz' reconstructed hymns initially intended for the third volume of the *Papyri Graecae Magicae*,

their own sake and within their historical context, but mainly in relation to their hypothetical originals of which they were supposed to be a degraded form after many centuries of textual transmission.

As a basic tool for the now growing field, all Greek magical texts from Egypt were compiled under the directorship of Karl Preisendanz into one scholarly corpus, known as the 'Papyri Graecae Magicae', which was published in 1928 and 1931.[46] Each manuscript was given a number in Roman numerals whereby its lines were continuously numbered with Arabic numerals, so that, for example, P. Leiden 384 verso 1/15–3/22, a recipe to acquire control over a person with the help of Eros, became PGM XII.14–95. The magical handbooks of the Theban Magical Library form the principal part of the PGM, but are not included in their entirety. Whereas the Old-Coptic sections are given in full and provided with philological commentary, the Demotic spells are consistently left out. In his introduction, Preisendanz keeps silent about the reasons for this exclusion; in fact, he does not mention the existence of the Demotic columns at all.[47] This has led to the awkward situation that the extensive P. London-Leiden, which contains 29 columns on the recto and 33 on the verso, mostly written in Demotic, is reduced to three pages with 27 lines of Greek as PGM XIV. In the same way, the thirteen Greek columns of P. Leiden I 384 verso, collected as PGM XII, appear without the two preceding and four following Demotic spells. The PGM reference system established itself easily as standard, with the result that the Demotic spells, which could not be given a PGM number because they are not Greek,[48] disappeared

---

which never appeared. They can now be found as an appendix to the second edition of the *Papyri Graecae Magicae*, vol. 2.

[46] Karl Preisendanz, *Papyri Graecae Magicae. Die griechischen Zauberpapyri* 2 vols. (Leipzig 1928–1931). The planned third volume with indices was lost during an air raid on Leipzig during World War II. The present study refers always to the improved second edition: Karl Preisendanz [and Albert Henrichs ed.], *Papyri Graecae Magicae. Die griechischen Zauberpapyri* 2 vols. (Stuttgart 1973–1974).

[47] If the exclusion of the Demotic sections were to be attributed to insurmountable technical difficulties in printing Demotic script or transliteration, one would expect Preisendanz giving a short explanation in his introduction. His complete silence on the Demotic spells suggests rather a Helleno-centric perspective on the magical papyri.

[48] The Demotic spells were only given a PDM number with the comprehensive translation of the magical corpus in 1986; see footnote 56. Despite the fact that the introduction of the PDM numbering system demonstrates the final acknowledgement that the Demotic spells form part of the corpus, the system is otherwise of limited use. Bilingual spells are now given separate numbers for their Demotic and Greek parts, as for example in the case of P. London-Leiden 4/1–22, which has become PDM xiv.93–

from sight: no PGM number meant no attention from students of the magical papyri. It goes without saying that the publication of the PGM in this particular form fixed the parameters of future research on the Theban Magical Library. The exclusion of the Demotic spells logically suggested or even dictated concentration on Greek cultural elements. For example, the thirteen Greek columns known as PGM XII are key texts in the study of the *Greek Magical Papyri* and have continuously been studied since Albrecht Dieterich's pioneering dissertation on these spells, which was published in 1888.[49] However, none of these studies has taken the remaining Demotic spells (PDM xii) into account. As such, it is a perfect example of the danger of a scholarly discourse being narrowed down to one discipline: not only does such a one-sided approach run the risk of obscuring the object of study, it also blinds subsequent researchers, dictates the questions to be posed and, as a consequence, the answers to be found.[50]

To a large extent, the general absence of the Demotic spells in the study of the magical papyri can also be attributed to a general lack of interest in these Demotic texts on the part of Egyptology. Reuvens' intuition that the bilingual papyri would be of great help in the decipherment of the Demotic script, proved to be correct. Nevertheless, the Demotic spells did not provoke an energetic debate on the magical techniques, mythology, religious beliefs and the poetics of the invocations among early Egyptologists. As in the case of classicists, this was probably due to a general negative judgement on the mixing of cultures in the Hellenistic and Roman period.[51] Even in the introduction to the final publication of P. London-Leiden (PDM xiv) in 1904, the edi-

---

[114] [PGM XIVa.1–11]. This particular form of numbering fails to do justice to instances of code switching, a regular phenomenon in the corpus. It remains unclear to me why the PGM number is given in capitals and the PDM number in small letters. Does this suggest in a subtle way a Helleno-centric perspective on the part of the editors of the comprehensive translation volume?

[49] See footnote 44.

[50] A telling example of recent date is Fritz Graf, 'Prayer in Magical and Religious Ritual', in: Christopher A. Faraone and D. Obbink eds., *Magika Hiera. Ancient Greek Magic and Religion* (New York/Oxford 1991) 188–213, 193. He considers PGM XIV to be prayers without any accompanying ritual prescriptions. However, these prescriptions are quite detailed, but not included in the PGM because they are written in Demotic.

[51] See again Heinen, 'L'Egypte dans l'historiographie moderne du monde hellénistique', esp. 130–133. See on the 'biological model' and the underlying value judgements of its metaphors also Robert K. Ritner, 'Implicit Models of Cross-Cultural Interaction: a Question of Noses, Soap, and Prejudice', in: Janet H. Johnson (ed.), *Life in a Multi-Cultural Society. Egypt from Cambyses and Beyond* (SAOC 51; Chicago 1992) 283–294.

tors F.Ll. Griffith and Herbert Thompson wrote: 'though the subject-matter of the manuscript is not without its interest for the history of magic and medicine, its chief claim to publication lies in its philological interest'.[52] A further excuse for neglecting the study of the Demotic spells must have been the apparent discrepancy in theme and aims between pharaonic and Demotic magical spells. Whereas the former is mainly apotropaeic in nature, a fair number of Demotic spells are rather aggressive and aimed at acquiring control over a person or deity. Because of this difference the Demotic spells were not considered to be of interest for the study of pharaonic magic and easily fell into oblivion.[53] The remaining three Demotic magical handbooks were published at large intervals in 1936, 1975 and 1977, which demonstrates again the scant attention for this genre within Egyptology.[54] Janet H. Johnson, who published the Demotic spells on the Leiden manuscript containing the thirteen columns of Greek (PGM XII) in 1975 and the Louvre Demotic magical handbook in 1977, put an end to this trend and has done important work to bring the Demotic spells to the attention of Demotists.[55]

---

[52] F.Ll. Griffith and H. Thompson, *The Demotic Magical papyrus of London and Leiden*, 3 vols. (London 1904–1909), vol. 1, 7. The manuscript has indeed served as the basis for a study of Demotic grammar: Georges Ort-Geuthner, *Grammaire démotique du Papyrus Magique de Londres et Leyde* (Paris 1936). The following quote is noteworthy: 'Mais l'intérêt du papyrus de Londres et Leyde reside surtout dans sa langue', page xii.

[53] For example, see, J.F. Borghouts, 'Magical Texts', in: *Textes et Langages de l'Égypte Pharaonique* 3 Vol. (BibEt. 63: Cairo 1972–1974) vol. 3, 7–19, esp. 16–17. Note that François Lexa, as an exception to the rule, made extensive use of the Demotic and Old-Coptic spells in his general study on Egyptian magic: François Lexa, *La magie dans l'Égypte antique de l'ancien empire jusqu'à l'époque copte* (Paris 1925). Theodor Hopfner included partly the Demotic spells in his study *Griechisch-ägyptischer Offenbarungszauber* 2 vols. (Leipzig 1921–1924; 2nd ed. Amsterdam 1974, 1983, 1990).

[54] The publications are: H.I. Bell, A.D. Nock and H. Thompson, *Magical texts from a Bilingual Papyrus in the British Museum* (London 1933), Janet H. Johnson, 'The Demotic Magical Spells of Leiden I 384' *OMRO* 56 (1975) 29–64 and Idem, 'Louvre E3229: A Demotic Magical Text' *Enchoria* 7 (1977) 55–102. The latter handbook contains in fact also a spell in Greek, although largely effaced nowadays, see: William M. Brashear, *Magica Varia* (Papyrologica Bruxellensia 25; Brussels 1991) chapter 3, 'A charitesion', 71–73 and plates 4+5.

[55] Apart from the text publications (see foregoing footnote), Janet H. Johnson studied the dialect of P. London-Leiden and included the manuscript as a key text in her study of the Demotic verbal system. It is not without importance that the frontispiece of the latter publication shows a drawing of the god Seth that is taken from Demotic column 4 of P. Leiden I 384 verso. Janet H. Johnson, *The Demotic Verbal System* (SAOC 38; Chicago 1976) and 'The Dialect of the Demotic Magical Papyrus of London and Leiden', in: *Studies in Honor of George R. Hughes* (SAOC 39; Chicago 1976) 105–132.

With the majority of the extant Demotic and Greek magical material finally available in modern publications at the end of the 1970s, a first bridge was established between the two distinct disciplines making it possible to study the Greek and Egyptian spells in combination. An important step in this direction is the comprehensive translation of the magical papyri under the editorship of Hans Dieter Betz, which was published in 1986.[56] A joint team of classicists translated the Greek spells, while the Egyptologist Janet H. Johnson was in charge of the Demotic sections. Robert K. Ritner, another Egyptologist, aided with annotating the translated Greek and Demotic spells, giving earlier Egyptian parallels or explaining Egyptian religious concepts and images that underlie the mechanics of the rituals. In this way, the edition testifies to the linguistic and cultural complexity of the magical material.

However, the volume still advocates in a subtle but telling way the supremacy of the Greek spells over the Demotic sections as reveals its title 'The Greek Magical Papyri in translation', with the subtitle, in a significantly smaller font, 'Including the demotic spells'. In recent years, Robert K. Ritner has frequently objected to a prevalent Helleno-centric perspective by stressing the fact that, in his view, both the Greek and Demotic spells were embedded in earlier pharaonic magical practices and should be studied in the light of pharaonic ritual.[57] A slightly different position is taken by Christopher A. Faraone, who likewise stresses the multicultural character of the magical corpus, but argues for a combined study of Greek, Egyptian and Semitic

---

[56] Hans Dieter Betz (ed.), *The Greek Magical Papyri in Translation. Including the Demotic spells* (Chicago 1986).

[57] His most fervent and lucid plea for an acknowledgement of the underlying pharaonic tradition in the Demotic and Greek magical papyri is Robert K. Ritner, 'Egyptian Magical Practice under the Roman Empire: the Demotic Spells and their Religious Context' *ANRW* II.18.5 (1995) 3333–3379, esp. 3358–3371. In his dissertation on Egyptian magical practices he treats pharaonic, Demotic and Greek magical spells on an equal footing, thereby suggesting that, in a sense, they formed part of one and the same Egyptian ritual tradition: *The Mechanics of Ancient Egyptian Magical Practice* (SAOC 54; Chicago 1993). See also his rather polemic critique on the cultural hierarchies underlying most classicist's studies of Greco-Roman Egypt: Ritner, 'Implicit Models of Cross-Cultural Interaction'. Ritner's views have been characterised as overestimating the Egyptian side of the corpus; see for some critique: Graf, *Magic in the Ancient World*, 5; Christopher A. Faraone, *Ancient Greek Love Magic* (Cambridge 1999) 35–36; Idem, 'The Ethnic Origins of a Roman-Era *Philtrokatadesmos* (PGM IV.296–434)', in: Marvin Meyer and Paul Mirecki (eds.), *Magic and Ritual in the Ancient World* (Religions in the Graeco-Roman World 141; Leiden 2002) 319–343, 322f.

religion instead of sole focus on the Egyptian background.[58] Both perspectives have found adherents and opponents among scholars. In certain cases, arguments for identifying a particular cultural tradition in a religious image or prescribed rite have met with strong opposition, showing that the parameters of the intercultural study of the magical papyri have not yet been settled satisfactorily.[59] Nonetheless, the cultural and linguistic diversity of the corpus seems to be no longer a matter of debate, nor an impediment to a more comprehensive study of the magical papyri, so that questions about the social and cultural identity of the users of the Theban Magical Library are beginning to force themselves on scholars of today.[60] The present study is an inves-

---

[58] Exemplary for his approach is the analysis of the so-called Philinna Papyrus (PGM XX) in: Christopher A. Faraone, 'The Mystodokos and the Dark-Eyed Maidens: Multicultural Influences on a Late-Hellenistic Incantation', in: Marvin Meyer and Paul Mirecki (eds.), *Ancient Magic and Ritual Power* (Religions in the Graeco-Roman World 129; Leiden 1995) 297–333, see the table on pages 325–326 for a summation of the wide range of his data. Ritner critiqued severely Faraone's identification of Mesopotamian influence in the Philinna Papyrus: Robert K. Ritner, 'The Wives of Horus and the Philinna papyrus (PGM XX)', in: W. Clarysse, A. Schoors and H. Willems (eds.), *Egyptian Religion. The Last Thousand Years. Fs. Quaegebeur* 2 vols. (OLA 85; Leuven 1998) vol. 2, 1027–1041.

[59] An illustrative case in point is the debate, taken up in several articles, between Ritner and Faraone on the origins of the ritual techniques of a pierced magical clay figurine of the Roman period found near Antinoopolis in a clay jar with a lead lamella inscribed in Greek. Ritner argues for a late example of an execration ritual, the techniques of which are firmly rooted in Egyptian religious beliefs and attested since the third millennium BCE. Faraone, on the other hand, emphasises the use of magical figurines as intermediaries in destructive rituals in both Egypt and Greece, allowing a more complex history of cultural influences for the clay effigy and its accompanying spell. See: Christopher A. Faraone, 'Binding and Burying the Forces of Evil: The Defensive Use of "Voodoo Dolls" in Ancient Greece' *Classical Antiquity* 10 (1991) 165–205; Ritner, *The Mechanics of Ancient Egyptian Magical Practice*, 112–190; Faraone, 'The Ethnic Origins of a Roman-Era *Philtrokatadesmos*'. This debate demonstrates that it is extremely difficult to trace specific cultural or ethnic origins for ritual techniques. Moreover, such an undertaking easily runs the risk of ending up in an essentialistic debate on who was first.

[60] That the linguistic and cultural diversity of the magical papyri is generally accepted nowadays is borne out by the steady stream of conference volumes on ancient magic that appear since the middle of the nineties of the last century. These volumes include almost as a rule articles on Egyptian, Near Eastern, Jewish and Christian aspects of the corpus. Marvin Meyer and Paul Mirecki (eds.), *Ancient Magic and Ritual Power* (Religions in the Graeco-Roman World 129; Leiden 1995); David R. Jordan, Hugo Montgomery, Einar Thomassen (eds.), *The World of Ancient Magic* (Papers from the Norwegian Institute at Athens 4; Bergen 1999); Marvin Meyer and Paul Mirecki (eds.), *Magic and Ritual in the Ancient World* (Religions in the Graeco-Roman World 141; Leiden 2002); Scott B. Noegel (ed.), *Prayer, Magic, and the Stars in the Ancient and Late Antique World* (Pennsylvania 2003).

tigation into the sphere of production and use of the Demotic and Greek spells of the Theban Magical Library. It takes the bilingual character of the library as its starting point instead of as an accidental and inconvenient phenomenon and hopes to exploit its complex language situation as a means to track down the possible social and cultural contexts of the composers, compilers, editors and users of the spells.

### 1.3. *Aims and methods of the investigation: reading magic*

The foregoing section has shown that:

1. Any reconstruction of the Theban Magical Library must remain tentative on account of an irreparable lack of information about its archaeological context.
2. The study of the Theban Magical Library has been hindered by a disciplinary division of the bilingual material on ethno-linguistic grounds.
3. The question about the origins of ritual techniques, religious images, idiomatic expressions and text passages is far from settled.

In the light of the above given three observations, the present line of approach can be described in the following terms. First, as the core material for study serve two manuscripts that form a subgroup within the library, both of which can be assigned with certainty to the Theban Magical Library. In this way, problems about the exact make-up of the library can be avoided. These manuscripts are P. London-Leiden (PDM xiv and PGM XIV) and P. Leiden I 384 verso (PGM XII and PDM xii). They can be considered a unity, not only because the Demotic hand is identical, but also because fragments of the Leiden part of P. London-Leiden were discovered within the folded P. Leiden I 384 during their first examination in the National Museum of Antiquities in Leiden in 1829 and 1830.[61] Their Theban provenance is certain since, according to sparse information provided by Anastasi, the Leiden part of P. London-Leiden was acquired in Luxor, which agrees with the dialect of the Egyptian sections. Because both manuscripts contain substantial parts in Demotic and Greek, and make use of Demotic, hieratic, Old-Coptic and Greek script, the two manuscripts together contain all lan-

---

[61] For a more detailed account of these and the following arguments, see, chapter 2.

guages and scripts that are represented in the complete Theban Magical Library. As such, an investigation of the two manuscripts could serve as a case study, the conclusions of which might possibly hold as well for the entire library.

It goes without saying that the present study does not allow for any disciplinary division of the material: the extant manuscripts themselves set the limits for, and give direction to, the investigation. Demotic, Greek as well as Old Coptic spells are included in the research and the diversity of scripts will be fully taken into account. In fact, the variation in language and script is a first indicator of the social and cultural context of production and use of the two manuscripts, since the Demotic and hieratic scripts were only in use among Egyptian priests in the Roman period.[62] This means that the authors, editors and readers of the manuscripts must have gone through a priestly scribal training and, secondly, that the two extant manuscripts must derive somehow or other from an Egyptian temple milieu. If a native temple context cannot be proven for the phases of storage and burial of the manuscripts, it must nonetheless hold for the phases of composition, compilation and editing of the spells.

This conclusion carries important consequences for the methodology of the present investigation. Since this study is primarily about the identity of the producers and users of the magical spells, I give preference to an Egyptian reading attitude; this is to say that I attempt to reconstruct the reading experience of the Egyptian owner(s) of the two extant manuscripts in the course of my analyses. This does not imply that I believe that the magical spells, the Greek ones in particular, were by necessity unknown outside native priestly circles; it means that the *extant versions* of the spells functioned within a native temple context and will be studied as such. At this point it is instructive to quote Stephen Emmel, who recently proposed a similar approach for the study of the Nag Hammadi Library, a collection of religious texts translated from Greek into Coptic, which was stored in a large jar and buried around 400 CE in the hills of Nag Hammadi.[63]

---

[62] W.J. Tait, 'Demotic Literature and Egyptian Society', in: Johnson (ed.), *Life in a Multi-Cultural Society*, 303–310.

[63] For a general introduction to the content and discovery of this collection, see, James M. Robinson (ed.), *The Nag Hammadi Library in English* (3rd ed.; Leiden 1988) 1–26. Note that the Nag Hammadi Library is an intriguing parallel to the Theban Magical Library, because both were buried around the same period in roughly the same region. See also Fowden, *The Egyptian Hermes*, 170ff.

The attraction of what I am calling a 'Coptic reading' of the Nag Hammadi Codices is that the codices are our primary data, and presumably they were read by someone—or at least they were laboriously created for that purpose. Hence such a 'Coptic reading' takes us (in theory) the shortest distance into the minefield of the texts' complex history of transmission, and therefore it should provide us with more certain—albeit quite different—results than other readings. It is, in a sense, the first task of investigation that such artefacts call for, now that the manuscripts have been fully conserved and the texts published.[61]

Central to this undertaking is to reconstruct the valorisation of the different languages, scripts and religious images on the part of a possible Egyptian user. I assume that the composers and compilers of the spells made use only of those scripts, languages, divine names and textual formats that they considered to be efficacious in a magical ritual. This implies for example that I regard variation in languages and scripts within a single spell as meant to be meaningful to the ritual and thus reflecting a particular perspective on ritual techniques and the workings of nature. Moreover, I believe that only those marketing techniques, such as fictions about authors and miraculous discoveries, could survive several phases of redaction that were in line with the readers and editors' ideas about magicians and ritual power. A close reading of the spells along these lines will thus provide insight in the cultural and social identities of the producers and users of the magical spells.

---

[61] Stephen Emmel, 'Religious Tradition, Textual Transmission, and the Nag Hammadi Codices', in: John D. Turner and Anne McGuire (eds.), *The Nag Hammadi Library after Fifty Years. Proceedings of the 1995 Society of Biblical Literature Commemoration* (Nag Hammadi and Manichaean Studies 44; Leiden 1997) 34–43, 42f.

CHAPTER TWO

# PRESENTATION OF THE SOURCES
## P. LEIDEN I 384 AND P. LONDON-LEIDEN

### 2.1. *Two bilingual manuscripts from the Anastasi collection*

This study takes two magical handbooks of the Theban Magical Library as its primary source material, namely P. Leiden 384 I verso and P. London-Leiden (consisting of P. BM 10070 and P. Leiden I 383). Both manuscripts derive from the collection of Giovanni Anastasi, but were sold separately. The Dutch National Museum of Antiquities in Leiden acquired Anastasi's first large collection of Egyptian antiquities including the Leiden part of P. London-Leiden[1] (P. Leiden I 383) and the first half of P. Leiden I 384[2] after several rounds of serious bargaining in Livorno in 1828. Because Anastasi wanted to stimulate the slack negotiations between his agents and the Dutch government, he added, at a certain moment, a Byzantine military helmet, a papyrus codex in Greek and a bilingual papyrus scroll to the collection.[3] However, his agents Tossizza and De Castiglione were reluctant to carry out his orders at the moment that the negotiations entered their final stage. It was therefore only after the deal had been sealed, that the Dutch agent Jean Emile Humbert heard about the additional three items. After threatening the agents with a lawsuit Humbert acquired the antiquities and sent them afterwards to Leiden, where they arrived about a year later than the main load of the collection, which had arrived on New Year's Day 1829. Upon inspection of the supplement to the collection,

---

[1] This part contains the columns 10–29 on the recto and 1–24 on the verso.
[2] This part contains the columns II*-I* (Demotic) and 1–6 (Greek). The obverse side of this part of the manuscript contains the columns 13–22 of the *Myth of the Sun's Eye*.
[3] Halbertsma, *Le solitaire des ruines*, 106f. Note that his footnote 179 on page 106 contains two errors: the Greek papyrus is actually the codex P. Leiden I 395 (PGM XIII) and not P. Leiden I 384; the additional bilingual papyrus is the other half of P. Leiden I 384 and not P. Leiden I 383, which was part of the first shipment that arrived in Leiden on New Year's Day 1829. Cf. Reuvens, *Lettres à M. Letronne*, 145 and 151ff.

C.J.C. Reuvens found that the bilingual papyrus scroll fitted exactly to the Demotic-Greek magical handbook that was in the first shipment: it was the second half of P. Leiden I 384.[1]

The British Museum acquired a magical handbook similar to the Leiden manuscripts at the auction of 1857 in Paris, where Anastasi's complete collection was put up for sale after he had died earlier that year. The manuscript entered the British Museum collection under the number P. BM 10070, but remained unnoticed for a long time. Many years later Willem Pleyte, keeper and eventually director of the National Museum of Antiquities in Leiden (1869–1903), discovered that the London handbook is actually not a discrete composition, but fits exactly to the Leiden magical handbook P. Leiden I 383.[5] The two parts contain together 98 recipes, thus forming the largest Egyptian magical handbook to be preserved, and is nowadays better known as P. London-Leiden or merely P. Magical.[6]

## 2.2. *A subgroup within the Theban Magical Library*

The manuscripts P. London-Leiden and P. Leiden I 384 verso constitute clearly a discrete subgroup within the Theban Magical Library because of their remarkable bilingual character and their evident unity. Even at a first glance one cannot escape the impression that the manuscripts show a number of notable similarities. Both manuscripts are magical handbooks that bring together a considerable number of magical spells, in Demotic and Greek, of unequal length without any obvious thematic ordering. Several Demotic spells incorporate a Greek invocation of which one even recurs in two versions on P. Leiden I 384 verso and in an alternative version on P. London-Leiden.[7] Moreover, in both manuscripts occurs the device to provide magical names (*voces*

---

[1] This part contains the columns 6–13 (Greek) and IV–I (Demotic) of the magical handbook and columns 1–12 of the *Myth of the Sun's Eye*.

[5] The London portion of the manuscript contains the columns 1–10 on the recto and 25–33 on the verso. Pleyte's discovery was published by Hess, who made a photographic edition of the London part in 1892: Hess, *Der gnostische Papyrus von London*, (Freiburg 1892).

[6] The name P. Magical is used in the Chicago Demotic Dictionary, see, Janet H. Johnson, 'Text Abbreviations Used by the Chicago Demotic Dictionary. Including all references cited as of June 20, 1988' *Enchoria* 21 (1994) 128–141.

[7] These versions are PGM XII.365–375; 453–465 and PGM XIVc.16–27. See chapter 4.4.3 for a detailed discussion.

2.1 Two 'cipher' alphabets (photo RMO, Leiden)

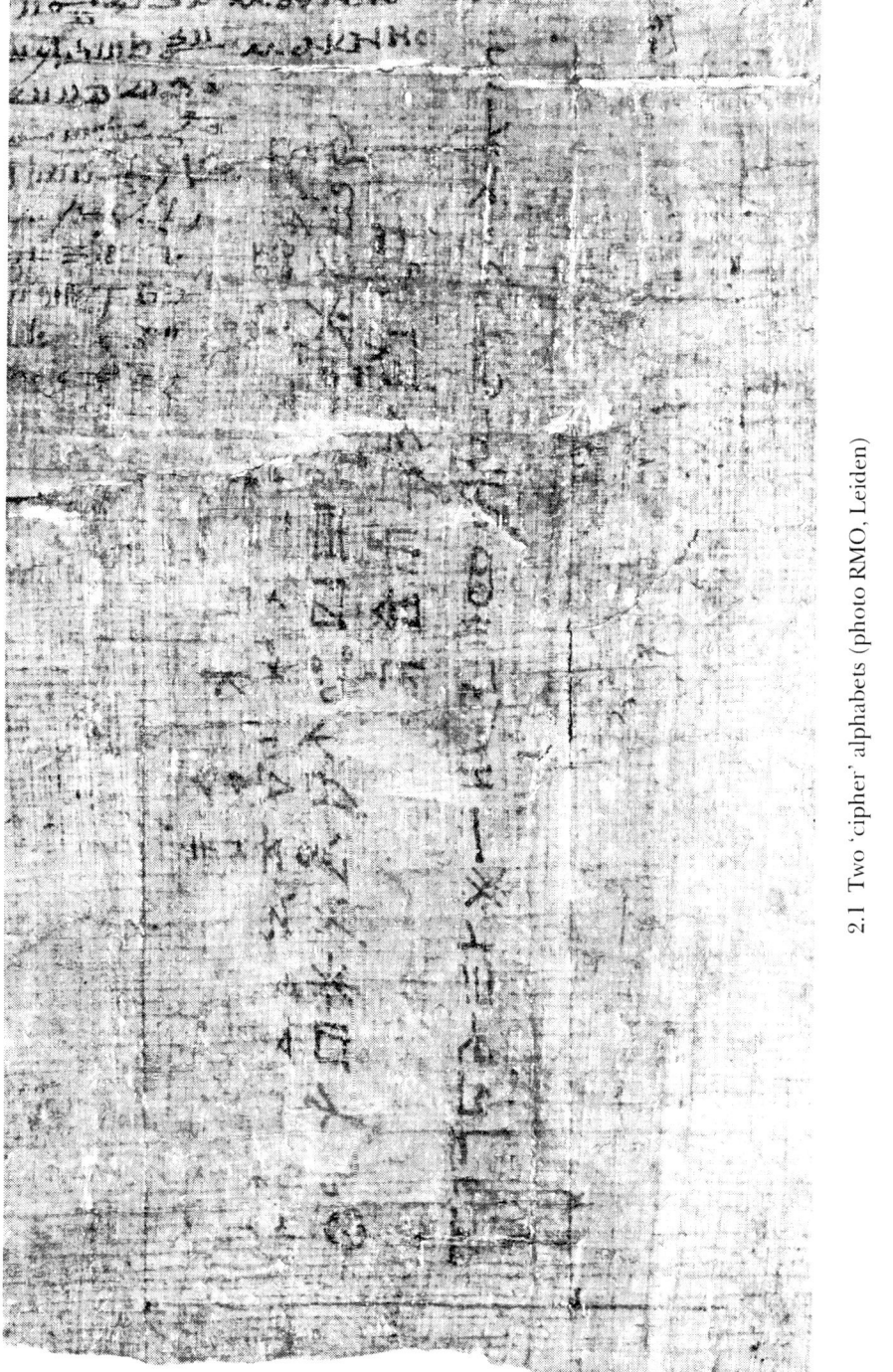

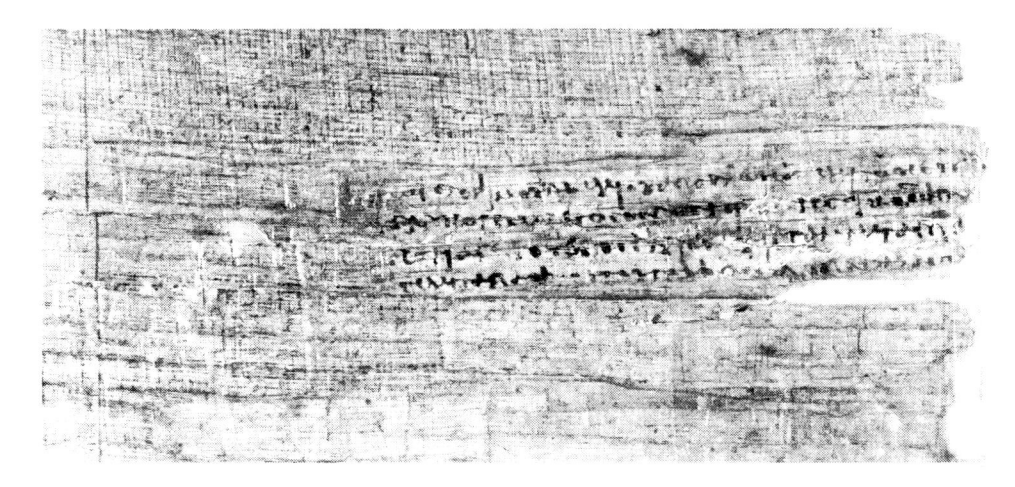

2.2 Scrap of papyrus pasted on the verso, under column 19, to London-Leiden manuscript; Leemans nr. 1 (photo RMO, Leiden)

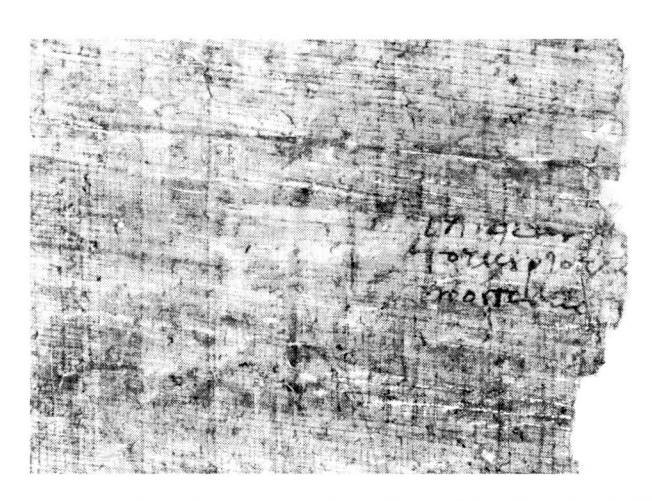

2.3 Scrap of papyrus pasted on the verso, under column 13, to London-Leiden manuscript; Leemans nr. 6 (photo RMO, Leiden)

*magicae*) written in alphabetic Demotic script with glosses above the line in Greek and Old-Coptic script as a means to ensure correct pronunciation.[8]

As C.J.C. Reuvens examined the first portion of P. Leiden I 384 in January 1829, he discovered within the folds of the manuscript papyrus fragments of about two columns that he thought belonged in fact to P. Leiden I 383, the Leiden portion of P. London-Leiden.[9] His guess was confirmed when the second half of P. Leiden I 384, which arrived about a year later in Leiden, happened to contain similar fragments within its folds that were undoubtedly part of P. Leiden I 383. These enfolded fragments led Reuvens to assume that the two manuscripts were actually found together, probably 383 enveloped within 384, but taken apart after their discovery and sold separately to Anastasi's agents in Luxor.[10] With Pleyte's discovery that P. Leiden I 383 forms with P. BM 10070 one large bilingual magical handbook, it has become further clear that, whoever discovered the two manuscripts, they took the scrolls apart, tore both into halves and sold the four separate parts as discrete manuscripts on three different occasions,[11] with the result that three parts ended up in Leiden and one in London.

The two manuscripts were in fact not only related at the phase of burial, but formed already a unity at the phase of compilation and

---

[8] The Old-Coptic glosses that are added above the magical names spelled in alphabetic Demotic signs were a convenient help for recitation, because the Old-Coptic script contains vowel signs unlike the Demotic script. In antiquity the glosses were meant to ensure correct pronunciation of the powerful names, whereas, in the nineteenth century, the glosses proved to be of considerable help in establishing the correct values of demotic signs.

[9] Reuvens, *Lettres à M. Letronne*, 6 and 145. Reuvens numbered the fragments provisionally as A(nastasi) 75a, because they were found within manuscript A 75 (=P. Leiden I 384).

[10] Reuvens, *Lettres à M. Letronne*, 145–148. P. Leiden I 384 was not rolled like P. Leiden I 383 but folded and could therefore very well have contained a papyrus roll between its sheets. Reuvens uses the image of a purse to explain the possible situation of the two manuscripts.

[11] The successive stages of the sales could possibly be reconstructed as follows. On the first occasion, sometime before 1828, the Leiden part of P. London-Leiden and the first half of P. Leiden I 384 were sold to Anastasi's agents. A little later, probably in 1828, the second half of P. Leiden I 384 was sold together with the Hermetic codex PGM XIII. Thereupon, Anastasi added both manuscripts as supplements to the collection that the National Museum of Antiquities in Leiden bought in 1828. The London part of P. London-Leiden came probably into Anastasi's possession between 1839, the second public auction, and 1857, the year of his death and the final auction in Paris, where the British Museum acquired the Demotic magical manuscript.

copying of the magical spells, since the Demotic sections are evidently written in the same scribal hand. A careful study of the orthography of the demotic and hieratic spellings reveals that the hands of P. London-Leiden and P. Leiden I 384 verso are identical to such an extent that the conclusion is warranted that the texts were written in the same workshop and in all likelihood even by the same scribe.[12] It is unclear whether this scribe wrote the Greek sections as well, albeit highly probable for practical reasons.[13] Whatever the case was, the scribe wrote also the Greek glosses above the *voces magicae* in the Demotic spells and it is clear that he had initially difficulties in finding a suitable method to transcribe the Demotic names, which are written from right to left, in Greek script which is read in the opposite direction, from left to right. Janet H. Johnson has argued convincingly that he decided from line 15 of Demotic column IV* of P. Leiden I 384 verso onwards to write the glosses in Greek characters from left to right above the Demotic magical names instead of putting the corresponding Greek letter immediately above the Demotic sign as he did in the previous lines.[14] Since this method is persistently applied in the following columns and in P. London-Leiden as well, it follows that P. London-Leiden must have been written sometime after P. Leiden I 384 verso.

The fact that the two manuscripts derive from the same workshop and were buried together in antiquity is highly significant in the light of a study that is concerned with the sphere of production and use of these manuscripts. On the one hand, it justifies viewing the two manuscripts as a subgroup within the Theban Magical Library and, on the other hand, it provides solid proof that the editors and owners of the two manuscripts, who might be identical, considered the magical spells to form a unity, despite the variety in language, script and style. In the phase of compilation and edition, the present spells were selected from an unknown but most likely a considerable number of magical spells available in Demotic and Greek and combined on two separate

---

[12] See for a detailed analysis: Johnson, 'The Demotic Magical Spells of Leiden J 384', 51–53, the glossary is on pages 54–64. Brashear ('The Greek Magical Papyri', 3404) states erroneously in his overview article of the *Greek Magical Papyri* that all Demotic magical handbooks were written by one and the same scribe: P. London-Leiden, P. Leiden I 384, P. BM 10588 (PGM LXI/PDM lxi) and P. Louvre 3229 (PDM Suppl.). This is however incorrect. The latter two manuscripts are unmistakably written in two distinct hands.

[13] The Greek sections are less homogeneous regarding orthography than the Demotic texts. At least three different hands can be identified.

[14] Johnson, 'The Demotic Magical Spells of Leiden J 384', 48–50.

papyrus scrolls, whereas, in the phase of use and burial, the manuscripts were carefully kept together. The question to be posed is thus: what were the criteria of inclusion and to whom did the result of the selection make sense?

### 2.3. *Description of the manuscripts and their textual contents*

#### 2.3.1. *P. Leiden I 384*

The manuscript that is nowadays catalogued in the National Museum of Antiquities in Leiden as P. Leiden I 384 contains on its recto side part of a mythological narrative in Demotic, known today as the *Myth of the Sun's Eye* or *Mythus*, and, on its verso, a bilingual (Demotic and Greek) magical handbook. The manuscript measures about 3,60 metres in length and 22 centimetres in height on average. Both the right and left side of the manuscript are broken and it is impossible to be certain about the number of columns missing on each side. When C.J.C. Reuvens examined the manuscript, he found six small papyrus fragments (a-f)[15] glued to the recto side as a means to repair small slits and reinforce the papyrus roll.[16] Since these fragments were carelessly placed over the Demotic writing of the mythological narrative, the manuscript must have been restored at a moment that the text of the *Myth of the Sun's Eye* was no longer of importance to the owner of the papyrus scroll. When the fragments were removed they appeared to contain Demotic writing on both sides, one side of which preserves writings that once had belonged to the broken last column of the mythological narrative. Reuvens noticed also that the recto side of the manuscript showed several effaced spots in the middle of its height caused by fingers unrolling the papyrus scroll while reading the obverse side.[17] These traces of use demonstrate that the magical handbook, which is on the verso, was regularly consulted in antiquity. As a conservation measure the manuscript was pasted between sheets of *papier végétal*,[18] which, despite Reuvens' good intentions, varnished and turned the papyrus dark and shiny in the course of several decades, with the

---

[15] Fragment c is nowadays broken into two small pieces between lines 8 and 9.
[16] Reuvens, *Lettres à M. Letronne*, 5.
[17] Reuvens, *op. cit.*, 4–5.
[18] Reuvens, *op. cit.*, 147, footnote (b).

result that the black and red ink are hard to read today. The lithography made by T. Hooiberg and published by Reuvens' successor Conrad Leemans in 1856 will therefore remain an important tool for the study of the Demotic sections.[19]

The recto side of the papyrus preserves 23 columns of the *Myth of the Sun's Eye* in a careful and trained Demotic hand written with a reed pen.[20] Each column is set between two vertical guidelines in black ink, a method only in use since the Roman period.[21] As the Demotic line surpasses regularly the ink border with a few signs, the scribe must have drawn the guidelines before he started copying the text itself. Of the first column only the left end of the lines are preserved, whereas the fragments that were pasted to the papyrus for strength contain parts of column 23, which was likely the final column of the composition. The text is written in black ink with the occasional use of red ink to indicate new chapters, a change of speakers in the narrative and directions for use of the voice meant for a reader who read the text aloud in front of an audience. Occasional editorial comments regarding alternative phrases demonstrate that the extant version is a compilation from several older versions that are lost.[22]

The *Myth of the Sun's Eye* is a complex narrative, set somewhere in Nubia, about a dog-ape, the animal of Thoth, who attempts to persuade the goddess Tefnut to leave Nubia and return to Egypt.[23] The goddess turned her back on Egypt, because she was angry with her father Re for reasons probably told in the missing opening columns. The dog-ape relates animal fables and explains proverbs in order to make the goddess recognize that each living being has its own particu-

---

[19] Conrad Leemans, *Papyrus égyptien démotique I. 384 du Musée d'Antiquités des Pays-Bas à Leide* (Leiden 1856). Because T. Hooiberg was not able to read Demotic, he traced the signs and the effaced spots as he saw them. The plates should therefore be used with caution.

[20] The standard edition of the text is still Wilhelm Spiegelberg, *Der ägyptische Mythus von Sonnenauge (der Papyrus der Tierfabeln—'Kufi') nach dem leidener demotischen Papyrus I 384* (Straßburg 1917) with a hand copy of the text by J.-J. Hess. Photos of the text can be found in: Françoise de Cenival, *Le mythe de l'oeil du soleil* (Demotische Studien 9; Sommerhausen 1988).

[21] See W.J. Tait, 'Guidelines and Borders in Demotic Papyri', in: M.L. Bierbrier (ed.), *Papyrus: Structure and Usage* (British Museum Occasional Papers 60; London 1986) 63–89.

[22] Spiegelberg, *Mythus*, 10.

[23] See for a general introduction to the text: Mark Smith, 'Sonnenauge, demotischer Mythos vom' *LdÄ* 5 (1984) 1082–1087.

lar place to live and that beautiful Egypt is her true home.[24] When the goddess acquiesces, turning from a fierce lioness into a friendly cat, and returns home, she is welcomed in Thebes and Memphis by hymns to her, the longest of which is preserved on column 22 and continues on the broken column 23, possibly the end of the composition. The *Myth of the Sun's Eye* was probably a popular text among Egyptian priests of the Roman period, since parts are preserved on two other manuscripts and a rather free translation in Greek of the second or third century CE is partly extant.[25] The underlying mythological theme about an angry goddess leaving for Nubia has pharaonic roots and is also treated in contemporary hieroglyphic temple texts in a number of temples situated in southern Egypt and Lower Nubia.[26]

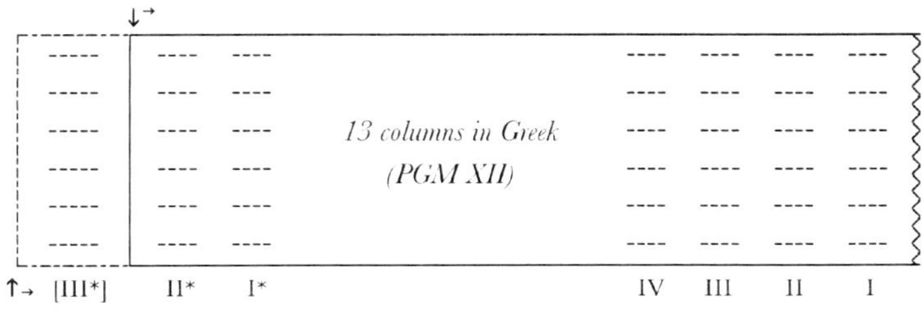

Fig. 2.4. P. Leiden I 384 verso: PDM xii & PGM XII

[24] See on the nationalistic motive: Edda Bresciani, 'L'Amore per il paese natio nel mito egiziano dell' 'Occhio del Sole' in demotico' *CRIPEL* 13 (1991) 35–38.

[25] A fragment, 2nd century CE, from the Tebtunis temple library preserves a version of the fable of the Seeing bird and the Hearing bird (= P. Leiden I 384 13/24–15/28): W.J. Tait, 'A Duplicate Version of the Demotic *Kufi* Text' *AcOr* 36 (1974) 23–37; see also Idem, 'The Fable of Sight and Hearing in the Demotic *Kufi* Text' *AcOr* 37 (1976) 27–44. The University of Lille possesses fragments of another manuscript, likewise dated to the second century CE, that is of unknown provenance, possibly the Fayum: Françoise de Cenival, 'Les nouveaux fragments du mythe de l'oeil du soleil de l'Institut de Papyrologie et d'Egyptologie de Lille' *CRIPEL* 7 (1985) 95–115 and Idem, 'Les titres des couplets du Mythe' *CRIPEL* 11 (1989) 141–146. See for the Greek translation: Stephanie West, 'The Greek Version of the Legend of Tefnut' *JEA* (1969) 161–183; the Greek text can also be found in: Maria Totti, *Ausgewählte Texte der Isis- und Sarapis-Religion* (Subsidia Epigraphica 12; Hildesheim 1985) 168–182. The Demotic and Greek text are compared in: M.C. Betrò, 'L'alchimia delle traduzioni: Il *Mito del Occhio del Sole* e il P.BM Inv. No. 274', in: *Atti del XVII congresso internazionale di papirologia* 3 vols. (Naples 1984) vol. 3, 1355–1360.

[26] See Hermann Junker, 'Auszug der Hathor-Tefnut aus Nubien' *AkPAW* (Berlin 1911) appendix 3; Idem, *Die Onurislegende* (DAW Wien 59/1–2; Vienna 1917), the Demotic text is discussed on pages 162–165; Danielle Inconnu-Bocquillon, *Le mythe de la Déesse Lointaine à Philae* (BdE 132; Cairo 2001). Note that the Demotic version of the myth is remarkably absent from the latter publication.

The verso side of the manuscript preserves a diverse collection of magical spells in Demotic and Greek. In its present state the manuscript consists of 13 consecutive columns in Greek set between two Demotic columns on the left side and four Demotic columns, which incorporate two Greek invocations and several *voces magicae* in Greek letters, on the right side. The verso side of the fragments that were pasted to the manuscript for reinforcement have so far been neglected in the study of the spells. However, this negligence is unjustified, because a careful inspection of the small and effaced fragments reveals that the Demotic writing is identical to the Demotic hand of the magical spells.[27] The fragments could hence be remnants of another column of Demotic spells (column III*) that preceded the extant Demotic column II*. Oddly enough, when the fragments are put into place in accordance with the *Myth of the Sun's Eye* on the obverse side,[28] the reconstructed column III* stands upside down in relation to the other magical columns. This can only be explained by assuming that the scribe of the magical spells started his work with writing the Demotic column III* on the far right end of the manuscript as is customary for Egyptian papyrus scrolls.[29] After finishing the column he realised that it would be difficult to fit in the many Greek spells that are read in the opposite direction. As a solution he turned the papyrus scroll 180 degrees and started to copy the Greek spells in consecutive columns from left to right, eventually filling 13 columns. Subsequently he added two Demotic columns on the left side and four (or more) other Demotic columns on the right side, which, contrary to Egyptian custom, have to be read from left to right like the Greek columns. Janet H. Johnson was able to establish the consecutive order of the Demotic columns with the help of the shift in

---

[27] Line 6 of fragment c preserves the word *wnw.t*, 'hour', in a spelling that occurs in P. London-Leiden 4/21, 25/26, 37 as well; see F.Ll. Griffith and Herbert Thompson, *The Demotic Magical Papyrus of London and Leiden* 3 vols. (Oxford 1921) vol. 3, 20, nr. 199 (third spelling).

[28] Fragment a is especially helpful in reconstructing the position of the fragments, because, although just a thin strip, it preserves the beginning of each line of the *Myth's* broken column 23. These lines open with the interrogative particle *ìn*, thus continuing the hymn to the returning goddess of the previous column 22.

[29] It is very likely that the fragments preserve the last or second last column of the *Myth of the Sun's Eye*, because they contain a hymn sung to the goddess at the moment that she returns from Nubia in Memphis where her father Pre, the sun god, awaited her. If this were correct, the column of the obverse side of the fragments would be the first or second column of the verso of the manuscript, counted from its left side.

the method for glossing the *voces magicae*.[30] Contrary to Leemans, who had numbered the Demotic columns from right to left in accordance with standard Egyptian practice (I, II, III, IV -to the right of the Greek columns- and I*, II* -to the left of the Greek columns-), the true order of the columns is II*, I* and IV, III, II, I, with column III* upside down preceding column II*.[31] This shows that the scribe of the magical spells started out with a traditional Egyptian layout, but quickly changed his mind and gave preference to a Greek layout, probably for practical reasons only.

The columns of the verso side are written only in black ink without the help of guidelines. Several spells are headed by a title, either written in the middle of an empty line above the spell or directly connected with the first line of the recipe itself. In three cases, a title in Demotic is added to a recipe in Greek that contains a Greek title as well.[32] A spell to foretell by way of numerology whether a sick person will die or recover from her or his ailment (PGM XII.351–364) is followed by a diagram with numbers, the so-called 'Demokritos' sphere' (Greek column 11). Four times a recipe is provided with a sketchy drawing that should be copied in the course of a ritual: a divine figure sitting on a throne (Greek column 12; fig. 2.2),[33] a standing Seth animal holding two spears (Demotic column IV; fig. 2.3),[34] Anubis standing at the mummy's bier (Demotic column I, top; fig. 2.4)[35] and a figure standing on a basket (Demotic column I, bottom; fig. 2.5).[36] The style and iconography are unmistakably Egyptian despite their somewhat clumsy character.[37] The

---

[30] Johnson, 'The Demotic Magical Spells of Leiden J 384', 48–50.
[31] Since the extant manuscript is not complete, it is very well possible that other columns were written to the right of column I. It would therefore be correct to number the preserved columns as x+IV, x+III, x+II, x+I, but, since the present numbering system is well-established among scholars of today, this numbering is not used in the book.
[32] PGM XII.201–269; 270–350; 365–375. See chapter 5.1 for more details.
[33] PGM XII.376–396.
[34] PDM xii.62–75 [PGM XII.449–452].
[35] PDM xii.135–146 [PGM XII.474–479].
[36] This drawing is badly preserved and only the basket can be clearly recognised. The standing figure is drawn in side view and represents possibly a mummified deity. The drawing is not given in *GMPT*; it is part of spell PDM xii 147–164 [PGM XII.480–495].
[37] The quality of the drawings can certainly not stand the test with vignettes of the Book of the Dead, but such sketchy drawings were not uncommon in magical texts of the pharaonic period. See for examples Peter Eschweiler, *Bildzauber im Alten Ägypten. Die Verwendung von Bildern und Gegenständen in magischen Handlungen nach den Texten des Mittleren und Neuen Reiches* (OBO 137; Freiburg and Göttingen 1994) plates 1–5.

representation of Anubis standing at the mummy's bier continues in fact a tradition in funerary iconography of more than 1500 years.[38]

Fig. 2.5. Figure sitting on stool

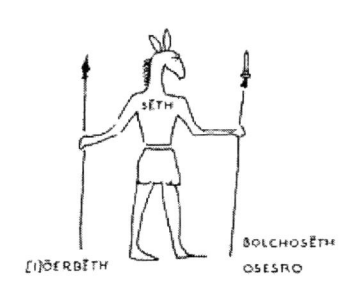

Fig. 2.6. Seth holding two spears

Fig. 2.7. Anubis standing at the mummy bier

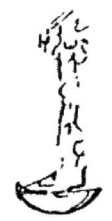

Fig. 2.8. Figure (Osiris?) standing on basket

Both the Demotic and Greek spells show a sophisticated use of script. The Greek spells are written in standardised Greek script, but abbreviated spellings, symbols and paragraph markers are frequently used

---

[38] This drawing was a popular image in Egyptian funerary culture from the New Kingdom until the Roman period. The image derives from the vignette to spell 151 of the Book of the Dead and retained its standard iconography in the course of its long history of transmission and adaptation. In the Greco-Roman period, the image could occur on sarcophagi, mummy masks, mummy wrappings, tomb walls, steles and, as a vignette to religious texts, on papyrus. See for a short description: Barbara Lüscher, *Untersuchungen zu Totenbuch Spruch 151* (SAT 2; Wiesbaden 1998) 31–33. Note that this particular drawing is actually a mirror image of the common representation: Anubis and the mummy's head are facing to the left instead of to the right. A similar mirrored image can be found on the north wall of the burial chamber of Sennedjem in Deir el-Medineh (19th dynasty): Abdel Ghaffar Shedid, *Das Grab des Sennedjem. Ein Künstlergrab der 19. Dynastie in Deir el-Medineh* (Mainz 1994), the image is on page 74, an overview of the tomb on pages 30 and 31. One of the latest examples is found

throughout the texts. The main Greek columns and the short Greek sections embedded in the Demotic spells are in the same hand. The Demotic script shows an intricate mixing with hieratic signs, while words or phrases in hieratic are occasionally intertwined with Demotic clauses, especially so in divine epithets. The *voces magicae* are spelled in alphabetic demotic signs and provided with glosses in Greek letters starting from Demotic column IV*. In the preceding Demotic column II the *voces magicae* are written either in alphabetic demotic or in Greek letters. It is customary to say that the *voces magicae* are actually written or glossed in Old-Coptic script instead of in Greek letters,[39] but the spellings of P. Leiden I 384 do not yet contain additional Demotic signs like the Old-Coptic glosses in P. London-Leiden. This may add further proof that P. London-Leiden was written after P. Leiden I 384 verso: in P. Leiden I 384 verso the scribe was not only experimenting with the writing direction of the glosses, he had also not yet determined the precise set of signs for the glosses. One Greek spell (PGM XII.397–400) contains a series of *charaktêres*, fanciful magical signs that were deemed very powerful, and in one case a Demotic recipe prescribes an ingredient written in cipher (IV/2).

The manuscript contains in total 29 magical spells, of which 19 are in Greek, 8 in Demotic and 2 partly in Demotic and partly in Greek. The recipes are concerned with such diverse topics as divination, magical rings, alchemy, love spells of attraction and separation, sending dreams, procuring a divine assistant and foretelling a sick person's fate. An overview of the spells is given in appendix 2.1 to this chapter.

2.3.2. *P. London-Leiden*

The magical handbook that is today generally known as P. London-Leiden preserves an extensive and varied collection of magical spells, which were grouped together without apparent order. The extant papyrus measures about 5 metres in length and 24 cm in height on average. Unfortunately, its original length can no longer be determined because

---

in Petosiris' tomb in Qaret el-Muzawwaqa (Dachleh oasis), 2nd century AD: Ahmed Fakhry, *Denkmäler der Oase Dachla* (Archäologische Veröffentlichungen des DAIs 28; Mainz 1982) Plates 26b, 28a, 29b, 33c. The image occurs in Greco-Egyptian style in the central burial chamber of the Kom el-Shuqafa catacombs in Alexandria: Jean-Yves Empereur, *Alexandria Rediscovered* (London 1998) 164.

[39] Johnson, 'The Demotic Magical Spells of Leiden I 384', 48–51.

both beginning and end are lost. It preserves 29 columns of text on its recto side and 33 short columns on its verso, the sequence of which runs from right to left according to standard Egyptian usage. The London part of the manuscript has columns 1–10 on the recto and columns 25–33 on the verso, whereas the larger Leiden part contains the remaining columns 10–29 on the recto and 1–24 on the verso. The columns of the verso are short and tend to cluster in small groups that are randomly distributed along the length of the papyrus roll. They occupy only the top of the page leaving the middle and bottom remarkably empty, which was possibly meant as a precaution against fingers rubbing the text when the scroll is held in the middle of its height at the moment that a person consults the recto side.[40] At several places of the verso, small scraps of papyrus, occasionally with effaced Greek or Demotic writing, are pasted to the manuscript for reinforcement.[41] Since the Leiden part was pasted between sheets of *papier végétal*, which turned the papyrus rather dark and shiny, the London part is in a better state of preservation.

Before the scribe started copying the spells he had selected, he drew two horizontal guidelines in black ink along the top and bottom of the manuscript and, until column 14, divided the manuscript up into neat squares by drawing vertical borders in black ink at a fairly regular distance.[42] Despite these preparations, he crossed the guidelines frequently as he copied the spells. The Demotic hand is consistent throughout the manuscript and identical with the Demotic hand of P. Leiden 384 verso. However, the Greek hand differs considerably from the one in P. Leiden 384 verso. The hand is much more careful, avoids ligatures and renders the letters slightly bigger; it is almost like a literary book hand.[43] The text is written in black ink with red ink reserved for headings, numbers, structuring key words that indicate the start of a recipe or invoca-

---

[40] Reuvens, *Lettres à M. Letronne*, 4–5.

[41] The scraps with writing that were attached to the Leiden part can be consulted in facsimile in Conrad Leemans, *Papyrus égyptien à transcriptions grecques du Musée d'Antiquités des Pays-Bas à Leide (Description raisonnée I 383)* 2 vols. (Leiden 1839) plate 14, nrs. 1–2 and 4–7.

[42] From column 15 onwards the vertical borders are generally missing, although they reappear between columns 27 and 28 and between columns 28 and 29. The horizontal guidelines are missing for the columns 24 to 26.

[43] Note that the hand of the Greek invocation of column 4/9–19 [PGM XIVa.1–11] differs slightly in appearance from the Greek invocations of 15/25–28 [PGM XIVb.12–15] and 23/9–20 [PGM XIVc.16–27].

tion,[14] and verse points.[15] Although the verse points were carefully copied onto T. Hooiberg's facsimile of 1839 and Herbert Thompson's hand copy of 1921, they never attracted scholarly attention despite the fact that their function within the manuscript is far from self-evident. Their presence is remarkable, since the application of verse points seems to be a rather marginal phenomenon in Demotic texts,[16] in contrast to their abundant appearance in hieratic texts of the pharaonic period.[17] Moreover, they are applied in the invocations, which are poetically structured to some degree, as well as in the rather mundane and straightforward recipe-like prescriptions to the rituals.[18] It is noteworthy that they occur only on the recto and are not even consistently applied there.[19]

The base language of the manuscript is Demotic, but at three occasions a short invocation in Greek is inserted between the Demotic lines of a recipe. In another case, a spell is said to be in Nubian and spelled in alphabetic Demotic signs. The Demotic script shows an intricate mixing with hieratic signs, while complete words or word groups in hieratic are frequently incorporated within Demotic clauses. The *voces*

---

[14] These key words are *ḏd mdw.t*, 'words to recite', or *pꜣ ꜥš nty-i-ir=k ꜥš=f*, 'the spell that you have to recite', at the start of an invocation, and *pꜣy=f swḥ-iḫ*, 'its gathering of things / preparation' at the start of a recipe.

[15] Verse points or *Gliederungspunkte* are dots in red ink set at regular intervals above the line. They are attested in Egyptian manuscripts since the 12th dynasty and were probably used as a device to structure a text in semantic units, since they always appear at the end of a (subordinate) clause. They appear mainly in texts of a poetic nature, although not exclusively. Since a number of texts are provided with verse points in one manuscript and lack verse points in the other, it has been suggested that verse points were used only by students. This is however very unlikely in the light of the available evidence. The exact meaning and function of the verse points remain therefore a matter of debate. See: Günter Burkard, 'Der formale Aufbau altägyptischer Literaturwerke: Zur Problematik der Erschliessung seiner Grundstrukturen' *SAK* 10 (1983), 79–118 and Nikolaus Tacke, *Verspunkte als Gliederungsmittel in ramessidischen Schülerhandschriften* (SAGA 22; Heidelberg 2001) 146-171.

[16] The only presently known example is *The Harpist's Song*. In the extant version of this composition each verse line is split up in two units by two dots in red above the line; see: Heinz-J. Thissen, *Der verkommene Harfenspieler. Eine altägyptische Invektive (P. Wien KM 3877)* (Demotische Studien 11; Sommerhausen 1992).

[17] Verse points are particularly common in literary and didactic texts of the New Kingdom.

[18] This phenomenon occurs at times also in magical texts of the New Kingdom; for example, P. BM EA 9997+10309, P. BM EA 10042 (Harris Magical Papyrus), P. Turin CG 1966, 1993, 1995, 1996, P. Chester Beatty VII.

[19] The verse points are only applied in columns 1, 2, 3 (lines 1–20), 5 (lines 3–24), 6, 7, 8 (lines 1–11), 12 (lines 15–18), 14, 15 (lines 1–20), 16, 17, 24, 25, 27, 28, 29 (lines 6–16).

*magicae* are spelled in alphabetic Demotic signs and, in the majority of cases, provided with glosses written in Old-Coptic, a script that consists of the Greek alphabet and a few additional Demotic signs to render sounds that the Greek alphabet does not provide.[50] Several sections of the manuscript contain a fair number of words written in an encrypted script, generally referred to as 'cipher', which is otherwise unattested outside the Demotic magical papyri.[51] Two sets of another encrypted script are found on the verso side written within a rectangular frame of three thin lines in black ink (fig. 2.6–7).[52] It is evident that both sets encrypt the Greek alphabet, because the first set contains the corresponding Greek letter above each sign as a transcription key and the second set consists of 24 signs, the total number of signs of the Greek alphabet. Except for four random signs, neither of these sets contains encrypted signs that are used in the spells, so that it remains a mystery to what aim they were written on the backside of the manuscript.[53]

---

[50] See on the development of the Coptic language and script out of ancient Egyptian: Daniel R. McBride, 'The Development of Coptic: Late-Pagan Language of Synthesis in Egypt' *JSSEA* 19 (1989) 89–111; Jan Quaegebeur, 'De la préhistoire de l'écriture copte' *OLP* 13 (1982) 125–136; David Frankfurter, *Religion in Roman Egypt. Assimilation and Resistance* (Princeton 1998) 248–256.

[51] P. Leiden 384 verso contains one word in cipher (IV/2) and P. Louvre 3229 one as well (2/25). This is very meagre when compared with the 93 words in cipher of P. London-Leiden.

[52] The frame with the set of signs is located in the middle of the page under the verso columns 1 and 2. Strangely enough, it is written at right angles in relation to the Demotic columns at the top of the page. See for a facsimile of this text: Leemans, *Papyrus égyptien à transcriptions grecques*, plate 14, nr. 3. The signs are also treated in Jean Doresse, 'Cryptographie copte et cryptographie grecque' *Bulletin de l'Institut d'Égypte* 33 (1952) 115–129, 224 and table III.

[53] For these four signs, see, Griffith, Thompson, *The Demotic Magical Papyrus of London and Leiden*, vol. 3, 108.

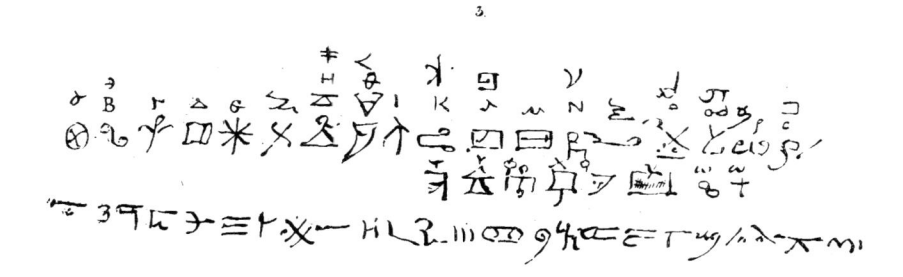

Fig. 2.9. Facsimile of two 'cipher' alphabets, Leemans nr. 3

The extant collection of spells is clearly the result of one or several phases of compilation and editing. In two cases a recipe refers to an invocation that is actually not given in the manuscript and must therefore, in all likelihood, have been forgotten in the course of editing and copying the texts.[54] In a few cases complete sections recur slightly changed in different spells demonstrating that spells were recycled and adapted at a certain moment during the phase of compilation and editing.[55] Editorial comments like 'otherwise said' (*ky dd*) and 'according to another manuscript' (*ky dmꜥ*) followed by alternative words or phrases occur regularly and are evenly distributed over the texts. They reveal that the copyist made use of several older manuscripts that could differ from each other in wording and prescribed ingredients. In one case, a recipe does not give the words of a prayer, but merely refers to it by giving its title in a mix of Demotic and hieratic: 'You have to recite the writings of *Adoring Re in the Morning at his Rising*' (6/3; PDM xiv 153).

The manuscript contains 98 spells in total, of which 5 are merely short lists and descriptions of plants, minerals and a salamander. The

---

[54] In 22/1–5 [PDM xiv.670–674] a powerful spell is recommended without the spell being given. After line 5 the column is empty as if the copyist initially meant to include the spell but forgot about it. A prescription for a lamp divination [PDM xiv.805–840] orders the practitioner to recite 'this spell in Greek' (27/35) without giving the Greek spell.

[55] Clear examples are 1/13–16 = V27/1–8 [PDM xiv 12–17 = 1172–1179]; 5/11–20 = 7/8–15 = 17/1–7 [PDM xiv 127–137 = 194–204 = 489–499]; 10/22–35 = 27/1–12 [PDM xiv 295–306 = 805–816]. The fancy hieroglyphs of column 5 recur in columns 6 and 27.

thematic scope of the recipes is varied, although spells for vessel or lamp divination clearly dominate. Other topics are love spells (both attraction and separation), dream sending, spells for charm and success and medicinal recipes for bites of poisonous animals, eye diseases and gout. An overview of the spells can be found in Appendix 2.2 to this chapter.

## 2.4. *Provenance*

According to the scarce information provided by Anastasi's catalogue, P. Leiden I 383 was acquired in Luxor.[56] There is no information about the provenance of P. BM 10070, the London part, and of P. Leiden I 384, but, since the two manuscripts were buried together, it follows automatically that both P. London-Leiden and P. Leiden I 384 were found somewhere in the Luxor region. For two reasons it is highly likely that the manuscripts were composed in the same region as where they were found in the 19th century. First, the orthography and grammar of the Demotic spells is very similar to the hand and grammar of the so-called *Demotic Gardening Agreement*, a little understood composition written on the outer surface of a small jar that was found *in situ* in the temple of Medinet Habu.[57] Second, Janet H. Johnson studied the phonetic relationship between the Old-Coptic renderings of the *voces magicae* and their transcription in alphabetic Demotic script and concluded that the vocalised glosses show signs of a Theban dialect (Coptic dialect P).[58] According to Helmut Satzinger, the language of the manuscript is rather an archaic Achmimic, a Coptic dialect spoken between Aswan and Akhmim, with Thebes as place of origin.[59] Since the *Myth of the Sun's Eye* shows characteristics of a southern dialect as

---

[56] Reuvens, *Lettres à M. Letronne*, 4.

[57] Richard A. Parker, 'A Late Demotic Gardening Agreement. Medinet Habu Ostracon 4038' *JEA* 26 (1940) 84–113. See also Janet H. Johnson, 'The Dialect of the Demotic Magical Papyrus of London and Leiden', in: *Studies in Honor of George R. Hughes* (SAOC 39; Chicago 1976) 105–132, 107–109.

[58] Johnson, 'The Dialect of the Demotic Magical Papyrus of London and Leiden'. For Coptic dialect P (= P. Bodmer VI), see, Rodolphe Kasser, 'Dialect P (or Proto-Theban)' *The Coptic Encyclopedia* 8 (1991) 82a–87b.

[59] Helmut Satzinger, 'Die altkoptischen Texte als Zeugnisse der Beziehungen zwischen Ägypten und Griechen', in: Peter Nagel (ed.), *Graeco-Coptica. Griechen und Kopten im byzantinischen Ägypten* (halle 1984) 137–146, 143; see also fn. 22. For the Akhmimic dialect, see, Peter Nagel, 'Akhmimic' *The Coptic Encyclopedia* 8 (1991) 19a–27b.

well, the manuscripts were clearly a product of the Theban region.[60] The identification of Thebes as place of origin may be corroborated by the occurrence in P. London-Leiden of the deities Montu, Khonsu and Opet, who were particularly prominent as objects of cult in the Theban region, among the otherwise rather 'national' gods as Osiris, Isis, Nephthys, Anubis and Thoth[61]

## 2.5. *Date*

There are unfortunately no extra-textual or absolute dating criteria available to date the two manuscripts under study. The spells do not contain dates, names of rulers, nor references to historical events that would help to situate the spells and the manuscripts in a more precise historical context. As a consequence, one has to resort to grammar and palaeography to establish a relative date for respectively the spells and the manuscripts. It remains problematic to date by palaeography the phase of copying the extant spells onto the manuscript, because the Greek hands show very few distinctive criteria and the palaeography of Demotic hands of the Roman period is still far from precise.[62] The hieratic signs and words interspersed with the Demotic are neither of help in establishing a date for the Egyptian hand.[63] P. London-Leiden

---

[60] Spiegelberg, *Der ägyptische Mythus vom Sonnenauge*, 380–382.

[61] Montu: P. London-Leiden 9/20, 10/26, 27/5. Khonsu: P. London-Leiden 9/1; Opet: 6/18, 19. The 'national' gods occur frequently throughout the manuscript. Note also that the god Imhotep is mentioned in a spell's title to validate the rite's efficacy (P. London-Leiden 4/1 = PDM xiv 93–114 [PGM XIVa.1–11]) and invoked as god of medicine (P. Leiden I 384 verso I*/1–29 = PDM xii.21–49). Although this god originated in Memphis, his cult was very popular in Thebes during the Greco-Roman period; László Kákosy, 'Probleme der Religion im römerzeitlichen Ägypten' *ANRW* II 18.5 (1995) 2894–3049, 2973–2977.

[62] A major impediment in establishing a precise palaeography of Roman Demotic is the fact that there are few literary texts and that the geographical range of provenance of the texts is too wide. It is practically impossible to trace the development of Demotic hands for Roman Thebes, because the number of sources is far too few.

[63] The hieratic palaeography of P. London-Leiden can conveniently be studied in B.H. Stricker, 'Het grafisch systeem van de magische papyrus Londen & Leiden' *OMRO* 36 (1955) 92–132. The hieratic signs are certainly close in form to the hieratic hands of a number of the Theban Books of Breathing, which are usually dated to the first and second century CE. However, Roman dates are now seriously challenged for certain of these manuscripts in favour of a Ptolemaic date; see, Jan Quaegebeur, 'Books of Thoth Belonging to Owners of Portraits? On Dating Late Hieratic Funerary Papyri', in: M.L. Bierbrier, *Portraits and Masks. Burial Customs in Roman Egypt* (London 1997) 72–77.

is generally dated to the third century CE by the palaeography of the three short Greek invocations.[64] However, the Greek hand of P. Leiden I 384 verso has until now been dated to the first half of the fourth century.[65] Strangely enough, no scholar has yet drawn attention to the fact that it is very unlikely that, given the unity of the manuscripts, the Greek hands diverge considerably in date. In fact, as the glosses written above the *voces magicae* in the Demotic spells demonstrate, P. Leiden I 384 verso should have been written *before* instead of several decades *after* P. London-Leiden.

A *terminus post quem* for the magical spells is provided by the Demotic *Myth of the Sun's Eye*, which is written on the recto of P. Leiden I 384 and must therefore be prior to the magical spells on its verso. The Demotic hand of the narrative is generally dated by palaeography to the beginning of the second century CE.[66] This means that the spells were copied onto the verso side of the discarded manuscript P. Leiden I 384 not earlier than the beginning of the second century CE. The small written scraps of papyrus that were pasted for reinforcement to the verso side of P. London-Leiden could indicate approximately when the papyrus roll was in use.[67] Although the writing is effaced and difficult to read, a date in the first half of the third century CE seems secure, although late second century CE cannot be ruled out (Fig.2.8–11).[68]

---

[64] F.Ll. Griffith, 'The Date of the Old Coptic Texts and their Relation to Christian Coptic' *ZÄS* 39 (1901) 78–82, 78 and 80; Griffith, Thompson, *The Demotic Magical Papyrus of London and Leiden*, 10. *GMPT*, xxiii gives the third century CE as date.

[65] Preisendanz, *Papyri Graecae Magicae*, vol. 2, 57 gives 300–350 CE. In the recent photographic edition of PGM XII, the editor followed Preisendanz' suggestion: Robert Daniel, *Two Greek Magical Papyri in the National Museum of Antiquities in Leiden. A Photographic Edition of J 384 and J 395 (= PGM XII and XIII)* (Papyrologica Coloniensia 19; Cologne 1990) x. *GMPT*, xxiii gives the fourth century CE as date.

[66] Spiegelberg, *Der ägyptische Mythus vom Sonnenauge*, 1. Françoise de Cenival dates the hand to around 100 CE: 'Obscurités et influences dans le Mythe de l'Oeil du Soleil', in: Kim Ryholt (ed.), *Acts of the Seventh International Conference of Demotic Studies* (CNI Publications 27; Copenhagen 2002) 39–43, 39.

[67] These two fragments are nrs. 1 and 6 in Leemans, *Papyrus égyptien à transcriptions grecques*, plate 14.

[68] For matters of Greek palaeography I rely heavily on the expertise of Klaas A. Worp and Robert W. Daniel. I thank them for their willingness to discuss with me the dating of the hands. In fragment 1, line 2, the group τοῦ κυρίου is clearly visible. In fragment 6 the phrase -μου δικαίου Ἀπόλλωνός can be read in line 1; the word γράμματα occurs at the end of line 3.

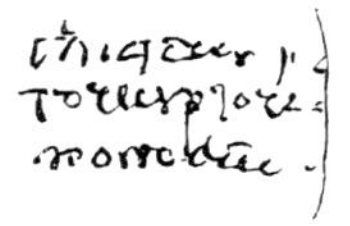

Fig. 2.10. Facsimile of scrap of papyrus pasted on the
verso to London-Leiden manuscript, Leemans nr. 1

It remains unclear whether the scraps were pasted to the papyrus before or after the spells were copied, but, since P. London-Leiden does not show any signs of being a palimpsest, it is conceivable that the scraps were applied when the magical handbook had already been in use for several years. This would mean that the spells of P. London-Leiden were copied onto the papyrus roll sometime in the late second or early third century CE. If this were correct, it follows that P. Leiden I 384 verso has to be dated to this period likewise instead of to the second half of the fourth century as has been customary until now. The palaeography of the Greek hands of the spells of P. Leiden I 384 verso and P. London-Leiden does certainly not exclude such an early dating.[69] It is therefore justified to conclude that the manuscripts were copied sometime after the beginning of the second century CE (*Myth of the Sun's Eye*) and before 250 CE at the latest (papyrus fragments), in all likelihood sometime at the turn of the second to the third century CE.[70]

---

[69] I thank Robert W. Daniel and Fabian Reiter for discussing with me the palaeography of the Greek hands of P. Leiden I 384 verso and P. London-Leiden. The Greek hands of the manuscripts are similar but not identical. Both can nonetheless be dated to the second half of the second century or early third century CE.

[70] This date does not conflict with the date of the *Demotic Gardening Agreement*. Like the two manuscripts under study, the *Demotic Gardening Agreement* can only be dated by palaeography. Parker has suggested that the text contains a *terminus post quem* in the phrase 'I will give [the gold pieces; jd] to you in gold of the infamous(?) queen, "Old Woman"' (C, 5–7). This would refer to gold pieces with the head of queen Zenobia of Palmyra, who invaded and gained control over Egypt in 271 CE. Parker argues that native Egyptians saw the queen as a conqueror and therefore called her an infamous queen. However, it is very unlikely that the phrase refers to coins minted in the days of Zenobia, because she never issued gold coins. In fact, the only gold coins with the head of a queen that were minted in Egypt date to the period between Ptolemy II and Ptolemy VI (285–145 BCE). The phrase refers probably to gold coins with the head of Arsinoe II, Arsinoe III, Berenike II or Cleopatra I, which were already old when this Roman-period text was written, but far more solid than the contemporary

6.

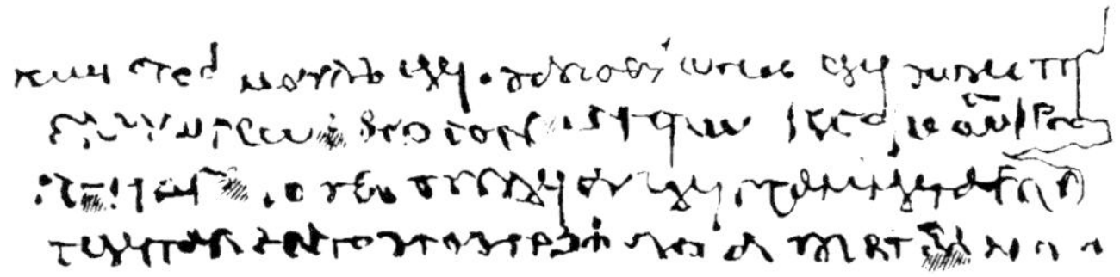

Fig. 2.11. Facsimile of scrap of papyrus pasted on the verso to London-Leiden manuscript, Leemans nr. 6

A date for the phase of composition of the spells can be gained from the grammar of the Demotic spells. The verbal paradigm of the Demotic spells displays certain distinctive 'late' features that do not yet occur in Demotic texts of the Ptolemaic period, but point already ahead to the Coptic verbal system.[71] This means that the extant spells must have been composed sometime in the Roman period, possibly not earlier than the late first or early second century CE. This would mean that the phase of compilation and editing of the extant spells lasted about a hundred years.

### 2.6. *Facsimiles and photos*

Due to its bilingual character the magical handbook of P. Leiden I 384 verso has never been published as a coherent manuscript. The Demotic sections were first published in lithography in 1856: Conrad Leemans, *Papyrus égyptien démotique I. 384 du Musée d'Antiquités des Pays-Bas à Leide* (Leiden 1856), plates 226–227. Photos of these columns, albeit hard to read due to the darkened *papier végétal*, are now available in: Janet H. Johnson, 'The Demotic Magical Spells of Leiden I 384' *OMRO* 56 (1975) 29–64. The Greek columns were first published in lithography as Papyrus V in: Conrad Leemans, *Papyri Graeci Musei Antiquarii Publici*

---

coins, which hardly contained precious metal. F.M. Heichelheim, 'On Medinet Habu Ostracon 4038' *JEA* 27 (1941) 161. See on the Ptolemaic gold coins: Susan Walker and Peter Higgs, *Cleopatra of Egypt from History to Myth* (London 2001) 83–84.

[71] Significant 'late' grammatical features are the general use of periphrastic verb forms and the occasional use of the progressive formed of the present tense, a qualitative of the verb *nj/nꜣ*, 'to go', and infinitive, which developed into the ϥ-ⲚⲀ-ⲤⲰⲦⲘ paradigm in Coptic. Johnson, *The Demotic Verbal System*, 4, footnote 14 and 94–99.

*Lugduni Batavi* Tomus II (Leiden 1885). Photos with transcriptions can nowadays be consulted in: Robert W. Daniel, *Two Greek Magical Papyri in the National Museum of Antiquities in Leiden. A Photographic Edition of J 384 and J 395 (= PGM XII and XIII)* (Papyrologica Coloniensia 19; Cologne 1990).

P. Leiden I 383, the Leiden part of P. London-Leiden, was first published in: Conrad Leemans, *Papyrus égyptien à transcriptions grecques du Musée d'Antiquités des Pays-Bas à Leide (Description raisonnée I 383)* 2 vols. (Leiden 1839). The London part, P. BM 10070, is available in a photographic edition: J.J. Hess, *Der gnostische Papyrus von London* (London 1892). The complete manuscript can be consulted in an exemplary hand copy made by Herbert Thompson: F.Ll. Griffith and Herbert Thompson, *The Demotic Magical Papyrus of London and Leiden* 3 vols. (Oxford 1904–1909). A photo of columns 4–7 can be found in Richard Parkinson, *Cracking Codes. The Rosetta Stone and Decipherment* (Berkeley and Los Angeles 1999) 101. A photo of column 15 is available in Maarten J. Raven, *Papyrus: van bies tot boekrol: met een bloemlezing uit de Leidse papyrusverzameling* (Zutphen 1982) 69. Column 33 on the verso is reproduced in photo in Geraldine Pinch, *Magic in Ancient Egyptian* (Austin 1994) 67.

CHAPTER THREE

# THE USE OF SCRIPT

## 3.1. *Introduction*

A very remarkable characteristic of the two manuscripts under study is the occurrence and mixing of multiple scripts, some of which were common and had been in use since very long, whereas others had only recently been invented or were restricted in use to these manuscripts. The following table lists the seven scripts that can be distinguished in the manuscripts. The second column indicates in what way the different scripts are marked in the translations of the present study.

| | | |
|---|---|---|
| 1. | Demotic | normal |
| 2. | Hieratic | italicised |
| 3. | Alphabetic Demotic | small capitals |
| 4. | Old-Coptic | bold[1] |
| 5. | Greek | normal |
| 6. | 'Cipher' script | small capitals, written between two * |
| 7. | *Charaktēres* | not transcribed |
| – | *Captions in red ink* | **bold, italicised** |
| – | *Verse point in red ink* | ° |

An analysis of the function of, and relationship between, the different scripts is of paramount importance to the current investigation, because script does not only serve as a vehicle or medium to convey a message in language, it can also operate as a tool to define a highly specific readership, since it excludes those who do not know the code. Spells written in a mixture of scripts presuppose therefore a highly skilled readership that had gone through an institutionalised scribal training, of whatever sort this may have been. To gain an understanding of the form and cultural context of this scribal training, it is necessary to

---

[1] This script occurs only in P. London-Leiden.

determine which scripts the ancient compilers deemed most suitable for conveying which message, this is to say, to discover the functional specialisation of each script.

### 3.2. *Native scripts mixed-up*

On a quantitative basis, one could easily argue that Demotic is the base script of P. London-Leiden and of the six columns that precede and follow the thirteen Greek columns of P. Leiden I 384 verso. It has already been said that a detailed analysis of the orthography and palaeography of both manuscripts has revealed that the hands resemble each other in closest detail.[2] The similarity is the more conspicuous as both hands make use of a particular and intricate mixing of Demotic and hieratic signs throughout the manuscripts. The idiosyncratic form of mixing certainly betrays an individual hand, so that it is warranted to assume that both manuscripts were written by the same scribe. This mixing of hieratic and Demotic script deserves close attention as an extraordinary phenomenon, because Egyptian texts are usually characterised by a concern for clear generic divisions as regards content, script and language variant, the specific combination of which is mainly determined by a text's function.[3]

From the end of the Ptolemaic period onwards, Demotic became gradually accepted as a language and script suitable to write texts of a more traditional and religious nature. Texts that would earlier have been written in Classical Egyptian with the hieratic script, such as ritual handbooks, funerary spells, mortuary liturgies, hymns, scientific works,

---

[2] Johnson, 'The Demotic Magical Spells of Leiden I 384', 29–64, 51.

[3] One could roughly make the following distinctions for the pharaonic period: hieroglyphs were used for carving religious or royal texts on a stone surface (temple wall or stele) or for inscribing wooden or metal luxury objects for ornamentation. These texts were written in Classical Egyptian. Hieratic, the cursive handwriting, was written with a brush on papyrus and initially developed for documentary purposes (receipts, letters, inventory lists, etc.). From the Late Period onwards, hieratic had become restricted to the priestly domain as a medium for writing texts containing traditional sacred knowledge (rituals, hymns, scientific works). Hieratic texts could be written in Classical Egyptian as well as Late Egyptian, although Classical Egyptian predominated because of its sacred character. From the Late Period onwards, administrative and legal texts were written in Demotic, a distinctive language phase and script. Note that these generic boundaries were never rigidly fixed, so that transgressions occurred, albeit limited.

were now also composed in Demotic.[4] This development was due to a general decline in proficiency in hieratic among the native priesthood whose authority and training was gradually weakened by a decrease in, and eventual lack of, state subsidies.[5] Hieratic and the Classical Egyptian language were undoubtedly perceived by the priesthood as prestigious and well suited for priestly literature out of tradition, but daily reality was such that the Hellenistic administration forced them increasingly to adopt Greek at the expense of the native languages and scripts. It is likely that Classical Egyptian fell the first victim to this development because it had existed only as an artificial language, requiring extensive training, for about two thousand years. As Demotic was closer to spoken language and therefore less difficult to learn, it became inevitably used where hieratic had previously been obligatory. In certain cases, hieratic texts were merely translated and reworked into Demotic, but the introduction of Demotic into the religious domain also gave a stimulating impetus for new compositions.[6] In the light of these developments, it comes as no surprise that the two scripts were occasionally combined.

In certain manuscripts, Demotic phrases serve merely as reading aides or explanatory glosses to the main text in hieratic without interfering substantially with the hieratic text. The insertion of explanatory glosses in Demotic proves that a thorough knowledge of the traditional languages and scripts was no longer self-evident in Greco-Roman Egypt. In a well-preserved Roman manuscript of the *Book of the Fayum*, for example, Demotic numbers are written in the vignettes, probably intended as an aid for a scribe to facilitate copying the hieroglyphic texts of each vignette in correct sequential order.[7] In one case,

---

[4] For a general overview, see, Friedhelm Hoffmann, *Ägypten: Kultur und Lebenswelt in griechisch-römischer Zeit. Eine Darstellung nach den demotischen Quellen* (Studienbücher Geschichte und Kultur der Alten Welt; Berlin 2000) 101–175 and Mark Depauw, *A Companion to Demotic Studies* (Papyrologica 28; Brussels 1997) 85ff.

[5] For a detailed historical overview, see, László Kákosy, 'Probleme der Religion im römerzeitlichen Ägypten' *ANRW* 18.5 (1995) 2894–3049, 2898–2948. See also Roger S. Bagnall, *Egypt in Late Antiquity* (Princeton 1993) 261–273 and Frankfurter, *Religion in Roman Egypt*, 27–30.

[6] Examples of Demotic texts that are (free) translations from hieratic texts are the alternative version on the verso side of the *Apis Embalming Ritual*, the abbreviated version of the *Book of Traversing Eternity*, certain spells of the *Book of the Dead* and the Amun hymn on O. BM 50601 (formerly known as O. Hess). The *Book of the Temple* is attested in both hieratic and Demotic versions. A new composition is, for example, the *Liturgy of Opening the Mouth for Breathing*.

[7] This is the Boulaq/Hood/Amherst manuscript: Horst Beinlich, *Das Buch vom*

a hieratic phrase is inserted to explain a cryptographic group, while the name 'Osiris' is once written in Demotic to clarify the cryptographic spelling of the name.[8] Something similar is found in another mythical-topographical manuscript from the Ptolemaic period in which the hieroglyphic text is accompanied at certain places by a hieratic or Demotic explanatory gloss written above and below the carefully drawn framework.[9] Some of the pictures are explained by a short Demotic note describing who is depicted.[10] The Tebtunis Onomasticon of the Roman period is entirely written in hieratic, but amply provided with Demotic glosses that give parallel or alternative words to the hieratic wordlists.[11] In the funerary compositions P. Rhind 1 and 2, from the reign of Augustus, interference is more substantial and of a different kind, because the funerary text is given in hieratic on the upper half of the column, while a parallel version is written in Demotic on the lower half.[12] It is difficult to discern which version is the translation of the other, as earlier versions of the funerary text are not known and neither the hieratic nor the Demotic version shows clearly identifiable misunderstandings that might have come about in the process of translation. The main difference between the two versions lies therefore not in an explicit hierarchy between a prestigious and a secondary redaction, but is solely of a grammatical and idiomatic nature. The hieratic version, written in Classical Egyptian, contains a fair amount of archaic religious terminology, whereas the Demotic version conforms grammatically and idiomatically more or less to contemporary written language.[13] However, the act of translation is indeed discernable in

---

*Fayum. Zum religiösen Eigenverständnis einer ägyptischen Landschaft* (Wiesbaden 1991) 46. The *Book of the Fayum* is known from several Roman period versions of which the most elaborate contain detailed vignettes accompanied by carefully drawn hieroglyphic texts. The versions without illustrations are solely written in hieratic. See for a full discussion and plates of the hieroglyphic version, Beinlich (1991), 15–26; for photos of the hieratic version, see, Guiseppe Botti, *La glorificazione di Sobk e del Fayyum in un papiro ieratico da Tebtynis* (AnAe VIII; Copenhagen 1959).

[8] Hieratic phrase: line 40; B/H/A 189/24,5. Demotic word: line 187; B/H/A 385/14,7.

[9] Plates are published in Jacques Vandier, *Le Papyrus Jumilhac* (Paris 1961).

[10] See plates 6 (bottom), 7 (bottom), 11 (bottom), 19 (in frame).

[11] Jürgen Osing, *The Carlsberg papyri 2: Hieratische Papyri aus Tebtunis I, Text* (CNI Publications 17; Copenhagen 1998).

[12] G. Möller, *Die beiden Totenpapyrus Rhind des Museums zu Edinburg* (Leipzig 1913).

[13] In this respect, the main difference between hieratic and Demotic is a matter of archaizing and innovative tendencies. Epithets and geographical names are rendered in a less traditional and elaborate form in Demotic than in hieratic. On a lexical

P. Carlsberg 1 and 1a (first century CE), which is a copy of a cosmological treatise already known from the New Kingdom.[14] As a possible help for readers less proficient in hieratic, each hieratic sentence is followed by a translation into Demotic.[15] The text is thus made accessible to a Greco-Roman period readership without discarding the ancient, and probably highly prestigious, format. In all of these cases, hieratic and Demotic are juxtaposed to the extent that they correspond without merging into a syntactic and semantic unit. Differently, a thorough and unusual movement of merging can be observed in the unique case of the *Apis Embalming Ritual*[16] and the *Demotic Magical Papyri*. In these manuscripts, hieratic and Demotic are integrated to form a single and coherent text, thereby obliterating the clear-cut generic divisions so characteristic of Egyptian textual practice. The following pages will deal in more detail with the particular form of mixing in the two manuscripts under discussion.

Demotic and hieratic are combined in three different ways in the two manuscripts.[17] First, hieratic signs may occur as an independent

---

level, the hieratic version uses traditional religious vocabulary, whereas the Demotic version adopts consistently a modernizing lexicon (for example, traditional $k3$, 'soul', is rendered in Demotic by $rn$, 'name'; the epithet $m3'.t.y$, 'the righteous', is given in Demotic as $ḥs.y$, 'the praised one'). It is tempting to assume that the Demotic version is a modernizing translation of an older and more traditional hieratic text that is unfortunately preserved in a single copy. However, the hieratic version displays instances of demoticism and several passages in the Demotic version are structured according to alliteration, which is completely lost in the hieratic parallel. See also Möller, *Die beiden Totenpapyrus Rhind*, 8–11.

[11] H.O. Lange and O. Neugebauer, *Papyrus Carlsberg No. 1, ein hieratisch-demotischer kosmologischer Text* (Copenhagen 1940) and O. Neugebauer and R.A. Parker, *Egyptian Astronomical Texts* 3 Vols. (London 1960–1969) vol. 1, 43–94. See also J.F. Quack, 'Kollationen und Korrekturvorschläge zum Papyrus Carlsberg 1', in: P.J. Frandsen and K. Ryholt (eds.), *The Carlsberg Papyri 3: A Miscellany of Demotic Texts and Studies* (CNI Publications 22; Copenhagen 2000) 165–171. The earliest version of the cosmological treatise, known as the *Book of Nut*, is found on the ceiling of the burial chamber in the cenotaph of Sethos I in Abydos. Abridged versions are in the tomb of Ramesses IV and Mutirdis (TT 410, unfinished).

[15] An early example of a similar Classical Egyptian-Demotic text is P. BM EA 69574 from the Saite or Persian period: J.F. Quack, 'A New Bilingual Fragment from the British Museum (Papyrus BM EA 69574)' *JEA* 85 (1999) 153–164. Each Classical Egyptian sentence is followed by its Demotic translation as in P. Carlsberg 1 and 1a. A crucial distinction between the two manuscripts is that the Saite papyrus is entirely written in the hieratic script, which was still widely in use during the Saite period.

[16] R.L. Vos, *The Apis Embalming Ritual. P. Vindob. 3873* (OLA 50; Leuven 1993).

[17] For a careful study of the palaeography of the Demotic and hieratic script in

scriptural and lexical cluster within a larger demotic unit. This means that a Demotic sentence incorporates a hieratic word or phrase without breaking up the sentential and semantic order of the Demotic unit. In these cases, the hieratic elements are mainly archaic, religious terms or traditional divine epithets. Second, a word can be made up of hieratic signs used in combination with demotic characters to form a hybrid unit. Again, in this case, the treatment is mostly limited to religious vocabulary. Third, hieratic is occasionally used for transcribing and glossing secret magical names, the so-called *voces magicae*. Principally, these *voces magicae* are transcribed and glossed in respectively alphabetic demotic and Old Coptic, but, in one case, a hieratic gloss is added above an epithet in Demotic.

The first above-mentioned type, interference of Demotic and hieratic script on a sentential level, can be illustrated with the help of a few examples. Egyptian magical spells or medicinal recipes are frequently accompanied by the standard closing phrase *nfr.wy pw* 'it is very good', which was added to spells as some sort of proof of efficacy or advertisement from as early as the Middle Kingdom.[18] In P. London-Leiden, the phrase occurs occasionally likewise as an addition to a recipe. In the majority of these cases, the clause is markedly written in hieratic in spite of the fact that the foregoing recipe is otherwise in Demotic.[19] For example, a spell to make a woman desire a man closes with the following prescription:

> (Recite it) seven times. You must do it on the fourteenth (day) of the lunar month. (It is) *very good*! [P. London-Leiden 25/37]

---

P. London-Leiden, see, B.H. Stricker, 'Het grafisch systeem van de Magische Papyrus Londen & Leiden' *OMRO* 31 (1950) 64–71; *OMRO* 36 (1955) 92–132; *OMRO* 39 (1958) 80–103; *OMRO* 42 (1961) 25–52; *OMRO* 45 (1964) 25–55.

[18] For the medical texts, see, W. Westendorf, *Handbuch der altägyptischen Medizin* I (Handbuch der Orientalistik I. Abt., Bd. 36; Leiden, Cologne, New York 1999) 98–99. A helpful discussion on the use of the phrase in magical spells can be found in: Adhémar Massart, *The Leiden Magical Papyrus I 343 + I 345* OMRO 34 (1954) 109, n.25 and Serge Sauneron, *Un traité égyptien d'ophiologie. Papyrus du Brooklyn Museum nos. 47.218.48 et 85* (PIFAO, Bibliothèque Générale 11; Cairo 1989) 198 and 235 (*nfr-nfr*). The nature of this phrase in the Demotic magical spells is discussed in more detail in chapter 7.4, under the heading 'proof of efficacy'.

[19] P. London-Leiden: 16/1, 17/1, 23/8, 24/17, 25/37, 27/30, V.11/7, V.25/8 (in hieratic); 3/26, 14/31, 24/14 (in Demotic script). The phrase is not attested in P. Leiden J. 384 verso. It occurs also in the other two Demotic magical papyri: P. Louvre E 3229: 1/18.27, 4/15.30, 5/22, 6/5 (hieratic). P. BM. 10588: 5/6, 6/16, 7/11 (hieratic).

It would thus seem that the copyists of the spells were very familiar with ritual texts in hieratic and added the standard clause in hieratic as they were accustomed to, even though the spell itself was actually in Demotic.

A more complex form of interference can be observed in a number of lengthy invocations that had to be recited in the course of a divination ritual. The poetic structure of these invocations conforms to the generic rules of traditional Egyptian hymns: each verse line consists of a divine name accompanied by a description of a deity's cultic topography or attributes.[20] It occurs frequently that a verse line is made up of a mixture of clauses in hieratic and Demotic script with the traditional and age-old epithets usually rendered in hieratic. In this way, the invocations appear as a close-knit patchwork of phrases in Demotic and hieratic script. The following three examples are meant to illustrate this point.

A  Hail *Nut, mother*[21] *of water; Hail Opet, mother of fire* °
   *Come to me, Nut, mother of water* °
   Come, *Opet, mother of fire* °
   *Come to me* IAHO °                    [P. London-Leiden 6/18–19][22]

B  I am the face of *the Ram* °
   *Youth is my name* °
   I was born under the venerable Persea-tree ° in Abydos °[23]
   I am the *soul of the great chief who is in Abydos* °
   I am *the guardian* of the great corpse *which is in Wu-Poke* °
   I am the one whose eye is an eye of a hawk watching over Osiris
      *by night* °
   I am '*He-who-is-upon-his-mountain*' upon the necropolis *of Abydos* °
   I am *the one who* watches over the great corpse *which is in* Busiris °
   I am *the one who* watches for *Re-Khepri-Atum* °
   *Whose name* is hidden in my heart °
   '*Soul-of-souls*' is his name °         [P. London-Leiden 6/22–26][24]

---

[20] Jan Assmann, *Ägyptische Hymnen und Gebete* (OBO, 2nd ed.; Freiburg, Göttingen 1999) 17–30.

[21] The word *mw.t*, 'mother' is written unetymologically with the hieratic group *Mw.t*, '(the goddess) Mut' in this and the following three instances.

[22] Tr. Janet H. Johnson, with minor modification.

[23] The adverbial clause 'in Abydos' is set apart by two verse points. I assume that the preceding verse point is a typo caused by the fact that the scribe mistakenly took the end of the line with the word *šps*, 'venerable', for the end of the verse. When he wrote 'in Abydos' in the following line he added the second and correct verse point.

[24] Tr. Janet H. Johnson, with minor modifications.

54                           CHAPTER THREE

> C  *Hail* the one whose form is of […] his great and mysterious[25] form
> from whose begetting a god came forth
> *who rests in the midst* of Thebes
> I am […]
> [I am …] *of the great Lady under whom* Hapy comes forth
> I am the face of *great* awe […]
> [I am …] soul in his *protection*
> I am the noble child *who is in the house* of Re
> I am *the* noble dwarf *who is in the cavern* […]
> [I am] the ibis of true *protection who rests in Heliopolis*
> I am *the master of the great foe, the lord* who obstructs semen
> The very strong one […] is my [name]
> I am *the Ram, son of the Ram*
> *Lotus-Lion-Ram (and vice versa)* is my name
> *Re-Khepri-Atum* is my true name         [P. London-Leiden 11/4–9][26]

Example C is taken from a spell to acquire charm and success as is made explicit in the example D, the lines that follow immediately example C. The instruction itself is rendered in Demotic but the standard closing phrase is again written in hieratic.

> D  Give me *praise and love* [before NN, son of] NN today, so that he give me all good things, so that he give me food and nourishment, and so that he do everything which I [shall desire. And do not let him] injure me so as to do any harm, so that he say to me a thing which [I] hate, *on this day, in this night, this month, this year, [this] hour* […]
> [P. London-Leiden 11/9–11][27]

Examples A and B are extracts from an invocation that has to be recited to a lit oil lamp in the course of an elaborate divination ritual that makes use of a youth to serve as medium. The ritual has to be carried out at dawn in a dark, clean room with the lamp facing the east. At the rising of the sun, the practitioner has to recite hymns to the sun god, which are not written out in the handbook but merely mentioned by their generic title as if the practitioner was expected to

---

[25] Note that the two determinatives of *št*, 'mysterious', are actually in hieratic script (Gardiner Q6 and G7). The hieratic signs are to be explained as an unetymological borrowing from the word *štyt*, the chapel of the god Osiris-Sokar.

[26] Tr. Janet H. Johnson, with minor modifications. Since this section lacks verse points, the division into verse lines is tentative. Note that the use of the third person singular suffix as the possessive after *ḥbr* (twice in line 4) is a grammatical construction typical of Classical Egyptian, which gives the hymn an archaic touch.

[27] Tr. Janet H. Johnson. The phrase *m hrw pn m grḥ pn m ibd pn m rnp.t tn m wnw.t [tn]* or parallel phrases occur frequently in texts of a ritual or magical nature: P. Louvre E 3229 3/18, see also 2/7.10 (similar mixing of Demotic and hieratic).

know them by heart. The title of this collection of hymns is written in a mixture of hieratic and Demotic: '*Adoring* Re in the morning *at his rising*' (P. London-Leiden 6/3). The title itself is not known from other late sources but resembles titles of ritual books that were kept in the House-of-Life, the cultic temple library.[28] Since the combination 'adoring Re' (*dwꜣ Rꜥ*) served also as a generic technical term for sun hymns,[29] it is very well possible that the present title refers to, or was even extracted from, a once existing compilation of sun hymns that was generally known in priestly circles. The distribution of hieratic and Demotic words in the title seems to be random and not governed by any hierarchical order between the two scripts. The following example is taken form the same recipe and confirms that the mixing of hieratic and Demotic script was not strictly determined by hierarchical considerations of any kind. The short passage contains two phrases that are coordinated in a *parallelismus membrorum*, the first member of which is written in Demotic and the second in hieratic.

E  *Hail* Osiris (and) the lamp; it will let (me) see *those things* that are above,[30] °
   *it will let (me) see those things that are below (and vice versa)*. °
                                                    [P. London-Leiden 6/28–29]

The second type of mixing occurs when a *single* word is written as a combination of Demotic and hieratic characters. It might therefore be more appropriate to speak of interference rather than mixing of scripts. In the majority of cases, these words are somewhat archaic and religious in nature, the use of which was restricted to ritual texts, hymns, spells, etc. The intricate mixing of hieratic and Demotic was therefore probably the result of an in-depth familiarity with religious texts in hieratic on the part of the ancient copyist. It goes without saying that it presupposes an equal familiarity with hieratic on the part of the reader. A selection of the hybrid words is listed below in transliteration and translation; the numbers refer to the Demotic glossary of P. London-Leiden by Griffith and Thompson.

---

[28] Siegfried Schott, *Bücher und Bibliotheken im alten Ägypten* (Wiesbaden 1990). See for titles containing the generic term *dwꜣ* nrs. 1718–1774, of which nrs. 1753–1759 are specifically connected with Re. See also: nrs. 1135, 1150–1172, 1212 and 1364. The present book title is omitted from Schott's lists. See for the House-of-Life: Alan H. Gardiner, 'The House of Life' *JEA* 24 (1938) 157–179 and Philippe Derchain, *Le papyrus Salt 825 (B.M. 10051). Rituel pour la conservation de la vie en Egypte* (Brussels 1965).

[29] Assmann, *Ägyptische Hymnen und Gebete*, 4.

[30] The ancient scribe had mistakenly written *hrw*, 'day', but corrected himself by

| | | |
|---|---|---|
| *iḥ* | joy, joyful | nr. 115 |
| *itef* | Atef crown | nr. 148 |
| *ꜥrk-ḥḥ* | Ark-Heh (toponym) | nr. 113 |
| *wyn* | light | nr. 183 |
| *wꜣḏ* | green | nr. 231 |
| *wḏꜣ.t* | Udjat eye | nr. 240 |
| *by-ꜥꜣ-n-p.t* | goat | nr. 250; P. Leiden I 384 verso II*/7 |
| *pḥṱ* | mighty | nr. 316a |
| *nm* | dwarf | nr. 435 |
| *rsw.t* | to watch, a dream | nrs. 513 & 514 |
| *ḥwne* | youth, boy | nr. 556 |
| *ḥyt* | fury, spell | nr. 646 |
| *ḫbr* | companion, friend | nr. 649 |
| *ḥm-ḥl* | servant, boy | nr. 658 |
| *ḫrt-ꜥnḥ* | Kherti-ankh, mother of Imhotep | P. Leiden I 384 verso I*/3,10,17 |
| *swr* | to drink | nr. 727 |
| *smi* | to paint [the eyes] | nr. 750 |
| *šḥn-ḏr.t* | fingers, hand | nr. 772 |
| *šw* | to be dry | nr. 834 |
| *šn-dꜣ.t* | circuit of the underworld | nr. 859 |
| *št* | secret, mysterious | nr. 876 |
| *ḳꜥ(i)* | the lofty one | nr. 939 |
| *kꜣ* | bull | nr. 886 |

The third type of mixing Demotic and hieratic script occurs when hieratic signs are used to transcribe and gloss *voces magicae*. This is remarkable because the alphabetic Demotic and Old-Coptic script are more apt than hieratic to render the sounds of the secret names by way of spelling out consonants and vowels, instead of following a rigid orthography like the hieratic script, which lacks vowel signs altogether.[31] Occasionally hieratic is used to add a gloss above a common phrase or name in Demotic. The reason for this particular use of hieratic remains unclear, because, unlike Old-Coptic glosses above *voces magicae*, a gloss in hieratic does not convey any additional information about a correct pronunciation, as hieratic is even less equipped for conveying vowels than Demotic. To learn more about the form and reasons of this third type of mixing it is helpful to analyse the transcriptions and glosses in a recipe for a vessel divination ritual that allows the practitioner to question the moon at the fifteenth day of the lunar

---

adding a gloss *ḥry* above the line.

[31] For more details, see, chapter 3.3.3.

month. The invocation is rather short and straightforward, but highly complex regarding its use of Demotic, hieratic and Old-Coptic. I have added numbers to the verse lines to distinguish between the actual verse lines and the glosses above the line.

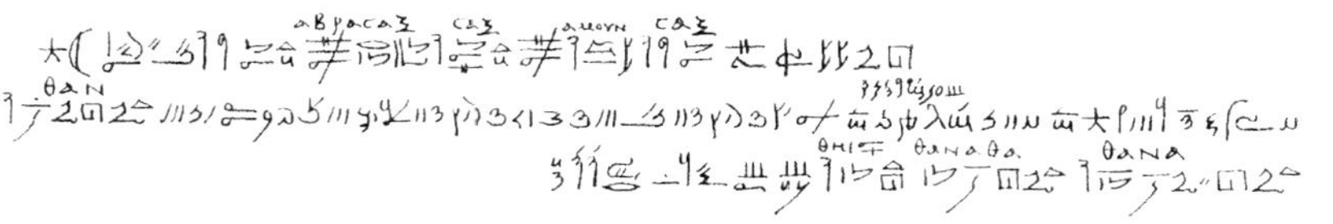

Fig. 3.1. P. London-Leiden 23/24–26

    **sax amoun sax abrasax**
F 1) *Hail,* *saks,* *Amun,* *saks,* *abrasaks,*
                  *he who gave birth to them*
  2) for you are *the moon*, the great one of the stars, he who gave birth to them.
  3) Listen to these things which I said.
  4) Walk in accordance with the (words) of my mouth.
  5) May you reveal yourself to me,
   **than thana thanatha;** another (manuscript) says **thêi**.
  6) *tahanu, taheanuna, tahnuatha*
  7) *This is my correct* name.    [P. London-Leiden 23/24–26][32]

The function of the hieratic signs in the current passage F is fundamentally different from that in the above-given passages A-E. In this case, the hieratic signs are used to spell out the *sounds* of the *voces magicae* contrary to the general rule that alphabetic Demotic signs were used for this. As usual, these *voces magicae* are provided with glosses in Old-Coptic script to indicate the correct vowels. Furthermore, contrary to regular usage, the Demotic clause 'he who gave birth to them' in line two is glossed above the line with a hieratic equivalent. Both phrases follow the rules of the standard grammar of their respective language phases. The Demotic phrase reads *p₃ i.ir ms.t̲=w*, while the hieratic gloss is rendered in correct Classical Egyptian as *p₃ ir ms=w*, which must have sounded rather awkward and archaic to Roman-period ears. This complex mixing resulted in all likelihood from the frequent consultation of multiple manuscripts during the phase of compilation and editing, as is actually made explicit in the final gloss above verse line 6:

---

[32] Tr. Janet H. Johnson, with minor modifications. The division in verse lines is tentative because the section lacks verse points.

'another (manuscript) says **thêi**'. The *vox magica* **thanatha** was apparently spelled **thanathêi** in an alternative manuscript, which reveals that the extant invocation was composed with the help of at least two manuscripts containing *voces magicae* in Old-Coptic script. A similar reasoning may hold true for the *voces magicae* and gloss in the hieratic script: they were taken from an older manuscript and 'pasted' into the extant spell without being transcribed or translated into Demotic. This argument might find substantial support in the peculiar scriptural form of the standard closing phrase '*This is my correct* name' in line 7, wherewith the practitioner confirms his identification with the foregoing divine names and epithets. Except for this sole example, which is almost completely written in hieratic, the clause is always given in Demotic in P. London-Leiden. It seems that no other line of reasoning than a slavish copying from an older hieratic manuscript can explain this irregular writing.

The relationship between, and the status of, the transcriptions in alphabetic Demotic, hieratic and Old-Coptic script can be studied in more detail by comparing two parallel versions of an invocation to the sun god, one version of which contains glosses in hieratic instead of in Old-Coptic that are added above *voces magicae* spelled in alphabetic Demotic signs. Both versions belong to a divination ritual that claims to establish contact with Re, when the god is navigating his bark across the sky.[33] The invocation is written in a mixture of Demotic and hieratic word groups according to the same method as applied in the examples A-E. The given translation follows the version of column 27.

G   Open to me, O *heaven*, mother of the gods °
    Let me see the bark of Pre, he *going up and going down* in it[34] °
    For I am Geb, heir of the gods °
    Praying is what I am doing before Pre, my father °
    On account of the thing which went forth from me °
    O Heknet, the great one, lady of the shrine, *the Rishtret* °
    Open to me, O mistress of spirits °
    Open to me, O primal *heaven* °

---

[33] The parallel versions are P. London-Leiden 10/22–35 and 27/1–12. The version of 27/1–12 is translated in *GMPT* as part of a rather elaborate ritual that fills the whole column (27/:–36 = PDM xiv 805–840). However, from line 13 onwards, the bark of Re is no longer mentioned, whereas the ritual suddenly requires a youth to serve as medium. The extant ritual text is therefore probably the result of a rather ill-succeeded combination of two originally separate spells for divination.

[34] The final 'it' refers to the heaven of verse 1.

Let me worship the messengers °
For I am *Geb*, heir of the gods °
O you seven kings °
*Hail* you seven Montus °
Bull who engenders, lord of awe °
*The one who illuminates the earth* °
Soul of *the primeval waters* °
*Hail, lion like a lion of the primeval waters, bull* of the darkness °
*Hail*, foremost one of *the people of the east* °
Nun, great one °
*The lofty one* °
*Hail*, soul of *the ram* °
Soul of *the people of the west* °
*Hail, soul of souls* °
Bull of darkness °
*Bull of two bulls* °
*Son of Nut* °
Open to me °
I am *the opener of earth, who* came forth from *Geb* °
*Hail* °
I am E° E° E, Ê° Ê° Ê, HÊ° HÊ° HÊ °
HÔ° HÔ° HÔ °
I am ANEPO °
MIRI°-PO°-RE *Ma'at ib*° THIBAÏ-O[35] °
ARU°-UI °
UOU° IAHO °         [P. London-Leiden 27/1–9][36]

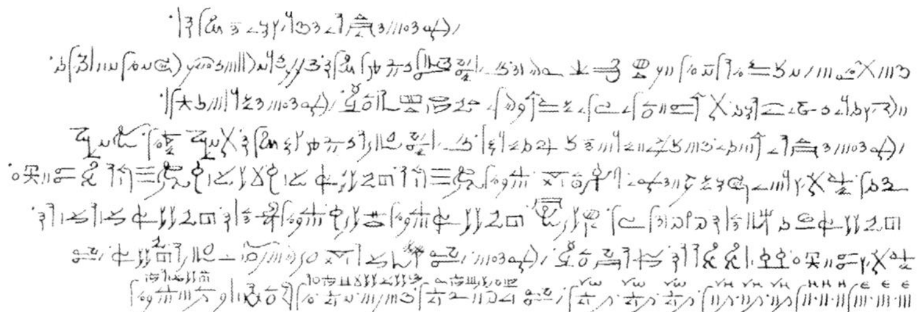

Fig. 3.2. P. London-Leiden 27/1–9

---

[35] The *vox magica* THIBAÏ-O could as well be read as 'THIBAÏ, the great one', because the final sound is in both the Demotic and hieratic version written as the word 'ꜣ, 'great' followed by divine determinative.

[36] Tr. Janet H. Johnson, with minor modifications.

The transcription of the *voces magicae* in the final lines of the current translation is but a modern attempt to vocalise the magical names according to the possible intentions of the ancient editor. In fact, this concluding set of *voces magicae* displays a complex mixture of garbled names in hieratic and alphabetic Demotic signs, which are glossed with names in hieratic in the current example and with Old-Coptic names in the parallel version. The following two tables juxtapose the *voces magicae* ANEPO, MIRI-PO-RE and THIBAÏ-O with their glosses as they are rendered in respectively column 10 and column 27 in order to gain insight into the correspondences and differences between the transcriptions.

**Column 10**

| *Vox Magica* | *Transliteration* | *Gloss* | Transcription |
|---|---|---|---|
| | rnep-ꜥ3 | ⲁⲛ\|ⲉⲡ\|ⲟ | ANEPO |
| | myry-p3-ꜥ3-Rꜥ | ⲙⲓⲣⲓ ⲡⲟⲣⲉ | MIRI-PO-RE |
| | thy-b3-ꜥ3 | — | THIBAÏ-O |

**Column 27**

| | ꜥnep-ꜥ3 | | ꜥne-ne-p-ꜥ3 |
|---|---|---|---|
| | Myry-p3-ꜥ3-Rꜥ | | My-rey-p-ꜥ3-Rꜥ |
| | thy-by-ꜥ3 | | thy-b3-ꜥ3 |

A comparison of the two tables reveals that no *vox magica* or gloss of any version is identical to the letter with its corresponding term of the parallel version. The differences are rather small, but sufficient to reveal that the ancient editors did not attach great value to a fixed orthography. Apparently, they did not believe that the efficacy of a given ritual was dependent on immutable writing conventions: it was sound that mattered in the communication with the gods, not orthography. For this reason, the Old-Coptic glosses of column 10 fulfilled an important function by virtue of their vowel signs, which are lacking in the Demotic (and hieratic) script. However, the presence of hieratic glosses in column 27 cannot be explained in a similar way, because they do not complement the alphabetic Demotic *voces magicae* in any way as regards information about etymology or factual pronunciation. Their occurrence remains therefore somewhat obscure.

A possible solution to this problem might be found in a tendency on the part of the ancient editors to be complete and to do justice to their various sources. Whenever they found an alternative writing, they were inclined to add it to their text irrespective of the fact whether it truly carried any additional information. In the case of the hieratic script, one could quite well understand that the ancient editors imbued alternative writings with a feeling of preserved tradition and established priestly knowledge, because the hieratic script had more or less been reserved for religious compositions since the Late Period, when Demotic was introduced as the new language and script for administrative documents. To these editors the hieratic script was simply more prestigious than Demotic, because it was older and had more affinity with religious language. Consequently, they were eager to include the magical names and glosses in hieratic. In the light of the age of the hieratic script, it seems reasonable to argue that glosses in hieratic script are liable to preserve the original orthography of the garbled *voces magicae*, from which the Demotic and Old-Coptic variants deviated as the result of misunderstood transcriptions. This is however not the case as far as the extant hieratic glosses are concerned. For example, neither the hieratic nor the alphabetic Demotic version of the *voces magicae* ANEPO, MIRI-PO-RE and THIBAÏ-O display any sign of understanding of the actual meaning and etymology of the divine names or epithets. The first vox, ANEPO, derives etymologically in all probability from *'Inpw '3* 'the great Anubis', but its original notation has not been preserved in the alphabetic Demotic nor the hieratic transcription. Both versions are nothing but a purely phonetic transcription of the *vox magica* without consideration for the correct orthography of the old divine epithet.[37] There is no question that whoever wrote the alphabetic Demotic and hieratic spelling did not understand the correct meaning of the word group. The same reasoning holds true for the second *vox magica*, MIRI-PO-RE, although a sound etymology cannot be given that easily. The part PO-RE is in both versions written as *p3 '3 R'*, which could be translated as 'the greatness of Re' or 'the Great One, Re', but the first part, MIRI, escapes interpretation.[38] The third *vox magica*, THIBAÏ-O, might betray an

---

[37] Although the *vox magica* ANEPO is not attested in the PGM, Ἀνουβις occurs occasionally.

[38] The hieratic gloss could possibly be interpreted as the imperative *mi*, 'come',

Egyptian phrase in its transcribed guise. The Demotic version is written as *thy-by ꜥꜣ*, while the hieratic reads *thy-bꜣ ꜥꜣ*. The final group *ꜥꜣ* is written as the adjective 'great', while the equivalent *by* and *bꜣ* are regular Egyptian words for 'soul, manifestation'. The preceding part, *thy*, is not accompanied by a determinative, which indicates that the scribe interpreted the group as a mere collection of sounds instead of as an existing Egyptian word. Nonetheless, it could derive from the verb *thj* that has among its meanings 'to attack an enemy'.[39] The *vox magica* could then tentatively be translated as 'The one who attacks the great soul' or 'The great attacker of the soul', although neither of both suggestions is known as an epithet from other Egyptian sources. To summarize the evidence presented by this analyse, the Demotic and hieratic version of the *voces magicae* are not complementary[40] and represent but attempts to vocalise magical names, the meaning of which was no longer understood.

Despite the traditional and religious character of the hieratic script, it seems warranted to suppose that there was no overt sacred hierarchy at work in the choice for a gloss in hieratic or Demotic script. The epithet *pꜣ it it.w n nꜣ ntr.w*, 'the father of the fathers of the gods', occurs twice in an invocation in P. London-Leiden (2/21 and 8/2). The first occurrence is written according to standard Demotic orthography, whereas the second attestation is a combination of hieratic and Demotic word groups: the hieratic 'the father of the fathers' is followed by 'of the gods' in Demotic. To ensure correct pronunciation of the former group, the hieratic clause is provided with an Old-Coptic gloss, which reads: ⲡⲓⲁⲧ-ⲓⲁⲧⲉ. The variety in writings shows that Demotic and hieratic could mutually be interchanged, which means that the choice between the two scripts was not strictly regulated or determined by a religious sanction. The Old-Coptic gloss indicates again that the essential aspect of the epithet was considered its sound, not its orthography.

---

followed by *rwy*, 'lion' (with cow's skin determinative). This does unfortunately not give any sense.

[39] WB 5, 320, 1; cf. Penelope Wilson, *A Ptolemaic Lexikon. A Lexicographical Study of the Texts in the Temple of Edfu* (OLA 78; Leuven 1997) 1148.

[40] Note however that in one instance, viz. P. London-Leiden 6/26, a hieratic word is provided with a Demotic gloss that could have had an explanatory purpose: the relative converter *nty-iw* is glossed with a demotic *iw*, for which there is no apparent reason other than philological comment. In Demotic magical papyrus P. Louvre E 3229 5/28 and 6/20, Demotic is similarly used for glossing a hieratic word. In 5/28 circumstantial *iw* is glossed by a similar Demotic *iw*, while in 6/20 hieratic *ḥꜣwty* is glossed with Demotic *ḥwt*, both meaning 'male'.

## 3.3. *Greek language inscribed*

The following section discusses the occurrence of the Greek script and the transcriptions of Greek sounds into alphabetic Demotic characters in the two magical handbooks. Considering the fact that Egyptian theology linked the Egyptian language and scripts innately with Egyptian mythology and, as a consequence, with traditional temple cult, it is highly remarkable that Greek script, which lacks the tradition and characteristics of Egyptian scripts, is taken up in an Egyptian ritual manual. In the light of the political and social realities of those days, the occurrence of the Greek script and language in Egyptian documents is not surprising, but nonetheless, it cannot have been self-evident that the common language and script of civil life entered the ritual domain, which functioned otherwise rather independent from daily reality. The following pages will therefore investigate the role of Greek script and sounds in the ritual texts of the manuscript.

### 3.3.1. *Greek script and language*

The Greek script appears as a matter of course first and foremost in the spells that are written in the Greek language: the thirteen columns in Greek of P. Leiden I 384 verso (PGM XII) and the three invocations inserted in the Demotic spells of P. London-Leiden (PGM XIVa–c). The thirteen Greek columns of P. Leiden I 384 verso make full use of abbreviations and stenographic symbols, which reveals that both editor and reader were familiar with the Greek scribal practices of the day and that their command of the Greek language and script was far greater than a working knowledge. The columns 1 to 5 on the verso of P. London-Leiden preserve short lists of plant and mineral names, which are given in their Greek and Egyptian form, thereby making these lists overtly bilingual by juxtaposing the Greek and Demotic script. In a few cases, glosses in Greek are added above Demotic words.[11]

---

[11] See chapter 4.3.1 for more details.

### 3.3.2. *Greek alphabetic devices in Egyptian guise*

The following passage is an excerpt of a spell, in Greek, for sending dreams (PGM XII.107–121), taken from the fourth Greek column of P. Leiden I 384 verso (4/1–15). According to the title of the spell, the author of the spell was a certain Agathokles, who is otherwise unknown.

> Come to me, NN, you who established the ⟨…⟩ by your own power, you who rule the whole world, the fiery god. Reveal to him, NN, THARTHAR THAMAR ATHATHA MOMMOM THANABÔTH APRANOU BAMBALÊA CHR[Ê]TH NABOUSOULÊTH ROMBROU THARAÊL ALBANA BRÔCHRÊX ABRANA ZOUCHÊL. Hear me, because I am going to say the great name, AÔTH, before whom every god prostrates himself and every demon shudders, for whom every angel completes those things which are assigned. Your divine name according to the seven (i.e. vowels; jd) is AEÊIOUÔ IAUÔÊ EAÔOUEÊÔIA. I have spoken your glorious name, the name for all needs. Reveal to NN, lord god. [PGM XII.114–121][12]

The practitioner compels the divine being to consider his case not only by saying the prestigious and all-powerful name AÔTH, but also by showing his knowledge of its name according to the seven Greek vowels. These vowels, α ε η ι ο υ ω, were considered powerful entities in the Hellenic world since the classical period and acquired great reverence in late antiquity.[13] From the archaic period, the Greek alphabet not only served as a medium to assign phonetic values, but was also a numerical system whose total number of 24 letters the Pythagoreans connected with the 24 sounds of the lute for musical notation. The correlation between letters, numbers and music notes was believed not to be accidental and soon led to philosophical speculations among the early Orphics and Pythagoreans. Greatest weight was laid upon the seven vowels whose relationship with the seventeen consonants was described in terms of soul and body.[14] With the advent of astrology in the Hellenistic period, the seven vowels were regarded as the cosmic sounds of the seven planets within the harmony of spheres, so that the vowels became bound up within the course of cosmic events. The

---

[12] Tr. W.C. Grese, with minor modifications.
[13] The classical work on this subject is still Franz Dornseiff, *Das Alphabet in Mystik und Magie* (2nd ed.; Berlin 1925). See also David Frankfurter, 'The Magic of Writing and the Writing of Magic. The Power of the Word in Egyptian and Greek Traditions' *Helios* 21 (1994) 189–221, 199–205.
[14] For references, see, Dornseiff, *Das Alphabet in Mystik und Magie*, 33.

following anecdote is illustrative of the hope and fear that were accordingly attached to the seven vowels in late antiquity.

> A young man was seen in the baths touching with the fingers of both hands alternately the marble and his chest while murmuring the seven vowels in the belief that it would bring healing to his stomach. Brought to court he was sentenced to die by the sword after being tortured.
> [Ammianus Marcellinus, *Res Gestae*, 29, 2.28]

In line with the Greco-Roman discourse on the acclaimed sacred character of the Egyptian priesthood, Egyptian priests were believed to hymn the seven vowels during their sacred rituals conducted in the native temple.

> In Egypt the priests, when singing hymns in praise of the gods, employ the seven vowels, which they utter in due succession; and the sound of these letters is so euphonious that men listen to it in preference to flute and lyre. [Ps. Demetrius, *On Style*, 71][45]

These seven vowels occur frequently in the *Greek Magical Papyri* as sounds that would allow the practitioner of a given ritual to compel the divine and to manipulate the workings of the cosmos.[46] The connection between the vowels and planetary spheres is occasionally even made explicit:

> You (Agathos Daemon) are the ocean, the begetter of good things and feeder of the civilised world. Yours is the eternal processional way in which your seven-lettered name is established for the harmony of the seven sounds (of the planets) which have their tones according to the twenty-eight forms of the moon, SARAPHARA ARAPHAIRA BRAARMARAPHA ABRAACH PERTAÔMÊCH AKMÊCH IAÔ OUEÈ IAÔ OUE EIOU AÊÔ EÊOU IAÔ.
> [PGM XIII.772–780][47]

---

[45] Tr. W. Rhys Roberts. Demetrius lived sometime in the period of the first century BCE until first century CE.

[46] For a useful discussion of the distribution of vowel sequences for each deity, see, Dornseiff, *Das Alphabet in Mystik und Magie*, 35–51.

[47] Tr. Morton Smith, with minor modifications. The connection between the numbers seven and twenty-eight on the one hand, and the number of the planets and moon phases on the other hand, is reminiscent of an account by Diodorus of Sicily of an exotic yet ideal society on a (fictional) island 'which has been discovered in the ocean to the south (of Arabia)' by a certain Iambulus; Diodorus II, 55.1–2. According to Diodorus, 'the inhabitants give attention to every branch of learning and especially to astrology; and they use letters which, according to the value of the sounds they represent, are twenty-eight in number, but the characters are only seven, each one of which can be formed in four different ways'; II 57, 4, tr. C.H. Oldfather.

Since the vowels were considered powerful entities in themselves, the recitation of these sounds had to be accompanied by specific ritual procedures as in the following passage.

> The instruction: Speaking to the rising sun, stretching out your right hand to the left and your left hand likewise to the left, say 'A'.
> To the north, putting forward only your right fist, say 'E'.
> Then to the west, extending both hands in front (of you), say 'Ê'.
> To the south, (holding) both on your stomach, say 'I'.
> To the earth, bending over, touching the ends of your toes, say 'O'.
> Looking into the air, having your hand on your heart, say 'U'.
> Looking into the sky, having both hands on your head, say 'Ô'.
> [PGM XIII. 823–835][48]

As a means to enhance the power of the signs, the vowels were frequently written out thrice—ⲀⲀⲀ ⲈⲈⲈ ⲎⲎⲎ ⲒⲒⲒ ⲞⲞⲞ ⲨⲨⲨ ⲰⲰⲰ—or written in succession with an increasing number—Ⲁ ⲈⲈ ⲎⲎⲎ ⲒⲒⲒⲒ ⲞⲞⲞⲞⲞ ⲨⲨⲨⲨⲨⲨ ⲰⲰⲰⲰⲰⲰⲰ.[49] This way of notation offered the possibility to arrange the vowels in geometrical patterns, in the belief that the characters draw their power from their visual representation as much as from their sound.[50] These *carmina figurata* were frequently arranged in the form of a pyramid (*klima*) or a wing (*pterugion*) as in the following two examples.

| | |
|---|---|
| Ⲁ | ⲀⲈⲎⲒⲞⲨⲰ |
| Ⲉ Ⲉ | ⲈⲎⲒⲞⲨⲰⲀ |
| Ⲏ Ⲏ Ⲏ | ⲎⲒⲞⲨⲰⲀⲈ |
| Ⲓ Ⲓ Ⲓ Ⲓ | ⲒⲞⲨⲰⲀⲈⲎ |
| Ⲏ Ⲏ Ⲏ Ⲏ Ⲏ | ⲞⲨⲰⲀⲈⲎⲒ |
| Ⲉ Ⲉ Ⲉ Ⲉ Ⲉ Ⲉ | ⲨⲰⲀⲈⲎⲒⲞ |
| Ⲁ Ⲁ Ⲁ Ⲁ Ⲁ Ⲁ Ⲁ | ⲰⲀⲈⲎⲒⲞⲨ |
| *klima*[51] | *pterugion*[52] |

It is highly significant, albeit extraordinary, that the device of the seven vowels was taken up in Demotic magical spells. From an Egyptian perspective, it is senseless to give paramount importance to precisely these seven sounds, since Egyptian phonology and script are rather

---

[48] Tr. Morton Smith. Cf. PGM V.24–30.
[49] For example PGM IV.1002–1007: 'Enter in, appear to me, lord, because I call upon you as the three baboons call upon you, who speak your name in a symbolic fashion, A EE ÊÊÊ IIII OOOOO UUUUUU ÔÔÔÔÔÔÔ.', tr. W.C. Grese
[50] Dornseiff, *Das Alphabet in Mystik und Magie*, 57–60; Frankfurter, 'The Magic of Writing and the Writing of Magic', 200.
[51] PGM V.83–90.
[52] PGM XIII.905–911.

THE USE OF SCRIPT 67

different from Greek.[53] The vowels had probably lost their original phonetic motivation for the Egyptian priests, so that they were deemed powerful characters in themselves. Take for example the concluding statement of an elaborate invocation in which the Greek vowels are summoned as a climax:

> Come to me at the mouths of my vessel °, my bandage °! Let my cup ° produce the [light] of *heaven* °. May the hounds of Phulot ° give me that which is just in the primeval waters. May they tell me that about which I am asking here today, in truth, truly °, there being no falsehood therein ⲁ° ⲉ° ⲏ° ⲓ̈° ⲟ° ⲩ° ⲱ° SPIRIT OF STRIFE.        [P. London-Leiden 14/14–16][54]

In this case, the copyist left the vowels in Greek script, attaching thus weight to a Greek concept that ultimately concerns the ordering of the cosmos. It is highly probable that he copied the set of vowels from a magical manuscript in Greek, because the divine name SPIRIT OF STRIFE, which follows the vowels, is Greek as well. It is spelled out in alphabetic Demotic signs as *mꜥkh-ꜥꜣ-pnewmꜥ* with foreign land determinative but glossed with (the probably original) ⲙⲁⲭⲟⲡⲛⲉⲩⲙⲁ. In all other cases, the vowels are transcribed into alphabetic Demotic signs to become, as it were, undercover Greek vowels, which proves that the vowels did not retain their visual prestige in the Egyptian manuals.[55] The following passages from two different divination rituals make use of such transcribed vowels:

> Open to me °
> I am *the opener of earth, who* came forth from *Geb* °
> Hail °
> I am ⲉ° ⲉ° ⲉ, ⲉ̂° ⲉ̂° ⲉ̂, ⲏⲉ̂° ⲏⲉ̂° ⲏⲉ̂ °
> ⲏⲟ̂° ⲏⲟ̂° ⲏⲟ̂ °                              [P. London-Leiden 27/7–8][56]
> BOEL BOEL BOEL ° ⲓ° ⲓ° ⲓ° ⲁ° ⲁ° ⲁ° ⲧⲁⲧ° ⲧⲁⲧ° ⲧⲁⲧ°, \the first servant of the great god/, he who gives light exceedingly °, the companion of the *flame*, \in whose mouth is the *flame*/, he of the *flame* which is never extinguished °, the god who lives, who never dies, \the great god/, he who sits in the

---

[53] The number seven was nonetheless considered extremely powerful in Egyptian theology. Ramses Moftah, 'Ära-Datierungen, Regierungsjahre und Zahlwortspiele' *CdE* 39 (1964) 44–60, 54–56.
[54] Tr. Janet H. Johnson, with minor modifications.
[55] A geometrical arrangement of the vowels does accordingly not occur in the Demotic spells.
[56] This passage is identical with P. London-Leiden 10/29–30. See the foregoing section for a translation of the entire invocation. The vowels are rendered in alphabetic demotic as *y y y*, *e e e*, *he he he*, *hꜥꜣ hꜥꜣ hꜥꜣ* and glossed as ⲉ ⲉ ⲉ, ⲏ ⲏ ⲏ, ⲩⲏ ⲩⲏ ⲩⲏ, ⲩⲱ ⲩⲱ ⲩⲱ.

*flame*, who is in the *midst* of the *flame* °, who is in the lake of *heaven*, in whose hand is the greatness and might of the god; \come into the *midst* of this *flame*/. [P. London-Leiden 17/1–3][57]

In several cases, the vowels have become independent from the alphabetical arrangement to occur as singular entities within a long string of magical names. Written in this way, a vowel starts acting as a *vox magica* in itself, having lost its primary phonetic bond.[58] Since the mechanism of the seven vowels can only be understood and become meaningful from the perspective of Greek phonetics, their presence in the Demotic spells is a testimony of the transference of culturally bound knowledge of one culture group to another. Undoubtedly, the Greek vowels had already become independent magical sounds in themselves by the time they were taken up in the Demotic manuals. They might never have had a phonetic function for Egyptian priests, but were seen, nonetheless, as extremely powerful.

A similar development could be sketched with respect to the function and transcription of palindromes in the magical papyri. Palindromes derive their singular character less from their phonetic quality than from their visual representation in an alphabetic script, because its symmetrical layout is principally lost when the word is pronounced. Palindromes are therefore not so much a phonetic device as a visual phenomenon. The palindrome ABΛANAΘANAΛBA was a popular magical name during the Roman period and occurs frequently on magical gems and in the *Greek Magical Papyri*.[59] The name recurs as well in the Greek spells of P. Leiden I 384 verso as one of many *voces magicae*. For example, the following prayer from column 6 takes recourse to the palindrome and, a few lines further, to a long string of vowel sounds.

Lord, be greeted, you who are the means to obtain favour for the universe and for the inhabited [world]. Heaven has become a dancing place (for you), ARSENOPHRÊ, O king of the heaven[ly gods AB]LANATHANALBA, you who posses righteousness, AKRAMMACHAMAREI, O gracious go[d,

---

[57] Tr. Janet H. Johnson. The passage is part of a larger invocation (17/1–7) that is paralleled in 5/12–19, 7/8–15 and 17/27–32. The vowels of the first line are transcribed as *y y y*, ' ' ', while being glossed as ï ï ï, ʌ ʌ ʌ.

[58] Take for example: P. London-Leiden 2/10, 5/11, 7/8, 25/6, 29/10, 29/13. In these cases, the vowels act as a mere play of sounds, cf. 16/1–3.

[59] On palindromes in ancient magic, see, Karl Preisendanz, 'Palindrom' *PRE* 18.3 (1949) 133–139; take notice also of D. Hagedorn, 'Zwei Spielverse' *ZPE* 2 (1968) 65–69. ABLANATHANALBA was by far the most common palindrome in ancient magic and was used in Greek, Egyptian and Aramaic spells; see Brashear, 'The *Greek Magical Papyri*: An Introduction and Survey', 3577.

sank]anthara, O ruler of nature, satraperkmêph, the origin of the heavenly [universe], aththannou aththannou astraphai iastraphai pakeptôth pa[...]êrintaskliouth êphiô marmaraôth. Let my outspokenness not leave me. [But] let every tongue and every language listen to me, because I am pertaô [mêkh khakh] mnêkh sakmêph iaôoueê ôêô ôêô ieouôêiêiaêa iêôuoie, give m[e gracious]ly whatever you want
[PGM XII.182–189][60]

In the Demotic spells of P. London-Leiden the following two palindromes occur as powerful magical names:

— ⲁⲃⲗⲁⲛⲁⲑⲁⲛⲁⲗⲃⲁ (1/16 and V.22/13)
— ⲁⲩⲉⲃⲱⲑⲓⲁⲃⲁⲑⲁⲃⲁⲓⲟⲱⲃⲉⲩⲁ (29/18)[61]

These names are rendered in alphabetic demotic while being glossed in Old-Coptic.[62] When written in this fashion, the palindrome's inherent ritual power is no longer motivated by its peculiar visual symmetry, since the symmetry is partly lost in the process of transcription. In the extant Demotic spells, the palindromes had ceased to serve as visual forms and acted merely as independent powerful names like the other *voces magicae*, which derived their prestige primarily from their widespread use in magical practices of the day. Both the occurrence of Greek vowels and palindromes make therefore clear that the Egyptian priesthood was not insensitive to ritual practices that lay outside its traditional framework.

### 3.3.3. *Alphabetic Demotic and Old-Coptic: transcription at work*

The process of transcribing Greek script and incorporating foreign sounds into the Demotic spells can best be studied with the help of the vast amount of *voces magicae*. *Voces magicae* constitute some sort of distinctive, yet heteroglossic, international code of divine names that

---

[60] Tr. R.F. Hock, with minor modifications. The palindrome ablanathanalba occurs in the same manuscript also in a spell for a divine revelation, PGM XII.153–160. The palindrome ôeaeô occurs in the same spell (line 156).
[61] auebôthiabathabaithôbeua recurs only in PGM IV.1941 and on a magical gem; for references, see, Brashear, 'The *Greek Magical Papyri*: An Introduction and Survey', 3581 and C. Bonner, *Studies in Magical Amulets chiefly Graeco-Egyptian* (Ann Arbor 1950) 203–204.
[62] ⲁⲃⲗⲁⲛⲁⲑⲁⲛⲁⲗⲃⲁ is ꜣbl'n'th'n'lb'; ⲁⲩⲉⲃⲱⲑⲓⲁⲃⲁⲑⲁⲃⲁⲓⲟⲱⲃⲉⲩⲁ is 'yeb-'ꜣ-thy'b'th'b'yth-'ꜣ-beγ'. The first transcription is not a correct palindrome because the first and last letters are different, whereas the second transcription left the second and last letter but one, ⲩ, untranscribed. This makes clear that the palindromes were originally conceived as names in Greek letters.

comprises elements of Egyptian, Semitic, Greek and Persian origin. In a few instances, the magical names may still bear traces of a traditional epithet or divine name, but in the majority of cases the sounds have become muddled due to incomprehension on the part of the ancient editors, so that most *voces magicae* are untranslatable.[63] *Voces magicae* first appeared in the first century CE and attained such an immediate and widespread dissemination that they became one of the main characteristics of late antique magic.[64] The names are not only found on gems and amulets as productive and apotropaic magical symbols, but, very often, they occur in long strings in the *Greek Magical Papyri* to serve as hidden and enigmatic names that can manipulate the supreme deity. Chanting these names will certainly have had an impressive effect within the ritual thanks to the frequent use of alliteration, euphony and repetition, as in this excerpt from a spell for a divine revelation, which is of Greek column 5 of P. Leiden I 384 verso.

PHTHA RA PHTHA IÊ PHTHA OUN EMÊCHA ERÔCHTH BARÔCH THO[RCH]THA THÔM CHAIEOUCH ARCHANDABAR ÔEAEÔ UNÊÔCH ÊRA ÔN ÊLÔPH BOM PHTHA ATHABRASIA ABRIASÔTH BARBARBELÔCHA BARBAIAÔCH; let there be de(pth), brea(dth), len(gth), brightness, ABLANATHANALBA ABRASIAOUA AKRAMMACHAMAREI THÔTH HÔR ATHÔÔPÔ. Come in, lord, and reveal.
[PGM XII.155–158][65]

Whereas Demotic spells mainly invoke traditional Egyptian deities, the invocations in Greek summon gods of a wide geographical range, but, nonetheless, the function and frequency of *voces magicae* are remarkably similar in both groups. Given the fact that quite a number of *voces* recur in the *Greek Magical Papyri*, in Demotic spells and on magical gems and

---

[63] See for a discussion and list of *voces magicae* that occur in PGM, together with suggested interpretations: Brashear, 'The *Greek Magical Papyri*: An Introduction and Survey', 3429–3438 and 3576–3603. As for suggested origins, for example the *ephesia grammata* or similar untranslatable words and phrases in pharaonic magical spells, see page 3429, n. 235. See also: Heinz J. Thissen, 'Ägyptologische Beiträge zu den griechischen magischen Papyri', in: U. Verhoeven and E. Graefe eds., *Religion und Philosophie in alten Ägypten. Fs. Derchain* (OLA 39; Leuven 1991) 293–302, who considers the Demotic magical spells as well.

[64] It has been suggested that *voces magicae* are nothing but the continuation of the (infrequent) practice to include untranslatable words and phrases in pharaonic magical spells. For useful references, see, Brashear, 'The *Greek Magical Papyri*: An Introduction and Survey', 3429, fn. 235.

[65] Tr. W.C. Grese. This section is part of the spell PGM XII.153–160.

amulets, there can be no question that *voces magicae* were a distinctive international code, the individual elements of which were not invented on the spot.

The main characteristic of the *voces magicae* in the Demotic spells is in the fact that they are not written in Greek script, but transcribed into alphabetic Demotic signs and, more often than not, provided with Old-Coptic glosses, possibly to indicate correct pronunciation. Alphabetic Demotic is a more or less artificial script that had been invented to render foreign words and personal names in Demotic.[66] The 'alphabet' consists of one-consonantal Demotic signs wherewith, to some extent, foreign words can be spelled out according to their factual pronunciation. On the other hand, Old-Coptic is an experimental and preliminary phase of the Coptic script, which only acquired wide usage and a more or less fixed alphabet from the second quarter of the fourth century CE onwards.[67] The Old-Coptic script comprises the Greek alphabet and a small, albeit variable, number of additional Demotic one-consonantal signs to represent sounds that are alien to Greek phonetics.[68] It arose from the desire to overcome the ever-growing discrepancies between factual pronunciation and the fixed orthography of the hieratic and Demotic script. The Old-Coptic texts that are known to date are primarily ritual in nature, possibly because the efficacy of a ritual was believed to rely on correct pronunciation of the magical names.[69]

The Old-Coptic script that is used in the manuscripts under study consists of the Greek alphabet and twelve additional alphabetic Demot-

---

[66] See also section 4.3 on the occurrence of Greek loan words in the Demotic spells.

[67] Bagnall, *Egypt in Late Antiquity*, 256. Next to coherent texts, onomastica are a vital source of information about the development of the Coptic script: Quaegebeur, 'De la préhistoire de l'écriture copte'. For a more sociological analysis of the rise of Coptic, see, McBride, 'The Development of Coptic'.

[68] For an overview, see, Rodolphe Kasser, 'Alphabets, Old Coptic' *The Coptic Encyclopedia* 8 (1991) 41a–45b.

[69] See for an overview, Helmut Satzinger, 'Old Coptic' *The Coptic Encyclopedia* 8 (1991) 169a–75b. The corpus of Old-Coptic texts is made up of the following manuscripts: 1) P. Schmidt, letter to the gods that was probably deposited at a tomb: H. Satzinger, 'The Old Coptic Schmidt Papyrus' *JARCE* 12 (1975) 37–50; 2) P. London 98 and P. Michigan 6131 (horoscopes); 3) PGM III.396–408 and 633–688; PGM IV.1–25 (partly translation of P. London-Leiden 21/1–9); PGM IV 86–153 (H. Satzinger, 'An Old Coptic Text Reconsidered: PGM 94FF' *OLA* 61 (1994) 213–224); PGM IV.1231–1239; PGM XLVIII.1–21. See also M. Meyer and R. Smith (eds.), *Ancient Christian Magic. Coptic Texts of Ritual Power* (San Fransisco 1994) nrs. 1–3., 13–25.; 4) a business letter (Iain Gardner, 'An Old-Coptic Ostracon from Ismant El-Kharab?' *ZPE* 125 (1999) 195–200).

ic signs. These additional characters do not yet appear in the Demotic spells of P. Leiden I 384 verso, possibly, as suggested in chapter 2.3.1, because the scribe had not yet found a suitable method for glossing the *voces magicae* when he wrote the manuscript. The script is occasionally used to gloss common Egyptian words such as religious vocabulary, prepositions and verbs,[70] but occurs mainly to write out the sounds of *voces magicae*, of which there are more than 700 in the two manuscripts. In those cases, the magical name is usually given in an alphabetic Demotic version with, above the line, the Old-Coptic rendering. These combined transcriptions allow investigating in more detail the complex process of adopting and incorporating the *voces magicae* in the Demotic spells. A substantial amount of these magical names derives definitely from age-old Egyptian epithets, but their alphabetic Demotic and Old-Coptic transcription hides or even distorts their etymology. These distortions can only be explained as resulting from the consultation of manuscripts in Greek script, in which the Egyptian phonetics of magical names had been distorted by necessity, as the Greek script lacks the means to represent adequately Egyptian sounds. This means that the editor of the extant alphabetic Demotic and Old-Coptic *voces magicae* did not recognize the Egyptian origin of a considerable number of magical names he found in the manuscript in Greek script and, instead of re-transcribing them in agreement with the rules of hieratic or Demotic orthography, spelled them out in alphabetic Demotic and Old-Coptic signs, thereby mangling the Egyptian sounds for the second time. In a number of cases, the editor did full justice to his parallel manuscripts by quoting alternatives, thereby demonstrating that he did not invent the names himself, but copied them indeed from various manuscripts.

> BOTH° THEU° IE° UE° O°-OE° IA° UA° \another manuscript [says] THEU° IE° OE° ON° IA° UA°/ PTHAKH° ELOE° \another manuscript [says] **elon**, very good/ IATH° EON° PERIPHAE° IEU° IA° IO° IA° IUE°, come down to the light of this lamp °      [P. London-Leiden 16/1–4].

In the foregoing passage, each magical name is spelled in alphabetic Demotic signs and provided with a gloss in Old-Coptic script.

The transcribed *voces magicae* and glosses in the following invocation illustrate rather well the various choices the editor made in incorporat-

---

[70] This method is not restricted to the Demotic magical papyri. It occurs frequently in the Tebtunis hieratic onomasticon of the Roman period: Osing, *Hieratische Papyri aus Tebtunis I*, 52–64.

ing the *voces magicae* into the Demotic spells. The passage is taken from a vessel divination rite.

**pnebbaï     oreidimbaei**
I am the lord of spirit°,[71] ORITSIMBAI° SONATSIR° EPISGHES° EMMIME° THO°-GOM°-PHRUR° PHIRIM°-PHUNI is your name°; MIMI soul of souls soul of souls° GTHETHO-NI°, I am Bastet° PTHA° BALKHAM° whom bore BINUI° SPHE PHAS°. I am BAPTHA° GAM°-MI°-SATRA is your name°, MI°-MEO° IA-NUME°.     [P. London-Leiden 28/1–4]

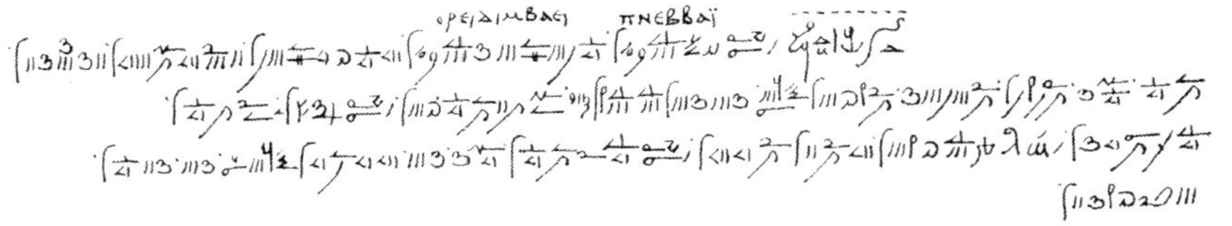

Fig. 3.3. P. London-Leiden 28/1–4

The first divine name, 'lord of spirit', is written in a correct Demotic spelling and provided with an Old-Coptic gloss, which vocalizes accurately the Egyptian name. The second name, ORITSIMBAI, is partly spelled in alphabetic Demotic signs (ORITSIM) and partly written in Demotic (BAI = *by*) as if the ancient editor interpreted the latter part of the name as an Egyptian noun (spirit, soul) as in the previous name, but was puzzled by his *Vorlage* with respect to the former part of the name. The gloss **oreidimbaei** may then very well represent the original form that he found in this manuscript and which he partly translated to Demotic. If this were correct, it would mean that the original name was spelled in Greek letters because the final i-sound of the group -BAI is written in the gloss as **baei** instead of Old-Coptic **baï**. The seventh magical name of this invocation, PHIRIM-PHUNI, may be a garbled form of the *vox magica* φιριμνουν known from similar sources (PGM XII.345 and XXI.25), which can be reduced to the very common Egyptian epithet *prj m Nwn*, 'He who came forth from Nun (the abyss)'.[72] Although the PHUNI part may very well represent something other than *PHNUN,

---

[71] Griffith/Thompson and Janet H. Johnson translate this name as 'lord of spirits', but I prefer to take BAÏ as a singular instead of a plural noun following Horapollo, *Hieroglyphika* I, 7. The noun in the Demotic version is likewise singular.
[72] *GMPT*, 165, fn. 87 and 259, fn. 5 [R.K.R.]; Thissen, 'Ägyptologische Beiträge zu den griechischen magischen Papyri', 299.

'the Nun',[73] the PHIRIM part derives certainly from the fixed clause *prj m*, 'He who came forth from', which the scribe knew very well judging by the frequent occurrence of the clause in the Demotic spells.[74] For example, the following two passages contain the common epithet in Demotic and a mixture of hieratic and Demotic.

> *ink p3 ḥf ir pyr n p3 nwn*
> I am the snake who came forth from the Nun
> [P. London-Leiden 9/15]

> *mtw=k p3y k3 km ḥyt ir pr n p3 nn.w*
> You are that black bull, the foremost one who *came forth* from the *Nun*
> [P. London-Leiden 21/33]

The fact that the name PHIRIM-PHUNI is spelled in alphabetic Demotic signs despite its clear Egyptian origin demonstrates that the ancient editor took it over slavishly from a manuscript in Greek script. This line of reasoning can also be applied to the *vox magica* PTHA, which occurs twice in the above quoted passage, once as an element in the longer form BAPTHA. This form is regularly employed in the *Greek Magical Papyri* as φθα as, for example, twice in the passage of P. Leiden I 384 verso quoted at the beginning of the present section. Although rendered in Greek script, it is actually a transcription of the name of the Egyptian god Ptah, written in Egyptian as *Ptḥ*.[75] The two magical names had therefore originally the meaning 'Ptah' and 'Soul of Ptah' (BAPTHA). Although the extant writings of the names still bear the traces of their etymology, the ancient editor did not follow Egyptian orthography, but gave preference to an alphabetic Demotic, distorted spelling, in all likelihood because his *Vorlage* did not have these magical names in a hieratic or Demotic writing, but in a Greek transcription. The same name occurs also in the last but one above quoted invocation, this time written as PTHAKH, still preserving the final uvular sound of original *Ptḥ*.[76]

To summarise the evidence presented thus far, in the course of editing the extant Demotic spells *voces magicae* in Greek script from

---

[73] If it would derive from ⲫⲟⲩⲱⲓⲛⲓ, 'the light' (B), the *vox magica* could be translated as 'He who came forth from the light', a phrase which is otherwise unknown as epithet.
[74] See for attestations the glossary of P. London-Leiden, page 30.
[75] See for forms of φθα: PGM II.118; IV.972,1585, 3013, 3015; V.22, 353; VII.362, 640; XII.81, 155; XXIII.6, 1056; LVII.20; LXI.26. See for regular forms of *Ptḥ* in the Demotic spells: P. London-Leiden 9/15 and P. Leiden I 384 verso I*/3, 6, 9, 14, 17.
[76] The vox is glossed with ⲫⲟⲗⲭ. In PGM LXI.26, a similar form φθααχε occurs.

manuscripts now lost were transcribed into alphabetic Demotic signs and incorporated into the Demotic spells.[77] In the majority of cases, the editors were unaware of possible etymologies and spelled the names out as they found them in the *Vorlage* without any concern for a consistent orthography.[78] However, the process of transcription was not always characterised by incomprehension, as the various writings of the *vox magica* ⲈⲔⲞⲘⲪⲐⲰ demonstrate. It occurs in P. London-Leiden 16/21 and 17/25 and once as ⲔⲞⲘⲦⲰ in 7/6. These Old-Coptic glosses are equivalent with the *voces* κομφθο in PGM IV.1323 and κμητο in PGM III.680, and can easily be interpreted as forms deriving from \**i̯.ir-ḳm3-p3-t3* (Demotic) or \**ḳm3-t3* (classical Egyptian), 'The one who created the earth'.[79] The peculiar spellings of these names reveal that the copyist was partly aware of the origin of the *vox magica*. By spelling the name twice in alphabetic Demotic, he acknowledged that he saw it as a *vox magica* instead of as a regular Egyptian epithet. In 17/25 he spelled EGOMTHO in alphabetic Demotic signs, which conforms to, and is clearly dependent upon, the Greek form; in 16/21, however, he made

---

[77] Three more examples can underpin the current hypothesis that the compilers were working with a text in Greek script at hand. Firstly, the term NYTSI, ⲚⲞⲨⲞⲒ, which occurs frequently as an element of a *vox magica*, is a transcription of Egyptian *nṯr*, ⲚⲞⲨⲞⲈ, 'god'. To spell this word in alphabetic Demotic signs is a remarkable thing to do for an Egyptian priest. Secondly, the *vox magica* PSHIBIEG (P. London-Leiden 10/6), glossed as ⲪⲒⲂⲒⲎⲔ, may be reduced to *Pa-bik*, 'He of the falcon' or *P3-bik*, 'The falcon', which were common personal names in the Ptolemaic and Roman period. See for standard transcription of Greek πφ+ι into Egyptian *p-sh*: Johnson, 'Dialect of the Demotic Magical Papyrus of London and Leiden', 123–124. See for regular writings of *bik* in P. London-Leiden: 3/17,18; 7/34; 9/7,34; 20/29; 21/4; V.25/2. See for *P3-bik* and *Pa-bik* as personal names: Dem.Nb. 182 and 363. PGM IV.3007–3086, a spell for exorcism, is attributed to a certain Πιβήχις, who should have been a famous Egyptian magician: Thissen, 'Ägyptologische Beiträge zu den griechischen magischen Papyri', 295 and K. Preisendanz, 'Pibechis' *PRE* 20 (1941) 1310–1312. A third argument is 'You are ITTH; THOUTSI is your name' (P. London-Leiden 14/13) of which the second name, glossed as ⲐⲞⲨⲞⲒ, contains the name of the god Thoth, *Ḏḥwty*. This god of writing and magic occurs frequently in the PGM, variously written as θωθ, θωουθ and θοωθ, e.g. PGM III.340; IV.317, 3020, 3159; VII.500; XII.110, 297. The unorthodox spelling in alphabetic Demotic signs can again only be explained by assuming an original text in Greek script.

[78] Compare also the many spellings in alphabetic Demotic signs of the most popular *vox magica*, IAO, in the glossary of P. London-Leiden (nr. 184–196); see also nrs. 401–403; 439–440; 449–450; 468–471; 478–481. These alternative spellings suggest that the transcription into alphabetic Demotic was done on the spot without much consideration for consistency.

[79] Thissen, 'Ägyptologische Beiträge zu den griechischen magischen Papyri', 300–302.

a mixture of alphabetic Demotic and regular Demotic signs by writing ⲈⲄⲞⲘ-*pꜣ-tꜣ*, so that the epithet becomes half-comprehensible (ⲈⲄⲞⲘ-the-earth). In 7/6 ⲔⲞⲘⲦⲰ is written as a gloss above a hieratic-demotic mixture *ḳmꜣ-tꜣ*, 'He who created the earth'. Given the fact that the epithet occurs in a long string of rather obscure *voces magicae*,[80] it is reasonable to assume that the ancient editor took it over with the whole passage from another manuscript, while recognising that this particular *vox magica* derives from a rather common Egyptian phrase. That he wrote the epithet in an unorthodox mixture of hieratic and Demotic only goes to prove the spontaneous character of his transcription.[81]

The assumption of an original text in Greek script cannot account for all peculiarities concerning the *voces magicae* in the Demotic spells. If such a text is postulated from the evidence, it can only have been one among many. Upon a total of 566 *voces magicae*, thirty contain one or more Egyptian sounds that are rendered by Old-Coptic letters. Although these magical names are as enigmatic as any other, their phonetic formation precludes a Greek origin or the involvement of a distorting Greek alphabet.[82] These *voces magicae* may as well derive from a manuscript in Old-Coptic script like the Roman-period P. BM 10.606, which preserves Middle Egyptian spells against fever transcribed into Old-Coptic letters.[83] Section 3.2 already touched upon the striking

---

[80] P. London-Leiden 7/6–7: 'ⲒⲞ ⲦⲀⲂⲀⲞ ⲤⲨⲄⲀⲘⲀⲘⲨ ⲀⲔϨⲀⲔϨⲀ-ⲚⲂⲨ ⲤⲀⲚⲀⲨⲀⲚⲒ ⲈⲦⲤⲒⲈ ⲔⲞⲘⲦⲰ ⲄⲈⲐⲞⲤ ⲂⲀⲤⲀ-ⲈⲐⲞⲢⲒ ⲐⲘⲒⲖⲀ ⲀⲔϨⲔϨⲨ, make for me [an] answer to everything about which I am asking here today'. Note that ⲈⲦⲤⲒⲈ may very well be a rendering of the Greek vocative θεέ, 'O god'.

[81] Consider in a similar way ⲈⲖⲒⲔⲞⲘⲦⲰ, gloss above ⲈⲦⲤⲒ-*ḳme-tꜣ* (P. London-Leiden 16/17). In the incantation of the footnote above, the same terms occur as successive but separate magical names. ⲈⲖⲒⲔⲞⲘⲦⲰ can therefore be taken as a mistake of the Egyptian copyist and should be read as two separate names. At all events, the copyist has again written the same epithet in a different way: in this case, he stuck to the Demotic script, although the language is Classical Egyptian. The gloss ⲔⲞⲘⲢⲎ, which is written above *ḳmꜣ-Rꜥ* (regular demotic), 'He who created Re' or 'He whom Re created', should be considered differently, as it does not occur among a string of *voces magicae*. This is probably a case of vocalising a traditional, still-understood epithet. As such, the form ⲔⲞⲘⲢⲎ is dependent upon the Demotic *ḳmꜣ-Rꜥ* and not upon a *vox magica* in Greek letters taken from a lost manuscript.

[82] It goes without saying that these thirty *voces magicae* do not appear in the *Greek Magical Papyri*.

[83] Only one column of the original manuscript is preserved, but the right margin of the papyrus sheet preserves scribbles of a previous column revealing that the original manuscript was actually a Demotic/Old-Coptic magical handbook; see Jacco Dieleman, 'Ein spätägyptisches magisches Handbuch: eine neue PDM oder PGM?', in: F. Hoffmann and H.-J. Thissen (eds.), *Res Severa Verum Gaudium. Fs Zauzich* (Studia Demotica VI; Leuven 2004) 121–128.

feature that a few *voces magicae* are rendered in hieratic instead of alphabetic Demotic script.[84] The following passage, which has also been discussed in section 3.2, illustrates that these hieratic *voces* are neither of Egyptian origin nor idiosyncratic inventions of the Egyptian copyist and, hence, must derive from again another *Vorlage*.

F 1) *Hail,* **sax** *saks,* **amoun** *Amun,* **sax** *saks,* **abrasax** *abrasaks,*
 *he who gave birth to them*
 2) for you are *the moon*, the great one of the stars, he who gave birth to them.
 3) Listen to these things which I said.
 4) Walk in accordance with the (words) of my mouth.
 5) May you reveal yourself to me,
 **than thana thanatha;** another (manuscript) says **thêi**.
 6) *tahanu, taheanuna, tahnuatha*
 7) *This is my correct* name. [P. London-Leiden 23/24–26][85]

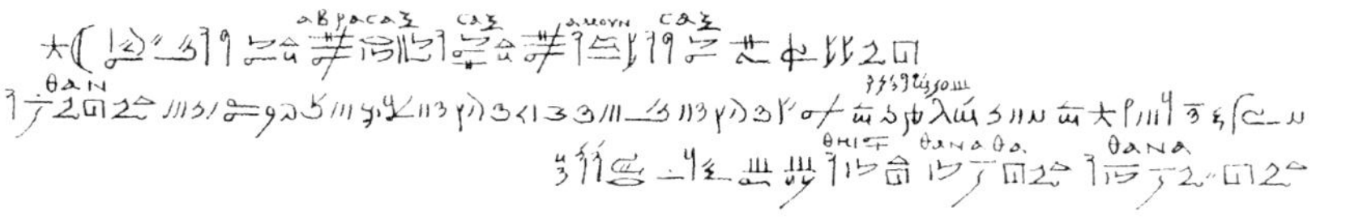

Fig. 3.4. P. London-Leiden 23/24–26

The elements sax of the first line are a play on the popular *vox magica* ABRASAX, which name is frequently summoned in the *Greek Magical Papyri* as a powerful divine being and whose name and image is inscribed on numerous magical gems.[86] The cultural and geographic origin of the name is unclear, but it certainly does not derive from an

---

[84] Not every Old-Coptic gloss above a hieratic word or epithet is a *vox magica*. In most cases, these glosses provide information about the correct pronunciation of a common Egyptian word. The same holds true for correct Demotic spellings that are provided with an Old-Coptic gloss. Take for example: *Ḥry-tȝ* (1/20), *Wn-tȝ* (1/28), *Tȝ-srpt* (2/17), *Pȝ-wr.tjw* (2/26), *Pȝ-hrd.t* (19/19), *'Imn* (23/24), *Srp.t* (29/6), *Pȝ-ym* (V.22/10). Two further possible examples of hieratic *voces magicae* are: *lḥ*, ⲁⲁⲧ (5/11) and *mȝʾ-ḥr* ?, ⲙⲟⲩⲓ *ḥ* ⲧⲁⲩⲓ (5/11).
[85] Tr. Janet H. Johnson, with minor modifications. The division in verse lines is tentative because the section lacks verse points.
[86] A vast amount of literature exists on the meaning of the name Abrasax. In antiquity the name was explained with the help of the numerical value of the Greek letters, which amounts to 365: 'You are the number of the days of the year, Abrasax' (PGM XIII.156; see also PGM VIII.49). For references to scholarly literature, see, Brashear, 'The *Greek Magical Papyri*: An Introduction and Survey', 3577. Because of the association with the 365 days of the year, Abrasax was seen as a solar deity. He is

Egyptian root, so that the name must be considered an import into the Egyptian ritual domain. It is therefore remarkable that the name is not spelled in alphabetic Demotic signs as customary with foreign names, but written in the highly traditional hieratic script. Moreover, instead of solely using one-consonantal signs, the Egyptian copyist chose to render the first sound of the first SAX group according to the principle of acrophony.[87] This is to say that a particular sound is expressed by means of a common Egyptian word, of which only the first consonant has phonetic relevance. In this case, the s-sound is rendered with the help of the verbs *sʒw* 'to walk slowly' in the first case and *stj* 'to pierce (through)' in the second and third case. Following such customs, proper to the native tradition and widespread in contemporaneous hieroglyphic temple inscriptions, the SAX renderings testify to a degree of incorporation that is much more profound than an alphabetic Demotic transcription would show at first sight.

The occurrence of the popular international *vox magica* ABRASAX is not the only indication that the Egyptian priesthood was willing to make use of foreign powerful names. The adaptation of Jewish material in the Demotic magical spells is testified by the frequent occurrence of IAO, the most attested *vox magica* in Roman period magical material.[88] The name can easily be interpreted as a vocalised rendition of the tetragrammaton YHWH. Greek borrowings can be found in an incantation of a divination ritual that contains the following series of names in alphabetic demotic: ARKHE-KHEM-PHE NSEY HELE SATRAPERMT (P. London-Leiden 17/18–19). Since the *vox* NSEY is glossed with ΖΕΟΥ, it is actually the vocative of Ζεύς, the supreme deity of the classical Greek pantheon.[89] Above the form HELE, a little sign is added that is frequently

---

frequently depicted on magical gems as an armoured figure with snake-feet and the head of a cock; A. Delatte and Ph. Derchain, *Les intailles magiques gréco-égyptiennes* (Paris 1964) nrs. 24–42.

[87] The principles of acrophony and rebus stand at the basis of the Ptolemaic hieroglyphic font and were thus well known in native priestly circles. Dieter Kurth, 'Die Lautwerte der Hieroglyphen in den Tempelinschriften der griechisch-römischen Zeit— zur Systematik ihrer Herleitungsprinzipien' *ASAE* 69 (1983) 287–309 and Serge Sauneron, *Esna VIII—L'Ecriture figurative dans les textes d'Esna* (IFAO, Cairo 1982), chapter 3, 'La philosophie d'une écriture', 47–80.

[88] See for references Brashear, 'The *Greek Magical Papyri*: An Introduction and Survey', 3588. For Demotic attestations, see, the glossary of P. London-Leiden nrs. 184–196; P. Leiden 384 verso 2/8; P. Louvre E 3229 Vo/9.

[89] Note that Zeus and the Egyptian god Amun were equated. The cultic presence of Zeus was otherwise rather limited in Greco-Roman Egypt.

used in Greek magical manuscripts as a symbol for Ἥλιος, 'sun (god)'.[90] HELE can therefore be interpreted as the vocative form of the Greek sun god. The opening vox is enigmatic although the first part ARKHE can certainly be read as Ἀρχή, 'beginning, sovereignty'. It is thus clear that this line contains material that ultimately derives from a Greek source.[91]

A final testimony of the international range of sources that were used for P. London-Leiden is the occurrence of the so-called Maskelli-Maskello formula. Although the *voces magicae* are rather enigmatic, undoubtedly already for the ancient compilers, and applied in quite a random way, some of them recur in fixed sequences, forming a so-called formula. In certain cases, a recipe in the *Greek Magical Papyri* merely gives the first word of the formula, because the magician was considered to know the formula by heart.[92] In P. London-Leiden V.15/2–4, the complete Maskelli-Maskello formula is given in alphabetic Demotic signs and Old-Coptic glosses with minor variation from the standard formula: 'MASKELLI MASKELLO PHNYGENTABAO HREKSIGTHO PERIGTHEON PERIPEGANEKS AREOBASAGRA (another manuscript [says]: OBASA-GRA)'.[93] In P Leiden J 384 verso, the formula returns in a Greek recipe for consecrating a ring for success and charm.[94] In this case, each name of the formula was considered a separate deity since an article precedes each name.

> O greatest god, who exceeds all power, I call on you, the IAÔ, the SABAÔTH, the ADÔNAI, ... the MASKELLEI, the MASKELLÔTH, the PHNOU, the KENTABAÔTH, the OREOBAZAGRA, the HIPPOCHTHÔN, the RÊSICHTHÔN, the PURIPÊGANUX ... [PGM XII.284–291]

To conclude, it has become clear by discussing the occurrence and transcription of the seven Greek vowels, palindromes and *voces magicae*

---

[90] It is used twice in P. London-Leiden: 17/19 and 23/8. In 23/8 it is used in a short Egyptian phrase in hieratic: *r-ḥr pʒ (Rʿ)*, 'in front of the sun'.

[91] The final magical name SATRAPERMT, which is glossed with ⲥⲁⲧⲣⲁⲡⲉⲣⲙⲏⲧ, contains the element *satrap* that was used as title for a governor of a province of the Persian Empire. With the military expansion of the Achaemenid Empire in the sixth and fifth centuries BCE, the title became a current term in the Near East. Cf. the *vox magica* σατραπερχμηψ (PGM XII.185).

[92] PGM VII.302. The complete Maskelli-Maskello formula is written in PGM IX.10; XXXVI.342–346.

[93] The standard formula is: MASKELLI MASKELLÔ PHNOUKENTABAÔTH OREOBAZAGRA RHÊXICHTÔN HIPPOCHTÔN PYRIPÊGANUX. See for possible etymologies: *GMPT*, 336 and Thissen, 'Ägyptologische Beiträge zu den griechischen magischen Papyri', 298.

[94] The spell is discussed in close detail in chapter 5.3.

that the Demotic spells are tightly linked with magical practices of the Greco-Roman *oikoumene*. The editors adopted the magical names to their own needs and scriptural possibilities without being aware of the origin of the names in many instances. In many cases a *vox magica* is but a garbled form of a common Egyptian epithet, but in as many other cases the etymological origin of a *vox magica* has to be sought outside the confines of Egyptian language and religion. In other words, the *voces magicae* found in the two handbooks under study derive from a variety of religious groups, of which traditional Egyptian religion is but one. Whereas the conclusion of the previous chapter situates the production and circulation of the Demotic spells firmly in the conservative Egyptian temple milieu because of the intricate mixture of Demotic and hieratic script, the present chapter argues consequently for a model of textual transmission which allows taking into account the dynamics of tradition and innovation, native and international. The current chapter has thus amply demonstrated that a sole focus on the Egyptian temple cannot be appropriate for a study of the sphere of production and use of the two manuscripts under study.

### 3.4. *Considering secrecy*

A peculiar phenomenon of P. London-Leiden is the occurrence of four different scripts that are encrypted. The verso side preserves two sets of an encrypted Greek alphabet written inside a rectangular frame in black ink. The first set has the corresponding Greek letter written above each enigmatic sign, while the other lists 24 signs in total, which equals the number of letters of the Greek alphabet (see figure 2.6). Strangely enough, neither script is used in any of the Demotic spells on the manuscript or in any other magical spell in Demotic, Greek or Coptic known to date. The third set of encrypted signs that occurs on the manuscript is well known from contemporaneous magical spells, amulets and lamellae, on which similar signs serve as a powerful 'sacred' writing that was believed to enable communication with the divine by virtue of its symbolic and mystical qualities. The signs were very popular in the eastern Mediterranean basin at large from the second century CE onwards and are known today as *charaktêres*. Differently, the fourth encrypted script seems to have been much more restricted in use as regards geographical range and attestations in magical material of that period. Although it occurs frequently in P. London-

Leiden to spell Egyptian and Greek words in recipes for drugs and potions, it recurs otherwise only once to spell a word in P. Leiden I 384 verso and once in P. Louvre E3229, a similar Demotic magical handbook from Thebes. Thanks to three parallel un-coded passages, Egyptologists have been able to decipher the script, which appeared to be some sort of encoded Old-Coptic alphabet. There can be no question that only a person who knew the correct key for decipherment could read words written in this idiosyncratic script, so that Egyptologists have coined the script merely 'cipher'. However, this term should be used with due caution, because it implies the idea of concealment, of purposely hiding information for others, wherewith Egyptologists may very well misrepresent the nature and function of this script. Since this study is concerned with the social context of the manuscripts, the relationship between script and secrecy has to be addressed in close detail.

It is of paramount importance to analyse whether scripts are used to hide information from others, because secrecy is socially highly productive.[95] A secret involves as a rule two or more persons who share and guard their knowledge trying to prevent their secret from being revealed to a third party.[96] As such, secrecy constitutes a complex social arena in which the members of the concealing party are characterised by a tension between the social obligation to conceal information and the desire to reveal it in order to gain social prestige for oneself. The other contesting party is defined precisely by its willingness to find out what the secret is. A defending in-group is thus defined as opposed to a desiring out-group based on the selective availability of knowledge. Given the desire of the dominant Greco-Roman culture to share in the secret knowledge and divine revelations of the Egyptian priesthood, such a sociological model of concealment might be a useful heuristic tool for situating the encrypted scripts in their textual and social context. Before doing this, a basic question is then: are these scripts indeed invented to hide information and, first, was secrecy an important characteristic of Egyptian religion?

---

[95] These ideas are based on a critique of Simmel's sociological model of concealment: Birgitta Nedelmann, 'Geheimhaltung, Verheimlichung, Geheimnis—Einige soziologische Vorüberlegungen'. in: Hans G. Kippenberg and Guy G. Stroumsa, *Secrecy and Concealment. Studies in the History of Mediterranean and Near Eastern Religions* (Leiden 1995) 1–16.

[96] This chapter is only concerned with so called relative secrecy. Absolute secrecy is defined as a secret that a person keeps to himself. It goes without saying that absolute secrecy is socially unproductive.

The latter question can be answered easily and firmly in positive terms. Secrecy was an important and recurring element of Egyptian theology and cultic practices.[97] In the ideology of the daily ritual, the officiating priest takes on the role of a god to participate in the thus enacted cosmic drama of the battle between chaos and order. His promotion to the rank of a deity is dependent upon his knowledge of the nature of the divine world. He should know the hidden names, attributes, and cultic topography of each specific god.[98] Cultic hymns regularly stress that this knowledge is not to be exposed to any other than the king or the priest who acts according to the king's cultic function. A ritual text for the conservation of life explicitly and frequently warns the reader of the manuscript never to reveal its contents on penalty of death, which is directly stated in the opening paragraph.

> ⟨Ritual of⟩ 'Finishing the Work' [...] it is not seen; it is not known. Life is in it; death is in it. You will keep yourself distant from it. Do not know it. Do not hear it, because it is one that turns into ashes, because it is a flame, because it is a quick death. Life is in it; death is in it for sure.
> [P. Salt 1/1–2][99]

> The book 'Finishing the Work' is conducted on that day. It is a secret book roll, which overturns magical charms, which binds binding-spells, which blocks binding-spells, which intimidates the whole universe. Life is in it; death is in it. Do not reveal it, because he who reveals it will die by a sudden death or by an immediate killing. You must be distant from it. Life is in it; death is in it.  [P. Salt 5/10–6/3][100]

Such secret cultic texts were kept in the House-of-Life or, in the case of the Books of the Netherworld,[101] laid out on the walls of the hidden and closed-off tombs of the New Kingdom pharaohs. Since secrecy was considered a precondition of cosmic order, these texts had to be

---

[97] Jan Assmann, 'Unio Liturgica. Die kultische Einstimmung in Götterweltlichen Lobpreis als Grundmotiv "esoterischer" Überlieferung im alten Ägypten', in: *Secrecy and Concealment*, 37–60.

[98] See for a selection of illustrative examples: Assmann, *op. cit.*, 48–49.

[99] Publication of the text: Philip Derchain, *Le Papyrus Salt 825 (B.M. 10051), rituel pour la conservation de la vie en Egypt* (Brussels 1965) and F.R. Herbin, 'Les premières pages du Papyrus Salt 825' *BIFAO* 88 (1988) 95–112.

[100] Cultic secrecy is as well an important precondition of the ritual. It has to be carried out in the dark (P. Salt 7/1) and Asiatics are not allowed to enter the room where the ritual is conducted (P. Salt 7/6).

[101] See for a useful overview of the various Books of the Netherworld: Erik Hornung, *The Ancient Egyptian Books of the Afterlife* (Ithaca, London 1999) 26–152.

defended against curious and malevolent beings.[102] However, secrecy was only an issue within the cultic context of the cosmic battle between the forces of evil and divine order. Differently, hymns, prayers and representations are often characterised by a concern for overt propaganda.[103] For example, hymns to the sun god were engraved on steles that were placed on clearly visible spots to be read by passers-by. The same holds true for statues and steles that were erected by private individuals in the forecourts of the temple.

Apart from a religious sanction, priestly secrecy can also be motivated by a concern to defend group interests, as in the case of priestly technical knowledge. For example, a rather enigmatic Old Kingdom title suggests that medicine was considered a secret art, at least during that early period,[104] while the large medical Ebers Papyrus, dating from the New Kingdom, contains a section entitled 'Beginnings of the secret (writings) of the physician' [P. Ebers 854]. One precept of this section makes clear that secrecy was not so much encouraged by a concern to protect untrained laymen from making failures, but motivated by a desire to protect professional knowledge and preserve group interests.

> Then you make for him medicines that are to be kept secret from underlings of the physician except for your own heir. [P. Ebers 206b][105]

It is important to stress that these texts of secret priestly knowledge were not encoded by means of an encrypted script: they were written in Classical Egyptian in the hieratic script. Nonetheless, the idea of coded script was existent and put to use in religious texts. For example, the *Enigmatic Book of the Netherworld* makes use of a cryptographic script for, so it seems, hiding information, or at least, giving the impression of secrecy.[106] The fanciful representations of demons, which are lined up in rows, are accompanied by their name and an explanatory note written in enigmatic hieroglyphs:

---

[102] Admonitions, 6/6–7 and Urk. VI, 2, 120–129
[103] Assmann, *op. cit.*, 51 and 57.
[104] Most recent treatment of the subject: Ludwig D. Morenz, '(Magische) Sprache der geheimen Kunst' *SAK* 24 (1997) 191–201. See also Westendorf, *Handbuch der altägyptischen Medizin* I, 99–100.
[105] Compare with P. Ebers 188b.
[106] Hornung, *Egyptian Books of the Afterlife*, 77–82; Alexandre Piankoff, *The Shrines of Tut-Ankh-Amon* Bollingen Series 40/2 (New York 1955) 121–125 and 127–131; John Coleman Darnell, *The Enigmatic Netherworld Books of the Solar-Osirian Unity. Cryptographic Compositions in the Tombs of Tutankhamun, Ramesses VI and Ramesses IX* (OBO 198: Fribourg, Göttingen 2004).

> These gods are like this in their caverns which are in the Place of Annihilation. Their bodies are in complete darkness when Re passes by, and their souls are behind his disk. His rays penetrate into their cavern.[107]

This passage is written in ordinary hieroglyphs, the phonetic value of which is different from regular usage. Following strict rules of acrophony and rebus, which are also the principles for the regular phonetic values, a hieroglyphic sign can be given differing values.[108] Texts written in this fashion spell the words alphabetically according to their contemporaneous pronouncement without the required determinatives, while they retain the Classical Egyptian syntax. The phenomenon occurs likewise in certain passages of the Books of the Netherworld that are recorded in the cenotaph of Sethi I in Abydos, and the tombs of Ramesses VI and IX in the Valley of the Kings. The above-mentioned *Ritual for preserving life* contains a passage in which the speech of the god Geb is quoted as a string of fancy hieroglyphs that cannot be translated. Similar signs recur on the manuscript in two vignettes and a list of ingredients.[109] In all likelihood, these enigmatic hieroglyphs were designed to enhance the secret and exotic nature of the ritual text.[110]

Cryptography was in use during all periods of pharaonic history, beginning as early as the Old Kingdom,[111] but remained always a

---

[107] Tr. Alexandre Piankoff, *Shrines of Tut-Ankh-Amon*, 123.

[108] An explanation of these phonetic rules together with a list of cryptographic hieroglyphs and their corresponding phonetic values can be found in E. Drioton, 'Essai sur la cryptographie privée de la fin de la 18e dynastie' *Rev.d'Egyptologie* 1 (1933) 1–50. See for the cryptographic hieroglyphs of the above quoted passage of the *Enigmatic Book of the Netherworld*: Idem, 'La cryptographie de la chapelle de Toutânkhamon' *JEA* 35 (1949) 117–122.

[109] A clear photo of the two columns together with explanation can be found in Richard Parkinson, *Cracking Codes. The Rosetta Stone and Decipherment* (Berkeley and Los Angeles 1999) 86–87. In the *Book of the Transformations*, preserved in a copy of 57–56 BCE, a number of lines are written in cipher, the signs of which are otherwise unknown: P. Louvre E 3452 6/5, 18–19 and 7/15. For a facsimile of the manuscript, see, G. Legrain, *Le Livre des Transformations (Papyrus démotique 3.452 du Louvre)* (Paris 1890).

[110] It has been suggested that the method occurs as early as the Coffin Texts: R.O. Faulkner, 'Abnormal or Cryptic Writings in the Coffin Texts' *JEA* 67 (1981) 173–174. Note Faulkner's word of caution: 'nowhere in the Coffin Texts is there a connected text in cryptic script, but only single signs or small groups of signs'. A very late example is a section of the *Book of Breathing* partly written in cryptographic hieroglyphs on a funerary shroud; text D in François-René Herbin, 'Une nouvelle page du Livre des Respirations' *BIFAO* 84 (1984) 249–302.

[111] E. Drioton, 'Un rébus de l'Ancien Empire', in: *Mélanges Maspero* I (MIFAO 66; Cairo 1935–1938), 697–704.

marginal phenomenon. Two separate methods are discernable: the use of fancy hieroglyphs that are invented for the occasion[112] or assigning alternative phonetic values to ordinary hieroglyphs in line with the above-mentioned principles of acrophony and rebus.[113] Unlike what may be expected from the above-mentioned *Enigmatic Book of the Netherworld*, texts in cryptographic script were actually always very much concerned with being read by a large audience. Therefore, cryptography should not be considered a strategy to hide and monopolize the access to information, but rather as a method to attract attention by way of an unfamiliar appearance. Cryptographic texts were usually displayed at an eye-catching spot with free access, while the reading of the enigmatic signs was more often than not facilitated by the presence of ordinary hieroglyphs or by a parallel text recorded in regular script.[114] This same concern for attention lies at the heart of the playful crossword texts from the late New Kingdom and Third Intermediate Period that are made up of a grid of squares, each of which is filled with a word, part of a word, or a phrase.[115] Their particular layout enables the reader to construct several different texts according to a horizontal or vertical combination of squares. The appearance of these documents might seem enigmatic at first sight, whether in the form of their layout or the use of cryptography, but has actually nothing to do with secrecy; on the contrary, they are begging for attention. The concern for attention is actually already apparent from their contents: for the main part, these texts are hymns to gods displaying an individual's piety to the outer world, while, in other cases, they are lists of pharaonic epithets or private titles.

[112] *Op. cit.* and tomb of Khety in Beni Hassan II, nr. 17, see 58–59, plate 14. See for the restored hieroglyph of a love making couple on a bed: Lise Manniche, *Sexual Life in Ancient Egypt* (London and New York 1987) 35, fig. 21. E. Drioton, 'Une figuration cryptographique sur une stèle du Moyen Empire' *Rev.d'Egyptologie* 1 (1933) 203–229.

[113] Drioton, 'Essai sur la cryptographie privée' and idem, 'Recueil de cryptographie monumentale' *ASAE* 40 (1940) 305–427.

[114] Consider text passages nrs. 1–3 given in Drioton, 'Recueil de cryptographie monumentale'.

[115] J.J. Clère, 'Acrostiches et mots croisés des anciens Egyptiens' *CdE* 13 (1938) 35–58. See for a complete edition of Clère's document B (hymn to the goddess Mut): H.M. Stewart, 'A Crossword Hymn to Mut' *JEA* 57 (1971) 87–104. J. Zandee, *An ancient Egyptian Crossword Puzzle: an inscription of Neb-wenenef from Thebes*. (Leiden 1966). A badly preserved crossword text can be found in TT 192: *The Tomb of Kheruef. Theban Tomb 192* (OIP 102; Chicago 1980) pl. 14 and 15. The so-called *Moschion Stele* of the Roman period preserves a crossword text in both Demotic and Greek: W. Brunsch, 'Die Bilingue Stele des Moschion (Berl. Inv. Nr. 2135 + Cairo JdE Nr. 63160)' *Enchoria* 9 (1979) 5–32 and

In the Ptolemaic and early Roman period, Egypt witnessed a phase of renewed temple building activity, financed by the foreign rulers who were keen on winning loyalty and confirmation of power from the part of the native priesthood. A characteristic of these temple buildings is the overwhelming amount of hieroglyphic texts and ritual scenes inscribed on the inner and outer walls, lintels and ceilings, as if the architects were driven by a sense of *horror vacui*. The temple texts were composed in the Classical Egyptian language as was customary for religious texts, but were written in a script, currently known as 'Ptolemaic', that exploits the phonetic and semantic possibilities of hieroglyphic signs to the extreme.[116] The script should not be termed cryptography, but nonetheless, it shares the indulgence in the rules of acrophony and rebus with cryptographic texts of the pharaonic period.[117] In all likelihood, the Egyptian priests did not invent this script of over more than 7000 hieroglyphic signs to protect their religious texts against possible foreign intruders, but used it as a means to multiply the meanings of a text by mixing the linguistic and iconic level. It is therefore best seen as an intellectual game, the rules of which were pursued persistently and seriously in order to improve upon the ways of expression and to develop an all-encompassing religious language.

The phenomenon of writing texts with some sort of encrypted script is also attested for Greek and Coptic texts of the Roman and late antique period.[118] As is the case for pharaonic cryptography, two methods were employed: either ordinary Greek or Coptic alphabetic letters were substituted for fantasy signs or the letters of the alphabet were ascribed a different phonetic value following a strictly defined rule. The occurrence of these enigmatic scripts is limited to magical, medical, astrological and Gnostic manuscripts and graffiti. In the case of

---

E. Bresciani, 'I testi demotici della stele "enigmistica" di Moschione e il bilinguismo culturale nell'Egitto greco-romano' *EVO* 3 (1980) 117–145.

[116] An introduction is given in Serge Sauneron, 'L'écriture ptolémaïque', in: *Textes et Langages de l'Égypte pharaonique I* (BdE 64; Cairo 1972) 45–56.

[117] There can be no question that the Ptolemaic script is rooted in pharaonic cryptographic writing. In fact, cryptographic texts occur in the native temples of the Ptolemaic and Roman period, in particular in the temple of Esna; see Serge Sauneron, *Esna I—Quatre Campagnes à Esna* (Cairo 1959) 51–52 and Idem, *Esna VIII*, 47–110.

[118] Jean Doresse, 'Cryptographie copte et cryptographie grecque' *Bulletin de l'Institut d'Égypte* 33 (1952) 115–129; Idem, 'Cryptography' *The Coptic Encyclopedia* 8 (1991) 65a–69a; Frederik Wisse, 'Language Mysticism in the Nag Hammadi Texts and in Early Coptic Monasticism I: Cryptography' *Enchoria* 9 (1979) 101–120. Of the *Greek Magical Papyri*, the spells PGM LVII and LXXII are written in a cryptographic script.

the manuscripts, the use of cryptography may have been motivated by a desire to conceal knowledge that a non-initiated was forbidden to know: a familiar element of the late antique discourse on divine revelations. The graffiti were undoubtedly encrypted to attract attention for a cliché message, as is the case for the majority of pharaonic cryptographic texts.

Summarizing the evidence presented thus far, the occurrence of enigmatic scripts in the *Demotic Magical Papyri* is not at odds with Egyptian tradition and contemporary magical texts in Greek. Since Egyptian and Greek cryptographic scripts were not necessarily put to use as a means to delude non-initiated readers, the following section has to study in detail whether the function of the 'cipher' script in P. London-Leiden was truly to encode information. It may as well represent an intellectual play on scripts, in a similar vein as in the majority of pharaonic cryptographic texts.

### 3.4.1. *'Cipher' script*

The so-called 'cipher' script of P. London-Leiden is an idiosyncratic alphabet of 36 signs, which is used 93 times to spell single words in the recipe part of a number of Demotic spells. The 'cipher' script behaves like the Greek and Coptic script, that is to say, it is written from left to right and, unlike the standard pharaonic scripts, includes vowel signs and does not make use of determinatives. In a few cases, the encoded words are arranged as a list of ingredients with their measures or weights, but in the majority of instances, the encrypted words are embedded in a running Demotic sentence. Since these words never occur in invocations, but are always concerned with the practical procedures of a given rite, their rationale was in all probability not a matter of theology but simply of selection of readership, that is to say, a means to control and limit the access to information about a rite's guidelines. Those who were not instructed in the code could not partake in the technical knowledge contained in the practical instructions of a number of spells of P. London-Leiden.

In total, 74 different words are spelled in 'cipher', which set comprises 10 Greek nouns, 11 Egyptian verbal forms and 53 Egyptian nouns (see appendix 3.2). A small number of the encoded Egyptian words recur in sometimes slightly varying spellings, which suggests that the script was far from conventionalised. The variance in spellings of the same word resulted from the fact that the alphabet allows in a few cases a phonetic value being represented by alternative 'cipher' letters. Conversely, certain letters can denote two different phonetic values without any clear-cut rule. The 36 'cipher' letters denote 27 phonetic values, 6 of which are distinctive Egyptian sounds that are represented by a standard corresponding Old-Coptic sign each (see appendix 3.1: xxxii-xxxv and xxix-xxxvi). This means that the 'cipher' alphabet is in fact an encrypted Greek alphabet enhanced with six standard and unaltered Old-Coptic letters to render sounds that are lacking in Greek phonetics. Of this original encrypted Greek alphabet, 5 signs are merely common Greek letters turned on the side or put upside down (ix, x, xii, xiii, xix), while 5 other characters derive from Demotic signs (xi, xv, xxv, xxvi, xxvii). Four of its signs (i, x, xxiii, xxxi) agree in shape and phonetic value with four signs that are listed in the second encrypted Greek alphabet on the verso side of the manuscript. It is therefore reasonable to assume that the extant Old-Coptic 'cipher' alphabet is an upgraded version of a similar Greek encrypted alphabet.

It remains unclear *who* designed the 'cipher' script as a tool against the curiosity of *which* linguistic or social group. According to Griffith and Thompson, probably a Greek invented the script, because:[119]

1. The Old-Coptic letters would only offer concealment in a text in Greek.
2. Three signs occur only in Greek words, possibly because they convey sounds that only a Greek could distinguish.
3. The sign for the aspirate is missing. As is known from Coptic texts, an Egyptian scribe would render this sound with the Coptic sign ϩ.
4. The sounds **т** and **ϫ** are not differentiated. Any native speaker of Egyptian would have distinguished these sounds.

A close inspection of the script and the manuscript reveals that the arguments are valid, but cannot account for all complexities of the encrypted script of P. London-Leiden. First of all, one has to acknowledge that the majority of encrypted words are Egyptian and not Greek and that the extant 'cipher' script must have been applied to delude those readers who were able to read Demotic but were not allowed to get acquainted with the specific instructions for certain drugs and potions. Since Greeks were not competent in the Demotic script anyhow, the editors of the extant manuscript cannot have regarded this

---

[119] Griffith and Thompson, *The Demotic Magical Papyrus of London and Leiden*, vol. 3, 108.

ethnic and linguistic group as the target of the security measures. If they had left the words in Demotic script, no Greek would ever have had access to the content of the spells. With respect to the first argument, as the Old-Coptic letters occur only in Egyptian words, it is hard to imagine that these signs would ever occur in an encrypted text in Greek. There is actually more reason to assume that these Old-Coptic signs were added to the 'cipher' alphabet not until an editor adopted the alphabet to spell Egyptian words in code as well. As he would have done in the case of modifying a regular Greek alphabet into an Old-Coptic alphabet, he added the exact same Demotic signs to the Greek 'cipher' alphabet to turn it into an Old-Coptic 'cipher' alphabet. It is true that the additional signs would offer no concealment to readers of Demotic, but possibly the editor did not aim exclusively for secrecy.

By distinguishing two separate stages in the creation of the extant 'cipher' script, the second and third argument can be explained as remnants of the first stage. These Greek words were copied out of a text in Greek 'cipher' script without any consideration for their new Egyptian textual environment. The following passage is a recipe for making a potion that makes a man sleep for two days. The 'cipher' words have been transcribed into Greek for convenience sake.

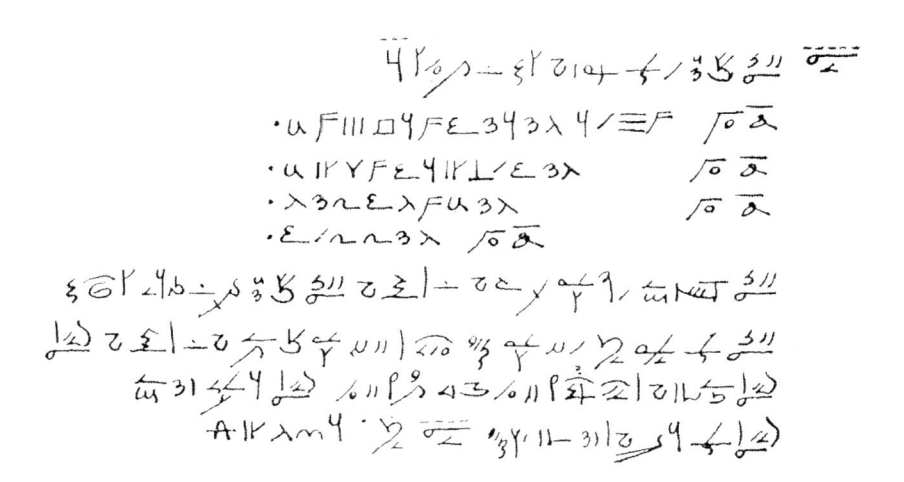

Fig. 3.5. P. London-Leiden 24/6–14

**Another**: If you wish to make a man sleep for **two** days:

| | | |
|---|---|---|
| ⁰ μανδραϰόρου ῥίζα | ο(ὐγϰία) ᾱ | [\*MANDRAKE ROOT\*, 1 ounce] |
| ⁰ μελαϰρετίϰου | ο(ὐγϰία) ᾱ | [1 ounce of \*QUINCES\*] |
| ⁰ ὑοσϰυάμου | ο(ὐγϰία) ᾱ | [1 ounce of \*HENBANE\*] |
| ⁰ ϰισσοῦ | ο(ὐγϰία) ᾱ | [1 ounce of \*IVY\*] |

You have to grind them with a *lok*-measure of wine. If you wish to do it in a sophisticated way, you have to put four portions to each one of them with a glass of wine. You have to moisten them from morning until evening. You have to strain them and let it be drunk. It is very good.

[P. London-Leiden 24/6–14]

The ingredients are not embedded in a running Demotic sentence as is usual, but written in 'cipher' and listed one above the other so as to form a separate text unit within the Demotic spell. The awkward layout suggests that the 'cipher' passage was slavishly taken over as one chunk out of an encoded text in Greek and pasted into the otherwise Demotic text without being translated or transcribed. This view is supported by the fact that the ingredients retained the genitive case endings in each but one instance, while the weight measure with its number are Greek and the third ingredient does not have a sign for the aspirate.[120] Written in this fashion, the text unit is an incongruity within the Demotic spell as regards its layout, scriptural appearance and linguistic form. However, the Egyptian editor knew how to incorporate Greek loan words into a Demotic text as is shown by a parallel spell only three lines farther, which prescribes mandrake root and ivy as well. In that case, the Greek names of the ingredients are transcribed into alphabetic Demotic signs, followed by a plant determinative and provided with Egyptian weights and numbers: 'root of MANDRAKE, 4 1/2 kite; GYSSOS (ivy), 4 1/2 kite' (P. London-Leiden 24/18–19).[121] Moreover, the K- and S- sounds are written in 'cipher' letters that do not occur in any of the Egyptian encoded words. It is very likely that the editor of the extant spells retained these 'cipher' signs for the Greek words only, because that is how he found them in his Greek encoded manuscript, but chose

---

[120] Compare this with a recipe for gout, whose list of Greek ingredients shows similar features, although the weights are in Demotic: P. London-Leiden V9/2–6; consider also the eroticon of P. London-Leiden V14/1–7.

[121] Note that the alphabetic Demotic transcription of 'mandrake', *m'ntr'grere*, preserves the Greek genitive case ending, which defined 'mandrake' as a partitive genitive in relation to the word 'root' in the original Greek compound. The case ending lost its function once the compound noun was transcribed into Egyptian. Note also that the transcription GYSSOS shows the nominative and not the genitive ending as in the passage above.

to replace them with alternative signs once he started encoding Egyptian words himself.[122] Therefore, Griffith and Thompson's arguments 2 and 3 are only valid with respect to the original Greek 'cipher' alphabet: in all likelihood, the script was invented to encode Greek words in texts that were written in Greek as a means to delude readers who were proficient in the Greek language and script. In other words, the script was initially not invented to serve as an encoding tool for texts in Egyptian such as the manuscript under study.

With respect to the fourth argument, it is indeed noteworthy that one sign, which is actually the Demotic sign for the sound $\underline{d}$, stands for both т and х in the extant 'cipher' alphabet. Strangely enough, there seems to be no strict rule that defines the distribution of the letter and its sounds within a word. This random correspondence between letter and sounds may have been the result of the fact that the script was originally designed to encrypt Greek words only. The Demotic $\underline{d}$ sign was then used to encrypt the T- sound in Greek words, because, to Greek ears, the $\underline{d}$- and T- sound were similar. When the script was adopted for spelling Egyptian words as well, an Egyptian editor maintained the rule of the 'cipher' script, but used the sign also to spell the sound $\underline{d}$ as he was used to when writing Demotic or Old-Coptic.

It remains a thorny issue to define in precise terms the function of the 'cipher' script within the extant manuscript. In fact, the exact purpose of the script escapes interpretation, because it is not applied consistently throughout the manuscript. First, the majority of spells are written entirely in Demotic and do not contain any word in 'cipher'. Secondly, certain passages with 'cipher' script have a parallel written without 'cipher' in the manuscript, which would have allowed an ancient reader to break the code quite easily.[123] Finally, even on the level of single spells with 'cipher' words, there seems to be no consistent effort to hide

---

[122] It is therefore highly unlikely that the encoded word *κεγορ* (P. London-Leiden 24/14) is a misspelling of the Greek κάρυα, 'kernels'; cf. Griffith and Thompson, *The Demotic Magical Papyus of London and Leiden*, vol. 3, 103 and 110. The word is written with the 'cipher' K- letter that is reserved for Egyptian words.

[123] William N. Groff and Herbert Thompson used these passages to decipher the 'cipher' script: William N. Groff, 'Étude sur la sorcellerie: ou, le rôle que la Bible a joué chez les sorciers' *MIE* 3 (1900) 337–415, esp. 358, 370; Griffith and Thompson, *The Demotic Magical Papyus of London and Leiden*, vol. 3, 105. Griffith gave pride of place to Thompson for deciphering the script: F. Ll. Griffith, 'The Old Coptic Magical Texts of Paris' *ZÄS* 38 (1900) 86–93, 93.

the overall meaning of the prescriptions. Nonetheless, certain rules of use can be discovered in spite of the apparent inconsistencies. As has already been said, encoded words occur only in those parts of a spell that are concerned with the practical procedures of the rite. In fact, the main bulk of 'cipher' words are ingredients like plants or animals for potions or drugs of a medicinal nature. In 16 cases, the script is used to encrypt the Egyptian verb that indicates the outcome of the rite.[124] It is remarkable that the meaning of these 6 verbs has nothing to do with recovery, but on the contrary, with deterioration of a person's physical condition:

| ⲗⲓⲃⲉ | 'to rave, be mad' (V32/1,9) |
| ⲙⲟⲩ | 'to die' (13/13,20,22,23; 23/7; 24/30; V32/10) |
| ⲙⲕⲁϩ | 'to suffer from pain' (24/5) |
| ϣⲉϥⲉ | 'to swell/ have a skin-disease' (13/13) |
| ⲭⲟⲩⲣ | 'to be violent' (13/25 [twice]) |
| ϭⲱⲛⲙ | 'to be blind' (13/12,26; 24/31) |

These verbs might suggest that the use of the script was reserved for spells that deal with the dark side of magic, but encrypted nouns occur as much in destructive as in productive and protective spells. The subject matter of the spells with encrypted nouns is actually quite diverse: making eye-ointments for divination, producing erotica, medical treatment, sending evil sleep, making blind and killing a person.

The following two passages are parallel prescriptions for making an eye-ointment, which the practitioner should apply to his eyes when conducting a divination ritual. The first passage has three nouns spelled in cipher, whereas the second excerpt writes them in Demotic.[125]

> ***Formula***: blood of a \*Nile goose\*, blood of a \*hoopoe\*, blood of a \*n[ightjar\*], '*Live-thereby*' plant, ['*Bread-of-heaven*' plant (=mustard?[126])], '*Great*-of-Amun' plant, ḳs-ʿnḫ stone, genuine lapis lazuli, myrrh, '*The-footprint-of-Isis*' plant. Pound ⟨them⟩; make ⟨them⟩ into a ball [and paint] your [eye] with it. *Put* a goat's-[tear] in a '*pleasure-wood*' of juniper or

---

[124] In the remaining two cases that an encrypted verb occurs, this does not apply. The first verb describes what the victim must do at a certain stage of the rite: '\*he will eat\* and \*he dies\*' (24/5). The other verb specifies an ingredient: 'the hair of a man who is \*dead\*' (V29/3).

[125] A number of the fancy plant names and ingredients recur in a Demotic recipe for sending evil sleep: P. Louvre E3229 3/27 (= PDM Suppl 60–101, 86). The nature of fancy plant names is treated in chapter 6.2.

[126] Griffith and Thompson, *The Demotic Magical Papyrus of London and Leiden*, vol. 1, 158, fn. to line 10.

ebony wood [and bind] (it) around you [with a] strip of male palm fibre in [an] elevated place opposite the sun after putting [the ointment as above on] your eye [...] according to what is written concerning it.
[P. London-Leiden 10/31–35][127]

**The preparation**: blood of *a Nile goose*, blood of a hoopoe°, blood of a nightjar°, '*Live-thereby*' plant°, '*Bread-of-heaven*' plant° (=mustard?), '*Great*-of-Amun' plant°. *ks-ꜥnḫ* stone°, genuine lapis lazuli°, myrrh°, '*The-footprint-of-Isis*' plant°. Pound ⟨them⟩; *make* ⟨them⟩ into a ball and *paint* your eye with it°. Place a goat's-tear° in a '\pleasure/-wood' of juniper° or ebony° and bind (it) around you with a strip of male palm fibre°.
[P. London-Leiden 27/9–12][128]

A comparison of these passages reveals that the 'cipher' script was indeed not consistently applied throughout the manuscript. Although the passages are separated from each other by 15 columns, this cannot be called a case of absolute secrecy on any account. With respect to the encoded ingredients of this recipe, it is noteworthy that not the substance itself but only the species' name is written in the 'cipher' script, a method that is characteristic of most encrypted ingredients. In those cases, the substance tends to be somewhat gory and repulsive, blood (*snf*), gall (*šḥy*) and dung (*ḥs*), as if the use of 'cipher' script was motivated by the phenomenon of the so-called *Dreck-Apotheke*.[129] However, if this would be the case, the rule has again not consistently been applied in the manuscript under study. The following passage from a love spell demonstrates that these inconsistencies even appear on the level of single spells. Three gory ingredients are encrypted as expected, but the editor did not consider it necessary to encode the placenta ingredient, which should have been encoded likewise following this rule.

> Dung of a *CROCODILE*, a little piece of a placenta of a she-ass with sisybrium, 7 'oipe' of dung of an *ANTELOPE*, gall of a male *GOAT* and first fruits of oil. You should heat them with flax stalks; you should recite to it seven times for seven days; you should anoint your phallus with it; and you should lie with the woman; and you should anoint the woman's breast (litt. heart) as well. [P. London-Leiden V13/6–9][130]

The excerpt below, taken from another love spell, describes a rather cruel and bloody rite to produce a drug for seducing a woman. The two

---

[127] Tr. Janet H. Johnson, with minor modifications (=PDM xiv 304–309).
[128] Tr. Janet H. Johnson, with minor modifications (=PDM xiv 812–815).
[129] See on *Dreck-Apotheke* chapter 6.2.
[130] Tr. Janet H. Johnson, with minor modifications (=PDM xiv 1043–1045).

animals for slaughter are written in 'cipher', but the base ingredients of the potion, blood of a male donkey and a black cow, are not encoded. Nonetheless, the subsequent lines do not divulge the encoded names, but refer consistently to them with personal pronouns and twice with the paraphrase 'the two'. In this way, no person would indeed have been able to conduct the ritual properly without knowledge of the key of decipherment.

> ***A method*** to put the heart of a woman after a man: done in one moment (?) and it comes to pass instantly°. You bring a *swallow* that lives° and a *hoopoe*, both being alive°. Ointment made for them°: blood of a male donkey°, blood of the tick of a black cow°. You should anoint their head**s** with lotus ointment° and cry out before the sun in his moment of rising°. You should cut off the heads of the two°; you should bring their hearts out from their right ribs° of the two° and anoint them with *the* donkey's blood and the *blood* of the tick of a black cow *that* are ⟨mentioned⟩ above°. You should put them into a donkey skin° and leave them in the sun until they dry up° in ***four*** days. When the ***four*** days have passed°, you should pound° them, put them into a box°, and leave it in your house°. [P. London-Leiden 25/23–31][131]

With respect to the encoded verbal forms, their occurrence seems to be motivated by a desire to hide the true nature of a given spell. Since the meaning of these verbs all imply an attack on a person's physical condition, the editors might have taken precautions against unwanted interference from the part of the civil authorities by using the 'cipher' script. In the following passage, which lists three methods to kill a man, the conjugated verbal form 'he dies' is encoded in each instance.[132]

> If you drown a *hawk* in a ⟨measure of⟩ wine, and you make the man *drink* it, ⟨then⟩ *he dies*. If you put the *gall* of an Alexandrian ⸢weasel⸣ into any piece of food, ⟨then⟩ *he dies*. If you put a two-tailed *lizard* into the oil, and [you cook] it, and anoint the man with it, ⟨then⟩ *he [dies*]. [P. London-Leiden 13/21–23][133]

The passage below is a similar collection of short recipes for lethal potions. In the first two prescriptions, the verbal forms are again encrypted, but in the third recipe, the clause *he is blinded* of the previous line is replaced by the euphemistic, and vague, expression 'this manner is it again'. The same textual strategy is applied in the fourth

---

[131] Tr. Janet H. Johnson, with minor modifications (=PDM xiv 772–780).
[132] Note that the verbal form, the so-called aorist, is only partially encoded. The particle *ḫr* is left in Demotic, whereas the *sḏm=f* form of the verb is spelled in 'cipher'.
[133] Tr. Janet H. Johnson (=PDM xiv 387–389).

text unit, which is actually a parallel to the previous example with this difference that it uses, instead of the recurring phrase *he dies*, the expression 'it does its work'.

> **Another**: if you put blood of a *camel*° with blood of a dead man into the wine and you make the man *drink* it, *he dies*°.
>
> **Another**: if you put blood of a nightjar° *to his eye*°, he is° *blinded*°.
>
> **Another**: if you put blood of a *bat*°, this manner is it again°.
>
> **Another**: if you drown a *hawk*° in a ⟨measure of⟩ wine and you make the man *drink* it, it does its work°. A *shrewmouse* in this manner again: it does its work also°. Its °*gall*° also: if you put it in the wine, it does its work very well. If you put the *gall* of an Alexandrian weasel on any food, it does its work. If you put a two-tailed *lizard* in the oil and cook it with it and anoint the man with it, it does its work.
>
> [P. London-Leiden 24/29–39][134]

These passages make it reasonable to believe that the editors were concerned about a possible distribution of these spells beyond their control. The use of 'cipher' and euphemistic expressions gave them the means to keep their readership in check. If this view would be correct, it is again remarkable to find that this rule does not apply for the verb ⲗⲓⲃⲉ/*lby*, 'to rave, be mad', which occurs twice in 'cipher' but seven times openly in Demotic.[135] A comparison of two parallel passages taken from a collection of recipes with the shrewmouse is again very instructive. The verb is consistently encoded in the first passage, but written in Demotic in the second excerpt, even in the caption to the recipe. Notice also the gender shift in the second procedure between the first and second passage.

> To make [a woman] *mad* after a man. You should bring a *live* *shrewmouse*, remove its *gall* and put it in one place; and remove its *heart* and put it in another place. You should take its whole body (*swm'* < σῶμα) and pound it carefully while it is dry. You should take a little of what is pounded with a little blood of your second finger and the little finger of your left *hand*; you should put it in a cup of wine and make the *woman drink* it. She is *mad* after you.[136]

---

[134] Tr. Janet H. Johnson, with minor modifications (=PDM xiv 739–749).

[135] *ⲗⲓⲃⲉ* occurs in V/32/1,9; *lby* is found in: 13/17, 19; 15/19; 21/37, 39; V12/9; V16/4. Note that the verb ⳓⲱⲛⲙ, 'to be blind', is written in Demotic script once, *gnm* (11/11). However, the Demotic writing occurs in an invocation, not in a recipe, and has nothing to do with the procedures of the rite.

[136] Note that the verbal form is the periphrastic aorist. It is only the infinitive form that is encrypted.

> If you put its *GALL* into a cup of wine, *SHE DIES* instantly. Or ⟨if you⟩ put it in meat or some food.
>
> If you put its *HEART* into a (seal) ring of gold and put it on your *hand*, it *gives* you *great praise, love* and respect. [P. London-Leiden V 32/1–13][137]
>
> If you do it to make a woman mad after a man, you should take its *BODY* (σῶμα) while it is dry and pound [it. You should] take a little of it together with a little blood from your second finger and the little finger of your left hand; you should mix it with it. You should put it in a cup of wine and give it to the woman so that she *drinks* it. She is mad after you.
>
> If you put its *GALL* into a ⟨measure of⟩ wine and the man *drinks* it, *HE DIES* instantly. Or ⟨if you⟩ put it in any piece of food.
>
> If you put its *HEART* into a (seal) ring of gold, you put it on your hand and go anywhere, it creates for you [*praise, love* and respec]t.
> [P. London-Leiden 13/17–21][138]

The foregoing pages have made it plausible that the 'cipher' script was meant as a means to control and limit the access to professional knowledge, even though the system was not applied with consistency. The target group of this concealing effort might have been competitors in the magic trade and, as make the encoded verbs conceivable, the civil authorities. The inconsistencies might be explained as resulting from the fact that the 'cipher' system was initially not invented for spells in Demotic. This means that a number of existing Demotic spells underwent a treatment of encoding not until an editor decided to adopt and modify the Greek 'cipher' script that he had found in a magical text in Greek. Given the tendency to be inclusive and to do justice to all available sources, the original Demotic spells were retained and found their way into the extant manuscript next to their encoded and secondary parallels.

### 3.4.2. *Mystery signs or charaktêres*

The other set of secret letters that occurs in P. London-Leiden is used not only in this manuscript, but enjoyed a wide popularity from the second century onwards in the eastern Mediterranean as a mystical and powerful 'sacred' script, the signs of which were called *charaktêres*.[139] David Frankfurter defines the category in the following terms:

---

[137] Tr. Janet H. Johnson, with minor modifications (=PDM xiv 1206–1218).
[138] Tr. Janet H. Johnson, with minor modifications (=PDM xiv 384–388).
[139] The best discussion of the nature and meaning of these signs is Frankfurter, 'The

*Charaktêr* is the general term for the small designs and figures found in lines or clusters on magical papyri and gems, having no apparent source in any known alphabet, and yet employed in such a way that a 'meaning' (albeit unutterable) is implied in their sequence or arrangement. The most common forms of magical *charaktêres* consist of asterisks and configurations of straight lines with small circles or lobes on each end. They appear in a variety of contexts, ranging from loose clusters inscribed on certain magical gems, to their integration with a larger drawing or *figura* on a magical text or tablet, to integration with a recognizably alphabetic text as if to suggest phonetic symbols 'transcendent' of the normal alphabet, much as *voces magicae* were supposed to be transcended of normal language.[140]

Unlike the 'cipher' script, these signs had a function in the ritual itself, that is to say, in the majority of cases they had to be written on a piece of papyrus, lead or bronze, which, for example, was subsequently worn around the neck as a phylactery or deposited at a hidden spot as a binding spell. The mysterious signs were supposed to represent 'sacred' writing intelligible only to demons and deities, so that its application would enable direct communication with the divine world.[141] Whereas the *voces magicae* served as a linguistic code to establish communication with the gods, the *charaktêres* functioned as an unutterable, and presumably untranslatable graphic code to convey a message to the gods.[142] In the following healing spell, the mystery signs are supposed to cure a patient who is bitten by a scorpion.

---

Magic of Writing and the Writing of Magic', 205–211. Instructive introductions are: Theodor Hopfner, 'Charaktêres' *PRE Suppl.* 4 (1924) 1183–1188; Brashear, 'The *Greek Magical Papyri*: An Introduction and Survey', 3440–3443; John G. Gager, *Curse tablets and Binding Spells from the Ancient World* (New York and Oxford 1992) 10–11. Illustrations are given in the latter publication, figs. 1 (Picatrix, medieval Arabic), 7 (Apamea); 8 (Carthage), 9, 10, 19 (Rome); 15 (Jewish, Cairo Geniza); 16, 25, 30 (Egypt); 20 (Athens). Consider also the magical signs on the divination apparatus from Pergamum; Richard Wünsch, *Ein antikes Zaubergerät aus Pergamon* (Berlin 1905).

[140] Frankfurter, 'The Magic of Writing and the Writing of Magic', 205.

[141] Frankfurter compares the nature of the *charaktêres* with the late antique concept of the 'heavenly books' whose writing was understandable only to divine beings and those enlightened; Frankfurter, 'The Magic of Writing and the Writing of Magic', 207. However, one has to bear in mind that the communication situation is opposite: heavenly books reveal a message of the divine world to humans, whereas the magical spells or gems with *charaktêres* are an attempt on the part of humans to address the divine world.

[142] In the late antique period, *charaktêres* became powerful entities of themselves who could be called upon as protectors or divine assistants. For example, a lead *defixio* to bind competitors in the chariot races from Apamea, Syria, dating from the 5th-6th century CE reads: 'Most holy Lord *Charaktêres*, tie up, bind the feet, the hands, the

> For scorpion sting. On a clean sheet of papyrus, write the *charaktêres*, place it on the place where the sting is and bind the sheet around it, and it will be painless immediately. These are the *charaktêres*: (a string of signs; jd). They make 11 *charaktêres*. [PGM VII.193–196]

The final clause demonstrates that the signs had to be copied carefully: one sign more or less would make the rite futile.

It remains unknown from where, by whom and through which channels the use of these signs spread over the eastern Mediterranean. Possibly, their popularity resulted from the awe that the hieroglyphs were generally afforded in Hellenistic circles.[113] Both scripts were seen as divine symbols transcending regular alphabetic scripts as regards semantic possibilities and imbued with great powers. Together with the rapid decline in knowledge of the hieroglyphic script in Egypt itself during the early Roman period, the Hellenistic perception may have provided fertile soil for these magical signs to develop into an alternative yet international 'hieroglyphic' script. For the same reason, it cannot be ruled out that Egyptian priests took an active part in spreading the belief in, and use of, the mystery signs.[114]

In P. London-Leiden, *charaktêres* occur once in a long string of 29 signs that, according to the Demotic instructions of the recipe, should be written on a reed leaf, whose subsequent treatment determines whether the practitioner will acquire dreams, send dreams or attract a woman.

---

sinews, the eyes, the knees, the courage, the leaps, the whip (?), the victory and the crowning of Porphuras and Hapsicrates ...'; Gager, *Curse tablets and Binding Spells*, 56–58, nr. 6. A Byzantine-period public inscription on the wall of the theater of Miletus, Asia Minor, addresses a set of seven *charaktêres* as protectors of the city; H. Grégoire, *Receuil des inscriptions grecques chrétiennes d'Asie Mineure* (Paris 1922) nr. 221.

[113] On the Hellenistic perception of hieroglyphs, see, chapter 1. The link between *charaktêres* and hieroglyphs has often been proposed; the most recent treatment is Frankfurter, *Religion in Roman Egypt*, 255–256.

[114] A study of the hieroglyphic texts on the so-called Horus-cippi of the Ptolemaic period revealed that the knowledge of the meaning of single signs rapidly declined in the course of this period and that only certain hieroglyphs or clusters of signs were copied to stand for the complete text. Written in this fashion, a hieroglyphic sign became an index of sacredness; Heike Sternberg-El Hotabi, 'Der Untergang der Hieroglyphenschrift. Schriftverfall und Schrifttod im Ägypten der griechisch-römischen Zeit' *CdE* 69 (1994) 218–245. According to Malcolm Mosher, a similar development is detectable in the *Book of the Dead* papyri from Akhmim; Malcolm Mosher, Jr, 'The Book of the Dead Tradition at Akhmim during the Late Period', in: A. Egberts, B.P. Muhs and J. van der Vliet (eds.), *Perspectives on Panopolis. An Egyptian Town from Alexander the Great to the Arab Conquest* (P.L.Bat. 31; Leiden 2002) 201–209. Note that both developments might reflect changes that were only valid for specific professional groups.

THE USE OF SCRIPT 99

Hence, the treatment of the *charaktêres* is in line with prescriptions from other Roman-period magical handbooks. Although a few signs resemble Greek letters, the majority are fanciful and not like any other contemporary 'official' script.[145]

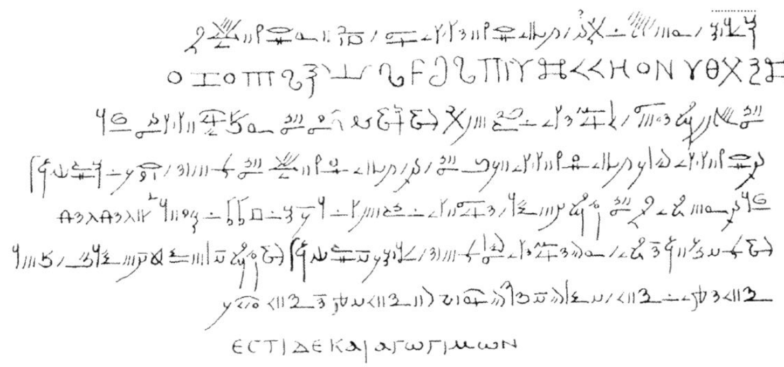

Fig. 3.6. P. London-Leiden verso 17/1–8

**A spell**[146] to bring [a woman] to a man (and) to send dreams (another ⟨manuscript⟩ says: to dream dreams) as well.

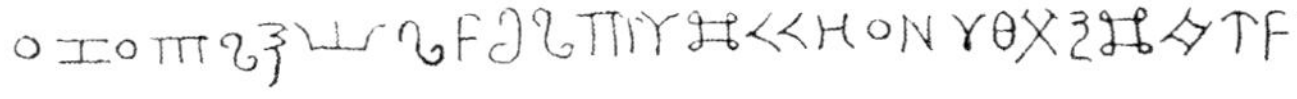

You should *write* these on a reed leaf and put (it) under your *head*. You should go to sleep; it makes dreams and sends dreams. If you will do it to send dreams, you should put it on the mouth of a mummy. It brings a woman also. You should write this name (*p3y rn*) on the reed leaf with blood of a *.?.* or a *ΗοοΡοΕ*; you should put the hair of the woman inside the leaf and put it on the mouth of the mummy. You should write on the ground this name (*p3y rn*), saying: 'Bring NN, the daughter of NN, to the house of the sleeping place in which is NN, the son of NN!'

Yet, it is also a fetching charm (ἔστι δὲ καὶ ἀγώγιμον)

[P. London-Leiden V17/1–8][147]

---

[145] The Greek letters are: ο (nrs. 1, 3, 19), π (nr. 12), υ (nrs. 14, 21), η (nr. 18), ν (nr. 20), ϑ (nr. 22). Several signs occur more than once: (nrs. 1, 3, 19), (nrs. 5, 8, 11), (nrs. 9, 28), (nrs. 14, 21), (nrs. 15, 25), (nrs. 16, 17).

[146] Herbert Thompson's hand copy does not reproduce that this caption is written in red.

[147] Tr. Janet H. Johnson, with modifications (= PDM xiv 1070–1077).

It is noteworthy that the Demotic text refers to the string of *charaktêres* as *p3y rn*, 'this name', as if the Egyptian editor interpreted the mystery signs as a magical name similar to *voces magicae* instead of as a secret message (in which case he would probably have written *n3y sḥ.w*, 'these writings'). The Greek clause at the end of the spell might be a gloss, which was added afterwards to the Demotic spell as a caption by a person who was less proficient in Demotic than in Greek, or a remnant of the original Greek spell that was translated into Demotic. If the clause is indeed a residue of the original spell in Greek, the Demotic clause 'It brings a woman also' (*ḥr ỉr=f ỉny sḥm.t ꜥn*; P. London-Leiden V17/5) is probably its direct translation. It is therefore well possible that the extant spell goes back to a version in Greek and that the *charaktêres* are a remnant of this lost Greek spell as well.

The twin manuscript, P. Leiden I 384 verso, preserves a Greek spell that prescribes a similar ritual technique, in this case to gain favour and friendship by carrying an amulet that has a series of *charaktêres* written upon it. The recipe gives 8 or 9 *charaktêres*, none of which is identical with a sign of the above given dream-sending recipe, to write with special ink on a pasithea or wormwood root.

> For favour and friendship forever. Take a pasithea or wormwood root, write this name (τὸ ὄνομα τοῦτο) on it in a holy way: ⳨ ⲧ ⲗ ⲋ ⳽ ⲙ ⲙ ⳌL and wear it and you will be an object of favour, friendship as well as admiration to those who see you. The formula ⟨for the ink⟩: 1 dram of myrrh, 4 drams of truffle, 2 drams of blue vitriol, 2 drams of oak gall, 3 drams of Arabic gum. [PGM XII.397–400]

The Greek text calls the mystery signs 'this name' (τὸ ὄνομα τοῦτο), as is the case in the Demotic dream-sending spell. This might suggest that the editors of the spells were familiar with the concept, but not aware of its correct technical term. This is however not correct. In fact, the term *charaktêr* occurs as a Greek loan word transcribed in alphabetic Demotic signs in an elaborate Demotic recipe for a lamp divination ritual (P. London-Leiden 5/1–32 = PDM xiv 117–149). Before the practitioner can truly start with the divinatory rite, he should get a white lamp, onto which no red lead or gum water has been applied.

> You should put a clean wick in it°; you should fill it with real oil°, after writing this name (*p3y rn*) and these CHARAKTÊRES (*gh'l'gter*) on the wick with ink of myrrh first°. [P. London-Leiden 5/4–5]

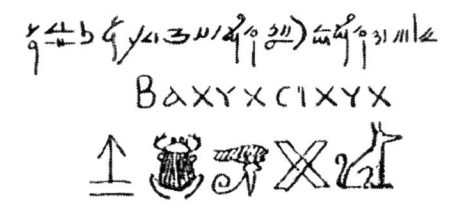

Fig 3.7. Pseudo-hieroglyphs, P. London-Leiden 5/8–10

In the right margin two lines below, the name and the *charaktêres* are carefully written one above the other and identified by the phrase 'here are (the) writings (*sḫ.w*) that you should write on the wick of the lamp' (P. London-Leiden 5/8; fig. 3.7). The name, which is spelled in Greek letters like a common *vox magica*, reads BACHUCHSICHUCH, possibly a transcription of *bꜣ kkw sꜣ kkw*, 'soul of darkness, son of darkness'.[148] The *charaktêres* that stand below this name are not like any of the signs that are called *charaktêres* today, but are carefully drawn and represent a geometric sign, a scarab (*ḫpr* hieroglyph), an *Udjat*-eye (*wḏꜣ.t* hieroglyph), a cross and a sitting dog in side-view. Despite their deviant shape (one is even tempted to speak of pseudo-hieroglyphs), the treatment of the signs corresponds otherwise with the use of *charaktêres*. These same 5 signs and the *vox magica* are repeated in two other recipes for fairly similar divination rituals (P. London-Leiden 6/1–8/11 = PDM xiv 150–231 and P. London-Leiden 27/1–32 =PDM xiv 805–840). The Demotic text refers to the *vox magica* and the signs in one case as 'the writings' (*nꜣ sḫ.w*)[149] and in the other case as 'this name' (*pꜣy rn*) as in the dream-sending recipe.[150]

---

[148] *GMPT*, 202, fn. 76 [R.K.R.].
[149] P. London-Leiden 6/25.
[150] P. London-Leiden 27/31.

CHAPTER FOUR

THE FORM AND FUNCTION OF BILINGUALISM

4.1. *Introduction*

One of the most remarkable characteristics of the two manuscripts under study is the combination of spells in Demotic and Greek on one and the same manuscript. As has been said in the introductory chapter, previous scholars never took the bilingual nature of the manuscripts fully into account, but chose to concentrate their attention either on the Greek or the Demotic sections, which eventually resulted in a disciplinary division of the material. By contrast, this chapter will take the bilingual nature of the manuscripts as point of departure for an investigation into the language attitude of the composers and compilers of the spells by studying in detail the relationship between Egyptian and Greek and their degree of interference in the spells. Before embarking on a close inspection, the interaction between Egyptian and Greek in the source material can be defined for the moment as follows:

1. On the level of the manuscripts, the distribution of Egyptian and Greek is rather clear-cut, this is to say, the use of a language is restricted to a self-contained section each. On P. Leiden I 384 verso, the Greek spells are grouped together in a section of 13 consecutive columns, which is flanked by a section of Demotic spells on both ends; the twin manuscript, P. London-Leiden, does not contain any separate Greek spells next to the Demotic spells.
2. On the level of individual spells, Egyptian and Greek are occasionally juxtaposed or combined as rather autonomous elements: three Greek spells contain a title in Demotic in addition to their Greek title (PGM XII.201–269; 270–350; 365–375) and seven Demotic spells include an invocation in Greek, to wit: PDM xii. 76–107 [PGM XII.453–465], PDM xii.135–146 [PGM XII.474–479], PDM xii.147–154 [PGM XII.480–495], PDM xiv.93–114 [PGM XIVa.1–11], PDM xiv.451–458 [PGM XIVb.12–15] and PDM xiv.675–694 [PGM XIVc.16–27].

3. The reverse side of P. London-Leiden contains a fair number of single Greek nouns in the Greek script, which serve mainly as headings to short Demotic descriptions of plants, minerals and animals. Their integration into Egyptian syntactical patterns is rather superficial.
4. In certain cases, the recipe part of a Demotic spell contains one or more Greek loanwords transcribed into alphabetic Demotic signs and fully integrated into the Egyptian syntax. The transcribed loan words may be accompanied by glosses in Greek script above the line.

As argued in the introductory chapter, there are reasons to believe that certain members of the Egyptian priesthood had, and propagated, a negative language attitude toward Greek to define their cultural superiority over the Hellenistic ruling elite. Therefore, it may come as a surprise to find that the two magical handbooks under study, which must have circulated among Egyptian priests, as demonstrated in the foregoing chapter, preserve a considerable number of spells in Greek next to those in Demotic. Why would an Egyptian priestly milieu put faith in spells written in Greek and treat them on a par with spells in the Egyptian language? The present chapter is an attempt to determine to what extent the incorporation of Greek spells and words truly meant a breach with traditional Egyptian religious concepts and practices. This detailed study of the bilingual phenomena in the two handbooks will hence put the general validity of the propagated priestly negative language attitude to the test.

### 4.2. *Language change and language attitude in Roman Egypt*

It is important to examine meticulously the form and degree of language interference in the magical spells, because modern sociolinguistic studies have made it abundantly clear that contact induced language change is not a self-evident and straightforward phenomenon. In fact, it is a prime indicator of the form and direction of cultural change, because it is governed by social and cultural constraints that are negotiated among the members of a speech community.[1] Roman Egypt was

---

[1] This and the next paragraphs are based on the following useful introductions to the study of language and cultural change in bilingual settings: René Appel and Pieter

a bilingual society in which Greek was the language of upward social mobility, dominant in the civil administration throughout the country as well as public life in the major cities. Consequently, the Egyptian language underwent substantial changes under the influence of Greek in the course of several centuries, very similar to the way native iconography, traditional notions of kingship and consumption patterns changed to a degree through contact with Hellenistic culture. By adopting lexical and grammatical forms from a prestigious donor language, in this case Greek, speakers of a recipient language of lesser cultural status, namely Egyptian, may express their wish to identify with the culture of the donor language's speech community, that is to say Hellenism. Changes of this nature are no autonomous developments, but the result of choices made by individuals who adjust to ever occurring shifts in the access to economic resources, while competing with other individuals for sources of power in the social arena. This means that any study of cultural change in Greco-Roman Egypt has to account for the creative impetus of individuals and the interests of various social groups, who adopt opportune social strategies and appropriate cultural identities depending on the situation and their aims. Any student of the ancient sources should therefore be prepared to take into account conflicting stands and contradictory perspectives articulated in the material.

The form and degree of contact induced language change is determined by a speech community's language attitude towards a donor language and the type of contact situation. Language attitude is the degree to which speakers of the recipient language valorise positively or negatively the donor language, its speakers and its associated cultural settings.[2] Since language and group identity are usually felt as closely related, speakers can perceive linguistic borrowing as corruption of their cultural traditions or, in contrast, as innovations that enable identification with a prestige language and its culture. Accordingly, language attitude determines to what extent a speech community is inclined to adopt foreign elements into its language. Suzanne Romaine formulates it as follows:

---

Muysken, *Language Contact and Bilingualism* (London 1987); Sarah Grey Thomason and Terrence Kaufman, *Language Contact, Creolization, and Genetic Linguistics* (Berkeley 1988); Suzanne Romaine, *Bilingualism* (Oxford 1989); William A. Foley, *Anthropological Linguistics* (Oxford 1997) 381–397.

[2] Most lucid discussion: Muysken and Appel, *Language Contact and Bilingualism*, 16–20.

> It is true of most multilingual societies that the differential power of particular groups is reflected in language variation and attitudes towards this variability. The study of language attitudes is important because attitudes represent an index of intergroup relations and they play an important role in mediating and determining them. [*Bilingualism*, 258]

With respect to language interference and the type of contact situation, the sociolinguist Pieter Muysken distinguishes three processes at work in bilingual speech:[3]

1.a. *Insertion* of single lexical elements from a donor language into a structure of a recipient language.
2.a. *Alternation* between structures from two or more languages within a single speech event.
3.a. *Congruent lexicalisation* of material from different lexical inventories into a shared grammatical structure.

These processes conform roughly to a particular contact situation each:[4]

1.b. Colonial settings and recent migrant communities, where there is a considerable asymmetry in the speaker's proficiency in the two languages involved.
2.b. Stable bilingual communities with a tradition of language separation.
3.b. Second generation migrant groups, dialect/standard and post-creole continua, and bilingual speakers of closely related languages with roughly speaking equal prestige and no tradition of language separation.

If one wants to apply this scheme to the society of Roman-period Egypt, it is necessary to differentiate between social groups on the basis of their ethnic origin, occupation, social position and place of residence, because not every Egyptian subject is likely to have been exposed to Greek language and culture to the same degree. Willy Clarysse has demonstrated with the help of Demotic and Greek documentary texts that, in the Ptolemaic period, Egyptians who were active in the administration and Hellenistic cultural life, took on a Greek name when dealing with Greeks, while retaining their Egyptian name in

---

[3] Pieter Muysken, *Bilingual Speech. A Typology of Code-Mixing* (Cambridge 2000) 3–10 and the respective chapters.
[4] *Op. cit.*, 8–9.

an Egyptian setting.[5] This practice of name switching suggests that the language situation of the upper layers of the native population could be described as under point 2.b, namely, as a stable bilingual community with a tradition of language separation. In all likelihood, the vast majority of the native population, especially in the countryside, was only occasionally required to deal with Greek language and if so, mainly through intermediaries, so that their knowledge of Greek will have been minimal, if extant at all.

To reconstruct the effect of these differing contact situations upon the true nature and degree of language change in the Roman period is nearly impossible, since the sources are written, the majority of which preserves rather a history of textual transmission than real life speech events. Nonetheless, the outcome of the process can be studied in Coptic, the successive language stage, while some information about its progression can be gained from analysing the Demotic ostraca from Narmuthis in the Fayum, dating from the second century CE. These ostraca were found near the temple of the goddess Triphis in a dump of what was probably once a temple school.[6] A high number of them served as exercises in copying legal documents, drafts of dispatches and vocalized word lists, so that they are likely to come close in lexicon and grammar to contemporary speech.[7] Coptic can assuredly be called a mixed language, because it contains Greek borrowings on the level of lexicon, phonology, syntax and even information structure.[8] In the light

---

[5] The best discussion of this social strategy is: Willy Clarysse, 'Ptolemaeïsch Egypte. Een maatschappij met twee gezichten' *Handelingen van de Koninklijke Zuidnederlandse Maatschappij voor Taal- en Letterkunde en Geschiedenis* 45 (1991) 21–38. See also Idem, 'Greeks and Egyptians in the Ptolemaic Army and Administration' *Aegyptus* 65 (1985) 57–66.

[6] To date, a total of 93 ostraca are published in two separate volumes: Edda Bresciani, Sergio Pernigotti, Maria C. Betro, *Ostraka demotici da Narmutti* (Pisa 1983) and Paolo Gallo, *Ostraca demotici e ieratici dall'archivio bilingue di Narmouthis II* (Pisa 1997). Three astrological ostraca are published in Richard A. Parker, 'A Horoscopic Text in Triplicate', in: Heinz-J. Thissen and Karl-Th. Zauzich (eds.), *Grammata demotika. Fs. Lüddeckens* (Würzburg 1984) 141–143.

[7] For a description of the material, see, Gallo, *Ostraca demotici e ieratici*, xli-lx.

[8] A lucid analysis of the bilingual phenomena in Coptic can be found in Chris Reintges, 'Code-Mixing Strategies in Coptic Egyptian' *LingAeg* 9 (2001) 193–237; see also John David C. Ray, 'How demotic is Demotic?' *EVO* 17 (1994) 251–265, 256–257. See for Greek loanwords in Coptic documentary texts: Hans Förster, *Wörterbuch der griechischen Wörter in den koptischen dokumentarischen Texten* (TU 148; Berlin and New York 2002). A study of the nature of Greek loanwords in Coptic literary and religious texts is still very much a *desideratum*. See for a definition of the term 'mixed language': Fredric W. Field, *Linguistic Borrowing in Bilingual Contexts* (Studies in Language Companion Series 62; Amsterdam, Philadelphia 2002) 13–15.

of the 'hierarchies of borrowability' that linguists established on the basis of comparative data as scales to study which linguistic categories are universally borrowed more freely than others, Coptic is evidently the result of long-standing and intense contact between Egyptian and Greek.[9] The Narmuthis ostraca corroborate this conclusion, because the Demotic texts incorporate a high number of Greek loanwords, which are written in the Greek script in an opposite direction to the Demotic reading direction.[10]

The majority of these loanwords are nouns, to wit, administrative titles, legal terms, objects of daily use and ingredients, that are embedded in Egyptian grammatical structures as object and genitive constructions (with loss of case endings), occasionally preceded by a Demotic possessive or demonstrative pronoun in correct gender. In a fair number of cases, a Greek infinitive occurs as a bare noun in direct object position to the agentive verb *ir*, 'to do', which is a common procedure in Coptic to incorporate a Greek verb into the Egyptian syntax.[11] One ostracon preserves the preposition κατά followed by a Greek noun phrase embedded in a Demotic sentence. The ostraca demonstrate hence that colloquial Egyptian of the Roman period was undergoing a process of significant re-lexification under the influence of Greek while retaining its Egyptian grammatical structure, with the result that Coptic evolved into a mixed language.[12]

This conclusion is highly relevant in the light of the general lack of Greek borrowings in Demotic texts that are contemporary or a little earlier than the Narmuthis ostraca. In a study of Greek loanwords in Demotic documentary texts of the Ptolemaic and Roman period, Willy

---

[9] See for a discussion of the 'hierarchies of borrowability': Muysken and Appel, *Language Contact and Bilingualism*, 170–172 and Field, *Linguistic Borrowing in Bilingual Contexts*, 34–40. The specific order of borrowed linguistic categories depends on the two languages involved, but one could say in general that content words (nouns, adjectives, verbs) are more easily borrowed than function words (prepositions, pronouns, articles, conjunctions), while nouns are universally borrowed most easily. The longer and more profound the contact between two languages is, the more grammatical categories of the donor language are likely to enter the recipient language.

[10] A representative, albeit not complete, list of Greek loanwords in the ostraca can be found in: E. Bresciani and R. Pintaudi, 'Textes démotico-grecs et greco-démotiques des ostraca de Medinet Madi: un problème de bilinguisme', in: S.P. Vleeming (ed.), *Aspects of Demotic Lexicography* (Studia Demotica 1; Leuven 1987) 123–126; see also Ray, 'How demotic is Demotic?', 257–258.

[11] A discussion of hybrid light-verb constructions in Bohairic and Sahidic Coptic is given in: Reintges, 'Code-Mixing Strategies in Coptic Egyptian', 196–207.

[12] See on re-lexification: Muysken, *Bilingual Speech*, 266–268.

Clarysse concludes, 'the Demotic vocabulary was remarkably free of Greek influence' and 'the Demotic scribes consciously tried to translate rather than to transliterate the Greek vocabulary'.[13] John Ray is therefore correct in questioning the widely held assumption that Demotic represents colloquial Egyptian of the Greco-Roman period by asking in reference to Herodotus' definition of the Egyptian script varieties, 'how demotic (< δημοτικά, "of the people") is Demotic?'.[14] His answer is that 'the true description of Demotic is not vernacular; it is a purified and filtered vernacular which was subject to its own rules'.[15] A close inspection of the Greek loanwords in the Demotic documentary texts reveals that they can be grouped into three main categories: honorific and official titles, administrative terms and objects of daily life. With only a few exceptions, these loanwords are additions to the Egyptian lexicon that only became relevant after the introduction of Greek administration. Together with the apparent preference for loan translations rather than loan words, the lack of substituting borrowings suggests that Demotic scribes were reluctant to adopt Greek borrowings into the written language, despite the fact that colloquial Egyptian was undeniably changing under the influence of Greek. These observations are reminiscent of speech strategies to disguise inevitable foreign influence in contact situations where the speakers of the recipient language have a negative language attitude towards the donor language and its associated culture.[16] Yet, one must refrain from extrapolating rashly from the Demotic documentary texts to the language attitude of Demotic scribes at large, because documentary texts were written in a highly specific and formulaic speech register, which by its nature was rather resistant to any sort of modifications. Nonetheless, Greek borrowings are also remarkably absent from letters and literary texts in Demotic. Therefore, the following section will study the Greek loanwords and Greek invocations

---

[13] W. Clarysse, 'Greek Loan-Words in Demotic', in: S.P. Vleeming (ed.), *Aspects of Demotic Lexicography* (Studia Demotica 1; Leuven 1987) 9–33; a list of 92 Greek loan words can be found on pgs. 21–32. An update to this list with 13 new loanwords can be found in: Katelijn Vandorpe and Willy Clarysse, 'A Greek Winery for Sale in a Fayum Demotic Papyrus', in: A.M.F.W. Verhoogt and S.P. Vleeming (eds.), *The Two Faces of Graeco-Roman Egypt. Fs. P.W. Pestman* (P.L.Bat 30; Leiden 1998) 127–139, the list is on page 139.

[14] Herodotus gives the following remark in his *Histories*: 'They (the Egyptians, jd) use two different kinds of writing; one of which is called sacred (ἱρά) and the other common (δημοτικά)' (II, 36). Herodotus' sacred writing is the hieroglyphic script.

[15] Ray, 'How demotic is Demotic?', 264.

[16] Romaine, *Bilingualism*, 56–58.

in the Demotic spells in the light of the general lack of Greek borrowings in Demotic texts. This is to determine in what way the spells relate to the contemporary process of re-lexification of the vernacular and the religiously motivated negative language attitude as articulated, for example, in treatise XVI of the *Corpus Hermeticum*.

### 4.3. *The process of insertion: Greek loanwords in the Demotic spells*

Unlike the Demotic sections of P. Leiden I 384 verso, the Demotic spells of P. Leiden-London contain a fair amount of Greek borrowings (see appendices 4.1–3). The total number of Greek loanwords (62, without magical names) may be quite low compared to the number of Demotic words in the manuscript (1121), but it is remarkably higher, both in absolute and relative terms, than in any other Demotic text known to date. The loanwords are without exception single nouns and occur only within the recipe sections of a spell or in the bilingual descriptions of medical and magical material on the verso side of the manuscript (columns 1–4). This means that the invocations are left free from linguistic borrowing—except for the incorporated *voces magicae*, which constitute a different class of linguistic interference and are left out of the present analysis. The borrowed nouns can be classified according to three categories:

1. Materials of medicine and magic
2. Medical terminology
3. House utensils

This tripartite distinction demonstrates that the religious and magical terminology of the related PGM spells, which carries overtones of ideas current in the Greek mystery religions, is absent from the language of the Demotic spells.[17]

---

[17] The occurrence of PGM terminology deriving from Greek mystery religions is discussed in Hans Dieter Betz, 'Magic and Mystery in the Greek Magical Papyri', in: Christopher A. Faraone and Dirk Obbink (eds.), *Magika Hiera. Ancient Greek Magic and Religion* (Oxford 1991) 244–259. Cf. Robert K. Ritner, 'Egyptian Magical Practice under the Roman Empire: the Demotic Spells and their Religious Context' *ANRW* 18.5 (1995) 3333–3379, 3365f.

4.3.1. *Materials of medicine and magic*

The category 'materials of medicine and magic' comprises 44 items, to wit: plants, solids (minerals and metals) and animals (see appendix 4.1), which occur as ingredients for drugs and potions or as lemmas in the bilingual descriptions of medical and magical material. The items are not specifically Greek in nature, but belong to an international pharmacological jargon that was current in scientific and occult texts of the Hellenistic and Roman period. This jargon occurs in classifications of the natural world,[18] medical texts,[19] alchemical treatises[20] and Hermetic technical literature,[21] which works were written in *koine* Greek and circulated throughout the Hellenistic *oikumene* at large. The contribution of ancient Egyptian medicine to this jargon cannot easily be overestimated, so that the occurrence of the loanwords in the Demotic spells should not be dismissed as an instance of slavish one-way borrowing from a dominant Hellenistic scientific paradigm.[22] Moreover, apart from the Demotic magical handbook, the same jargon is also used to a certain degree in a partly preserved Demotic Medical Book of the Greco-Roman period, which belongs otherwise to the pharaonic medical tradition.[23]

---

[18] The classical works were Theophrastus, *On Stones*, Dioskorides, *On the Materials of Medicine*, Pliny the Elder, *Natural History*.

[19] For example, in the works of Celsus, Galen, Soranus, Paul of Aegina.

[20] R. Halleux, *Les alchimistes grecs 1: Papyrus de Leyde, Papyrus de Stockholm* (Paris 1981).

[21] For example, the *Cyranides* and Thessalos of Tralles' astro-botanical treatise *On the plants governed by the twelve signs of the zodiac and the seven planets*. See A.-J. Festugière, *La révélation d'Hermès Trismégiste 1: l'astrologie et les sciences occultes* (2nd ed.; Paris 1950); Fowden, *The Egyptian Hermes*, 87–94; François Daumas, 'L'alchimie a-t-elle une origine égyptienne?', in: Günter Grimm, Heinz Heinen and Erich Winter (eds.), *Das römisch-byzantinische Ägypten* (Aegyptiaca Treverensia 2; Mainz 1983) 109–118.

[22] Robert K. Ritner, 'Innovations and Adaptations in Ancient Egyptian Medicine' *JNES* 59 (2000) 107–117, 116. The international range of this jargon is borne out by the synonyms added to Dioskorides' *On the Materials of Medicine*, which are grouped according to geographic and ethnic origin; see for a convenient list: Max Wellmann, *Pedanii Dioscuridis Anazarbei De Materia Medica Libri Quinque* 3 Vols. (Berlin 1907–1914) vol. 3, 327–358.

[23] The Medical Book is preserved in a manuscript of the second century CE, but was possibly composed in the Ptolemaic period; publication: E.A.E. Reymond, *From the Contents of the Libraries of the Suchos Temples in the Fayyum. Part I: A Medical Book from Crocodilopolis (P. Vindob. D. 6257)* (MPER 10; Vienna 1976). The ingredients of the recipes, Egyptian and international, are listed on pp. 244–292; Reymond's identifications have to be used with due caution: Didier Devauchelle and Michel Pezin, 'Un papyrus médical démotique' *CdE* 53 (1978) 57–66. For other necessary improvements upon Reymond's readings, see the following reviews: Mark Smith, *BiOr* 35 (1978) 53–57;

The loanwords tend to cluster in a limited number of spells, which suggests that the editors did not consider them standard terms and only included them when found in a particular source. They occur as follows:

1. Embedded in a running Demotic sentence, either as ingredient or term of comparison.
2. Grouped in a list of ingredients provided with Greek or Egyptian weights.
3. As lemma in short bilingual descriptions of medical and magical material.

1) When embedded in a running Demotic sentence, the loanwords are transcribed into alphabetic Demotic signs, except for one occurrence in 'cipher' script, and provided with an appropriate determinative for 'plant', 'stone', 'solid' or 'granular', so that the borrowings are truly integrated into the matrix language. The following three excerpts are taken from an appendix to an elaborate divination spell, which lists alternative methods as variants to the spell. The loanword is the ingredient and, in the first two cases, provided with a gloss in Greek script. The translation renders the Greek loanword in small caps and gives the original transcription between brackets.

> *If you wish* to bring in a living man°, you have to put copper vitriol/ ΚΑΛΑΚΑΝΘΙ
> CHALKANTHES (gɜlɜgɜntsy) on the brazier°.
>
> ΚΑΡΑΒ
> *If you wish* to bring in a drowned man, you have to put sea KARAB (gʿrb n yʿm)[24] on the brazier.
>
> *If you wish* to bring in a thief, you have to put CROCUS powder (ḥke n grwgws) with alum, put (it) on the brazier.
> [P. London-Leiden 3/24, 26, 29]

Transcribed Greek loanwords occur similarly as terms of comparison in the short descriptions of medical and magical material.

> ['Gold flower'/chrysanthemum] its flower is of gold; its leaf is like (that of) the lily flower/KRINANTHEMON (gryn'themwn)
> [P. London-Leiden V2/6]

---

W. Brunsch, *WZKM* 72 (1980) 155–160; Janet H. Johnson, *JNES* 41 (1982) 301–303.

[24] The material *karab* cannot be identified with certitude. The Demotic determinative suggests that it is a solid, either a metal or a mineral. If the word derives from the

[Lees of wine] It is a white stone, which is like 'all-heal resin'/GALBANUM (g'lb3n'). There is another that is made into LIME (sgewe).

[P. London-Leiden V3/5–7]

[Moon stone] It is a white *stone*, which is like glass (and) grinded into tiny fragments like orpiment/ARSENICON (3rsenygwn).

[P. London-Leiden V3/17–18]

2) When the loanword occurs as an item in a list of ingredients, it is transcribed into alphabetic Demotic signs in the case that the enumeration is written in a continuous line (horizontal), whereas it is written in the Greek or 'cipher' script when the items are written one above the other (vertical). Whenever the ingredients are provided with units of weight, the Egyptian units *stater* (*sttr.t*) and *kite* (*ḳd.t*) are used in the horizontal list,[25] whereas the abbreviations for the Greek units *drachma* and *ounce* are also used in the vertical arrangement.[26] The following two excerpts are lists of ingredients written in a continuous line, in which the loanword is transcribed in its nominative form, as is the rule with Greek loanwords in Coptic, next to common Egyptian ingredients, so that the loanword truly blends in with the Egyptian linguistic environment. The second passage has Egyptian weights.

---

Greek word κάραβος, which means 'horned or cerambycid beetle' or 'a pricky crustacean' (LSJ, 876b), it might be pulverised shell of a crustacean.

[25] The *kite* unit is attested since the 18th dynasty. The *stater* was originally a Greek weight, but introduced as a unit of currency and weight into Demotic around the fourth century BCE. By the time of the Roman period, the *stater* had become fully integrated into the Egyptian language.

[26] The units of weight are of particular interest, because pharaonic medicine made use of measures of volume, whereas pre-Alexandrian Greek medicine was rather unconcerned with measured quantity, as was the case in cuneiform medical texts. From the Alexandrian physician Herophilus onwards (3rd century BCE), Greek medical texts prescribe precise quantities as attested in both the 'high' medical literature and the medical papyri found in Egypt. For Egyptian medical texts, see, Westendorf, *Handbuch der altägyptischen Medizin*, vol. 1, 521–524. See on the lack of doses in the *Corpus Hippocraticum* and Mesopotamian medical texts: Dietlinde Goltz, *Studien zur altorientalischen und griechischen Heilkunde: Therapie—Arzneibereitung—Rezeptstruktur* (Wiesbaden 1974) 19, 116, 174–176. On Hellenistic and Roman medicine: Heinrich von Staden, *Herophilus: The Art of Medicine in Early Alexandria* (Cambridge, Mass. 1989) 19; John M. Riddle, 'High Medicine and Low Medicine in the Roman Empire' *ANRW* II 37.1 (1993) 102–120, 119.

Fragrance that you should *put* up (on the brazier): FRANKINCENSE,[27] balm°, AMMONIAC GUM INCENSE° (ꜣmwny‛k trymy‛m‛-tꜣ-s),[28] dates°. Pound them with wine, make them into a ball and offer it up°.

[P. London-Leiden 14/22–24]

**A prescription** to make a man fall asleep. Very *good*! *APPLE* seeds°, 1 stater, 1 half-kite°; MANDRAKE *root* (nn.t n m‛ntr‛gwnꜣ),[29] 4 half-kite°; ivy /KYSSOS (gyss-‛ꜣ-s), 4 half-kite°. *Grind* into one *substance*.

[P. London-Leiden 24/17–19]

In the following four passages, the ingredients are listed one above the other and provided with abbreviations for Greek units of weight (nos. 1, 2, 4) or Egyptian units (no. 3). When connected to Greek units of weight, the majority of loanwords are written in the genitive case following standard Greek grammar, so that the list is actually a Greek instead of an Egyptian text. In order to allow insight into the varying case endings, the lists are given in transcription and translation. The arrow in the left margin indicates the actual reading direction on the manuscript.

1. → ° σκαμουνάρι⟨ο⟩ν      (δραχμὴ) ā   [*SCAMMONY (ROOT)*, 1 drachma]
     ° ὀπίου               (δραχμὴ) ā   [1 drachma of *OPIUM*]
                                        [P. London-Leiden 24/2–3]

2. → ° μανδρακόρου ῥίζα    o(ὐγκία) ā   [*MANDRAKE ROOT*, 1 ounce]
     ° μελακρετίκου        o(ὐγκία) ā   [1 ounce of *QUINCES*]
     ° ὑοσκυάμου           o(ὐγκία) ā   [1 ounce of *HENBANE*]
     ° κισσοῦ              o(ὐγκία) ā   [1 ounce of *IVY*]
                                        [P. London-Leiden 24/7–10]

3. → ° εὐφορβίου           1.t ḳt.t     [1 kite of spurge]
     ° πεπ{τ}έρεως         1/2 ḳt.t     [1/2 kite of pepper]
     ° περήθου[30]         sttr.t 1.t   [1 stater of pellitory]

---

[27] This is a Semitic loanword (ꜣlbwnṯ < lebonah); Günter Vittmann, 'Semitisches Sprachgut im Demotischen' *WZKM* 86 (1996) 435–447, 438.

[28] Griffith & Thompson and Janet H. Johnson parse this compound noun incorrectly into two separate ingredients: ammoniac and incense. In fact, the second noun is connected to the first term in a genitive construction, whose case ending is retained in the alphabetic Demotic transcription. The ingredient occurs as ἀμμωνιακὸν θυμίαμα among the synonyms to Dioscorides III.84RV. Note that the first term is correctly provided with the plant determinative and the second with the powder determinative.

[29] This is actually a mixed compound, because it derives from μανδραγόρου ῥίζα. The hieratic group nn.t n, 'root of', is the Egyptian translation of ῥίζα followed by the genitive morpheme. Note that the transcription m‛ntr‛gwnꜣ retains the original genitive case, although standard Coptic grammar prescribes the nominative case for mixed compounds.

[30] This is probably πύρεθρος, Dioscorides III.73RV.

|   |   | ° αὐτάρχης[31] | sttr.t 1.t | [1 stater of salt efflorescence] |
|---|---|---|---|---|
|   | ← | °δῖον ἄπερον[32] | sttr.t 1.t | [1 stater, native sulphur][33] |
|   |   | ° mn irp | sttr 6 | [any wine, 6 staters] |
|   |   | ° nhe n mȝʿ.t | ? | [genuine oil, a measure?] |
|   |   |   |   | [P. London-Leiden V9/2–8] |
| 4. | ← | ° ȝbn | (δραχμὴ) ā | [alum, 1 drachma] |
|   |   | ° πίπιρ[34] | (δραχμὴ) ā | [*PEPPER*, 1 drachma] |
|   |   | ° mḫ-n-knwṱ iw=f šw | (δραχμὴ) δ̄ | [dry ?-plant, 4 drachmas] |
|   |   | ° sȝterw[35] | (δραχμὴ) δ̄ | [4 drachmas of SATYRION[36]] |
|   |   |   |   | [P. London-Leiden V14/2–5] |

The lists present clearly a mixture of scripts, reading directions, Egyptian and Greek units of weight and a combination of genuine Egyptian terms and loanwords. Given the genitive case endings in combination with Greek units of weight, the majority of the Greek terms cannot be called loanwords in the true sense of the word, that is to say, lexical items of a donor language imported and *integrated* into a recipient language. The degree of language interference is hence very limited in these passages. Since the excerpts do not record actual speech events, but are the result of textual transmission, it is perhaps better to speak of a donor manuscript and manuscript interference, instead of a donor language and language interference. Similar lists, albeit not bilingual, can be found in the Greek medical papyri from Egypt,[37] so that it is

---

[31] This is ἀδάρκη (F) or ἀδάρκης (M), 'salt efflorescence on marsh plants'; see Dioscorides V.119.

[32] This is θεῖον ἄπυρον, Dioscorides V.107. See also PGM VII.168.

[33] From this line onwards, the reading direction of the list changes. The four foregoing lines run from left to right, whereas the last three lines have to be read from right to left. This means that the list follows initially a Greek reading direction despite the Egyptian units of weight, but changes into a true Egyptian list from line 6 onwards. This could provide an explanation for the fact that δῖον ἄπερον is written in the nominative instead of the genitive case as the four foregoing ingredients. According to Coptic grammar, Greek loanwords are incorporated into Egyptian in their nominative form irrespective of their syntactical function. The first four ingredients follow the Greek grammatical rule that units of weight follow the genitive.

[34] This is πίπερι, Dioscorides II.159.

[35] This is the transcription of σατυρίου, genitive form of σατύριον; see Dioscorides III.128.

[36] Max Aufmesser identifies this plant with 'Ohnsporn', aceras anthropophorum: *Etymologische und wortgeschichtliche Erläuterungen zu* De Materia Medica *des Pedanius Dioscurides Anazarbeus* (Altertumswissenschaftliche Texte und Studien 34; Hildesheim 2000) 147.

[37] Instructive are P. Oxy. 1088 and P. Tebt. 273. See also ODN 43 and 54; a similar bilingual list, though very short, is O. Straßburg 619. See on the Greek medical papyri

plausible that the compilers of the extant manuscript copied parts of the extant lists from Greek texts, written either in Greek or 'cipher' script.

3) The first four columns of the verso side of P. London-Leiden preserve an apparently random collection of short descriptions of materials of medicine and magic. These short texts are headed by the name of a plant or mineral and describe the item's outward appearance, its treatment and the place where it can be obtained. The rationale of their inclusion is unclear, because none of the items is called for in the spells on the manuscript. The lemmas are Greek nouns, written in Greek script, whereas the descriptions are in Demotic. In the majority of cases, the Greek loanword is followed by its name in Egyptian. This name can take on the following forms:

a) A transcription of the Greek term in alphabetic Demotic signs
b) An equivalent with identical meaning[38]
c) An equivalent with different meaning

The following passages illustrate this breakdown:

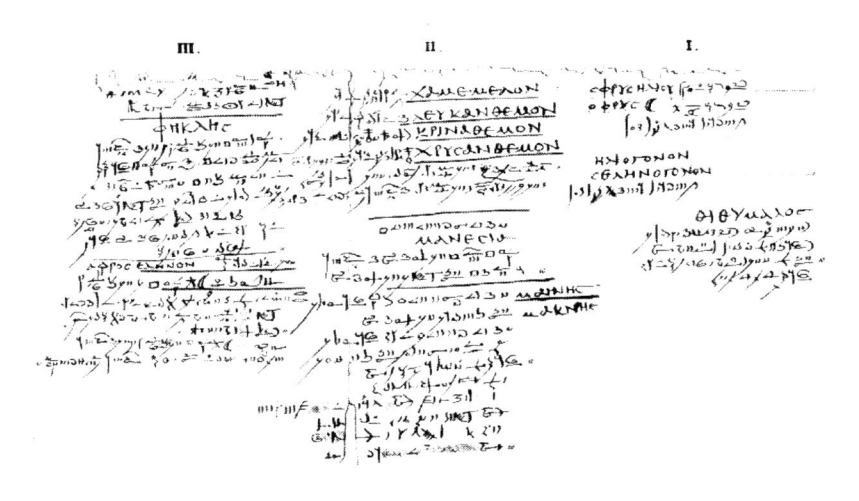

Fig. 4.1. P. London-Leiden verso 1–3

---

in general: Marie-Hélène Marganne-Mélard, 'La Médicine dans l'Égypte romaine: les sources et les méthodes' *ANRW* II 37.3 (1996) 2709–2740, 2718–2725.

[38] In these cases, it cannot be determined which of the terms is the translation of the other or, in other words, which is the original and which the secondary name.

a) The ΜΑΚΝΗϹΙΑ (pꜣ mꜥknesy)
   ΜΑΝΕϹΙΑ
   A *stone* of *stone*, which is black like galena (stem). You should *grind* it while it is black.
   ΜΑΓΝΗϹ / ΜΑΚΝΗϹ The *living* ΜΑΚΝΗϹ.(pꜣ mꜥknes nty ꜥnḫ): it is imported; you should scrape it while it is black. The human ΜΑ⟨Κ⟩ΝΕϹ (pꜣ mꜥnes n rmṯ): it is imported from India (tꜣ ꜥntsyke); you should scrape it; it makes blood come out. [P. London-Leiden V2/7–15][39]

b) ΟΦΡΥϹ ΗΛΙΟΥ   ꜣnḫ n Rꜥ   [eyebrow of the sun: eyebrow of the sun]
   ΟΦΡΥϹ ☾       ꜣnḫ n Iꜥḥ   [eyebrow of the moon: eyebrow of the moon]
   ḥyn.w sym.w nꜣw              [These are herbs]
                                     [P.London-Leiden V1/1–3]

   Its name in Greek: ΑΦΡΟϹΕΛΗΝΟΝ [foam of the moon/ moon-stone]
   Foam of the moon (dꜣḥ n iꜥḥ): it is a white *stone*.
                                     [P.London-Leiden V3/12–13]

c) ΧΑΜΕΜΕΛΟΝ    'Clean-straw' (thw wꜥb) is its name
   ΛΕΥΚΑΝΘΕΜΟΝ  '..?.-*horse*' (šk ḥtr)[40] is its name
   ΚΡΙΝΑΘΕΜΟΝ   'There-is-none-*better*-than-I' is its name
   ΧΡΥϹΑΝΘΕΜΟΝ  '*Beautiful-of-face*' is its name, another (manuscript) says: 'The-golden-flower' of the wreath seller. Its leaf is strong; its stem is cold; its flower is golden; its leaf is like (that of) the lily flower/ΚΡΥΝΑ⟨Ν⟩-ΘΕΜΟΝ (gryn ꜥthemwen).   [P. London-Leiden V2/1–6]

   '*Ram's*-horn'   ΚΕΦΑΛΕΚΗ is its name.
   A *herb* that is like a wild fennel bush; its leaf and its stem are incised like the 'Love-man' plant. You should *grind* it, while it is *dry*; sift ⟨it⟩; make into a DRY POWDER (kser-ꜣ-n). You put it on any wound; it stops.
                                     [P. London-Leiden V4/10–15]

As becomes clear from these passages, the Greek terms are barely integrated into the Egyptian syntax. The short descriptions represent rather a bilingual dictionary or herbal, which allows the reader to identify plants by their local and international name.

## 4.3.2. *Medical terminology*

The medical terminology used in P. London-Leiden is, though limited in number, in line with the terminology of the medical papyri of the pharaonic period, except for seven Greek loanwords [see appendix 4.2]. The occurrence of these loanwords is remarkable, because Egyp-

---

[39] See also the description of ivy in P. London-Leiden 24/22–25.
[40] Griffith and Thompson suggest reading the name of this plant as 'prick horse': *The Demotic Magical Papyrus of London and Leiden*, vol. 1, 171, fn. to line 2.

tian medical terminology was well developed and therefore not in need of foreign borrowings. The Demotic Medical Book is accordingly free of foreign loanwords with respect to its medical terminology.[11] Since the use of Greek medical terms is restricted to a single spell each, every instance is an isolated one-time usage rather than a completely accepted loanword.[12] The Greek terms are spelled in alphabetic Demotic signs, or in one case in cipher, and integrated into a running Demotic sentence. The term ⲡⲟⲇⲁⲕⲣⲁⲛ (V8/1), written in Greek script, serves as heading to a Demotic prescription against gout. Since the loanword is written in the accusative case without apparent grammatical reason, it might be a remnant of a spell in Greek used as *vorlage* to the extant spell, where the term served as object to a verb.

### 4.3.3. *House utensils*

P. London-Leiden contains 6 Greek loanwords that belong to the category 'house utensils' [see appendix 4.3]. Like the Greek medical terms, these borrowings occur only in a single spell each. Reasons for their inclusion do not present themselves readily.

### 4.3.4. *Mixed compounds*

Mixed compounds or loan blends combine a native noun or morpheme with a noun from a donor language.[13] Unlike loan translations, which coin a foreign word in native terms, mixed compounds testify to a close and neutral contact between the two languages involved. In Demotic and Coptic, compounds are usually constructed by linking two nouns through the genitive morpheme *n*. In the following three excerpts, an Egyptian noun is combined in this way with a Greek loanword,

---

[11] Note that Reymond's identification of *gꜥm.t* (P. Vindob. D. 6257 11/10 and 14/23) with καῦμα, 'fever' is incorrect. Since the word is written with the flesh determinative, it refers in all probability to a body part. The Chicago Demotic Dictionary suggests a derivation from *gmꜣ*, 'temple of the head', WB 5, 170.2. I thank Janet H. Johnson for this reference.

[12] The word σῶμα occurs in two separate spells (13/17 and V32/5), but these are parallels.

[13] Muysken sees mixed compounds as cases of borrowing through congruent lexicalisation: *Bilingual Speech*, 150–151.

thereby forming a mixed compound. The Greek words are transcribed into alphabetic Demotic signs and provided with appropriate determinatives.

iw=s n iwn n kʾlyne (< καλαίνη)
It is BLUE-GREEN in colour                    [P. London-Leiden V4/8][14]

wʿ.t šmwꜣ.t n ḥt n tphn° (< δάφνη)
A peg of LAUREL wood°                         [P. London-Leiden 27/15]

nn.t n mʿntrʿgwrw (< μανδραγόρου)
MANDRAKE root                                 [P. London-Leiden 24/18][15]

The term 'lupine-seller' represents a true loan blend, since it combines the agentive prefix s-n (+ noun), 'man of –', which is used to denote craftsmen and dealers, with the Greek loanword θέρμος, 'lupine', to refer to the lupine seller.

ḫr gm=k s n pꜣ mꜣʿ n pꜣ s-ḵlm ky dd pꜣ s-trmws (< θέρμος)

You will find them in the place of the wreath-seller, another [manuscript] says: the lupine-seller             [P. London-Leiden 5/25]

ḫr gm=k s n pꜣ mꜣʿ n pꜣ s-trmws°

You will find it in the place of the lupine-seller°
                                              [P. London-Leiden 27/25]

4.3.5. *Conclusions*

The foregoing pages have demonstrated that the degree of interference between Egyptian and Greek is rather limited with respect to the process of insertion. In the light of the process of re-lexification of the Egyptian language during the Roman period, the conclusion is warranted that the Demotic spells do not reflect colloquial language, but, to speak with John Ray, represent 'a purified and filtered vernacular which was subject to its own rules'.[16] The categories of loanwords that have been identified above accord well with Willy Clarysse's conclusions regarding the occurrence of Greek loanwords in Demotic documentary texts, this is to say, the loanwords are mainly specialised international jargon and objects of daily life. The adoption of Hellenis-

---

[14] Although καλαίνη is morphologically an adjective, it is used as a noun following Demotic grammar.
[15] Note that the alphabetic Demotic transcription retains the genitive case ending of the original μανδραγόρου ῥίζα.
[16] Ray, 'How demotic is Demotic?', 264.

tic pharmacological jargon demonstrates that the compilers were not ignorant of contemporaneous developments in the Hellenistic centres of learning, but there are no reasons to assume that the occurrence of Greek loanwords in the Demotic spells is motivated out of a desire to identify with Hellenistic culture or to include Greek currents of thought in the ritual procedures. In fact, the restricted use of Greek loanwords, both in quantitative and qualitative terms, points rather at a conscious effort of linguistic purism.

In a few cases, there are indications that the Greek terms were copied from texts used by the compilers of the extant spells. A main argument is the observation that several loanwords are written with case endings that are without use in the Demotic linguistic environment.[17] In all likelihood, the case endings were retained when the words were copied from a Greek *Vorlage*. The following short passage contains two Greek words in the right margin and three Demotic terms in the main text that are best explained as literal translations of Greek words.

> ⲘⲀⲄⲚⲎⲤ / ⲘⲀⲔⲚⲎⲤ The *living* MAKNES.(*pꜣ mꜥknes nty ꜥnḫ*): it is imported; you should scrape it while it is black. The human ⲘⲀ⟨Ⲕ⟩ⲚⲈⲤ (*pꜣ mꜥnes n rmṯ*): it is imported from India (*tꜣ ꜥn-tsyke*); you should scrape it; it makes blood come out.     [P. London-Leiden V2/7–15]

The 'living magnes' is probably the Egyptian translation of μάγνης ζῶν, while 'human magnes' derives from μάγνης ἀνδρεῖος.[18] Since the common Demotic term for India is *Hntw*, the present form *tꜣ ꜥn-tsyke* can only be explained as a transcription of ἡ Ἰνδική under the influence of a Greek manuscript. It is therefore likely that the entire passage is a translation of a Greek pharmacological description, of which the two Greek terms ⲘⲀⲄⲚⲎⲤ and ⲘⲀⲔⲚⲎⲤ were copied into the extant text. These observations conform to the conclusion of the previous chapter, that the multiplicity of scripts is the result to a large degree of the consultation of manuscripts in different languages and scripts. Hence, the occurrence of Greek loanwords is less a matter of language interference than of manuscript interference.

---

[17] Examples are: ⲎⲖⲒⲞⲄⲞⲚⲞⲚ and ⲤⲈⲖⲎⲚⲞⲄⲞⲚⲞⲚ (V1/4–5), ⲪⲎⲔⲀⲎⲤ (V3/4), ⲀⲪⲢⲞ-ⲤⲈⲖⲎⲚⲞⲚ (V3/12), ⲠⲞⲖⲀⲔⲢⲀⲚ (V8/1).

[18] See for references Griffith and Thompson, *The Demotic Magical Papyrus of London and Leiden*, vol. 1, 172, fn. to lines 11 and 13.

4.4. *The process of alternation: the ritual power of foreign languages*

The lack of Greek loanwords in the Demotic spells could easily be explained as a reflection of a negative language attitude towards Greek and thus as in support of nationalistic priestly beliefs. However, this assumption is seriously challenged by the presence of seven discrete Greek invocations incorporated into seven Demotic spells. Unlike the Greek loanwords, which occur only in the recipe part of the spell, the Greek invocations had to be pronounced in the course of the rite, so that they played an active and significant role in the ritual itself. If the editors of the spells had considered Greek invocations ineffective on account of the fact that Greek is 'empty speech' (CH 16/2.16), they would not have included these seven invocations as means to address the divine and manipulate the workings of nature. In other words, the presence of the Greek prayers demonstrates that the editors of the Demotic spells attributed ritual power to the Greek language notwithstanding the clear-cut message of *Corpus Hermeticum* XVI.

In imitation of Peter Muysken, I define this bilingual phenomenon as alternation between languages within a single, self-contained magical prescription.[49] The languages remain separate insofar that they maintain their linguistic structure, form a discrete section and serve each a distinct function within the text and ritual. At the same time, the discrete sections are related to the extent that they are both subservient to the same magical goal and cannot do without the other to attain this goal. Any recitation of a Greek invocation will be futile as long as the requirements regarding ingredients and ritual acts as prescribed in the accompanying Demotic recipe are not met. Words, ingredients and ritual acting are connected with each other through mythological allusions and the rules of *sympatheia* and *antipatheia*. Therefore, in the following pages, the relationship between the Greek invocations and their accompanying Demotic recipes is analysed to determine the degree of coherence and, if possible, the causes and rules of language alternation.

Apart from these seven instances of language alternation within a single spell, there is one instance of language alternation within a single speech event.[50] In an elaborate Demotic invocation of a vessel

---

[49] Muysken, *Bilingual Speech*, 3–10; see also chapter 5.2. Pieter Muysken is only concerned with alternation between structures of languages within a single *speech event*.

[50] I leave out of the discussion Greek clauses that might possibly be mangled and hidden in *voces magicae*. Two cases in point can be found in P. London-Leiden 28/1 and

divination ritual, the practitioner identifies himself with a wide range of divine beings and urges the light repeatedly to enter before the youth, who is used as a medium (P. London-Leiden 1/1–3/35 = PDM xiv 1–92). The language, style and imagery of the invocation are in accord with traditional Egyptian religion and ritual throughout, but in one instance a Demotic clause switches into a Greek adverbial phrase. The adverbial phrase comprises three words, which are spelled in alphabetic Demotic signs, followed by the foreign land determinative and provided with a gloss in Greek.

> [Dem.] O great god whose name is great°,
> [Dem.] Appear to this youth°
> [Greek] WITHOUT CAUSING FEAR° (or) DECEIVING°, TRUTHFULLY°.
>
> *p3 nṯr ꜥ3 nty-ı̓w n3e-ꜥ3y.w rn=f* °
> *wnḥ r p3y ꜥlw* °
> ΑΦΟΒѠC        ΑΦΕΥCΤѠC        ΕΠΑΛΗΘΕΙΑ
> *rph-ꜥ3-b-ꜥ3-s* °   *ꜥpsewst-ꜥ3-s* °   *epꜥletsy*ꜥ °        [P. London-Leiden 2/13–14]

The adverbial phrase ἀφόβως ἀψεύστως ἐπ' ἀληθείᾳ is embedded in a Demotic clause as an independent foreign constituent that follows Greek grammatical rules. It derives its adverbial function primarily from Greek morphology, even if its position at the end of the clause conforms to Demotic syntax. A close comparison of the alphabetic Demotic spellings with their associated glosses reveals that each alphabetic Demotic character constitutes a pair with a corresponding Greek letter, which suggests that the Demotic rendering is a faithful transcription of the Greek spelling instead of an attempt to reproduce in writing the factual pronunciation of the Greek expression. It is therefore likely, that the adverbial phrase was adopted from a text in Greek and transcribed into alphabetic Demotic characters while retaining the original spelling as supralineal glosses.

---

V13/6; see Griffith and Thompson, *The Demotic Magical Papyrus of London and Leiden*, vol. 1, 163, fn. to line 1 and 186, fn. to line 6. The Demotic scribe showed his unawareness of the etymology of these groups by providing them with god determinatives like any other *vox magica*. For another instance of language alternation, see the discussion of P. London-Leiden V17/1–8 in chapter 3.4.2 (fig.3.6).

4.4.1. *The ritual power of Greek*

The fourth column of P. London-Leiden preserves a prescription for a divination ritual, commonly termed *ph-ntr* in Demotic,[51] which claims to make a god appear in a dream, who will answer any question the practitioner poses (P. London-Leiden 4/1–22 =PDM xiv.93–114 [PGM XIVa. 1–11]; translation given in Appendix 4.3.A).[52] The recipe is entirely written in Demotic and occupies lines 1–8 and 20–22; the Greek invocation breaks up the Demotic section in lines 9–19.

The title defines the ritual as a *sš-mšt*, of which the great god Imhotep made frequent use (line 1).[53] The term *sš-mšt* escapes accurate interpretation, because it is not known from any other text to date. Robert Ritner suggested translating it as 'casting for inspection', because the ritual finally entails the drawing up of a horoscope;[54] Heinz-J. Thissen prefers the more neutral 'Entwurf einer Untersuchung'.[55] Despite this initial ambiguity, the Demotic recipe is fairly easy to follow and prescribes ritual techniques that are well known from similar divination rituals from the *Demotic* and *Greek Magical Papyri* and fit in with earlier pharaonic magic.[56] The practitioner is ordered to place a bench of olivewood in a clean room and to cover it from foot to top with a linen cloth. Having placed four bricks under the bench, the practitioner should throw a little ball made of goose fat, myrrh and *ks-'nh*-stone onto a clay censer, while reciting 'this spell in Greek' (line 7). When he goes to sleep without having spoken to anyone, the god will appear to him in the guise of an Egyptian priest wearing clothes of byssus and sandals and answer all his questions. The second component of the ritual is the placement of an astrological hour table (πίναξ *n 'š wnw.t*: line 21) together with a papyrus sheet containing a specific question upon one of the bricks. The god will then take care that the stars are favourable with respect to the practitioner's business.

---

[51] Ritner, *The Mechanics of Ancient Egyptian Magical Practice*, 214–220.
[52] An alternative German translation with notes can be found in: Reinhold Merkelbach and Maria Totti, *Abrasax. Ausgewählte Papyri religiösen und magischen Inhalts. Band 2: Gebete (Fortsetzung)* (Papyrologica Coloniensia 17.2; Cologne 1991) 77–82.
[53] On these advertising introductions, see chapters 6.1 and 4.
[54] *GMPT*, 200, fn. 59; compare with Griffith and Thompson, *The Demotic Magical Papyrus of London and Leiden*, vol. 3, 77, # 786.
[55] Merkelbach and Totti, *Abrasax. Band 2: Gebete*, 78.
[56] Several of the techniques are discussed in John Gee, 'The Structure of Lamp Divination', in: Kim Ryholt (ed.), *Acts of the Seventh International Conference of Demotic Studies* (CNI Publications 27; Copenhagen 2002) 207–218.

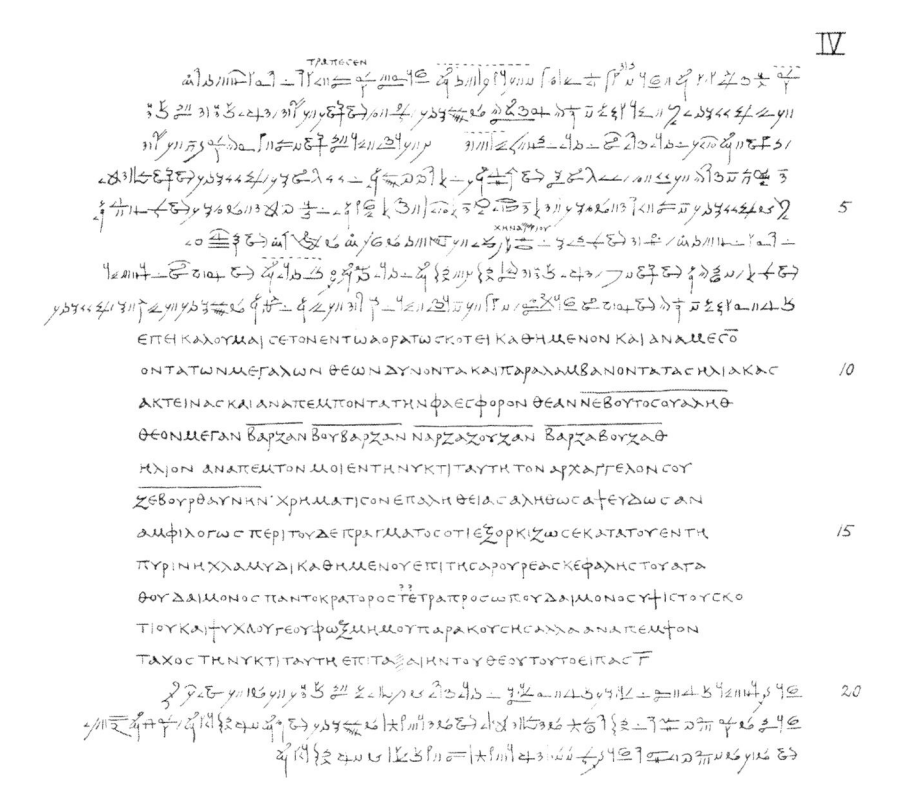

ΕΠΙΚΑΛΟΥΜΑΙ CΕ ΤΟΝ ΕΝ ΤΩ ΑΟΡΑΤΩ CΚΟΤΕΙ ΚΑΘΗΜΕΝΟΝ ΚΑΙ ΑΝΑΜΕCΟ
ΟΝ ΤΑΤΩΝ ΜΕΓΑΛΩΝ ΘΕΩΝ ΔΥΝΟΝΤΑ ΚΑΙ ΠΑΡΑΛΑΜΒΑΝΟΝΤΑ ΤΑC ΗΛΙΑΚΑC
ΑΚΤΕΙΝΑC ΚΑΙ ΑΝΑΠΕΜΠΟΝΤΑ ΤΗΝ ΦΑΕCΦΟΡΟΝ ΘΕΑΝ ΝΕΒΟΥΤΟCΟΥΑΛΗΘ
ΘΕΟΝ ΜΕΓΑΝ ΒΑΡΖΑΝ ΒΟΥΒΑΡΖΑΝ ΝΑΡΖΑΖΟΥΖΑΝ ΒΑΡΖΑΒΟΥΖΑΘ
ΗΛΙΟΝ ΑΝΑΠΕΜΨΟΝ ΜΟΙ ΕΝ ΤΗ ΝΥΚΤΙ ΤΑΥΤΗ ΤΟΝ ΑΡΧΑΓΓΕΛΟΝ COY
ΖΕΒΟΥΡΘΑΥΝΗΝ· ΧΡΗΜΑΤΙCΟΝ ΕΠ ΑΛΗ ΘΕΙΑC ΑΛΗΘΩC Α†ΕΥΔΩC ΑΝ
ΑΜΦΙΛΟΓω C ΠΕΡΙ ΤΟΥΔΕ ΤΟΥ ΠΡΑΓΜΑΤΟC ΟΤΙ ΕΞΟΡΚΙΖΩ CΕ ΚΑΤΑ ΤΟΥ ΕΝ ΤΗ
ΠΥΡΙΝΗ ΧΛΑΜΥΔΙ ΚΑΘΗΜΕΝΟΥ ΕΠΙ ΤΗC ΑΡΟΥΡΕΑC ΚΕΦΑΛΗC ΤΟΥ ΑΓΑ
ΘΟΥ ΔΑΙΜΟΝΟC ΠΑΝΤΟΚΡΑΤΟΡΟC ΤΕΤΡΑΠΡΟCωΠΟΥ ΔΑΙΜΟΝΟC ΥΨΙCΤΟΥ CΚΟ
ΤΙΟΥ ΚΑΙ †ΥΧΛΟΥ ΓΕΟΥ ΦωΞ ΜΗ ΜΟΥ ΠΑΡΑΚΟΥCΗC ΑΛΛΑ ΑΝΑΠΕΜΨΟΝ
ΤΑΧΟC ΤΗ ΝΥΚΤΙ ΤΑΥΤΗ ΕΠΙΤΑΞΑΙ ΗΝ ΤΟΥ ΘΕΟΥ ΤΟΥΤΟ ΕΙΠΑC F

Fig. 4.2. P. London-Leiden 4/1–22

The Greek invocation starts with a standard phrase 'I call upon you who …' (Ἐπικαλοῦμαι σε τόν …: line 9) as a plea to the sun god, who is addressed as the master of light and darkness. During daytime, he travels across the sky and sends his solar rays to the earth, while, in the evening and night, the moon goddess NEBOUTHOSOUALÊTH[57] brings light upon his command. He is called 'great god, BARZAN BOUBARZAN NARZAZOUZAN BARZABOUZATH Helios' (lines 12–13) and asked to send up, most probably from the underworld, his archangel ZEBOURTHAUNEN.

---

[57] The etymology of this name, which occurs frequently in the *Greek Magical Papyri*, remains unclear. Nebouthosoualeth is associated with the moon and the underworld and seems to make up a triad with the goddesses Aktiôphis and Ereschigal. She is also connected with Selene-Hekate. K. Preisendanz, 'Nebutosualeth' *PRE* 16 (1935) 2158–2160; C. Bonner, *Studies in Magical Amulets Chiefly Graeco-Egyptian* (Ann Arbor 1950) 197–198.

In the following lines, the focus shifts to the archangel, who is urged under threat of the anger of the demon PHÔX[58] to give reliable answers to the practitioner. Unlike the lengthy invocations of the numerous Demotic divination rites preserved on the manuscript, this invocation does not address the divine by recognizable traditional Egyptian names and places of worship. Instead, it mainly takes recourse to *voces magicae*, whose etymology is far from clear and possibly not Egyptian.[59] The connection between the sun god and the moon goddess NEBOUTHOSOUALÊTH is also suggestive of an origin outside the traditional parameters of Egyptian religion. The alien character of the invocation is reinforced by the fact that the interaction between the Demotic prescription and the Greek invocation is rather limited. Were it not for line 7, 'you have to pronounce this spell in Greek to it (the clay censer)', the textual parts would seem to function independently from each other: neither does the invocation refer to the prescribed ritual action, nor can ritual techniques and ingredients be linked to the demons invoked. It is hence conceivable that the extant spell is actually not an organic unit, but a composite of text units of different origins, which were combined during the phase of compilation.

This hypothesis finds support in two Greek glosses written above two common Demotic words in the recipe text. The word *tks* 'throne, chair, boat' is glossed with ΤΡΑΠΕϹΕΝ from τράπεζα, 'table', (line 1), while *sriw.t* 'goose' is accompanied by the gloss ΧΗΝΑ[Γ]ΡΙΟΥ from χὴν ἄγριος 'wild goose' (line 6). In this particular instance, the glosses do not reproduce a vocalised version of the Demotic word, as is usually the case with glosses, but give the Greek lexical equivalent of the Demotic term. They are provided with case endings, respectively accusative and genitive, that perfectly match with the syntactic function of their Demotic equivalents, respectively object and possessive. It seems odd that an Egyptian scribe would take pains to supplement regular Demotic words, which are not to be pronounced, with Greek glosses provided with correct and corresponding case endings, which are without meaning in the Egyptian syntax. It is therefore more likely that the scribe proceeded the other way around: he used a ritual text in

---

[58] Heinz-J. Thissen suggests to derive this name from Egyptian *pȝ ḥḳȝ*—ⲠϨⲰⲔ-Ⲥ, 'the ruler': Merkelbach and Totti, *Abrasax. Band 2: Gebete*, 82, note to line 18. This etymology cannot be considered secure.

[59] See for the *vox magica* Barza, PGM IV.2891–2942. According to Hopfner, it is a Persian word, 'shining light'; Hopfner, *Griechisch-ägyptischer Offenbarungszauber*, vol. 2, 100.

Greek as one of his sources and, in the course of translating the Greek into Demotic, decided to add the original Greek terms, without rewriting them in the nominative case, to limit the semantic field of the rather general Demotic terms.[60] A Greek *Vorlage* would also help to explain the alphabetic Demotic transcriptions of the Greek loanword πίναξ (lines 21 and 22), which owe more to the letter combination of the original Greek term than to factual pronunciation (*pyngs* / *pynˁks*: πίναξ).[61] Since astrology is factually foreign to Egyptian religion, Egyptian vocabulary could not offer the Egyptian scribe an equivalent Demotic technical term. He had no other choice than to transcribe the loanword into alphabetic Demotic signs.

To summarise what has been said in the foregoing, it is likely that the extant Demotic-Greek spell is a heterogeneous amalgam, compiled from an indeterminable number of *Vorlagen*, among which were texts in Greek. In the recipe part of the spell, the Greek glosses and the alphabetic Demotic transcriptions of the loanword πίναξ testify to the act of translating Greek into Demotic. However, the invocation, whose desired effect was considered dependent upon correct pronunciation,[62] had to be kept in its original language, lest the entire rite would be stripped of its ritual power. The alternation of languages in this particular spell is therefore less determined by socio-pragmatic rules of code switching than by an inhibition to translate magical sounds. Sounds that are, in this case, not Egyptian but Greek. This does not mean that the spell derives from a Greek cultural background, because the ritual procedures are clearly in accord with traditional Egyptian ritual techniques. By ascribing the ritual to 'the great god Imhotep' (line 1) the ritual text was inscribed into the traditional parameters of Egyptian religion and any possible doubt on the part of a contemporary reader about the spell's efficacy taken away.

---

[60] Note that the scribe's procedure is nowadays still of help to a modern scholar. Thanks to the Greek glosses it is clear that *tks* refers to something like a bench, while *srw.t* appears to signify more specifically a 'wild goose'.

[61] See for variant Demotic transcriptions of this Greek term in documentary texts: ODN 56/4, 60/2, 82/4, 85/1, 90/4; O.dem. Leiden 336, line 11; O.dem. BM 30258, line 2.

[62] See chapter 1 on the prohibition to translate.

### 4.4.2. *Translating from Greek into Demotic*

The process of translating from Greek into Demotic can be seen at work in a short spell to appease one's overseer, which is preserved in a Greek and Demotic version, written one above the other (P. London-Leiden 15/24–31 = PDM xiv.451–458 [PGM XIVb.12–15]). The text opens with a title in Demotic (line 24), which indicates the purpose of the spell, to give the invocation in Greek (lines 25–28) and, subsequently, an identical version in Demotic preceded by the words 'Its invocation in Egyptian again is this which is below' (lines 28–31). In the right margin of the column, on the level of line 27, is written in red ink a hieratic *ḏd md.wt*, 'words to be said'.[63]

[Dem.]  [***A spell***] for going before a superior[64] if he fights with you and he will not speak with you:

[Greek]  '*Do not pursue me, you, so-and-so*,[65] **I am**[66] PAPIPETOU METOUBANES, *I am carrying the mummy of Osiris, and I go to take it to Abydos, to take it to Tastai, and to bury it at Alkhah. If he, NN, causes me trouble, I will throw it at him*'.

[Dem.]  Its invocation in Egyptian again is this which is below:
ΠΑΠΙΠΕΤ[.]
'Do not run after me, NN.[67] I am PAPIPETU METUBANES, carrying the mummy of Osiris, going to take it to Abydos to let it rest in ALKHAH. If NN[68] fights with me today, I shall cast it out' (Say seven times!)                    [P. London-Leiden 15/24–31][69]

---

[63] The hieratic group is not reproduced on Thompson's hand copy, but clearly visible on Hooiberg's lithography.

[64] Note that the word *ḥry*, 'superior' is provided with the same determinatives as the word *pr-ʿ3*, 'pharaoh': the god's determinative followed by the abbreviation for the standard salutation for pharaoh, *ʿnḫ.w wḏ3.w snb.w*, 'may he live, be whole and healthy'. This suggests that the spell is aimed against influential people on the highest levels of society.

[65] Masculine.

[66] The Greek text writes the word ⲀⲚⲞⲔ and the following vox magica PAPIPETOU as one group as if they form a compound magical name. In fact, ⲀⲚⲞⲔ is the Old-Coptic independent pronoun, first person singular, meaning 'I am'. The Demotic version has accordingly *ink*.

[67] Either feminine or plural.

[68] Either feminine or plural.

[69] Tr. Janet H. Johnson (Demotic); R.F. Hock (Greek).

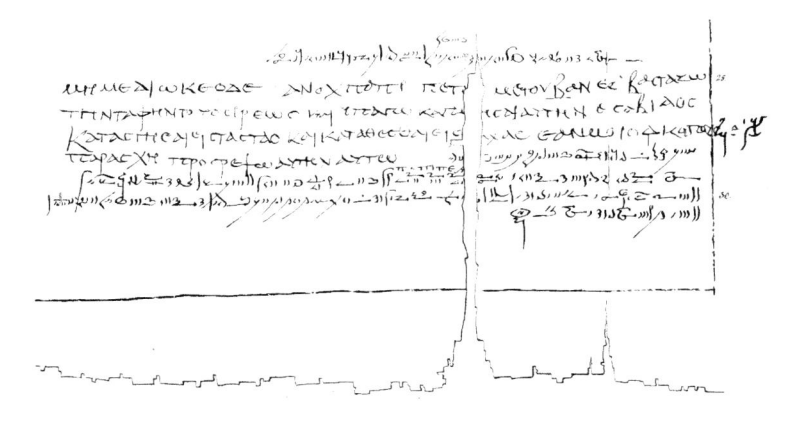

Fig. 4.3. P. London-Leiden 15/24–31

The magical rationale of the spell is the threat to discard the mummy of Osiris, the god of the dead who fell victim to his evil brother Seth, whom the practitioner claims to carry for interment in the holy burial ground of the Abydos region, if the opponent maintains his negative attitude. Since the spell plays consciously with the Osiris myth and displays a detailed knowledge of the ritual topography of the Abydos region, the spell must be the product of an Egyptian priestly environment. The most natural conclusion would hence be that the Demotic version, albeit written in secondary position, is the original rendering and the Greek spell a faithful translation. However, a close comparison of the spellings of the *voces magicae* and the topographical names in both versions reveals that, in fact, the extant Demotic version is translated from the Greek text (see the two following tables). For example, in the Greek version, the group *PAPIPETOU* serves with certitude as a vocalised, albeit garbled, reproduction of an Egyptian nominal predicate to the foregoing Old-Coptic independent pronoun **ⲁⲛⲟⲕ**, 'I am'.[70] It is noteworthy that the extant Demotic version does not provide the original meaning of the group by means of regular orthography, as might be expected, but parallels, by way of an alphabetic Demotic rendering, the Greek spelling letter by letter. Although the Egyptian scribe recognised the Old-Coptic independent pronoun **ⲁⲛⲟⲕ** and translated it accordingly into its Demotic equivalent *ỉnk*, he did not identify the Egyptian origin of the following group and, instead, interpreted it as a *vox magica*, so that, as was customary, he transcribed it into alphabetic

---

[70] The exact etymology of the group escapes interpretation. Griffith and Thomp-

Demotic signs and provided it with a god's determinative.[71] This means that the gloss ΠΑΠΙΠΕΤ[.] above the alphabetic Demotic transcription derives directly from the extant Greek text. The primacy of the Greek version is also borne out by the anomalous alphabetic Demotic rendering of the traditional place name Arkhah, the burial ground of Osiris in Abydos. Instead of writing it according to standard hieratic-Demotic orthography as he did in other spells, the scribe spelled the name in alphabetic Demotic signs following the Greek rendering.[72] A further argument is the fact that the clause with the place name Tastai does not occur in the Demotic version: it is more likely that a passage is lost than added in the process of translation.

|         | *Greek*   | *Demotic* | *Transliteration* |
|---------|-----------|-----------|-------------------|
| Line 25 | ΑΝΟΧ      |           | *ı͗nk*            |
| Line 25 | ΠΑΠΙΠΕΤΟΥ |           | *P'pypetw*        |
| Line 25 | ΜΕΤΟΥΒΑΝΕC |          | *metwb'nes*       |
| Line 27 | [ΑΛ]ΧΑC   |           | *'lgh'h*          |

Transcribing Greek into Demotic

| 1/6  | *ȝrk-ḥḥ* |
| 9/15 | *ʿrk-ḥḥ* |
| 9/23 | *ʿrk-ḥḥ* |
| 19/2 | *ȝrk-ḥḥ* |

Regular Demotic / hieratic orthography of *Arkheh* in P. London-Leiden

It cannot easily be established in what way the Greek and Demotic version relate to the intended ritual action, because the text does not

---

son's suggestion is problematic for a number of morphological reasons: *The Demotic Magical Papyrus of London and Leiden*, vol. 1, 108, fn. to line 25.

[71] The same holds true for the following group ΜΕΤΟΥΒΑΝΕС, which hides an Egyptian clause as well. A possible etymology of this group might be: *my tȝ-wbn=s*, 'Let her appear!' Cf. Griffith and Thompson, *The Demotic Magical Papyrus of London and Leiden*, vol. 1, 108, fn. to line 25.

[72] The scribe wrote the place name according to standard orthography in 1/6; 9/15, 23; 19/2.

give any information whatsoever, apart from the title, about the spell's mode of application. Since an editor took the trouble over translating the Greek spell into Demotic, the conclusion seems warranted that the Demotic version was certainly meant to be put to use. This is also borne out by the short instruction 'Say seven times!' added to the Demotic version. A similar direction for use is remarkably missing from the Greek version. The hieratic *ḏd md.wt* group in red ink, which is the customary keyword in Egyptian ritual texts to introduce the words that should be recited, is written to the right outside the vertical black ink border of the column suggesting that it was added afterwards. It was placed on the level of line 27, the last but one line of the Greek version and just above the Demotic introductory phrase 'Its invocation in Egyptian again is this which is below', which starts in the right margin of line 28. Hence, the hieratic group is either meant, being placed halfway, as introducing both versions or, since placed close to the start of the Demotic version, as indicating that the Demotic version is the portion to be pronounced. The latter interpretation would explain why only the Demotic version is provided with a direction for use. The Greek version should then be seen as a large gloss, which was retained to do justice to the sources or, possibly, out of respect for the inhibition to translate magical sounds.

### 4.4.3. *Invoking Seth—Typhon*

The first half of column 23 of P. London-Leiden preserves a spell to send evil sleep or, if the rite is repeated over seven days, to kill the intended victim, which offers a beautiful example of the meaningful interplay between ritual action, which is prescribed in a Demotic recipe, and the words addressed to the god, which is given in Greek (P. London-Leiden 23/1–20 = PDM xiv.675–694 [PGM XIVc.16–27]; translation given in Appendix 4.3.C). Words and acts are closely knit in an intricate web of connections between Egyptian mythology and native temple ritual. The Demotic recipe occupies lines 1–8 and prescribes a rite that has to be conducted twice a day, at sunrise and sunset, for four days to make the victim suffer from evil sleep or for seven days to make him die.[73]

---

[73] Note that the verb 'to die' is spelled in 'cipher' script. The victim is male according to the Demotic text, male or female according to the Greek invocation.

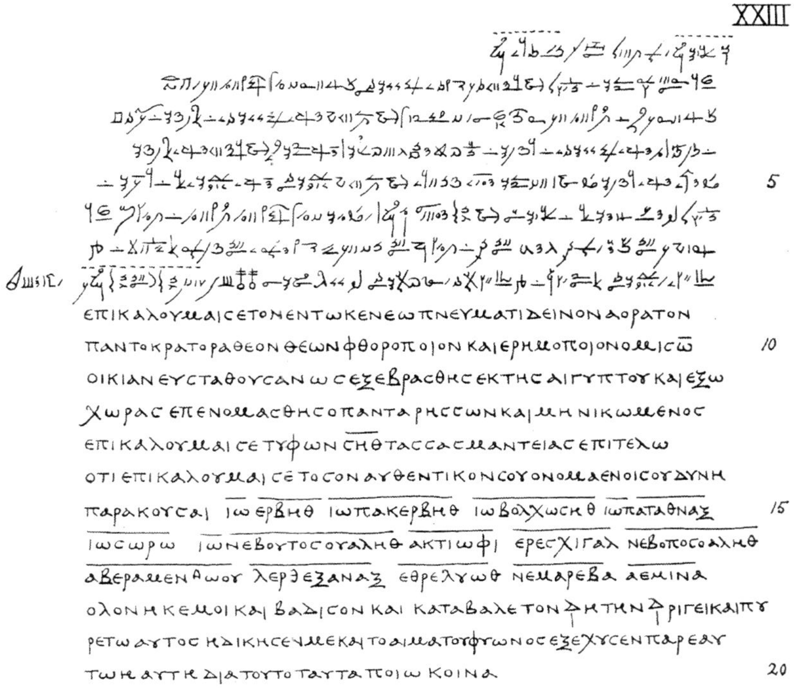

XXIII

[Demotic text lines 1–8]

ΕΠΙΚΑΛΟΥΜΑΙ ϹΕ ΤΟΝ ΕΝ ΤΩ ΚΕΝΕΩ ΠΝΕΥΜΑΤΙ ΔΕΙΝΟΝ ΑΟΡΑΤΟΝ
ΠΑΝΤΟΚΡΑΤΟΡΑ ΘΕΟΝ ΘΕΩΝ ΦΘΟΡΟΠΟΙΟΝ ΚΑΙ ΕΡΗΜΟΠΟΙΟΝ Ο ΜΕΙϹⲰ  10
ΟΙΚΙΑΝ ΕΥϹΤΑΘΟΥϹΑΝ Ω ϹΕ ΞΕΒΡΑϹΘΗϹ ΕΚ ΤΗϹ ΑΙΓΥΠΤΟΥ ΚΑΙ ΕΞΩ
ΧΩΡΑϹ ΕΠΕΝΟΜΑϹΘΗϹ Ο ΠΑΝΤΑ ΡΗϹϹΩΝ ΚΑΙ ΜΗ ΝΙΚΩΜΕΝΟϹ
ΕΠΙΚΑΛΟΥΜΑΙ ϹΕ ΤΥΦΩΝ ϹΗΘ ΤΑϹ ϹΑϹ ΜΑΝΤΕΙΑϹ ΕΠΙΤΕΛΩ
ΟΤΙ ΕΠΙΚΑΛΟΥΜΑΙ ϹΕ ΤΟ ϹΟΝ ΑΥΘΕΝΤΙΚΟΝ ϹΟΥ ΟΝΟΜΑ ΕΝ ΟΙϹ ΟΥ ΔΥΝΗ
ΠΑΡΑΚΟΥϹΑΙ ΙΩ ΕΡΒΗΘ ΙΩ ΠΑΚΕΡΒΗΘ ΙΩ ΒΟΛΧΩϹΗΘ ΙΩ ΠΑΤΑΘΝΑΞ  15
ΙΩϹΩΡΩ ΙΩ ΝΕΒΟΥΤΟϹΟΥΑΛΗΘ ΑΚΤΙΩΦΙ ΕΡΕϹΧΙΓΑΛ ΝΕΒΟΠΟϹΟΑΛΗΘ
ΑΒΕΡΑΜΕΝΘΩΟΥ ΛΕΡΘΕΞΑΝΑΞ ΕΘΡΕΛΥΩΘ ΝΕΜΑΡΕΒΑ ΑΕΜΙΝΑ
ΟΛΟΝ Η ΚΕ ΜΟΙ ΚΑΙ ΒΑΔΙϹΟΝ ΚΑΙ ΚΑΤΑΒΑΛΕ ΤΟΝ Δ(ΕΙ)ΝΑ Η ΡΙΓΕΙ ΚΑΙ ΠΥ-
ΡΕΤΩ ΑΥΤΟϹ Κ(ΑΙ) ΙΚΗϹΕΥ ΜΕ ΚΑΤΟ ΑΙΜΑΤΟ ΦΡΩΝΟϹ ΕΞΕΧΥϹΕΝ ΠΑΡ ΕΑΥ
ΤΩ Η ΑΥΤ Κ ΔΙΑ ΤΟΥΤΟ ΤΑΥΤΑ ΠΟΙΩ ΚΟΙΝΑ  20

Fig. 4.4. P. London-Leiden 23/1–20

While facing the rising or setting sun, the practitioner should place the head of a donkey between his feet and position his right hand in front of, and his left hand behind, the animal's head. While he is seated on his heels above the head,[74] he has to recite the invocation that is given in Greek in lines 9–20. Before starting the rite, he has to anoint his right foot with yellow ochre from Syria, his left foot and soles with clay and to put donkey's blood on one of his hands and the two corners of his mouth. As a phylactery, he should bind a thread of palm fibre to his hand and a piece of male palm fibre to the head and phallus. The accompanying Greek invocation runs as follows:

> I call upon you who are in the empty air, you who are terrible, invisible, almighty, a god of gods, you who cause destruction and desolation,

---

[74] If this is the correct interpretation of the instructions, the donkey's head is shut in by a limb on each of the four quarters of the compass and by the practitioner's body on top. This bodily arrangement was possibly meant to express in a magical way that the practitioner has total control over the donkey's head and its associated god.

you who hate a stable household, you who were driven out of Egypt and have roamed foreign lands, you who shatter everything and are not defeated. I call upon you, Typhon SETH; I command your prophetic powers because I call upon your authoritative name, to which you cannot refuse to listen, IÔ ERBÊTH IÔ PAKERBÊTH IÔ BOLCHÔSÊTH IÔ PATATHNAX IÔ SÔRÔ IÔ NEBOUTOSOUALÊTH AKTIÔPHI ERESCHIGAL NEBOUTOSOALÊTH ABERAMENTHÔOU LERTHEXANAX ETHRELUÔTH NEMAREBA AEMINA (the whole formula). Come to me and go and strike down him, NN, (or her, NN) with chills and fever. That very person has wronged me and he (or she) has spilled the blood of Typhon in his own (or her own) house. For this reason I am doing this (add the usual)
[P. London-Leiden 23/9–20 = PGM XIVc. 16–27][75]

The rite and the invocation are linked together through the Egyptian god Seth, who was identified, at the latest from the fifth century BCE onwards, with the Greek chthonic deity Typhon, whom Zeus had punished for insurrection by throwing him into the Tartarus.[76] The rite evokes a connection with Seth by means of the manipulation of the head and blood of a donkey, which animal was the symbol *par excellence* of the god Seth in Egyptian temple ritual throughout the Late and Greco-Roman period.[77] During the later stages of the pharaonic religion, the god's role had become restricted to representing the archetypical enemy of the ordered world, the 'god of confusion', who was not only seen as the murderer of Osiris and contester of the son and righteous heir Horus, but also as a thunder god and ruler of the desert and foreign countries.[78] To keep Seth's destructive powers ritually at bay, priests manipulated and destroyed small wax dolls or other inanimate objects as magical substitutes for Seth and his group

---

[75] Tr. R.F. Hock.

[76] See for Typhon in general: J.W. van Henten, 'Typhon' *DDD* 879–881. Ancient sources: Hesiod, *Theogony*, 820–868; Homeric hymn to Apollo, 305–355. Earliest testimony of association between Seth and Typhon: Herodotus, II 144 and 156; see A.B. Lloyd, *Herodotus Book II. Commentary 99–182* (Leiden 1988) 111.

[77] An almost exhaustive list of sources related to the donkey as a symbol of evil in Egyptian and Greco-Roman sources is B.H. Stricker, 'Asinarii I–IV' *OMRO* 46 (1965) 52–75; 48 (1967) 23–43; (1971) 22–53; 56 (1975) 65–74.

[78] The function of Seth in the Egyptian pantheon is discussed in H. te Velde, *Seth, God of Confusion: a study of his role in Egyptian mythology and religion* (Leiden 1967). The process of demonisation after the New Kingdom is discussed on pp. 138–151. Te Velde updated the bibliography in his contribution 'Seth', in: *Oxford Encyclopedia of Ancient Egypt*, 269a–271a. Note that a cult for Seth remained nonetheless existent in certain parts of Egypt during the later periods, which is well documented for the Dakhleh and Kharga oases; Frankfurter, *Religion in Roman Egypt*, 112–115.

of enemies in the daily temple ritual.[79] However, contrary to the state temple ritual, the present rite invokes the potentially dangerous powers of Seth and, instead of averting these for the sake of the wellbeing of the country, attempts to direct the destructive energy against a particular individual in a private matter.

The reversed nature of the present rite manifests itself most explicitly in the donkey's head. According to an account of Herodotus, Egyptian priests never offered an animal's head up to the god, but cursed it and took it outside the sacred precinct of the temple.[80]

> After leading the marked beast to the altar where they [Egyptian priests] will sacrifice it, they kindle a fire; then they pour wine on the altar over the victim and call upon the god; then they cut its throat, and having done so sever the head from the body. They flay the carcass of the victim, then invoke many curses on its head, which they carry away. Where there is a market, and Greek traders in it, the head is taken to the market and sold; where there are no Greeks, it is thrown into the river. The imprecation, which they utter over the heads, is that whatever ill threatens those who sacrifice, or the whole of Egypt, fall upon that head. In respect of the heads of sacrificed beasts and the libation of wine, the practice of all Egyptians is the same in all sacrifices; and from this ordinance no Egyptian will taste of the head of anything that had life.
> [Herodotus, *The Histories*, II, 39]

Therefore, by making use of the head of a donkey, the rite does not only establish a close relationship with Seth, but also it defines itself as a rite opposed to the rules of regular temple ritual, which is in accord with Seth's role as enemy to the ordered world. When the practitioner applies the donkey's blood to one of his hands, he trespasses in the same way another rule of Egyptian temple ritual. Since blood was seen as impure, the flowing of the sacrificial victim's blood symbolized the triumph over the enemies in regular temple ritual. In this particular

---

[79] Yvan Koenig, *Magie et magiciens dans l'Égypte ancienne* (Paris 1994) 147–149. The curses recited during such an execration ritual are preserved in a fourth century BCE manuscript: Urk. VI, Siegfried Schott, *Bücher und Sprüche gegen den Gott Seth* 2 Vols. (Leipzig 1929–1939). As late as the fourth century CE the corporation of Hermonthis ironworkers sacrificied a donkey in the Deir el-Bahari temple; A. Lajtar, '*Proskynema* Inscriptions of a Corporation of Iron-Workers from Hermonthis in the temple of Hatshepsut in Deir el-Bahari: New Evidence for Pagan Cults in the 4th Cent. A.D.' *JJP* 21 (1991) 53–70, esp. 66ff.

[80] See for a critical review of Herodotus' account in the light of Egyptian sources: Alan B. Lloyd, *Herodotus, Book II* 3 Vols. (EPRO 43; Leiden 1975–1988) vol. 2, 173–179; see also Philippe Derchain, *Le sacrifice de l'oryx* (Rites égyptiens I; Brussels 1962) 17.

case, the practitioner does not cast the blood away, but smears it on his hand and, in the act, identifies with the enemies by way of contiguity.

Next to Seth, the rite is also concerned with the sun god Re, since the invocation has to be recited to the sun, while the practitioner faces the rising and setting sun disk. Daybreak and evening were probably considered opportune moments for this rite, because they are the beginning and end of the sun god's nightly travel through the underworld, where he has to enter into battle with the forces of chaos and evil, who attempt to bring the sun boat to a standstill in their effort to subdue the forces of creation and rejuvenation. By reciting at these critical moments between light and darkness, the practitioner takes full advantage of the intensified activity of the forces of disorder. Moreover, according to pharaonic sun theology, the god Seth, part of the sun boat's crew as a servant to Re, exerted his destructive powers now to combat the snake Apopis, the sun god's arch-rival in the underworld.[81] Seth and the sun god were consequently believed to be in each other's presence at these moments.

The Greek invocation develops the Sethian elements of the rite further by calling the deity the god of cosmic upheaval, who is hostile to the social order[82] and dwells in foreign countries.[83] As outsider to the divine pantheon, the social world and the land Egypt, he is the appropriate candidate to take up the anti-social task. In the final lines of the invocation, the practitioner prompts the deity to come to his aid by accusing the victim of having 'spilled the blood of Typhon in his own (or her own) house' (line 19–20). This language act establishes a meaningful link between the rite and the words, for, within the parameters of

---

[81] Coffin Text spell 160 and Book of the Dead spell 108 situate the battle between Seth and Apopis at sunset. According to the *Book of Gates*, the forces of evil intensify during the twelfth hour of the night, just before daybreak, in a final attempt to stop the sun boat. In the *Amduat*, Seth fights Apopis with his magical charms in the seventh hour, at the turn of the night. See in general: Erik Hornung, *Die Nachtfahrt der Sonne. Eine altägyptische Beschreibung des Jenseits* (Düsseldorf and Zürich 1991) 111–133.

[82] This trait derives from Seth's role as enemy of the Osirid family. Curse formulae on stelae dating from the Third Intermediate Period combine this trait with the symbolism of the donkey: 'May asses have intercourse with him and his wife and may his wife have intercourse with his son!'; example taken from W. Spiegelberg, 'Die Tefnachtosstele des Museums von Athen' *RecTrav* 25 (1903) 190–198. On Egyptian threat formulae in general, see, Scott Morschauser, *Threat-Formulae in Ancient Egypt. A Study of the History, Structure and Use of Threats and Curses in Ancient Egypt* (Baltimore 1991), the Third Intermediate and Late Period are treated on pp. 203–245.

[83] For Seth as foreigner, see, te Velde, *Seth, God of Confusion*, 109–151.

Egyptian myth and ritual, the donkey's blood on the practitioner's hand is synonymous with Typhon's blood. The blood functions in fact as evidence of the unjust and blasphemous behaviour of the intended victim: the practitioner puts the blame for the slaughter of the god's animal on the victim in order to direct the deity's anger at him.[84] The god is addressed as Typhon SETH and coerced to listen by speaking out his true name, a string of *voces magicae* that recurs now and again in Greek spells dealing with Seth Typhon.[85] Like the *voces magicae*, the name SETH is provided with a horizontal supralineal line in black ink, which indicates that the editor considered the Egyptian name a *vox magica*, a hidden name granting great powers to those who know it.[86] Since the name Typhon lacks the horizontal stroke, it functions as the ordinary name of the god, a tag to identify the god on the level of colloquial language. Considering the ancient views on the ritual power of language, the common Egyptian name, albeit placed in secondary position, must then have precedence over the Greek term, representing the efficacious hidden essence of the god. It is therefore warranted to conclude that, like the prescribed acts, the invocation draws on traditional Egyptian notions of myth and ritual, notwithstanding its Greek linguistic form. This conclusion is borne out by the Greek invocation's close similarity to the words of the following curse in hieratic taken from an execration ritual conducted in the state temples to subdue Seth's destructive forces.

> ⟨O you⟩ thief, lord of lies, ruler of deceit;
> Leader of criminals is he;
> Who is content with desertion and hates brotherhood;
> Whose heart is haughty amidst the gods;
> Who creates enmity and causes destruction;
> The 'Evil One' (*dbḥꜣ* < *tbḥ*) who creates rebellion       [Urk. VI, 7/13–18]

---

[84] This ritual technique is called a *diabolè* and occurs more often in the PGM, for example PGM IV.2441–2621, 2622–2707 and PGM VII.593–619. See for the Egyptian roots of this ritual technique: Ritner, 'Egyptian Magical Practice under the Roman Empire', 3368–3371.

[85] Instructive are PGM III.1–164, 71*–79* and IV.154–285, 260–285, which is a hymn to Typhon recited before the sun. See for a discussion of these names: Christine Harrauer, *Meliouchos. Studien zur Entwicklung religiöser Vorstellungen in griechischen synkretistischen Zaubertexten* (Wiener Studien, Beiheft 11; Vienna 1987) 23, fn. 19. The occurrence of these magical names in PGM XII is discussed below.

[86] Note that this horizontal supralineal line is missing in the god's name in a Greek spell on the twin manuscript P. Leiden I 384 verso (PGM XII.121–143). In this spell, the name is written σηϑ (4/32 = PGM XII.138).

As it seems, the editors of the manuscripts regarded the invocation of Seth Typhon an efficacious charm, since it occurs twice on P. Leiden I 384 verso in a slightly different version in two spells to separate two persons. The first spell (PGM XII.365–375) is entirely in Greek, though provided with an additional Demotic title in the left margin (διακοπός = *wʿ prḏ*; line 365); in the second spell, four columns farther on the manuscript, the Greek invocation is again combined with a recipe in Demotic (PDM xii.76–107 [PGM XII.453–465]). The latter spell is part of a cluster of four Demotic separation spells, the other three of which make only use of the string of *voces magicae*, mentioned above, that is reserved to invoke the demonic powers of Seth Typhon (PDM xii.50–61; 62–75; 108–118).[87] All five spells prescribe to write the invocation or the magical names on a sheet of papyrus or an ostracon and to bury it in a place where the couple meets or passes by. One of them orders to draw on an ostracon an image of a standing man with a donkey's face together with four Sethian *voces magicae* (PDM xii.62–75; see fig. 2.2). In PDM xii.76–107, the connection with Seth is made explicit through the ink of donkey's blood. The Greek spell (PGM XII.365–375) evokes a relation with Seth by ordering to write the invocation on a potsherd of a vessel used for storing smoked or pickled fish.[88] Since fish had eaten Osiris' male member after Seth had thrown his body into the river, fish were often considered impure, chaotic and evil beings.[89] A potsherd that had been in contact with fish could therefore serve as an appropriate writing medium for a Sethian curse formula. The last part of the invocation exploits the Osiris myth again by equating the couple to be separated with Osiris and Seth or Isis and Seth depending on the gender of the intended victims.

> I call upon you who are in the empty air, you who are terrible, invisible, great god, you who afflict the earth and shake the universe, you who love disturbances and hate stability and scatter the clouds from one another, IAIA IAKOUBIAI IÔ-ERBÊTH IÔ-PAKERBÊTH IÔ-BOLCHOSÊTH BASDOUMA PATATHNAX APOPSS OSESRÔ ATAPH THABRAOU ÊÔ THATHTHABRA BÔRARA AROBREITHA BOLCHOSÊTH KOKKOLOIPTOLÊ RAMBITHNIPS; give to him, NN, the son of her, NN, strife, war; and to him, NN, the son of her, NN,

---

[87] All three spells write the *voces magicae* in alphabetic Demotic signs together with supralineal glosses in the Greek script. Preisendanz included these glosses in the corpus of the Greek Magical Papyri as PGM XII.445–448, 449–452, 466–488 respectively.

[88] R.F. Hock translates ταρίχου ὄστρακον (line 366) with 'a pot for smoked fish', *GMPT*, 166. I prefer to translate 'potsherd (of a vessel) for smoked fish' in accordance with the ritual instructions of the parallel Demotic spells, which have *blḏʿ*, 'potsherd'.

[89] See on this mytheme: Plutarch, *On Isis and Osiris*, 358B.

odiousness, enmity, just as Typhon and Osiris had (but if it is a husband and wife, 'just as Typhon and Isis had'). Strong Typhon, very powerful one, perform your mighty acts. [PGM XII.367–375][90]

The following variant does not explicitly mention Seth or Typhon, but the Demotic recipe prescribes to write the Greek spell on some sort of strip or an ostracon with donkey's blood.

> I call upon you who are in the empty air, you who are terrible, invisible, a god who causes destruction and desolation, you who hate a stable household and you who do mischief. I call upon your great name; cause him, NN, to be separated from him NN, IÔ IÔ IÔ-BRACH KRABROUKRIOU BATRIOU APOMPS STROUTELIPS IAK[OUBIAI] IAÔ [PAK]ERBÊTH PAKERBÊTH, THEOU AIÊ god of gods, .?. at the gate of Iao. Separate him, NN, from him, NN, because I am the XANTHIS demon OUBAEME[...] TEBERETERRI [...]. Separate [him, NN from] him, NN. [PGM XII.454–465][91]

On comparison the Demotic variants turn out to be rather straightforward and to restrict themselves to transcribing the Sethian string of *voces magicae* into alphabetic Demotic signs with the appropriate glosses in Greek script (which are not rendered in the translation).

> IO-ERBETH[92] IO-SETH IO-BOLGHOSETH IO-PAKERBETH IO-PATATHNAGS LE-EME-NKT-..RE IO-OSESRO IO-GHLONTOEPS, separate NN, born of NN, from NN, born of NN! [P. Leiden I 384 verso IV/8–11 = PGM XII.445–448]

> BRAG GRAB BRAGH HOSPERTHNAKS BHRIENTHE(?)GH BASPHETHOI ATHRUPH PATATHNAG APOPS IO-ERBÈTH IO-BOLGOSETH IO-PAGERBETH, separate NN, born of NN, from NN, born of NN!
> [P. Leiden I 384 verso IV/15–19 = PGM XII.449–452]

> IAKUMBIAI IAO IO-ERBETH IO-BOLGHOSETH BASELE OM GITATHNAGS APSOPS O.EL.T, separate NN, born of NN, from NN, born of NN; hurry, hurry, be quick, be quick!
> [P. Leiden I 384 verso II/8–11 = PGM XII.466–468]

The foregoing discussion of the Sethian invocation has made abundantly clear that the invocation is firmly embedded in traditional Egyp-

---

[90] Tr. R.F. Hock, with minor modifications.
[91] Tr. R.F. Hock, with minor modifications. The *voces magicae* are transcribed according to Robert Daniel's edition: *Two Greek Magical Papyri*, 28.
[92] Unlike the other transcribed *voces magicae*, this name is not provided with the god's determinative, but with the foreign country determinative.

138 CHAPTER FOUR

tian ritual practices. The recurrence of variant versions demonstrates that it was used freely and adapted easily for various destructive rites. The writing rites of P. Leiden I 384 verso make no distinction in terms of prestige or presumed efficacy between writing a Sethian spell in Greek or Demotic, as if the languages were regarded as interchangeable. This observation seems corroborated by the instruction in a common lamp divination ritual with a youth as medium to 'recite to his head this spell in Greek' (P. London-Leiden 27/35).[93] Although other lamp divination rituals preserved on the manuscript make only use of invocations in Demotic, the present recipe does not in any way indicate the exceptional nature of this instruction. Apparently, the compilers of the spells did not consider it outstanding at all.

### 4.4.4. *Fear of Nubia*

Next to the three Greek invocations discussed above, P. London-Leiden preserves yet another invocation in a language other than Egyptian. The spell, which is basically in Demotic, alleges to cure a man who suffers from a 'bad eye' by means of applying an ointment of oil, salt and nasturtium seed to the patient (P. London-Leiden V20/1–7 = PDM xiv 1097–1101; translation given in Appendix 4.3.D).

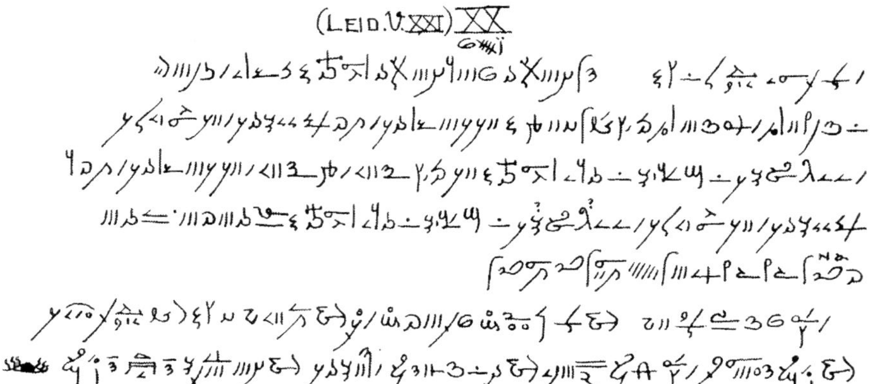

Fig. 4.5. P. London-Leiden verso 20/1–7

---

[93] The Greek spell itself is not given in the manuscript. It was probably forgotten in the course of editing and copying the texts.

While preparing the ointment, the practitioner should recite over it an invocation, which incorporates 'three spells in the Nubian language' (3 rʒ n md.t 'Ikš; line 3, 4). Together with the words 'you are this eye of the heaven' and the image of an eye,[94] the invocation should be written on a new papyrus sheet, which will serve as amulet on the patient's body (line 7). It cannot be made out with certitude whether the recipe is concerned with curing an eye-ailment or breaking the spell of the 'evil eye', because the title says merely '[**Spell**] to make a man's bad eye cease' (line 1).[95] As the word 'bad eye' is written ir.t, 'eye', with dying warrior determinative, it could be interpreted as ir.t bin.t, the common term for the 'evil eye' in personal names and apotropaeic spells.[96] On the other hand, remedies against eye-diseases, which are abundantly attested in medical papyri from as early as the Middle Kingdom, frequently prescribe similar ointments against an ailing eye.[97] However, unlike these medical recipes, the present spell does not give precise instructions on how to apply the medicament to the patient's eyes; in fact, the text suggests that the patient's whole body has to be

---

[94] The drawing on the manuscript represents possibly a sun's eye, because it is provided with six short ray-like lines on its top. It is certainly not an 'Abbild einer Sonnenscheibe mit Strahlen'; Westendorf, *Handbuch der altägyptischen Medizin*, vol. 1, 156.

[95] Griffith and Thompson, *The Demotic Magical Papyrus of London and Leiden*, vol. 1, 192, fn. to line 1. Johnson (*GMPT*, 247) translates 'ophthalmia' following Griffith and Thompson, whereas Koenig and Westendorf prefer 'the evil eye'; Yvan Koenig, 'La Nubie dans les textes magiques. "L'inquiétante étrangeté"' *RdE* 38 (1987) 105–110, 109; Westendorf, *Handbuch der altägyptischen Medizin*, vol. 1, 156. Thissen considers the spell a remedy against an eye-ailment; Heinz-Josef Thissen, 'Nubien in demotischen magischen Texten', in: Daniela Mendel and Ulrike Claudi (eds.), *Ägypten im afro-orientalischen Kontext: Aufsätze zur Archaeologie, Geschichte und Sprache eines unbegrenzten Raumes: Gedenkschrift Peter Behrens* (Cologne 1991) 369–376, 371.

[96] See on the 'evil eye' in general, J.F. Borghouts, 'The Evil Eye of Apopis' *JEA* 59 (1973) 114–150, esp. 142–148. See for an apotropaeic spell, Siegfried Schott, 'Ein Amulet gegen den bösen Blick' *ZÄS* 67 (1931) 106–110 and Sylvie Cauville, 'La chapelle de Thot-Ibis à Dendera édifiée sous Ptolémée Ier par Hor, scribe d'Amon-Rê' *BIFAO* 89 (1989) 43–66, esp. 52–56. The occurrence of the term in personal names is discussed in W. Spiegelberg, 'Der böse Blick im altägyptischen Glauben' *ZÄS* 59 (1924) 149–154. Overcoming the 'evil eye' was apparently considered a task of the *Kherep-Serqet* priest: Jean-Claude Goyon, 'Un parallèle tardif d'une formule des inscriptions de la statue prophylactique de Ramsès III au Musée du Caire (P. Brooklyn 47.218.138)' *JEA* 57 (1971) 154–159, 155 fn. 5.

[97] Westendorf, *Handbuch der altägyptischen Medizin*, vol. 1, 146–156. See also the charms for protection of the eyes on P. Turin 54003, dating from the Middle Kingdom: Alessandro Roccati, *Papiro Ieratico n. 54003. Estratti magici e rituali del Primo Medio Regno* (Catalogo del Museo Egizio di Turino I,2; Turin 1970) 28–35.

rubbed. Furthermore, the eye that should be drawn on the papyrus amulet is reminiscent of the *wḏ3.t* eyes found on an amulet against the 'evil eye'.[98]

The Nubian language was spoken in the region neighbouring Egypt's southern border, which was called *Kush* (*k3š* or *ikš*) in Egyptian texts since the second millennium BCE. Contact between Egypt and the people of this region started at least in the third millennium BCE, so that the social and cultural interaction between these two regions had become fairly complex by the time of the Greco-Roman period. In the course of time, Egypt had more than once exercised military and economic control over the region for substantial time periods. However, at the end of the Third Intermediate Period (around 730 BCE), rulers from Kush invaded Egypt and established their political and religious supremacy for about seventy years. During the Greco-Roman period, the Nubian Kingdom of Meroe gradually developed into a serious political entity that regularly threatened and questioned the southern border of the Ptolemaic and subsequent Roman Empire.[99] These historical developments resulted in a multi-layered image of Nubian culture and topography among the Egyptian elite, floating between the extremes of anxiety and respectful admiration.[100] On the one hand, Nubia was seen as a dwelling place of the gods, so that substantial temple building programs were carried out in the region;[101] on the other hand, its people were feared for their character and knowledge

---

[98] Schott, 'Ein Amulet gegen den bösen Blick'; see also Borghouts, 'The Evil Eye of Apopis', 148.

[99] Derek A. Welsby, *The Kingdom of Kush. The Napatan and Meroitic Empires* (Princeton 1996) 65–71.

[100] The complexities of the pharaonic discourse on Nubia have not yet been treated in a sophisticated way by taking the differing perspectives and interests of specific social groups in particular places and times into account. Useful contributions are: Chr. Onasch, 'Kusch in der Sicht von Ägyptern und Griechen', in: E. Endesfelder eds., *Ägypten und Kusch. Fs. Hintze* (Berlin 1977) 331–336 and L. Török, *Meroe: six studies on the cultural identity of an ancient African state* Studia Aegyptiaca 16 (Budapest 1995) 172–180. See for a discussion of the Greek and Latin sources: S.M. Burstein, *Graeco-Africana. Studies in the history of Greek relations with Egypt and Nubia* (New Rochelle 1995). A somewhat impressionistic description is: L. Kákosy, 'Nubien als mythisches Land im Altertum' in: Idem, *Selected Papers (1953–1976)* Studia Aegyptiaca 8 (Budapest 1981) 131–138.

[101] In the New Kingdom, the cult for Amun became particularly prominent in the region, because *Djebel Barkal* at the fourth cataract was seen as his dwelling place. For the link between Egyptian royal ideology and the temple building program in Nubia, see, Kákosy, 'Nubien als mythisches Land', 132–135. It was not until the Greco-Roman period that Nubia became a location in Egyptian myth, e.g. the Onuris and Tefnut myth and the Horus myth of Edfu. In both cases, Nubia is negatively connoted.

of destructive magic, as pharaoh Amenhotep III brought poignantly to the fore in a letter to his son, the viceroy of Nubia:[102]

> Do not trust the land of Nubia,
> Guard yourself against its people and its charmers!
> [Urk. IV 1344/11–12]

The magical rationale of the present Demotic spell should be understood in the light of these ancient Egyptian views on Nubia.

The spell's title and the ritual instructions are in Demotic (lines 1 and 6–7), while the invocation comprises a short *historiola* in Demotic about Horus and the Nubian Amun (lines 1–4)[103] and a sequence of five allegedly Nubian words or divine names transcribed in alphabetic Demotic signs (lines 4–5). The invocation runs as follows:

> O Amun, this lofty male, this male of Nubia who came down from Meroe to Egypt and found Horus, my son. He hurried on his feet and beat him (= Horus) on his head with three spells in the Nubian language. He found NN, whom NN bore, hurried on his feet, and beat him on his head with three spells in the Nubian language: 'gntjini TNTJINA QUQUBI [A]KHE AKHA'. [P. London-Leiden V20/1–5][104]

The *historiola* provides the mythical rationale for the application of the spell: as Amun of Meroe once came down from Nubia to Egypt to cure Horus with three spells in the Nubian language, the patient will be cured similarly when the three spells are said over the ointment. The *historiola* contains two levels of narration. The first level is characterised by emotive language use ('O Amun, this lofty male') spoken by Horus' mother, the goddess Isis, whose name is not mentioned but can be inferred from the phrase 'Horus, my son' (line 2). By describing the scene in her words, Isis acts as focaliser of the *historiola*, meaning that Amun's behaviour is presented to the reader through the eyes of

---
[102] Koenig, 'La Nubie dans les textes magiques', 105–110.
[103] On *historiola* in the magical papyri, see, David Frankfurter, 'Narrating Power: the Theory and Practice of the Magical Historiola in Ritual Spells', in: Marvin Meyer and Paul Mirecki (eds.), *Ancient Magic and Ritual Power* (Leiden 1995) 434–476.
[104] The tense of all verbal forms is obscure, so that the translation can only be tentative. For grammatical comments, see, Griffith and Thompson, *The Demotic Magical Papyrus of London and Leiden*, vol. 1, 193 and Thissen, 'Nubien in demotischen magischen Texten', 373–374. Compare the expression 'he hurried on his feet' (iw=f fy.t=f r hn rd.wy.t=f) with P. d'Orbiney 6/3, 10/6, 13/1 and P. Amherst 20/1; W. Spiegelberg, *OLZ* 5 (1907) 199. The four final words of the Nubian invocation are rendered as *voces magicae* in the translation, because they are provided with the god's determinative.

Isis, the greatest magician among the gods according to Egyptian theology.[105] On the second level of narration, Isis passes the word to Amun of Meroe by quoting the spell he said to Horus. The quotation, which is purportedly in Nubian, has resisted translation until today, possibly because the invocation is but a collection of sounds that could serve as an icon of Nubian speech in the perception of an Egyptian audience. Whatever the authenticity of the Nubian quote, the text claims that the spell's ritual power is contained in the un-Egyptian sounds, since Amun of Meroe once pronounced them to cure successfully the child Horus.

The present spell takes recourse to the Nubian language to share in, or take advantage of, the large potential of Nubian spells and powerful sounds, which the Egyptian elite feared and admired. For this same reason, Egyptian gods were frequently addressed in their Nubian aspect in magical spells since the New Kingdom.[106] The so-called *Chapitres supplémentaires* of the Book of the Dead, first attested since the early Third Intermediate Period, contain a fair number of incomprehensible names borrowed from Nubian, as is made explicit in the following passage from spell 164.[107]

> Hail to thee, Sakhmet-Bastet-Re! (…) you are the great fire breath of *Sknk.t* at the prow of your father's bark. *Ḥrpgkšršb* is your name as the Nubian man of the archers of Bow-Land says.   [BD 164, lines 1, 5–6][108]

In a contemporary Demotic-Greek magical handbook, a spell to acquire love and respect resorts similarly to a spell in Nubian.

> **Spell of giving praise** ⟨and⟩ love in Nubian (*mdw ikš*): 'SUMUTH KESUTH HRBABA BRASAKHS LAT son of (?) NAPH son of (?) BAKHA'. Say these, put gum on your hand, kiss your shoulder twice, and go before the man whom you desire.   [P.BM. 10588 7/1–5 =PDM lxi.95–99]

---

[105] Maria Münster, *Untersuchungen zur Göttin Isis vom Alten Reich bis zum Ende des Neuen Reiches* (MÄS 11; Berlin 1968) 192–196; Jan Bergman, *Ich bin Isis. Studien zum Memphitischen Hintergrund der griechischen Isisaretalogien* (Acta Universitatis Upsaliensis—Historia Religionum 3; Uppsala 1968) 286–289

[106] Koenig, 'La Nubie dans les textes magiques', 106–107; Thissen, 'Nubien in demotischen magischen Texten', 370–375.

[107] The *chapitres supplémentaires* are published in W. Pleyte, *Chapitres supplémentaires au Livre des Morts, 162 à 174* 3 Vols. (Leiden 1881). On the dating of the corpus, see: J. Yoyotte, 'Contribution à l'histoire du chapitre 162 du Livre des Morts' *RdE* 29 (1977) 194–202. On the names, see also Pascal Vernus, 'Vestiges de langues chamito-sémitiques dans les sources égyptiennes méconnues', in: James Bynon (ed.), *Current Progress in Afro-Asiatic Linguistics. Papers of the Third International Hamito-Semitic Congress* (Amsterdam 1984) 477–481.

[108] Translation based on Lepsius' edition. See for variant versions: Pleyte, *Chapitres*

In all these cases, code switching is motivated out of a desire to put fearful, though powerful, exotic spells to use, a want fuelled by the common Egyptian image of Nubia and its people. It is therefore significant to observe that the Egyptian goddess Isis keeps the Nubian spell ultimately in check, since she is the primary internal narrator of the *historiola*. In this fashion, Nubia remains as it were under Egypt's command.[109]

4.4.5. *The pragmatics of language alternation in the Demotic spells*

The foregoing discussions have demonstrated that language alternation is a fairly limited phenomenon in the Demotic magical spells, but that when language alternation occurs, the process of incorporation does not pose serious problems to the internal cohesion of the spell. In these cases, the functional specialization of the two languages, and hence their separation, is stringent: a recipe or invocation in a mixture of Demotic and Greek or Nubian never occurs. A degree of interference between the languages concerned can only be observed on the level of the symbolic properties of prescribed acts and ingredients on the one hand and, on the other, the mythical configuration of invoked deities and demons. The presence of Greek invocations in otherwise Demotic spells can be attributed to a generally felt inhibition to translate magical sounds into a second language. The spells were composed with several *Vorlagen* in various languages and scripts at hand and, when an editor thought a Greek invocation to be appropriate, he copied it without translating it into a recipe that he wrote in Demotic irrespective of the language of its sources. In case the invocation lent itself for multiple purposes, it could be adapted without apparent problems, the *voces magicae* could even be spelled in alphabetic Demotic signs if necessary.

In the light of the negative language attitude, propagated most explicitly in tractate XVI of the *Corpus Hermeticum*, these conclusions are far-reaching. The relative lack of Greek loanwords in the Demotic spells might corroborate the message of the tractate, but the present discussions reveal that the nationalistic propaganda was not followed in all priestly circles, if authoritative at all. The inhibition to translate

---

*supplémentaires*, vol. 2, 6 and Ursula Verhoeven, *Das Saitische Totenbuch der Iahtesnacht. P. Colon.Aeg. 10207* 3 Vols. (Papyrologische Texte und Abhandlungen; Bonn 1993) vol. 1, 335 and vol. 2, 138*.

[109] Compare this with the discussion of the Demotic narrative *Setne and Sa-Osiris* (Setne II) in chapter 6.3.3.1.

magical sound was certainly alive among the editors of the magic handbooks under study, but for them it also counted for spells in 'the language of empty speech'. Nonetheless, there is one example where translation did occur: in this particular case from Greek into Demotic. None of the Demotic spells pass a negative value judgement with regard to ritual efficacy on Greek invocations. In fact, the spells seem to be rather indifferent with respect to language attitude. In the case of the Nubian invocation, its presence can be explained out of a desire to include exotic sounds that long since were deemed powerful. This socio-cultural explanation is of no value with respect to the Greek invocations, because no Greek deities are invoked as powerful beings and no Egyptian text ever passes a judgement on Greek ritual and magic. The presence of the Greek invocations is rather motivated out of respect for the *Vorlagen*. It is therefore a matter of textual transmission instead of real-life sociolinguistics.

Whatever the exact degree of language alternation in the Demotic spells, it is always high in comparison with the Greek spells preserved in the thirteen consecutive columns on P. Leiden I 384 verso (PGM XII). These spells never incorporate a Demotic section, except for an occasional additional title in Demotic. Therefore, with respect to scripts and languages, the Demotic spells are far more flexible than the Greek prescriptions. However, the Greek spells combine religious imagery and textual formats of various cultural origins in their addresses to the divine, quite different from the Demotic spells. For that reason, after studying in the last two chapters the 'diversity of scripts and languages' in the Demotic spells, the following chapter will analyse the 'diversity in rhetoric' in the Greek spells.

CHAPTER FIVE

DIVERSITY IN RHETORIC

5.1. *Alternation of writing traditions in the Greek spells*

The thirteen Greek columns preserved on the reverse side of the Leiden manuscript J 384 contain eighteen spells that deal with divination, sending dreams, procuring charm and success, and the like. The section is concluded with a list of code words provided with an equivalent term for each entry, which is presented as a translation of secret knowledge of the Egyptian temple scribes (P. Leiden 384 verso 12/17–13/30 = PGM XII. 401–444).[1] The issues treated in these spells are thus similar to those in the Demotic charms discussed so far. However, from a cross-cultural perspective, the Greek spells are more complex, because they incorporate overtly cultural elements from a wide geographic area, ranging from Egypt, to Greece, the Near East and Persia. Given this syncretistic flavour, they fit perfectly in with the corpus of *Greek Magical Papyri*, of which they have been an established part since the beginnings of PGM scholarship.[2] Apart from the various cross-cultural influences, the spells share with other PGM material the attribution of spells to a famous, though often fictitious, author, and the occurrence of Greek deities, who have merged with Egyptian gods more often than not. Since these elements can occasionally be observed in the Demotic spells as well, the difference between the two linguistic corpora is really a matter of degree. Nevertheless, the difference must be taken into account when studying the sphere of production and use of the magical handbooks.

---

[1] This text will be treated in detail in chapters 6.1 and 2.
[2] Albrecht Dieterich, who is one of the 'founding fathers' of the study of the PGM, wrote his dissertation on PGM XII in 1888: 'Papyrus magica musei Lugdunensis Batavi, quam C. Leemans edidit in papyrorum Graecarum tomo II etc.', in: *Jahrbücher für klassische Philologie* Suppl. Bd. 16 (Leipzig 1888) 749–830; see also 'Papyrus magica musei Lugdunensis Batavi, prolegomena', in: Albrecht Dieterich, *Kleine Schriften* (Leipzig and Berlin 1911) 1–47.

From a linguistic point of view, the Greek spells are less complex than the Demotic texts, because here alternation between Greek and a different language occurs minimally. None of the Greek recipes contains a prayer in Demotic or any other language. Language alternation is only at stake when an additional Demotic title is inserted above a Greek spell, which occurs three times. In one case, an elaborate spell for consecrating a ring that will endow its wearer with charm and success is headed by a Demotic and Greek title (PGM XII.201–269). Its Greek title, which reads 'A little ring [useful] for every [magical] operation and for success', is preceded by Demotic *wꜥ gsmr*, 'a ring', which is added above the line in the small space left after the last line of the preceding ritual text (P. Leiden I 384 verso 6/26 =PGM XII.201). Although the Demotic term does not contain any information that the Greek title does not provide, the scribe deemed it for an unknown reason necessary to add it. The second instance occurs in the subsequent spell, which describes a ritual of a similar nature, where the Demotic title is neatly written in the middle of an empty line above the Greek ritual text (PGM XII.270–350; title in P. Leiden I 384 verso 8/23). In the third case, a separation spell (PGM XII. 365–375), the Greek title 'Charm for causing separation' is preceded by a scribbled Demotic *wꜥ prd* 'a separation [spell]' in the left margin (P. Leiden I 384 verso 11/15 = PGM XII.365). In all three cases, the spells, albeit written in Greek, came to be categorised under a Demotic heading. Whatever the actual origins of the Greek spells, in the extant manuscript they were obviously read by a person proficient in the priestly Demotic script and, as a consequence, versed in Egyptian theology. Since the present study is concerned with the producers and users of the *extant* manuscripts, the Demotic titles call for an interpretive attitude which takes an Egyptian temple milieu as its starting point, even if the spells are written in Greek. Therefore, the analyses presented in this chapter try to read the spells with an Egyptian user (preferably a priest) in mind.[3] How would he have made sense of the various ritual techniques and religious ideas when reading and using the Greek texts?[4]

---

[3] It goes without saying that such a reading of the spell is restrictive, because it reduces the text to a univocal interpretation, whereas, in fact, the text itself invites multiple readings, thus enabling it to be used and appreciated in various religious settings, be it with minor adaptations. However, the person who decided to include the spell in this particular collection of Demotic and Greek spells, was in all likelihood an Egyptian priest.

[4] Note that this approach leaves aside the question whether or not the Egyptian

In comparison with the Demotic spells, the phenomenon of code mixing is evidently less attested in the Greek section of P. Leiden I 384 verso. However, several Greek spells combine prayers that derive from various cultural and linguistic settings, a few of which are possibly direct translations from Egyptian into Greek. In this way, it would not be correct to speak of 'alternation of languages', even though some passages may still reflect their linguistic origin. In these spells, passages that give the impression of being translated from Egyptian or that have an unmistakable Egyptian character alternate with Greek hexametrical hymns or with sections that testify to a sophisticated mastery of Greek language and style. To account for this peculiar phenomenon, it is useful to coin the phrase 'alternation of writing traditions' in imitation of 'alternation of languages'. This phrase makes clear that code mixing merely takes on a different form in the Greek spells. The present chapter will trace the alternation of genres and styles by studying an elaborate prayer that is part of a ritual for consecrating a ring to acquire success (PGM XII.201–269)—the first spell with a Demotic heading. In the manuscript, this spell is immediately followed by another ring spell, also provided with a Demotic title, which reveals an alternative way of mediating between traditional Egyptian temple ritual and the shifting demands of private religious life in the Roman period. Both analyses will reveal the complexity of cultural interference and, at the same time, raise questions concerning the representation of the Egyptian priesthood. These questions will only be addressed in chapters 6 and 7; the present chapter focuses on the diversity of writing styles.

### 5.2.1. *Consecration of the ring (PGM XII.201–216)*

For those who wished to aggrandise their social position, the magical handbook P. Leiden I 384 verso preserves a rather complex spell for consecrating a magical ring that might have been of help (PGM XII. 201–269). Even 'kings and governors m[ake use of it]' its introductory lines want the reader to believe. The spell comprises a detailed recipe, which, different from ancient Egyptian magical spells, comes first, and a lengthy prayer addressed to the All-Lord, which will be analysed in

---

temple was the true place of origin for these spells. Whatever the case, at a certain moment an Egyptian priest considered the spells to be worthy of inclusion.

depth in the following section. The recipe prescribes the use of a golden ring with a blue coloured jasper gem, which the practitioner should engrave with a detailed design. The design represents a snake holding its tail in its mouth, within whose circular posture a crescent moon with a star on both its horns should be engraved. Above the moon, a sun (Helios) together with the name ABRASAX must be inscribed. The reverse side of the stone should have the names ABRASAX, in the centre, and IAÔ-SABAÔTH along the rim of the stone. Since gems with similar designs have been found in Egypt and throughout the Mediterranean, rituals of this kind were indeed conducted in antiquity.[5] This combination of the snake design, the Egyptian so-called Ouroboros snake,[6] with the Semitic names IAÔ-SABAÔTH is of particular interest and characteristic of the multi-layered and cross-cultural nature of the *Greek Magical Papyri*. Once the stone has been engraved and is set into the golden ring, it must be induced with power by a strict succession of ritual actions consisting of burnt offerings and recitations.

The ritual consist of two separate offerings conducted above two separate altars. On a sacred spot suitable for religious ceremonies or next to a purified tomb, a pit (βόθρος) has to be dug above which an altar (βωμός) has to be erected of the wood of fruit trees. On the altar the practitioner should make a burnt offering of an unblemished goose, three roosters, three pigeons and all sorts of incense, the fumes of which will rise up into the sky. Next he must stand near the pit and make a libation of wine, honey, milk and saffron, which substances will penetrate the soil.[7] While holding the ring in the smoke of the offering, the lengthy prayer has to be said.

---

[5] For examples, see, Campbell Bonner, *Studies in Magical Amulets chiefly Graeco-Egyptian* (Ann Arbor 1950) and Delatte and Derchain, *Les intailles magiques*.

[6] The snake who eats its own tail (*sd m r3*) is a symbol of regenerative time. It contains and protects within the circle formed by its body the ordered cosmos as created by the sun god; see B.H. Stricker, *De grote zeeslang* (Leiden 1953) and L. Kákosy, 'Uroboros', *LdÄ* VI, 886–893. In the Greco-Roman period it had become a favoured symbol in esoteric circles.

[7] Note that the directions of the two offerings are opposite. In all likelihood, the burnt offering is directed towards the heavenly powers, whereas the libations are aimed at the powers in the earth. Together with the use of the two Greek technical terms βωμός and βόθρος, this ritual structure evokes the idea that the Greek Olympian and chthonic offering are combined into one ritual setting. However, the distinction between Olympian and chthonic in Greek religion has recently seriously been challenged; for the latest opinions and relevant literature, see, Renate Schlesier, 'Olympian versus Chthonian Religion' *Scripta Classica Israelica* 11 (1991–1992) 38–51 and Scott Scullon, 'Olympian and Chthonian' *Classical Antiquity* 13 (1994) 75–119.

At first sight, the interaction between invocation and described ritual actions is not evident. It is only towards its end that the invocation refers to the ring held in the smoke of the burnt offering as 'this power' (δύναμις; 259, 260) and 'this object' (πρᾶγμα; 266). A possible interplay between prayer and ritual actions might be detected in the prayer's opening address to the three personified aspects of the sun god who might correspond with the threefold name IAÔ-SABAÔTH-ABRASAX and the tripartite design of sun, moon and stars on the stone. Other than that, the invocation is a self-contained prayer to the All-Lord, which draws its effect upon its own phraseology.

### 5.2.2. *Close reading of the prayer (PGM XII.216–269)*

The invocation can be divided into five distinct parts according to its content and textual form. As a sharp divide between each section serves a concluding address that explicitly asks the invoked god to come to the aid of the practitioner. Before embarking on a close analysis of each section in the light of the cultural traditions from which it borrows imagery and idiom, the structure of the invocation can be outlined as follows:

i. Address to the three suns (=IAÔ-SABAÔTH-ABRASAX?) (lines 216–227)
ii. Self-presentation of practitioner by identifying with a range of deities and divine attributes that can easily be traced back to traditional Egyptian theology (lines 227–238)
iii. Prose hymn to the All-Lord (lines 238–244+252–263)
iv. Hexametrical hymn incorporated into iii. (lines 244–252)
v. Invocation of deity according to his 'Names of the Nations' (lines 263–267)

The invocation is an address to the All-Lord, the pantocrator, whose plurality is repeatedly stressed without ever mentioning explicitly his name in the text. The idea of a cosmotheistic being who is self-engendered and governs nature, for having created it himself, was widespread in the Roman period. Several religious groups of diverse origin turned their attention to a deity of this kind without necessarily discarding the multiplicity of polytheistic theology. In their view, the All-Lord stood above, and ruled, the lesser gods who were still believed to exert their influence on life on earth. Such religious currents were popular among the newly founded movements such as Hermetists, Gnostics,

Neo-Platonists, while more traditional communities such as Jews and Egyptians had already developed similar ideas at a much earlier stage.[8] In Egypt the idea can be traced back to the Ramesside period (about 1300–1100 BCE) and a foregoing formative period starting with Amenhotep III (1391–53 BCE).[9] The priesthood of Amun promoted its deity, who had originally been a wind god, to the status of ruler over the whole cosmos who was One among the many and from whom life came forth.[10] After a short interruption that celebrated a monotheistic sun god at the expense of all other deities, known as the Amarna period, the Amun-Re theology flourished and its ideas were put into words in the form of hymns executed on temple walls or written on papyrus rolls. This practice continued into the Roman period, with this restriction that its ideas were often transferred to local deities to fit local demands.

An important argument in favour of the inclusive instead of restrictive character of the invocation is the absence of an explicitly named deity or references to a well-established mythology. In accordance with the inscription on the reverse side of the stone, the invoked deity is probably IAÔ-SABAÔTH-ABRASAX, but these names are not mentioned in the invocation itself. Even the otherwise so pervasive *voces magicae* are almost entirely absent in this particular case. The few occurrences are all idiosyncratic, so that they are of no help in tracing the precise identity of the invoked deity. The divine being is only identified with such vague and in those days current terms as 'Agathos Daemon' (244) and 'Aiôn' (247, 248) that are merely personified abstract nouns. In certain cases they were identified with images so as to become personalized as independent divine beings, otherwise they served as attributes applica-

---

[8] See for a portrait of the interplay between these diverse religious communities in Late-Antique Alexandria: Chr. Haas, *Alexandria in Late Antiquity. Topography and Social Conflict* (Baltimore, London 1997).

[9] Jan Assmann, *Egyptian Solar Religion in the New Kingdom. Re, Amun and the Crisis of Polytheism* (London, New York 1995) 156–210; translated from *Re und Amun. Die Krise des polytheistischen Weltbilds im Ägypten der 18.-20. Dynastie* (OBO 51; Freiburg, Göttingen 1983) 189–277.

[10] Egyptological literature on the concept of One and the Many in Egyptian theology is vast. The fundamental study is still: E. Hornung, *Der Eine und die Vielen. Ägyptische Gottesvorstellungen* (Darmstadt 1971), which is translated as *Conceptions of God in Ancient Egypt. The One and the Many* (Ithaca, New York 1982). A recent re-assessment of the topic from an interdisciplinary perspective is: Barbara Nevling Porter (ed.), *One God or Many? Concepts of Divinity in the Ancient World* (Chebeague 2000).

ble to more than one particular god.[11] Although both names can be attributed to Sarapis, the patron god of Alexandria, the most likely place within Egypt where texts as these were composed, there is no strict reason to do so in this particular case.[12] The invocation is rather directed towards a more or less anonymous but, nevertheless, powerful All-Lord, whose hidden and mysterious aspect is only stressed by the absence of a regular name.

The first section of the prayer is what follows:[13]

> I invoke and beseech the consecration,
> O gods of the heavens, O gods under the earth, O gods circling in the middle region, three suns, ANOCH MANE BARCHUCH, who daily come forth in part from one womb.
> O masters of all living and dead,
> [O] heedful in many necessities of gods and men.
> O concealers of things now seen,
> O directors of the Nemeseis who spend every hour with you,
> O senders of the Fate who travels around the whole world,
> O commanders of the rulers,
> O exalters of the abased,
> O revealers of the hidden,
> O guides of the wind,
> O arousers of the waves,
> O bringers of fire (at a certain time),

---

[11] See for Agathos Daemon: P.M. Fraser, *Ptolemaic Alexandria* (Oxford 1972) 209–211 and Jan Quaegebeur, *Le dieu égyptien Shaï dans la religion et l'onomastique*, (OLA 2; Leuven 1975) 170–176, who argues convincingly for an Egyptian origin of the particular form of the cult in Alexandria and other parts of Egypt. For Aiôn, see, Arthur D. Nock, 'A Vision of Mandulis Aion', in: Z. Stewart (ed.), *Essays on Religion and the Ancient World* I (Cambridge 1972) 357–400; H.J.W. Drijvers, 'Aion' *DDD* 13b–14b; Günther Zuntz, *Aion, Gott des Römerreichs* (Heidelberg 1989); Idem, *Aion im Römerreich: die archäologischen Zeugnisse* (Heidelberg 1991) and Idem, *Aiṓn in der Literatur der Kaiserzeit* (Wien 1992); Helena Maria Keizer, *Life Time Entirety: a Study of αἰών in Greek Literature and Philosophy, the Septuagint and Philo* (unpubl. dissertation, University of Amsterdam 1999).

[12] Nonetheless Merkelbach and Totti include the present spell in their collection of texts they think derive from the Sarapis religion: R. Merkelbach and M. Totti, *Abrasax. Ausgewählte Papyri religiösen und magischen Inhalts—Band 1: Gebete* (Papyrologica Coloniensia 17.1; Opladen 1990) 155–178, §67–69. See also: R. Merkelbach, *Isis Regina—Zeus Sarapis. Die griechisch-ägyptische Religion nach den Quellen dargestellt* (Stuttgart and Leipzig 1995) 195–198, §371–374.

[13] The translation given follows Morton Smith in Betz, *GMPT*, 161–163 provided that the suggestions of the re-edition of PGM XII have been taken into account: Daniel, *Two Greek Magical Papyri*, xxi–xxii. For each section of the prayer, a vertical line marks the translation of the actual prayer to distinguish it from the quotations added to support the line of reasoning.

> O creators and benefactors of every race,
> O nourishers of every race,
> O lords and controllers of kings,
> Come, benevolent, for that [purpose] for which I call you, as benevolent assistants in this rite for my benefit. [PGM XII.216–227]

The opening address of the invocation is directed towards 'three suns' to ask them to assist in the rite. These gods are in heaven, underworld and the region in between, daily coming forth from one womb. This imagery is strictly in line with traditional Egyptian cosmography, according to which the goddess Nut gives daily birth to the sun god in the early morning, so that he can make his journey along the firmament, which is Nut's body, to be swallowed up again by Nut's mouth in the evening, thus entering the underworld. During this trip the sun god takes on three different forms: youth or scarab in the morning, vigorous disk or falcon at noon and old man or ram in the evening.[11] Just like the Egyptian sun god who shines upon the living on earth and the deceased and demons in the underworld, the three suns are called 'the masters of all living and all dead'. The invocation continues with a repetitive list of greetings to the deities with each line attributing a different function or sphere of influence to them. The list celebrates their power over the physical world: they not only direct the fate of men, but exert influence as well over forces in nature, such as wind, waves and fire. In this way several elements of the image of the All-Lord are taken up. By portraying them as controllers of the Nemeseis and Fate, the invocation is clearly set in the Hellenistic and Roman period, when the idea of a preordained human lot developed and became widespread. In spite of this, the textual form of the prayer, a list of epithets, each entry of which is introduced by an exclamatory greeting, with a direct address to come over to the worshipper as a conclusion, was already an old and common Egyptian hymnic device. This device is well illustrated by a passage from a funerary composition dated to the Augustan period.

> O Re; O Atum; O Shu; O Tefnut; O Geb; O Nut; O Osiris; O Isis; O Nephthys; O Horus; O Hathor; O great Ennead; O small Ennead; O Indefatigable-Ones (*jḥm(w)-wrṯ*; stars of the southern constellation); O Imperishable-Ones (*jḥm.w-sge.w*; stars of the northern constellation); O

---

[11] Since each aspect corresponds with a name, Khepri in the morning, Horakhti at noon and Atum in the evening, it is tempting to associate the three *voces magicae* ANOCH MANE BARCHUCH with these names. It is however very unlikely that this is correct. The suggestion to translate the *voces* as 'rising one, midday sun and soul of darkness' is

Orion of the southern sky; O Big Dipper of the northern sky; O Sopdet, queen of the stars; great Bastet, mistress of Bubastis; the noble *djed*-pillar; the great *neshmet* barque; Hathor, lady of the underworld; Geb, prince [of the] gods; Thoth, lord of ma'at, bull in the underworld; come to the Osiris, brother of the family of pharaoh[ph], the artisan Sauef.

[P. Rhind I 10d/6–12][15]

As in the quoted funerary text, the prayer to the sun gods is concluded by an appeal to come to the aid of the practitioner. This address serves at once as a transition to the next section of the invocation in which the practitioner identifies himself as a divine being to enable interaction with the All-Lord whom he is about to call upon.

> I am a plant named Baïs,[16]
> I am an outflow of blood from the tomb of The Great One (surrounded by) Baïs trees,
> I am Faith found in men, and he who declares the holy names,
> I am ⟨the lotus⟩,[17] which came forth from the abyss,
> I am {So}krates who came forth from the Udjat-Eye,
> I am the god whom no one sees or rashly names,
> I am the sacred bird Phoenix,
> I am Krates the holy who is called MARM⟨AR⟩AUÔTH,
> I am Helios who showed forth light,
> I am Aphrodite who is called TUPHI,
> I am the holy sender of winds,
> I am Kronos who showed forth light,
> I am mother of gods who is called Heaven,
> I am Osiris who is called water,
> I am Isis who is called dew,
> I am ÊSENEPHUS who is called spring,
> I am the Image resembling the true images,

---

untenable for phonetic reasons: Merkelbach, Totti, *Abrasax I*, 169. A suggestion is 'I am enduring, the soul who made darkness' (*ink mn bꜣ-ỉr-kkw*).

[15] The translation given is the Demotic version of the funerary text that is preserved in a Classical Egyptian (in hieratic script) and Demotic version on one and the same manuscript. The hieratic version of this passage replaces 'underworld' by 'land of the west' and gives 'pharaoh's brother' instead of 'brother of the family of pharaoh'— P. Rhind I 10h/5–10. Georg Möller, *Die beiden Totenpapyrus Rhind des Museums zu Edinburg* (Dem.St. 6; Leipzig 1913). Another good example of this textual form is P. Leiden I 346, 1/1–4 in which the practitioner first greets all the malevolent divinities who roam the earth during the final five days of the year, in order to repel them thereafter; see Martin Bommas, *Die Mythisierung der Zeit* (GÖF IV.37; Wiesbaden 1999) and for an English translation: J.F. Borghouts, *Ancient Magical texts* (Nisaba 9; Leiden 1978) nr. 13.

[16] Baïs is a branch of a date palm. In Coptic ⲃⲁ (Crum, 27b); derives from *bꜣ* 'palm leaf' (WB I, 446). See also LSJ, 302b and 303a.

[17] See Daniel, *Two Greek Magical Papyri*, xxi, note to line 229.

154                           CHAPTER FIVE

> I am Souchos ⟨resembling⟩[18] a crocodile,
> Therefore, I beseech (you, pl.), come as my helpers,
> Because I am about to call on the hidden and ineffable name,
> The forefather of gods, overseer and lord of all.      [PGM XII.227–238]

Egyptian ritual works on the assumption that the practitioner is not so much communicating with the gods from a humble position as interacting with the gods on equal terms. Consequently, the practitioner must claim a status similar to that of the god by taking on the roll of a god. In other words, he must become an actor in the cosmic drama.[19] The procedure to do so consists of identifying oneself with a range of deities and giving the correct epithets to show that one possesses the necessary hidden knowledge. This scheme recurs in all sorts of ritual texts and was thus not at all viewed as blasphemous or confined to the darker side of magic. The first spell of the Book of the Dead, which kept being copied down into the Ptolemaic period, is illustrative of the technique. Only the first lines are given.

> Greetings to you, Osiris, bull of the west (spoken by Thoth), king of eternity,
> I am the great god on the side of the divine boat,
> I have fought for you,
> I am one of the gods of the tribunal,
> Who make Osiris triumph over his enemies on that day of judgement,
> I belong to your entourage,
> I am one of these gods whom Nut gave birth to,
> Who slays the enemies of Re and arrests the rebels,
> I belong to your entourage, Horus,
> I have fought for you; I have acted on your behalf.
> I am Thoth,
> Who makes Osiris triumph over his enemies on that day of judgement in the great mansion of the prince which is in Heliopolis.
>                                                    [Book of the Dead, spell 1][20]

Something similar occurs in a New Kingdom magical text to ward off evil spirits during the final five days of the year. The practitioner defies the spirits because he has taken on the roll of more powerful deities.

---

[18] The ὡμοιωμένος of the previous line is probably to be taken as an erroneous haplography. The scribe mixed up the line a bit.

[19] Jan Assmann, *Theologie und Frömmigkeit einer frühen Hochkultur* (2nd ed.; Stuttgart 1991) 58–63, translated as *The Search for God in Ancient Egypt* (Ithaca, New York 2001).

[20] See for an analysis of this particular chapter Wilhelm Czermak, 'Zur Gliederung des 1. Kapitels des ägyptischen "Totenbuches"' *ZÄS* 76 (1940) 9–24.

> Because I am Re who [appe]ars in his eye,
> I have risen as Sakhmet and I have risen as Ouadjet,
> Because I am Atum who is behind his heads, I am Atum who is in the midst of the lands,
> I am Atum in the house,
> Lord of mankind, creator of the gods,
> Lord of slaughter, who creates respect,
> Because I am this *shm*-scepter that rejoices and gladdens.
> [P.Leiden I 346 1/7–9][21]

The Greek invocation reflects not only Egyptian ritual procedures, but also it takes recourse solely to Egyptian gods, even if some of their names have been translated into a Hellenistic idiom. The section resounds with imagery taken over from Osiris theology and accounts of the daily birth of the sun out of the primeval waters.[22] The first two lines play on the image of the Osirian funerary complexes such as those in Abydos, Busiris and Philae, that had vineyards and palm tree gardens situated along the processional way and around the very tomb of 'The Great One'.[23] References to Krates, the abyss, the *Udjat*-eye and Phoenix have all to do with the rising of the sun god in the morning. The correct connections between names and appropriate epithets or attributes surely testify to a level of knowledge of Egyptian religion that goes beyond name-dropping, of which the following lines are even a stronger proof. At a certain point (PGM XII.232ff.), the succession of names outlines the genealogy of the Heliopolitan ennead in correct order as shown in the two given family trees. An identical list is preserved in the opening lines of the above quoted excerpt from the Augustan period funerary document.[24]

---

[21] Bommas, *Mythisierung der Zeit*. Further examples in Borghouts, *Magical Texts*, nrs. 115, 133, 145.

[22] The section is analysed in Merkelbach, Totti, *Abrasax I*, 171–176, who trace each line back to Egyptian mythology. Their conclusions have to be used with due caution.

[23] P. Koemoth, *Osiris et les arbres. Contribution à l'étude des arbres sacrés de l'Égypte ancienne* (Aegyptiaca Leodiensia 3; Luik 1994) 237–250, see for this passage and discussion 270–274.

[24] Note that the name Seth (Typhon) is missing in both the PGM XII and P. Rhind I list.

```
              Atum (Amun-Re)
                    |
          ┌─────────┴─────────┐
         Shu                 Tefnut
                    |
          ┌─────────┴─────────┐
         Geb                  Nut
                    |
     ┌────────┬─────┴────┬──────────┐
   Osiris    Isis     (Seth)     Nephthys
```

Heliopolitan genealogy

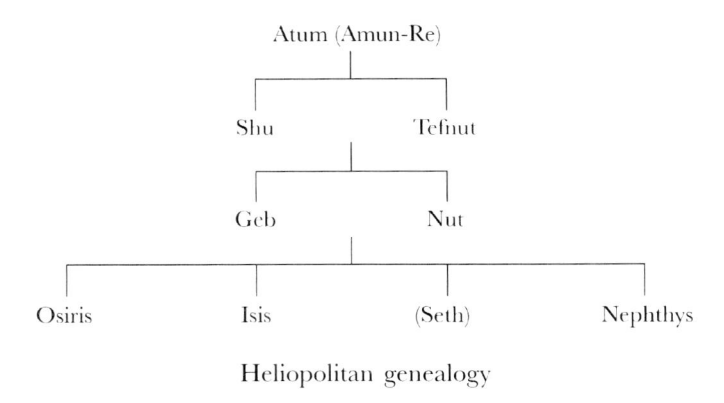

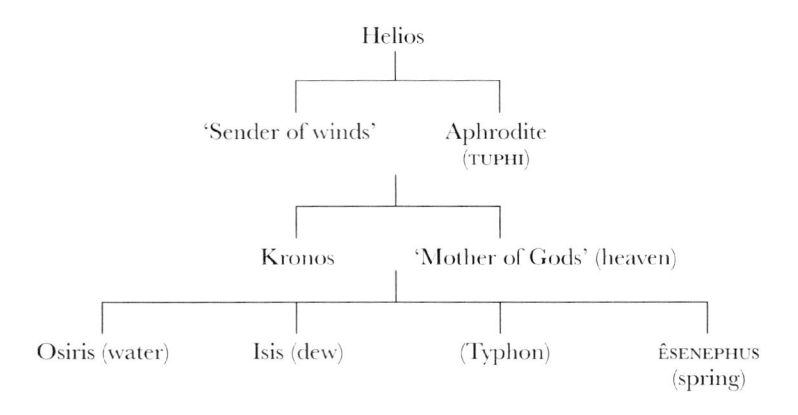

```
                 Helios
                    |
          ┌─────────┴─────────┐
   'Sender of winds'       Aphrodite
                           (TUPHI)
                    |
          ┌─────────┴─────────┐
        Kronos         'Mother of Gods' (heaven)
                    |
     ┌──────────┬────┴─────┬──────────┐
  Osiris      Isis      (Typhon)    ÊSENEPHUS
  (water)    (dew)                   (spring)
```

PGM XII genealogy

According to the cosmology of Heliopolis, the creator god Atum, partly relegated in the New Kingdom by Amun-Re (Helios), emerged from the primeval waters on a mound on which the temple of Heliopolis ('city of the sun', Egyptian *'Iwn.w*) would later be built. By an act of masturbation and spitting, he produced a couple that brought gender into being and constituted the ether. Shu, the male, is the god of air and wind ('Sender of winds'), while his consort Tefnut (TUPHI) represents fire. Together they brought forth another couple, Geb and Nut, who set borders to the physical world. By outstretching his body, Geb (Kronos)[25] formed the earth above whom Nut stood on her hands and

---

[25] The epithet given to Geb-Kronos in the Greek invocation repeats Helios' epithet:

feet to form the sky, the abode of the stars, which were considered gods in Egypt ('mother of gods who is called Heaven'). The result of their union was a third generation consisting of two couples: Osiris with his consort Isis and Seth with his wife Nephthys. The Greek invocation has undoubtedly deleted Seth (Typhon) because of the destructive qualities of this god, having become the ultimate symbol of disorder in Egyptian theology since the Late Period.[26] His wife Nephthys is primarily referred to in Egyptian sources as Isis' sister and companion in grief while mourning the deceased body of Osiris (ÊSENEPHUS).[27] In this fashion, the practitioner is not only taking on a set of divine names, he is also conveying a specific Egyptian religious discourse that explains the creation of nature and provides the legitimacy of pharaonic kingship, regardless of the fact that it is partly disguised by its Hellenistic idiom.[28] It remains open to question whether the author was really aware of these implications and whether he intended to reshape this theology towards contemporary needs.

The section closes again with an address to the gods to come to the aid of the practitioner. He forces them by the threat to invoke the

---

'who showed forth light'. Since Geb is never provided with a similar epithet in ancient Egyptian texts, it is well possible that the editor of the extant text mistakenly copied the epithet twice.

[26] H. te Velde, *Seth, God of Confusion: a study of his role in Egyptian mythology and religion* (Leiden 1967). See also chapter 4.4.3 of the present book.

[27] The form ÊSENEPHUS probably derives from *S.t-Nb.t-Hw.t*, 'Isis and Nephthys'. The name is also mentioned in PGM CXXII.52 (dating from the first century CE).

[28] An intriguing tension between Egyptian imagery and Hellenistic idiom can be seen in line 229 where the scribe mistakenly wrote Σόκρατης instead of ὁ Κράτης, changing Harpocrates, *Ḥr-pꜣ-ḥrd*, symbol of the sun god as a youth, into a Classical Greek name, well known as that of the fifth century Athenian philosopher (o instead of ω). Despite the established identification of Krates with the Egyptian Harpocrates, it is interesting to note that the name Κράτης was also wide-spread as a personal name of philosophers, poets and scholars in the Greco-Roman period; for a list consisting of 21 entries, see, *PRE* 11 (1921) 1622–1642 (entry 17 discusses the present passage). The uses of the word εἴδωλον in line 235, 'I am the Image resembling the true images', opens up a huge intertextual field. In Greek religion it denotes the soul of the deceased (Homer, Orphics), while Plato and Epicures also use the term to refer to the material imprint made in the mind by observation. At the same time, the clause reminds of the idea of Amun-Re emanating into all other gods: 'The Ennead is assembled in your limbs; every god is your image (*tj.t=k*) united with your being (*ḏ.t=k*)' [P. Leiden I 350 4/1]. Note also that εἴδωλον is the translation of the word *bꜣ*, 'manifestation' of a god or deceased, on a Roman period mummy label; Jan Quaegebeur, 'Mummy Labels: an Orientation', in: E. Boswinkel and P.W. Pestman (eds.), *Textes grecs, démotiques et bilingues* (P.L.Bat 19; Leiden 1978) 232–259, 253f. For a discussion of the concept Πίστις (line 228) in antiquity, see, Dieter Lührmann, 'Glaube' *RAC* 11, 48–122, esp. 54.

hidden and unspeakable name of the supreme deity, the One-and-All. These lines (237–239) serve as a transition to the hymn to a pantheistic god that is attested in three spells of the *Greek Magical Papyri*. Apart from the present invocation (PGM XII.240–269), the hymn can also be found as a prayer to serve as phylactery (PGM XXI) and in a spell for acquiring the hidden and powerful name of the supreme deity (PGM XIII.732–1056).[29] Regardless of minor differences between the versions, the hymn testifies to the fact that the editors of the Greek magical spells made use of, and adapted, existing hymns that were available to them. The parallel texts of PGM XIII.732–1056 and XXI are almost identical, whereas the version under discussion has inserted a more or less independent hexametrical hymn, elaborates upon the terrifying effects of speaking out the name of the All-Lord[30] and leaves out a section on the eight Egyptian primeval gods.[31] The first part of the hymn is what follows.

> Come to me, you from the four winds, god, ruler of all, who have breathed spirits into men for life, master of the good things in the world.
>
> Hear me, lord, whose hidden name is ineffable. The demons, hearing it, are terrified—the name BARBAREICH ARSEMPHEMPHRÔTHOU—and of it the sun, of it the earth, hearing, rolls over;[32] Hades, hearing, is shaken; rivers, sea, lakes, springs, hearing, are frozen; rocks, hearing it, are split.
>
> Heaven is your head; ether, body; earth, feet; and the water around you, ocean.
>
> [O] Agathos Daimon, you are the lord, the begetter and nourisher and increaser of all.   [PGM XII.238–244]

This passage presents several themes, for which parallels are extant, both in more ancient and contemporary texts. For the sake of convenience, the following three themes will be treated separately:

---

[29] See for comparison and discussion of these three versions: Merkelbach, Totti, *Abrasax I*, 127–222, §59–72 and Merkelbach, *Isis Regina—Zeus Sarapis*, 196–197, §372.

[30] This is PGM XII.241–242.

[31] The eight primeval gods are Nun—Naunet, Huh—Hauhet, Kuk—Kauket, Amun—Amaunet, see PGM XIII.787–788 and PGM XXI.18–20. The section corresponds with Merkelbach's section S. One could only speculate about the reasons why the scribe left these out. Nevertheless, the occurrence of these eight divine entities is another strong argument for reading the invocation in the light of Amun-Re theology, since they were an essential part of its cosmology; see, K. Sethe, *Amun und die Acht Urgötter von Hermopolis* (Berlin 1929).

[32] The papyrus gives ελευσεται, which is either to be emendated to ἑλίσσεται or ἀνοίγεται (see Merkelbach, Totti, *Abrasax I*, 176 and Daniel, *Two Greek Magical Papyri*, xxii, note to line 241). I have given preference to the former suggestion.

1. Lord of the wind
2. The god's ineffable name
3. Divine body parts equated with physical nature

(1) The first line addresses the cosmocrator as beneficent ruler of the winds who gives enlivening breath to mortal men. The image of the god who controls the winds and dispensates vivifying breath is recurrent in hymns for Amun since the New Kingdom.[33] Originally a god of the winds, the ambiguous distinction in Egyptian between wind and breath became meaningful after Amun had acquired a pantheistic character.[34] In a passage from the above quoted funerary text P. Rhind I, dated to the first years of Roman rule, the connection between Amun, wind and vivifying breath is made explicit by a gloss that is added to the Demotic version of the text.[35]

> *May your ba live with the lord of the winds;*
> May your ba live with the lord of the wind, who is Amun.[36]

The imagery of wind and breath is exploited in the following poetic passage from an elaborate hymn to Amun dating from the days of Amenhotep III, which gives an explicit and vivid description of Amun's role as dispensator of enlivening breath.[37]

> Your breath (*t3w=k*) comes to the noses of everyone,
> They breathe (*ḥnm=sn*) of the warm whiff (*hh*) from your [mouth];
> When you come forth towards heaven, one lives under your command.
> [P. Leiden I 344 verso 5/10]

---

[33] This connection was still known among Greco-Roman authors, who translated Amun's name into Zeus: Diodorus I 12,2; Plutarch, *On Isis and Osiris*, 36; Eusebius, *Prae-paratio evangelica* III, 2, 6.

[34] Sethe, *Amun und die Acht Urgötter von Hermopolis*, 90–102 and Assmann, *Re und Amun*, 246–250.

[35] Two other Roman period Demotic references to Amun in connection with the (four) winds are P. Spiegelberg 1/6 and P. Berlin 8279. The Berlin papyrus is an astronomical text in which the planet Jupiter, which is presided over by Zeus in Greek astronomical texts, is rendered in Demotic by *t3w* 'wind' instead of Amun, the common equivalent of Zeus. The short passage P. Spiegelberg 1/5–7 describes the sacred bark of Amun and refers to Amun's diadem as the four winds.

[36] P. Rhind I 6h/4 and P.Rhind I 6d/3–4. The mortuary text consists of a Classical Egyptian (in hieratic script) and a Demotic version rendering the same text with minor variation in phraseology.

[37] J. Zandee, *Der Amunhymnus des Papyrus Leiden I 344, Verso I–III* (Rijksmuseum van Oudheden; Leuven 1992). The manuscript is dated by palaeography to the

The next passage, which refers to Amun-Re's control over the four winds,[38] is an important testimony, since it occurs in a cultic hymn that is attested in three hieroglyphic versions on temple walls and in a Demotic version on an ostracon.[39] Although this passage is only known from the temple of Amun-Re in Hibis, the occurrence of multiple variants, which even cross linguistic borders, testify that the hymn must have circulated among the native priesthood between at least the Kushite and early Roman period. The occurrence of parallels in a late New Kingdom magical papyrus, the so-called *Harris Magical Papyrus*, suggests that parts of the hymn even go back several centuries earlier.[40]

> You are Amun, you are Shu,
> You are the one who is more exalted than the other gods,
> You are holy of forms in the four winds of the sky,
> Which, as they say, come forth from the mouth of your majesty.[41]

---

19[t] dynasty, but its date of composition must go back to the middle of the 18th dynasty, because parallel passages occur in Kheruef's tomb (TT 192), which dates to the reign of Amenhotep III. See for this tomb: *The Tomb of Kheruef. Theban Tomb 192* (OIP 102; Chicago 1980).

[38] On the image of the four winds in Greco-Roman Egypt in general, see, Adolphe Gutbub, 'Die vier Winde im Tempel von Kom Ombo (Oberägypten). Bemerkungen zur Darstellung der Winde im Ägypten der griechisch-römischen Zeit', in: Othmar Keel, *Jarwe-Visionen und Siegelkunst. Eine neue Deutung der Majestätsschilderungen in Jes 6, Ez 1 und 10 und Sach 4* (Stuttgarter Bibelstudien 84/85; Stuttgart 1977) 328–353.

[39] The hieroglyphic versions are found in the so-called *Edifice of Taharqa* next to the sacred lake of Karnak (Kushite period), the temple of Amun-Re in Hibis, El Khargeh oasis (Persian period) and the temple of Opet in Karnak (Ptolemaic period). The Demotic rendition of the hymn is O. BM. 50601 (late Ptolemaic or early Roman). The relationship between the material from Hibis and Karnak is discussed by David Lorton, 'The Invocation Hymn at the Temple of Hibis' *SAK* 21 (1994) 159–217. See for the Demotic ostracon: Mark Smith, 'A New Version of a well-known Egyptian Hymn' *Enchoria* 7 (1977) 115–149 and for important corrections Idem, 'O.Hess=O.Naville= O. BM 50601: an Elusive Text relocated', in: E. Teeter and J.A. Larson (eds.), *Gold of Praise. Fs. E. Wente* (SAOC 58; Chicago 1999) 397–404.

[40] J.F. Quack, 'Kontinuität und Wandel in der spätägyptischen Magie' *SEL* 15 (1998) 77–94, 87–89. For the parallel extracts, see, Christian Leitz, *Magical and Medical Papyri of the New Kingdom* (Hieratic Papyri in the British Museum 7; London 1999) 35–38.

[41] Sethe, *Amun und die Acht Urgötter von Hermopolis*, 97, §205. A facsimile of the Hibis version is given in Norman de Garis Davies, *The Temple of Hibis in El-Khargeh Oasis III, The Decoration* (PMMA 17; New York 1953) plate 31; comments to the text: Eugene Cruz-Uribe, *Hibis Temple Project I; translations, Commentary, Discussions and Sign List* (San Antonio 1988) 119–123. The version of the *Edifice of Taharqa* is discussed in Richard A. Parker (eds.), *The Edifice of Taharqa by the Sacred Lake of Karnak* (Brown Egyptological Studies VIII; Providence, London 1979) 70–76. See also: Assmann, *Ägyptische Hymnen und Gebete*, 297–304 (nr. 128).

(2) The topic of the hidden and ineffable name of the invoked deity, which is recurrent in the *Greek Magical Papyri*,[12] is characteristic of hymns for Amun, motivated by a pun on his name, which can be translated as 'the hidden one'. The following passage occurs in an elaborate hymn consisting of several 'chapters', which combines the secrecy of Amun-Re's being and name with its dreadful character.

> Unique is Amun, who is hidden from them,
> Who conceals himself from the gods, so that they do not know his being,
> Who is more remote than the sky, who is deeper than the underworld,
> None of the gods knows his true character,
> His image is not explained (*prḫ*) in the writings,
> One learns (*mtr*) nothing certain (*dr.y.t*) about him,
> He is too mysterious to fathom (*kfꜣ*) his majesty,
> He is too big to inquire him, too strong to know him,
> One falls immediately dead because of terror,
> When his secret name is spoken, knowingly or ignorantly,
> No god can call him with it,
> (He is a) ba, whose name is hidden as his secret.
> [P. Leiden I 350 4/17–21]

The idea of unleashing destructive powers when pronouncing the god's hidden name was apparently known in traditional Egyptian religious thought. The Greek hymn under discussion turns this ancient theme into a lively image of disordered nature (240ff.): demons are shivering, earth and underworld are collapsing, rivers, sea, lakes, springs are frozen and rocks are bursting. The theme and the imagery of the upheaval of social and natural order was well known in Egyptian literature, but not in connection with the theme of the ineffability of the god's name.[13] It is therefore plausible that this imagery, which is missing from the variant hymns in PGM XIII and XXI, derives from sources other than those deeply rooted in Egyptian tradition.[14]

---

[12] PGM IV.243ff.; 356ff.; 1019ff.; XII.117ff.

[13] The theme of cosmic and social disorder is particularly recurrent in prophetic works such as *The Words of Neferti, The Words of Chacheperreseneb, The Dialogue of Ipuur and the Lord of All* and, in Demotic literature, the so-called *Demotic Chronicle, The Lamb of Bocchoris* and *Nectanebo's Dream* (was extant in both a Demotic and Greek version). *The Oracle of the Potter* is preserved only in a Greek version, but a Demotic version must have been extant. For this theme in Egyptian literature of the Greco-Roman period, see, A. Blasius and B.U. Schipper (eds.), *Apokalyptik und Ägypten. Eine kritische Analyse der relevanten Texte aus dem griechisch-römischen Ägypten* (OLA 107; Leuven 2002).

[14] This suggestion could be substantiated by the description of the physical world, which evokes a landscape different from Egypt by way of a multiplicity of rivers and springs and the idea of frost.

(3) The next line of the Greek hymn equates the deity's body parts with different elements of the cosmos: heaven, ether (wind), earth, (primeval) water. In this way the cosmos is portrayed as the physical manifestation of the hidden god. Although the image of an anthropomorphic cosmos was widespread among religions in the Hellenistic period, it is very plausible that the Greek hymn falls back again on older Egyptian hymns to Amun-Re.[15] The following example is again taken from the Persian period temple in Hibis.

> His body is the wind,
> Heaven rests on his head,
> Nun (the primeval waters) carries his mystery.
> [...]
> You are Nun, who stretches himself over the earth,
> You enliven the land with your spring water.
> You are heaven, you are earth, you are underworld,
> You are the water, you are the wind between them.[16]

The same image is found in the oracular response that was allegedly sent by the priests of Sarapis to Nikokreon, king of Cyprus, sometime between 321 and 311 BCE.[17] Nikokreon had asked the oracle whether the Egyptian Sarapis could be compared with any other deity. Although the medium of the message is clearly Greek (hexametrical verses as a god's answer), the imagery betrays familiarity with traditional Egyptian theology rather than positing a superficial theoretical idea.

> I am the god who can be known as such as I am saying:
> The heavenly world is my head, my stomach is the sea,
> The earth is feet to me, my ears are set in the ether,
> My far-shining eyes are the bright light of the sun (Helios).
> [Macrobius, *Saturnalia*, I 20, 17]

The god Sarapis, who was believed to have given this oracle, was often equated with the *Agathos Daimon*, whose name is mentioned in line 244 of the Greek hymn under discussion and functioned as city god of

---

[15] See for a useful overview including Egyptian, Orphic, Stoic and Indian material: J. Assmann, 'Primat und Transzendenz. Struktur und Genese der ägyptischen Vorstellung eines "Höchsten Wesens"', in: W. Westendorf, *Aspekte der spätägyptischen Religion* (GOF IV, 9; Wiesbaden 1979) 7–42, esp. 7–13.
[16] For commentaries to the translation, see, footnote 39.
[17] R. van den Broek, 'The Sarapis Oracle in Macrobius *SAT.*, I, 20, 16–17', in: Margreet B. de Boer and T.A. Edridge (eds.), *Hommages à Maarten J. Vermaseren* 3 Vols. (EPRO 68; Leiden 1978) vol. 1, 123–141.

Alexandria in the form of a snake.[48] In this way, a meaningful link is established between the oracular verses and the PGM XII hymn.

At this point the PGM XII hymn changes its poetical form: hitherto the sentences are arranged by *parallelismus membrorum* or associative oppositions of thought as in Egyptian poetry, but for lines 244-252 the verses are characterised by their hexametrical form. At a certain moment, a redactor must have incorporated this poetic hymn into the invocation, since it is missing from the parallel texts in PGM XIII and XXI.

> Who moulded the forms of the beasts (of the Zodiac)? Who founded
>   (their) routes?
> Who was the begetter of fruits? Who raises up the mountains?
> Who commanded the winds to hold to their annual tasks?
> What Aiôn nourishing an Aiôn rules the Aiôns?
> You, the one and deathless god; you are the begetter of all,
> And you assign souls to all and control all,
> King of the Aiôns and lord, (before) whom tremble
> Mountains and plains together, springs and streams of rivers,
> And valleys of earth, and spirits, and all things that are.
> High shining heaven trembles before you, and every sea,
> Lord, ruler of all, holy one and master of all.
> By your power the elements exist and all things come into being,
> – the route of sun and moon, of night and dawn –
> By air and earth and water and the breath of fire.   [PGM XII.244-252]

Given the hexametrical form and the fact that it is missing in the parallel hymns, this section is a self-contained hymn incorporated into the larger prose hymn to the pantheistic deity.[49] The foregoing discussion made it plausible that the hymn to the All-Lord was composed with the help of an Egyptian text like the one of which versions can be found in Hibis and Luxor. Similarly, the incorporation of the hexametrical hymn makes clear that the composers of the extant invocation employed sources other than Egyptian and did not feel restricted to Egyptian generic forms.[50] The reference to the beasts of the zodiac, which image developed in the Hellenistic period outside of Egypt, points in a similar

---

[48] See for a visual equation of Sarapis with Agathos Daimon (snake with Serapis' head): *Égypte Romaine. L'autre Égypte*, exhibition catalogue of Musée d'Archéologie méditerranéenne, Marseille, 1997; object nr. 227. See also: P.M. Fraser, *Ptolemaic Alexandria* (Oxford 1972) 209-211.

[49] The hymn is included into the collection of hymns that are attached as appendix to the PGM: Preisendanz, PGM II, 237, hymn 1.

[50] Merkelbach, Totti want to see Zarathustran elements in the hymn: *Abrasax I*, 16-19.

direction. The wordplay with the concept of Aion[51] and the grouping of the four elements of the cosmos as a given set into a single verse line are also indicative of a highly Hellenised milieu.[52] The hymn itself consists of a series of rhetorical questions whose expected answer introduces a list of glorifying epithets to the All-Lord. The epithets merely develop upon the recurring theme of the god for whom all nature shivers and who has brought everything into existence.

The following lines 252–263 complete the prose hymn to the pantheistic god:

> Yours is the eternal processional way (of heaven), in which your seven-lettered name is established for the harmony of the seven sounds (of the planets) which utter (their) voices according to the 28 forms of the moon.
>
> Yours are the beneficent effluxes of the stars, demons and fortunes and fates. You give wealth, good old age, good children, strength, food.
>
> You, lord of life, ruling the upper and lower realm, whose justice is not thwarted, whose glorious name the angels sing, who has truth that never lies, hear me and complete for me this operation so that I may wear this power in every place, in every time, without being smitten or afflicted, so as to be preserved intact from every danger while I wear this power. Yea, lord, for to you the god in heaven, all things are subject, and none of the demons or spirits will oppose me because I have called on your great name for the consecration. [PGM XII.252–263]

These lines contain again elements that originated outside Egypt. The first above line can be understood only within Hellenistic cosmology, which teaches that the seven planets circle around the earth emitting the seven sounds that have their effect upon earthly events.[53] The 'seven-lettered name' that is established within this constellation refers to the idea of the Greek seven vowels whose powerful qualities have been discussed in chapter 3.3.[54] In these lines, accrediting the deity

---

[51] The idea of a plurality of Aions developed mainly among gnostic (pagan and Christian) circles, see: H. Sasse, 'Aion' *RAC* 1, 193–204.

[52] The idea of the four elements as constituents of the cosmos was incessantly discussed by Greek philosophers starting with Heraclitus and Empedocles and became widely influential in antiquity, especially in Stoic cosmogony; see, L.J. Alderink, 'Stoicheia' *DDD*, 815a–818a. The idea was probably not unknown in pharaonic Egypt but became never articulated in a consistent manner; cf. the list of examples in J. Assmann, *Egyptian Solar Religion in the New Kingdom. Re, Amun and the Crisis of Polytheism* (London, New York 1995) 180–186.

[53] See also chapter 3.3.2 on the power accorded to the seven vowels.

[54] Merkelbach and Totti interpret the 'seven-lettered name' to be of Sarapis, whose name consists indeed of seven letters: Merkelbach, Totti, *Abrasax* I, 147.

with power over the stars and, consequently, fate solves the theological problem of determinism raised by astrology. The closing line brings the purpose of the ritual finally to the fore: the deity is asked to consecrate the ring that will serve as a powerful phylactery to its wearer. The reason given to the god reveals again the preoccupation with the 'hidden name': 'because I have called on your great name'.

As if this name would not be sufficient, the closing line of the complete invocation lists another five names:

> And again I call upon you,
> according to Egyptians, PHNÔEAI IABÔK;
> according to Jews, ADÔNAIE SABAÔTH;
> according to Greeks, 'the king of all, ruling alone';
> according to the high priests, 'hidden, invisible, overseer of all';
> according to Parthians, OUERTÔ 'master of all'.
> Consecrate and empower this object for me, for the entire and glorious
>     time of my life! [PGM XII.263–267]

These names, grouped along ethnic lines except for the high priests, bring three important new elements to the discussion, which will be of central concern in the next chapter: ethnicity, translatability of cultures and high priests as a distinct class and discrete concept. The section takes up again the idea that the deity can be compelled to act in accordance with the practitioner's will, if the correct names and epithets are called upon. In this case, however, the names do not allude to hidden knowledge confined to a specific mythic constellation, but, on the contrary, they are concerned with a multiplicity of religious manners, opening up a wide geographical area that is thought to be the deity's realm. The underlying idea of the invocation is that different peoples living in different areas give their supreme deity differing names, although these are ultimately only varying denominators of one and the same All-Lord. This topic, which Jan Assmann coined the 'Names of the Nations' motif, was very popular in connection with the concept of the pantheistic deity in the Hellenistic and Roman period.[55] An encomium of Isis in Greek, preserved on a papyrus from Oxyrhynchus (P. Oxy 1380) which is dated to the early second century CE, glorifies the goddess as the mistress of the cosmos and gives a long list of names and epithets in a geographical arrangement before enumerating

---

[55] Jan Assmann, *Moses the Egyptian. The memory of Egypt in western monotheism* (Harvard University Press; Cambridge, London 1997) 47–54. see also Idem, 'Translating gods: religion as a factor of cultural (un)translatability', in: S. Budick and W. Iser eds., *The Translatability of Cultures. Figurations of the Space Between* (Stanford 1996) 23–36.

all her beneficent qualities. The lost columns that preceded the extant manuscript undoubtedly dealt with Upper Egypt, since the beginning of the papyrus contains only place names of Lower Egypt.[56] After this detailed section the text lists the different names and epithets under which Isis is known abroad and among foreign people.

> [They call you] in Arabia 'great, goddess'; in the Island 'giver of victory in the sacred games'; in Lycia 'Leto'; at Myra in Lycia 'sage, freedom'; at Cnidus 'dispeller of attack, discoverer'; at Cyrene 'Isis'; in Crete 'Diktynnis'; at Chalcedon 'Themis'; at Rome 'warlike'; in the Cyclades islands 'of threefold nature, Artemis'; ... among the Thracians and in Delos 'many-named'; among the Amazons 'warlike'; among the Indians 'Maia'; among the Thessalians 'moon'; among the Persians 'Latina'; among the Magi 'Korè, Thapseusis'  [P.Oxy 1380 Col iv, 76–105][57]

One of the native guiding principles leading to this rhetorical device was certainly the habit of compiling word lists, today known as 'onomastica', that catalogue all physical and metaphysical phenomena of the cosmos.[58] These texts are replete with lists of divine names and their geographical distribution. The author of the opening lines of the divine decree about the Abaton on emperor Hadrian's gate at Philae may have had such a text at his disposal. This text restricts the device to a regional instead of the international scheme of the contemporary Oxyrhynchus papyrus.

> Hail to you holy *ba* of Osiris Wennefer,
> Divine phoenix, who came into being by himself,
> The only one, who created what exists,
> Holy primeval one of the *ba*'s of the netherworld,
> 'Holy *ba*' is your name in the Abaton,
> 'Divine phoenix' is your name in Biggeh,
> 'Strong *ba*' is your name in 'House of Sekhmet',

---

[56] Compare this geographical arrangement with a Demotic onomasticon (Ptolemaic period) that lists place names of the Delta while providing a long list of deities with their specific epithets: P. Cairo 31168+31169, see: F. Hoffmann, *Ägypten. Kultur und Lebenswelt in griechisch-römischer Zeit. Eine Darstellung nach den demotischen Quellen* (Akademie Verlag; Berlin 2000) 104–106.

[57] Translation: B.P. Grenfell and A.S. Hunt.

[58] The onomasticon of Amenope starts thus: 'Beginning of the teaching for clearing the mind, for instruction of the ignorant and for learning all things that exist: what Ptah created, what Thoth copied down, heaven with its affairs, earth, and what is in it, what the mountains belch forth, what is watered by the flood, all things upon which Re has shown, all that is grown on the back of earth': Alan H. Gardiner, *Ancient Egyptian Onomastica* I–III (Oxford 1947); for Greco-Roman period material, see, Osing, *Hieratische Papyri aus Tebtunis*.

'*Ba* [*spd*] *irw*' is your name on Philae,
'*Ba* that is mourned' is your name in the temple of Isis (on Philae),
'Living *ba*' is your name in *Hp.t*,
Your are the *ba* that is above the divine *ba*'s.
[Decree concerning Abaton ll. 1–11][59]

The motif is also taken up in the final book of Apuleius' *Metamorphoses*. The unfortunate Lucius, who was transformed into an ass on account of his unbridled curiosity about the magical arts, seeks refuge with the goddess Isis after many misadventures and having lost all hope to become human again. After he has prayed to her and laid himself down on the beach, she appears to him in a dream consoling him that she is the cosmocrator and nourisher of all living beings and will relieve him of his troubles. Her self-identification is replete with epithets known from the Isis aretalogies and cosmotheistic hymns. She explains that she is worshipped in many different forms and manners, but that, in the end, all her many names come down to her true name, *verum nomen*, by which she is only known among the Ethiopians and Egyptians. She affords these two ethnic groups this prestige because of the presumed antiquity of their customs and religious knowledge. By stressing the antiquity of their doctrines, her discourse touches upon, and responds to, the Greco-Roman fascination for Egypt as the land of ancient wisdom. However, apart from this intertextual motif, Ethiopians and Egyptians could also be considered the true guardians of Isis worship, because they conducted her cult in Philae, the goddess' southernmost cult place and popular pilgrimage site in the Greco-Roman period.[60]

> My name, my divinity is adored throughout all the world, in diverse manners, in variable customs, and by many names. For the Phrygians that are the first of all men[61] call me 'the Mother of the gods at Pessinus'; the Athenians, which are sprung from their own soil, 'Cecropian Minerva'; the Cyprians, which are girt about by the sea, 'Paphian Venus'; the Cretans which bear arrows, 'Dictynnian Diana'; the Sicilians, which speak three tongues, 'infernal Proserpine'; the Eleusinians 'their ancient goddess Ceres'; some 'Juno', other 'Bellona', other 'Hecate', other 'Rhamnusia', and principally both sort of the Ethiopians which dwell

---

[59] H. Junker, *Das Götterdekret über das Abaton* (Vienna 1913).

[60] By the Ethiopians are meant the people living south of the Egyptian border in modern Sudan. For the temple of Philae as pilgrimage site, see, Ian Rutherford, 'Island of the Extremity: Space, Language, and Power in the Pilgrimage Traditions of Philae, in: D. Frankfurter ed., *Pilgrimage and Holy Space in Late Antique Egypt* (Religions in the Graeco-Roman World 134; Leiden 1998) 229–256.

[61] See Herodotus II, 2 for an explanation of this assumption.

in the Orient and are enlightened by the morning rays of the sun, and the Egyptians, which are excellent in all kind of ancient doctrine, and by their proper ceremonies accustom to worship me, do call me by my true name (*vero nomine*), 'Queen Isis'. [Apuleius, *Metamorphoses*, Book XI, 4][62]

This passage not only illustrates the 'Names of the Nations' motif, but establishes also a hierarchical relationship between the different ethnicities. Pride of place is given to the Ethiopians and Egyptians because they know the *verum nomen* and the proper rites whereas the other nations have only artificial access to the goddess. This tension between the *verum nomen* and the multitude of variant names of one and the same god is precisely what occupies the magical texts to the utmost: the search for the hidden, all-encompassing name of the divine being.

The short concluding 'international' invocation of the PGM XII spell is thus part of a larger theological discourse that comes to light in several Roman-period compositions made for the goddess Isis.[63] The presence of these lines in PGM XII has far-reaching effects for the intercultural character of the manuscript as a whole. Ethnicity has now become a productive category of thought with positive connotations, in contrast to the nationalistic message of tractate XVI of the *Corpus Hermeticum*. There seems to be no overt hierarchy among the different ethnicons as in Apuleius' text, unless the enumeration must be taken as strictly and purposefully ordered: Egyptians, Jews Greeks, high priests, Parthians. If so, the text does not give any clue as to whether the list is arranged from lesser to higher prestige or vice versa. It is remarkable that the high priests are treated as a distinct category in a list enumerating ethnic groups. However, the underlying principle of the list is not so much ethnicity as it is religious discourse. Sole criterion for inclusion into this list is the group's possession of a distinct fitting name or epithet for addressing the divine. Although there is no hierarchy among these groups, they certainly had a value attached to them because of which they were included in the list. The Egyptians and Jews were seen in the Greco-Roman period as great magicians who were able to do great feats. The same holds true for the Magi, the Persian priests of the fire ritual, who are undoubtedly meant by the otherwise remarkable ethni-

---

[62] Tr. W. Adlington

[63] See also Isidoros' first hymn to Isis, ll. 14–24 (= SB 5.8138) that is one of four that were inscribed on both side pillars of the entrance to the temple of Renenutet in Narmuthis in the Fayum and is dated to the late Ptolemaic period. V.F. Vanderlip, *The Four Greek Hymns of Isidorus and the Cult of Isis* (American Studies in Papyrology 12: Toronto 1972) 17–34; see also Frankfurter, *Religion in Roman Egypt*, 98–106.

con 'Parthians'. The Parthians, originating from Northern Iran, were for more than two centuries the enemy of the Roman Empire in the Near East until their defeat in the 220s CE by the Persian Sassanids. Could the ethnicon therefore be a terminus ante quem for the composition of the spell? Such a straightforward explanation cannot be given for the Greeks who were never viewed as experts in rituals and magic as a group.[61] The occurrence of this group should however not be surprising given the overall presence of Hellenised communities in the eastern Mediterranean. However, one could be somewhat surprised that the list does not contain 'the Romans', whose presence was clearly visible in the landscape throughout the Near East. The inclusion of the high priests, which is a social instead of ethnic category, is, as said, remarkable. Something similar can be observed in the Isis encomium from Oxyrhynchus where the list ends with the Magi, the Persian priests of the fire ritual. These Magi are set off against the Persians as the high priests against the Egyptians in the PGM spell, although both fall within the ethnic category:

> among the Persians 'Latina'; among the Magi 'Korè, Thapseusis'

Both these groups were seen as privileged among their ethnic group and therefore set apart as being highly specialized masters of the magical arts.

The names that are laid into the mouths of these groups seem to be a mixture of Greek epithets and *voces magicae* that are not always in accord with their respective languages. This mystification of languages recurs in other *Greek Magical Papyri*, although not always explicitly connected with the 'Names of the Nations' motif. The languages mentioned are primarily Hebrew, Syrian (which is missing in the PGM XII spell), and Egyptian. In the latter case, language and script are usually not clearly distinguished, presumably on account of the mystical qualities ascribed to the hieroglyphs in the Hellenistic world. Examples are:

> I conjure you in the Hebrew language (PGM III.119)

> I am the one who calls upon you in Syrian, great god: ZAALAÊRIFFOU; and you should not ignore my utterance in Hebrew: ABLANATHANALBA ABRASILÔA. (PGM V.472–475)

---

[61] Note that several subgroups could be viewed as being particularly inclined towards the magical arts. For example, literary sources portray the region Thessaly frequently as the home of magic and members of the Pythagorean or Neo-Platonic

> I call on you, lord, in 'birdglyphic': ARAI; in hieroglyphic: LAÏLAM; in Hebrew: ANOCH BIATHIARBATH BERBIR ECHILATOUR BOUPHROUMTROM; in Egyptian: ALDABAEIM; in 'baboonic': ABRASAX; in 'falconic': CHI CHI CHI CHI CHI CHI CHI TIPH TIPH TIPH; in hieratic: MENEPHÔÏPHÔTH CHA CHA CHA CHA CHA CHA CHA
> (PGM XIII.81–86, cf. 149–160, 454–470 and 593–598)[65]

> I call upon you who encompasses everything in every tongue and every dialect (PGM XIII.138–139)

Irrespective of any ethnic claim, each epithet of the 'international' list can generally be applied to a pantheistic deity who governs the cosmos as sole-ruler. The Greek epithets 'the king of all, ruling alone; hidden, invisible, overseer of all; master of all' speak for themselves. The *voces magicae* ADÔNAIE SABAÔTH are indeed of Jewish origin. ADÔNAIE means in Hebrew 'Lord' and SABAÔTH occurs often attached to the word Yahweh in the Hebrew Bible.[66] The Egyptian PHNÔEAI IABÔK cannot be interpreted that easily, unless PHNÔ can be derived from ⲫⲚⲞⲨⲦ (Bohairic) meaning 'God' in its monotheistic form. The Parthian OUERTÔ may be Egyptian *wr-tꜣ*, 'the great one of the land', if it is not true Persian or simply bogus. As such, the epithets fall within and continue the general theme of this elaborate invocation: an address to the sole-ruler of the universe who transcends the limits imposed on physical nature and is above geographical, ethnic and linguistic boundaries.

## 5.3. *Appropriation of a ritual: 'Opening the Mouth'*

In line with the catalogue-like nature of the handbook, the ritual just discussed is immediately followed by an alternative spell for consecrating a ring (PGM XII.270–350). As in the first spell, the Greek text is headed by a Demotic title, *wʿ gswr*, 'a ring [spell]', which, in this case, is not jotted between the lines but carefully written in the middle of the empty line dividing the text of the first from the second ring spell. These identical Demotic headings suggest that the two spells were

---

movements could be accredited with knowledge of the magical arts. See also chapter 6.3.3.2.

[65] The passage clearly plays with the iconic nature of the hieroglyphic sign and the mystical qualities generally afforded to the hieroglyphic sign among the Hellenistic elite.

[66] K. Spronk, 'Lord' *DDD*, 531a–33b and T.N.D. Mettinger, 'Yahweh Zebaoth' *DDD*, 920a–24b.

regarded as forming some sort of unity, which is corroborated by the fact that the second spell refers back to the prescriptions of the first spell: 'when you are performing the rite, with each recitation libate the things that are written above' (lines 309–310). Despite these links, the two spells are fairly different in their way of conducting the consecration, both with respect to the ritual action and address to the god. Next to the recipe for consecrating the ring, the second spell provides two additional invocations, called the *Ouphôr*, that should be recited each time the practitioner wishes to put the ring to use. Its textual structure is accordingly as follows:

| i | Description of the ring and its possibilities | (lines 271–284) |
|---|---|---|
| ii | Invocation of the 'greatest god' | (lines 284–307) |
| iii | Prescription of the *Ouphôr* ritual | (lines 307–322) |
| iv | Invocations of the *Ouphôr* | (lines 323–350) |

The text claims to provide the practitioner with a ring that is capable of executing virtually all magical operations, because 'it contains an excellent name' (line 273): it bestows its wearer with respect and admiration, makes friends, creates wealth, restrains anger, opens doors, breaks chains, bursts rocks and exorcises demons.

The prescribed stone and its design are different from the previous spell. In the present spell, a heliotrope stone has to be engraved with an image of the sun as *Ouroboros* snake containing within its circular body the image of a scarab with sunrays.[67] The reverse side of the stone should be inscribed with Helios' name 'in hieroglyphs, as the prophets say' (line 276).[68] The consecration of the ring consists of invoking 'the greatest god, who exceeds all power' (line 284), while facing the sun, in the third, sixth and ninth hour, during fourteen days, starting from the third day of the moon month with, preferably, the moon in the zodiacal sign of Bull, Virgin, Scorpion, Water Carrier or Fishes (lines 307–309). While reciting, the practitioner should pour libations as specified in the first spell and burn all kinds of perfumes except frankincense. After

---

[67] For a detailed discussion of the stone's design and the prescribed time of execution, see, Ian Moyer and Jacco Dieleman, 'Miniaturization and the Opening of the Mouth in a Greek Magical Text (*PGM* XII.270–350)' *JANER* 3 (2003) 47–72.

[68] The prophets are the highest class of the Egyptian priesthood; for detailed discussion, see chapter 6.3.1. I do not follow Morton Smith's translation (*GMPT*, 163) 'as the prophets pronounce [it]', but prefer to take the standard construction ὡς λέγουσιν as an editorial comment on the origin of the information to prove the validity of the ritual technique.

fourteen days a white or yellow double-combed rooster must be cut open alive, into whose guts the ring has to be placed for one day (lines 311–315).[69] In the ninth hour of the night, the ring can be taken out and is ready to be used as soon as the need makes itself felt.

The invocation of the 'greatest god' is a hybrid collection of about 100 magical names, each of which is preceded by the definite article, as if each name serves as an independent tag or aspect of the pluralistic god. The majority of these names are garbled *voces magicae*, but the string begins with the Jewish names IAÔ SABAÔTH ADÔNAI EILÔEIN (line 285), incorporates the names of the patriarchs Abraham, Isaac and Jacob (line 287), the name 'the opponent of Thoth' (line 289), the entire Maskelli-Maskello formula (lines 290–291), the Jewish name 'Cherubi[m]' (line 296), the Egyptian name 'Soul-of-Darkness' (line 296; βαινχωωχ), one of the Greek *Ephesia Grammata*, 'Damnameneu[s]' (line 299), and closes with the seven vowels (line 301).[70] In this fashion, the supreme deity is summoned through an amalgam of powerful names, which originally derive their power and prestige from different currents of thought. Having invoked the god in these terms, the practitioner should beg the god 'that you may give divine and supreme power to this statue (ξόανον) …' (line 302). It is highly significant that the object of consecration is called ξόανον instead of δακτυλίδιον, 'a little ring', as in the spell's title, because the former term's usage indicates that the magical ring functions as a divine statue within the rite.[71] According to Egyptian theology, a statue does not merely represent a physical image of the divinity, but truly incarnates the god on earth, after the requisite ritual of Opening the Mouth has been conducted onto the statue.[72] In the following, it will be shown that this ritual of

---

[69] This technique is probably meant to make the animal's pulse enter the ring. A similar technique is found in the 'Sword of Moses': Moses Gaster, *Studies and Texts in Folklore, Magic, Medieval Romance, Hebrew Apocrypha, and Samaritan Archaeology* 3 vols. (London 1925–1928) vol. 1, 324–325. I thank C.H. Faraone for this reference.

[70] On the Maskelli-Maskello formula and the seven vowels, see chapter 3.3. On the *Ephesia Grammata*, see Frankfurter, 'Magic of Writing and Writing of Magic', 195f.

[71] The word ξόανον is the Greek technical term to denote divine images or objects made of various materials, not just of wood as Pausanias' usage of the word suggests. The exact nature of the word is discussed in A.A. Donuhue, *Xoana and the Origins of Greek Sculpture* (American Classical Studies 15; Atlanta 1988) 9–174. I thank Ian Moyer for this reference. In line 302 the ring is called a ξόανον as well: 'I have called upon you greatest god{s} and through you upon everything in order that you give divine and greatest power to this carved object (ξοάνῳ)'.

[72] Assmann, *Ägypten, Theologie und Frömmigkeit*, 55–58.

Opening the Mouth provides a meaningful framework to understand the subsequent invocations of the *Ouphôr*. The present invocation closes with the exhortation 'Verily, lord {lord}, bring to perfection a perfect rite (τέλει τελείαν τελετήν)', which presents a subtle variant on the traditional Greek coda to end hexametrical incantations, 'bring to perfection a perfect incantation (τέλεσον τελέαν ἐπαοιδήν)' attested since Aristophanes (4th century BCE) and still operative in early Greek magical spells found in Egypt (PGM XX and CXXII; late Ptolemaic or early Roman period).[73] By using this closing line, the editor of the prose invocation inscribed the hybrid prayer into a long-standing tradition of poetic charms that originated outside Egypt.

As was said above, whenever the practitioner wishes to put the ring to use, he should 'recite the greatest *Ouphôr*' (line 316), which consists of two separate invocations. Unlike the most recent translation of the spell suggests, *Ouphôr* is not the name of an unknown deity, but, as Joseph Vergote demonstrated as early as in 1961, a vocalised reproduction of Egyptian *wp.t-r3*, the traditional name of the age-old ritual of Opening the Mouth.[74] The occurrence of the word ξόανον and the name *Ouphôr* reveal hence that the ritual framework of the present ring spell is Egyptian in nature, regardless of the hybrid character of the invocation of 'the greatest god'.

The ritual of Opening the Mouth, referred to as early as in the fourth dynasty tomb of Meten and the Pyramid Texts, was originally a means to enable statues to perform certain life-preserving actions, like breathing, eating, drinking.[75] Prior to installation in a temple, a statue had to be consecrated in the workshop to appoint it an owner

---

[73] According to Faraone, the traditional Greek coda was used in the early Greek spells from Egypt, because 'the user of the collection or his clients expected that any [love] spell intoned in the Greek language, regardless of its origin, need to end with this traditional Greek coda'; Christopher A. Faraone, 'Handbooks and Anthologies: The Collection of Greek and Egyptian Incantations in Late Hellenistic Egypt' *AfR* 2 (2000) 195–214, 209.

[74] Morton Smith's translation amends the text unnecessarily: 'saying the greatest [name] *Ouphôr*' and 'this *Ouphôr* is the [god] whom Ourbikos used', *GMPT*, 164. The second invocation is actually not 'the invocation to *Ouphôr*' (*GMPT*, 165), but 'the invocation of *Ouphôr*'. On the etymology of *Ouphôr*, see, J. Vergote, 'Sur les mots composés en Egyptien et en Copte' *BIOR* 18 (1961) 208–214, 213–214.

[75] The standard edition of the ritual is E. Otto, *Das ägyptische Mundöffnungsritual* (ÄgAbh. 3; Wiesbaden 1960) who gathered the existing sources. See for translation also: Jean-Claude Goyon, *Rituels funéraires de l'ancienne Égypte. Introduction, traduction et commentaire* Littératures anciennes du Proche Orient, 4 (Les Éditions du Cerf; Paris 1972) 87–182. For the Pyramid Texts, see Utterances 20–22 (§§ 11–15) and 35ff. (§ 27ff.).

and instil it with 'life' through a succession of rites like purification, touching the statue with certain implements, sacrificing an ox, goose and a goat, clothing it and feeding it. The available sources make clear that, from early onwards, its use was extended to the funerary realm as a rite to be conducted onto the mummy before it was laid to rest in its tomb to enable the deceased to take the offerings and lead a life in the hereafter.[76] Temple texts of the Ptolemaic Period indicate that the ritual was even performed to consecrate the entire temple building in order to imbue its divine statues and wall reliefs with life.[77] Similarly, amulets or statuettes that served in magical rites had to be 'opened the mouth' as well.[78] The introduction to the two *Ouphôr* invocations does not give an explicit instruction to perform the ritual of Opening the Mouth on the ring. Instead, it claims to be a condensed version of the ritual itself—which amounts to the same thing, albeit a bit more pretentious. Since the text gives a correct definition of the ritual, there can be no doubt about the authenticity of this claim:

---

[76] The majority of sources for this ritual derive from a number of New Kingdom tombs on whose walls a selection of scenes display the proceedings of the ritual as performed, in most cases, onto the mummy. The most famous and most elaborate of these is found in Rekhmire's tomb from the 18th dynasty (TT 100). Although the ritual text was only occasionally copied onto the walls of the tomb in the Late Period, the ritual text is still attested on three hieratic papyri of the Roman period: P.Louvre 3155, P. Cairo CG 58036 and a papyrus from Saqqara mentioned in M.G. Daressy, 'Fragments d'un livre de l'ouverture de la bouche' *ASAE* 22 (1922), 193–198; for the first two manuscripts, see, E. Schiaparelli, *Il libro dei funerali degli antichi Egiziani*, 2 vols. (Rome, Turin 1881–1890) text C, pls. 19–49 and W. Golénischeff, *Papyrus hiératiques CG 83* (Cairo 1927) 231–268 and pls. 36–39. The Demotic mortuary *Liturgy of Opening the Mouth for breathing* is a composition unknown before the Roman period preserved in several copies from the first century CE, probably all coming from Akhmim (Panopolis). Apparently, the ritual was still meaningful enough in the Roman period to be abridged and transformed into a new funerary text; for the manuscripts, see, Mark Smith, *The Liturgy of Opening the Mouth for Breathing* (Oxford 1993).

[77] A.M. Blackman and H.W. Fairman, 'The consecration of an Egyptian temple according to the use of Edfu' *JEA* 32 (1946) 75–91; Dieter Kurth, *Treffpunkt der Götter. Inschriften aus dem Tempel des Horus von Edfu* (Zürich, Munich 1994) 153–156; according to a note on page 355 a similar text is preserved in Philae. A variant adaptation of the ritual of Opening the Mouth for the temple building can be found in the Hibis temple (27th dynasty); Eugene Cruz-Uribe, 'Opening of the Mouth as Temple Ritual', in: E. Teeter and J.A. Larson (eds.), *Gold of Praise. Fs. E.F. Wente* (SAOC 58; Chicago 1999) 69–73.

[78] For example, the magical brick with the human figure described in *Book of the Dead* spell 151 and a Horus statue in a healing rite (P. Vienna ÄS 3925); Barbara Lüscher, *Untersuchungen zu Totenbuch Spruch 151* (Studien zum Altägyptischen Totenbuch 2; Wiesbaden 1998) 259 and Helmut Satzinger, '"Horus auf den Krokodilen": Stele

> Whenever you want to command the god, give command after you have said the great *Ouphôr* and he (i.e. the god[79]) will fulfil: you have the rite of the greatest and divine execution (ἐνεργήματος). This is the *Ouphôr* of which Ourbikos made use. The holy *Ouphôr*, the true one, has carefully (ἀληθῶς) been written down in all brevity, through which all moulded figures (πλάσματα) and engraved images (γλυφαί) and carved statues (ξόανα) are kindled to life (ζωπυρεῖται): because this is the true one, the others, that carry on at great length, bring lies while containing idle length. So keep it in secrecy as a great mystery. Conceal, conceal.
> [PGM XII.316–322]

These introductory lines are exemplary for the phenomenon, which, in contrast with the Demotic spells, is almost a distinctive feature of the *Greek Magical Papyri*, to advertise explicitly rituals by ascribing the techniques and prayers to famous authors and magicians, while praising the qualities and trustworthiness of the spell at length. Although these marketing techniques can already be found in pharaonic ritual and magical texts and were also occasionally used in the Demotic spells, the editors of the Greek spells were seemingly obsessed with the technique and applied it almost as a rule.[80] In this particular case, the text posits the idea that it competes with alternative texts for the reader's confidence by stressing its genuine character and brevity at the expense of the alternative spells. Apart from these qualities, the ritual text also assumes authority and prestige by asserting that a certain Ourbikos, who is otherwise unknown, made use of it.[81] In other words: if Ourbikos made use of it, how could it possibly be wrong?

The *Ouphôr* rite prescribes none of the many ritual acts that make up, and are essential to, the ritual of Opening the Mouth, so that it is in effect a purely oral affair.[82] Both invocations are different from any of the recitations prescribed for the ritual of Opening the Mouth, although they share a few distinctive features with the classical ritual which prove the authentic roots of the *Ouphôr* rite. The first invocation runs as follows:

---

oder Statue?', in: Bettina Schmitz (ed.), *Festschrift Arne Eggebrecht* (HÄB 48; Hildesheim 2002) 85–88, 86.

[79] The ring itself could be meant as well.

[80] This topic is treated in detail in chapter 6.4.

[81] The name derives probably from Egyptian *Ḥr-bik*, 'Horus-the-falcon' (DN, 799): see, Moyer and Dieleman, 'Miniaturization', 60 fn. 53.

[82] The Roman-period mortuary *Liturgy of Opening the Mouth for Breathing* is also devoid of ritual instructions, thus relying solely on the power of the word.

Beginning

| The gates of the heaven were opened | the gates of the earth were opened |
| The course of the sea was opened | the course of the rivers was opened |

My spirit (πνεῦμα) was heard by all gods and demons;
My spirit was heard by the heavenly spirit (πνεύματος);
My spirit was heard by the earthly spirit;
My spirit was heard by the marine spirit;
My spirit was heard by the riverine spirit;
Give, therefore, spirit (πνεῦμα) to the mystery that has been prepared by me,
[O] gods whom I have named and called upon,
Give breath (πνοήν) to the mystery that has been prepared by me.

[PGM XII.323–333][83]

The contents and structure of the opening lines are reminiscent of the first line of the 'Opening of the Mouth' closing prayer, which was recited when the statue was finally put into its shrine. In this prayer, opening the wooden doors of the shrine is likened to the opening of heaven:

> Words to be spoken:
> Both gates of heaven are opened (*wn*); both gates of the god's house are opened (*sš*):
> The house is opened (*wn*) for its lord,
> Who goes out when he wants to go out,
> Who enters, when he wants to enter.
> Go inside, you lord.
> I am Thoth who is ignorant of who entered; I am an ignorant;
> I know that not knowing the *ba* is to be ignorant of its abomination.
> 
> [Otto, scene 74A]

The notion of 'opening the gates of heaven and earth' was central to the imagery and ritual techniques of the liturgy of the morning ritual. Conducted on a daily basis in the innermost shrine of the temple, this ritual served as the morning toilet for the divinity, who, present in the form of its statue, was woken up, washed, clothed and fed in the course of the rite. Since this ritual was concerned with preserving the vitality of the divine statue, it is not surprising that its procedures, known from sources of the New Kingdom and the Greco-Roman period,[84] agree

---

[83] The layout of the present translation follows the actual layout of the text on the manuscript.

[84] The main New Kingdom sources are the ritual scenes in the chapels of the

to a large extent with those of the ritual of Opening the Mouth.[85] At the moment that the wooden doors of the holy shrine holding the divine statue were opened, the following prayer, taken from the ritual of Amun-Re, was recited:

> **Spell for** revealing the face (*wn-ḥr*) of the divinity.
> **Words to be spoken:**
> Both gates of heaven are opened (*wn*); both gates of the earth are
>     opened (*sš*);
> Geb is greeted with the speech of the gods, who are firmly established
>     on their[86] thrones;
> Both gates of heaven are opened (*wn*); the Ennead is shining;
> Lofty is Amun-Re, lord of the throne[s] of the two countries, on his
>     great throne;
> Lofty is the great Ennead on its throne;
> Your beauty belongs to you, Amun-Re, lord of the throne[s] of the two
>     countries;
> O naked one, be clothed! O you, who must be girded, gird yourself!
>                                                    [P. Berlin 3055 4/3–6][87]

Apart from the imagery of the opening lines of the first *Ouphôr* invocation, the text's layout recalls Egyptian texts as well. The scribe carefully juxtaposed the first two lines so as to suggest their interdependence and poetic structure (the layout is retained in the translation). Its layout is identical to, for example, the Demotic *Harpist's Song*, an invective preserved on a second century CE manuscript, which follows an age-old model of Egyptian verse-making. In the *Harpist's Song*, each verse

---

funerary complex of Sethi I in Abydos (19th dynasty) and the hieratic ritual texts of the liturgy for Amun (P. Berlin 3055) and his consort Mut (P. Berlin 3053, beginning P. Berlin 3014), both dated to the 21st-22nd dynasty. All relevant versions are synoptically listed in Waltraud Guglielmi and Knut Buroh, 'Die Eingangssprüche des Täglichen Tempelrituals nach Papyrus Berlin 3055 (I,1-VI,3)', in: Jacobus van Dijk (ed.), *Essays on Ancient Egypt in Honour of Herman te Velde* (Egyptological Memoirs 1; Groningen 1997) 101–166, 134–166; see also Alexandre Moret, *Le rituel du culte divin journalier en Égypte* (BdE 14; Paris 1902). The daily temple ritual of the Greco-Roman period is depicted on the walls of all major temples of this period; see for a useful translation of the Edfu version: Dieter Kurth, *Treffpunkt der Götter*, 89–93. The similarities between the New Kingdom and the Greco-Roman material reveal that the procedures had hardly changed during the intermediate 1000 years.

[85] In fact, the layout of the text of the ritual of Opening the Mouth in the Edfu temple juxtaposes and combines the two rituals in an ingenious and meaningful way; Blackman and Fairman, 'The consecration of an Egyptian temple according to the use of Edfu', 86.

[86] I emend the 3rd singular feminine suffix pronoun (=*s*) to 3rd plural (=*sn*).

[87] Guglielmi and Buroh, 'Die Eingangssprüche des Täglichen Tempelrituals', 122–124; Moret, *Culte divin journalier*, 113.

line is a self-contained semantic unit that falls apart into two complementary or contrasting phrases separated by a red dot, the verse point.[88]

By its play on the word πνεῦμα, the densely composed invocation evokes a wide range of religious and philosophical currents of thought that were widespread in the Roman period. The basic meaning of πνεῦμα is 'wind in motion' but as early as the fifth century BCE it was developed in Greek medicine and philosophy into a concept that denotes 'breath of life' or 'spirit of the cosmos'.[89] It became even the central concept of Stoic physics as referring to the divine soul that pervades the whole cosmos and acts as its cohesive principle. In the *Septuagint*, it refers to the soul of God and in the *New Testament* it became the concept of the Holy Spirit.[90] At the time of the Roman period, the term had consequently become a multi-layered concept that could appeal to philosophical and religious communities of a different kind. However, given the Egyptian context of the spell, the Egyptian idea of the *ba*, the essence or manifestation of the divinity present in the statue, will have prevailed for the editors, regardless of the possible interpretations of their readers. In the final line, the text makes clear that the rite is concerned with πνοή (breath), a synonym of πνεῦμα, although without the same broad range of metaphorical connotations. As in the first ring spell, the practitioner wants his ring (the mystery) to be imbued with enlivening breath through the help of the gods and powerful spirits, which pervade the whole cosmos (heaven, earth, sea and river).[91]

The second *Ouphôr* invocation (lines 336–350) is a list of *voces magicae* consisting of 15 entries written on a separate line each. The text is laid out in three uneven columns separated by a blank space,

---

[88] See the plates in H.-J. Thissen, *Der verkommene Harfenspieler. Eine altägyptische Invektive (P. Wien KM 3877)* (Demotische Studien 11; Sommerhausen 1992). Note that the layout of the first ring spell does not reproduce the verse structure of the hexametrical hymn (lines 244–252) by writing each verse line on a separate line as in Homeric papyri from Egypt.

[89] See for a useful summary of this complex development: T. Tieleman, 'Pneuma' *DNP—Altertum* 9, 1181–1182.

[90] J. Reiling, 'Holy Spirit' *DDD* 418a–424a.

[91] Note that the netherworld region is lacking in this list. According to pharaonic conceptions the cosmos consisted of sky, earth and netherworld, together surrounded by the primeval ocean, called Nun.

the first two columns positioned fairly close to each other. The text of the first and second column is the same throughout the list, but the third column contains a different name for each line. The list is separated from the first *Ouphôr* invocation by a short remark that repeats the essential qualities mentioned in the introduction: secrecy, truth and conciseness.

> Hide, hide the true Ouphôr that, in a concise form (ἐν συντομείᾳ), contains the truth    Invocation of Ouphôr:
> 
> | ÊI | IEOU | MAREITH |
> |---|---|---|
> | ÊI | IEOU | MONTHEATHIMONGITH |
> | ÊI | IEOU | KHAREÔTHMONKÊB |
> | ÊI | IEOU | SÔKHOUSÔRSÔÊ |
> | ÊI | IEOU | TIÔTIÔ OUIÊR |
> | ÊI | IEOU | KHARÔKHSIKHARMIÔTH |
> | ÊI | IEOU | SATHIMÔOUEÊOU |
> | ÊI | IEOU | RAIRAI MOURIRAI |
> | ÊI | IEOU | AMOUNÉEI OUSIRI |
> | ÊI | IEOU | PHIRIMNOUN |
> | ÊI | IEOU | ANMORKHATHI OUER |
> | ÊI | IEOU | ANKHEREPHRENEPSOUPHIRIGKH |
> | ÊI | IEOU | ORKHIMOROÎPOUGTH |
> | ÊI | IEOU | MAKHPSAKHATHANTH |
> | ÊI | IEOU | MOROTH |
>
> [PGM XII.334–350][92]

Robert Ritner has suggested to read the repetitive group of the first two columns as a phonetic transcription of Egyptian *'I îȝw*, a greeting formula meaning 'O hail'.[93] Heinz J. Thissen added substantial weight to this identification by pointing out that the Demotic sign for *'I* is indeed glossed ÊI in P. London-Leiden.[94] The second *Ouphôr* invocation is hence merely a list of magical names, each of which is introduced by an Egyptian greeting formula. In fact, the repetition of greeting formula with divine name defines the text as an Egyptian litany, a list-like hymn, addressed to the sun god in particular, which enumerates the deity's names, epithets and cult places, all arranged in a sequence

---

[92] The layout of the present translation reproduces the layout of the text on the actual manuscript.

[93] GMPT, 165, fn. 86.

[94] P. London-Leiden 7/24 and 15/9; Thissen, 'Ägyptologische Beiträge zu den griechischen magischen Papyri', 299.

of fixed opening greetings.[95] Take for example the following litany addressed to the sun god Re preserved on a 21st dynasty funerary manuscript.[96]

> Adoring Re-Harakhti by [titles omitted] Nesitanebtasheru:
> Hail to you (*i.nd-ḥr=k*) Re in your beautiful rising (*wbn*),
> Hail to you Re who rises (*ḫʿj*) beautifully,
> Hail to you Re in your beautiful shining,
> Hail to you Re who is beautiful,
> Hail to you Re who is strong,
> Hail to you Re who is great,
> Hail to you Re who shines forth,
> Hail to you Re who is respected (*šfj.tı̓*),
> Hail to you Re who is honoured (*wšš.tı̓*),
> Hail to you Re who is divine,
> Hail to you Re who is complete (*ḥtm.tı̓*),
> Hail to you Re who is perfect (*ı̓p.tı̓*),
> Hail to you Re who is enduring (*dd.tı̓*),
> As a litany (*[w]dnw*) for Re-Harakhti,
> A litany (*wdnw*) of all his names that are in heaven and on earth.
> [P. Greenfield sheet 66 (plate 77)]

In the light of the other borrowings from the ritual of Opening the Mouth in the *Ouphôr* rite, it is not without importance that one of the

---

[95] According to Jan Assmann, listing and a combination of repetition with variation are formal criteria of the litany, see 'Litanei' *LdÄ* III 1062–1066 and also Idem, *Liturgische Lieder an den Sonnengott. Untersuchungen zur altägyptischen Hymnik, I* (MÄS 19; Munich 1969) 90 for discussion and 70–71 for an example. The Egyptian generic term for litany, *wdn*, means originally 'to bring food offerings accompanied by recitations', see S. Schott, 'Eine ägyptische Bezeichnung für Litaneien', in: O. Firchow (ed.), *Ägyptologische Studien. Fs. Grapow* (Berlin 1955) 289–295, 294. See also E. Hornung, *Das Buch der Anbetung des Re im Westen (Sonnenlitanei) nach den Versionen des Neuen Reiches* (AH 2–3; Genf 1975–1977).

[96] The Greenfield papyrus is an impressive collection of funerary spells made for Nesitanebtasheru, daughter of Pinudjem II, who lived during the tenth century BCE. It is impressive for its size, its richness in *Book of the Dead* spells, litanies, vignettes and its excellent state of preservation. Publication: E.A. Wallis Budge, *The Greenfield Papyrus in the British Museum. The funerary papyrus of princess Nesitanebtasheru, daughter of Painetchem II and Nesi-Khensu, and priestess of Amen-Ra at Thebes* (London 1912); recent re-analysis of the texts: C. Zaluskowski, *Texte ausserhalb der Totenbuch-Tradierung in Pap. Greenfield* (Bonn 1996) [non vidi]. A glance over the plates of P. Greenfield reveals immediately, even to the untrained eye, the importance of litanies and lists in the manuscript. The correspondence between the layout of the Ouphôr invocation and the lists and litanies of P. Greenfield is striking; litanies, plates 30, 31, 50, 75–77, 80, 83, 85, 87, 88; lists, plates 40–44, 70, 76–79, 85, 86, 113, 114. See also Jean-Claude Goyon, *Le Papyrus d'Imouthès fils de Psintaés au Metropolitan Museum of Art de New York (Papyrus MMA 35.9.21)* (New York 1999) plates 1 and 41–43.

closing scenes of the traditional Opening the Mouth ritual (scene 71) contains a similar litany for the sun god Re:

> O (*i*) Re [lord of ma'at], O Re [who lives on ma'a]t,
> O Re [who rejoices] in ma'at, O Re [who ...] in ma'at, O Re [who ... ma'at],
> O Re [who is effective in] ma'at, O Re [who is enduring in] ma'at, O Re who exults in ma'at,
> O Re [who is established through ma']at, O Re who is strong through ma'at, O Re [who is ... through ma'at],
> O Re who is adorned with ma'at, O Re [who is ...] with ma'at,
> O Re who rises with ma'at, O Re [who shines] with ma'at, O Re who sets with ma'at,
> O Re who feeds on ma'at, O Re who unites with ma'at, O Re who unites with ma'at as first,
> O Re whose occasions endure, whose plans are excellent, whose character is sincere, who founded ma'at after he had created it,
> I have come to you (because) I am Thoth who is your equal
> [Otto, scene 71]

The identification of ÊI IEOU as *'I ȝw* is rather convincing for phonetic and generic reasons, but it has to be taken into account that in none of the many Egyptian litanies a greeting formula like *'I ȝw*, which should be reconstructed as 𓀀𓇋𓄿𓅱𓀢 or 𓇋𓄿𓅱𓀢, can be found. The standard greeting formulas are *dwȝ n=k, ȝw n=k, i.nḏ-ḥr=k, ṯs=k m ḥtp* or *iy.wy m ḥtp*. Nonetheless, the formal generic criteria of listing, repetition and variation combined with a layout in three separate columns are persuasive enough to define the *Ouphôr* invocation as an Egyptian litany in Greek. As in the first two lines of the preceding invocation, the scribe was again eager to retain the traditional textual format in the layout of the text, which reveals that he was aware of the text's Egyptian roots. The names that follow after each greeting formula are nothing but *voces magicae* as they can be found throughout the PGM. Although some can be interpreted as deriving from Egyptian epithets or phrases, they were part of an international current of magical thought, which, in this particular case, are fitted in into a traditional Egyptian textual format.

To conclude the foregoing analysis, it is warranted to state that the *Ouphôr* rite, besides its name, shows striking similarities with the Egyptian ritual of Opening the Mouth, even if none of the requisite ritual acts are prescribed in the Greek text. Those priests participating in the Egyptian ritual of Opening the Mouth and the daily ritual in the temple, tried through a fixed succession of ritual acts to make contact with the divine energy potentially present in the statue. Likewise, the *Ouphôr* rite creates a setting in which the practitioner addresses the potent energy that is contained in his ring. If the ring and its stone are imagined as a miniature shrine containing its statue, similar to those set up in an Egyptian temple, the practitioner changes into an Egyptian priest who is opening the wooden doors of the divine shrine, adoring the divine statue and motivating it to bestow its life-generating powers upon earth. In this fashion, the *Ouphôr* rite is no less than a miniaturized cosmic drama such as those rituals that were enacted in the Egyptian temples on a daily basis. The pharaonic ritual of Opening the Mouth was tightly bound to an Egyptian temple complex or, in the case of performing it onto the mummy, to the forecourt of the tomb chapel, but the *Ouphôr* rite has been adapted to a portable, cheap and easily performed ritual believed to work anywhere and anytime 'because this is the true one' (line 320).

### 5.4. *Once again the 'Paradox of Translation'*

The two ring spells discussed in the foregoing are complex rites, which combine in a meaningful way ritual techniques, textual forms and religious vocabulary and imagery that originate from different culture groups. In the first spell, the stone should be inscribed with a design combining Jewish names and an Egyptian *Ouroboros* snake and is consecrated with an invocation of a more or less anonymous pantheistic deity. The invocation's imagery and stylistic devices derive to a large extent from ancient Egyptian sources except for the hexametrical hymn, the idea of the seven heavenly spheres and the 'Names of the Nations' motif. In the second spell, a similar combination of traditional Egyptian and Hellenistic ideas is at work. The ritual instructions stress the importance of the zodiac in determining the right moment of consecration, whereas the *Ouphôr* rite is clearly an appropriation of a traditional Egyptian ritual, irrespective of the fact that only the name was left unchanged. The two *Ouphôr* invocations imitate ancient Egyptian ritual hymns as far as their textual form is concerned, but, on the level of phraseology, include idiom and magical names that open up a wide intertextual and intercultural field.

The recurrence of the prose hymn to the anonymous All-Lord in PGM XIII and XXI illustrates rather well that these kind of spells were composed with the help of other texts, some of which were considered quite prestigious judging from their reuse towards different ritual aims. This practice of collecting religious texts to use them as sourcebooks to compose new spells came also to light in the analysis of the Demotic magical spells in chapters 3 and 4. In that case, however, it resulted in a complex combination of languages and their scripts. The stylistic devices and imagery used in the Demotic spells remain well within the boundaries of Egyptian religious thought, even in those rare cases when an invocation in Greek is inserted. This is an important distinction between the Demotic and Greek spells which needs to be stressed. Although the two ring spells are entirely written in Greek, they rely heavily on sources from different cultural backgrounds, which makes them into complex products of an intercultural environment.

The reader will have noticed that the discussion of the 'Names of the Nations' motif returned to issues that have been dealt with in the introductory chapter. Celsus and Porphyry advocate the idea that the various appellations for the gods in different languages are but variants of one and the same name, a view to which Origen, Iamblichus and *Corpus Hermeticum* XVI oppose vehemently, all three for different reasons. The spell PGM XII 201–269 takes clearly issue in this debate by addressing the All-Lord with his variant names as they are used among different religious groups. It thus acknowledges that the variants are meaningful and magically potent, but, at the same time, that they are merely weak parallels of the *nomen verum*, 'your great name for the consecration', that is not explicitly given. This debate was taken up in the introduction to coin the phrase 'paradox of translation' and to show that the Demotic spells are governed by this tension between translation and prohibition. The *Ouphôr* rite is an illustrative case in which the prohibition to translate is clearly trespassed. It is certainly not a slavish translation of the ritual of Opening the Mouth, since none of the essential ritual acts of the original ritual appear in the *Ouphôr* rite, but, notwithstanding, the advertising introduction plays upon the ritual's Egyptian origin by referring to this Ourbikos who probably was a well-known Egyptian priest among the intended audience. Even more convincing of its genuine Egyptian roots are the litany and the imagery of 'opening the gates of heaven and earth', which must be the result of a direct consultation of hieratic or Demotic ritual texts. It is therefore intriguing to see that the ring spells, which occur together with Demotic spells on one and the same manuscript, bring us back, from a different perspective, to this 'paradox of translation', although, for the Greek texts, the paradox' spell had been broken.

CHAPTER SIX

## OF PRIESTS AND PRESTIGE
## THE NEED FOR AN AUTHORITATIVE TRADITION

### 6.1. *Introduction*

The Greek section of P. Leiden I 384 verso closes with a text that is likely to draw immediate attention on the part of a modern reader due to its rather bizarre contents (PGM XII.401–444). Unlike the foregoing eighteen spells, the text is not concerned with procuring a magical effect itself, but claims to provide a translation key for a proper understanding of the ingredients prescribed in magical recipes. The text, which will be given in full in the following section, is actually a catalogue listing a fair number of rather repulsive bodily fluids and body parts of animals and gods like crocodile dung, lion semen, a hawk's heart, semen of Hermes, and Kronos' blood. These items occur only in the left column of the list, whereas the right column consists of herbs, minerals and animal substances that are known from other contemporary magical and medicinal sources. The list, consisting of thirty-seven entries, presents thus nothing more than encoded ingredients with their respective decoded solutions. In this way, crocodile dung appears to be Ethiopian soil, while semen of Hermes is a code name for the herb dill: the unusual character of the ingredients is thus only superficial. In fact, these ingredients must have been easily available in Egypt or in any flourishing harbour town of the Roman Empire. In this respect, the text should have been an indispensable tool for any magician who did not want to be misled by the encoded recipes of his magical books.

The catalogue is preceded by a short introduction that not only explains the function of the list, but also tries to take away any suspicion on the part of the reader about the nature and reliability of the list. It runs as follows.

> Interpretations (ἑρμηνεύματα) translated (μεθηρμηνευμένα) from the holy (writings), of which the temple scribes (ἱερογραμματεῖς) made use. Because of the nosiness (περιεργίαν) of the masses, they (the temple scribes) wrote the (names of the) herbs and other things that they made use of

> on statues of gods in order that they (the masses), since they do not take precautions (μὴ εὐλαβούμενοι), do not meddle (περιεργάζωνται)[1] at all, due to the inevitable result of their mistake. However, we have collected the solutions (λύσεις) from many copies, all of them secret.
>
> [PGM XII.401–407]

The rather densely written introduction claims that the list derives from holy writings that were in use by the *hierogrammateis*, a common technical term for Egyptian priests who wrote the native language and scripts.[2] The reader is made to believe that these priests used to encode the names of necessary ritual ingredients to prevent untrained laymen from performing any kind of ritual activity. Since the lay masses would be excessively curious about rituals, the priests encoded the ingredients and wrote them on statues of gods. If then, for whatever reason, any uninitiated might ever get hold of the ritual texts, he would nonetheless be unable to perform any magical feat, since he would only make harmless errors out of ignorance. To counter this problem, the present list pretends to give the necessary solutions as they were found in an impressive amount of secret, and thus authentic, Egyptian documents. Who could still mistrust the authenticity of the list after having read the introduction?

These introductory lines and its following list raise some fundamental questions about the social and cultural embedding of the magical manuscripts that have been studied so far. First of all, statues engraved with the names of ingredients for magical rituals as described in the introductory text are not attested in Egypt for any time period. Egyptian statues were indeed provided with texts in the majority of cases, but, in the case of private statuary, only the owner's name, titles and sometimes a biographical account were written on the statue, whereas cult statues were only provided with their name, if at all, or attributes. The so-called healing statues and *Horus cippi* were written all over with magical spells for curing snakebites and scorpion stings, but none of the preserved specimens contains a list of ingredients. In fact, these statues could do without ritual prescriptions, because the patient was only required to drink the water that he or she had first poured over the

---

[1] The verb περιεργάζειν has a derived meaning 'assiduously investigating and performing rituals', the overtones of which are certainly brought into play in the present passage; cf. 'Zauberei treiben', Preisendanz, *PGM II*, 84, and 'practice magic', Betz and Scarborough in *GMPT*, 167. In 1Ep.Cor.9.13 ἐργάζειν denotes 'performing rituals'.

[2] See for a more detailed description of the duties of these priests section 6.3.1.

statue.[3] It is therefore warranted to conclude that the present introductory lines attribute to the Egyptian temple scribes a custom that was factually not extant in antiquity.[4]

It is clear that the introductory lines serve for the intended reader as a validation of the decoded list's trustworthiness. As with the introductory text to the *Ouphôr* rite, the present text tries to impress and to take away any suspicion on the reader's part by stressing the Egyptian origin and secret character of the list. Since the advertising text refers to a priestly custom that was not extant in historical reality, it should be considered a fiction, a marketing technique, which anticipates the client's needs, aspirations and expectations. The question is then who this client or intended reader was. In view of the false claim about Egyptian statues, it is very unlikely that the text aims at convincing Egyptian priests, who would of course have known that ingredients were not written on statues of gods. However, this observation seems at odds with the conclusion of the previous chapters that the two handbooks must have circulated among Egyptian priests. Who else than Egyptian priests could have consulted these bilingual manuscripts with their multiple Egyptian scripts?

To complicate matters further, the narrator of the introductory lines sets Egyptian priests apart from himself and his readership by speaking about 'them', the temple scribes, and 'us', the compilers and readers of the present text. According to the text, 'we' have collected a number of 'their' secret books to translate them and share their content with other members of 'our' group. In this fashion, the text constructs an image of the temple scribes that is based on notions of separation, secrecy, translation and professional knowledge—knowledge that the narrator and his in-group deeply desire. A similar dichotomy seems to be evoked in a recipe that describes the ritual techniques for a correct picking of plants (PGM IV.2967–3006), which is preserved in the Great Magical Papyrus of Paris, which manuscript formed part of the Theban Magical Library

---

[3] A valuable overview is given in László Kákosy, *Egyptian Healing Statues in Three Museums in Italy (Turin, Florence, Naples)* (Catalogo del Museo Egizio di Torino, Serie prima—monumenti e testi IX; Turin 1999) 9–34.

[4] Nonetheless, it is very likely that the author of the text meant to refer to the *Horus cippi*, because this type of magical statues was very popular in the Late and Greco-Roman period. Any inhabitant of Egypt, regardless of his or her religious inclinations, must have been generally familiar with their design. The *Horus cippi* known to date are collected in Heike Sternberg-El Hotabi, *Untersuchungen zur Überlieferungsgeschichte der Horusstelen. Ein Beitrag zur Religionsgeschichte Ägyptens im 1. Jahrtausend v. Chr.* 2 Vols. (ÄgAbh 62; Wiesbaden 1999).

with certitude. A purification ritual, a libation of milk and an invocation of all deities involved in the growth of the plant must precede the picking of the plant to ensure the effectiveness of the herb.[5] The following statement introduces the description of the ritual techniques:

> Among the Egyptians, herbs are always obtained in the following manner  [PGM IV.2967f.]

Written in this fashion the clause seems to posit 'the Egyptians' as a category distinct from the narrator and his implied audience, who are willing to adopt, or learn about, the idiosyncratic ritual techniques of this ethnic category.

In order to come to a better understanding of the underlying mechanisms of the marketing strategy, it is necessary to examine the introductory text and its wider cultural and historical context, a task taken up in the present chapter. The contents and form of the text belong to a current of thought that was widespread in the Roman period, so that it will not suffice to concentrate fully on the Egyptian priests themselves. Greek and Roman sources will have to be taken into account as well, since they throw light on the existence and the form of widespread stereotyped images of the Egyptian priesthood. The topic will be addressed from a variety of angles in order to subdivide the problem and to discuss a range of suggestions. Four questions will serve as pillars to the discussion and, at the same time, as successive stages of the line of argument.

1. What is this text about?
2. About whom is the text speaking?
3. In what way does the text acquire authority and prestige for what kind of reader?
4. Who is speaking?

The first three questions will be considered in the following three sections of the present chapter. Since this book is not only concerned with Egyptologists, the discussion of the tasks and concepts of the Egyptian

---

[5] Knowledge of the rituals to preserve a plant's magical power when picking it was considered indispensable for any magician of the Greco-Roman period. The Great Magical Papyrus of Paris contains two more recipes that give ritual directions for the picking of plants: PGM IV.286–295 and 3172–3208. For a collection and analysis of ancient sources, see, A. Delatte, *Herbarius. Recherches sur le cérémonial usité chez les anciens pour la cueillette des simples et des plantes magiques* (3rd ed.; Brussels 1961). The techniques described in this spell are undoubtedly of Egyptian origin, see, Ritner, *The Mechanics of Ancient Egyptian Magical Practice*, 39f.

priesthood is given ample attention. These three fairly independent sections will finally enable a discussion of the pertinent and most tenacious question that haunts this study from the outset: who is speaking, or, to whom did this all make sense? The next chapter will address this subject and present a hypothesis as conclusion to this study of the sociological context of the *Demotic* and *Greek Magical Papyri*.

### 6.2. *Compound plant names and ancient botany*

> In my youth, I met Apion the Grammarian, who informed me that the herb *Dog's Head* (cynocephalia), known in Egypt as *Osiritis*, was a source of divination and a protection against all black magic.
> [Pliny the Elder, *Natural History*, 30.6.18][6]

The text in question, PGM XII.401–444, consists of an explanatory introduction (401–407) and a list of ingredients (408–444), which is made up of thirty-seven entries that are conveniently arranged on the manuscript in two straight columns, of which the left contains the encrypted name and the right the decoded equivalent. The text starts in about the middle of the twelfth Greek column and occupies in its entirety the following column thirteen, which, being the final Greek column of the manuscript, is followed by four more columns in Demotic before the papyrus breaks off. In relation to the margin of the column, the text is markedly indented as if the scribe meant to add a drawing as he did at the top of the column next to a list of *voces magicae* that are identically indented (PGM XII.386–395; the drawing in question is fig. 2.2). The present section will study the nature of the list and demonstrate that it is not an idiosyncratic second or third century invention, but that, in fact, it contains remnants of botanical jargon that Egyptian priests of the pharaonic period used in their medical and magical texts. Parts of this jargon are also preserved in the book *On Botany* written in the first century CE by Pamphilus, a lexicographer

---

[6] Tr. John F. Healey. Apion the Grammarian was a scholar in Alexandria, born in El-Kharga Oasis, who wrote on Egypt and Homer. He was sent to Rome as member of a delegation of Greek citizens to plead their cause in front of emperor Caligula after severe anti-Jewish riots in Alexandria. Jospehus critiqued him severely in *Against Apion*. For similar plant synonyms, see, Plutarch, *On Isis and Osiris*, 37, 365E and 62, 376B.

from Alexandria, whose botanical glossary was used by an anonymous redactor of Dioscorides' *On the Materials of Medicine*. This link with pharaonic botany and Pamphilus reveals that the PGM list fits in with a discourse on botany and pharmacology that exceeds the historical and geographical borders of Roman Thebes and the discursive boundaries of the *Greek Magical Papyri*. This conclusion sheds of course an intriguing light on the statements made in the Greek introduction about the secret and priestly character of the list.

The list runs as follows:

| | | |
|---|---|---|
| Here they are: | | (407) |
| A snake's head: | a leech | |
| A snake's 'ball of thread': | this means soapstone | |
| Blood of a snake: | hematite | (410) |
| A bone of an ibis: | this is buckthorn | |
| Blood of a hyrax: | truly of a hyrax | |
| 'Tears' of a baboon: | dill juice | |
| Crocodile dung: | Ethiopian soil | |
| Blood of a baboon: | blood of a spotted gecko | (415) |
| Lion semen: | human semen | |
| Blood of Hephaistos: | wormwood | |
| Hairs of a baboon: | dill seed | |
| Semen of Hermes: | dill | |
| Blood of Ares: | purslane | (420) |
| Blood of an eye: | tamarisk gall | |
| Blood from a shoulder: | bear's breach | |
| From the loins: | camomile | |
| A man's bile: | turnip sap | |
| A pig's tail: | scorpion's tail[7] | (425) |
| A physician's bone: | sandstone | |
| Blood of Hestia: | camomile | |
| An eagle: | wild garlic (?) | |
| Blood of a goose: | a mulberry tree's 'milk' | |
| Kronos' spice: | piglet's milk | (430) |
| A lion's hair: | 'tongue' of a turnip | |
| Kronos' blood: | .?. of cedar | |
| Semen of Helios: | white hellebore | |
| Semen of Herakles: | this is mustard-rocket | |
| A Titan's ⟨blood⟩:[8] | wild lettuce | (435) |

---

[7] I prefer to translate literally unlike Scarborough who replaces it with 'leopard's bane' on the basis of ancient parallels, *GMPT*, 168, fn. 101.

[8] The copyist mistakenly omitted the word 'blood' in this line (435), but wrote it two lines further below (437) to delete it again and replace it with the correct word 'semen' ('a bull's semen' instead of 'a bull's blood'). Scarborough puts the wording 'a Titan's'

| | | |
|---|---|---|
| Blood from a head: | lupine | |
| A bull's semen: | egg of a blister beetle | |
| A hawk's heart: | heart of wormwood | |
| Semen of Hephaistos: | this is fleabane | |
| Semen of Ammon: | houseleek | (440) |
| Semen of Ares: | clover | |
| Fat from a head: | spurge | |
| From the belly: | earth-apple | |
| From the foot: | houseleek | [PGM XII.408–444][9] |

The title of the introduction calls the items in the list ἑρμηνεύματα (interpretations), which was otherwise used as a generic term for Greek-Latin school texts that present lists of words (alphabetically or thematically arranged), idiomatic expressions, proverbs and exercise material.[10] A papyrus fragment of the third century BCE testifies that Greek-Egyptian wordlists for everyday purposes were in use as well, probably among Greek mercenaries who were forced to settle in the Egyptian countryside.[11] Each entry consists of a Greek word, mainly household items like 'door', 'bed', 'talent', 'axe', 'iron', 'sword/knife', 'footstool' and 'pigeon', followed by its Egyptian equivalent, in this case its most literal translation, written phonetically in Greek characters. The PGM XII list should thus be read as a lexicographical study with this difference that it principally lists 'mysterious' and decoded terms that were in use in the field of magic and medicine. The items given in the left column (A) are said to derive from ancient temple texts as compiled by temple priests, whereas the right column (B) contains the solutions. It is not possible to discover an overall order in the list except for certain alphabetic and thematic groupings, which suggests that the list is compiled from several older manuscripts (or fragments of manuscripts?).[12] The reading direction of the list is unmistakably from left to right as follows from additions like 'this means' and 'this is' in column B.

---

incorrectly between square brackets in his translation, thus suggesting it is a restoration of a lacuna (*GMPT*, 168). In fact, the words are well preserved.

[9] tr. John Scarborough, GMPT, 157–169 (with explanatory notes), slightly modified.

[10] Johannes Kramer, *Glossaria Bilinguia Altera (C. Gloss. Biling. II)* (AfP Beiheft 8; Leipzig, Munich 2001) 15–18. The earliest known text of this kind dates to the early Roman Principate.

[11] Hans Quecke, 'Eine griechisch-ägyptische Wörterliste vermutlich des 3. Jh. v. Chr. (P. Heid. Inv.-Nr. G 414)' *ZPE* 116 (1997) 67–80.

[12] Three thematic groupings can be found in column A: 408–410 (snake), 420–423 (blood), 439–441 (semen). Column B contains three alphabetically arranged clusters: 414–423/4, 433–440, 441–444.

Despite the apparent disordered arrangement of the list, the forms of the names of column A exhibit a clear pattern: inner organs and bodily fluids of man, animal or god, preferably items that have a strong stench or are tabooed in daily life.[13] The inclusion of animals such as ibis, baboon, crocodile, lion and hawk demonstrates that the Egyptian fauna served as a source of inspiration to the devisers of the encoded names.[14] These animals were not only visibly present in Egypt, they were also venerated as aspects or terrestrial images of gods since early times.[15] Moreover, each of the Greek god names of the list has an Egyptian equivalent, except for the 'Titan' that is mentioned in line 435. These observations make it plausible that the items mentioned in column A have indeed an Egyptian origin.

In a recent study Lynn R. LiDonnici wishes to demonstrate that the claims about the indispensability of the list made in the introduction, are senseless pretensions.[16] She argues that none of the items of column A save one occur in recipes of the *Greek Magical Papyri*, whereas several items of column B are openly called for. In other words, 'the list provides explanation where explanation is not needed, and provides mystification rather than clarity'.[17] If applied to the available evidence this conclusion is correct, and she continues suggesting 'that the list "interprets" substances from a formulary that is lost, or that it does not interpret PGM-style materials at all, but belongs in a quite different

---

[13] Because of its rather bizarre items, the list is reminiscent of the so-called *Dreck-Apotheke*, which was particularly popular from the seventeenth century CE onwards and has its roots in medieval and classical sources. Take for example the title of a highly influential treatise: Kristian Frantz Paullini, *Neu-vermehrte, heilsame Dreck-Apotheke, wie nehmlich mit Koht und Urin fast alle, ja auch die schwerste, gifftigste Kranckheiten, und bezauberte Schaeden vom Haupt biss zun Fuessen, inn- und aeusserlich, gluecklich curiret worden* ... (Frankfurt am Main 1699). The term is also used in egyptology by W. Westendorf, *Handbuch der altägyptischen Medizin* I (Handbuch der Orientalistik 1. Abt., Bd. 36; Leiden, Cologne, New York 1999) 515.

[14] The 'hyrax' (412) and the 'eagle' (428) were not particularly well known in Egypt. In fact, the Greek word for hyrax is only known from the LXX: *GMPT*, 168, fn. 96. The eagle became a symbol of authority and kingship in Egypt only after its introduction by Alexander the Great and his Ptolemaic successors, who saw it as the sacred bird of Zeus, king of the gods: Emma Brunner-Traut, 'Adler' *LÄ* I, 64f.

[15] Dimitri Meeks and Christine Favard-Meeks, *Daily Life of the Egyptian Gods* (Ithaca, London 1996) 60–63 [translated from: *La vie quotidienne des dieux égyptiens* (Paris 1993)].

[16] Lynn R. LiDonnici, 'Beans, Fleawort, and the Blood of a Hamadryas Baboon: Recipe Ingredients in Greco-Roman Magical Materials', in: Paul Mirecki and Marvin Meyer (eds.), *Magic and Ritual in the Ancient World* (Religions in the Graeco-Roman World 141; Leiden 2002) 359–377.

[17] DiLonnici, 'Beans, Fleawort, and the Blood of a Hamadryas Baboon', 374–375.

context, one that remains unknown'.[18] This second conclusion, however, is in need of substantial refining, since it does not do justice to the cultural and textual context of the list. The following three arguments can be raised against the second conclusion:

1. Only a fraction of the magical literature of antiquity is preserved. What cannot be found in the extant sources could very well have been present in manuscripts now lost.
2. The disguising device is in fact attested in PGM XIII.1066–1067.[19] The items 'blood of a baboon' (415) and 'semen of Helios' (433) are attested in respectively PGM XIII.316 and PGM III.332, PDM xiv.889 (= P. London-Leiden verso 1/4).[20]
3. The information provided by the introduction should certainly not be taken at face value, but, at the same time, it should not be dismissed too rashly as pretentious bogus, since the method of using fanciful and repulsive names for plant and mineral species was already in use among priests in ancient Egypt and Mesopotamia.

A direct parallel to the PGM XII list is not known from ancient Egypt as might be expected from the introduction to the list, but a similar device is attested in a cuneiform botanical treatise called Uruanna=*maštakal*, which, according to its introduction, was compiled from older texts during the reign of the Assyrian king Assurbanipal (668–627 BCE).[21] The handbook, preserved in several redactions, is a list of *materia medica* consisting of plants, minerals, dairy products and animals. Each entry gives a name in Sumerian or Akkadian followed by a second term, which is probably a so-called *succedaneum*, an alternative with identical medicinal properties that could be applied in case the

---

[18] Op. cit.
[19] 'Taking the navel of a male crocodile (it means pondweed) and the egg of a scarab and a heart of a baboon (it means myrrh, perfume of lilies), put these into a blue-green faïence vessel' [PGM XIII.1065–1069].
[20] LiDonnici mentions these occurrences, but concludes from the low number of attestations that the use of the device was negligible. Given the limited number of preserved manuscripts, I hesitate to accept this conclusion and prefer to stress the fact that it was indeed in use.
[21] The majority of the texts is published (without translation) in R.C. Thompson *Cuneiform Texts from Babylonian Tablets in the British Museum* 14 (1902) and Franz Köcher, *Keilschrifttexte zur assyrisch-babylonischen Drogen- und Pflanzenkunde* (1955). See also Köcher, 'Ein Text medizinischen Inhalts aus dem neubabylonischen Grab 405', in: R.M. Boehmer, F.Pedde, B. Salje (eds.), *Uruk: die Gräber* (Deutsches Arch. Institut, Baghdad 1995) 203–217. I am highly indebted for this paragraph to professor M. Stol who generously translated the text for me and patiently answered my questions.

first mentioned plant or mineral was not available.[22] The third tablet contains a list of 138 entries that differ in character from the *succedanea*. Instead of the usual determinative for 'plant, herb, drug', a Sumerogram meaning 'secret' precedes each entry of the second column, indicating that the second column does not provide alternatives but secret code names or *Decknamen*.[23] These code names are similar in design to, but save for one item never identical with, the code names of PGM XII: for example, tail of a mongoose (III, 1), faeces of man (III, 5), dust of crossroads burnt in fire (III, 19), bone of man (III, 34), tongue of a multicoloured snake (III, 59), tallow of chameleon (III, 67), head of a male sheep (III, 108), scorpion tail (III, 122 = PGM XII.425, column B!), saliva of a dog (III, 128). Each of these items is followed by the name for an ordinary herb, mineral or liquid as in the PGM XII list. Given this exact correspondence between the device of the PGM XII list and the third tablet of the Uru-anna=*mastakal*, it might seem obvious to assume that the Greek text is a reflection of Mesopotamian influence in the *Greek Magical Papyri*. However, this conclusion is probably not correct: if Mesopotamian influence were to be found in the Greek text, it might probably only be circuitous via Egyptian priests (who were particularly receptive to new ideas from Mesopotamia since the first period of Persian domination[24]). In fact, Egyptian priests made already use of fanciful names to describe plant species since at least the New Kingdom. In one case, even an exact parallel between the PGM XII list and a pharaonic text is available. To understand correctly the relevance of the Egyptian priesthood to the subject, it is necessary to deal first with pharaonic botany before continuing the discussion.

---

[22] The *succedanea* were an important field of research in ancient medicine. Lists can be found in Galen, *Book on the Substitutes* [C.G. Kühn (ed.), *Claudii Galeni Opera Omnia* (Leipzig 1830) vol. 19, 721–747] and Paul of Aegina [I.L. Heiberg (ed.), *Corpus Medicorum Graecorum* (Leipzig 1924) vol. 19.2, 401–408]. Scarborough is wrong in calling these lists similar to the PGM XII list, since the latter's entries do not consist of alternatives but of encoded and decoded terms (*GMPT*, 167, fn. 95).

[23] Köcher, 'Ein Text medizinischen Inhalts', 204.

[24] See on the reform of the House-of-Life and the introduction of astrology in Egypt during the Persian period: Jacco Dieleman, 'Claiming the Stars: Egyptian Priests facing the Sky' *Aegyptiaca Helvetica* 17 (2003) 277–289.

## EXCURSUS: PHARAONIC BOTANY & PHARMACOLOGY

In the light of the present discussion, the following observations regarding pharaonic botany and pharmacology are particularly relevant:[25]

1. It can be concluded from the fact that medical and magical texts frequently prescribe plant and mineral substances as ingredients for offerings, potions, unguents, or amulets, that a form of botany was existent in pharaonic Egypt.
2. Plant species are occasionally given names similar in form to those in column A of the PGM XII list.
3. Medical and magical texts were written and consulted by priests, so that the fanciful plant names were known, if not invented, by Egyptian priests.

Testimonies of pharaonic botany are very few as regards detailed descriptions or meticulous drawings of plants, but occasional descriptions in medical books demonstrate that priests had at least developed a rudimentary descriptive format.[26] Nonetheless, pharaonic drug therapy relied heavily on the use of plants and minerals, so that it is justified to conclude that priests of the pharaonic period were knowledgeable in the identification and use of plant species. It is only from the Roman period that a botanical treatise systematically listing descriptions of herbs is preserved. The manuscript, now in a very fragmented state, dates to the second century CE, is written in Demotic and once formed part of the Tebtunis temple library.[27] Each heading is provided with a number, of which 86 is the highest to be recognised (possibly even 99), and the name of a herb, after which the herb's outward appearance, florescence, place of growth, medicinal properties and use are given. The herb and plant names, of which only about a dozen are

---

[25] Introductions to pharaonic botany and pharmacology are: W.R. Dawson, 'Studies in medical history: (a) The origin of the herbal, (b) Castor-oil in antiquity' *Aegyptus* 10 (1929) 47–72; M.C. Betrò, 'Erbari nell'antico Egitto' *EVO* 11 (1988) 71–110 and Lise Manniche, *An Ancient Egyptian Herbal* (London 1989). A useful bibliography can be found in: W.J. Tait, 'P. Carlsberg 230: Eleven Fragments from a Demotic Herbal', in: P.J. Frandsen (ed.), *The Carlsberg Papyri 1: Demotic Texts from the Collection* (CNI Publications 15; Copenhagen 1991) 47–92, 54f.

[26] Westendorf, *Handbuch der altägyptischen Medizin*, 492. See for pharaonic botanical descriptions: P. Ebers §§28, 128, 294; P. Berlin 3038 §118; P. Brooklyn 47.218.48+85 §§65c, 66a, 90a.

[27] Publication: Tait, 'P. Carlsberg 230: Eleven Fragments from a Demotic Herbal'.

preserved,[28] seem genuinely Egyptian without showing any act of translation from the Greek as is the case in the first five columns on the verso of P. London-Leiden, which preserve a bilingual collection of short descriptions of plants and minerals.[29] Despite this bilingual flavour, the magical handbook belongs undoubtedly to the same priestly current of botanical thought as the Demotic herbal from the Tebtunis temple library. Firstly, the two texts share an identical descriptive format and, secondly, the remarkable plant name 'Great-inundation' occurs in both manuscripts (PDM xiv 953–955 = P. London-Leiden V 5/1–3 and P. Carlsberg 230, fragment 8/x+7).

Some of the herb or plant names given in botanical descriptions or medicinal recipes are rather figurative or evocative like the names in column A of the PGM XII list. Such names occur already in medical texts of the New Kingdom as in the Edwin Smith Surgical Papyrus, the Berlin Medical Book and Papyrus Ebers, and continue to be used in the Snake Book of the 26th dynasty[30] and the Demotic Herbal and P. London-Leiden of the Roman period. An arbitrary selection of these names is given in the following table to gain an idea of their nature and form.[31]

| | |
|---|---|
| Ear-of-the-ḥḏr.t animal | P. Smith 20/18 |
| Phallus-of-a-donkey | P. Berlin 3038 §124 (= 10/12) |
| Head-of-a-donkey | P. Ebers §106 (= 25/15) |
| Tail-of-a-mouse | P. Ebers §160 (=33/11); frequently in the Snake Book[32] |
| My-arm-grasps-my-arm-seizes | P. Ebers §166 (= 34/5) |

---

[28] *Op. cit*; an overview of these names is given in tables 1 and 2 on pages 52 and 55.

[29] For these first five columns, see, chapter 4.3.1.

[30] See for the Snake Book: Serge Sauneron, *Un traité égyptien d'ophiologie: papyrus du Brooklyn Museum 47.218.48 et 85* (PIFAO BibGén. 11; Cairo 1989). Ursula Verhoeven argues convincingly for a date in the second half of the 26th dynasty instead of the early Ptolemaic period as suggested by Sauneron: Ursula Verhoeven, *Untersuchungen zur späthieratischen Buchschrift* (OLA 99; Leuven 2001) 306.

[31] The occurrences of such fancy names in pharaonic medical and magical texts are few. The editors of the *Grundriß der Medizin* list only 13 names, from which *t3 msḥ* has to be deleted: H. von Deines, H. Grapow and W. Westendorf, *Ergänzungen. Drogenquanten, Sachgruppen, Nachträge, Bibliographie, Generalregister* (Grundriss der Medizin der alten Ägypter 9; Berlin 1973) 55. See also H. Grapow, *Von den medizinischen Texten. Art, Inhalt, Sprache und Stil der medizinischen Einzeltexte sowie Überlieferung, Bestand und Analyse der medizinischen Papyri* (Grundriss der Medizin der alten Ägypter 2, Berlin 1955) 79. See for a few additions to this list: Joachim F. Quack, 'Das Pavianshaar und die Taten des Thoth (pBrooklyn 47.218.48+85 3,1–6)' *SAK* 23 (1996) 305–333, 313 fn. 32.

[32] For attestations in the Snake Book, see, Sauneron, *Un traité égyptien d'ophiologie*, 229.

| | |
|---|---|
| *Pḥt*-of-a-donkey[33] | P. Ebers §334 (= 55/17); |
| | Snake Book §61a (= 4/7) |
| Ear-of-a-donkey | P. Ebers §770 (= 92/6) |
| Scorpion-herb | P. Turin CG 54051 (dupl. 1993) rt. 4/4 |
| | Snake Book §46g (= 3/15) |
| Image-of-Horus | Snake Book §65a (= 4/12) |
| Image-of-Seth | Snake Book §65b (= 4/12) |
| Daughter-of-the-one-who-is-asleep | P. Carlsberg 230 fr. 1/10 |
| My-name-cannot-be-found | P. Carlsberg 230 fr. 4+5/x+2/13 |
| Great-of-Amun | P. London-Leiden 10/32 |
| | (= PDM xiv 305) |
| The-footprint-of-Isis | P. London-Leiden 10/32 |
| | (= PDM xiv 305) |
| There-is-none-better-than-I | P. London-Leiden V 2/3 |
| | (=PDM xiv 899) |

The table shows that the plant names are either short clauses or compounds consisting of a body part in combination with the name of an animal or god. Identification of the plant species is hardly possible and greatly hindered by the lack of descriptions or explanatory glosses. Only in two cases the figurative name is provided with such a gloss. The first example is taken from the Snake Book; the second is from a New Kingdom magical spell.

'Living-Flesh' is the name of the *iṯrw.t* plant   [Snake Book §90b = 5/25]

A 'Hair-of-the-chin-of-Osiris', which is called 'twig' by its name
[P. Leiden I 348 recto 11/9]

It is unclear whether the names were popular designations like 'forget-me-not', 'sunflower' and 'wolf's claw' or institutionalised jargon that was meant to exclude outsiders from participating in priestly medical knowledge. The two above given glosses might indicate that the figurative names were indeed not generally known, although both passages are seemingly not concerned with keeping the glosses secret. Whatever the case, according to the introduction to the collection of medical recipes of P. Ebers, medical knowledge was considered secret knowledge.[34]

Unlike the names in column A of the PGM XII list, none of the compound plant names contains substances like bile, blood, dung, se-

---

[33] The word *pḥ.t* has the phallus determinative in P. Ebers. See also Sauneron, *Un traité égyptien d'ophiologie*, 85.
[34] Morenz, '(Magische) Sprache der geheimen Kunst'; Westendorf, *Handbuch der altägyptischen Medizin* I, 99 f.

men, or fat as element. However, these substances are frequently called for as ingredients in medical or magical recipes of the pharaonic period.[35] In analogy with the PGM XII list, one might now be inclined to interpret these ingredients likewise as code names for ordinary herbs or minerals, but there are no reasons to distrust a literal reading of those recipes and to assume an ingredient in disguise. First, none of these bodily items are connected with a god's name as in 'Semen of Hermes' in the PGM XII list and, secondly, the animal substances seem to be practical and reasonable components for potions and unguents in each case, irrespective of any scientifically proven medical effect. The following recipe from the snake book testifies unequivocally to the application of goat's blood, since it prescribes to lead the goat back to its mother.

> ***Remedy against (the bite of) a female snake***. *Qebu* plant, ***1/4***; mix with honey, ***1/4***; blood of a young goat, ***1/8***; he has to be taken alive without being slaughtered; beer, ***2*** hin; absorb; give freedom to the said goat (to let him return) to his mother; very good, (tested) a million times; it is used against any snake.  [Snake Book §70 = 4/18–19]

END OF EXCURSUS

It has been said above that, in all probability, the PGM XII list draws directly on Egyptian priestly knowledge instead of on the Mesopotamian Uru-anna=*maštakal*. This conclusion follows not only from the Egyptian fauna mentioned in the list, but is also confirmed by the fact that the item 'hairs of a baboon' mentioned in line 418 of column A occurs already in the Snake Book, which is dated to the 26th dynasty, about eight centuries earlier than PGM XII.[36]

> ***Another prescription that is made for a man who suffers from a bite of whatever snake***: 'Hair-of-a-baboon' plant ***1/8***; cumin ***1/8***; *s3-wr* resin ***1/64***; honey ***1/8***; sweet beer ***1/32***; filter and to be swallowed by him who suffers from the bite. [Snake Book §43a = 3/1–2]

---

[35] A helpful tool to study Egyptian drugs is H. von Deines and H. Grapow, *Wörterbuch der ägyptischen Drogennamen* (Grundriss der Medizin der alten Ägypter 6; Berlin 1959). See for bile: pp. 145–146 (*wdd*), 170–171 (*bnf*), 460–461 (*shw*); for blood: 444–448 (*snf*) and for dung: 358–363 (*ḥs*). See also the indices in Sauneron, *Un traité égyptien d'ophiologie* and E.A.E. Reymond, *A Medical Book from Crocodilopolis. P. Vindob. D. 6257* (Vienna 1976).

[36] Joachim F. Quack already pointed out the occurrence of hair-of-a-baboon in both the PGM XII list and the snake book: Quack, 'Das Pavianshaar und die Taten des Thoth', 313.

Although the term Hair-of-a-baboon can be identified with certitude as a plant name because of the hieratic plant determinative, it remains uncertain whether the name refers to dill seed as the PGM XII list dictates. Anyhow, the link between hairs-of-a-baboon and dill is not an idiosyncratic invention of the copyist of the P. Leiden I 384 verso manuscript, since both occur also as synonym in the alphabeticalised revision of Dioscorides' *On the Materials of Medicine* (written around 65 CE). This work, a five-book catalogue in Greek of about 700 plants and 1000 drugs employed in medicine, is the culmination of a scientific trend, which started with Theophrastus' *Inquiry into Plants* around 300 BCE, that tried to classify the natural world by a strict appliance of rational and empirical methods.[37] The revision of the treatise, which was undertaken sometime at the end of the first century CE, consisted on the one hand of the alphabetisation of Dioscorides' ingenious arrangement of materials according to drug affinities and, on the other, the interpolation of long lists of synonyms that were excerpted from Pamphilus' lexicographical work *On Botany*.[38] Very little is known of Pamphilus, a resident of Alexandria in the first century CE, who wrote a number of lexica of which not much more than the title is preserved.[39] His work *On Botany*, consisting of six books, was an alphabetically arranged collection of plant names, each entry provided with synonyms, descriptions of outer appearance, discussions of medicinal properties, methods of application and folklore knowledge. The famous physician Galen (129-ca.216 CE) accused him of having written a book on botany full of uncritical observations and fairytales without ever

---

[37] The *On the Materials of Medicine* is published in Max Wellmann, *Die Schrift des Dioskurides Περὶ ἁπλῶν φαρμάκων: ein Beitrag zur Geschichte der Medizin* 3 volumes (Berlin 1914). A useful historical overview of Greco-Roman botany and pharmacology is given in John Scarborough, 'The Pharmacology of sacred Plants, Herbs, and Roots', in: C.A. Faraone and D. Obbink (eds.), *Magika Hiera. Ancient Greek Magic and Religion* (New York, Oxford 1991) 138-174 and F. Pfister, 'Pflanzenaberglaube' *PRE* 19.2 (1938) 1446-1456. Theophrastus' followers are discussed in John Scarborough, *Pharmacy's Ancient Heritage: Theophrastus, Nicander, and Dioscorides* (The distinguished lectures, College of Pharmacy, University of Kentucky 1984).

[38] See for a discussion of the original arrangement of Dioscorides' botanical treatise: John M. Riddle, *Dioscorides on Pharmacy and Medicine* (Austin 1985) 176-180. Max Wellmann was able to establish the date of the redaction and to identify Pamphilus' *On Botany* as source of the numerous synonyms: Max Wellmann, 'Die Pflanzennamen des Dioskurides' *Hermes* 33 (1898) 360-422, 369f.

[39] The available material is collected in Hans Diller, 'Pamphilos [25]' *PRE* 18.2 (1949) 336-349.

having seen the described plants himself and having properly tested their medicinal properties.[40] Whatever the scientific merit of Pamphilus' work, the long lists of synonyms found their way into the revised edition of Dioscorides' botanical treatise and allow identifying with certitude the Egyptian priestly character of the list of ingredients in PGM XII.

In the revised edition of Dioscorides' treatise, each entry is provided with an arbitrary number of synonyms that can be distinguished into three categories:[11]

1. Language or dialect of origin
   i.e. Greeks, Romans, Egyptians, Syrians, Africans, Spaniards, Gauls, people from Dacia, from Armenia, from Boeotia, Cappadocia, Sicily, etc.
2. Authoritative Greek physicians and botanists
   i.e. Andreas, Erasistratus, Hippocrates, Krateuas, Nikandros, Theophrastus, etc.
3. Authoritative masters of the occult arts (Greco-Roman perception)
   i.e. Demokritos, Ostanes, Pythagoras, Zoroaster and the prophets

The following two passages illustrate the descriptive format. The added strings of synonyms are put between square brackets to bring Pamphilus' contribution to light.

> Dill [manageable dill, some call it Polyeidos, others Aniketon, the prophets call it Semen-of-a-baboon, also Hairs-of-a-baboon, others Semen-of-Hermes, the Egyptians say Arachou, the Romans say Anatum, the Africans say Sikkiria, the Dacians say Polpum]
>
> Drinking the decoction of the foliage and the fruit of dry dill draws down milk, stops twisting of the bowels and flatulence, eases the belly and suppresses slight vomiting, stimulates urinating and soothes hiccup. When drinking it continually, it produces loss of eyesight and suppresses the libido. Its decoction is also of use to hysterical women as sitz bath. Its burnt seed applied as poultice stops distensions.
>
> [Dioscorides, *On the Materials of Medicine*, III.58]
>
> Ironwort, some call it Herakleia [the prophets call it Semen-of-a-scorpion, some Blood-of-a-Titan, others Tail-of-a-scorpion; Pythagoras calls it Parmoron; Andreas calls it Xanthophaneia; Ostanes calls it Bouphthalmon; the Egyptians say Senôdionôr; the Romans say Vertumnus, some

---

[40] Galen gives a description of the contents and method of Pamphilus' *On Botany* in the introduction to *De Simpl. Med. Temp. ac Fac.* (XI 792–798 Kühn).

[11] The number of categories adds up to 25. They are listed in Wellmann, *Die Schrift des Dioskurides*, 327–358 (notice that number 3 is mistakenly skipped).

Mulcetrum, others Soleastrum, others Intubum Silbatikum; the Africans say Oudodonni].

It is a herb with leaves like horehound, but longer like those of the salvia or the oak although smaller and rougher. It grows square stems measuring a span or longer, not distasteful, although somewhat astringent, on which are by intervals wreaths (of flowers) in which a black seed. It grows on rocky spots. The leaves have the power as a poultice to close up wounds and prevent inflammation.

[Dioscorides, *On the Materials of Medicine*, IV.33]

The two passages demonstrate clearly that the category of the terms coined by the 'prophets' contains compound plant names that are similar in design to those of the pharaonic medical texts and the PGM XII list that were discussed above. In fact, three pharaonic and seven PGM XII compound plant names recur in the revised *On the Materials of Medicine* as synonyms that were in use among these circles. It will be demonstrated with the help of administrative documents in section 6.3.1 that the category 'prophets' refers to the highest class of Egyptian priests, the so-called 'god's servants', not in the least to Biblical prophets. Given this specific professional designation and the correspondence of the plant names, it is justified to conclude that Pamphilus' synonyms reflect Egyptian priestly knowledge. In the case of Hairs-of-a-baboon the tradition reaches back for about 800 years, as was said above; in the case of Feather-of-ibis/Thoth and Tail-of-a-mouse the tradition even goes back for more than 1600 years.

The following two compound plant names are attested in both pharaonic medical texts and in the revised *On the Materials of Medicine* (Dioscorides' name and the modern scientific designation are given in the right column):

| | | |
|---|---|---|
| Tail of a mouse | P. Ebers 160 + Snake Book | Diosc II.118<br>mallow (Malva silvestris) |
| Hair of a baboon | Snake Book 43a | Diosc III.58<br>dill (Anethum graveolens) |

Compound plant names that are attested in both the list of ingredients in PGM XII and the revised *On the Materials of Medicine* are:

| | | |
|---|---|---|
| Hairs of a baboon | PGM XII.418 | Diosc III.58<br>dill (Anethum graveolens) |
| Semen of Hermes | PGM XII.419 | Diosc III.58 & III.139<br>dill & ox-eye<br>(Anacyclus radiatus) |

| Blood of Ares | PGM XII.420 | Diosc I.10 & III.102 |
| | | Hazelwort (Asarum europaeum) & |
| | | white lily (Lilium candidum) |
| Blood of an eye | PGM XII.421 | Diosc II.178 |
| | | pimpernel |
| | | (Anagallis arvensis) |
| Tail of a scorpion | PGM XII.425 | Diosc IV.33 |
| | | ironwort (Sideritis romana) |
| Semen of Herakles | PGM XII.434 | Diosc IV.144 & IV.148 |
| | | butcher's broom (Ruscus aculeatus) & |
| | | white hellebore (Veratrum album) |
| ⟨Blood⟩ of a Titan | PGM XII.435 | Diosc II.136; IV.33; IV.37 |
| | | wild lettuce (Lactuca scariola) & |
| | | ironwort (Sideritis romana) & |
| | | bramble (Rubus ulmifolius) |

In the case of 'Hairs of a baboon', 'Semen of Hermes' and 'Blood of a Titan', not only the compound plant name is identical, but also Dioscorides' name corresponds with the respective decoded ingredient given in column B of the PGM XII list, which proves that Pamphilus and the editor of the PGM XII list made use of similar priestly sources that were rooted in an Egyptian tradition reaching back for more than one and a half millennium.[12] One should therefore beware of dismissing the list of interpretations too rashly as material irrelevant to the study of the PGM. Instead, we must acknowledge that the list of PGM XII opens up a textual field with an extensive geographical and historical reach. It was certainly not idiosyncratic bogus confined to the Theban hills, because at least parts of it were already known among Hellenistic scholars in Alexandria in the first century CE and, in all likelihood, through Pamphilus' *On Botany* and the revised edition of *On the Materials of Medicine* also in other scholarly centres of the Roman world such as Athens, Rome, Ephesus and Antioch.

The foregoing pages have provided an answer to the first of the four questions that were formulated in the introductory section, that is, to the question 'what is this text about?' The text is a list of encoded and decoded names of plants, minerals and animal material similar to the Mesopotamian Uruanna=*maštakal*. Despite the correspondence with a Mesopotamian treatise, it reflects authentic Egyptian priestly

---

[12] It is also noteworthy that one herb mentioned in P. London-Leiden recurs as well in the *On the Materials of Medicine*. This is Semen of Helios (PDM xiv 889 = P. London-Leiden V1/4 and Diosc III 140).

knowledge as is demonstrated by the indigenous fauna of which the compound names are made up and the occurrence of similar or even identical names in pharaonic medical texts. In the light of these Egyptian roots, the introduction to the list is actually a highly peculiar piece. On the one hand, it is indeed correct in its claiming to introduce a list of pharmacological jargon that was in use among Egyptian priests, but, on the other hand, its allegation that this jargon was inscribed on the statues of gods is nonsense. The latter claim betrays that the author of these lines was either ill-informed himself as regards the origin of his authentic word list or that he wanted to address a reader who was only partly familiar with Egyptian priestly practice. Whatever the case, the text exploits the idea that Egyptian priestly knowledge is highly valuable and, simultaneously, evokes the idea that the narrator and reader do not belong to the inner-circle of temple scribes, as I argued in the introduction to this chapter. To gain an understanding of how Egyptian priests can function as prestigious marketing elements to promote magical knowledge, the following section will study the Egyptian priesthood's duties and obligations in Egyptian society and its perception in the imagination of the day.

## 6.3. *Temple scribes, prophets and the like*

In the introduction to the list of interpretations, the narrator ascribes the idea of disguising the names of ritual ingredients to the 'temple scribes' (ἱερογραμματεῖς), who, as he says, have devised the method to delude the curious and uninitiated masses. The somewhat bizarre compound plant names that were added posthumously to Dioscorides' *On the Materials of Medicine*, deriving from a lost botanical treatise by Pamphilus, are consistently regarded as jargon of the 'prophets' (προφῆται), who figure as an autonomous category among linguistic groups, Greek botanists and famous masters of the occult arts. In chapter 5.2.2 a long invocation to the anonymous All-Lord was studied that contains as its climax a list of divine names (PGM XII.263–267). The list, which was discussed in connection with the motif of 'the Names of the Nations', consists of five entries of which all but one are specifically ascribed to an ethnic or linguistic group, making it therefore comparable in design to Pamphilus' catalogue. In the case of this spell, the category 'high priests' (ἀρχιερεῖς) occurs next to the Egyptians, Jews, Greeks and Parthians.

In each of these three sources, the priestly titles are treated as autonomous categories of considerable prestige that are self-evident. Apparently, the sole occurrence of these titles was sufficient to convince the readership of the day of the efficacy of the spell or wording given by the text. In this respect, the titles are an essential part of the text's rhetorical structure, aimed at silencing from the outset any possible critical comment on the reader's part. This marketing strategy of investing the text with overwhelming authority could only have been effective if the values attached to these titles were widely shared within the intended group of readers. What were these values and to which culture group do these values appeal? It goes without saying that these complex questions can only be answered after having established the precise meaning of the titles and their cultural origin. Fortunately, this is not a difficult task and it can be made quite clear that the titles refer to specific ranks within the Egyptian priesthood with the help of trilingual priestly decrees that were set up in Egyptian temples during the Ptolemaic period. These decrees can only provide a description of the administrative structure of the priestly institution in historical reality, so that, to know more about the values and judgements attached to the native priesthood, religious and literary sources have to be taken into account as well. By studying these texts, the present section will answer the second question formulated in the introductory section: about whom is this text speaking?

This chapter consists of four separate sections. The first studies the Egyptian priestly titles as administrative categories so as to gain an understanding of the priestly hierarchy and the obligations pertaining to the titles. The next section focuses on the specific duties of Egyptian priests in the temple as well as in their local community by way of analysing temple texts and steles that priests set up in the vicinity of the temple building. The information provided by these texts should be regarded as a conscious effort on the part of the priests to construe an ideal and official image of priestly life for the outer world. The section is thus concerned with issues of priestly self-presentation. The inner view or the way Egyptian priests imagined their own position and qualities can be studied with the help of Egyptian literary narratives, in which priests play a prominent role—the subject of the third section. The fourth section assesses the images of Egyptian priests in Greek and Latin literary texts of the Roman period to make out in what way the governing elite of the day perceived the Egyptian priesthood.

6.3.1. *Egyptian priestly titles as social classes*

The Greek titles 'temple scribe', 'prophet' and 'high priest' can easily and unambiguously be interpreted as Egyptian priestly titles that were precisely defined within the hierarchy of the native priesthood and carried on a tradition of more than two millennia.[13] The priestly titles mentioned in the magical texts can thus firmly be situated within historical reality. The correspondence between the Egyptian and Greek form of the priestly titles can be studied at best with the help of the trilingual decrees that were set up as steles in the main native temples by order of the Ptolemaic king to record decisions taken at priestly synods convened by the king to discuss matters of cult and state.[14] The decrees were inscribed on a stone slab in a hieroglyphic, Demotic and Greek version, from top to bottom, uniting the language of religion and tradition, the vernacular and the language of the conqueror within one frame. In all three versions, an elaborate dating formula and a hierarchical listing of the different classes of the Egyptian priesthood precedes the actual account of the decisions taken. The introduction

---

[13] The priestly titles discussed in this section were in use from the Old Kingdom until the disappearance of the Egyptian temple religion in late antiquity. Information about the form and nature of priestly titles in the Old and Middle Kingdom can be gained from the Abusir archive, a collection of administrative documents from the mortuary temple of king Neferirkare-Kakai (5$^{th}$ dynasty) and from administrative documentation found in the Middle Kingdom workman's village of Lahun. An overview is given in: Wolfgang Helck, 'Priester, Priesterorganisation, Priestertitel' *LdÄ* IV, 1084–1097 and B.J.J. Haring, *Divine Households. Administrative and economic aspects of the New Kingdom royal memorial temples in Western Thebes* (Egyptologische Uitgaven 12; Leiden 1997) 3–7. For the New Kingdom, the *Onomasticon of Amenemope* (earliest manuscripts dated to the end of the New Kingdom) is of help. It gives the following succession of priestly titles: god's servant (*ḥm-nṯr*), god's father (*it-nṯr*), priest (*wꜥb*), lector priest (*ḥry-ḥb*), temple scribe (*sš ḥwt-nṯr*) and scribe of the god's book (*sš mḏꜣt-nṯr*): Gardiner, *Ancient Egyptian Onomastica*, vol. 1, 47*–59*. The Tebtunis onomastica of the second century CE are unfortunately in a sad state of preservation; only one fragmentary manuscript preserves a list of regional priestly titles: Osing, *Hieratische Papyri aus Tebtunis I*, 157–162. The survival of the titles into the Byzantine period is testified by the Demotic and hieroglyphic graffiti inscribed in the temples of the Dodecaschoenus, 'Twelve Mile Land', a region to the south of Aswan: F. Ll. Griffith, *Catalogue of the Demotic Graffiti of the Dodecaschoenus* Vol. 1 (Oxford 1937).

[14] Trilingual decrees, of which seventeen are known to date, are attested from Ptolemy II Philadelphos until the end of the second century BCE. See for an overview of the sources and relevant literature: W. Huß, 'Die in ptolemäischer Zeit verfaßten Synodal-Dekrete der ägyptischen Priester' *ZPE* 88 (1991) 189–208. For the political and cultural context of the decrees, see, Joachim Kügler, 'Priestersynoden im hellenistischen Ägypten. Ein Vorschlag zu ihrer sozio-historischen Deutung' *GM* 139 (1994) 53–60.

identifies thus the legal parties of the decree and attempts to create the impression that the decisions were taken with one accord and were, therefore, legally valid and binding for the Egyptian priesthood as a group. The following three passages give the hierarchical listing of the native priesthood in respectively the hieroglyphic, Demotic and Greek versions as found on the Memphis Decree (March 27, 196 BCE).[15]

> [Hieroglyphic] ¹The leaders of the temple complexes (*ỉmy.w-r3 gs.w-pr.w*) and ²the god's servants (*ḥm.w-nṯr*) and ³the overseers of secrets, the purified ones of the god, who enter into the sanctuary to dress the gods with their clothing and ⁴the scribes of the divine book (*sš.w mḏ3.t-nṯr*) and ⁵the staff-members of the House-of-Life (*ṯty.w Pr-ꜥnḫ*) and ⁶the other priests (*wꜥb.w*) who have come from the temples of Egypt to Memphis (…) have said:

> [Demotic] ¹The lesônes (*mr-šn.w*) and ²the god's servants (*ḥm.w-nṯr*) and ³the priests who enter the sanctuary to perform clothing rituals for the gods and ⁴the scribes of the divine book (*sḥ.w mdy-nṯr*) and ⁵the scribes of the House-of-Life (*sḥ.w Pr-ꜥnḫ*) and ⁶the other priests (*wꜥb.w*) who have come from the temples of Egypt [to Memphis] (…) have said:

> [Greek] ¹The high priests (ἀρχιερεῖς) and ²prophets (προφῆται) and ³the (priests) who enter the holy shrine to clothe the gods and ⁴feather bearers (πτεροφόροι) and ⁵temple scribes (ἱερογραμματεῖς) and all ⁶the other priests (ἱερεῖς) who had come from the temples throughout Egypt to Memphis (…) have said: [Rosetta Decree 6–7]

The hierarchical listing makes a division into six distinct classes, declining in importance, among which, in the Greek version, the titles 'high priest', 'prophet' and 'temple scribe' appear as equivalents to traditional Egyptian titles as they are given in the hieroglyphic and Demotic version:[16]

| *Greek* | *Hieroglyphic* | *Demotic* |
|---|---|---|
| High priest | leader of the temple complex | lesônis |
| Prophet | god's servant | god's servant |
| Temple scribe | staff member of the House-of-Life | scribe of the House-of-Life |

The administrative and ritual functions of each of the six priestly positions can be briefly described in the following terms.[17] The high priest

---

[15] The Canopus Decree (March 7, 238 BCE) gives an almost identical list.

[16] The Greek titles and their corresponding Egyptian terms are studied in detail in François Daumas, *Les Moyens d'expression du grec et de l'égyptien comparés dans les décrets de Canope et de Memphis* (ASAE Suppl. 16; Cairo 1952) 179–185.

[17] An important overview, although out of date in many respects, of the functions

(leader of the temple complex, lesônis[18]) was responsible for the administration of the temple complex, in which function he was assisted or supervised by an ἐπιστατής, 'overseer', who was appointed by the king, while religious authority lay in the hands of the prophets (god's servant) who conducted the cult on the main festival days. The third rank, those who were responsible for clothing, washing and anointing the divine statues, called in Greek documentary sources στολισταί, 'clothing priests',[19] were important actors in the daily ritual and during religious festivals when processions were held and a number of rituals had to be performed. The hieroglyphic description, 'The overseers of secrets, the purified ones of the god, who enter into the sanctuary to dress the gods with their clothing' explicates the crucial role of these priests in the temple cult by stressing the notions of secrecy and purity. The lector priests (scribes of the divine book, feather bearers) assisted these clothing priests in the performance of the ritual as those responsible for the ritual texts and guardians of a correct performance of rites and a faultless recitation of hymns and invocations.[50] The fifth title, temple scribe (staff-member of the House-of-Life, scribe of the House-of-Life), refers to those who took care of the religious and scholarly literature that was composed and copied in the temple libraries and the House-of-Life, the cultic library that housed those texts that were seen as the emanations of the sun god Re, magical and medical texts among others.[51] The sixth

---

and obligations of the individual native priestly classes in Ptolemaic Egypt is: Walter Otto, *Priester und Tempel im Hellenistischen Ägypten: ein Beitrag zur Kulturgeschichte des Hellenismus* 2 vols. (Leipzig and Berlin 1905–1908; reprint Rome 1971) 17–172. A general presentation is given in Serge Sauneron, *The Priests of Ancient Egypt* (Ithaca, London 2000) 51–74 [translated from *Prêtres de l'ancienne Égypte* (Paris 1957)].

[18] For the etymology of this word and the nature of this priestly function, see, K.-Th. Zauzich, 'Lesonis' *LÄ* III, 1008–1009 and F. de Cenival, *Les associations religieuses en Égypte d'après les documents démotiques* (BdE 46; Cairo 1972) 154–159.

[19] G. Vittmann, 'Stolist' *LÄ* VI, 63–65; Daumas, *Moyens d'expression du grec et de l'égyptien*, 182, fn. 2.

[50] In earlier periods the lector priest was usually called 'he who is in charge of the festival roll' (ḥry-ḥb). The Greek title 'feather bearer' is derived from the two feathers that these priests wore on their head as distinctive markers of their profession in the Late Period. See for a representation of such a priest: Dendera, Mammisi, plate 87. Note that the accompanying hieroglyphic text speaks of a lector priest (ḥry-ḥb). In a temple text from Esna, this priest is described as having only one feather: Esna V, 134 (284, 11). See also Olaf E. Kaper, *Temples and Gods in Roman Dakhleh. Studies in the indigenous cults of an Egyptian oasis* (unpublished PhD thesis, Groningen 1997) 113.

[51] Gardiner, 'The House of Life'. The hieroglyphic version of the Canopus Decree calls this priestly position rḫ-ḫ.t, a title that is already attested since the Middle Kingdom. The title means merely 'he who knows things', but is better translated as 'scholar'

and final class of the list in the Memphis decree is more or less a rest category. It groups together the priests of lower rank by means of a general term for priest, in Greek as well as in Egyptian.

These priestly titles were kept in use during the following Roman period as is testified by an important administrative document that defined the legal and societal position of the native priesthood in more detail: the so-called *Gnomon of the Idios Logos* (Regulations of the emperor's private account). The *Idios Logos* was a department (or the title of its main functionary) in the administration of the Ptolemaic and Roman Empire charged with supervision over the sale of government property as well as confiscated or abandoned private property.[52] It constituted some sort of parallel account of irregular income to the royal treasury: so to say, the private account of the king or emperor. Substantial parts of the *Gnomon of the Idios Logos* are preserved in a document of the late second century CE, which an anonymous scribe wrote as an aide-mémoire for an anonymous friend or colleague (BGU 5 1210).[53] These regulations of Greek, Roman and Egyptian law make up a legal compendium of rules and jurisprudence concerning disputes between heirs over legacies, charges of ritual impropriety, and infractions against the laws and ordinances regulating civil privileges.[54] Paragraphs 71–97 deal specifically with the sale or inheritance of priestly positions, the requirements for holding these ranks and some ritual and procedural infractions that were liable to fines due to the treasury of the *Idios Logos*.[55] A study of these paragraphs reveals that the duties, requirements and rules of admission were narrowly defined to such an extent that, in the Roman period, the native priestly class had factually become a closed-off and marked-out community without civil duties in society. That this Roman policy of subordination and marginalisation was a

---

or 'intellectual'. It denotes a person who is not only versed in writing, but more importantly, has a broad knowledge of scholarly literature in general; see, Ludwig D. Morenz, *Beiträge zur Schriftlichkeitskultur im Mittleren Reich und in der 2. Zwischenzeit* (ÄAT 29; Wiesbaden 1996) 142–143.

[52] Paul R. Swarney, *The Ptolemaic and Roman Idios Logos* (ASP 8; Toronto 1970), see on temple and priests pp. 57–59 and 83–96; See also Strabo, *Geography*, 17.1.12.

[53] The text is published in W. Schubart, *Der Gnomon des Idios Logos* vol. 1 (BGU 5,1; Berlin 1919) 29–35; the accompanying commentary can be found in Woldemar Graf Uxkull-Gyllenband, *Der Gnomon des Idios Logos* vol. 2 (Berlin 1934). A section is also preserved in P.Oxy. XLII 3014, first century CE.

[54] Swarney, *op. cit.*, 123.

[55] Swarney, *op. cit.*, 83–96.

conscious act, is demonstrated by emperor Augustus' decision to place the office of high priest in the hands of a Roman official, resident in Alexandria, as a means to keep tight control over the activities and organization of the native priesthood.[56] Applications for membership to the native priesthood had to be submitted to his bureau together with proofs of priestly descent, circumcision and an unblemished physical appearance.[57] The rules were stringent since admission to the priesthood meant exemption from the poll tax. Next to the installation of a Roman civil servant as head of the native priesthood, emperor Augustus decreed as well the abolishment of the system of temple-owned estates, which had provided the main income of the Egyptian temples in the pharaonic period.[58] In the Roman period, all land fell to the state and the native temples were dependent on state intervention, either in the form of small plots of land or subsidies, which diminished rapidly from the third century CE onwards.[59]

The opening paragraph of the section on Egyptian priests interdicts the priestly class activities outside the religious sphere and obliges them to wear white linen clothing and to go baldhead.[60] Given the extraordinary high rate of the charged fine in the following piece of jurisprudence, the authorities took these regulations very seriously.

> 71 For priests (ἱερεῦσ[ι]) it is not allowed to have another occupation than the cult of the gods, neither to go forth in woollen clothing and neither to have long hair, even not when they are away from the divine procession.
> [BGU 5 1210, 181–187]

---

[56] Otto, *Priester und Tempel im Hellenistischen Ägypten*, 58–72.

[57] Two applications for permission to circumcise are found in BGU 1 347 (Primer, nr. 48); see also M. Kaimio in P. Rainer Cent. P. 340; applications for permission to circumcise are P. Tebt 292 and 293 (cf. 314), see also BGU 82, P. Strassb. 60: Wilcken Archiv, ii, 4ff.; Otto, *Priester und Tempel im Hellenistischen Ägypten*, 213ff. Take also note of text 10 in Klaas A. Worp, 'Short Texts from the Main Temple', in: Colin A. Hope and Gillian E. Bowen (eds.), *Dakhleh Oasis Project: preliminary reports on the 1994–1995 to 1998–1999 field seasons* (Dakhleh Oasis Project: Monograph 11; Oxford 2002) 333–349, 346.

[58] László Kákosy, 'Probleme der Religion in römerzeitlichen Ägypten' *ANRW* II 18.5 (1995) 2894–3049, 2904.

[59] Bagnall, *Egypt in Late Antiquity*, 262ff.; Frankfurter, *Religion in Roman Egypt*, 27ff.

[60] White linen clothing and a shaven head were originally meant as outward signs of purity, resulting from the idea that bodily hair attracts lice and that clothes made of living beings would pollute its wearer, see Sauneron, *The Priests of Ancient Egypt*, 35–42. However, in the mind of the Roman administrators, the possibility to mark out native priests as a distinctive group within society might have taken precedence.

76 A priest (ἱερεύς) who wore woollen clothing and had long hair (was fined) 1000 drachmas. [BGU 5 1210, 188]

Of major importance to the Roman authorities were the rules pertaining to the conveyance of priestly positions. The position of prophet could ideally only be transferred by inheritance (§§77–78), whereas the rank of *stolistes* was sellable (§80). This means that some of the upper ranks of the native priesthood were reserved for a small circle of candidates: relatives and persons with a certain amount of wealth. Since priests of the Greek and Roman cults were not professionals, but affluent laymen performing a tour of duty,[61] the organisation of the Egyptian priesthood contrasted sharply with the customs of the ruling elite, in particular with respect to its closed-off character. A letter from Tebtunis, written in 162 CE, indicates that membership of the priestly class, because of its financial benefits, was carefully monitored by the authorities. The text is the official account of a judicial examination in which three priests of Soknebtunis had to give proof of their priestly status. Two persons handed over written proofs of priestly descent, while one of them was even able to produce a document proving circumcision. The third candidate was handed over a divine book to show competence in the Egyptian language and scripts (hieratic and Demotic).[62]

> Marsisouchos, son of Mar[sisouchos?], whose mother is Thenkebkis, has given proof of being proficient in the sacred ([ἱε]ρατικά) and Egyptian (Αἰγύπτια) scripts from a sacred book which the priestly scribes (ἱερογραμματεῖς) had given, in conformity with the memorandum of the 12th of the month Tybi of the present second (regnal) year.
> [P. Tebt. 291, 40–45]

The *Gnomon of the Idios Logos* makes thus clear that the native priesthood had become entirely subordinate to the Roman administration. First of all, a Roman administrator, appointed by the prefect, held the function of high priest, so that this previously highest priestly position had become an extension of Roman bureaucracy. One of his tasks was to keep tight control over the transference of priestly positions. In case of conveyance or sale of these functions the parties had to show proofs of

---

[61] Otto, *Priester und Tempel im Hellenistischen Ägypten*, 133f. A general overview is given in Walter Burkert, *Greek Religion* (Cambridge 1985) 95–98. See also Alan K. Bowman, *Egypt after the Pharaohs, 332 BC–AD 642 from Alexander to the Arab Conquest* (London 1986) 183.

[62] See also S. Sauneron, 'Les conditions d'accès à la fonction sacerdotale à l'époque gréco-romaine' *BIFAO* 61 (1962) 55–57.

priestly descent, circumcision and the absence of any physical defect. The Roman authorities had not invented these regulations. On the contrary, they were traditional elements of native priestly identity that had already been in use during the pharaonic period. However, they had acquired a new meaning and usage in the eyes of the Roman administration. Instead of elements of prestige they were turned into tools to mark out and subjugate the Egyptian priestly class.

### 6.3.2. *Egyptian priests as actors in cult and community*

The preceding section dealt with the position of Egyptian priests within the administration of the Ptolemaic and Roman period. The documentary sources concerned are silent about the active role Egyptian priests played within their own circles or about the terms in which the priests defined their own position. The following two sections will survey the ways in which the native priesthood presented itself in texts that were written and transmitted within its own circle. The present section will primarily be concerned with texts that were part of the official temple ideology. These texts could be termed 'official' as far as they were inscribed in stone (temple wall, stele or statue) and written in Classical Egyptian in hieroglyphs. These texts were thus meant to be preserved and to create and confirm traditional Egyptian ideas, imagery and values.

First and foremost, Egyptian priests were ritual experts who conducted their rituals in the innermost chambers of the temple to ensure the preservation of the cosmic order. According to Egyptian theology, purity was of central concern to the effectiveness of any ritual.[63] Since Egyptian state religion consisted mainly of a regular performance of rituals and sacrifices, strictly scheduled by a festive calendar, to guarantee the vitality of the divine cosmic order, purity was of major importance to the institution.[64] In Egyptian terms, purity could be defined as the physical and mental condition required to enter a sacred place, either a temple, tomb, palace or any spot where a ritual is conducted

---

[63] See for a general discussion of the term and concept 'purity' in Egyptian culture: Dimitri Meeks, 'Pureté et purification en Égypte', in: *Dictionnaire de la Bible*, Supplément 9 (Paris 1979) 430–452.
[64] See for a comprehensive description of Egyptian cult: Assmann, *Ägypten. Theologie und Frömmigkeit*, 25–66.

for the occasion.⁶⁵ The Egyptian term for purity is *wꜥb*, the opposite of *bwt*, which latter entails everything the gods abominate, ranging from a certain conduct to specific food products, animals, regions, peoples, etc.⁶⁶ On a cosmic level, a similar distinction is at work between the divine order (*mꜣꜥ.t*) established by an act of creation, either by a god (cosmos) or a king (temple building), and the primordial chaos (*isf.t*) and everything associated with it. Since the gods are the creators of the ordered cosmos, they are pure by definition and live on *ma'at*. Moreover, according to temple doctrine, each temple building stands on the primeval mound on which creation was enacted; a pure place *par excellence* thus. As a result, Egyptian temple architecture is mainly a translation into stone of the anxiety for pollution: fortifications with a sequence of entrance towers, in which the sacred shrine is enclosed on three sides by a succession of defensive layers of chapels and ambulatories.⁶⁷ In the Late Period instruction text of Onkhsheshonqi it is put as bluntly as:

> Purity (*wꜥb*) is the essential element (*rnn.t*) of a temple (*hwt-ntr*)
> [P. BM. 10.508 8/18]

It goes without saying that those who were interacting with the divine, who were ritually enacting the perpetual cosmic battle against chaos, were required to be pure when entering the temple building. The general Egyptian term for priest presupposes this requirement from the outset. The word for priest derives from the same root as the word for purity, *wꜥb*, meaning in this case 'a pure one', thus making clear

---

⁶⁵ The *locus classicus* for this definition is the victory stele of king Piye/Piankhi in which two Egyptian kings are forbidden entrance to the royal palace for not having been circumcised and eating fish: 'They could not enter the palace because they were not circumcised and eat fish. King Nimlot, however, entered the palace because he was a clean one (*wꜥb*) and did not eat fish. They stood (there) and (but) one entered the palace' [lines 150–153 = Urk. I, 50/16–51/1]. See for a full publication of the stele: N.-C. Grimal, *La stèle triomphale de Pi(ꜥankh)y au Musée du Caire, JE 48862 et 47086–47089* (PIFAO; Cairo 1981). See also: Elke Blumenthal, 'Die "Reinheit" des Grabschänders', in: U. Verhoeven and E. Graefe (eds.), *Religion und Philosophie im Alten Ägypten* Fs. Derchain (OLA 39; Leuven 1991) 47–56. See for discussions about a definition of ritual purity in Egyptian terms: R. Grieshammer, 'Reinheit, kultische' *LÄ* V 212–213; John L. Gee, *The Requirements of Ritual Purity in Ancient Egypt* (unpublished dissertation; Yale University, May 1998).

⁶⁶ P. Montet, 'Le fruit défendu' *Kêmi* 11 (1950) 85–116; Paul John Frandsen, 'On the Origin of the Notion of Evil in Ancient Egypt' *GM* 179 (2000) 9–34, 12f.

⁶⁷ This architectural idea finds its culmination in the Ptolemaic and Roman period, but developed out of a format from the pharaonic period: Assmann, *Ägypten. Theologie und Frömmigkeit*, 39–43.

that purity is indeed the defining criterion of the function or profession. Since it is at the same time a designation for the lowest priestly rank, specific knowledge and skills were apparently only necessary for promotion to a higher rank and contributed thus less to priestly identity as such. In the temple of Edfu, on the doorpost of a side entrance in the eastern wall, through which priests entered the building to bring the god offerings, a text is inscribed to remind the priests again of the requirement.

> Everybody who enters through this gate, beware of entering in impurity because god loves purity more than a million precious objects or hundred thousand gold pieces. His food is *ma'at*; he is satisfied with that. His heart is content with great purity. [Edfu VI: 349/4–6]

Ritual purity was regarded as a physical and moral state of being that could be attained by a combination of observing a number of commandments and abstaining from certain conduct.[68] To be allowed entrance to the holy shrine, the body had to be in a healthy condition, free from physical or mental illness or any form of pollution.[69] Priests were therefore required to wash themselves in the temple lake before entering the temple and had to have all bodily hair removed. From the Late Period onwards, and maybe even earlier, circumcision was obligatory as well. Because the ritual in the temple consisted of presenting offerings and reciting hymns, hands and mouth had to be washed carefully. Chewing on a piece of natron salt and spitting it out cleansed the mouth. The route from the entrance gate to the innermost shrine was characterised by a gradual increase in severity of the requirements. The deeper a priest had to enter the temple, the longer he should have abstained from sexual intercourse. Animal products were not allowed as material for clothing: sandals were made of papyrus while clothes had to be made of white linen. The priestly diet was also subject to strict rules. Each province, city, temple had its own food taboos that found their justification in a myth. Animals like fish and donkeys were by and large forbidden to the priesthood, although local divergences did occur.[70] A text on a pillar in the pronaos of the temple of Esna,

---

[68] See for a general overview: Sauneron, *The Priests of Ancient Egypt*, 35–42.
[69] The Egyptian views on circumcision and food taboos are discussed and compared with religious customs in ancient Israel in P. Galpaz-Feller, 'The Piye Stela: a brief Consideration of "Clean" and "Unclean" in Ancient Egypt and the Bible' *RB* 102 (1995) 506–521.
[70] See Ingrid Gamer-Wallert, 'Fische, religiös' *LdÄ* II, 228–234.

inscribed during the reign of emperor Trajan, illustrates the present description rather well. It is an account of rituals to be performed at the 19th of the month Epiphi. Participants have to observe a number of intriguing rules, of which only a selection is given here:[71]

> All men have to be purified (twr.tw) from female contact for a (period of) purity of one day. They have to be purified, they have to be washed, they have to be clothed (as is ordained). Do not let anybody enter it (the temple) who is possessed or under a curse[72] (...).   [Esna III, n° 197/16]
>
> Shave (your) body, cut (your) nails, shave (your) head, you who enter it (the temple). Be clothed in fine linen, you who go inside it. (Purify) with natron water, you who dwell in it.   [Esna III, n° 197/18]

These liturgical rules were translated into a more personal and societal morality in texts of priestly self-presentation. Central to this ethical discourse is again the distinction between pure and impure, in this case defined in the following terms and oppositions:

| To act justly | ir nfr | : | to do evil | ir dw |
| The wise man | rmt rh | : | the fool | swg / lg |
| The godly man | rmt ntr | : | the impious man | s3b3 |

These three oppositions can best be illustrated with the help of a temple text from Edfu and a short passage from an instruction text whose principal manuscript is known as P. Insinger. Both texts are structured according to a well-articulated paradigmatic polarity of good and evil, each in its own way. The Edfu text is inscribed on a door lintel in the eastern face of the forecourt and belongs to a ritual scene of the Offering of Ma'at (m3'.t).[73] The scene presents the standard image of the king offering the symbol of Ma'at to a god, in this case Horus the

---

[71] Serge Sauneron, *Les fêtes religieuses d'Esna aux derniers siècles du paganisme* [Esna V] (PIFAO; Cairo 1962) 340–349.

[72] Sauneron takes this passage as a reference to people suffering from epilepsy: S. Sauneron, 'Les possédés' BIFAO 60 (1960) 111–115.

[73] H.W. Fairman, 'A Scene of the Offering of Truth in the Temple of Edfu' *MDAIK* 16² (1958) [Fs. H. Junker] 86–92. The ritual's primary importance is illustrated by the central position afforded to the relief scenes in the temple building, see Sylvie Cauville, *Essai sur la théologie du temple d'Horus à Edfou* 2 vols. (BdE 102; Cairo 1987) 6 and figure 2. See for a discussion of the meaning and history of the ritual in the light of New Kingdom and Third Intermediate Period material: Emily Teeter, *The Presentation of Maat. Ritual and Legitimacy in Ancient Egypt* (SAOC 57; Chicago 1997). A translation of a cultic text of the Offering of Ma'at scene, found on the inner side of the north wall of the naos of the Edfu temple, can be found in Kurth, *Treffpunkt der Götter*, 94–96, [nr. 4], notes on p. 341 f.

Behdetite accompanied by his consort Hathor. Behind the king stands Seshat, the goddess of writing, who addresses Horus with the following words:

> [I have] come [to thee], O Behdetite, (you) with the dappled plumage to set down in writing for you the evildoer (*ir ḏw*) and who acts justly (*ir nfr*):
> (1) He who leads inside (initiates) wrongfully,
> (2) [He who enters] when unclean (*s3t*),
> (3) He who speaks falsehood in your house,
> (4) He who knows right (*gs-ḏb*) from wrong (*isf.t*),
> (5) He who is pure (*ʿb*),
> (6) He who is accurate and walks in accordance with the divine order (*m3ʿ.t*),
> (7) [He who does every good] deed [for] your servants in your city,
> (8) He who loves your staff exceedingly,
> (9) He who takes bribes,
> (10) He who discriminates between [a rich man] and a poor man,
> (11) He who covets property of your house,
> (12) He who is careful,
> (13) He who does not take rewards or the share of any man.
> I write down good for the one who acts justly in your city, (whereas) I reject the character of the evildoer […]. You [do not harm your] people. [He who acts justly] in [your] house is enduring forever, (but) who does evil perishes everlastingly.           [Edfu V: 334/1–6]

In this text the evildoer is placed in opposition to the one who does good. Lines 1–3 and 9–11 define the evildoer as one who trespasses the moral rules of the temple doctrine, whereas his opposite, described in lines 4–8 and 12–13, respects its rules. The opposition between the two characters is defined by a set of taboos and is ultimately about ritual purity and impurity, defining who is allowed to enter the temple.[74] By

---

[74] Compare this text with the addresses to the officiating priests in the Ptolemaic temples; Maurice Alliot, *Le culte d'Horus à Edfou au temps des Ptolémées* 2 Vols. (BdE 20; Cairo 1969) 181–195; Adolphe Gutbub, *Textes Fondamentaux de la théologie de Kom Ombo* 2 Vols. (BdE 47; Cairo 1973) 146–148; Hermann Junker, 'Vorschriften für den Tempelkult in Philä', in: *Studia Biblica et Orientalia III: Oriens Antiquus*, Analecta Biblica 12 (Rome 1959) 151–160. Relevant are also the so-called 'negative confession' of *Book of the Dead* spell 125 and the priestly oath; Jan Assmann, *Das kulturelle Gedächtnis. Schrift, Erinnerung und politische Identität in frühen Hochkulturen* (München 1992) 185–190; J. Gwyn Griffiths, *The Divine Verdict. A Study of Divine Judgement in the Ancient Religions* (Studies in the History of Religions 52; Leiden 1991) 218–222. Recently the Egyptian version of the priestly oath, which is only known in a Greek version to date, has come to light: J.F. Quack, 'Ein ägyptisches Handbuch des Tempels und seine griechische Übersetzung' *ZPE* 119 (1997) 297–300. For the Greek version of the oath, see, Maria Totti, *Ausgewählte Texte der Isis- und Sarapis-Religion* (Hildesheim 1985) 24 [nr. 9]. Totti's collection of texts includes P. Oslo 2 (4th century CE) as a second priestly oath [text nr.10]. The text is mistakenly known among the *Greek Magical Papyri* as PGM XXXVII.

saying these words over the pharaoh's head the goddess implies that he is a pure person worthy to be accepted by Horus. However, the final lines go beyond a strict cultic interpretation by introducing the idea of punishment and reward in terms of failure and success in life. This idea is central to the instruction texts, a corpus of texts belonging to the generic category of rhetorical-didactic literature.[75] The main aim of the instruction texts is to teach its reader to lead a successful life within his family and local community. It is therefore more concerned with wisdom, knowledge about life and society, than with temple religion, knowledge about the taboos. P. Insinger, an impressive Demotic manuscript of 35 extant columns dating from the end of the Ptolemaic period[76] and originating from native priestly circles,[77] explicates this wisdom discourse by building its arguments consistently upon the distinction between the 'man of knowledge' (*rmṯ rḫ*) and the 'man of stupidity' (*rmṯ swg, lḫ, ḫne*).[78] The wise man is the one who is successful in life, whereas the fool fails because of his character. Main characteristic of the wise man is his reliance on god as a guide in life, so that he can also be called the 'godly man' (*rmṯ nṯr*) in opposition to the 'impious man' (*sꜣbꜣ*), shifting the emphasis from knowledge to piety. The following passage illustrates well the distinction between the two types and assigns a pivotal role to god as the judge of good and evil characters.

> God places the heart (*ḥꜣ.t*) on the scales opposite the weight.
> He knows the infamous man (*sꜣbꜣ*) from the godly man (*rmṯ nṯr*) because of his (their) heart.
> Curse and blessing are in the character (*smy.t*) that was given to him.
> The commandments that god ordained for those who are good are (to be found) in the character.   [P. Insinger 5/7–10]

---

[75] For the generic term rhetorical-didactic literature, see, Gerald Moers, *Fingierte Welten in der ägyptischen Literatur des 2. Jahrtausends v. Chr. Grenzüberschreitung, Reisemotiv und Fiktionalität* (PdÄ 19; Leiden 2001) 167–188.

[76] Until recently P. Insinger was dated to the first century CE; see now, K.A. Worp, 'The Greek Text on the P.Dem.Insinger: A Note on the Date' *OMRO* 63 (1982) 39–41 and Friedhelm Hoffmann, 'Neue Fragmente zu den drei grossen Inaros-Petubastis-Texten' *Enchoria* 22 (1995) 27–39, 38f.

[77] John Tait, 'Demotic Literature and Egyptian Society', in: Janet H. Johnson (ed.), *Life in a Multi-Cultural Society. Egypt from Cambyses to Constantine and beyond* (SAOC 51; Chicago 1992) 303–310.

[78] Miriam Lichtheim, *Late Egyptian Wisdom Literature in the International Context. A study of Demotic Instructions* (OBO 52; Freiburg, Göttingen 1983) 116–121; see pp. 1–12 for a discussion of the specific character of Demotic instruction texts compared to earlier ones of the pharaonic period.

God and character are pivotal notions in the biographical inscriptions of the Late and Greco-Roman period.[79] Piety pervades these accounts as the right attitude to life, the sole guarantee and cause of a successful life. These texts can only be considered private documents in so far as that they were commissioned for an individual as part of a person's burial equipment. Instead of being private accounts of an individual's life, the majority of the texts present a collection of fixed topics like prayers for offerings, an address to the living to exhort them to give offerings, and an enumeration of the virtues of the deceased, made up of stock phrases that are part of a longstanding native funerary and literary tradition. In those rare cases that an individual elaborates on his personal achievements, the boundaries of the generic norms and values are never transgressed. This means that these texts allude to an idealised image of an Egyptian (mainly male) elite and can only provide insight into the conscious effort of this elite to construct an identity. In her study of a collection of priestly biographical inscriptions on statues and funerary stelae from Ptolemaic Akhmim, Edfu and Dendera, Maria-Theresa Derchain-Urtel distinguishes twelve topics that recur in a variety of combinations in the inscriptions.[80] Statements about the priestly virtues of the deceased abound next to invocations of the gods, prayers for offerings, genealogies, addresses to colleague priests, and excerpts from Book of the Dead spell 15. These priestly virtues are a combination of formal requirements and additional moral achieve-

---

[79] A systematic collection of funerary biographies of the Late and Greco-Roman period is not available. The most important, although selective, collection of translated biographies is E. Otto, *Die biographischen Inschriften der ägyptischen Spätzeit. Ihre geistesgeschichtliche und literarische Bedeutung* (PdÄ 2; Leiden 1954); See also Ph. Derchain, *Les impondérables de l'hellénisation. Littérature d'hiérogrammates* (Monographies Reine Elisabeth 7; Turnhout 2000). A discussion of the genre within Egyptian literature is Andrea M. Gnirs, 'Die ägyptische Autobiographie', in: Antonio Loprieno (ed.), *Ancient Egyptian Literature. History and Forms* (Leiden1996) 191–241. Note that she pays minimal attention to the Late and Greco-Roman period, which is regrettable. A convenient grouping of the standard themes, although limited to the Old Kingdom, is given in Nicole Kloth, *Die (auto-) biografischen Inschriften des ägyptischen Alten Reiches: Untersuchungen zu Phraseologie und Entwicklung* (SAK Beiheft 8; Hamburg 2002).

[80] M.-Th. Derchain-Urtel, *Priester im Tempel: die Rezeption der Theologie der Tempel von Edfu und Dendera in den Privatdokumenten aus ptolemäischer Zeit* (GOF IV/19: Wiesbaden 1989) 103–245. Note that she groups these topics together under the heading of 'the Akhmim formulary' as if all of these themes were specific to the Akhmim region, which is not the case. See for some important philological corrections to the translations: A. Egberts, *BiOr* 51 (1994) 536–544.

ments like voluntary presence in the temple and providing teaching for posterity. Concerning the formal requirements, Derchain-Urtel identifies the following recurring topics:[81]

1. Purity
2. Rectitude in performing priestly duties
3. Denial of theft from offerings
4. Righteousness (social solidarity)
5. Proper speech

Accordingly, these five points can be considered the main constituents of priestly self-presentation in the Late and Greco-Roman period.[82] Each of the five topics was already common in earlier periods, albeit less pronounced, but the underlying morality of Late Period biographies stresses human responsibility and accountability as never before. Much stress is laid on one's individual achievements in such a way that personal responsibility and accountability are suitable key-terms to describe its discourse. The royal institution has almost completely disappeared from these accounts. Instead, the deceased presents himself as a capable leader of his local community on whose initiative all kinds of works were undertaken. The deceased even takes all the credit for having built or renovated temple structures, which earlier formed part of the cultic role of the pharaoh. The city god has also replaced pharaoh as the point of reference in life. The biographies emphasise the deceased's piety and propagate, often in digressions of a general moral nature, the reliance on god as guide in life, as in the instruction texts. In this way, the deceased portrays himself as a wise man, successful in life and knowledgeable in rhetorical-didactic literary forms (proper speech), and, ultimately, as a godly man, whose success in life is entirely dependent upon his piety and respect for his city god. In this way, self-presentation and didactic literature collide, both propagating the idea that social cohesion within the community is ultimately also about god.

---

[81] Derchain-Urtel, *Priester im Tempel*, 198.
[82] See also Stele Manchester Museum n° inv. 2965, dated to the Saite period, in which this sequence occurs already. Lines 5–7 contain a series of four negations concerning priestly duties in the temple which are reminiscent of the earlier *Book of the Dead* spell 125 and the addresses to the priests of the Ptolemaic temples. Olivier Perdu, 'Exemple de stele archaïsante pour un prêtre modèle' RdE 52 (2001) 183–216; the four negations are discussed on pgs. 200–207.

Since entrance to the temple was not allowed to laity, a local community's access to the divine was seriously restricted. In such a setting, priests could function as intermediaries between temple and laity by means of their mastery of traditional idiom and knowledge of scripts and language. As a result of this, the local community could very well accredit them with a prestige or charisma that went beyond a strict interpretation of their priestly duties within the temple hierarchy. Moreover, their distinctive physical appearance and way of life made them into models of divine contiguity and reciprocity. They could therefore serve as ritual experts with considerable prestige.[83] Local needs were primarily concerned with issues of daily life such as fertility, childbirth, protective amulets, blessings and curses, and charms against demons and sorcerers. All sorts of forms of applied magic that testify to these activities have been found in abundant numbers. Unfortunately, the scattered sources do not allow a precise identification of the priests who took on this role. Moreover, it remains unclear through which channels and in what way the magical lore of the temple reached the world outside the *temenos* wall. Some information can be gleaned from the concluding words on the healing statue of the priest Djed-Hor from Athribis.[84] Healing statues portray the private individual who commissioned the statue and are covered with magical spells against bites and stings of venomous animals. They provided a means for the uninitiated and illiterate to share in the magical knowledge of the priests, because drinking the water that had been poured over the statue was believed to cure poisonous bites and stings.[85] The priest (*ḥm*) Wah-ib-Re

---

[83] See for a similar sociological model: Frankfurter, *Religion in Roman Egypt*, 210–214. However, Frankfurter is far too positive in assigning these roles to the priestly office of lector priest. The ancient sources provide a much more complex and even conflicting picture.

[84] For this statue, see, E. Jelínková-Reymond, *Les inscriptions de la statue guérisseuse de Djed-Her-le-Sauveur* (BdE 23; Cairo 1956). The Oriental Institute in Chicago houses the base of a parallel statue that was placed in the necropolis of Athribis: Elizabeth J. Sherman, 'Djedhor the Saviour Statue Base OI 10589' *JEA* 67 (1981) 82–102. A naophoric statue representing Djedhor has also been preserved, Cairo 4/6/19/1. The three sources are also listed in Pascal Vernus, *Athribis. Textes et documents relatifs à la géographie, aux cultes et à l'histoire d'une ville du Delta égyptien à l'époque pharaonique* (BdE 74; Cairo 1978) 193–195 [documents 160–162].

[85] Note that Djed-Hor's biographical account contains all the elements of the priestly self-presentation outlined above. He presents himself as a righteous and god-fearing man, who acted as a leader for his local community. On account of these qualities, Djed-Hor embodies the ritual purity required for the efficacy of the spells.

states proudly that he inscribed Djed-Hor's statue conforming what was found in the books:

> I put the writings on this statue conforming to what is written in *The excerpts*[86] *from the Bau of Re* and in *Every work of the Kherep-Serket* to bring all humans and animals back to life with them.
> [Djed-Hor, Biography §14, ll. 161f.]

By inscribing the statue with spells taken from two priestly handbooks, a bridge between the ritual world of the temple and the needs of the local community is established.

The passage does not specify which priestly class was concerned with composing and copying these handbooks. Two of the six titles mentioned in the trilingual decrees qualify. The lector priests, known in the trilingual decrees as 'scribes of the divine book' (in Egyptian) and 'feather bearers' (in Greek), played in all likelihood a major role in the transfer and translation of temple knowledge, because they were in charge of the ritual texts used in the cult. During public religious festivals and funerals they displayed their knowledge of ritual language and acts in front of the laity, possibly with the result that the local community recognized them as masters of the occult arts. Since the House-of-Life, the institutionalised cultic library in service to the temple, functioned as archive of magical and medical texts, its members, the 'scribes of the House-of-Life' (in Egyptian) or 'temple scribes' (in Greek), may also have acted as providers of charms and amulets to the lay public. It is therefore noteworthy that the introduction to the list of bizarre ingredients (PGM XII.401–444) pretends that it makes available information of exactly this class of priests.[87]

---

[86] This is a tentative translation of the technical term *inj-r*. See on book titles with this term: Siegfried Schott, *Bücher und Bibliotheken im Alten Ägypten. Verzeichnis der Buch- und Spruchtitel und der Termini technici* (Wiesbaden 1990) 13 [nr. 25].

[87] Egyptian sources from the pharaonic until the Late Period indicate that the House-of-Life knew a more refined disciplinary division than the term 'scribe of the House-of-Life' suggests. In the case of medicine, at least three different classes with a distinctive hierarchy were recognized: *swnw* priests, *ḥrp* priests of the goddess Serket and *wʿb* priests of the goddess Sekhmet. The exact division of tasks between these professional groups remains a matter of debate, although the *ḥrp* priests of the goddess Serket seem to have been particularly involved with curing venomous snake bites. Sources pertaining to the *ḥrp* priests of Serket and the *wʿb* priests of Sekhmet are collected in Frédérique von Känel, *Les prêtres-ouâb de Sekhmet et les conjurateurs de Serket* (Paris 1984); the titles are discussed in relation to the *swnw* on pp. 302ff. For the wab priest of Sekhmet, see also, Heinz Engelmann and Jochen Hallof, 'Der Sachmetpriester, ein früher Repräsentant der Hygiene und des Seuchenschutzes' *SAK* 23 (1996) 103–143. For the *ḥrp* priests of Serket, see also, Sauneron, *Un traité égyptien d'ophiologie*; 198–201.

## 6.3.3. *Egyptian priests as characters in the literary imagination*

The following two sections are concerned with the images of Egyptian priests in respectively Egyptian literature and Greek and Latin texts of the Roman period. In both traditions, the Egyptian priest was a favoured literary type that acts according to a limited number of generic conventions. These images should be understood as verbal representations, a way of speaking about, or referring to, Egyptian priests. As such, they are not directly related to reality, but mediated by an author, who passes a judgement on reality or, in the case of fictional narratives, creates a new (textual) reality altogether. It is therefore inevitable that societal interests, prejudices and power relations of the author or the group he represents influence the form and content of the representation. In the case of Egyptian literary works, it is highly probable that literary production and reception was more or less confined to priestly circles, so that these texts in all likelihood provide information about the way Egyptian priests viewed themselves.[88] The Greek and Latin texts were produced outside Egypt for an audience that was only aware of the country along the banks of the Nile by way of hearsay, imperial propaganda and classical literary and historiographical texts such as Homer's *Iliad* and *Odyssey* and Herodotus' *Histories*. In the Roman period texts, Egyptian priests tend to be portrayed as outsiders who are feared or revered for their outstanding knowledge of ritual texts, which tension betrays a pervasive Hellenistic debate on defining self and otherness.

---

For the *swnw* priests, see, John F. Nunn, *Ancient Egyptian Medicine* (London 1996) 113–135, take notice of appendix B on pp. 211–214 for a chronological listing of known doctors. See also Westendorf, *Handbuch der altägyptischen Medizin*, vol. 1, 472–481 and Joachim F. Quack, 'Das Buch vom Tempel und verwandte Texte: ein Vorbericht' *ARG* 2 (2000) 1–20, 13f.

[88] Due to a lack of relevant sources, the sociology of literary production in ancient Egypt is still far from understood. For example, virtually nothing is known about authorship in Egypt: Philippe Derchain, 'Auteur et société', in: A. Loprieno (ed.), *Ancient Egyptian Literature. History and Forms* (PdÄ 10; Leiden 1996) 83–94. In the Greco-Roman period, literary life was probably restricted to the native temple: Tait, 'Demotic Literature and Egyptian Society' and Idem, 'Demotic Literature: Forms and Genre', in: Loprieno (ed.), *Ancient Egyptian Literature*, 175–187, 178–180.

6.3.3.1. *Egyptian priests in Egyptian literary texts*

> If you desire to read writings, come along with me and I will let you be taken to the place where that book is that Thoth wrote with his own hand when he came down following the gods [Setne I, 3/12]

Egyptian priests are prominent characters in Egyptian literary texts. These fictional characters can be distinguished into two separate literary types, complying with two generic text categories. In rhetorical-didactic texts, Egyptian priests function as sages who, on account of their knowledge of religious texts and rhetorical forms, act as guardians of morality and just speech.[89] The priest functions as an embedded narrator who instructs a pupil in proper rules of conduct or converses with his heart or pharaoh about the state of affairs in Egypt.[90] In this way, the priest remains outside the story told and his textual role is restricted to rendering the message of the embedded text trustworthy, authoritative and prestigious for its audience by means of his priestly title. In fictional narratives, Egyptian priests act as miracle workers who are concerned with solving their own particular problems or satisfying their curiosity for magical texts, thereby frequently trespassing ideal rules of conduct. An external narrator recounts the course of events that are undergone and influenced by the priestly character. These stories could conveniently be called 'Tales of Wonder', because of the high number of episodes entailing magical tricks and miraculous objects.[91] Both textual categories are attested for the early as well as later phases of ancient Egyptian history. The extant record of tales, however, suggests a fair increase in popularity of the ritual expert type in the Greco-Roman period.

---

[89] For the term rhetorical-didactic literature, see, Moers, *Fingierte Welten in der ägyptischen Literatur des 2. Jahrtausends v. Chr. Grenzüberschreitung, Reisemotiv und Fiktionalität* (PdÄ 19; Leiden 2001) 167–188.

[90] The narratological terminology used in the present and the following section is taken from Mieke Bal, *Narratology. Introduction to the Theory of Narrative* (2nd ed.; Toronto 1997).

[91] See for a rather impressionistic discussion of such tales in Egyptian literature: Susan Tower Hollis, 'Tales of Magic and Wonder from Ancient Egypt', in: Jack M. Sasson, *Civilizations of the Ancient Near East* 4 vols. (New York 1995) 2255–2264. One must beware of considering this designation a generic literary term with heuristic value.

This section discusses the role of the ritual expert type in the fictional narratives. Three stories have been selected as instructive examples for their relative length, detailed descriptions and fairly well preserved state: *Tale of King Khufu's Court*, *Setne and the Book of Thoth* (Setne 1), *Setne and Sa-Osiris* (Setne 2). Before treating each story in more detail, the following tenets as regards the literary construct of the ritual expert can be listed:

1. The figures are related to the Egyptian priesthood.
2. The royal court is the arena of display and conflict.
3. Magic is not condemned on moral grounds.
4. Egyptian ritual experts are decent members of society.
5. The priest's knowledge is based on the consultation of books.
6. Effective magical texts are written by the god Thoth.
7. Books written in Thoth's own hand are carefully kept from mortals.
8. Powerful ritual experts are of the past.
9. The described magical techniques are also prescribed and explained in extant contemporary magic handbooks.

The *Tale of King Khufu's Court* is a cycle of wondrous stories partly preserved on a manuscript from the late Second Intermediate Period (around 1640–1532 BCE).[92] King Khufu's sons take turns telling their father of some miraculous feat done in the past. Each story evolves around a figure that holds the title 'chief lector priest' (*ḥry-ḥb ḥry-tp*), perhaps better translated in this context as 'magician'. One of them, Ubainer, made a crocodile out of wax to seize the man who seduced his wife,[93] while another, Djadjaemankh (who is also 'scribe of the book'), put one side of a lake on top of the other to retrieve a fish-pendant that one of the king's rowing girls had dropped into the water. After each embedded story, king Khufu orders to give copious funerary offerings to the deceased ritual expert, because 'I have seen his deed of wisdom (*sp=f n rḫ*)' (P. Westcar 1/16, 4/16–7 and 6/21). To outdo his royal

---

[92] The manuscript is known as P. Westcar: A.M. Blackman, *The Story of King Kheops and the Magicians. Transcribed from Papyrus Westcar (Berlin Papyrus 3033)* (Reading 1988).

[93] The manipulation of human or animal figurines made out of wax or mud was a common technique in Egyptian ritual. The method is attested for execration and funerary rituals from the Middle Kingdom onwards. See for an overview and relevant sources: M.J. Raven, 'Magic and Symbolic Aspects of Certain Materials in Ancient Egypt' *VA* 4 (1988) 237–242 and Idem, 'Wax in Egyptian Magic and Symbolism' *OMRO* 64 (1983) 7–47.

brothers, Prince Hordedef chooses not to tell his father a story about the past, because 'truth cannot be known from falsehood' (P. Westcar 6/23f.). Instead, he prefers to lead a contemporary before his father, a certain Djedi.

> He is a commoner (*nḏs*), a hundred and ten years old.
> He eats five hundred loaves of bread,
> A shoulder of ox for meat,
> And also drinks a hundred jars of beer,
> Up to this day.
> He knows how to rejoin a severed head.
> He knows how to make a lion walk behind him with its leash on the ground.
> He knows the number of the Chambers of the Sanctuary of Thoth.
> [P. Westcar 7/1–6][94]

Khufu orders his son Hordedef to bring this man to the court immediately, whereupon Djedi arrives with his children and books in due course. Although Djedi does not have a priestly title, he knows 'his words of magic' (*ḏd.w.t=f m ḥkꜣ.w*; P. Westcar 8/20 and 25) like the lector priests in the foregoing stories, so that he is able to perform all feats with ease. Instead of telling pharaoh the number of the Chambers of the Sanctuary of Thoth, he reveals that the text is kept in a flint casket in a room in Heliopolis, where only the first three kings of the following dynasty will find it. At this point the tale relates in detail the wondrous birth of these children but, unfortunately, the physical manuscript breaks off before anything further has been said about the Sanctuary of Thoth.

In the above quoted passage, the embedded narrator prince Hordedef, who was not only a historic but also a celebrated figure with his own literary tradition for the audience of the day,[95] introduces the

---

[94] Tr. R.B. Parkinson.

[95] Prince Hordedef was also known as the author of an instruction text and was remembered as a classical author of high merit at least until the end of the New Kingdom (the *Harper's Song* from the tomb of king Antef [preserved in three New Kingdom copies] and P. Chester Beatty IV verso 3/5; see D. Wildung, *Imhotep und Amenhotep. Gottwerdung im alten Ägypten* (MÄS 36; Munich 1977) 21–29). In *Hori's Satirical Letter* (time of Ramsesses II), knowledge of the exact wording of one of Hordedef's verses serves as a criterion of education in an intellectual contest between two scribes (P. Anastasi I 11/1): H.-W. Fischer-Elfert, *Die Satirische Streitschrift des Papyrus Anastasi I* (ÄgAbh 44; Wiesbaden 1986) 94–96. He was also remembered as the discoverer of *Book of the Dead* spells 30B, 64, 137A and 148; see for collected sources (17th dynasty until Ptolemaic period): D. Wildung, *Die Rolle ägyptischer Könige im Bewußtsein ihrer Nachwelt* (MÄS 17; Berlin 1969) 218–221 and P. Vernus, *Essai sur la conscience de l'histoire dans l'Égypte*

magician Djedi by enumerating a number of interesting constituents. Djedi is set off from ordinary humans by his old age (110 years) and his extraordinary income or appetite (500 loaves of bread, a shoulder of ox, 100 jars of beer).[96] He knows a number of magical tricks and holds secret knowledge about the sanctuary of Thoth, the god of magic. Djedi is brought from his residential town Djed-Sneferu[97] in the vicinity of modern Meidum to the royal court in Memphis together with his books. Djedi's mastery of script and language and his connection with Thoth make him a prototypical Egyptian intellectual.[98] Apparently, an Egyptian audience considered these the constitutive elements of a person knowledgeable in the occult arts.

For the Late and Greco-Roman Period, the number of preserved narratives featuring ritual experts increases considerably, possibly indicating a rise in popularity of this literary type among the audience of Egyptian narratives. Like all the fictional narratives composed in this later period, the stories are set in a glorious past when Egypt was still traditionally ruled by an indigenous pharaoh. The scattered sources allow identifying two favoured historical and priestly settings for the events to take place: the high priests of Ptah in Memphis around the time of

---

*pharaonique* (Paris 1995) 113f. According to the introductions or postscripts to these spells, Hordedef made his discoveries in the course of an inspection of the temples in the country. In the Greco-Roman period he was accredited with having discovered the *Book of the Temple*: J.F. Quack, 'Der historisch Abschnitt des Buches vom Tempel', in: Jan Assmann and Elke Blumenthal (eds.), *Literatur und Politik im pharaonischen und ptolemäischen Ägypten* (BdE 127; Cairo 1999) 267–278, 274f. and 277.

[96] Djedi's age and daily diet were probably not randomly chosen. In fact, 110 years was considered in ancient Egypt to be the ideal life span reserved for righteous persons. These 110 years make Djedi a member of a generation of a bygone age. In this respect, it may not be coincidental that the bread, ox and beer are reminiscent of common funerary offerings. In other words, Djedi is a figure of the past although still alive. Note that the same holds true for Sa-Osiris, the main character in *Setne and Sa-Osiris* (Setne 2).

[97] Djed-Sneferu was the priestly settlement attached to king Snefru's pyramid in Meidum. King Snefru was remembered as a beneficent king who ruled Egypt in a time of prosperity. The author of the tale intended in all likelihood to associate Snefru's beneficial character and the fictional character Djedi. See on the Egyptian memory of king Snefru: Dietrich Wildung, *Die Rolle ägyptischer Könige im Bewußtsein ihrer Nachwelt* (MÄS 17; Berlin 1969) 114–124 and E. Graefe, 'Die gute Reputation des Königs Snofru', in: S. Israelit-Groll (ed.), *Studies in Egyptology Presented to Miriam Lichtheim* 2 vols. (Jerusalem 1990) vol. 1, 257–263.

[98] A detailed discussion of Djedi as *homme de lettres* can be found in Morenz, *Beiträge zur Schriftlichkeitskultur*, 107–123.

pharaoh Ramesses II (1290–1224 BCE) and the priesthood of Atum-Re in Heliopolis in a yet undefined past. The literary characters either hold the priestly title 'high priest' (ḥm nṯr) or 'chief' (ḥry-tp), an abbreviated form of the common title 'chief lector priest' (ḥry-ḥb ḥry-tp) that the ritual experts featuring in the *Tale of King Khufu's Court* held.[99] Main characters of the stories of the priesthood of Heliopolis that could be identified so far are Petese, son of Petetum, a certain Horpaouensh, who appears as well in an Aramaic version, and Hareus, son of Tjainefer.[100] However, the stories of the high priests of Ptah, evolving around the character Setne Khamwase, are better suited for a discussion, because of the good state of preservation of two manuscripts that contain the stories *Setne and the Book of Thoth* and *Setne and Sa-Osiris*.[101] The priestly title 'Sem' or, since the nineteenth dynasty, 'Setem', which the high priest of Ptah traditionally held in addition to the title 'chief of the leaders of the craftsmen', had become a fixed name 'Setne' in the Demotic narratives about the Memphite priesthood.[102]

---

[99] The exact reading of the Demotic group ḥry-tp was settled by Wilhelm Spiegelberg, 'Demotica I' *SBAW* 6. Abhandlung (1925) 4–7. See also Gardiner, 'The House of Life', 164 and Idem, *Ancient Egyptian Onomastica*, vol.1, 56*. Also take notice of Ritner, *The Mechanics of Ancient Egyptian Magical Practice*, 220f., fn. 1025.

[100] See for Petese, son of Petetum: Kim Ryholt, *The Carlsberg Papyri 4, The Story of Petese son of Petetum and Seventy Other Good and Bad Stories* (CNI Publications 23; Copenhagen 1999). The story of Horpaouenesh is still unpublished: Karl-Th. Zauzich, 'Neue literarische Texte in demotischer Schrift' *Enchoria* 8.2 (1978) 33–38, 36. The story featuring Hareus, son of Tjainefer is partly published in Kim Ryholt, 'An Elusive Narrative belonging to the Cycle of Stories about the Priesthood at Heliopolis', in: Kim Ryholt (ed.), *Acts of the Seventh International Conference of Demotic Studies* (CNI Publications 27; Copenhagen 2002) 361–366.

[101] The story *Setne and the Book of Thoth* (Setne I) is preserved complete except for the first two columns on P. Cairo 30646 (of Ptolemaic date). The second Setne tale, *Setne and Sa-Osiris*, only misses the opening of the story. It is preserved on P. BM. 10822 [604 verso] (of Roman date). Both texts are published in F. Ll. Griffith, *Stories of the High Priests of Memphis* 2 vols. (Oxford 1900).

[102] A story badly preserved on a manuscript from the Tebtunis temple library evolves around a certain Setne: W.J. Tait, 'P. Carlsberg 207: Two Columns of a Setna Text', in: Frandsen (ed.), *The Carlsberg papyri 1*, 19–46 and J.F. Quack and K. Ryholt, 'Notes on P. Carlsberg 207', in: Frandsen and Ryholt (eds.), *The Carlsberg Papyri 3*, 141–164. Another setem priest, a certain Ptahhotep, appears in P. Cairo CG 30758 and P. Dem. Saq. 1. See for the former manuscript: W. Spiegelberg, *Demotische Denkmäler II* (Cairo 1906–1908) 145–148, pl. LVIII; the latter can be found in H.S. Smith and W.J. Tait, *Saqqâra Demotic Papyri I* (EES Texts from Excavations 7; London 1983) 1–69, pls. 1–3. Setne Khamwase occurs possibly in one of the short stories contained in the cycle of Seventy Good and Bad Stories in the Story of Petese, son of Petetum: K. Ryholt, *The Carlsberg Papyri 4, The Story of Petese son of Petetum and Seventy Other Good and Bad Stories* (CNI Publications 23; Copenhagen 1999) 84f.

For an Egyptian audience of the Late and Greco-Roman period, Setne Khamwase was as much a celebrated historic figure as the embedded narrator prince Hordedef in the *Tale of Khufu's Court* was for an audience of the Middle and New Kingdom. The fictional character Setne Khamwase was based on the historical prince Khaemwaset, who lived in the thirteenth century BCE as fourth son of pharaoh Ramesses II the Great and served as high priest of Ptah in Memphis.[103] His father reigned for about 66 years, built or renovated dozens of temples and claimed as many military successes, which were lavishly laid out in text and relief on the outside walls of the major temples of Egypt. At the time of his death, Ramesses left Egypt scattered with statues and monumental texts glorifying his name and deeds, which guaranteed his endurance in Egypt's collective memory.[104] Like his father, Khaemwaset remained in the minds of the literate elite. He was not remembered as a conqueror and powerful ruler, but as a scholar and collector of ancient texts on account of his activities as high priest of Ptah in the Memphite area. First, he ordered the construction of an underground burial complex for the Apis bulls in the Saqqara desert, nowadays known as the Serapeum, which complex remained in use until the Roman period. Secondly, in his name renovation works were undertaken at the millennium-old pyramid complexes of the pharaohs of the Old Kingdom that were located in the vicinity of Memphis. Both activities were commemorated in monumental texts that remained clearly visible for the generations to come.[105] As a result, he entered the imagination as a sage and scholarly priest anxious for old texts of sacred knowledge. For example, Book of the Dead spell 167 *supplémentaire*, preserved on two manuscripts from the Ptolemaic period, is presented as a text found by Khaemwaset under the head of a mummy in the Memphite desert.[106]

---

[103] See for sources relating to the historical Khaemwaset and a detailed account of his life: Marjorie M. Fisher, *The Sons of Ramesses II* 2 vols. (ÄA 53; Wiesbaden 2001) 89–105 [vol. 1] and 89–143 [vol. 2]. See also: Farouk Gomaà, *Chaemwese. Sohn Ramses II. Und Hoherpriester von Memphis* (ÄgAbh 27; Wiesbaden 1973) and K.A. Kitchen, *Pharaoh Triumphant. The Life and Times of Ramesses II, King of Egypt* (Warminster 1982) 103–109.

[104] See as introduction to this topic: Robert S. Bianchi, 'Graeco-Roman uses and abuses of Ramesside traditions', in: E. Bleiberg and R. Freed (eds.), *Fragments of a Shattered Visage: the proceedings of the international symposium of Ramesses the Great* (Memphis 1991), 1–8.

[105] See for translations of these texts: Gomaà, *Chaemwese*, 44, 63 (hieroglyphic transcriptions are found on pages 110f. and 101–106) and Kitchen, *Pharaoh Triumphant*, 105–107.

[106] The date of composition of spell 167 and the other *chapitres supplémentaires* is

> The writings of the ointment bowl (*mḥ.t*) that had found the king's son, the chief [lector priest] (*ḥry-tp*) Khaemwaset under the head of a blessed spirit (*ꜣḫw*) to the west of Memphis.
>
> It is more divine than any (other) bowl from the House-of-Life. It was made in the gate of fire between the blessed spirits and the dead in order to prevent the aggressor (*pḥ-sw*) reaching them there. [Tested] a million times.
>
> The book (*šꜥ.t*) 'Secret of forms' that had found the king's scribe, the chief [lector priest] (*ḥry-tp*) Amenhotep son of Hapu, true of voice. He made (it) for himself (as) an amulet (litt. protection for (his) members).

It remains a matter of debate whether the advertising introduction is a posthumous fiction to render the spell authentic and prestigious or a historically correct record of the discovery of an ancient text by Khaemwaset during his renovation works in the Memphite desert. The reference to Amenhotep son of Hapu in the final paragraph indicates rather a Theban instead of Memphite origin of the spell. After his death, Amenhotep son of Hapu, a favourite official of pharaoh Amenhotep III (1391–1353 BCE), had become an object of cult in the Theban region, which became particularly prominent in the Greco-Roman period.[107] Whatever the case, the Book of the Dead tradition continued the image of Khamwaset as a priest, antiquarian and bibliophile into the Ptolemaic period.

The tale *Setne and the Book of Thoth* (Setne 1) tells the unfortunate love story of Naneferkaptah and Ihweret, son and daughter of pharaoh Mernebptah, who were untimely separated in death due to Naneferkaptah's obsessive desire to posses the Book of Thoth. The extant version of the story starts in the burial chamber of Naneferkaptah's tomb in the Memphite desert, where Ihweret's ghost, as embedded narrator,

---

unclear. Yoyotte argues for a Ramesside date, whereas Lesko proposes the 21st dynasty: Jean Yoyotte, 'Contribution à l'histoire du chapitre 162 du Livre des Morts' *RdE* 29 (1977) 194–202 and Leonard H. Lesko, 'Some Further Thoughts on Chapter 162 of the *Book of the Dead*', in: E. Teeter and J.A. Larson (eds.), *Gold of Praise. Fs. E.F. Wente* (SAOC 58; Chicago 1999) 255–259. Pleyte's edition of spell 167 *suppl.* is based on two manuscripts from the Ptolemaic period (P. Leiden T 30 and P. hiérat. Louvre Inv. 3248): W. Pleyte, *Chapitres supplémentaires du Livre des Morts, 162 à 174* 3 vols. (Leiden 1881–1882); see for a hieroglyphic transcription of the hieratic text: Gomaà, *Chaemwese*, 134, plate 34.

[107] See for sources pertaining to Amenhotep son of Hapu: Dietrich Wildung, *Imhotep und Amenhotep. Gottwerdung im alten Ägypten* (MÄS 36; Munich 1977) 251–297, the present text is discussed on pages 272f. (§ 176).

tries to keep Setne from taking the Book of Thoth. Setne had discovered the book in the burial chamber and the ghost tells him about the misfortune that befell her family on account of the book. Many years ago, an old priest had talked to her husband Naneferkaptah in vivid terms about a magical book written by Thoth himself. In exchange for a fee amounting to the costs of a proper burial, the old priest gave away that the book was hidden on an island in the vicinity of Coptos, whereupon Naneferkaptah decided to travel with his wife Ihweret and newly born son Merib from Memphis to southern Coptos to take possession of the book. In Coptos, the priests of Isis welcomed them warmly and took care of them. After the prerequisite offerings to Isis and Harpocrates and four days of feasting with the priests, Naneferkaptah made a boat and its crew out of wax to set off to the island where the book was kept. On the island, the book was defended by the pre-eminent chthonic enemies: a six mile barrier of snakes, scorpions and worms, and an ever living serpent coiled around the box in which the book was kept. Naneferkaptah overcame the defences of the book by the use of his magical tricks.[108] On the way back to Memphis, however, the god Thoth punished him severely for his intrusion. His son and wife drowned in the Nile and were buried in Coptos, while Naneferkaptah drowned as well afterwards and was buried together with the book in Memphis. When Ihweret finishes her story, Setne is still determined to take the book from the tomb. In a final desperate effort to keep the book, Naneferkaptah proposes to play a game of *Senet* over the book, which Setne willingly accepts.[109] However, Setne is easily outplayed and is only saved in the nick of time with the help of his amulets and magic handbooks, which his foster brother Inaros brings to the tomb. When Setne escapes from the tomb with the book of Thoth, he leaves Naneferkaptah and Ihweret's ghost in darkness and distress. Thereupon, Naneferkaptah sends Setne a bad dream in which he is seduced and humiliated by Tabubu, the daughter of the high priest of

---

[108] The number of attested spells to repel venomous animals is small. Unfortunately, the sources have not yet been collected systematically. See for some relevant literature: Christian Leitz, 'Die Schlangensprüche in den Pyramidentexten' *Orientalia* 65 (1996) 381–427. Charms to ward off these animals occur as early as the Pyramid Texts (spells 226–243, 276–299, 314, 375–399, 499–500, 502, 538, 549–551, 727–733) and continue through the Coffin Texts into the Book of the Dead (spells 31–40).

[109] For the identification of the game as *Senet*, see, Peter A. Piccione, 'The Gaming Episode in the *Tale of Setne Khamwas* as Religious Metaphor', in: David. P. Silverman, *For his Ka. Fs. Klaus Baer* (SAOC 55; Chicago 1994) 197–204, 199f.

Bastet, who forces him to sign a maintenance contract and to throw his children to the dogs.[110] When Setne wakes up from this nightmare in the street, naked and lying in front of pharaoh (Naneferkaptah in disguise), he understands his mistake. He returns the book and orders the corpses of Merib and Ihweret to be transferred from Coptos to Memphis, so that the family is reunited, now forever.

The main theme of this Demotic narrative is the inevitable failure of any human endeavour to get hold of divine knowledge for reasons of sheer curiosity. The tale's message is that Books of Thoth are not meant to be readings for mortals. The division between the divine and human spheres should be respected and maintained. This division is clearly specified in the distribution of space in both the primary and secondary fabula. The divine sphere is located on the island in the Theban region (line 4/19) and in the tomb of Naneferkaptah in the desert to the west of Memphis, whereas the royal court in Memphis represents the human sphere. The respective spheres of actions are ideally separated and their borders become blurred the moment a human, Naneferkaptah or Setne, introduces into the human world an object from the divine realm, in this case the Book of Thoth. The underlying structure of the literary topography in the embedded narrative is given in the following table. It clearly shows that transgressing the spatial rule blurs the established oppositions and, as a consequence, is doomed to bring trouble.

| *Court in Memphis* | *Island beyond Coptos* |
| --- | --- |
| pharaoh | Thoth |
| human sphere | divine sphere |
| order | chaos (animals) |
| safety | danger |
| life | death |

By bringing the Book of Thoth back to the court in Memphis, Naneferkaptah and Setne intermingle the two separate spheres and thus pose a potential threat to the social order at the royal court. This idea is most clearly brought into the open at the moment that, after his son

---

[110] Spells to send a (bad) dream or to obtain a revelatory dream abound in the *Demotic* and *Greek Magical Papyri*, see Brashear, 'The *Greek Magical Papyri*', 3502. Examples in the two manuscripts under discussion are PGM XII.107–121; 121–143; 144–152; 190–192 and PDM xiv.706–749 (12 short recipes); 912–916; 917–919; 1070–1077.

Merib and wife Ihweret drowned, Naneferkaptah understands his mistake and, on the way back home, explicates the dichotomy between Memphis and the Theban region in terms of life and death.

> 'Could I return to Coptos and dwell there also? If I go to Memphis now and Pharaoh asks me about his children, what shall I say to him? Can I say to him, 'I took your children to the region of Thebes; I killed them and stayed alive, and I have come to Memphis yet alive?'
> [P. Cairo 30646 4/17–19]

The Book of Thoth is thus literature reserved to gods (the island) and the deceased (Naneferkaptah's tomb). Whenever mortals take the book out of its secluded context into the world of the living, they call down interference from the world of the gods or deceased upon themselves. Only by restoring the dichotomy between human and divine spheres, the tale can come to a happy ending.

Both the external narrator and the embedded narrator Ihweret present their story from a Memphite perspective. They perceive the Theban region as a dangerous place of magic and wonder opposed to the human conditions in Memphis. Ihweret brings this view to the fore when she describes her reaction to her husband's plan to seize the Book of Thoth. In all likelihood, Ihweret's comments are meant to articulate the audience's thoughts, so that it can identify with her and feel the rise of tension within the story.

> He [said] to me: 'I will go to Coptos, I will bring this book, hastening back to the north again'. But I chided the priest, saying: 'May Neith curse you for having told him these [dreadful things. You have brought] me combat, you have brought me strife. The region of Thebes, I now find it [abhorrent]'. I did what I could with Naneferkaptah to prevent him from going to Coptos; he did not listen to me.
> [P. Cairo 30646 3/21–22][111]

This passage may thus be a reflection of a shared view among the native priesthood of the Late and Greco-Roman period that the Theban region in the south was an extraordinary place of magic and wonder.

The tale exhibits a number of prominent similarities with the *Tale of King Khufu's Court* with respect to the handling of books. First of all, Djedi's concern for his books is paralleled in Naneferkaptah's roaming through the western desert of Memphis to read the texts on the ancient tombs and steles until the priest tells him of the Book of Thoth in

---

[111] Tr. M. Lichtheim.

Coptos. In both tales, the magician is portrayed as an intellectual whose knowledge is based on the consultation of texts. Unlike Djedi, who is also aware of a book kept in a flint box in the temple of Heliopolis but does not collect it, Naneferkaptah does not respect the set borders between the human and the divine. Djedi makes use of his books to perform magical feats at pharaoh Khufu's court, while Setne draws on his magic books to save himself from Naneferkaptah's attacks in the *Senet* game episode. This means that the possession and consultation of magic books was not considered forbidden as such. Naneferkaptah and Setne are punished because they breach a religious law and act contrary to the ideal rules of conduct set out in rhetorical-didactic texts, which have been discussed in the previous section.[112] However, the Book of Thoth is not a recipe book for a variety of apotropaeic and healing rites, but rather reminiscent of mortuary literature.[113] Mortuary texts were placed in the deceased's tomb to enable him or her, having become god-like after the glorification rites,[114] to participate in the mysteries of the daily journey of the sun barge through the sky and the netherworld.[115] The funerary character of the Book of Thoth is borne out first by the way it is defended against mortals on the island and, second, by its content. The episode in which Naneferkaptah finds the book on the island is full of funerary imagery.

> He not only found a span of six miles of serpents, scorpions and worms around the place in which the book was, he also found an ever-living serpent around the said chest (*tby.t*[116]). (... he defeats the animals; jd ...) Naneferkaptah went to the place where the chest was [and found that

---

[112] The behaviour of Naneferkaptah and Setne is reminiscent of the portrayal of the fool (*swg*, *lg*) in contemporary Demotic instruction texts. They do not listen to advice, do not respect hierarchy and act on impulse. In his relationship to Tabubu, the following maxim is well applicable to Setne: 'The [fool] brings danger to his life because of his phallus' [P. Insinger 8/1]. The tale held thus a moral lesson for its audience.

[113] Ritner interprets the Book of Thoth likewise as a collection of funerary spells: Ritner, *The Mechanics of Ancient Egyptian Magical Practice*, 63f. Ritner refers to *Book of the Dead* spells 133–134 as instructive parallels to the fictive spells of the tale. However, these *Book of the Dead* spells prescribe ritual manipulation of objects and images unlike the fictive spells. The fictive spells are less about ritual as about knowledge.

[114] See on these rites: Jan Assmann, *Tod und Jenseits im Alten Ägypten* (Munich 2001) 321ff.

[115] See for an overview of the texts: Erik Hornung, *The Ancient Egyptian Books of the Afterlife* (Ithaca, London 1999) 26ff. [translation from: *Altägyptische Jenseitsbücher. Ein einführender Überblick* (Darmstadt 1997)]. The possible use of these texts by a selected group of initiates during lifetime is discussed by Edward F. Wente, 'Mysticism in Pharaonic Egypt?' *JNES* 41 (1982) 161–179 and Assmann, *Tod und Jenseits*, 504–517.

[116] Note that the first meaning of the word *tby.t* is 'sarcophagus'.

it was a chest of] iron. He opened it and found a chest of copper. He opened it and found a chest of juniper wood. He opened it and found a chest of ivory and ebony. [He opened it and found a chest of] silver. He opened it and found a chest of gold. He opened it and found the book inside it.  [P. Cairo 30646 3/30–35]

To an Egyptian audience the image of the island may have evoked an association with Osiris' tomb that was located on an island.[117] The protective ever-living serpent is reminiscent of the Ouroboros snake, which played in different functions, and under different names, an important role in mortuary texts and was occasionally depicted along the rim of royal sarcophagi.[118] The series of chests corresponds with a burial assemblage of several sarcophagi.[119]

The Book of Thoth is not used as a recipe book for magical rites, but treated as a container of knowledge. The characters read the text aloud and share its contents with others (lines 3/40 and 4/38). Naneferkaptah even incorporates its contents literally by way of drinking the water in which the ink of the freshly written spells has been dissolved (lines 4/3–4).[120] This stress on knowledge is highly reminiscent of mortuary literature, which operated on the basis that knowledge of the workings of nature enabled participation in the cosmic cycle of death and rebirth. The opening of the *Book of the hidden Room* (Amduat) explicates this notion clearly.[121]

> To know the souls (*b3.w*) of the netherworld,
> To know the secret souls,
> To know the gates and the roads on which the greatest god goes,
> To know what is done,
> To know what is in the hours together with their gods,
> To know the course of the hours together with their gods,
> To know their glorifications for Re,
> To know what he says to them,
> To know the honoured ones and the damned ones
>  [*Amduat*, title, ll. 3–8]

---

[117] Hans Bonnet, *Reallexikon der ägyptischen Religionsgeschichte* (Berlin 1952) 576a–77a.

[118] L. Kákosy, 'Uroboros', *LdÄ* VI, 886–893 and Piccione, 'Gaming Episode in the *Tale of Setne Khamwas*', 201f.

[119] Piccione, 'Gaming Episode in the *Tale of Setne Khamwas*', 201f.

[120] The connection between ritually eating or swallowing and knowledge is attested since the Pyramid Texts, see: Ritner, *The Mechanics of Ancient Egyptian Magical Practice*, 102–110.

[121] See for a philological commentary on this passage: Siegfried Schott, *Die Schrift der verborgenen Kammer in Königsgräbern* (NAWG 4; Göttingen 1958) 342ff.

The two spells of the fictive Book of Thoth provide its reader knowledge about the cosmos in a similar vein, as illustrated in the following passage:

> He (Naneferkaptah) put the book in my hand (Ihweret). I recited a written spell (*hpe n sẖ*) from it. I charmed (*pḥr*) the heaven, earth, underworld, the mountains and the waters. I discovered (*gmj*) all that the birds of the sky, the fish of the deep and the beasts were saying. I recited another written spell. I saw (*nwj*) Pre appearing in the sky with his Ennead. I saw the Moon rising with all the stars of heaven in their form. I saw the fish of the deep, although there were twenty-one divine cubits of water over them. [P. Cairo 30646 3/40–4/3]

The central verbs of this passage—*pḥr*, *gmj*, *nwj*—indicate the nature of the Book of Thoth. The latter two verbs ('to discover' and 'to see') describe a moment of recognition and insight, a personal experience. The first verb is translated as 'to charm', but means actually something like 'to have ritual control over an object so as to make it work properly'.[122] The two spells thus allow the practitioner to have control over the cosmos and to witness the mystery of the travels of the divine heavenly bodies. According to one of the closing statements of the *Book of the hidden Room* it was prohibited to share this kind of knowledge with ordinary humans:

> The choice guidebook (*ꜥjt.t ꜥnd.t*),[123] the secret transcript of the underworld that is unknown to any human except for the select few (*ꜥnd*).
> [*Amduat*, short version, 292f.][124]

It is exactly this rule that Naneferkaptah and Setne violate.

The tale *Setne and Sa-Osiris* (Setne II) is the story of Setne's wondrous son Sa-Osiris, who saved Egypt from a loss of face by winning a magic contest between Egypt and Nubia. An external narrator relates that Sa-Osiris was conceived after Setne's wife Mehsehet had received divine directions, possibly from Imhotep, in an incubation dream.[125] The boy

---

[122] Ritner, *The Mechanics of Egyptian Magical Practice*, 57–67.

[123] The translation is tentative; Schott, *Die Schrift der verborgenen Kammer*, 348–350.

[124] Erik Hornung, *Das Amduat. Die Schrift des verborgenen Raumes* 3 vols. (ÄA 13; Wiesbaden 1963–1967) vol. 3, 25–26.

[125] Temple incubation was a common institution in Greco-Roman Egypt. Compare this episode with the biographical account of Tayimhotep's funerary stele (BM EA147) dated to 42 BCE. Tayimhotep relates that she was granted a male child, after her husband, the high priest of Ptah Pasherenptah, had fulfilled the directions given by Imhotep in a dream: E.A.E. Reymond, *From the Records of a Priestly Family in Memphis*

was exceptional for his fast intellectual growth and his talent for the sacred writings, which he discussed with the scribes of the House-of-Life. After an episode in which Sa-Osiris guides his father through the netherworld to show him the fate of men after the divine judgement, the tale shifts to the court of pharaoh Ramsesses II in Memphis where a Nubian chieftain is challenging the Egyptian court to read a sealed letter without opening it.[126] In case no Egyptian will be able to perform the feat, he threatens to bring the shame of Egypt back to Nubia. Sa-Osiris saves his father Setne, who is assigned the task but does not know how to carry it out, by reading out loud the unopened letter. As embedded narrator, Sa-Osiris tells the story of a magic contest between Nubia and Egypt in the bygone days of pharaoh Menkh-Pre-Siamun.[127] A Nubian king started the contest as he allowed one of his chieftains (ꜣte) to execute his evil plans against Egypt. The chief, Horus-son-of-the-Nubian-woman, modelled a bier and four bearers out of wax and, after having recited a magical spell, sent them off to Egypt in order to collect pharaoh and beat him with 500 blows of the stick in front of the Nubian ruler. The morning after, the beaten and frightened pharaoh, meanwhile returned to his own palace, asked his ritual expert (ḥry-tp) Horus-son-of-Paneshe to find a remedy against these attacks. The ritual expert went to the temple of Thoth in Hermopolis and was told by Thoth in a dream about a magical handbook for amulets written by the god himself hidden in the library of the temple. The following evening the amulets proved able to ward off the Nubian threats, while the Egyptian ritual expert inflicted identical punishment on the Nubian ruler for the next three days. Thereupon, the Nubian chieftain came

---

2 Vols. (ÄgAbh 38; Wiesbaden 1981) vol.1, cat. nr. 20. Spells to acquire dream revelations abound in the PGM: S. Eitrem, 'Dreams and Divination in Magical Ritual', in: Faraone and Obbink (eds.), *Magika Hiera*, 175–187. Manuals for dream interpretation are attested for the Ramesside (P. Chester Beatty IIIa) and the Greco-Roman period (best known are P. Carlsberg XIII and XIV verso). See: A. Volten, *Demotische Traumdeutung (Pap. Carlsberg XIII und XIV Verso)* (AnAe 3; Copenhagen 1942) and K.-Th. Zauzich, 'Aus zwei demotischen Traumbüchern' *AfP* 27 (1980) 91–98. The institution of temple incubation in Roman Egypt is discussed in Frankfurter, *Religion in Roman Egypt*, 162–169. See for an early Roman incubation structure attached to the temple of Denderah: F. Daumas, 'Le Sanatorium de Dendera.' *BIFAO* 56 (1957) 35–57.

[126] Spell PGM V.213–303, a recipe to make a magical ring, claims to enable the practitioner to read sealed letters (line 301). The Demotic spell PDM Suppl. 168–184 has probably the same purpose.

[127] The pharaoh's name is in all likelihood a corruption of pharaoh Thutmoses III's throne name Men-Kheperu-Re (1479–1425 BCE). This king lived actually only about 200 years instead of 1500 years earlier than pharaoh Ramesses II.

down to the Egyptian court where he engaged in a magic contest with Horus-son-of-Paneshe. The Nubian chieftain set fire in court, clouded the sky over and placed a great vault of stone above pharaoh and his court, but Horus-son-of-Paneshe undid each trick. In the end, the mother of the Nubian chieftain came flying from Nubia to her son's aid to no avail. When a fowler was about to kill her and her son who had assumed the form of a goose and a gander, she asked for mercy and promised not to return to Egypt for 1500 years. When Sa-Osiris finishes reading the letter, he explains that the 1500 years have passed and that the Nubian letter carrier is nobody else but Horus-son-of-the-Nubian-woman who has come back to Egypt for revenge. Thereupon Sa-Osiris reveals that he is actually Horus-son-of-Paneshe having returned to earth to counter the Nubian sorcerer. He slays the Nubian with fire and vanishes while leaving Setne and the court at a loss.

In *Setne and Sa-Osiris*, magic from an unfamiliar environment poses a threat to the stable social community at the royal court in Memphis as in the first tale of Setne. In this case, the threat is not the result of an infraction of a religious rule but of a foreign intruder with malicious intent. The god Thoth acts therefore not as an antagonist but as a helper who willingly shares his magical spells with the Egyptian protagonist. For an Egyptian audience, Nubia was a credible aggressor, since the Nubian kingdom of Meroe was a continuous menace to the territory of Ptolemaic and Roman Egypt in historical reality.[128] Moreover, Nubia was traditionally considered one of the nine traditional foes in Egyptian religion.[129] The tale is thus not only an exciting story about two contesting magicians in a distant yet glorious past, but can also be read as an attempt to confirm Egypt's territorial integrity and cultural superiority vis-à-vis an intruding foreign power in a fictive setting that bears on a historical and ideological reality. In the light of contemporary Greco-Roman hegemony, this subtext plausibly addressed pertinent political questions of the day for a native audience.[130] The magical tricks and the glorious past should therefore not

---

[128] Josef Locher, 'Die Anfänge der römischen Herrschaft in Nubien und der Konflikt zwischen Rom und Meroe' *Ancient Society* 32 (2002) 73–133.

[129] For the image of Nubia in pharaonic and Greco-Roman Egypt, see, chapter 4.4.4.

[130] A similar idea is expressed in Richard Gordon, 'Reporting the Marvellous: Private Divination in the *Greek Magical Papyri*', in: Peter Schäfer and Hans G. Kippenberg (eds.), *Envisioning Magic. A Princeton Seminar and Symposium* (Studies in the History of Religions

be dismissed as mere folklore motives, but be regarded as the stake of a serious priestly effort to define Egypt's uniqueness and supremacy. For the author and his audience magic was not a silly and improper category, but a means to compel admiration and respect: magic as national pride. This notion is plainly present in the following passage, which is included in the embedded story to raise tension about the outcome of the impending encounter between the Nubian and Egyptian magician. At the same time, it resonates with the nationalistic discourse. The chieftain's mother warns her son for the power of Egyptian magic before he embarks on his trip to Egypt.

> If you go down to Egypt to do sorcery there, guard yourself against the people of Egypt. You will not be able to fight (*tꜣ irm*) with them. Do not get caught in their hands (?), lest you cannot retreat to the land of Nubia ever. [P. BM. 10.822 6/1–2][131]

In both the primary and secondary fabula, the Egyptian hero (Sa-Osiris and Horus-son-of-Paneshe) is called a 'good scribe and wise man' (*sḫ nfr rmṯ rḫ*), a man of high moral and intellectual standing. The wording of this idiomatic expression is notably reminiscent of the ethical discourse in the priestly self-presentation that was discussed in the foregoing section. The Egyptian hero is thus a character similar to the image that the contemporary priestly audience of the tale propagated in biographies and temple texts. The occurrence of the expression in the following passage is highly instructive as regards the valorisation of magical knowledge among the native priesthood. Horus-son-of-Paneshe explains to pharaoh's court why he came back as Sa-Osiris to Egypt after 1500 years.

> When I found out in the Netherworld that the Nubian fiend (*sꜣbꜥꜣ n ꜣIgš*) was going to cast his sorceries (*ḥkꜣ.w*) here, while there was not a good scribe and wise man (*sḫ nfr rmṯ rḫ*) in Egypt at this time who would be able to contend with him, I begged Osiris in the Netherworld to let me come up again, so as to prevent him from taking the shame of Egypt to the land of Nubia. [P. BM. 10822 6/35–7/1][132]

The passage brings two important points to the fore. First of all, the Nubian magician is defined as an aggressor, whereas the Egyptian magician acts as a 'good scribe and wise man'. This implies that knowledge of magic is not condemned in itself: the criterion is the goal

---

75; Leiden 1997) 65–92, 76.
[131] Translation modified from M. Lichtheim.
[132] Tr. M. Lichtheim.

towards which the knowledge is applied. Because the Nubian sorcerer uses his knowledge in an attempt to subvert pharaonic rule, he acts as the villain in the story. His Egyptian opponent is a man of god, highly educated in the temple writings, who, by virtue of his way of life, acquires apotropaeic magical spells from the god Thoth. In this way, the contest is elevated to the level of a battle, in Egyptian theological terms, between good and evil or order and chaos. Egypt's answer to chaotic upheaval within the ordered community of men and gods is a priest who sticks strictly to the religious taboos and moral rules. The second point of importance is the fact that no good scribe and wise man was available in the days of Ramesses II. The same expression is used in *Setne and the Book of Thoth* for Naneferkaptah, who is likewise a skilful magician from a distant past. Both tales express thus the idea that highly skilled ritual experts belong to the past. Could this be interpreted as a reflection of a pessimistic view on contemporary society?

The foregoing pages have demonstrated that magic and miracle workers were favoured topics in Egyptian fictional narratives. The priestly morality as set forth in the 'official' temple texts, biographies and instruction texts governs the stories' plot and its outcome to a large degree. The characters are portrayed as well educated priests, whose engagement with books and ritual texts is repeatedly emphasised. Their knowledge of magic is not rejected on moral grounds, neither by a narrator, nor a character within the story. On the contrary, magic is perceived as a category that bestows prestige on the person who is knowledgeable about it. In the case of the tale *Setne and Sa-Osiris*, magic operates even as a category to construct a national priestly identity in response to foreign intrusion. The god Thoth plays a prominent role as the provider of effective magical texts. However, his texts are not self-evidently available to humans: Thoth will only share his texts with righteous priests who will make use of the knowledge to come to the aid of pharaoh or the country. Djedi's reluctance to collect the flint casket in the temple of Heliopolis and the punishment of Naneferkaptah and Setne demonstrate that sheer curiosity for secret knowledge was considered inappropriate. The ritual expert was thus a reality for an Egyptian audience, but not an ordinary type.

6.3.3.2. *Egyptian priests in Greek and Latin texts of the Roman period*

> In a word, there was nothing Egyptian into which they did not inquire, for anything heard or told of Egypt has a special charm for Greek listeners.
> [Heliodorus, *Aithiopika* 2, 27.3][133]

> We had heard of Alexandria, now we know it! It is the home of all tricks, the home, I say, of all deceits. Yes, it is from its inhabitants that writers of farces draw all their plots.
> [Cicero, *Pro C. Rabirio Postumo*, 12.35][134]

The idea of Egyptian priests being ritual experts was persistent and widespread among Hellenised elites during the Roman period as the frequent occurrence of such images in texts written in Greek or Latin testify. This image consists of a number of stereotypes on Egypt, its religion and its priests. The arrangement of these stereotypes or, so to say, the structure of the representation, is governed by a dominant Hellenistic perspective that observes from without phenomena that are actually specific for, and only meaningful within, an Egyptian context, without giving voice to the subordinate Egyptian object itself. Consequently, images of Egyptian priests in Hellenistic texts reveal a Hellenistic debate on defining self and otherness. Depending upon the rules of the genre, the author's intention, and his religious or philosophical inclinations, the image was positively or negatively coloured: either the Egyptian priest was represented as a philosopher who had acquired close contact with the divine by renouncing earthly pleasures or he was constructed as a wandering fraudulent wizard who deceived his credulous clientele willing to pay for healings and contact with the divine. This distinction lays bare a fundamental trait of the Roman-period preoccupation with Egypt in Hellenistic elite circles: the oscillation between the opposing attitudes 'fascination' and 'rejection'.[135] The

---

[133] Tr.: M. Hadas.
[134] Translation taken over from K.A.D. Smelik and E.A. Hemelrijk, "'Who know not what monsters demented Egypt worships?" Opinions on Egyptian animal worship in Antiquity as part of the ancient conception of Egypt' *ANRW* II 17.4 (1984) 1852–2000, 1921f.
[135] The major themes of the Greco-Roman discourse on Egypt are summarized in Assmann, *Weisheit und Mysterium*, 31–73. The antique fascination for Egypt is discussed by Iversen, *The Myth of Egypt*, 38–56 and by Siegfried Morenz, *Die Begegnung Europas mit Ägypten* (2nd ed.; Zürich 1969) 67–105; also of interest is James Stevens Curl, *Egyptomania*.

aim of this section is to trace the constitutive elements of these widely shared Hellenistic images of the Egyptian priest and to compare it with the conclusions of the foregoing section on the images of Egyptian priests in Egyptian literature. Ultimately, both images will have to be confronted with the ideas on Egyptian priests found in the introductions to the magical recipes in the *Greek Magical Papyri*. In which way and to what extent do they relate to the Egyptian and Hellenised stereotypes?

Two well-known passages will serve as examples to the discussion.[136] The first passage is taken from an embedded story in Apuleius' *Metamorphoses* (written around 170 CE[137]). A certain Thelyphron relates the embedded story to Lucius, the main character of the *Metamorphoses*, during a supper with some notables of the city of Hypata in Thessaly, 'the native land of those spells of the magic art which are unanimously praised throughout the entire world' (2.1). He tells the story of a young widow in Thessalian Larissa who poisoned her husband to inherit his wealth and to share her bed with her new lover. To find out the truth, the deceased's father called for an Egyptian priest, a certain Zatchlas, to raise his son briefly from the dead.

> Consequently the old man spoke up again. 'Let us put the judgement of the truth,' he said, 'into the hands of divine Providence. There is a man here named Zatchlas, an Egyptian prophet of the first rank (*Aegyptius propheta primarius*), who has already contracted with me for a great price to bring my nephew's spirit back from the dead for a brief time and reanimate his body as it was before his death.' At this point he

---

*The Egyptian Revival: a Recurring Theme in the History of Taste* (2nd ed.; Manchester 1994) 1–56. See for the Roman negative attitude towards Egypt: Smelik and Hemelrijk, '"Who know not what monsters demented Egypt worships?"' and M.J. Versluys, *Aegyptiaca Romana. Nilotic Scenes and the Roman Views of Egypt* (Religions in the Graeco-Roman World 144; Leiden 2002) 422–443. See on the general issue of the Hellenistic attitude towards foreign cultures: Arnaldo Momigliano, *Alien Wisdom. The Limits of Hellenization* (Cambridge 1975) and Paul Cartledge, *The Greeks: a Portrait of Self and Others* (2nd ed.; Oxford 2002) 36–77.

[136] These passages have been chosen because they are short though explicit. Three further instructive examples are (1) Paapis, the villainous priest in Antonius Diogenes' novel *The Incredible Wonders beyond Thule* (first century CE), (2) pharaoh Nectanebo II in Ps-Callisthenes' *Alexander-Romance* (sometime before third century CE) and (3) the Memphite priest Kalasiris in Heliodorus' *Aithiopica* (probably third century CE). See for a discussion and bibliographical references: Fulvio De Salvia, 'La figura del mago egizio nella tradizione letteraria Greco-romana', in: A. Roccati and A. Siliotti (eds.), *La magia in Egitto ai tempi dei faraoni* (Mailand 1987) 343–365.

[137] See for a discussion on dating the Metamorphoses: J. Gwyn Griffiths, *Apuleius of Madauros. The Isis-Book (Metamorphoses, Book XI)* (EPRO 39; Leiden 1975) 7–14.

introduced a young man dressed in long linen robes and wearing sandals woven from palm leaves. His head was completely shaven. The old man kissed his hands at length and even touched his knees. "Mercy, priest, mercy!", he begged, 'In the name of the stars of heaven and the spirits of hell, in the name of the elements of nature and the silences of night and the sanctuaries in Coptos (*adyta Coptitica*), in the name of the Nile's risings (*incrementa Nilotica*) and Memphis' mysteries (*arcana Memphitica*) and Pharos' sistra (*sistra Pharaica*): grant a short borrowing of the sun and pour a little light into eyes closed for eternity. We make no resistance, nor do we deny the Earth her property; we beg only for a tiny period of life to furnish the consolation of revenge.' [Apuleius, *Metamorphoses* II.28][138]

The second example is a passage from Lucian's *Philopseudes* (written in the second half of the second century CE), a satirical dialogue between adherents of different philosophical schools on supernatural phenomena and on the existence of spirits and phantoms. One of the conversation partners, Tychiades, is sceptical about the existence of these phenomena, so that the others try to convince him by telling fanciful stories that they believe occurred in reality. In this passage, Eucrates tells Tychiades about his encounter with the priest Pancrates in Egypt. This same priest appears to be the teacher of Arignotus, another member of the conversation.

'When I was living in Egypt during my youth (my father had sent me travelling for the purpose of completing my education), I took it into my head to sail up to Coptos and go from there to the statue of Memnon in order to hear it sound that marvellous salutation to the rising sun. (…) But on the voyage up, there chanced to be sailing with us a man from Memphis, one of the scribes of the temple (ἀνὴρ τῶν ἱερῶν γραμματέων), wonderfully learned, familiar with all the culture of the Egyptians. He was said to have lived underground for twenty-three years in their sanctuaries, learning magic from Isis.' 'You mean Pancrates,' said Arignotus, 'my own teacher, a holy man (ἄνδρα ἱερόν), clean shaven, in white linen, always deep in thought, speaking imperfect Greek, tall, flat-nosed, with protruding lips and thinnish legs.' 'That self-same Pancrates,' he replied: 'and at first I did not know who he was, but when I saw him working all sorts of wonders whenever we anchored the boat, particularly riding on crocodiles and swimming in company with the beasts, while they fawned and wagged their tails, I recognised that he was some holy man (ἱερόν τινα ἄνθρωπον), and by

---

[138] Tr. J.A. Hanson. See for a philological commentary on this passage: D. van Mal-Maeder, *Apuleius Madaurensis, Metamorphoses, Livre II* (Groningen Commentaries on Apuleius; Groningen 2001) 367–375.

degrees, through my friendly behaviour, I became his companion and associate, so that he shared all his secret knowledge (ἀπορρήτων) with me.' [Lucian, *Philopseudes*, 33–34][139]

Despite the fact that the function of Apuleius' and Lucian's images within their textual context differs,[140] certain constitutive elements recur, which are reflections as well of a social reality of wandering ritual experts of all sorts throughout the Roman empire[141] as of a Hellenistic discourse on Egypt in general and Egyptian priests in particular. Both texts make use of, and play upon, ideas about Egyptian priests that were shared among their Hellenistic audience. The features, by which the audience would have immediately recognised the literary type, are the priestly titles and the description of their outward appearance. Zatchlas is a 'prophet', which, as has already been shown, is a Greek translation of the Egyptian title 'god's servant' (ḥm-nṯr), while Pancrates is a 'scribe of the temple', holding the same title as the one used in the introduction to the list of ingredients (PGM XII.401–444), which is the Greek rendering of the title 'scribe of the House-of-Life (sẖ Pr-ʿnḫ). The description of their outward appearance is limited to the most conspicuous elements of the Egyptian priestly attire: bald-headed, white linen clothing and, in the case of Zatchlas, sandals of palm leaves.[142]

In these two passages, both priests function as wizards who are able to perform extraordinary magical feats because of their acquaintance with the divine. Zatchlas is represented as an object of divine contiguity by the wording of the old man's prayer, which is merely an instance of name-dropping that is supposed to convey the old man's intimate knowledge of the mysteries of Egyptian religion. The list shows that the image of Egypt as land of mysteries and miracles could be invoked for a Hellenistic audience by a limited number of stereotypes concerning cosmography, Egyptian topography and religious phenom-

---

[139] Tr. A.M. Harmon.

[140] In the *Metamorphoses*, Zatchlas is introduced to add suspense to the story and to heighten the idea of the miraculous, one of the main themes of the novel, whereas Lucian uses Pancrates to parody the priestly type and the credulity of his contemporaries in general.

[141] The extant archaeological and textual sources provide little reliable information on itinerant ritualists within the Roman Empire. Ethnic origins, methods, gender, and social standing in local communities are far from clear. See for a sociological description (which has to be used with caution): M.W. Dickey, *Magic and Magicians in the Greco-Roman World* (London, New York 2001) 202–250.

[142] See for sandals of palm leaves in Egyptian religion: Griffiths, *The Isis-Book*, 136.

ena. The rather arbitrary association between topography and religious phenomenon, itemized in the table below, demonstrates the metonymic character of each individual term. Every term for itself would have been sufficient to call Egypt to mind; in combination, the terms evoke an exotic image of a country condensed into the toponyms Alexandria, Memphis and Coptos, flooded by the Nile, and filled with temples where mysterious rites are conducted. Each pair was possibly meant to suggest a link with the Isis cult, as is indicated by the bold lettering.[143]

| *religious phenomena* | *topography* | *associated deity* |
|---|---|---|
| sanctuaries | **Coptos** | **(Isis)** |
| **flooding** | the Nile | (Osiris) |
| mysteries | **Memphis** | (Isis) |
| **sistra** | **Pharos** (Alexandrian Lighthouse) | (Isis) |

Of major importance to the present discussion is Zatchlas' economic relation with the Greek old man. It is only for a considerable fee that the Egyptian priest performs necromancy, in this case by placing some herb on the corpse's mouth and chest, while invoking the sun. The priest sells off his knowledge to those in need of assistance from the divine.

The image of Pancrates should first be understood as a weapon in Lucian's attack on the credulity and superstition of his contemporaries. By exaggerating and ridiculing stereotypes on Egyptian magicians, he ridicules the conversation partners, thereby criticizing the intellectualism and presumed rationality of their respective philosophical schools.

---

[143] Coptos was widely known for its temple dedicated to Isis, Min and Horus; C. Traunecker, *Coptos: hommes et dieux sur le parvis de Geb* (OLA 43; Leuven 1992) 333–335; note that it are the Isis priests of Coptos who welcome warmly Naneferkaptah in *Setne I* (3/25f.). The flooding of the Nile was associated with, and attributed to, Osiris, especially so in Elephantine which became a major cult place of Isis in the Greco-Roman period; Hermann Junker, *Das Götterdekret über das Abaton* (Vienna 1913) 37–44. Memphis played an important role in the dissemination and Hellenisation of the Isis cult; M. Malaise, 'Le problème de l'hellénisation d'Isis', in: L. Bricault (ed.), *De Memphis à Rome. Actes du Ier colloque international sur les études isiaques* (Religions in the Graeco-Roman World 140; Leiden 2000) 1–19, 17f. The sistrum was a musical instrument used as rattle in religious ceremonies. It was closely connected with the goddesses Isis and Hathor, so that, with the spread of the Isis cult throughout the Roman Empire, it became a typical feature of the Isiac religion in the Greco-Roman perception. As for the lighthouse, in Alexandria Isis was venerated as Isis Pharia, the protector of the harbour and navigation.

In doing so, he confirms the existence of these stereotypes and gives insight into his audience's expectations and fixed ideas regarding Egyptian priests. His mockery could hardly have been successful if the images he ridicules were not widely shared and immediately recognised by the readership of the day. The stereotypic motives he makes use of are the following:

1. Memphis as home of the magician.
2. The Egyptian temple as a place of learning and initiation.
3. Isis as mistress of magic.
4. The Egyptian priest as holder of secret knowledge.

The ironic and singular part of the representation is the exaggerated length (23 years) and place of initiation (in an underground structure) and Pancrates' application of his arcane knowledge towards riding on crocodiles and turning a door bar, broom or pestle into a house servant (*Philopseudes*, 35).

Two further elements of Lucian's description deserve particular attention. First, by mentioning Pancrates' imperfect command of Greek, the priest is firmly placed outside the social group of the author and his audience whose common identity is based to a large degree on their knowledge of Greek language and culture. Pancrates is an alien in the Greek language as Zatchlas is an alien in a Greek region. Both representations touch thus upon the Hellenistic debate on otherness. A discourse that reveals a tension between the desire for magical feats, occult knowledge, and initiations situated outside one's one culture group on the one hand, and the prohibition to transgress fixed social and cultural borders on the other. Second, Eucrates calls Pancrates a 'holy man' indicating that he attaches much value to the priest's knowledge and morality. Lucian introduces the term 'holy man' into the text to take position in the debate about magic and miracles, which was lively discussed among Hellenistic authors of the Roman period. The central issue of this debate was the question whether persons who performed magical feats or pretended to be able to do so were frauds or genuine sages and miracle workers touched by the divine. It goes without saying that this debate cannot be disconnected from the Roman-period discourse on otherness. Lucian's use of the term 'holy man' is highly ambivalent in this particular context. Within Eucrates' and Arignotus' embedded focalisation the term is positively connoted, reflecting their belief in, and reverence for, Oriental wisdom, but within the context of the complete dialogue Eucrates' tale stands out as an outrageous story unworthy of any credibility. From the author's perspective, the term becomes thus synonymous with false pretence, a crucial term denoting, but also proving, Eucrates' and Arignotus' credulity.

Lucian ridicules another type of miracle worker in the figure of Arignotus, who shortly interrupted Eucrates' story, to inform the conversation partners of the fact that the Egyptian priest was actually his teacher. This type is a key figure to understand Roman-period ideas on magicians. The sceptical Tychiades describes him in the following words at the moment that Arignotus joined the conversation, a few minutes before Eucrates started telling his story.

> At this juncture Arignotus the Pythagorean came in, the man with the long hair and the majestic face—you know the one who is renowned for wisdom (τῇ σοφίᾳ), who is called the holy (man) (τὸν ἱερόν). As I caught sight of him, I drew a breath of relief thinking that this one came to me as an axe against (their) lies. 'For,' I said, 'the wise man (ὁ σοφὸς ἀνήρ) will put a stop to them telling such prodigious yarns.' As the saying is, like a *deus ex machina* I considered him to be brought in to me by Fortune (Τύχης). [Lucian, *Philopseudes*, 29][144]

Arignotus is represented as a philosopher of the Pythagorean School, recognisable by his long hair, a symbol of reason and wisdom. Tychiades hopes that the presence of a man of learning will bring some reason and sense to the discussion. However, these expectations appear to be illusory as soon as Arignotus takes an active part in the conversation, because he tells that he once expelled a spirit from a house by use of spells in the Egyptian language from his Egyptian books (*Philopseudes*, 31) and confesses to be one of Pancrates' students. The elements of wisdom, study in Egypt, and occult knowledge would have evoked for a Hellenistic audience a familiar type. The well-known author and rhetorician Apuleius of Madaura, or shadowy figures known for their compilations of occult lore such as Bolos of Mendes, Anaxilaus of Larissa, and Nigidius Figulus, or a fictional character like Thessalos of Tralles fall within this category.[145] The constitutive elements of this type are the following:

---

[144] Translation modified from A.M. Harmon.

[145] Dickey has coined the term 'learned magician' for this category, which inappropriately foregrounds the element of 'magic' over learnedness or curiosity (for the workings of nature); M.W. Dickey, 'The Learned Magician and the Collection and Transmission of Magical Lore', in: Jordan (eds.), *The World of Ancient Magic*, 163–193 and Idem, *Magic and Magicians in the Greco-Roman World*, 117 f. (note that Dickey calls the term 'something of a misnomer' here).

1. Hellenistic identity: The identity is based on a set of shared Hellenistic cultural forms; the persons are not necessarily ethnically Greek or Roman. From a Hellenistic perspective, such a person is hence culturally not a foreigner or outsider. He is knowledgeable in general Hellenistic cultural forms and expresses himself in a Hellenistic idiom.
2. Philosophy: Adherent of Neopythagorean or Platonic movement.[146]
3. Initiation: Knowledge is taught by a sage, in most cases an Egyptian priest. It was a persistent Greco-Roman conception that esoteric knowledge could only be acquired by travelling to foreign religious masters, as there were the Persian Magoi, the Indian Brahmans, the Babylonian Chaldaeans or, particularly popular in the Roman period, Egyptian priests. The tradition that Pythagoras, Plato, Eudoxos, and Democritus spent several years in Egypt studying the Egyptian teachings from the priests provided the basis for this idea.[117]
4. Books: Knowledge is based on the consultation and collection of texts of revealed occult knowledge.

Lucian introduces Arignotus into the dialogue to pass his negative judgement on this intellectual type. Arignotus may have the air of wisdom and learning because of his adherence to philosophy, but from Lucian's perspective he is a quack and as credulous as the other conversation partners. Arignotus' characterization as 'holy man' and *deus ex machina* is thus charged with irony from the outset.

Lucian's negative judgement of the magical abilities of Egyptian priests and Hellenistic 'purveyors of the occult' should be contrasted

---

[146] Neopythagoreanism was an eclectic current of thought that became popular from the Hellenistic period onwards basing its teachings, influenced by Platonic, Aristotelian and Stoic philosophy, on texts supposed to have been written by Pythagoras, whose authority was undisputed. The movement had a strong religious component and prescribed certain rules of conduct like asceticism and vegetarianism. Platonism remained popular during the Roman period and, due to a strong religious inclination, developed an interest in theurgy as a way to contact the divine (Neoplatonism).

[117] The main sources for this literary tradition are: Strabo, *Geography*, 17.1.29; Diogenes Laertius, *Lives of the Philosophers*, 3.6; 8.3; 8.87; 9.35; Iamblichus, *On the Mysteries of Egypt*, I 1 (2, 10–12). Note that there are no historical records to support the literary tradition.

with Philostratus' account of the life of Apollonius of Tyana, written sometime during the first decades of the third century CE.[148] The aim of the work is to rehabilitate Apollonius, citizen from Tyana in Cappadocia, modern Turkey, who had been active as a Neopythagorean wandering sage and miracle worker during the second half of the first century CE, and to defend him against the charge that he had been a fraud and sorcerer. In the introduction to the actual account of Apollonius' travels and wonders, Philostratus touches upon several points that belong to the above described type. Unlike Lucian, Philostratus does not use these elements to discredit his subject, but, instead, to underscore Apollonius' remarkable and sincere character. Philostratus' argumentation is as follows:[149]

1. Apollonius was no wizard because he never resorted to the black arts (and was never interested in financial gain [VA 8.7.3]): his interest into the divine was *religiously* motivated.
2. The argument that his visits to Babylonian, Indian and Egyptian priests turn him into a quack does not hold, because several Greek philosophers of high esteem made similar travels: his interest in foreign wisdom was *philosophically* motivated.

> For quite akin to theirs [Neopythagorean philosophers, jd] was the ideal which Apollonius pursued. Being more god-like (θειότερον) than Pythagoras, he wooed wisdom and soared above tyrants; and lived in times not long gone by nor again quite of our own day; yet men know him not because of the true wisdom, which he practised as a sage and sanely. One person praises this, another that (aspect) of the man, while others, because he had interviews with the wizards (μάγοις) of Babylon and with the Brahmans of India, and with the nude ascetics (Γυμνοῖς) of Egypt, put him down as a wizard (μάγον), and spread the calumny that he

---

[148] A general assessment of the antique interest in Apollonius of Tyana is given in E.L. Bowie, 'Apollonius of Tyana: Tradition and Reality' *ANRW* II 16.2 (1978) 1652–1699 and M. Dzielska, *Apollonius of Tyana in Legend and History* (Problemi e ricerche di storia antica 10; Rome 1986). Morton Smith discusses Philostratus' biography in the light of the Hellenistic debate on magicians: *Jesus the Magician: Charlatan or Son of God?* (San Francisco 1978) 111–123. Lucian and Philostratus are also compared in F. Gascó, 'Magia, religion o filosofia, una comparacion entre el *Philopseudes* de Luciano y la *Vida de Apolonio de Tiana* de Filostrato' *Habis* 17 (1986) 271–281 [non vidi].

[149] Philostratus' line of reasoning is very similar to Apuleius' argumentation in the *Apologia* or *Defence Against Magic* (about 158 CE). Apuleius defends himself against the accusation of magic not by denying the charges brought in against him, but by stressing the religious and philosophical character of his interest into the divine, thereby accusing his litigants of irreligiosity and ignorance. See: F. Graf, *Magic in the Ancient World* (Revealing Antiquity 10; Cambridge Mass. 1997) 83f.

was a sage (σοφόν) of an illegitimate kind, judging of him ill. However, Empedocles and Pythagoras himself and Democritus consorted with wizards (μάγοις) and uttered many supernatural truths, but they were never subsumed under (the category of) black art (οὔπω ὑπήχθησαν τῇ τέχνῃ). Moreover, Plato went to Egypt and mingled with his own discourses much of (what he heard from) the prophets and priests there; and though, like a painter, he laid his own colours on to their rough sketches, yet he never passed for a wizard, but, instead, was envied above all mankind for his wisdom.

[Philostratus, *The Life of Apollonius of Tyana*, 1.2][150]

The underlying question of this short passage, which summarizes the essential elements of the Greco-Roman perceptions of magic and magicians, is that for the nature of true wisdom. Philostratus responds to a view widely accepted during the Roman period that constructs a rigid distinction between *magos* (wizard) and *sophos* (sage), of which the latter is the positive member, associated with Greek philosophy and Hellenic culture in general. The former member is coupled with foreignness that is rejected on the ground of a general dislike towards cultural forms and religious views that are alien and felt to be dangerous to Hellenic culture. This view is strongly opposed against otherness and defines an oriental culture like Egypt in terms of decadence, trickery, deceit, treachery, cruelty and abstruse religious customs. Philostratus counters this view by introducing the element of personal intentions: a sage is only of the illegitimate sort when he turns towards the black arts and sells off his knowledge.[151] In his view, interest in oriental wisdom is very positive since it stood at the basis of Greek philosophy itself. For him, Apollonius of Tyana is a holy man leading a contemplative life of a high moral standard and combining Greek and oriental wisdom in one person, thereby emulating the ancient Greek philosophers. Philostratus is thus not necessarily opposed against foreignness; on the contrary, he holds the foreign sages in high esteem for their particular knowledge that is lacking in Hellenic culture.

---

[150] Translation modified from F.C. Conybeare.

[151] This argument is as well taken up by Heliodorus in his *Aithiopika*, when he makes the fictional Memphite priest Kalasiris explain to a Greek the twofold nature of Egyptian wisdom (*Aithiopika*, 3.16). The vulgar form is concerned with idols, herbs, incantations and necromancy producing illusion instead of reality, whereas the second form, 'the true Egyptian wisdom', is directed towards companionship with the gods. The second form 'is remote from the earthy matters of our world, and concerns itself with all that is noble and profitable for mankind' (*Aithiopika*, 3, 16.4; tr. M. Hadas).

It has become clear by now that, in the Greco-Roman writings on magic and miracles, advocates and opponents alike based their arguments on a stereotypic image of Egypt and its priests. Depending on their viewpoint, Egyptian priests were either perceived as fraudulent wizards solely interested in financial gain or as prestigious philosophers who had served as teachers to the famous Greek philosophers (and still served as teachers to those interested in esoteric lore) deriving their wisdom from their ancient texts stored in their temples. When this image is compared with the images of Egyptian priests found in Egyptian texts, a number of important differences can be observed:

1. In Egyptian texts, the discussion whether the priest is a fraud or genuine religious master is absent.
2. The idea of performing magical feats for financial gain is likewise absent.
3. In Egyptian literary texts, ritual experts are respected members of society, whereas in Greek or Latin texts Egyptian priests are alienated from society and function as exotic gurus or miracle workers.
4. The royal court as the arena of display and contest is absent in the Greco-Roman texts.
5. In Egyptian literary texts, ritual experts are mostly projected back into the remote past, whereas they are set in a time period more or less contemporary with the reader's time in Greek or Latin texts.
6. In Egyptian fictional narratives, magicians are actors who focalise and speak, whereas in Greek or Latin texts Egyptian priests are mainly passive objects subordinated to a Hellenistic view-point.

Despite these differences, the Egyptian and Greco-Roman images have certain elements in common as well:

1. The priest is recognised by his title (prophet, temple scribe) and dress (white linen clothing, sandals of palm leaves or papyrus, baldhead).
2. Priestly knowledge is based on the consultation of books.
3. This knowledge is kept secret from laity.

In the light of these correspondences, the question wherefrom Hellenistic authors drew their knowledge about Egypt becomes highly relevant. Unfortunately, little is known about the nature of the transfer of this knowledge and its actors. The following four sources could at least be suggested:

1. Classical Greek literature.
2. Egyptian priests writing in Greek.
3. Spread of the Isis-Sarapis cult throughout the Roman empire.
4. Tourism to Egypt.

The first two members of this list are solely discursive in nature, whereas the other two imply actual contact between the two different culture groups, either in the form of an Egyptian Isis or Sarapis priest working for Greco-Roman adherents outside Egypt or in the form of Greco-Roman tourists travelling through Egypt. The opinions on Egypt of classical Greek authors like Homer, Herodotus and Plato remained authoritative during the Hellenistic and Roman period, which led to an image of the country and its priests detached from contemporary reality.[152] Unfortunately, very little is preserved of the works in Greek written by Egyptian priests, of whom Manetho (third century BCE) and Chaeremon (first century CE) are best known,[153] so that it is almost impossible to judge whether these works responded to the distorted although highly influential classical Greek image.[154] As little is known about the reception of these Greco-Egyptian works in Hellenistic elite circles.[155] Chaeremon's description of Egyptian priestly life (first century CE) was probably well known among scholarly elites, since it was quoted as an authoritative text in Porphyry's *On Abstinence* (second half of third century CE).[156] Chaeremon's text should be seen as an active attempt to inscribe Egyptian priestly culture into Hellenistic thought by way of casting his account in Stoic terms. He describes Egyptian priestly life as an ascetic life in seclusion characterised by notions such

---

[152] See for the image of Egypt in classical Greek literature: C. Froidefond, *Le mirage égyptien dans la littérature grecque d'Homère à Aristote* (Paris 1971); S.M. Burstein, *Graeco-Africana: Studies in the History of Greek Relations with Egypt and Nubia* (New Rochelle 1995) 3–27; Idem, 'Images of Egypt in Greek Historiography', in: Loprieno (ed.), *Ancient Egyptian Literature*, 591–604; Phiroze Vasunia, *The Gift of the Nile. Hellenizing Egypt from Aeschylus to Alexander* (Classics and Contemporary Thought 8; Berkeley 2001).

[153] A useful overview is given in Fowden, *The Egyptian Hermes*, 52–57.

[154] One of Manetho's works is called *Against Herodotus*, suggesting a polemic stance on the part of the Egyptian priest. See also: Verbrugghe and Wickersham, *Berossos and Manetho*, 100 f.

[155] Manetho and Apion were severely attacked in Flavius Josephus' *Against Apion* (shortly after 94 CE), which testifies to the fact that their works were known outside Egypt. See for Manetho's reception in Josephus and the Christian chronographers: R. Laqueur, 'Manetho' *PRE* 27 (1928) 1060–1101; see also: Verbrugghe and Wickersham, *Berossos and Manetho*, 115–118.

[156] Van der Horst, *Chaeremon. Egyptian Priest and Stoic Philosopher*.

as self-control, contemplation, strict observance of religious rules, and vision of the divine.[157] He presents Egyptian priests as Stoic philosophers whose secluded life is directed towards the divine and who show no interest in such mundane matters as erotic magic or necromancy. The following two fragments are illustrative of Chaeremon's endeavour at connecting Egyptian and Hellenic culture: he combines the notion of philosophy (characteristic for the Greco-Roman discourse on Egyptian priests and magic) and the idea of purification (characteristic for Egyptian priestly self-presentation). The second fragment contains again the Egyptian priestly titles in Greek that were found in the trilingual priestly decrees of Canopus and Memphis.

> Chaeremon the Stoic tells in his exposé about the Egyptian priests, who, he says, were considered also as philosophers (φιλοσόφους) among the Egyptians, that they chose the temples as the place to philosophise. For to live close to their shrines was fitting to their whole desire of contemplation, and it gave them security because of the reverence for the divine, since all people honoured the philosophers as if they were a sort of sacred animals. [Porphyry, *On Abstinence* 4.6]

> The true philosophising was found among the prophets (προφήταις), the priests who had charge of the sacred vestments (ἱεροστολισταῖς), the temple scribes (ἱερογραμματεῦσιν) as well as hour-priests (ὡρολόγοις). However, the rest of the priests, the crowd of shrine bearers, temple wardens and assistants, perform the same purification rites for the gods, although not with such precision and self-control.
> [Porphyry, *On Abstinence* 4.8][158]

These written accounts will certainly have had their effect on the Hellenistic image of Egypt and its priesthood, but the actual presence of Egyptian priests in centres of the Hellenistic world like Athens, Antioch, Rome, will probably have been more important. With the spread of the Isis-Sarapis cult throughout the Hellenistic world, which became particularly predominant in the Roman period, Egyptian priests, temples, artefacts and iconography entered the Hellenistic *oikumene* in large num-

---

[157] Chaeremon's account of Egyptian priestly life is highly reminiscent of *On the Contemplative Life* by Philo of Alexandria (lived within the period of 25 BCE – 45 CE) that describes a Jewish ascetic group called the Therapeutae living in seclusion south of Alexandria near Lake Mareotis. See: R. Barraclough, 'Philo's Politics. Roman Rule and Hellenistic Judaism' *ANRW* II 21.1 (1984) 417-553, 544-550. Both works should be seen as attempts to explain in favourable terms familiar to a Hellenistic audience the particularities of Egyptian and Jewish religious thought.

[158] Translations slightly modified from P.W. van der Horst.

bers.[159] This will certainly have stimulated direct contact between Egyptian priests and Greco-Romans interested in Egyptian religion, but the form and frequency of such contacts is mostly unknown. Book 11 of Apuleius' *Metamorphoses* and Plutarch's *On Isis and Osiris* (written around 120 CE) reveal a sincere interest and detailed knowledge of Egyptian religious thought, although cast in a Hellenistic idiom.[160] Both works testify to the wide interest in Egyptian mysteries and initiations among Hellenistic elites during the Roman period. This fascination for Egyptian religious experiences led some to undertake a journey to Egypt to witness the wonders of the country of the Nile. It appears from historical accounts and Greek graffiti left by these tourists on Egyptian monuments that the tourists followed a standard route from Alexandria in the north to Philae in the far south via Memphis, Abydos and Thebes.[161] These visits had a strong religious component as is testified

---

[159] See for a general overview of the Isis-Sarapis cult in the Greco-Roman world: Sarolta A. Takacs, *Isis and Sarapis in the Roman World* (Religions in the Graeco-Roman World 124; Leiden 1995) and, although rather idiosyncratic, Reinhold Merkelbach, *Isis Regina—Zeus Sarapis. Die griechisch-ägyptische Religion nach den Quellen dargestellt* (Stuttgart and Leipzig 1995). An important assessment of the legend about the discovery of the Sarapis cult statue and its installment in Alexandria in the light of historical sources is Philippe Borgeaud and Youri Volokhine, 'La formation de la légende de Sarapis: une approche transculturelle' ARG 2 (2000) 37–76. See for a discussion of the theology and spread of the cult of Sarapis and Isis in the Greco-Roman world: Ladislav Vidman, *Isis und Sarapis bei den Griechen und Römern. Epigrafische Studien zur Verbreitung und zu den Trägern des ägyptischen Kultes* (RGVV 29; Berlin 1970); John E. Stambaugh, *Sarapis under the Early Ptolemies* (EPRO 25; Leiden 1972); F. Dunand, *Le Culte d'Isis dans le basin oriental de la Méditerranée* 3 Vols. (EPRO 26; Leiden 1973) and on Egyptian cults in general: M. Malaise, *Les conditions de pénétration et de diffusion des cultes égyptiens en Italie* (EPRO 22; Leiden 1972). A collection of sources pertaining to the cult and testimonies of reverence can be found in: Ladislaus Vidmann, *Sylloge inscriptionum religionis Isiacae et Sarapiacae* (RGVV 28; Berlin 1969) and Maria Totti, *Ausgewählte Texte der Isis- und Sarapis-Religion* (Subsidia Epigraphica 12; Hildesheim 1985). Egyptian and egyptianizing artefacts in the Greco-Roman world are discussed in: A. Roullet, *The Egyptian and Egyptianizing Monuments of Imperial Rome* (EPRO 20; Leiden 1972); G.J.F. Kater-Sibbes, *Preliminary Catalogue of Sarapis Monuments* (EPRO 36; Leiden 1973); Versluys, *Aegyptiaca Romana*, 32–139 (Nilotic scenes) and 182–230 (Aegyptiaca Romana). Also of interest is: E.A. Arslan (ed.), *Iside. Il mito, il mistero, la magia* (exhibition catalogue; Mailand 1997).

[160] J. Gwyn Griffiths, *Plutarch's De Iside et Osiride* (Cardiff 1970) and Idem, *Apuleius of Madaura. The Isis-Book (Metamorphoses, Book XI)* (EPRO 39; Leiden 1975).

[161] An account of this tour is given in Strabo's *Geography* 17.1 and 2, 1–5. He undertook this tour in the reign of Augustus as companion to the Roman prefect of Egypt Aelius Gallus, see: Jean Yoyotte and Pascal Charvet, *Strabon—Le Voyage en Égypte. Un regard romain* (Paris 1997) 47–57. Prince Germanicus (during the reign of Tiberius; Tacitus, *Annals* II, 59) and Emperor Hadrian (130 CE) made a similar trip through the country to visit the ancient sites. Their travels are confirmed by graffiti and ostraca mentioning the preparations made for them in Thebes, see: Chrest.Wilck., 412 (=

by the graffiti that record prayers, thanksgivings for healings or religious experiences and hopes for oracular utterances. As in the Greek or Latin fictional narratives, the relationship between Greek subject and Egyptian priest was unequal and largely economic in nature: religious experiences could be obtained from Egyptian priests, either for money or for supplications,[162] as Thessalos of Tralles found out when he wanted an Egyptian priest to arrange for him an encounter with the god Asclepius.[163] In the perception of some tourists, if not the majority, Egyptian priests will have functioned as religious masters and miracle workers very similar to the images found in Hellenistic literary works.

It is difficult to trace the provenance of the Greco-Roman image of Egyptian priests as ritual masters and wizards, but it seems justified to see it as the result of an interaction between ideas expressed in texts on the one hand and experiences of actual encounters between Egyptian priests and Greco-Roman elites on the other. It is important to note that a dominant Hellenistic perspective determines the Greco-Roman images of Egyptian priests, but nevertheless Egyptian priests may have played an active role in formulating this image. Egyptian priests like Manetho and Chaeremon wrote apologetic works for the Hellenistic elite, while priests of Isis and Sarapis were actively present outside Egypt itself. Inside the country, Egyptian priests met the demands of Greco-Roman tourists, who came in search of revelations and initia-

---

O. Stras. 452) and 413; Pestman, Prim., 34. See for a general discussion of tourism in Roman Egypt: J. Grafton Milne, 'Greek and Roman Tourists in Egypt' *JEA* 3 (1916) 76–80, N. Hohlwein, 'Déplacements et tourisme dans l'Égypte romaine' *CdE* 30 (1940) 253–278 and Smelik, Hemelrijk, '"Who know not what monsters demented Egypt worships?"', 1938–1945.

[162] See also the quotation from Pseudo-Clement, *Recognitions* 1.5 in Frankfurter, *Religion in Roman Egypt*, 218.

[163] This act of divination is described in the narrative introduction to an astrobotanical treatise *On the Plants Governed by the Twelve Signs of the Zodiac and the Planets*, which is preserved in several Greek and Latin redactions. The treatise is fictitiously ascribed to Thessalos of Tralles, who is historically attested as a physician of the Methodist school living in Rome during the first half of the first century CE. In the introduction, the fictive Thessalos claims having obtained his information from Asklepius himself, after an Egyptian priest in Thebes had carried out a bowl divination ritual; Moyer, 'Thessalos of Tralles and Cultural Exchange'. For the Greek and Latin texts, see, Hans Veit Friedrich, *Thessalos von Tralles: griechisch und lateinisch* (Meisenheim am Glan 1968). The introductory letter is translated, together with philological commentary, in: A.-J. Festugière, 'L'expérience religieuse du médecin Thessalos' *RevBibl* 48 (1939) 45–77. The translation is reprinted in: idem, *L'astrologie et les sciences occultes*, 56–58.

tions. It is well possible that these native priests were prepared to act in accordance with the preconceived ideas these tourists had about Egyptian religion and its priests, in order to guarantee a reasonable fee from the tourists. David Frankfurter has introduced the term 'stereotype appropriation' to describe this mechanism.[164] According to Frankfurter the term refers 'to the manifold ways indigenous cultures embrace and act out the stereotypes woven by a colonial or otherwise dominant alien culture. While the latter creates its images of the exotic out of its own needs, aspirations, and insufficiencies (and only to some degree the realia of the indigenous culture), the indigenous cultures appropriate those same images as a means of gaining political and economic status in a broader culture now dominated by, in this case, Rome'.[165] It has to be shown in the remaining part of this chapter whether this term is applicable to the images found in the introductions to the *Greek Magical Papyri*.

### 6.4. *Packaging the text: rhetorical strategies in the introductions to the recipes*

> It has been tested
> [P. London-Leiden 4/23]
>
> The world has had nothing greater than this
> [PGM XII.277]

This section is a study of the rhetorical techniques that are used in the *Demotic* and *Greek Magical Papyri* as means to make their implied reader to believe from the outset in the reliability, trustworthiness and efficacy of a magical recipe. As such, it deals with the third question formulated in the introductory section to this chapter: how does the text succeed in acquiring authority and prestige, and for what kind of reader? The goal of the section is to gain an understanding of the social formation and cultural make-up of the intended readers by way of analysing what Wolfgang Iser calls the repertoire and strategies of the text, two heuristic terms that describe the conventions and procedures

---

[164] Frankfurter, *Religion in Roman* Egypt, 225ff. and Idem, 'The Consequences of Hellenism in Late Antique Egypt', 162–194. See also chapter 1.1 of the present book.
[165] *Op. cit.*, 225.

which enable communication between reader and text.[166] Iser defines the two terms and their interaction as follows:

> Das Textrepertoire bezeichnet das selektierte Material, durch das der Text auf die Systeme seiner Umwelt bezogen ist, die im Prinzip solche der sozialen Lebenswelt und solche vorangegangener Literatur sind. Eingekapselte Normen und literarische Bezugnahmen setzen den Horizont des Textes, durch den ein bestimmter Verweisungszusammenhang der gewählten Repertoire-Elementen vorgegeben ist, aus dem das Äquivalenz-system des Textes gebildet werden muß. Zur Konkretisierung dieser virtuell gebliebenen Äquivalenz des Repertoires bedarf es der Organisation, die von den Textstrategien geleistet wird.  [*Der Akt des Lesens*, 143]

This section, then, presents an analysis of the set of social, historical and cultural norms that the magical text and reader share and of the textual procedures by means of which these conventions are communicated from text to reader. Therefore, the central question is here: to what kind of reader is the text speaking? In which way do the magical recipes address the implied reader's expectations and aspirations and do they make use of culturally specific text formats and knowledge? The most obvious sources to provide clues for answering these questions are the 'marketing' statements contained in the magical spells. A considerable number of magical recipes are introduced by short advertising texts stressing the reliability of the following recipe, its efficacy and its extraordinary character. These guarantees, or quality marks, can easily be disguised as utter instances of window-dressing aimed at rendering the recipe beyond all doubt and critique. The texts are, so to speak, wrapped in an attractive package as an appeal to impress their readers and to attract attention among the many alternative spells that must have been available in antiquity. Since these advertisements could only have been successful if they address the expectations and aspirations of the intended readers and share the audience's ideas and values regarding magic and ritual, they provide valuable information about the social and cultural identity of their implied audience.

The *Demotic* and *Greek Magical Papyri* make use of a uniform set of rhetorical techniques to mystify magical recipes. Each of these methods was already known in pharaonic Egypt, but in many cases the items that were deemed prestigious and authoritative fall outside a specific

---

[166] Wolfgang Iser, *Der Akt des Lesens. Theorie ästhetischer Wirkung* (Uni-Taschenbücher 636; Munich 1976) 87–175. Translated as *The Act of Reading. A Theory of Aesthetic Response* (Baltimore 1978); for a loose translation of the quote, see, page 86.

Egyptian framework.[167] One could thus say that the outer form was in line with an existing tradition, while the contents of this form could diverge from it. In a few instances an advertising introduction even combines motifs deriving from separate cultural traditions that would strictly speaking be mutually exclusive, as if the author of the spell intended an (cross-cultural) accumulation of prestige. In the following pages the different methods and motifs will be discussed by means of tables listing the occurrences in the magical spells. Since the two manuscripts under study do not deviate in this respect from the other manuscripts contained in the corpus of Magical Papyri, the entire corpus is taken into account, so that it is possible to study the mechanism of mystification in more detail. Ultimately, the conclusions will be confronted with the conclusions of the previous sections to determine to which degree the implied reader of the Demotic and Greek magical spells is identical with the implied reader of any of the literary traditions.

### 6.4.1. *Advertising introductions to the actual magical recipes*

To gain an idea of the nature and the possible textual formats of the advertising introductions one might consider the following six passages, which have been selected for their explicitness and relative length. The different methods and motifs will be considered in more detail later.

(a) The first passage is the one that triggered the questions of the present chapter. According to this short explanatory preface, the following list of encoded ingredients is the result of the consultation and translation of a considerable number of secret temple texts kept and written by the Egyptian temple scribes.

> Interpretations (ἑρμηνεύματα) translated (μεθηρμηνευμένα) from the holy (writings), of which the temple scribes (ἱερογραμματεῖς) made use. Because of the nosiness (περιεργίαν) of the masses, they (the temple scribes)

---

[167] An overview of the different textual techniques employed in the PGM to inscribe magical recipes with authority is given in Hans D. Betz, 'The Formation of Authoritative Tradition in the *Greek Magical Papyri*', in: Ben F. Meyer and E.P. Sanders (eds.), *Jewish and Christian Self-Definition. Volume Three: Self-Definition in the Graeco-Roman World* (London 1982) 161–170. Note that Betz does not take the Egyptian background of the magical spells fully into account.

wrote the (names of the) herbs and other things that they made use of on statues of gods in order that they (the masses), since they do not take precautions (μὴ εὐλαβούμενοι), do not meddle (περιεργάζωνται)[168] at all, due to the inevitable result of their mistake. However, we have collected the solutions (λύσεις) from many copies, all of them secret.

[PGM XII.401–407]

(b) The second example is the introduction to the *Ouphôr* rite, which has already been discussed as part of an elaborate and complex ring spell in chapter 5.3. The passage claims the Ouphôr to be a holy rite, which has been written down carefully, devoid of lies or verbosity unlike alternative spells. A certain Ourbikos, who is otherwise unknown, is said to have made use of the spell. The reader is ordered to keep the text secret.

> Whenever you want to command the god, give command after you have said the great Ouphôr and he (i.e. the god[169]) fulfills: you have the rite of the greatest and divine execution (ἐνεργήματος). This is the Ouphôr of which Ourbikos made use. The holy Ouphôr, the true one, has carefully (ἀληθῶς) been written down in complete conciseness, through which all moulded figures (πλάσματα) and engraved images (γλυφαί) and carved statues (ξόανα) become imbued with life (ζωπυρεῖται): because this is the true one, the others, that carry on at great length, bring lies while containing idle length. And keep it in secrecy as a great mystery. Conceal, conceal. [PGM XII.316–322]

(c) The following passage is taken from a spell to acquire a divine assistant (PGM I.42–195).[170] The recipe is packaged into a letter written by a temple scribe Pnouthis, whose name is correct Egyptian although unattested,[171] addressed to a certain Keryx, who is related to Pnouthis as a student to a mentor. The priest tells that the spell has been chosen from an infinite number of (sacred) books, implying that this specific

---

[168] The verb περιεργάζειν has a derived meaning 'assiduously investigating and performing rituals', the overtones of which are certainly brought into play in the present passage; cf. 'Zauberei treiben', Preisendanz, *PGM II*, 84, and 'practice magic', Betz and Scarborough in *GMPT*, 167. In 1Ep.Cor.9.13 ἐργάζειν denotes 'performing rituals'.

[169] The ring itself could be meant as well.

[170] For this passage, see also, Gordon, 'Reporting the Marvellous', 73ff.

[171] Thissen suggests that the name is rather an invention than a real personal name. Its meaning 'The-god' or 'He-of-the-god' (< *P3-ntr* or *Pa-ntr*) would render a sense of trustworthiness to the text; Thissen, 'Ägyptologische Beiträge zu den griechischen magischen Papyri', 295.

spell is of exceptional quality. Moreover, he seems to suggest in a poorly preserved part of the passage that the spell is god-given.

> The spell of Pnouthis, the temple scribe (ἱερογραμματέως), for acquiring an assistant: [...] Pnouthios greets Keryx, the god-[fearing man]. As one who knows, I have prescribed for you [this spell for acquiring an assistant] to prevent your failing as you carry out [this rite]. After detaching all the prescriptions [bequeathed to us in] countless books (βίβλοις μυρίαις), [one out of all ...] I have shown (you) this spell for acquiring an assistant [as one that is serviceable] to you [...] that you (pl.) take this holy [assistant] and only [...]. O friend of aerial spirits that mo[ve ...] having persuaded[172] me with god-given (θεολογουμένοις) spells [...] but [now] I have dispatched this book so that you may learn thoroughly; for the spell of Pnouthis [has the power] to persuade the gods and all [the goddesses]. [I shall write] you from it about [acquiring] an assistant.
> [PGM I.42–54][173]

The elaborate ritual instructions are concluded by a demand to keep the contents of the spell concealed and a farewell greeting.[174]

> Therefore share these things with no one except [your] legitimate son alone when he asks you for the magic powers imparted [by] us. Farewell.
> [PGM I.192–194][175]

(d) The fourth citation introduces a spell for bowl divination (PGM IV. 154–285). A certain Nephotes, who is probably an Egyptian priest given his Egyptian name,[176] recommends the magical recipe in a letter addressed to a certain king Psammetichos, under which name three pharaohs of the 26th dynasty (664–525 BCE) are known. The reliability and efficacy of the spell is suggested by Nephotes' assurance that Psammetichos will be amazed after having tested the spell. Near the end of the recipe Nephotes exhorts the king to keep the spell secret.

---

[172] This participle refers to the aerial spirits.
[173] Tr. E.N. O'Neil, with slight modifications.
[174] The demand for secrecy occurs already several lines earlier in a short address to the reader as a conclusion to a long, detailed and fanciful description of the possibilities offered by the spell: 'Share this great mystery with no one [else], but conceal it, by Helios, since you have been deemed worthy by the lord [god]' [PGM I.130f.]. It occurs again in a prescription to engrave a magical name on a stone [PGM I.146].
[175] Tr. E.N. O'Neil. See for the translation 'legitimate son' GMPT, 8, fn. 37.
[176] Thissen, 'Ägyptologische Beiträge zu den griechischen magischen Papyri', 295. The name (< *Nfr-ḥtp*) is actually only known as epithet to Osiris or, in later periods, as a divine name.

> Nephotes greets Psammetichos, immortal[177] king of Egypt. Since the great god has appointed you immortal king and nature has made (you) the best wise man (ἄριστον σοφιστήν), I too, with a desire to show the industry in me, have sent you this rite that, with complete ease, produces a holy power. And after you have tested it, you too will be amazed at the miraculous nature of this magical operation. [PGM IV.154–162]
>
> Let this spell, mighty king, be transmitted to you alone, guarded by you, unshared. [PGM IV.254–256][178]

(e) The fifth passage is the opening to the so-called *Mithras Liturgy*, an elaborate spell for an initiatory accession through several heavenly layers to meet the supreme god Helios Mithras (PGM IV.475–829). The text is laid out as a teaching of an anonymous religious master to a female initiate. The address to the divine entities Providence and Psyche to come to the aid of the author is reminiscent of the invocation of the muses in classical literature. The text is said to derive from the supreme god himself.

> Be Gracious to me, O Providence and Psyche, as I write these mysteries handed down ⟨not⟩ for gain; and for an only child I request immortality, O initiates of this our power (furthermore, it is necessary for you, O daughter, to take the juices of herbs and spices, which will ⟨be made known⟩ to you at the end of my holy treatise), which the great god Helios Mithras ordered to be revealed to me by his archangel, so that I alone may ascend into heaven as an inquirer and behold the universe.
> [PGM IV.475–485][179]

At two instances the narrator bears witness to the efficacy of the given spell.

> I have not found a greater spell than this in the world [PGM IV.776]
>
> Many times have I used the spell, and have wondered greatly
> [PGM IV. 790f.][180]

---

[177] The Greek αἰωνοβίῳ is a literal translation of Egyptian *(nty) 'nḫ ḏ.t*, 'who lives forever', an epithet attached to the name of the reigning pharaoh in Demotic documentary texts of the Ptolemaic period; F.Ll. Griffith, *Catalogue of the Demotic Papyri in the John Rylands Library Manchester* 3 vols. (Manchester, London 1909) vol. 3, 127, fn. 4. For a list of occurrences, see, Mark Depauw, *The Archive of Teos and Thabis from Early Ptolemaic Thebes. P.Brux.Dem.Inv. E 8252–8256* (Monographies Reine Élisabeth 8; Brussels 2000) 134f., note (h).

[178] Tr. E.N. O'Neil, with slight modifications.

[179] Tr. M.W. Meyer. Meyer translates 'mysteries handed down ⟨not⟩ for gain but for instruction', although the clause 'but for instruction' is not present in the Greek text. For this reason I have deleted the clause from the translation given here.

[180] Tr. M.W. Meyer.

(f) The sixth excerpt is an anecdote incorporated into a spell of attraction (PGM IV.2441–2621). Before giving the instructions for a burnt offering, the text relates how the Egyptian high priest Pakhrates[181] was given a double fee by emperor Hadrian (who indeed visited Egypt in 130 CE) because of the miraculous effect of the spell.[182]

> Pakhrates, the high priest (προφήτης) of Heliopolis, revealed [it] to the emperor Hadrian, revealing the power of his very own divine magic (τῆς θείας αὐτοῦ μαγείας). For it attracted in one hour; it made someone sick in 2 hours; it destroyed in 7 hours, sent the emperor himself dreams as he thoroughly tested the whole truth of the magic within his power. And marvelling at the prophet, he ordered double fees to be given to him.
> [PGM IV.2446–2455][183]

This short narrative interruption of the recipe serves as evidence to the claims made by the text in the advertising introduction.

> It attracts those who are uncontrollable, requiring no magical material, within one day. It inflicts sickness excellently and destroys powerfully, sends dreams beautifully, accomplishes dream revelations marvellously and in its many demonstrations has been marvelled at for having no failure in these matters. [PGM IV.2442–2446][184]

These passages stand out among the available advertising introductions because of their explicitness and relative length. The texts make use of several textual strategies: they can take the form of a justifying, almost philological, preface, a letter or an anecdote, while the invoked communication situation is one between an Egyptian priest and an Egyptian king or between a mentor and a student in the occult arts. However, in most cases, a spell is made attractive only by its title, like, for example, *Charm of Agathokles for sending dreams* (PGM XII.107–121), *Zminis' of Tentyra's spell for sending dreams* (PGM XII.121–143), *Charm of Solomon that produces a trance* (PGM IV.850–929), *Apollonius of Tyana's old serving woman* (PGM XI.a.1–40), *Hidden stele* (PGM IV.1115–1166) or *'Great is the mistress Isis'; Copy of a holy book found in the archives of*

---

[181] This character may be identical with the Pancrates described in Lucian's *Philopseudes* 34 (see the preceding section). However, there are no historical documents to support this claim. The name derives from *Pa-hrd*, 'He-of-the-(divine)-child (= Harpokrates)', Thissen, 'Ägyptologische Beiträge zu den griechischen magischen Papyri', 296.

[182] The passage has attracted considerable scholarly attention as a testimony of Egyptian cultural pride vis-à-vis Roman economic and political hegemony; R. Gordon, 'Reporting the Marvellous', 77ff. and Frankfurter, *Religion in Roman Egypt*, 227ff.

[183] Tr. E.N. O'Neil.

[184] Tr. E.N. O'Neil, with slight modifications.

*Hermes* (PGM XXIVa.1–25). The sole reference to a famous magician, a hidden Egyptian text or a divinity was apparently deemed sufficient to impart to the reader a feeling of confidence in the efficacy of the spell.

### 6.4.2. *Analysis of the mystifying motifs*

The advertising introductions make use of four motifs to mystify a magical recipe. These motifs have here been separated for clarity's sake, but recur in a variety of combinations in the actual spells.[185]

1. Origin of the text (pseudepigraphy)
   a. God-given or attributed to a god
   b. Famous author (philosopher, magician)
2. Authenticity of the message
   a. 'Original' letter, suggesting actual correspondence between two magicians
   b. Testimony of text's discovery in temple or on stele
   c. Testimony of text's translation from Egyptian into Greek
3. Proof of efficacy
4. Importance to maintain secrecy

In the following, the distribution and the nature of each of the above listed motifs will be considered in closer detail by means of tables listing the occurrences in the *Demotic* and *Greek Magical Papyri*. The following conclusions can be given beforehand:

1. The idea to render a text authoritative and prestigious by means of mystification was already known in the pharaonic period.
2. There seems to be no strict relationship between the rite's purpose and authorship.
3. The pseudepigraphy motif makes use of several distinct cultural traditions (Egyptian, Greek, Jewish, Persian).

---

[185] This breakdown by subjects diverges slightly from the subdivision proposed by Wolgang Speyer, whose theoretical work on pseudepigraphy and literary forgery in antiquity remains the standard. Wolfgang Speyer, *Die literarische Fälschung im heidnischen und christlichen Altertum. Ein Versuch ihrer Deutung* (Handbuch der Altertumswissenschaft I.2; Munich 1971); for his subdivision, see, chapter A.IV 'Die Mittel der Echtheitsbeglaubigung' pp. 44–84.

**1a.** 1. The text is god-given

| Spell | Subject Matter | God |
|---|---|---|
| PGM III.424–466 | Foreknowledge and Memory | Osiris (440) |
| PGM IV.475–829 | Initiation (Mithras Liturgy) | Helios Mithras (482 ff.) |
| PGM IV.850–929 | Exorcism | Hermes Trismegistos (885 ff.) |
| PGM VII.862–918 | Lunar spell (of attraction) | The Twelve Olympic Gods and Aphrodite Urania (863 ff.) |

**1a.** 2. The text is attributed to a god[186]

| Spell | Subject Matter | God |
|---|---|---|
| PGM X.36–50 | Restraining spell | Apollo (36) |
| PDM xiv.93–114 | Divination | Imhotep (93)[187] |
| PDM lxi.100–105 | Spell of attraction | Nephthys (100)[188] |

These two tables demonstrate that both the *Demotic* and *Greek Magical Papyri* contain spells that are said to have a divine origin. The Demotic spells refer solely to Egyptian divinities, whereas the Greek spells make also use of gods of Hellenic origin (the twelve Olympic gods, Apollo) and syncretistic divinities that were particularly popular during and throughout the Roman Empire (Helios Mithras, Hermes Trismegistos).

The idea of religious pseudepigraphy was well known in Egypt since early pharaonic times.[189] In theory, all cultic texts were viewed as cre-

---

[186] Not included in this table are spells of which the title contains a god's name to identify the god addressed in the rite. These are: *Oracle of Kronos* (PGM IV.3086–3124), *Saucer divination of Aphrodite* (PGM IV.3209–3254), *Oracle of Sarapis* (PGM V.1–53), *Stele of Aphrodite* (PGM VII.215–218), *Hermes's ring* (PGM V.213–303), *Request for a dream oracle from Besas* (PGM VII.222–249), *Hermes' wondrous victory charm* (PGM VII.919–924), *Vessel inquiry of Khonsu* (PDM xiv.239–295), *Vessel inquiry of Osiris* (PDM xiv.627–635), *Spell of the Geat One of Five* (PDM xiv.670–674), *God's arrival of Osiris* (PDM Suppl. 130–138), *God's arrival of Thoth* (PDM Suppl. 149–162), *God's arrival of Imhotep* (PDM Suppl. 168–184).

[187] P. London-Leiden 4/1.

[188] P. BM 10588 7/6.

[189] See for the concept of religious pseudepigraphy: Wolfgang Speyer, 'Religiöse Pseudepigraphie und literarische Fälschung im Altertum' *JAC* 8/9 (1965/66) 88–125, 91f. [reprinted in: Norbert Brox (ed.), *Pseudepigraphie in der heidnischen und jüdisch-christlichen Antike* (Darmstadt 1977) 195–263]. See also Speyer, *Die literarische Fälschung im heidnischen und christlichen Altertum*, 35–37.

ations of Thoth, the god of language and writing,[190] but, in certain cases, texts were explicitly ascribed to a divinity. For example, Book of the Dead spells 30b, 101 and 184 are presented as compositions of Thoth himself, whereas Book of the Dead spell 148 is called 'Wennefer's roll' in certain redactions. The so-called *Oracular Amuletic Decrees*, which were worn rolled-up around the neck as phylacteries, were considered written records of a god's promise to ward off evil.[191] Certain *Documents of Breathing*, a class of mortuary compositions dating to the Greco-Roman period, were explicitly ascribed to Isis or Thoth.[192]

**1b.** The text is attributed to a famous author (magician or philosopher)

This motif is frequently attested in the two manuscripts under study as shown by the following table, in which the attestations are presented in their order of appearance. The authors attested in the other *Greek Magical Papyri* are distinguished into ethnic categories below.

| *Spell* | *Subject* | *Author* | *Known as* |
|---|---|---|---|
| PGM XII.96–106 | spell to acquire business | Himerios (96) | unknown[193] |
| PGM XII.107–121 | dream sending | Agathokles (107) Apollobex (121) | unknown[194] famous magician[195] |

---

[190] Patrick Boylan, *Thoth, the Hermes of Egypt. A Study of Some Aspects of Theological Thought in Ancient Egypt* (Oxford 1922) 92ff. C.J. Bleeker, *Hathor and Thoth. Two Key Figures of the Ancient Egyptian Religion* (Studies in the History of Religions 26; Leiden 1973) 140ff. Highly instructive is Siegfried Schott's collection of Egyptian book titles: *Bücher und Bibliotheken im Alten Ägypten*, a long list of references to Thoth can be found in the index on page 536.

[191] Edwards, *Oracular Amuletic Decrees of the Late New Kingdom*.

[192] See for a classification of this group of mortuary texts: Mark Coenen, 'Books of Breathing. More than a Terminological Question?' *OLP* 26 (1995) 29–34 and Martin A. Stadler, 'The Funerary Texts of Papyrus Turin N. 766: A Demotic Book of Breathing (part II)' *Enchoria* 26 (2000) 110–124, 114f.

[193] Preisendanz suggests to identify the author with a fourth-century physician, see *GMPT*, 156, fn. 24. This identification is a mere guess.

[194] No magician or priest of this name is known to date. The name was widely used as a personal name during the Roman period.

[195] Apuleius (*Apologia* 90) and Plinius (*Nat.Hist.* 30.9) include Apollobex in a list of famous magicians next to Persian Magoi, Greek philosophers and Jewish magicians. If the name were indeed a free Greek rendering of the Egyptian name *Ḥr-bik* 'Horus-the-falcon' (the god Apollo was identified with Horus), Apollobex might be identical with Pibechis (< *P3-bik* 'The-Falcon' or *Pa-bik* 'He-of-the-falcon', see, Thissen, 'Ägyptologische Beiträge zu den griechischen magischen Papyri', 295) who is mentioned in

| Spell | Subject | Author | Known as |
|---|---|---|---|
| PGM XII.121–143 | dream sending | Zminis of Tentyra (121) | unknown[196] |
| | | Ostanes (122) | Persian magos[197] |
| PGM XII.316–350 | Ouphôr | Ourbikos (318) | unknown[198] |
| PGM XII.351–364 | 'Sphere', prognostic of life and death | Demokritos (351) | Greek philosopher[199] |
| PDM xiv.1–92 | vessel divination | [A physician] in the Oxyrhynchite nome (1)[200] | anonymous[201] |

PGM IV.3007–3086 as author of a spell for exorcism. Hopfner, *Griechische Offenbarungszauber*, vol. 1, §210, 102; Karl Preisendanz, 'Pibechis' *PRE* 20 (1941) 1310–1312.

[196] Given this person's name (Zminis < *Ns-Mn* 'He-who-belongs-to-(the-god)-Min', Demot.Nb., 647) and his stated origin from the city Dendera, 60 kilometres to the north of Thebes, he is likely to be Egyptian.

[197] Ostanes, together with his fellow magoi Zoroaster, Hystaspes and Astrampsouchos, was considered an authority in the field of magic and alchemy by the Hellenistic elite. It was thought that he had accompanied the Persian king Xerxes during the second Persian campaign against Greece (480/79 BCE). A large body of pharmacological and alchemical literature circulated under his name during the Roman period. He was particularly well known for knowledge in the field of necromancy. In general, see, Jack Lindsay, *The Origins of Alchemy in Graeco-Roman Egypt* (London 1970) 131–158. For a list of secondary literature, see, Hopfner, *Griechische Offenbarungszauber*, vol. 2, §370, 160–161. See for an overview and ancient sources: Joseph Bidez and Franz Cumont, *Les mages hellénisés. Zoroastre, Ostanès et Hystaspe d'après la tradition grecque* 2 vols. (Paris 1938) vol.1, 167–212 and vol. 2, 267–356. For the nature and function of the pseudepigraphy of the Persian magoi, see, Roger Beck, 'Thus Spake not Zarathuštra. Zoroastrian Pseudepigrapha of the Greco-Roman Period', in: M. Boyce and F. Grenet, *A History of Zoroastrianism* 3 vols. (HdO, 1. Abt., VIII.1,2,2,3; Leiden 1975–1991) vol. 3, 490–565.

[198] See also chapter 5.3.

[199] In the Hellenistic and Roman period Demokritos of Abdera (second half of the fifth century BCE), was promoted from philosopher particularly known for his atomic theory of matter to renowned alchemist and purveyor of the magical arts and considered a follower of Pythagoras. Like Plato, Pythagoras and Eudoxus, he was thought to have studied with the Egyptian priests. Festugière, *L'Astrologie et les sciences occultes*, 25–26; Lindsay, *The Origins of Alchemy*, 90–100; Dickie, *Magic and Magicians in the Greco-Roman World*, 119–123, 195.

[200] P. London-Leiden 1/1

[201] See for the connection between physicians (*swn.iw*) and magic and a table of Egyptian physicians holding priestly titles: John F. Nunn, *Ancient Egyptian Medicine* (London 1996) 120f. Oxyrhynchus was the capital of the 19th Upper Egyptian nome, about 280 kilometres to the north of Thebes. Nothing is known about the perception of Oxyrhynchus regarding magic and mystery. Several magical texts were found in Oxyrhynchus, see, Brashear, 'The *Greek Magical Papyri*', 3485 s.v. Not included in Brashear's list is P. BM 10808, an Egyptian magical text dating to the second century CE, of

| Spell | Subject | Author | Known as |
|---|---|---|---|
| PDM xiv.232–238 | divination (*ph-ntr*) | Paysakh, the priest from Cusae (232)[202] | unknown[203] |
| PDM xiv.309–334 | spell for honour and praise | pharaoh [Dariu]s (334)[204] | Persian ruler over Egypt[205] |
| PDM xiv.528–553 | Vessel divination | A physician in the Oxyrhynchite nome (528)[206] | Anonymous |

PGM XII presents an international mix of authoritative magicians (Egyptian, Greek, Persian), whereas the persons referred to in P. London-Leiden are firmly rooted in Egypt itself, geographically or historically. It is unclear whether the highly specific references to 'a physician in the Oxyrhynchite nome' and 'Paysakh, the priest from Cusae' are instances of fictitious window dressing or historically correct records of factual exchange of magical texts between priests. Such exchange is testified by a Demotic letter of Ptolemaic date, in which a certain Miysis asks a priest of Thoth to return a medical and pharmacological book.[207] A similar clause occurs twice rather casually in PGM V.370–

---

which only one column is preserved, belonging to the corpus of *Demotic Magical Papyri*; Dieleman, 'Ein spätägyptisches magisches Handbuch'.

[202] P. London-Leiden 8/12.

[203] The name Paysakh is otherwise unattested. The name, which is written without the seated man determinative, consists of the demonstrative or possessive article *p3y* and the substantive *sh*, 'gall' (the alternative meaning 'bitterness' is less likely given the flesh determinative). Since the name's meaning 'He-of-the-gall' is rather odd, it is doubtful whether this reading is correct. Cusae (*k3s* in Egyptian) was the capital of the 14th Upper Egyptian nome in Middle Egypt, about 200 kilometres to the north of Thebes. Nothing is known about its economic, political or religious significance in the Greco-Roman period.

[204] P. London-Leiden 11/26. See for the restoration of the name Griffith and Thompson, *The Demotic Magical Papyrus of London and Leiden*, vol. 1, 86, fn. to line 26.

[205] The Persian king Darius I (521–486 BCE) ruled over Egypt as second pharaoh of the 27th dynasty (521–486 BCE); Georges Posener, *La première domination perse en Égypte: receuil d'inscriptions hiéroglyphiques* (BdE 11; Cairo 1936) 175–190. He was remembered by the Egyptians as law-giver, pious king and, eventually, magician; see Diodorus of Sicily I.95, 5 and Porphyrius, *On Abstinence*, IV.16. His name is possibly also mentioned in a Demotic text on solar and lunar omina (2nd century CE); Richard A. Parker, *A Vienna Demotic Papyrus on Eclipse- and Lunar-Omina* (Brown Egyptological Studies 2; Providence 1959) 21 [text A, IV, 10].

[206] P. London-Leiden 18/7.

[207] Karl-Th. Zauzich, 'Zwei Briefe von Bücherfreunden', in: Frandsen and Ryholt (eds.), *The Carlsberg Papyri 3*, 53–57. The text in question is P. Carlsberg 21. Compare this with a fourth century CE Coptic letter from Kellis, the Dakhleh Oasis, which

446, a recipe for a dream divination of the god Hermes. The clauses are meant to give trustworthiness to alternative ingredients: 'But I have heard from a certain man from Herakleopolis, that he takes 28 new sprouts from an olive tree, which is cultivated, the famous one' (372–375) and 'Again, just (as I heard) from the man from Herakleopolis' (383).[208] It is very probable that such clauses refer to real individuals, testifying to a lively exchange of books and information about rituals among Egyptian priests. As such, these clauses are fundamentally different from the introductions mentioning highly acclaimed magicians. The individuals are not accredited with authorship but with advice based on empirically established knowledge.

As in PGM XII, pseudepigraphy is very frequent in the other *Greek Magical Papyri*. The instances are classified according to ethnicity in the following tables to gain a clear insight into the favoured groups.

Egyptian priest

| Spell | Subject Matter | Author |
| --- | --- | --- |
| PGM I.42–195 | Acquiring an assistant | Pnouthis, the sacred scribe (42)[209] |
| PGM III.424–466 | Foreknowledge and charm | Manetho (440)[210] |
| PGM IV.154–285 | Bowl divination | Nephotes (154)[211] |
| PGM IV.1928–2005 | Necromancy | (King) Pitys (1928)[212] |

---

contains a copy of a magical spell: Paul Mirecki, Iain Gardner, and Anthony Alcock, 'Magical Spell, Manichaean Letter', in: Paul Mirecki and Jason BeDuhn (eds.), *Emerging from Darkness. Studies in the Recovery of Manichaean Sources* (Nag Hammadi and Manichaean Studies 43; Leiden 1997) 1–32.

[208] Tr. E.N. O'Neil.

[209] See example *c* and footnote 171.

[210] Egyptian high priest of, in all probability, Heliopolis (native of the town Sebennytos in the eastern Delta) who wrote in Greek about Egyptian history and religion in the early Ptolemaic period. He is also accredited with having played a decisive role in the establishment of the Sarapis cult in Alexandria (Plutarch, *About Isis and Osiris*, 28; 362A). In the Roman period a book on astrology circulated under his name. Verbrugghe and Wickersham, *Berossos and* Manetho, 95–102 and Heinz-J. Thissen, 'Manetho' *LdÄ* 3, 1180f.

[211] See example *d* and footnote 176.

[212] Pitys is probably identical with the Egyptian high priest (προφήτης) Bitys who, according to Iamblichus (*On the Mysteries of Egypt*, VIII.5 and X.7), translated hieroglyphic hermetic texts into Greek. The name derives from *Pa-t3*; 'He-who-belongs-to-the-country (Egypt)', see Thissen, 'Ägyptologische Beiträge zu den griechischen magis-

| Spell | Subject Matter | Author |
|---|---|---|
| PGM IV.2006–2125 | Acquiring an assistant | Pitys (2006) |
| PGM IV.2140–2144 | Necromancy | Pitys (the Thessalian) (2140) |
| PGM IV.3007–3086 | Exorcism | Pibechis (3007)[213] |
| PGM V.96–172 | Exorcism | Ieu, the painter (96)[214] |

Greek philosopher or holy man

| Spell | Subject Matter | Author |
|---|---|---|
| PGM IV.1716–1870 | Spell of attraction | Dardanos (1716)[215] |
| PGM VII.167–186 | Table tricks | Demokritos (167) |
| PGM VII.795–845 | Dream divination | Demokritos (795) |
| Idem | Request for dream oracle | Pythagoras (795) |
| PGM VII.862–918 | Lunar spell (of attraction) | Claudianus (862)[216] |
| PGM XIa.1–40 | Acquiring an assistant | Apollonius of Tyana (1)[217] |
| PGM XX.13–19 | Remedy against headache | Philinna the Thessalian (13)[218] |

---

chen Papyri', 295. His identification as king or Thessalian should probably be understood as secondary buildings.

[213] Pibechis (< *P3-bîk* 'The-Falcon' or *Pa-bîk* 'He-of-the-falcon'; Thissen, 'Ägyptologische Beiträge zu den griechischen magischen Papyri', 295) was a famous magician and alchemist. He may be identical with Apollobex who is mentioned in PGM XII.121 (see footnote 195). As alchemist he was associated with the Persian magos Ostanes; Preisendanz, 'Pibechis'.

[214] Ieu's professional title, ζωγρ(άφος), is usually translated as 'hieroglyphist', but it means actually 'painter'; cf. *GMPT*, 103 fn. 11 and Preisendanz, *Papyri Graecae Magicae*, vol.1, 184f. fn. to lines 96–171. The term 'hieroglyphist' occurs in the tale *The Dream of King Nectanebo*, which is partly preserved in a Greek and Demotic version. The Demotic version has *ḥmw-n-s'nḫ*, whereas the Greek version has ἱερόγλυφος. See also P. Oxy 1029, 5–8. It is therefore improbable that Ieu's professional title should be translated as 'hieroglyphist'. It is more likely that the title refers to a painter of mummy masks or portraits.

[215] Dardanos is the mythical ancestor of the Trojan kings and was considered to be the founder of the mystery rites of the Kabeiroi on Samothrace, see: Diodorus of Sicily, 5.48–49 and A. Hermann, 'Dardanus' *RAC* 3 (1957) 593f. Pliny the Elder considers him a great magician, *Nat. Hist.* 30,9.

[216] This same name is mentioned in a list of alchemists in Berthelot and Ruelle, *Collection des anciens alchimistes grecs*, 26, 1.1 (taken from *GMPT*, 141, fn. 140).

[217] See chapter 6.3.3.2.

[218] This woman is otherwise unknown. The name is attested in a Late-Hellenistic collection of magical spells nowadays generally known as the 'Philinna Papyrus' (PGM XX). Faraone argues to see the collection as one of the earliest preserved specimens

## Semitic magician

| Spell | Subject Matter | Author |
|---|---|---|
| PGM IV.850–929 | Divination through medium | Solomon (850)[219] |
| PGM VII.619–627 | Invisibility or love spell | Moses (619)[220] |
| PGM XX.4–12 | Remedy against inflammation | Syrian woman of Gadara (4)[221] |
| PGM XXIIb.1–26 | Prayer for protection | Jacob (1, 26) |

## Persian magos

| Spell | Subject Matter | Author |
|---|---|---|
| PGM VIII.1–63 | Spell of attraction | Astrampsouchos (1)[222] |

Except for the Semitic magicians, the international range of presumed authors is identical with PGM XII.[223] Noteworthy is the absence of a

---

of Greco-Egyptian magic handbooks, which still preserves certain distinctly Greek conceptions of a magical charm: Christopher A. Faraone, 'Handbooks and Anthologies: The Collection of Greek and Egyptian Incantations in Late Hellenistic Egypt' *ARG* 2 (2000) 195–214, 209ff.

[219] King Solomon was known as a sage, astrologer and magician among the Hellenised elites of the Greco-Roman period, see, Pablo A. Torijano, *Solomon the Esoteric King. From King to Magus, Development of a Tradition* (JSJS 73; Leiden 2002) and Karl Preisendanz, 'Salomo' *PRE* Suppl. 8 (1956) 660–704.

[220] Moses was promoted from a culture hero to a powerful magician in the Greco-Roman period, see, John G. Gager, *Moses in Greco-Roman Paganism* (SBL Monograph Series 16; Nashville 1972) 134–161.

[221] This woman is otherwise unknown. See also footnote 218.

[222] In the actual manuscript the name 'Astrapsoukos' is given. This must be a corrupted writing of the name Astrampsouchos, a famous Persian magos. In Diogenes Laertius I.2 he is listed as magos next to Ostanes, Gobryas and Pazatas. See E. Riess, 'Astrampsouchos' *PRE* 2 (1896) 1796f. An oracle book containing answers to a set of 90 to 110 different questions pertaining to issues of private life circulated in the third to fifth century CE under the name of Astrampsouchos (*Sortes Astrampsychi*), see on this oracle book and its method of devining the appropriate answer to a question: Frankfurter, *Religion in Roman Egypt*, 181ff. Frankfurter calls Astrampsouchos incorrectly a 'legendary Egyptian seer' (p. 182). See for relevant literature to the *Sortes Astrampsychi*: *GMPT*, 265.

[223] Despite the fact that PGM XII lacks titles mentioning Moses or king Solomon, the manuscript contains clear reflections of a great reverence for Jewish magic, which was widespread in the Roman Empire. As in PDM xiv, references to Moses and the Holy Mount occur in coercive invocations: PGM XII.92f. and PDM xiv.130f., 1031f. See also Gager, *Moses in Greco-Roman Paganism*, 140–146. For discussions on the form and nature of Jewish influence on the *Greek Magical Papyri*, see, Morton Smith, 'The Jewish Elements in the Magical Papyri', in: Idem, *Studies in the Cult of Yahweh* (Religions in the Graeco-Roman World 130; Leiden 1996) vol.2, 242–256 [improved version of

category of Chaldaeans, the name under which the astronomer priests of Babylonia were known among the Hellenistic elites. Like Persian magoi, Egyptian priests and Jewish magicians, the Chaldaeans were highly esteemed as ritual experts, mainly in the field of astrology and theurgy.[224] Nonetheless, the widely shared respect for their knowledge did not find its way into the *Greek Magical Papyri*.

**2a.** The text is presented as an original letter

| Spell | Subject | Sender | Addressee |
|---|---|---|---|
| PGM I.42–195 | Acquiring an assistant | Pnouthios, the temple scribe[225] | Keryx[226] |
| PGM IV.154–285 | Bowl divination | Nephotes[227] | King Psammetichus |
| PGM IV.2006–2125 | Acquiring an assistant[228] | Pitys | King Ostanes |
| PGM V.96–172 | Exorcism | Ieu, the painter | – Not mentioned – |

---

the same article in *SBL Seminar Papers* 25 (1986) 455–462]; Hans Dieter Betz, 'Jewish Magic in the *Greek Magical Papyri*' (PGM VII.260–271)', in: Schäfer and Kippenberg (eds.), *Envisioning Magic*, 45–63 and Gideon Bohak, 'Greek, Coptic and Jewish Magic in the Cairo Genizah' *BASP* 36 (1999) 27–44.

[224] Dicky, *Magic and Magicians in the Greco-Roman World*, 110f.

[225] See example *c* and footnote 171.

[226] Keryx is actually not a personal name but a designation of the herald at a procession or sacrifice in ancient Greece. In the Eleusinian Mysteries the sacred herald (ἱεροκῆρυξ) played an important role and was chosen exclusively from the *Kerykes* family. The link with the mystery rites is significant in this particular case, because Pnouthios addresses his student Keryx, while describing the extraordinary character of the rite, as 'bl[essed] *initiate* of the sacred magic' (PGM I.127) and commands him to 'share with no one [else] (…) this great *mystery*' (PGM I.130f.). See on the use of language deriving from mystery religions in the PGM: Hans Dieter Betz, 'Magic and Mystery in the *Greek Magical Papyri*', in: Faraone and Obbink (eds.), *Magika Hiera*, 244–259. However, Ritner regards these Greek terms as mere translations of Egyptian concepts like *sštз* that do not carry any of the connotations of Greek mystery-cult theology. Note that he does not explain the personal name Keryx. Ritner, 'Egyptian Magical Practice under the Roman Empire', 3365f.

[227] See example *d* and footnote 176.

[228] Although the spell's title is 'Pitys' spell of attraction', the rite is meant to procure a daimôn who is capable of fulfilling a variety of commands. The spell is the second in a cluster of three dealing with necromancy and the interrogation of skulls, which are ascribed to Pitys. On this cluster, see, Christopher A. Faraone, 'When Necromancy goes Underground: Skull- and Corpse-Divination in the Paris Magical Papyrus (PGM IV.1928–2144)', in: P. Struck and S. Johnston (eds.), *Greek and Roman Divination* (Leiden, forthcoming 2004).

The custom to ascribe fictitious letters to a famous person of an earlier period was a widespread phenomenon in the Hellenistic and Roman period. Collections of letters attributed to figures such as Socrates, Plato, Apollonius of Tyana circulated throughout the Roman Empire.[229] The method was particularly popular in Christian, Hermetic and alchemical circles as a means to render new texts and opinions authoritative by giving them the air of tradition and authenticity. The idea of fictitious letters was already extant in pharaonic Egypt as is testified by the literary *Wermai's Letter* (beginning 21$^{st}$ dynasty) and the semi-literary school letters of the so-called *Late Egyptian Miscellanies* (late New Kingdom).[230] Of particular interest are two letters out of a set of Demotic fictional letters written on the outer surface of three jars dating to the late Ptolemaic or early Roman period.[231] The first letter (O. Krug. A,a), of which the sender's name is lost, is addressed to pharaoh and relates the tale of a certain magician (*ḥry-tp*) Hyhor who was detained in prison and received help from two birds. The second letter (O. Krug. A,d) is sent by the king of Arabia to pharaoh and contains a fable of a swallow and the sea.[232] The format of these letters is very similar to the letters in the PGM: in the first letter, pharaoh functions as the receiving partner in the exchange of knowledge on magic, while the second letter is an instance of correspondence between kings as in the case of Pitys and Ostanes (PGM IV.2006–2125).[233]

---

[229] Speyer, *Die literarische Fälschung*, 79–81.

[230] For *Wermai's Letter*, see, Ricardo A. Caminos, *A Tale of Woe. Papyrus Pushkin 127* (Oxford 1977) and Moers, *Fingierte Welten*, 101, 273ff. The *Late Egyptian Miscellanies* can be found in Alan H. Gardiner, *Late Egyptian Miscellanies* (Bibliotheca Aegyptiaca 7; Brussels 1937). Translations of certain texts can be found in Miriam Lichtheim, *Ancient Egyptian Literature. Volume II: The New Kingdom* (Berkeley 1976) 110–114 and 168–175 and Nikolaus Tacke, *Verspunkte als Gliederungsmittel in ramessidischen Schülerhandschriften* (SAGA 22; Heidelberg 2001).

[231] Since only jar A is completely preserved, the total number of letters cannot be established. The first jar (A) contains four letters (a-d), of the second jar (B) two letters are partly preserved. See: Wilhelm Spiegelberg, *Demotische Texte auf Krügen* (Leipzig 1912). Note that the opening address of the letters should be read as *ḫrw bꜣk* NN *m-bꜣḥ* NN, 'the voice of the servant NN to NN'; Mark Depauw, 'The Demotic Epistolary Formulae' *EVO* 17 (1994) 87–94.

[232] A re-edition of this text considerably improved Spiegelberg's publication: Philippe Collombert, 'Le conte de l'hirondelle et de la mer', in: Ryholt (ed.), *Seventh International Conference of Demotic Studies*, 59–76.

[233] Pitys is not called king in this spell, but is so in the preceding spell (PGM IV.1928–2005).

**2b.** Testimony of text's discovery in temple or on stele

| Spell | Subject Matter | Original Location |
|---|---|---|
| PGM III.424–466 | Foreknowledge and memory | Holy book (424)[234] |
| PGM IV.850–929 | Spell for exorcism | Hermes Trismegistos wrote the holy name in Heliopolis in hieroglyphs (885f.) |
| PGM IV.1115–1166 | Prayer | Hidden stele (1115)[235] |
| PGM IV.1167–1226 | Prayer for protection and blessing | Stele (1167) |
| PGM V.96–172 | Spell for exorcism | Stele (96) |
| PGM VII.862–918 | Lunar spell (of attraction) | Found in temple in Aphroditopolis next to statue of Aphrodite Urania (864f.)[236] |
| PGM VIII.1–63 | Business spell to attract customers | True name was inscribed on sacred stele in the innermost shrine (of temple) in Hermopolis (41f.) |
| PGM XII.401–444 | List of encoded ingredients | Statues of the gods in temple (404) |

---

[234] The term 'holy book' ἱερὰ βίβλος is a designation for a papyrus roll containing an Egyptian ritual text (mdꜣ.t nṯr). These texts were written in hieratic or, from the Roman period onwards, in Demotic by the lector priests and temple scribes and kept in the House-of-Life and temple library. Therefore, the use of the word 'holy book' in the title of a magical spell in Greek implies an act of appropriation and translation.

[235] A stele is a stone slab inscribed with a commemorative text. In Egypt, steles were usually inscribed with a hieroglyphic text and erected in temples or at the entrance to a tomb.

[236] Three cities were under the name Aphroditopolis in Greco-Roman Egypt: (1) Atfih, lying about 400 kilometres to the north of Thebes at the height of the Fayum region, (2) Kom Ishqaw, about 200 kilometres to the north of Thebes and (3) Dzjebelein (Pathyris), about 30 kilometres to the south of Thebes. All three of them had a cult for the goddess Hathor (Aphrodite in Greek). The magical spell refers in all probability to Atfih, which was known, nation-wide, for its cult of the white cow *Hesat*, which goddess was assimilated with Isis-Hathor; R. Grieshammer, 'Atfih' *LdÄ* I, 519. The main character of the tale *Nectanebo's Dream*, which is partly preserved in both Demotic and Greek, is a resident of this same Aphroditopolis (in Demotic *Pr-nb.t-tp-ỉḥ*). Since this character is fond of wine and women, the city of Hathor, goddess of love and merriment, is probably deliberately chosen in this tale. For the texts, see, Jörg-Dieter Gauger, 'Der "Traum des Nektanebos"—die griechische Fassung –', in: Blasius and Schipper (eds.), *Apokalyptik und Ägypten*, 189–219 and Kim Ryholt, 'Nectanebo's Dream or the Prophecy of Petesis', *op. cit.*, 221–241.

| Spell | Subject Matter | Original Location |
|---|---|---|
| PGM XXIVa.1–25 | Description of oracular rite | Holy book found in the archives of Hermes (2 ff.) |
| PGM CXXII.1–55 | Magic handbook | Holy book called *Hermes* found in innermost shrine of the temple in Heliopolis (1 ff.) |

The fiction of the discovery of an old and lost ritual text does not occur in the *Demotic Magical Papyri*, but is frequent in the *Greek Magical Papyri*. In each case, an Egyptian ritual text is concerned, either written on a papyrus roll or inscribed on a stele, which had been found in a temple shrine or a temple library.[237] The geographical location of the temple, Heliopolis, Hermopolis or Aphroditopolis, is not arbitrarily chosen but determined by the religious prestige the city held within Egypt and even abroad. The god Thoth (Hermes, in Greek) and his cult centre Hermopolis are clearly favoured topics. This rhetorical strategy was already in use in religious and magical texts of the pharaonic period. The idea is attested as early as in spell 577 of the *Coffin Texts* where it is stated that the spell was found under the flank of (a statue of) Anubis. It is also prominent in the *Book of the Dead* and texts of technical priestly knowledge of different periods.[238] The so-called *Memphite Theology*, a cos-

---

[237] Speyer distinguishes between books fallen from heaven, books found in tombs (written either on a papyrus roll or a stele) and books found in temple archives or libraries: Wolfgang Speyer, *Bücherfunde in der Glaubenswerbung der Antike* (Hypomnemata 24; Göttingen 1970). In the case of the *Greek Magical Papyri*, the Egyptian temple is the sole place of discovery of ritual papyri or steles. Nonetheless, the other motifs were also used in pharaonic Egypt (see next footnote).

[238] Certain *Book of the Dead* manuscripts have postscripts to spells that attribute the discovery of spells to prince Hordedef, son of pharaoh Khufu, who would have found the spells during an inspection of temples in the time of pharaoh Menkaure: BD 30B, 64, 137A, 148; for the sources, see, Dietrich Wildung, *Die Rolle ägyptischer Könige im Bewußtsein ihrer Nachwelt I* (MÄS 17; Berlin 1969) 217–221. Variant manuscripts set the discovery of spells BD 64 and 130 back to the times of king Khasti, the fifth king of the first dynasty: Wildung, *op. cit.*, 25–28. BD Pleyte 166 is said to be found around the neck of the mummy of king User-Ma'at-Re (Ramses II); the introduction to BD Pleyte 167 claims that Khamwaset, son of Ramses II, found the spell under the head of a mummy and that it had earlier been used by Amenhotep son of Hapu. A portion of the so-called *Vessel Book*, preserved in two varying redactions in the New Kingdom medical compendia P. Ebers (§§854–855 and 856) and P. Berlin 3038 (§163) was purportedly found in a manuscript lying under the feet of a statue of the god Anubis in Letopolis (Egyptian *Khem*) in the days of pharaoh Khasti, see: Wildung, *op. cit.*, 21–25. The second section of the Brooklyn Snake Book was discovered in the time of pharaoh Neferkare (probably Pepi II): Sauneron, *Un traité égyptien d'ophiologie*, 60. The so-called *Book-of-the-*

mogonical account inscribed on the Shabaka Stone, brings the significance of this rhetorical strategy in Egyptian religious discourse most prominently to the fore. The introduction to the actual cosmogony does not only state that pharaoh Shabaka (first king of the 25th dynasty) ordered that a faithful copy of the ancient worm-eaten papyrus must be made, the orthography and grammar of the text display as well as a number of archaising features. Despite these archaic elements the text is clearly the product of the 25th dynasty (c. 715–657 BCE) and thus represents an attempt on the part of the Memphite priesthood to acquire prestige and authority by means of presumed tradition.[239]

In the Greek-speaking world the motif of discovery became popular only from the fourth century BCE onwards, to become pervasive in the Roman period, particularly so in works of occult knowledge.[240] In the majority of cases the fictitious discovery is situated on the periphery of the Greco-Roman world, for example, in Egypt or Mesopotamia, where temples and graves were thought to abound in magical charms

---

*Temple*, a treatise on the ideal arrangement of the temple building and its institution, which is preserved in a large number of hieratic and Demotic redactions, is said to be found by prince Hordedef in the temple of the god Atum in Heliopolis in the days of pharaoh Khufu: Joachim F. Quack, 'Der historische Abschnitt des Buches vom Tempel', in: Jan Assmann and Elke Blumenthal (eds.), *Literatur und Politik im pharaonischen und ptolemäischen Ägypten* (BdE 127; Cairo 1999) 267–278, 274. The idea of a text fallen from heaven is attested in a New Kingdom medical prescription (London Medical Papyrus §60) in which is stated that the spell descended into the court of the temple of Coptos the moon shining upon it in the days of king Khufu. According to a passage in the foundation account of the temple of Edfu, the architectural plan of the temple had fallen from heaven to the north of Memphis (Edfu VI, 6,4).

[239] Friedrich Junge, 'Zur Fehldatierung des sog. Denkmals memphitischer Theologie oder Der Beitrag der ägyptischen Theologie zur Geistesgeschichte der Spätzeit' *MDAIK* 29 (1973) 195–204. This text is not the sole example of the Egyptian priesthood employing the mystifying technique with the aim of religious propaganda. The *Bentresh Stele* and the *Famine Stele* are two obvious cases in point. The *Bentresh Stele* is a forgery of the Persian or Ptolemaic period, which relates the miraculous cure of a princess Bentresh of Bakhtan by the Theban god Knonsu-the-provider-in-Thebes in the time of pharaoh Ramses II, see: Michèle Broze, *La princesse de Bakhtan. Essai d'analyse stylistique* (Monographies Reine Élisabeth 6; Brussels 1989). The *Famine Stele*, composed in the Ptolemaic period, pretends to be a decree of pharaoh Djoser of the third dynasty to grant revenues of Nubia to the temple of Khnum-Re in Elephantine as a reward for Khnum's willingness to end a seven year period of drought, see, Paul Barguet, *La Stèle de la Famine à Séhel*, (BdE 24; Cairo 1953). Both texts are translated in Miriam Lichtheim, *Ancient Egyptian Literature. Volume III the Late Period* (Berkeley 1980) 90–103.

[240] Speyer, *Bücherfunde*, 110ff. and Idem, *Die literarische Fälschung*, 67–70. On the occurrence of this motive in esoteric texts, see, Speyer, *Bücherfunde*, 72ff. and R.P. Festugière, *La révélation d'Hermès Trismegiste I. L'astrologie et les sciences occultes* (Paris 1943) 319–324.

and steles in the native languages and scripts.[241] Therefore, the motif of translation was closely related to the motif of discovery.[242]

**2c.** Testimony of text's translation from Egyptian into Greek

| *Spell* | *Subject Matter* | *Language Concerned* |
|---|---|---|
| PGM III.424–466 | Foreknowledge and memory | Copy of holy book (Egyptian) (424) |
| PGM IV.850–929 | Spell for exorcism | Holy name was written in hieroglyphs (885f.) |
| PGM XII.401–444 | Encoded ingredients | Holy books (Egyptian) (407) |
| PGM CXXII.1–55 | Magic handbook | Holy book called *Hermes* was written in hieroglyphs and translated into Greek (1ff.) |

One should beware of dismissing too rashly all claims of Greek translations from Egyptian as Hellenic attempts to appropriate Egypt's prestige and authority regarding the occult, because the motif of translation was equally important in the propaganda of Egyptian cults in the Hellenistic world. Since Egyptian priests were important and active partners in this enterprise, accounts of translations of Egyptian hymns into Greek could be genuine in certain cases.[243] Moreover, that the transla-

---

[241] The story of Euhemerus (preserved in Diodorus of Sicily, VI, 1.4–7) is a case in point. Euhemerus sailed southward from Arabia and reached an island called Panchaea where he found a stele of gold, set up in the sanctuary of Zeus Triphylius. The stele contained, in the script and language of the Panchaeans, an account of the deeds of the Greek creator gods.

[242] Speyer, *Die literarische Fälschung*, 70f.

[243] Cases in point are the famous Isis aretalogy and the four hymns to Isis of Isidorus of Narmuthis. The Isis aretalogy, preserved in several redactions (Kyme, Thessaloniki, Ios, Andros and a variant version in Diodorus of Sicily I, 27.3–6), is said to be copied from the stele that stood next to the Ptah temple in Memphis. For the texts, see, Totti, *Ausgewählte Texte der Isis- und Sarpis-Religion*, nrs. 1 and 2. For an attempt to translate back into Demotic, see, Joachim F. Quack, '"Ich bin Isis, die Herrin der beiden Länder" Versuch zum demotischen Hintergrund der Memphitischen Isisaretalogie', in: Sibylle Meyer (ed.), *Egypt—Temple of the Whole World. Fs. Jan Assmann* (Studies in the History of Religions 97; Leiden 2003) 319–365, 336ff.; see also, Thomas M. Dousa, 'Imagining Isis: on some Continuities and Discontinuities in the Image of Isis in Greek Isis Hymns and Demotic Texts', in: Ryholt (ed.), *Seventh International Conference of Demotic Studies*, 149–184. Isidorus' hymns to Isis were inscribed on a stone placed in the temple of the goddess Renenutet in Narmuthis, the Fayum, sometime in the late Ptolemaic period. In the fourth hymn, Isidorus relates that he got his information from those who read the sacred scripts; Vera F. Vanderlip, *The Four Greek Hymns of Isidorus and the Cult of Isis* (American Studies in Papyrology 12; Toronto 1972).

tion of Egyptian texts into Greek was not merely a topos but a reality as well is proven by a number of priestly texts of which sections are preserved in both an Egyptian and Greek version.[244] Egyptian priests were thus engaged in translation work and it is highly probable that they consciously used the motif of translation as a means to impress their Greek-speaking public and to render their message authentic, irrespective of the fact whether the claim to translation was genuine or made up.[245]

## 3. Proof of efficacy

In the *Demotic* and *Greek Magical Papyri*, proofs of a spell's efficacy are numerous and standardised to such an extent that there is no need to list the occurrences in a table. These proofs can take the following forms:

1. Addition to the title or recipe of an adjective such as 'tested' or a clause such as 'nothing is better in the world'[246]

---

[244] These texts are the *Myth of the Sun's Eye* (a mythological narrative), *Nectanebo's Dream* (a prophetic text of Egyptian nationalistic character) and the *Book of the Temple* (treatise on the ideal arrangement of the temple). See for the *Myth of the Sun's Eye*: S. West, 'The Greek Version of the Legend of Tefnut' *JEA* 55 (1969) 161–183. For *Nectanebo's Dream*, see, Gauger, 'Der "Traum des Nektanebos"', in: Blasius and Schipper (eds.), *Apokalyptik und Ägypten*, 189–219 and Ryholt, 'Nectanebo's Dream or the Prophecy of Petesis', *op. cit.*, 221–241. For the *Book of the Temple*, see, Joachim F. Quack, 'Ein ägyptisches Handbuch des Tempels und seine griechische Übersetzung' *ZPE* 119 (1997) 297–300.

[245] The extent to which Egyptian priests were actively involved in the production of Greek texts glorifying Egyptian gods is still a matter of debate. In recent years scholarship tends to give major credit to the Egyptian priesthood arguing that these Greek texts should be viewed as part of an Egyptian discourse for the benefit of a Greek-speaking audience. Important contributions to the discussion are: Jan Bergman, *Ich bin Isis. Studien zum Memphitischen Hintergrund der griechischen Isisaretalogien* (Acta Universitatis Upsaliensis, Historia Religionum 3; Uppsala 1968); Fowden, *The Egyptian Hermes*, 45–74; Frankfurter, *Religion in Roman Egypt*, 241–248.

[246] In P. London-Leiden a spell is said to be tested by the wordings 'it has been tested' (*iw=f dnṱ*), 'tested' (*ip(.w)*), 'good' (*nfr*), 'very good' (*nfr nfr*), 'excellent' (*m-šs*). In P. Louvre E3229 and P. BM 10588 the wording '(it is) very good' (*nfr nfr (pw)*) is used. In the *Greek Magical Papyri* the idea is expressed by δόκιμος, which is probably a litteral translation of Egyptian *iw=f dnṱ* or *ip(.w)*. Advertising clauses claiming there is nothing better in the world can be found in P. London-Leiden 3/35, 11/26, 22/1 (=PDM xiv 92, 334, 671) and P. Louvre E3229 6/6 (=PDM Suppl. 149). Greek spells make use of clauses such as 'a great work', 'there is nothing better', 'excellent', 'accomplishes everything', 'the power of the spell is strong', etc. In PGM XII are used: 'Apollobex used this as well' (121), 'according to Ostanes' (122), 'an exact method for everything' (145), 'very effective' (203), 'it contains a first-rate name' (273), 'the world has had nothing greater than this' (277).

2. Listing of possible applications[247]
3. Eyewitness account[248]
4. Anecdote[249]

This method was also common in magical and medical texts of the pharaonic period.[250]

**4.** Importance of maintaining secrecy

Commands to keep a spell concealed from laity often occur in the *Greek Magical Papyri*, but are remarkably missing in the Demotic spells.[251] Such orders to keep a recipe secret are either given in the form of an imperative like 'hide, hide!' or as a short clause explaining that the spell may not be shared with any uninitiated because of its divine character. Since secrecy was an important constituent of Egyptian cultic life, directives about concealing magical spells are frequent in magical texts of the pharaonic period.[252]

### 6.4.3. *Combination of separate cultural traditions*

It has already been said that an advertising introduction may combine a number of the mystifying motifs listed above. The motifs are

---

[247] This method is very frequent in the Greek spells of the corpus, but lacking in the Demotic spells. It can take the form of a short and straightforward listing of alternative applications or be transformed into an elaborate and fanciful catalogue as in PGM I.96–130 or IV.2152–2178; see Gordon, 'Reporting the Marvellous', 70–76. In PGM XII a listing occurs only once in 277–282.

[248] See above examples *d*, *e* and *f*; see also, Gordon, 'Reporting the Marvellous', 86ff.

[249] See above example *f*.

[250] J.F. Borghouts, 'The Magical Texts of Papyrus Leiden I 348' *OMRO* 51 (1972) 105, note 202. Examples are *Book of the Dead* spells 17, 68, 71, 72, 86, 91, 99B, 100, 125, 134, 137A, 144, 148, 155, 156 and 175; Borghouts, *Ancient Egyptian Magical Texts*, nrs. 46, 53, 68, 71, 72, 81, 84. For the medical texts, see, Westendorf, *Handbuch der altägyptischen Medizin*, 98f.

[251] The Demotic spells are only interested in secrecy as far as the ritual itself is concerned. Several spells prescribe to conduct a divination ritual in a secret room or to store a magical potion in a hidden spot: P. London-Leiden 16/23 (hidden place for divination); P. London-Leiden 5/26.29; 12/12.31; 23.31; 27/26.29 (to keep a substance on a secret spot). For the warnings of secrecy in the Greek spells, see, Hans Dieter Betz, 'Secrecy in the *Greek Magical Papyri*', in: Kippenberg and Stroumsa, *Secrecy and Concealment*, 153–175.

[252] See also chapter 3.4. Examples can be found in the following magical spells: BD spells 137A, 147, 148, 156, 161, 190; Borghouts, Ancient Egyptian Magical Texts, nr. 126. See for the medical texts: Westendorf, *Handbuch der altägyptischen Medizin*, 99f.

not strictly kept separate and, in combination, aim at reinforcing the authority of the spell. However, a few Greek spells combine elements which, from a modern historian's viewpoint, would be mutually exclusive. These cases need to be addressed, because they demonstrate conclusively that the advertising statements do not relate to historical reality, but to a universe of preconceived ideas about authority and ritual power. Moreover, they testify to the fact that the compilers and authors of the Greek magical spells were not striving for exclusive cultural or ethnic categories when composing the spells. According to them, a spell's efficacy did not depend on upholding a rigid separation between ritual traditions. This attitude is paralleled in the practice in the Demotic magical spells to combine occasionally scripts and languages that derive from different generic and cultural contexts.

(1) A cluster of magical spells (PGM IV.1928–2144) dealing with necromantic rites is attributed to a certain Pitys, who is variably identified as king (1928), writer of a letter to king Ostanes (2006) and as originating from Thessaly (2140).[253] These varying designations indicate that Pitys' identity was changeable, thus raising a legitimate modern mistrust of the veracity of the statements. In fact, contrary to the information provided by the magical text, it is tempting to identify Pitys with a certain Bitys who was neither a king nor originated from Thessaly, but an Egyptian priest who translated Egyptian hermetic texts into Greek.[254] If this were true, the various attributions reveal a preference for an accumulation of prestige that trifles with cultural and ethnic boundaries. For example, the designation 'Pitys of Thessaly' (PGM IV.2140) combines the prestige and authority that was granted to Egyptian priests in both the Egyptian and Greco-Roman mind with the Hellenistic image of Thessaly as the home of all efficacious herbs, potions, spells and witches.[255] What could be better than a magical spell written by an Egyptian priest from Thessaly? Pitys' letter to king Ostanes is also a

---

[253] On the relationship between the different spells within this cluster, see, Faraone, 'When Necromancy goes Underground'.

[254] Iamblichus, *On the Mysteries of Egypt*, VIII.5 and X.7; Thissen, 'Ägyptologische Beiträge zu den griechischen magischen Papyri', 295f.; Fowden, *The Egyptian Hermes*, 150–153. See also footnote 212.

[255] Thessaly was notorious for its witches and serves in a number of Greek and Latin literary works as the home of all magic. For example, it is the action place in Apuleius' *Metamorphoses* and it is the homeland of the witch Erichto who performs necromancy on Pompey's son's order in Lucan, *The Civil War*, 6.413–830. See also Ovid, *Metamorphoses* VII.221–233.

case in point. Ostanes was not a king but a Persian magos who, according to tradition, had accompanied the Persian king Xerxes on the second Persian campaign against Greece in 480/79 BCE.[256] In the Roman period, Ostanes was remembered among Hellenistic elites as one of the greatest magicians and alchemists so that, in alchemical circles, he could be called 'the prince of all the magoi' or 'king of the seven vowels'.[257] Several antique works on alchemy relate that Ostanes shared his knowledge with Egyptian priests in Memphis after the Persian king had sent him to Egypt as supervisor to its priests.[258] In this way, the title 'Pitys' letter to king Ostanes' draws for its effect upon the combination of, on the one hand, the image of Egyptian priests and, on the other, the Roman period tradition according to which the great Ostanes had resided in Egypt: a magical spell given by an Egyptian priest to Ostanes can only be of the highest quality.

Like Pitys' identity, the necromantic recipes themselves are composite, betraying several layers of redaction and containing excerpts that recur in other parts of the PGM.[259] This shows that the spells are not unique compositions and that compilers of magical lore were willing to edit spells and manipulate information about the spell's origin.

(2) Egyptian and Jewish traditions are combined in a divination spell that claims to establish communication with Osiris by means of an ecstatic seizure of an adult or boy medium (PGM IV.850–929). The spell's title ascribes the procedure to the Old Testament king Solomon: 'Solomon's collapse' (850) and 'the procedure of Solomon' (853). However, the ritual techniques, mythological references and *voces magicae* are unmistakably Egyptian in nature. The medium should be seated on unbaked bricks (as in the majority of the Demotic divination spells), while holding an 'Anubian ear of corn' and a 'falconweed plant' in

---

[256] See footnote 197.

[257] Bidez, Cumont, *Les mages hellénisés*, I 169. The title 'king of the seven vowels' has come down to us in a citation given by Porphyry in his *Philosophy from Oracles*. The passage is fragment 11 in Bidez, Cumont, *Les mages hellénisés*, II 284. See for the 'seven vowels' chapter 3.3.2. Pliny the Elder blames Ostanes for having introduced the vile art of magic to the Greeks: *Natural History*, 28.6 and 30.7. Apuleius numbers Ostanes among Epimenides, Orpheus, Pythagoras, Socrates and Plato: *Apologia*, 27.

[258] This fictional account is preserved by Syncellus, Synesius and in the introduction to the standard antique alchemic work *Physika kai Mystika* (Ps. Demokritos). The relevant passages are collected as fragments A 3–7 in Bidez, Cumont, *Les mages hellénisés*, II 311–321.

[259] Faraone, 'When Necromancy goes Underground'.

his hands as phylacteries (900–903). Although nothing is known about these phylacteries, they are surely meant to invoke the guarding powers of the dog-faced god *Anubis*, god of the embalmment and guardian of Isis after the murder of Osiris,[260] and the *falcon* god Horus, son of Osiris. The link with Anubis is even reinforced by the prescription to awaken the medium from his trance by barking like a dog (929). The invocation calls upon Osiris as Hesies, a Greek transcription of the Egyptian epithet *ḥs.y*, 'the praised one' or 'the drowned one', which refers to Osiris' drowning in the Nile and subsequent resurrection.[261] The strings of *voces magicae* consist of a mix of incomprehensible names, muddled Osirian epithets and the repetition of Osiris' name, either on its own or in combination with another divine name.[262] According to the text, Hermes Trismegistos wrote the third and final string of these names in hieroglyphs in Heliopolis. Thus, given the purely Egyptian character of these ritual techniques and mythological references, the attribution to the Jewish king Solomon is rather remarkable. However, the occurrence of Solomon's name in a magical text of the Roman period is not unusual, since, among Hellenised Jewish circles in Alexandria of the second century BCE onwards, the Biblical figure Solomon had been transformed from a wise king to a powerful astrologer and magician who exerted control over a wide range of demons.[263] As a result of this, Solomon became a favoured pseudepigraphic author of magical and astrological treatises in Greek and Hebrew during the Roman period.[264] This particular magical spell thus has its roots in Egyptian ritual while, at the same time, it shares in the prestige that was attributed to the Jewish king Solomon among the Hellenistic elites of the Roman period.

---

[260] Plutarch, *On Isis and Osiris*, 14, 356F and 44, 368E–F.

[261] The epithet could be applied to any deceased after the necessary mortuary rituals by which the deceased was transformed into an Osiris were conducted. See for the term '(H)esies': *GMPT*, 334.

[262] See for the series of compound divine names whose second element is 'Osiris': *GMPT*, 55, fn. 120 [R.K.R.].

[263] For a chronology of this development, see, Torijano, *Solomon the Esoteric King*, 225–230.

[264] See for example the *Hygromanteia of Solomon* and *Testament of Solomon*. The *Sepher ha-Razim* (Book of Mysteries) was, according to its introduction, handed down from Noah to the patriarchs and finally to Solomon. *Hygromanteia of Solomon*: Torijano, *Solomon the Esoteric King*, 151–175 and 231–309 (translation and synopsis); *Testament of Solomon*: C.C. McCown, *The Testament of Solomon* (Leipzig 1922); *Sepher ha-Razim*: M.A. Morgan, *Sepher Ha-Razim: the Book of the Mysteries* (SBL Texts and Translations 25; Chico 1983).

(3) The reverse of what has just been said can be observed in a spell to drive out demons (PGM IV.3007–3086). According to the spell's title, the famous Egyptian magician Pibechis[265] is its author: 'A tested charm of Pibechis for those possessed by demons' (3007). However, the invocation itself contains but few Egyptian elements (restricted to the *voces magicae*), while abounding in Jewish and Biblical references.[266] The Jewish character of the spell is reinforced by the closing statement 'this charm is Hebraic'. Whatever the veracity of this statement, the spell combines the authority of the Egyptian priest Pibechis with the prestige that was afforded to Jewish magic.[267]

## 6.5. *What about priests and prestige?*

This chapter started out with a discussion of the advertising introduction to the list of encoded ingredients (PGM XII.401–407) and expanded to a wide-ranging study of the nature, function and perception of the Egyptian priesthood in the Greco-Roman period. This comprehensive discussion was necessary to bring out sharply the tension between what the text claims to be and historical reality. The results of the analyses are brought together and confronted with the conclusions of the chapters 1–5 in the following and final chapter. Before continuing, however, it is opportune to summarise and evaluate what has been said about Egyptian priests and the textual devices to bestow magical spells with prestige.

---

[265] See footnote 213.

[266] The Biblical references are given in *GMPT*, 96f. It goes without saying that the Jewish or Christian character of the spell has attracted considerable attention, not in the least because of the opening of the invocation 'I conjure you by the god of the Hebrews, Jesus' (3019f.). It is unclear whether the text is the product of a Jewish or pagan author, but scholars seem to favour the latter possibility because of certain inconsistencies in the text. An analysis of the invocation in the light of the New Testament can be found in S. Eitrem, *Some Notes on the Demonology in the New Testament* (Symb.Osloensis Suppl. 20; 2nd ed.; Oslo 1966) 15–30. A bibliography is given in Brashear, 'The Greek Magical Papyri', 3526f.; add to the list: Morton Smith, 'The Jewish Elements in the Magical Papyri', 250.

[267] A noteworthy parallel is PGM V.96–172, a spell to acquire a demon as assistant attributed to an Egyptian person named Ieu the painter. The practitioner identifies himself with 'Moses, your prophet to whom you have transmitted your mysteries celebrated by Israel' (109–111) and he claims to know the true name 'which has been transmitted to the prophets of Israel' (116f.).

The foregoing pages have demonstrated that, in the *Demotic* and *Greek Magical Papyri*, the rhetorical strategies used to invest a spell with prestige and authority are limited in number and were rooted in Egyptian priestly tradition. The repertoire of the Greek advertising texts, the set of social, historical and cultural norms, can be described as follows. Efficacious magical spells are either given directly by a god, found in a temple in Egypt, or were in the possession of persons who were in contact with the divine in their capacity as priest, physician, king or philosopher. These persons are preferably historic figures widely accepted as outstanding authorities in the fields of magic, alchemy, astrology or philosophy. The cultural or ethnic origin of these figures is not restricted to one particular category, but ranges from Egyptian priests, Jewish culture heroes and Persian magoi to Greek philosophers. Nor are the ritual traditions represented by these categories treated as mutually exclusive, but can be combined in an attempt to share in an abundance of authority. It is remarkable that this cultural and ethnic diversity holds solely for the motif of pseudepigraphy, whereas, in contrast, the discovery of a magical spell is always situated in a temple in Egypt, the Nile valley to be exact, and the act of translation is always from Egyptian into Greek.

When comparing these conclusions with the repertoire of the Demotic spells, a divergence in frequency and quality can be observed. In the Demotic spells, quality marks are short and limited to statements about a text's origin and proofs of efficacy, of which only the latter is frequently applied. In a few cases a spell's origin is explicitly ascribed to a god or mortal, but the attributions are never international. Even in the case of the Persian king Darius I (P. London-Leiden 11/26), the attribution is to be understood in the light of the fact that the Egyptian priesthood remembered Darius as a pious and righteous pharaoh. This divergence in repertoire between the Demotic and Greek spells cannot be without meaning in view of the question what kind of reader the magical texts address, since, as has been said in the introduction to this section, the structure and nature of the advertising statements is indicative of the social formation and cultural make-up of the audience. In case of the Demotic spells, knowledge of Egyptian culture is sufficient to rate the advertising statements at their true value. However, the Greek spells demand from their implied reader familiarity with international gods and authors. The spells take for granted that the reader knows of, and values highly, the authority of Egyptian priests, Jewish culture heroes, Persian magoi and Greek philosophers alike. Thus, the

282                    CHAPTER SIX

difference between the Demotic and Greek magical spells is not only a matter of language but also of implied audience. Given the fact that the two groups can be found together on one and the same manuscript, as in the case of P. Leiden 384 verso, this conclusion is highly significant. Were the Greek spells initially designed for an audience different from the users of the Demotic recipes?

It is important to emphasise that the international range of gods and authors is embedded in rhetorical devices in use in Egyptian ritual texts since as early as the redaction of the *Coffin Texts* (around 2100 BCE). Thus, the format as such did not change: it was the contents of the device that was adapted in the Greek spells. In addition to this link with older Egyptian rhetorical devices, the Greek advertising texts bear also a resemblance to Egyptian ideas and images of magic as expressed, for example, in the fictional narratives that were discussed earlier:

1. The Egyptian priest is a miracle worker
2. Efficacious magical texts are written by Thoth-Hermes and hidden from laity inside an Egyptian temple
3. The royal court is the receiving partner in the exchange of knowledge on magic

The resemblance with the Egyptian literary image of the ritual expert is evident and not in need of further comments. These elements were already productive in introductions or postscripts to magical or medical texts of the pharaonic period. The following two passages of the New Kingdom may serve to illustrate the effective use of the motifs of divine origin, discovery in a temple, secrecy and proofs of efficacy in such pedigrees of pharaonic date. In both cases, the royal court is the arena of display and the time of discovery is set in the remote past, that is to say, the Old Kingdom, a period that was perceived as ideal and exemplary since the Middle Kingdom. In the first passage, a historic figure is accredited with the discovery, whereas the second refers to the work of an anonymous temple scribe.

> This spell was found in Hermopolis on a brick of the ore of Upper Egypt, incised in real lapis lazuli, under the feet (of the statue) of this god in the time of the majesty of the king of Upper and Lower Egypt, Menkaure, by the king's son Hordedef,[268] who found it when he was going about to make inspections of the temples, a military force being

---
[268] On this historic figure, see, footnote 95 and chapter 6.3.3.1.

with him on that account. He obtained it by entreaty and brought it like a marvel to the king when he saw that it was a great secret, unseen and unbeheld. [Postscript to BD 30B][269]

Beginning of the collection (of prescriptions) to abate inflammations (ḥꜣ(i̯).t wḫd.w[270]), which was found in old writings in a chest for documents under the feet of (a statue of) Anubis in Letopolis in the time of the majesty of Upper and Lower Egypt Khasti, justified. After he had fallen ill, it was brought to the majesty of Upper and Lower Egypt Senedj, justified, because of its excellence. Thereupon this book loosened the feet that were bound (? ḥtm.w) through (the work of) a scribe of the divine book (sš md.w.t nṯr), chief physician, excellent one who satisfies the god.[271] (Because of) the book a procession was held at dawn and offerings (were given) of bread, beer and incense on the fire in the name of the great Isis, Horus-khenty-khety, Khonsu-Thoth, the god who is in the belly.
[P. Berlin 3038 15/1–5, §163a]

The presence of these same elements in the Greek spells suggests a familiarity with Egyptian ideas about ritual and magic on the part of the authors and users of the spells. However, there are also elements that are reminiscent of the Hellenistic discussions on magic, which were analysed in the previous section.

1. Authoritative magicians are not only to be found among Egyptian priests, but among Jewish culture heroes, Persian magoi and Greek philosophers as well
2. Objectification or even alienation of Egyptian priesthood
3. Pursuit of financial profit
4. Awareness of fraudulence and truly effective rituals

Despite these similarities with a Hellenistic discourse that was created and maintained outside Egypt, the *Greek Magical Papyri* originated in all likelihood in Egypt. Reasons for this are:

1. The advertising introductions reveal rather detailed knowledge of native cultic topography of the Nile Valley. In Greek and Latin texts, Memphis, to a lesser degree Thebes, function as the centre of occult knowledge.[272]

---

[269] Tr. Thomas G. Allen.
[270] For a discussion of the word *wḫd*, see, Westendorf, *Handbuch der altägyptischen Medizin*, vol. 1, 329 ff.
[271] For this list of titles, see, Hermann Grapow, *Kranker, Krankheiten und Arzt* (Grundriss der Medizin der alten Ägypter 3; Berlin 1956) 87 f.
[272] Memphis is given pride of place in these texts, because it was considered the place of origin of the Isis cult in the Greco-Roman world. The place name must therefore

2. The spells are always presented as being translated from Egyptian, never from another language.
3. Many texts contain truly Egyptian priestly knowledge; for example, the list of ingredients (PGM XII.401–444).

In view of what has been said above, it seems warranted to conclude that the *Greek Magical Papyri* address an audience, resident in Egypt, that views ritual and magic from a slightly different perspective than the users of the Demotic spells. The following chapter will address this apparent discrepancy and formulate a model of textual transmission to come to terms with the differences between the *Demotic* and *Greek Magical Papyri*.

---

have been widely known among Hellenised elites of the Roman Empire. Place names like Herakleopolis (PGM V.372 and 382) and Aphroditopolis (PGM VII.864) were probably unknown and therefore without advertising effect for an audience outside Egypt.

CHAPTER SEVEN

# TOWARDS A MODEL OF TEXTUAL TRANSMISSION

> For the most part, Demotic texts tend to be very different from Greek texts and to fulfil different functions; they are not simply Greek papyri in Egyptian.[1]

It has become abundantly clear in the foregoing chapters that, although similar in the type of spells, the Demotic and Greek sections on the two manuscripts under study differ in a number of important respects. The two corpora are not only different as far as their base language and script are concerned, but also with respect to the way the reader is made to believe in the efficacy of a given spell. The analysis of the 'marketing' techniques at work in the introductions to the spells has demonstrated that both text corpora make use of the same rhetorical devices, which are firmly rooted in pharaonic magical thought, but the realization of these devices or, their textual content for that matter, may differ for each corpus. For example, the Greek spells address as prestigious authors the same range of international miracle workers and gurus that occur in Greek and Latin texts of the Greco-Roman period: Persian magoi, Greek philosophers, Semitic magicians and Egyptian priests. However, pseudepigraphy is far less attested in the Demotic spells and, in those rare cases where it does occur, a spell is attributed to a person who fits into the local Egyptian tradition. It is therefore warranted to conclude that the Greek spells were written with a readership in mind that differs from that of the Demotic spells. Given the striking similarities between the text corpora regarding prescribed ritual techniques and claimed magical effects, their respective user groups cannot be differentiated on the basis of the type of spell; this is to say, the two groups had more or less similar magical aspirations, namely, contact with the divine, control over other persons and healing. It is primarily in their view on the nature and the origin of authoritative ritual specialists that they differ.

---

[1] Roger S. Bagnall, *Reading Papyri, Writing Ancient History* (London 1995) 21.

Egyptian ideas about ritual efficacy and ritual specialists were grounded in the conviction that an Egyptian priest is a servant of god, whose attitude to life is in agreement with the priestly ethos of purity and who, on account of this morality, is in close contact with the divine. Even in the fictional and somewhat burlesque narratives Setne I and II, the main character is only able to perform extraordinary magical feats because he is a 'good scribe and wise man'. Greco-Roman discourse on the nature of ritual experts takes a different approach: Egyptian priests are not admired because of their supposed high moral standing, but primarily on account of their otherness: like the Persian magoi, Greek philosophers and Semitic magicians, they are regarded as withdrawing from Hellenistic communal life and, through study, seclusion and initiation, being knowledgeable in the workings of nature and in ways to manipulate the course of events. As I argue in chapter 6.1, the introduction to the list of coded ingredients not only falsely attributes a non-existent custom to Egyptian temple scribes, but also represents these temple scribes as *outsiders* to the narrator and his intended readership. In this fashion, this short text aims at appealing to readers who are acquainted with, and believe in, the exoticised image of Egyptian priests as it is propagated in Hellenistic texts, rather than to readers who are truly versed in Egyptian priestly lore.

This observation is at odds with the conclusion of chapters 3 and 4, that the scribes engaged in editing and copying the Demotic spells of the two magical handbooks must have been native priests, who had gone through an Egyptian scribal training at an Egyptian temple school. The extant Demotic spells are clearly the result of a complex process of compiling, consulting, adapting, copying and editing religious and magical texts in hieratic, Demotic, Old-Coptic and Greek. The former two languages were taught and used only among the native clergy. The short titles in Demotic added to the two Greek ring spells and the Greek separation spell testify to the fact that the extant Greek spells were also edited and copied by a scribe literate in the Egyptian language and scripts. It then follows that any user of the manuscripts must also have been familiar with the Egyptian scripts and, as a consequence, with native priestly life. Therefore, it is remarkable to discover that the list of coded ingredients is validated by means of an image of the Egyptian priesthood that is not authentic to Egyptian culture. The Egyptian editors and users of the extant handbooks must have perceived this incongruity. How then to explain this incongruity?

Irrespective of the Hellenistic image of Egyptian priests, the introductory text is correct in claiming to provide authentic native priestly knowledge, as has been demonstrated in chapter 6.2. Similarly, the analysis of the two Greek ring spells in chapter 5 has revealed that the texts present genuine Egyptian ritual techniques, verse patterns and, in the case of the *Ouphôr* rite, even incorporate an adapted version of a vital Egyptian ritual. This means that the Greek spells were composed with the help of genuine Egyptian ritual, magical and medical texts, books which were traditionally written in the hieratic script and only accessible to Egyptian priests. Like the Demotic spells, the Greek spells are thus clearly the product of compiling, consulting, adapting and editing Egyptian priestly lore and must therefore, one way or another, originate from a native temple milieu. David Frankfurter's suggestion of reconciling the exotic Hellenistic image with the genuine Egyptian roots of the magical texts by applying the concept of stereotype appropriation onto the material has been mentioned a number of times in the foregoing chapters. He argues that Egyptian priests, bereft of their income by the economic measures taken by the Roman government, mimic the Hellenistic image of their profession to secure financial gain from the Hellenistic elite, which is interested in personal religious experiences and close contact with the divine through the agency of an Oriental guru. This explains why the Greek magical texts are packaged in pedigrees that appeal to a Hellenistic readership, while at the same time being firmly rooted in traditional Egyptian thought. As has been said in chapter 6.3.4, it is indeed very likely that native priests, expatriate and within Egypt, played an active role in constructing and confirming the exotic image among Hellenistic elite.

David Frankfurter's suggestion might apply when considering the Greek spells in isolation as an independent corpus, but is less obviously true for the two manuscripts under discussion, which combine Greek *and* Demotic spells. Why would a manuscript that was produced in a native temple scriptorium and could only be used by a person trained in an Egyptian temple school, contain passages in which Hellenistic stereotypes are appropriated? For whom would these stereotypes be included? A Hellenistic reader could not make use of the manuscript anyway. A solution to this problem might be considering the combination of Demotic and Greek sections as contrary to their editor's original intentions, this is to say, that the two parts were initially produced as two separate branches of magical literature and were only combined later in the course of their complex history of textual transmission.

Certainly, the two branches are closely related with respect to source material and social milieu of origin, but as end products they were not meant to fulfil the same functions.

At this point of the discussion it is instructive to consider the motto to this chapter, which is taken from a paragraph in which the Greek papyrologist Roger Bagnall explains the functional and sociological relationship between Demotic and Greek documentary papyri (contracts, petitions, tax receipts) in the Ptolemaic period. He concludes that an Egyptian's choice of language did not necessarily depend upon his or her ethnic or cultural background, but rather upon the specific circumstances of the case, for example, whether one sought access to an Egyptian or a Greek court, a choice that could be made for strategic reasons.[2] Although Bagnall limits himself to legal texts, the present study might gain something from his conclusion: 'All this suggests that the historian must pay considerable attention to questions of the use of different languages for particular purposes and certainly not assume that they are in any sense equivalent.'[3] In analogy with the language strategies at play in the legal system, it is quite possible to argue that the Demotic and Greek spells, though closely related in form, content and source material, addressed different social groups and functioned initially within different social contexts. It is then hardly surprising that the Greek spells, because directed towards a Hellenistic audience, display at times aspects of stereotype appropriation, whereas the social strategy is completely lacking in the Demotic spells, as they were not concerned with this social group, but with Egyptian priests only.

Before considering how it came about that the two text corpora ended up in combination on two associated manuscripts written in the Theban region, it is opportune to address the difference between the Demotic and Greek spells in more detail. The most fertile line of approach is to study the recurring tension between local and international aspects, on the one hand, and traditional and innovative elements on the other, a tension which surfaces in both corpora to varying degrees and in different ways. The Demotic spells are clearly rooted in a long tradition of Egyptian text production as is most evident from the use of red ink to mark headings, technical key terms and verse points, and from the standard phrases 'otherwise said' or 'another manuscript

---

[2] Bagnall, *Reading Papyri*, 20–21. Bagnall merely summarizes the important work done by P.W. Pestman and W. Clarysse; for the references, see, page 121.

[3] Bagnall, *op. cit.*, 21.

⟨says⟩' to introduce variant readings that the scribe found in parallel manuscripts. These scribal techniques had been in use for over two thousand years in Egypt. That a high number of spells displays an intricate mixing of Demotic and hieratic is a further indication that the spells originate from an Egyptian temple scriptorium, where the knowledge, the means and the textual sources for these kind of texts were available. Moreover, the rites and prayers always operate against the background of Egyptian ritual and mythology, except for the six short references to Moses and the great god upon the mountain. Apart from these traditional Egyptian roots, the editors were also receptive to innovations and international currents of thought concerning ritual power. The introduction of the seven Greek vowels and palindromes into the Demotic spells clearly testifies to a positive valorisation of magical concepts that are in essence foreign to Egyptian language and culture. The array of transcribed and glossed *voces magicae*, which include garbled divine names and epithets in Egyptian, Hebrew, Aramaic, Persian and Greek, is another testimony to the larger Hellenistic world entering the domain of Egyptian ritual. The most obvious example of the desire to share in the international world of Hellenistic magic and medicine is the occurrence of the Greek *materia medica et magica* jargon accompanied by transcriptions and explanations in Demotic on the verso side of P. London-Leiden. Of particular interest is that the jargon is only explained in Demotic, not in Greek, so that the insertion of this jargon cannot be interpreted as reflecting the ambition to open up the manuscript to a user group outside the native priestly milieu.

The Greek spells have an unmistakable Hellenistic character not only because of the frequent occurrence of *voces magicae*, palindromes and the seven vowels, but also because of the inclusion of cultural ideas that have direct parallels in other Greek or Latin texts that formed part of Hellenistic intellectual life, such as, for example, the already mentioned international range of ritual specialists or the 'Names of the Nations' motif discussed in chapter 5.2.b. In spite of this, the corpus contains several indications that the Egyptian component should not be underestimated. First of all, the testimonies of a text's discovery in a temple or on a stele, treated in chapter 6.4, always situate the discovery in the Nile valley, preferably in Hermopolis. Furthermore, the mythological references are almost always Egyptian, the Osiris myth in particular, albeit not as detailed or varied as in the Demotic spells. As far as the scribal techniques are concerned, it is remarkable that the rendition in writing or layout of the first *Ouphôr* invocation adheres to the traditional combination of the clauses about opening the doors of heaven and earth, while the second *Ouphôr* invocation mirrors the layout of a litany in hieratic script. Not only this striking similarity with the layout of Egyptian ritual texts, but also the fact that the *Ouphôr* rite itself is an adapted version of the Opening of the Mouth ritual makes evident that the influence of the Egyptian temple scriptorium is strong. The textual structure of the invocation to the All-Lord, discussed in chapter 5.2.b, strictly follows the pattern of an Egyptian ritual in so far as the practitioner identifies with a wide range of divine beings and shows his knowledge of their epithets and spheres of influence. As I have argued, several passages reveal a detailed knowledge of Egyptian mythology and develop religious ideas and imagery that can already be found in Egyptian texts dating to the New Kingdom. In one case, the parallel text is preserved in three hieroglyphic versions on temple walls, dating from the Kushite to the Ptolemaic period, and in a Demotic version on an ostracon of the Roman period, proving that these kinds of texts were still read and edited in the Roman period. Next to these Egyptian sections the prayer to the All-Lord contains a hexametrical hymn, which likely derives from a cultural tradition other than the Egyptian. This shows again that, firstly, a spell's Egyptian roots were not an impediment to the cross-cultural interests of the editors of the Greek spells and, secondly, that the editors were well versed in both the Egyptian and Hellenistic religious literature.

Thus, in terms of the oppositions tradition/innovation and local/international the Demotic and Greek spells do not diverge fundamentally; it is rather a matter of shifting emphasis. In fact, the two corpora meet in those few cases that a Greek invocation is inserted into a Demotic spell, a phenomenon that has been discussed in chapter 4.4. These short invocations fit in perfectly with the corpus of *Greek Magical Papyri* as regards wording, divine names and *voces magicae* and, accordingly, can be considered to be adopted from manuscripts which, if they had been preserved, would be counted among the *Greek Magical Papyri* today. As the language of the Demotic spells themselves lacks the expected number of Greek lexical and syntactical borrowings, it constitutes a purified speech register distinct from contemporary colloquial Egyptian. Despite this apparent concern for language purity, which accords well with the negative language attitude propagated in treatise XVI of the *Corpus Hermeticum*, the editors of the extant spells copied, edited and even translated Greek spells to fit them in with a number of Demotic spells. To find these Greek invocations among the Demotic texts is really remarkable in view of the close connection between tradition, authority and ritual power in this corpus and in Egyptian magic and ritual in general. Unlike in the case of the short Nubian spell, so far no known Egyptian text expresses any kind of value judgement on Hellenic religion, its practitioners and the Greek language. As a result, the socio-pragmatics of this type of language alternation escapes straightforward interpretation. But do we need such a text?

If we assume that the Greek invocations derive from the same priestly milieu as the Demotic spells, we could still make sense of these instances of code switching. As the foregoing paragraphs have demonstrated, there is every reason to do so. This means that the editors of the extant Demotic spells were simply incorporating texts that derived from their own circles, although initially designed for a user group different from the Demotic spells. This might be the reason that the editors did not find problems in translating parts of the Greek spells into Demotic: in a way, it was their own material and it would remain within their own circles. Nonetheless, the editors must have regarded the Greek spells as highly efficacious and of significant value in their own right; otherwise, they would not have made the effort to rework and incorporate the material. As a matter of fact, their high esteem is borne out by the recurrence of the Sethian invocation in Greek, which combines Egyptian mythology with Semitic *voces magicae*, in three Demotic-Greek spells and another spell entirely in Greek, which, interestingly enough, is provided with an additional Demotic title. The fact that the Greek *Vorlagen* were as highly regarded as the hieratic and Demotic, suggests that the Greek spells had acquired a ritual authority of their own by the time they were incorporated into the extant Demotic spells. This could only have come about after some period of time, during which the texts were disseminated and used among Egyptian priests like other, by now lost, Greek magical papyri.

The latter thought brings to the fore the question of when and where the Demotic and Greek spells were initially composed. The two text corpora were undoubtedly conceived in native priestly circles, but there is no compelling reason to assume that this must have happened in the same place and at the same time. As stated in chapter 2.4, the place of origin of the extant Demotic spells is undoubtedly the Theban region because of the Theban or archaic Akhmimic dialect and the orthography of the Demotic hand. Its grammar places the time of composition firmly in the Roman period, the late first century

CE at the earliest. Additional information might be deduced from the two spells that are said to be recommended by a physician from the Oxyrhynchite nome and from the spell that was allegedly praised by Paysakh, a priest of Cusae. If there is any truth in these statements, it corroborates the idea that the Demotic spells are the product of the Nile Valley, the region where pharaonic temple culture remained alive far into the Roman period.

Unfortunately, the language and orthography of the Greek spells is of no help in establishing their place and time of origin. Since their attached pedigrees are in line with the Roman-period Hellenistic discourse on ritual specialists, they can be dated, without being more precise, securely to the Roman period. An approximate *terminus post quem* provide the *voces magicae* and *charaktêres*, which are attested on amulets from respectively the first and second century CE onwards. Starting from the Hellenic overtones in the poetic structure of the incantations of PGM XX and CXXII, Christopher A. Faraone has recently argued that the compilation of Greek magical spells had commenced sometime in the late Hellenistic period, in a social milieu where the processes of Hellenisation and cultural assimilation were strongly felt.[1] Although he does not define the geographical location of origin more precisely than 'close to the Mediterranean', he is clearly inclined to accept Alexandria as the most likely candidate. In view of the fact that Alexandria was home to a mixed and, in a way, displaced population, the city must have been a melting pot, where various ethnic groups with differing cultural norms and religious outlooks were competing for power, prestige and identity. It is most certainly conceivable that it was a fertile environment for the production of cross-cultural texts that continue certain ritual and textual traditions of prestige and, at the same time, zero in on a new religious market, where phenomena such as astrology, initiation and personal contact with the divine are gaining ground at the expense of age-old types of communal religion.

The Greek spells preserved in the two manuscripts under study clearly present a later development than the two anthologies studied by Faraone. Nonetheless, it is also most likely that they originated in an environment where Egyptian and Hellenistic culture intertwined in a productive way and where a Hellenised clientele was to be found. In the Roman period, such settings existed in many places through-

---

[1] Faraone, 'Handbooks and Anthologies', 212f.

out the country, such as in the Fayum region and Hellenistic cities such as Hermopolis, Oxyrhynchus, Panopolis, Ptolemais and, of course, Alexandria. Since the lexicographer Phamphilus, who lived and worked in first century CE Alexandria, knew the coded ingredients as native priestly jargon, it is clear that the required source material was available in Alexandria. In addition, Pamphilus regarded the prophets as a category alongside Demokritos, Ostanes, Pythagoras and Zoroaster, which proves that the required readership could be found in Alexandria. Whatever the case, it is clear from found amulets and inscribed *lamellae* dating from the first century CE onward that these kind of spells must soon have become popular among the Hellenised population of the country and that the spells were reworked and expanded at will.

Since the development of the Greek spells started as early as the late Hellenistic period and the grammar of the extant Demotic spells dates to the late first century CE at the earliest, it cannot be ruled out that the Demotic spells originated sometime after the Greek spells. This suggestion is of particular significance, because one would expect spells written in the traditional Egyptian language and scripts to precede similar spells written in the language of the dominant foreign elite. It might simply be a matter of archaeological chance that earlier Demotic spells of this type have not been found, but it might also be true that they never existed until well into the Roman period. I like to argue that, contrary to the commonly held view, the Demotic spells did not develop organically from pharaonic magic over a long stretch of time, the stages of which cannot be followed due to a complete lack of preserved sources. Instead, they were written against the background of the Greek spells, which were composed by Egyptian priests anyway and circulated throughout the country starting in the Hellenistic period. This model of textual transmission explains why the Demotic spells, although firmly rooted in magical techniques of the pharaonic period, constitute a type of spell that was somewhat different from earlier, mainly apotropaeic, pharaonic magical spells. It also explains why a number of short Greek invocations were inserted in the Demotic spells without apparent problems on the part of editors and users: this was a matter of incorporating primary material into secondary material. As the base language of the genre, these Greek spells by definition carried ritual authority for this type of spells.

With this model of textual transmission, the peculiar combination of spells in Demotic and Greek in two associated manuscripts written in the Theban region can be explained as follows. At a certain moment in the early Roman period, Egyptian priests of the Theban region got acquainted with the new type of magical spells in Greek through their business travels to Alexandria or similar Hellenised cities in the Nile valley. They undertook, for example, the submission of temple accounts and petitions or assisted in religious festivals. On return to Thebes taking the Greek spells with them, they studied them and wrote similar spells in their own dialect and script for their own priestly circles. However, these Demotic spells were no slavish translations of the Greek spells. On the contrary, older texts in hieratic and Demotic were also taken into account to create a wholly new Demotic genre in the same vein as the Greek spells, without being identical. In this fashion, the Theban priests succeeded in bending the Hellenised Egyptian magic to their will. Since the Greek spells were the primary material, the Hellenised images of Egyptian priests were not deleted in the course of several stages of editing, so that, sometime in the second or third century CE, a scribe copied Greek spells that were actually composed for a Hellenised clientele next to Demotic spells that aimed at a more traditional native user group. There was truly no problem in doing so, because, in the end, the two text corpora present only two different realizations of the same phenomenon. Seen in this light the two manuscripts turn out to be not only a testimony of the multicultural society of the Hellenistic world in general and Greco-Roman Egypt in particular, but also a creative attempt on the part of a group of Egyptian priests in the Theban region of the second and third century CE to combine, incorporate and manipulate various cultural and religious traditions in order to create an identity that was appropriate for and meaningful within their time, when traditional social structures and religious viewpoints underwent important changes.

# APPENDICES

## Appendix 1

The following table provides an overview of the spells of P. Leiden I 384 verso in their order of occurrence in the manuscript. For each spell is given its position in the manuscript according to column and line numbers, its PDM or PGM number according to the *GMPT* and its title as found in the text itself.

| | | | |
|---|---|---|---|
| §1  | II*/1–5      | PDM xii.1–5       | (no title) Invocation |
| §2  | II*/6–20     | PDM xii.6–20      | A ring to cause praise |
| §3  | I*/1–29      | PDM XII.21–49     | (no title) Prayer for a revelation of a remedy for a disease |
| §4  | 1/1–13       | PGM XII.1–13      | Rite (to produce an epiphany of Kore) |
| §5  | 1/14–3/22    | PGM XII.14–95     | Eros as assistant daimon |
| §6  | 3/23–33      | PGM XII.96–106    | Himerios' recipes |
| §7  | 4/1–15       | PGM XII.107–121   | Charm of Agathokles for sending dreams |
| §8  | 4/15–5/3     | PGM XII.121–143   | Zminis of Tentyra's spells for sending dreams |
| §9  | 5/4–12       | PGM XII.144–152   | Request for a dream |
| §10 | 5/13–20      | PGM XII.153–160   | Spell for a divine revelation |
| §11 | 5/20–6/3     | PGM XII.160–178   | (no title) Spell to release from bonds |
| §12 | 6/4–6        | PGM XII.179–181   | (no title) Spell for restraining anger |
| §13 | 6/7–14       | PGM XII.182–189   | (no title) Spell for gaining favour |
| §14 | 6/15–17      | PGM XII.190–192   | Request for a dream oracle spoken to the Bear |
| §15 | 6/18–26      | PGM XII.193–201   | [To make] a tincture of gold |

| §16 | 6/26–8/23 | PGM XII.201–269 + Demotic. title | A ring |
| §17 | 8/24–10/38 | PGM XII.270–350 + Demotic. title | A little ring for success and favour and victory |
| §18 | 11/1–14 | PGM XII.351–364 | Demokritos' sphere |
| §19 | 11/15–25 | PGM XII.365–375 + Demotic title | Charm for causing separation |
| §20 | 11/26–12/12 | PGM XII.376–396 | Charm to induce insomnia |
| §21 | 12/13–16 | PGM XII.397–400 | To gain favour and friendship forever |
| §22 | 12/17–13/30 | PGM XII.401–444 | Interpretations |
| §23 | IV/1–12 | PDM xii.50–61 [PGM XII.445–448] | Spell for separating one person from another |
| §24 | IV/13–26 | PDM XII.62–75 [PGM XII.449–452] | Another (spell for separation) |
| §25 | III/1–20 | PDM xii.76–107 [PGM XII.453–465] | Another (spell for separation) |
| §26 | II/1–11 | PDM xii.108–118 [PGM XII.466–468] | A spell [to] cause a woman to hate a man |
| §27 | II/12–27 | PDM xii.119–134 [PGM XII.469–473] | A spell for it (fetching spell?) |
| §28 | I/1–12 | PDM xii.135–146 [PGM XII.474–479] | (no title) Love spell |
| §29 | I/13–30 | PDM xii.147–164 [PGM XII.480–495] | Another (love spell) |

## Appendix 2

The following table lists the spells of P. London-Leiden in consecutive order following the layout of the manuscript[1]. The table gives position according to column and line numbers, PDM and PGM number according to the *GMPT* and titles written in red ink.

| | | | |
|---|---|---|---|
| §1 | 1/1–3/35 | PDM xiv.1–92 | [A vessel divination] |
| §2 | 4/1–22 | PDM xiv.93–114 [PGM XIVa.1–11] | A (casting for inspection) |
| §3 | 4/23 | PDM xiv.115 | [Spell] (for vision?) |
| §4 | 4/24 | PDM xiv.116 | Another (spell for vision?) |
| §5 | 5/1–32 | PDM xiv.117–149 | A tested 'god's arrival' |
| §6 | 6/1–8/11 | PDM xiv.150–231 | An inquiry of the lamp |
| §7 | 8/12–18 | PDM xiv.232–238 | A 'god's arrival' |
| §8 | 9/1–22 | PDM xiv.239–295 | The vessel inquiry of Khonsu |
| §9 | 9/22–35 | PDM xiv.295–308 | [A] vessel [inquiry] |
| §10 | 11/1–26 | PDM xiv.309–334 | A spell for causing favour |
| §11 | 12/1–21 | PDM xiv.335–355 | (no title) Love spell |
| §12 | 12/21–31 | PDM xiv.355–365 | Another love spell |
| §13 | 13/1–10 | PDM xiv.366–375 | The method (for separating man and woman) |
| §14 | 13/11–29 | PDM xiv.376–394 | (no title) Various recipes with shrewmouse |
| §15 | 14/1–33 | PDM xiv.395–427 | [A vessel divination] |
| §16 | 15/1–23 | PDM xiv.428–450 | (no title) Two love potions |
| §17 | 15/24–31 | PDM xiv.451–458 [PGM XIVb.12–15] | [Spell] for going before a superior |
| §18 | 16/1–17 | PDM xiv.459–475 | (no title) Lamp divination |
| §19 | 16/18–30 | PDM xiv.475–488 | (no title) Lamp divination |
| §20 | 17/1–26 | PDM xiv.489–515 | Another (lamp divination) |
| §21 | 17/26–18/6 | PDM xiv.516–527 | Another (lamp divination) |

---

[1] This list is based on Janet H. Johnson's division in *GMPT*. See for slightly different divisions: Griffith, Thompson, *The Demotic Magical Papyrus of London and Leiden*, vol. 1, 15–18; Ritner, 'Egyptian Magical Practice under the Roman Empire', 3339–3342.

| | | | |
|---|---|---|---|
| §22 | 18/7–33 | PDM xiv.528–553 | [Another] vessel divination |
| §23 | 19/1–9 | PDM xiv.554–562 | (no title) Spell for dog bite |
| §24 | 19/10–21 | PDM xiv.563–574 | (no title) Spell for removal of poison |
| §25 | 19/21–32 | PDM xiv.574–585 | (no title) Spell for removal of bone stuck in the throat |
| §26 | 19/32–40 | PDM xiv.585–593 | Spell for dog bite |
| §27 | 20/1–27 | PDM xiv.594–620 | (no title) Spell for sting |
| §28 | 20/27–33 | PDM xiv.620–626 | Spell for removal of bone stuck in the throat |
| §29 | 21/1–9 | PDM xiv.627–635 | The vessel inquiry of Osiris |
| §30 | 21/10–43 | PDM xiv.636–669 | (no title) Love potion |
| §31 | 22/1–5 | PDM xiv.670–674 | (no title) Introduction to a collection of spells (?) |
| §32 | 23/1–20 | PDM xiv.675–694 [PGM XIVc.16–27] | A spell (to cause 'evil sleep') |
| §33 | 23/21–26 | PDM xiv.695–700 | (no title) Vessel divination |
| §34 | 23/27–31 | PDM xiv.701–705 | (no title) Vessel divination |
| §35 | 24/1a–5a | PDM xiv.706–710 | (no title) Spell against 'evil sleep' |
| §36 | 24/1–5 | PDM xiv.711–715 | Prescription (to cause 'evil sleep') |
| §37 | 24/6–14 | PDM xiv.716–724 | Another (spell to cause 'evil sleep') |
| §38 | 24/14–16 | PDM xiv.724–726 | Another (spell to cause 'evil sleep') |
| §39 | 24/17–26 | PDM xiv.727–736 | A prescription (to cause 'evil sleep') |
| §40 | 24/27–28 | PDM xiv.737–738 | A prescription (to cause 'evil sleep') |
| §41 | 24/29–30 | PDM xiv.739–740 | Another (spell to cause 'evil sleep') |
| §42 | 24/31 | PDM xiv.741 | Another (spell to cause 'evil sleep') |
| §43 | 24/32 | PDM xiv.742 | Another (spell to cause 'evil sleep') |

| § | | | |
|---|---|---|---|
| §44 | 24/33–39 | PDM xiv.743–749 | Another (spell to cause 'evil sleep') |
| §45 | 25/1–22 | PDM xiv.750–771 | (no title) Lamp divination |
| §46 | 25/23–26/18 | PDM xiv.772–804 | A method (love spells) |
| §47 | 27/1–36 | PDM xiv.805–840 | Another (vessel inquiry) |
| §48 | 28/1–10 | PDM xiv.841–850 | Another method (vessel inquiry) |
| §49 | 28/11–15 | PDM xiv.851–855 | Another (vessel inquiry) |
| §50 | 29/1–20 | PDM xiv.856–875 | (no title) Inquiry of the sun |
| §51 | 29/20–30 | PDM xiv.875–885 | Here is another (inquiry of the sun) |
| §52 | V1/1–11 | PDM xiv.886–896 | (no title) Recipes involving herbs |
| §53 | V2/1–15 | PDM xiv.897–910 | (no title) List of herbs and minerals |
| §54 | V2/16–20 | PDM xiv.911–916 | (no title) Spell to cause 'evil sleep' |
| §55 | V3/1–3 | PDM xiv.917–919 | Prescription (to cause 'evil sleep') |
| §56 | V3/4–13 | PDM xiv.920–929 | (no title) Information concerning mineral |
| §57 | V3/14–16 | PDM xiv.930–932 | A prescription (love spell) |
| §58 | V3/17–18 | PDM xiv.933–934 | (no title) Information concerning mineral |
| §59 | V4/1–5 | PDM xiv.935–939 | (no title) Prescription for a watery ear |
| §60 | V4/6–19 | PDM xiv.940–952 | (no title) Information concerning salamander and herbs |
| §61 | V5/1–3 | PDM xiv.953–955 | A prescription (to stop blood) |
| §62 | V5/4–8 | PDM xiv.956–960 | (no title) Test of pregnancy |
| §63 | V5/9–13 | PDM xiv.961–965 | A prescription (two prescriptions to stop blood) |
| §64 | V5/14–17 | PDM xiv.966–969 | (no title) Information concerning herbs |

| | | | |
|---|---|---|---|
| §65 | V6/1–8 | PDM xiv.970–977 | Prescription (two prescriptions to stop liquid in a woman) |
| §66 | V7/1–4 | PDM xiv.978–980 | Another (prescription to stop liquid in a woman) |
| §67 | V7/4–7 | PDM xiv.981–984 | Another (prescription to stop liquid in a woman) |
| §68 | V8/1–8 | PDM xiv.985–992 | Gout (prescription) |
| §69 | V9/1–10 | PDM xiv.993–1002 | Another (prescription for gout) |
| §70 | V10/1–12 | PDM xiv.1003–1014 | (no title) Amulet for gout |
| §71 | V11/1–6 | PDM xiv.1015–1020 | (no title) prescription for unidentifiable ailment |
| §72 | V11/7–9 | PDM xiv.1021–1023 | (no title) Prescription for a stiff foot |
| §73 | V11/10–11 | PDM xiv.1024–1025 | (no title) Another prescription for a stiff foot |
| §74 | V12/1–13/9 | PDM xiv.1026–1045 | (no title) Love spell |
| §75 | V13/10–11 | PDM xiv.1046–1047 | (no title) Love spell |
| §76 | V13/11–12 | PDM xiv.1047–1048 | (no title) Love spell |
| §77 | V14/1–7 | PDM xiv.1049–1055 | (no title) Love spell |
| §78 | V15/1–7 | PDM xiv.1056–1062 | (no title) Spells to bring in a thief |
| §79 | V16/1–7 | PDM xiv.1063–1069 | (no title) Love spell |
| §80 | V17/1–8 | PDM xiv.1070–1077 | (no title) Spell to send dreams and make a woman love |
| §81 | V18/1–12 | PDM xiv.1078–1089 | (no title) Request for a dream revelation |
| §82 | V19/1–7 | PDM xiv.1090–1096 | (no title) Fetching spell |
| §83 | V20/1–7 | PDM xiv.1097–1103 | (no title) Spell to heal an eye disease |
| §84 | V21/1–6 | PDM xiv.1104–1109 | (no title) Recipe concerning eye ointment |
| §85 | V22/1–20 | PDM xiv.1110–1129 | (no title) Spell to open eyes for divination |
| §86 | V23/1–12 | PDM xiv.1130–1140 | (no title) Love spell |
| §87 | V24/1–13 | PDM xiv.1141–1154 | (no title) Spell for lamp divination |

| | | | |
|---|---|---|---|
| §88 | V25/1–8 | PDM xiv.1155–1162 | (no title) Love spell |
| §89 | V26/1–27/8 | PDM xiv.1163–1179 | (no title) Spell for vessel divination |
| §90 | V28/1–2 | PDM xiv.1180–1181 | (no title) Fragment from invocation |
| §91 | V29/1–6 | PDM xiv.1182–1187 | (no title) Spell to cause madness |
| §92 | V30/1–2 | PDM xiv.1188–1189 | (no title) Love spell (?) |
| §93 | V30/3–6 | PDM xiv.1190–1193 | (no title) Another love spell |
| §94 | V30/7–8 | PDM xiv.1194–1195 | (no title) Another love spell |
| §95 | V30/9–11 | PDM xiv.1196–1198 | (no title) Another love spell |
| §96 | V31/1–7 | PDM xiv.1199–1205 | (no title) Spell for lamp divination |
| §97 | V32/1–13 | PDM xiv.1206–1218 | (no title) Love spell |
| §98 | V33/1–9 | PDM xiv.1219–1227 | (no title) Spell for fever |

## Appendix 3.1

The following table enumerates the 'cipher' signs with their corresponding phonetic values. The first column gives the 'cipher' sign, the second column the Greek or Old-Coptic letter and the third column presents the number according to the 'cipher' list in Griffith and Thompson, *The Demotic Magical Papyrus of London and Leiden*, 105–107. Note that the current arrangement is slightly different from Griffith and Thompson's to gain a better insight into the distribution of the Greek and Old-Coptic letters.

### Signs for the Greek alphabet

| Sign | Letter | No. |
|---|---|---|
| ⲧ | ⲁ | i |
| F | ⲁ | ii |
| F, F | ⲉ | iii |
| ⲓⲕ | ⲉ | iv |
| ⲧ | ⲉ, π(?) | v |
| h | Η | vi |
| / | ⲓ | vii |
| ⲥ | ⲓ | viii |
| 3 | ⲟ | ix |
| ⁓ | ⲟ | x |
| ⁂ | ⲱ | xi |
| R | ⲟⲩ | xii |
| λ | ⲩ (ⲉ) | xiii |
| τ | ⲩ | xiv |
| ȝ, ẏ | Β | xv |
| ⏍ | ⲇ (τ) | xvi |
| ≡ | Ζ (only once, in Greek word) | xxxi |
| ⳓ | κ | xxxvi |
| ⲁ | κ (only in Egyptian words) | xvii |
| ⲉ | κ, Γ (only in Greek words) | xviii |
| у | ⲗ | xix |
| h | ⲗ | xx |
| ɯ | Μ | xxi |
| η | Μ | xxii |
| ⲓⲓⲓ | Ν | xxiii |
| ✳ | Ν | xxiv |
| ⲓ⌐ | π | xxv |
| ⲩ, ẏ | ρ | xxvi |

## Signs for the additional Egyptian sounds[2]

| | | |
|---|---|---|
| ꜣ | ϣ | xxxii |
| ẏ | ϥ | xxxiv |
| ʿ | ḫ | xxxiii |
| ḅ (?) | ḫ | xxxv |
| λ | ẖ | xiii |
| ṯ | ẖ | xiv |
| ḏ | ϫ | xxix |
| ḡ | ϭ | xxxvi |

---

[2] Note that the signs xiii and xiv, used for the ẖ, are actually the 'cipher' signs for the upsilon. This means that the *h*-sound of the ẖ is represented by the aspirated upsilon and that the alphabet did not need an additional Demotic sign for this Egyptian sound. The upsilon is used in the same way in a number of transcriptions of *voces magicae*; see, for example, P. London-Leiden 27/8.

## Appendix 3.2

The following three tables list in alphabetical order the words written in the 'cipher' script in P. London-Leiden. They are concerned with Egyptian nouns, Egyptian verbs and Greek nouns. The first column gives the transcription of the encoded word in Coptic letters; the fourth column contains the corresponding term in Demotic, Coptic or Greek, unless otherwise indicated.

a. *Egyptian nouns*

| Transcription | Reference | Translation | Equivalent |
|---|---|---|---|
| *ⲁⲗⲃⲟⲩⲛⲟⲩⲧ* | 29/17.24 | frankincense | lebonah (Hebrew)[3] |
| *ⲃⲉⲗ* | 5/24 | eye | *bl* / ⲃⲁⲗ |
| *ⲃⲉⲉⲙⲡⲉ* | V.13/7 | goat | *by-ꜥ3-n-p.t* ⲃⲁⲁⲙⲡⲉ |
| *ⲃⲉⲱⲉ* | 25/24 | desert animal | ⲃⲟⲓⲱⲓ (B)[4] |
| *ⲃⲉⲱⲟⲩⲱ* | 19/20 | rue | *bšwš* / ⲃⲁⲱⲟⲩⲱ |
| *[ⲃ]ⲉϩⲱⲗ* | V.2/19 | a kind of dates | ⲃⲉϩⲱⲗ |
| *ⲃⲉϭ* | 4/23, 13/21, 24/33, V.29/4.6 | hawk | *bı͗k* / ⲃⲏϭ |
| *ⲉⲟ* | 3/27, V.30/11 | ass | *ꜥ3* / ⲉⲱ |
| *ⲉⲃⲱⲕ* | 5/25, 27/25 | raven | *ꜣbk̲* / *ꜥbk̲* / ⲁⲃⲱⲕ |
| *ⲉⲕⲓⲗ* | 24/4a | reed (?) | *ꜣkyr* |
| *ⲉⲙⲓⲙ* | 24/34, V.32/2 | shrewmouse | *ꜥmꜥm* / ⲁⲙⲏⲙ |
| *ⲉⲙⲓⲥ* | 3/23 | anise, dill | *ꜣmys* / ⲉⲙⲓⲥⲉ |
| *ⲉ[ⲙⲟⲩⲗⲭ]* | 10/31 | nightjar | *ꜣmwld̲* / ⲙⲟⲩⲗⲁⲭ(B) |
| *ⲉⲉⲛ* / *ⲉⲛ* | 11/21, 3/28 | ape | *ꜥn* / ⲉⲛ (B) |
| *ⲉⲡⲱⲉ* | V.2/17 | beetle | *pšy* |
| *ⲉⲣⲡ* | V.25/6 | wine | *ı͗rp* / ⲏⲣⲡ |

---

[3] Lebonah is a Hebrew loan word that had become part of the Egyptian lexicon sometime during the Persian period, see, Günter Vittmann, 'Semitisches Sprachgut im Demotischen' *WZKM* 86 (1996) 435–447, 438; Richard C. Steiner, 'Albounot "Frankincense" and Alsounalph "Oxtongue": Phoenician-Punic Botanical Terms with Prothetic Vowels from an Egyptian Papyrus and a Byzantine Codex' *Orientalia* 70 (2001) 97–103.

[4] Griffith and Thompson suggest *ⲃⲏⲛⲉ*, 'swallow', as alternative. However, the suggestion is not supported by the 'cipher' system; see Griffith and Thompson, *The Demotic Magical Papyrus of London and Leiden*, vol. 1, 155, fn. to line 24. According to Hess, a ⲃⲟⲓⲱⲓ is a canine desert animal: J.J. Hess, 'Bemerkungen zu einigen arabischen Wörtern des abessinischen Glossars (ZA XXI, 61ff.).' *Zeitschrift für Assyriologie* 31 (1918) 26–32, 28 fn. 2.

| Transcription | Reference | Translation | Equivalent |
|---|---|---|---|
| *ιετϥ* | 24/31 | his eye | r it.t̠=f / ειατϥ |
| *ιιΔ* / *ιιx* | 29/26, V.17/5 | a fish (?) | ? |
| *κογκογπετ* | 4/24, 10/31, 25/24, V.17/5 | hoopoe | ḳwkwpt κογκογϕατ(B) |
| *κελ* | V.30/4 | an animal | ? |
| *κλο* | 24/27, V.3/2 | a vegetable poison | kr'ꜣ / κλο |
| *κμε* | 13/9 | gum | ḳmꜣ / κομη (B) |
| *κνογμ* | 24/4 | food | nkt n wnm νκανογμ |
| *κεγορ* | 24/14 | (fruit) pit | (?)[5] |
| *κρογρ* | 3/22 | frog | ḳrr / κρογρ |
| *μοcε* | 13/12 | liver | mws [6] |
| *μcε2* | 3/21, V.13/6 | crocodile | msḥ / μcα2 |
| *μλογ* | 13/11 | water | mw / μοογ |
| *νενεβε* / *νενεεβ*(?) | 11/22, V.2/17 | styrax | nnyb |
| *νε2* | 19/28.32 | oil | nḥ / νε2 |
| *πλειϣε* | 13/24 | a skin-disease | pš [7] / πλιϣε |
| *ρωμε* | 24/1 | man | rmt̠ / ρωμε |
| *cμογνε* | 10/31, V.30/1 | Smun-goose | smnw / cμογνε |
| *cτημνκβτ* | V.18/8 | stibium of Koptos | stem n Gbtyw cτημνκεβτω |
| *cα2ε* / *cε2ε* | 13/19.22, 24/35.36 | gall | sḥy / cαϣε |
| *cιϥαc* | V.30/5 | an animal | ? |

---

[5] Griffith and Thompson suggest to take this word as a misspelling of κάρυα 'kernel': Griffith and Thompson, *The Demotic Magical Papyus of London and Leiden*, vol. 3, 110. Since the letter for the K- sound of the present spelling occurs otherwise only in Egyptian words, it is more likely that the word is Egyptian. Their second suggestion is to read it as κε-2ορ, deriving from kꜣ Ḥr, 'The-ka-of-Horus', which name is unknown from other sources.

[6] This word has long been taken as a misspelling of the word swm', wich equals σῶμα, 'body': Griffith and Thompson, *The Demotic Magical Papyrus of London and Leiden*, vol. 3, 110. See for the correct identifcation of the term: Tonio Sebastian Richter, 'Leib oder Leber? Zum Wort *MOCE* im demotischen P. Magical XIII, 12' *ZÄS* 125 (1998) 137–139.

[7] I.E.S. Edwards, *Oracular Amuletic Decrees of the Late New Kingdom* (British Museum, Hieratic Papyri, Fourth Series; London 1960) docs. L1, verso 43–44 and L6, verso 27.

| Transcription | Reference | Translation | Equivalent |
|---|---|---|---|
| *ϣⲱⲧⲉ* | 24/15 | flour | šd.t [8] / ϣⲱⲧⲉ |
| *ϩⲉⲗ* | 13/10 | myrrh | ḥl / ϣⲁⲗ |
| *ϩⲁⲧⲟⲩⲗ* | V.30/9 | ichneumon | štl / ϣⲁⲧⲟⲩⲗ (B) |
| *ϩⲭⲁⲛ* | 19/8 | garlic | ḥdn / ϣⲭⲏⲛ |
| *ϩⲁⲛⲧⲟⲩⲥ* | 13/24, V.18/9 | *Hantous*-lizard | ḥnṯs / ⲁⲛⲟⲟⲩⲥ (B) |
| *ϩⲁⲓⲧⲉ* | V.30/7 | hyena | ḥyṯ.t / ϩⲟⲉⲓⲧⲉ |
| *ϩⲉⲧ* | 13/20, V.32/4.12 | heart | ḥзṯ / ϩⲏⲧ |
| *ϩⲁϥⲗⲉⲗⲗ* / *ϩⲁϥⲗⲉⲗⲉ* | 13/23.24, 24/38 | *Hafleele*-lizard | ḥflel' / ϩⲁϥⲗⲉⲉⲗⲉ |
| *ϩⲉϥⲗⲉⲗⲉⲛⲥⲉⲧ* | 24/26 | (two-)tailed *Hafleele*-lizard | ϩⲁϥⲗⲉⲉⲗⲉ ⲛⲥⲁⲧ (ⲥⲛⲁⲩ) |
| *ⲭⲡⲟϩ* / *ⲭⲡⲱϩ* | 24/15.18, V.2/18 | apple | dph / ⲭⲙⲡⲉϩ |
| *ϭⲉⲗⲉ* | 24/25 | weasel | g'lз.t ⟨ γαλῆ |
| *ϭⲉⲙⲟⲩⲗ* | 24/29 | camel | gmwl / ϭⲁⲙⲟⲩⲗ |
| *ϭⲟⲙⲩ/ϩ* | 19/8 | gum (?)[9] | ḳmз / ⲕ(ⲟ)ⲙⲙⲉ |
| *ϭⲉⲛϭⲁⲱ* | 24/32 | bat | gnglз / ϭⲉⲛϭⲉⲗⲟ |
| *ϭϩⲉⲥ* | V.5/12, V.13/7 | gazelle | ghs / ϭϩⲟⲥ |
| *ϭⲁϭⲉ* | 24/16 | cake (?) | k'k' / g'g' / ϭⲁϭⲉ |

b. *Egyptian verbs*

| Transcription | Reference | Translation | Equivalent |
|---|---|---|---|
| *ⲗⲓⲃⲉ* | V.32/1.9 | to rave | lby / ⲗⲓⲃⲉ |
| *ⲙⲁⲟⲩⲧ* | V.29/3 | to be dead | mwt.ṯ / ⲙⲟⲟⲩⲧ |
| *ⲙⲕⲁϩ* | 24/5 | to suffer from pain | mkḥ / ⲙⲕⲁϩ |
| *ⲙⲟⲩ* | 13/13, 23/7 | to die | mwt / ⲙⲟⲩ |
| *ⲙⲟⲩⲛⲧⲟ* | 13/13 | to suffer from a skin-disease (?)[10] | ⲙⲟⲩ-ⲛ-ⲧⲟ |

---

[8] WB IV, 567, 3 and 569,5.

[9] The meaning of the term is unclear: *mtw=k nḏ* *ϩⲭⲁⲛ* *ḥr* *ϭⲟⲙⲩ/ϩ**: 'you have to pound garlic with gum (?)'. A derivation from ⲕ(ⲟ)ⲙⲙⲉ, ⲕⲟⲙϩ, ⲕⲟⲙⲓ, ⲕⲏⲙⲙⲉ, ⲕⲏⲙⲉ, *ḳmз*, 'gum' is well possible. See Griffith and Thompson, *The Demotic Magical Papyrus of London and Leiden*, vol. 1, 124, fn. to line 8.

[10] Probably a compound verb in a light verb construction: *mtw=k tī wnm=f s \pз rmt/ ḥr ir=f* ⲙⲟⲩⲛⲧⲟ*: 'you let him eat it and the man will suffer from a skin-disease'. See Griffith and Thompson, *The Demotic Magical Papyrus of London and Leiden*, vol. 1, 95, fn. to line 13.

| Transcription | Reference | Translation | Equivalent |
|---|---|---|---|
| *ⲙⲧⲉⲥ* | V.32/10 | she will die | mwet=s |
| *ⲙⲧⲉϥ* | 13/20.22.23, 24/30 | he will die | mwet=f |
| *ⲟⲩⲁⲙϥ* | 24/5 | he will eat | wnm=f |
| *ϣⲉϥⲉ* | 13/13 | to swell | šfj [11] / ϣⲁϥⲉ |
| *ⲭⲟⲩⲣ* | 13/25 (twice) | to be violent | dr / ⲭⲱⲱⲣⲉ |
| *ϭⲱⲛⲙ* | 13/12.26, 24/31 | to be blind | gnm / ϭⲱⲛⲙ |

c. *Greek nouns*

| Transcription | Reference | Translation | Equivalent |
|---|---|---|---|
| *ⲉⲣⲉⲕⲟⲥ* | V.22/5 | Vetch | ἄρακος (?) |
| *ⲕⲓⲥⲥⲟⲩ* | 24/10 | Ivy | κισσός |
| *ⲕⲣⲟⲕⲟⲥ* | V.18/7 | Saffron | κρόκος |
| *ⲙⲁⲛⲇⲣⲁⲕⲟⲣⲟⲩ ⲣⲓⲍⲁ* | 24/7 | Mandrake root | μανδραγόρου ῥίζα |
| *ⲙⲉⲗⲁⲕⲣⲉⲧⲓⲕⲟⲩ* | 24/8 | Cretan apples | μῆλα κρητικά? [12] |
| *ⲟⲡⲓⲟⲩ* | 24/3 | Opium | ὄπιον |
| *ⲡⲓⲡⲓⲣ* | V.14/3 | Pepper | πέπερι |
| *ⲥⲕⲁⲙⲟⲩⲛⲁⲣⲓⲛ* | 24/2 | Scammony (root) | σκαμμωνάριον [13] |
| *ⲥⲟⲙⲁ* | 13/17 | Body | σῶμα |
| *ⲩⲟⲥⲕⲩⲁⲙⲟⲩ* | 24/9 | Henbane | ὑοσκύαμος |

---

[11] WB IV, 455, 8–11.

[12] Griffith and Thompson suggest μελίκρητον (?), 'mixture of water and honey' or 'quinces' (⟨ κυδώνια) as possible meanings; see, Griffith and Thompson, *The Demotic Magical Papyrus of London and Leiden*, vol. 1, 149, fn. to line 8. Since the word occurs in a list of vegetable products; I consider the first suggestion improbable.

[13] I thank Klaas A. Worp for suggesting the following new interpretation to me. The word in 'cipher', *ⲥⲕⲁⲙⲟⲩⲛⲁⲣⲓⲛ*, is a garbled form of σκαμμωνάριον, which derives in turn from σκαμμωνία with the diminutive suffix -αριον. As in οἶνος/οἰνάριον, the suffix has lost its diminutive meaning, so that the word σκαμμωνάριον (thus far not attested in the Greek dictionaries) is basically a synonym for 'scammony'; for parallel constructions, see, Leonard R. Palmer, *A Grammar of the Post-Ptolemaic Papyri* (London 1945) 83, 88. For the loss of the double –μμ- and the change from ω to ου, see, F.Th. Gignac, *Grammar of the Greek Papyri of the Roman and Byzantine Periods* 2 Vols. (Milan 1976–1981) vol. 1, 157, 209ff. In Coptic medical texts the word is preserved as ⲥⲁⲕⲁⲙⲟⲩⲛⲓⲁ and ⲥⲕⲁⲙⲟⲩⲁⲓⲁⲥ; Walter Till, *Die Arzneikunde der Kopten* (Berlin 1951) 86. Griffith and Thompson emended the 'cipher' spelling to σκαμωνία ῥίζα, 'scammony root', following the more common term σκαμμωνίας ῥίζα; *The Demotic Magical Papyrus of London and Leiden*, vol. 1, 148, fn. to line 2. Note that σκαμμωνία and σκαμμωνίας ῥίζα are synonyms in Diosc. IV 170RV.

## Appendix 4.1

The Greek *materials of medicine and magic* that occur in the manuscript are listed in the following three tables divided into the categories plants, solids and animals. The first column gives the official Greek form according to LSJ or Dioscorides, *De Materia Medica*; the fourth column gives the transcription of the form as attested in the manuscript (in alphabetic Demotic, Greek or 'cipher' script). A modern identification, if possible, is given in the third column.

a. *Plants*

| greek term | Ref. | translation | Attested form |
|---|---|---|---|
| ἀμμωνιακή | V4/15 | styrax | (τ-) ΑΜΟΝΙΑΚΗ[14] |
| ἀμμωνιακὸν θυμιάματος | 14/23 | gum-ammoniacum incense | ꜣmwny'k trymy'm'-tꜣ-s |
| ἄρακος (?) | V22.5 | wild chickling | *ΕΡΕΚΟC* |
| ἀσφόδελος | V5/14 | asphodel | ΑCΦΟΔΕΛΟC |
| δάφνη | 27/15 | laurel | tphn |
| εὐφορβία | V9/2 | spurge | ΕΥΦΟΡΒΙΟΥ |
| ἡλιόγονος | V1/4 | safflower, cardamom[15] | ΗΛΙΟΓΟΝΟΝ |
| κεφαλική (?)[16] | V4/10 | name of an herb | ΚΕΦΑΛΕΚΗ |
| κισσός | 24/10 | ivy | *ΚΙCCΟΥ* |
|  | 24/19 |  | gyss-'ꜣ-s |
|  | 24/22 |  | (pꜣ) gyss-'ꜣ-s |
| κρινάνθεμον | V2/3 | martagon lily | ΚΡΙΝΑΘΕΜΟΝ |
|  | V2/6 |  | gryn'themwn |
| κρόκος | 3/29 | saffron | grwgws |
|  | V18/7 |  | *ΚΡΟΚΟC* |
| λευκάνθεμον | V2/2 | name of an herb[17] | ΛΕΥΚΑΝΘΕΜΟΝ |

---

[14] The word is preceded by the Coptic definite article τ- for feminine singular nouns.

[15] It might be a synonym for ϭογχ (Crum, *Coptic Dictionary*, 840b) as suggested by Griffith and Thompson, *The Demotic Magical Papyrus of London and Leiden*, vol. 1, 170, fn. to line 4.

[16] The Demotic equivalent is *tp-n-sr*, which means 'ram's horn'. Since κεφαλική means litterally 'of the head', it is conceivable that a copyist mistakenly omitted a noun constructed with κριός, 'ram'. Cf. Dioscorides II, 104.

[17] See for suggested readings Griffith and Thompson, *The Demotic Magical Papyrus of London and Leiden*, vol. 1, 171, fn. to line 2.

| greek term | Ref. | translation | Attested form |
|---|---|---|---|
| μαλάβαθρον | 12/1 | leaf of laurus cassia | ⲙⲁⲗⲁⲃⲁⲑⲟⲩ [gloss to *hb-ỉr-y*?[18]] |
| μανδραγόρου ῥίζα | 24/7 | mandrake root | *ⲙⲁⲛⲇⲣⲁⲕⲟⲣⲟⲩ ⲣⲓⲍⲁ* |
|  | 24/18 |  | *nn.t n mʿntrʿgwrw* |
| μῆλα κρητικά (?) | 24/8 | quinces[19] | *ⲙⲉⲗⲁⲕⲣⲉⲧⲓⲕⲟⲩ* |
| ὄπιον | 24/3 | opium | *ⲟⲡⲓⲟⲩ* |
| ὀποβάλσαμον | 12/1 | juice of balsam tree | *hepwbʿlsʿmw* [gloss to ⲏⲡⲟⲃⲁⲥⲁⲙⲟⲩ] |
| ὀφρὺς ἡλίου | V1/1 | name of an herb[20] | ⲟⲫⲣⲩⲥⲛⲁⲓⲟⲩ |
| ὀφρὺς σελήνης | V1/2 | name of an herb[21] | ⲟⲫⲣⲩⲥ ☾ |
| πενταδάκτυλος | V8/7 | potentilla | ⲡⲛⲧⲁⲕⲧⲁⲗⲟⲥ [gloss to *sym n gyḏ*] |
| πέπερι | V9/3 | pepper | ⲡⲉⲡⲧⲉⲣⲉⲱⲥ |
|  | V14/3 |  | *ⲡⲓⲡⲓⲣ* |
| πύρεθρον/ς | V9/4 | unidentified umbellifer | ⲡⲉⲣⲏⲑⲟⲩ |
| σατύριον | V14/5 | unidentified plant | *sꜣterw* |
| σεληνόγονος | V1/5 | peony | ⲥⲉⲗⲏⲛⲟⲅⲟⲛⲟⲛ |
| σκαμμωνάριον[22] | 24/2 | scammony (root) | *ⲥⲕⲁⲙⲟⲩⲛⲁⲣⲓⲛ* |
| σκευή | V3/7 | lime (?) | *sgewe* |
| τιθύμαλλος | V1/7 | spurge | ⲟⲓⲟⲩⲙⲁⲗⲟⲥ |
| ὑοσκύαμος | 24/9 | henbane | *ⲩⲟⲥⲕⲩⲁⲙⲟⲩ* |

---

[18] The Demotic rendering escapes interpretation. I assume that the final oblique stroke is part of the plant determinative, although it could also be read as the consonant *r*.

[19] Griffith and Thompson suggest μελίκρητον (?), 'mixture of water and honey' as alternative reading. I prefer to translate 'quinces', because the word occurs in a list of vegetable products. Cf. Griffith and Thompson, *The Demotic Magical Papyrus of London and Leiden*, vol. 1, 149, fn. to line 8.

[20] Literal translation: 'eyebrow of the sun'. In the manuscript, the word is juxtaposed with Demotic *ꜣnḥ n Rʿ*, which means exactly the same.

[21] Literal translation: 'eyebrow of the moon'. In the manuscript the word σελήνη is written with a sign representing the moon sickle, which occurs frequently in Greek magical papyri. Its Demotic equivalent in the manuscript reads *ꜣnḥ n ỉʿḥ*, which is identical in meaning.

[22] For this reading, see footnote 13.

| greek term | Ref. | translation | Attested form |
|---|---|---|---|
| χαμαίμηλον | V2/1 | earth-apple, camomile | ⲭⲁⲙⲉⲙⲉⲗⲟⲛ |
| χρυσάνθεμον | V2/4 | chrysanthemum coronarium | ⲭⲣⲩⲥⲁⲛⲟⲉⲙⲟⲛ |

### b. *Solids (minerals and metals)*

| greek term | Ref. | translation | Attested form |
|---|---|---|---|
| ἀδάρκη | V9/5 | salt efflorescence on marsh plants | ⲁⲩⲧⲁⲣⲭⲉⲥ |
| ἀρσενικόν | V13/18 | yellow orpiment | ꜣrsenygwn |
| ἀφροσέληνος | V3/12 | moon-stone | ⲁⲫⲣⲟⲥⲉⲗⲉⲛⲟⲛ |
| θεῖον ἄπυρον | V9/6 | blue vitriol / native sulphur | ⲇⲓⲟⲛⲁⲡⲉⲣⲟⲛ |
| κάραβος (?) | 3/26 | (sea) karab | gꜥrb (n yꜥm) [ⲕⲁⲣⲁⲃ] |
| μαγνεσία | V2/7 | magnesia | ⲙⲁⲛⲉⲥⲓⲁ / mꜥknesyꜥ |
| μάγνης | V2/11 | magnetite | ⲙⲁⲅⲛⲏⲥ / mꜥknes |
| | V2/12 | magnetite | ⲙⲁⲕⲛⲏⲥ / mꜥnes |
| φέκλη | V3/4 | lees of wine | ⲫⲏⲕⲗⲏⲥ |
| χαλβάνη | V3/6 | galbanum | gꜥrbꜣnꜥ |
| χαλκάνθη | 3/24 | sulphate of copper | gꜣlꜣgꜣntsy [gloss ⲕⲁⲗⲁⲕⲁⲛⲟⲓ] |
| ψιμύθιον | V6/2 | white lead | psymytsy |

### c. *Animals*

| greek term | Ref. | translation | Attested form |
|---|---|---|---|
| γαλῆ | 24/25 | weasel | *ⲥⲉⲗⲉ* |
| | 24/37 | | gꜣlꜣ.t |
| δέρμα ἐλάφιον | V10/5 | deer skin | ⲇⲉⲣⲙⲁⲉⲗⲁⲫⲓⲟⲛ |
| σαλαμάνδρα | V4/6 | kind of lizard | ⲥⲁⲗⲁⲙⲁⲧⲣⲁ |

Not included in the present tables, although occurring among the 'words of Greek origin', Griffith and Thompson, *The Demotic Magical Papyrus of London and Leiden*, vol. 3, 102–104.

| Attested form | Ref. | translation | derivation |
|---|---|---|---|
| ⲭⲉⲗⲕⲉⲃⲉ [equivalent to *ḥdn ḥwt̲*, 'wild garlic'] [23] | V.5/16 | garlic | γέλγις (?) |
| *ⲕⲉⲩⲱⲣ*[24] | 24/14 | kernel | κάρυα (?) |

---

[23] The same term occurs as βοτάνην χελκβει in PGM V.70. Since the term is not declined, I assume that it is not a genuine Greek term.

[24] The word is written with the K-letter of the 'cipher' script that occurs otherwise only in words of Egyptian origin. It is therefore very plausible that this word is actually Egyptian.

## Appendix 4.2

The following table lists, in a fashion similar to appendix 4.1, the Greek medical terminology that occurs in P. London-Leiden.

| greek term | Reference | translation | Attested form |
|---|---|---|---|
| καῦμα | V.33/4, 6, 7, 8 | fever | g'wm' |
| ξηρόν | V.4/14 | dry powder | kser-'ꜣ-n |
| πληγή | 20/1, 15, 17, 25, 26 | sting | plege, plꜣge |
| ποδάγρα | V.8/1 | gout | ⲡⲟⲇⲁⲕⲣⲁⲛ |
| ποδαγρῶν | V.10/1 | (a man) who suffers from gout | pꜣ-etꜣgrwn |
| σπλήν | V.9/9 | poultice | splelyn |
| σῶμα | 13/17 | body | *ⲥⲟⲙⲁ* |
|  | V.32/5 |  | swm' |

## Appendix 4.3

The Greek terms for house utensils that occur in P. London-Leiden are listed in the following table.

| greek term | Reference | translation | Attested form |
|---|---|---|---|
| ἀγγεῖον | 12/11 | vessel | ỉn-gen |
| ἀρκίον | 25/31 | box[25] | ꜣrky' |
| βατάνη | 3/9.10 | flat dish | bꜣtꜣne.t, b'ṭ'ne.t |
| λαμπάς | 28/5 | lamp | l'mps |
| λοπάς | V.7/4 | flat dish | lwps |
| πίναξ | 4/21.22 | writing tablet | pyngs, pyn'ks |

---

[25] According to Max Müller, this word derives from Latin 'arca': 'Einige griechisch-demotische Lehnwörter' *RecTrav* 8 (1886) 172–178.

## Appendix 4.4

**A. *P. London-Leiden 4/1–22 = PDM xiv.93–114 [PGM XIVa.1–11]*[26]**

***A*** casting for inspection (*sš-mšt*), which the great god Imhotep \made/.
***Its preparation***: You bring a stool (*tks*: ⲧⲣⲁⲡⲉⲥⲉⲛ) of olive wood having four legs, upon which no man on earth has ever sat, and you put it near you, it being clean. When you wish to make a god's arrival (*pḥ-nṯr*) with it truthfully without falsehood, ***here is*** its manner. You should put the stool in a clean *niche* in the *midst* of the place, it being near your head; you should cover it with a cloth from its top to its bottom; you should put four bricks under the table before it, one *above* another, there being a censer of clay before it (i.e. the table); you should put charcoal of olive wood on it; you should add *wild goose* (*srʾw.t*: ⲭⲏⲛⲁ[ⲅ]ⲣⲓⲟⲩ) fat pounded with myrrh and *ks-ʿnḥ* stone; you should make them into balls; you should put one on the brazier; you should leave the remainder near you; you should recite this spell in Greek to it. ***Words to be said***:[27]

[Greek]  I call upon you (sing.) who are seated in impenetrable darkness and are in the midst of the great gods; you who, when you set, take with you the solar rays and send up the light-bringing goddess ΝΕΒΟΥΤΟΣΟΥΑΛΗΘ; great god ΒΑΡΖΑΝ ΒΟΥΒΑΡΖΑΝ ΝΑΡΖΑΖΟΥΖΑΝ ΒΑΡΖΑΒΟΥΖΑΘ Helios.

Send up to me in this night your archangel ΖΕΒΟΥΡΘΑΥΝΗΝ, respond with truth, truly, not falsely, unambiguously concerning such-and-such a matter, because I conjure you by him who is seated in the fiery cloak on the serpentine head of the Agathos Daimon, the almighty, four-faced, highest demon, dark and conjuring, ΦΩΧ. Do not ignore me Do not ignore me, but send up quickly tonight ⟨in accordance with⟩ the command of the god.

(Say this three times)

You should lie down without speaking to anyone on earth; and you should go to sleep. You see the god, he being in the likeness of a priest wearing clothes of byssus on his back and wearing sandals on his feet. He speaks with you truthfully with his mouth opposite your mouth concerning anything that you wish. When he has finished, he will go away again. You place a tablet for reading the hours (πίναξ *n ꜥš wnw.t*) upon the bricks, and you place the stars

---

[26] See for relevant footnotes *GMPT*, 200–201 [Janet H. Johnson for Demotic section; W.C. Grese for Greek section] and Merkelbach and Totti, *Abrasax. Band 2: Gebete*, 77–82 [Heinz-J. Thissen for Demotic section].

[27] Following Merkelbach, I insert the Greek invocation at this point in spite of the fact that it occurs one line farther below in the manuscript.

upon it, and you write your business on a new roll of papyrus, and you place it on the tablet (πίναξ). It tells[28] you your stars, whether they are favorable for your business.

B. *P. London-Leiden 15/24–31* = *PDM xiv.451–458 [PGM XIVb.12–15]*

[Dem.]   [**A spell**] for going before a superior[29] if he fights with you and he will not speak with you:

[Greek]  '*Do not pursue me, you, so-and-so,*[30] **I am**[31] *PAPIPETOU METOUBANES, I am carrying the mummy of Osiris, and I go to take it to Abydos, to take it to Tastai, and to bury it at Alkhah. If he, NN, causes me trouble, I will throw it at him*'.

[Dem.]   Its invocation in Egyptian again is this which is below:

ⲠⲀⲠⲒⲠⲈⲦ[.]

'Do not run after me, NN[32]. I am PAPIPETU METUBANES, carrying the mummy of Osiris, going to take it to Abydos to let it rest in ALKHAH. If NN[33] fights with me today, I shall cast it out' (Say seven times!)

C. *P. London-Leiden 23/1–20* = *PDM xiv.675–694 [PGM XIVc.16–27]*[34]

**A spell** to cause 'evil sleep' to fall. **Words to be said**:
You bring a donkey's head; you place it between your feet opposite the sun at dawn when it is about to *rise*, opposite it again in the evening when it is going to set; you anoint your right foot with yellow ochre of Syria, your left foot with clay, the soles of your foot also; you place your right hand in front and your left hand behind, the head being between them; you anoint one of your two *hands* with donkey's blood, *and* the two corners(?) of your mouth; and you recite these writings before the sun at dawn and in the evening for four days. He sleeps.

---

[28] I take the compound verb *tἰ-ḥw* to mean 'to tell, to relate' instead of 'to make come, to send'. See DG, 20 and Crum, 442 (ⲦⲀⲨⲞ).

[29] Note that the word *ḥry*, 'superior' is provided with the same determinatives as the word *pr-ʿʒ*, 'pharaoh': the god's determinative followed by the abbreviation for the standard salutation for pharaoh, *'nḫ.w wdʒ.w snb.w*, 'may he live, be whole and healthy'. This suggests that the spell is aimed against influential people on the highest levels of society.

[30] Masculine.

[31] The Greek text writes the word **ANOK** and the following vox magica *PAPIPETOU* as one group as if they form a compound magical name. In fact, **ANOK** is the Old-Coptic independent pronoun, first person singular, meaning 'I am'. The Demotic version has accordingly *ink*.

[32] Feminine or plural.

[33] Feminine or plural.

[34] Translation following *GMPT*, 232 [Janet H. Johnson Demotic section; R.F. Hock Greek section].

If you wish to make him \*DIE\*, you should do it for seven days. If you do its magic, you should bind a thread of palm fiber to your *hand*, a piece of male palm fiber to your phallus *and* your head. *It is very good.*
**This spell which you should recite** *before the sun*:

[Greek]  I call upon you who are in the empty air, you who are terrible, invisible, almighty, a god of gods, you who cause destruction and desolation, you who hate a stable household, you who were driven out of Egypt and have roamed foreign lands, you who shatter everything and are not defeated.

I call upon you, Typhon SETH; I command your prophetic powers because I call upon your authoritative name, to which you cannot refuse to listen, IÔ ERBÊTH IÔ PAKERBÊTH IÔ BOLCHÔSÊTH IÔ PATATHNAX IÔ SÔRÔ IÔ NEBOUTOSOUALÊTH AKTIÔPHI ERESCHIGAL NEBOUTOSOALÊTH ABERAMENTHÔOU LERTHEXANAX ETHRELUÔTH NEMAREBA AEMINA (the whole formula). Come to me and go and strike down him, NN, (or her, NN) with chills and fever. That very person has wronged me and he (or she) has spilled the blood of Typhon in his own (or her own) house. For this reason I am doing this

(Add the usual)

D. *P. London-Leiden verso 20/1–7 = PDM xiv.1097–1103*

[**Spell**] to make a man's *bad eye* cease.
'O Amun, this lofty male, this male of Nubia who came down from Meroe to Egypt and found Horus, my son. He hurried on his feet and beat him (= Horus) on his head with three spells in the Nubian language. He found NN, whom NN bore, hurried on his feet, and beat him on his head with three spells in the Nubian language: "gntjini TNTJINA QUQUBI [A]KHE AKHA"'.
[**Say it**] to a little oil; put salt and nasturtium seed to it; rub the man who suffers from the *bad eye* with it. You should also write these on a new (piece of) *papyrus*, and make it into a papyrus roll on his body: 'You are this eye of the *heaven*' with the writings ⸗.

# BIBLIOGRAPHY

Only those works are listed to which is referred more than twice. The abbreviations used are in accordance with the *Lexikon der Ägyptology* (LdÄ) and the *Checklist of Editions of Greek, Latin, Demotic and Coptic Papyri, Ostraca and Tablets* (version used as of June 2004; http:/scriptorium.lib.duke.edu/papyrus/texts/clist.html) or listed as separate entries in the following bibliography.

Appel, René, and Pieter Muysken, *Language Contact and Bilingualism* (London 1987)
Assmann, Jan, *Re und Amun. Die Krise des polytheistischen Weltbilds im Ägypten der 18.–20. Dynastie* (OBO 51; Freiburg, Göttingen 1983)
——, *Theologie und Frömmigkeit einer frühen Hochkultur* (2nd ed.; Stuttgart 1991)
——, 'Unio Liturgica. Die kultische Einstimmung in Götterweltlichen Lobpreis als Grundmotiv "esoterischer" Überlieferung im alten Ägypten', in: Hans G. Kippenberg and Guy G. Stroumsa, *Secrecy and Concealment. Studies in the History of Mediterranean and Near Eastern Religions* (Leiden 1995) 37–60
——, *Hymnen und Gebete* (OBO, 2nd ed.; Freiburg, Göttingen 1999)
——, *Moses der Ägypter. Entzifferung einer Gedächtnisspur* (Frankfurt am Main 2000)
——, *Weisheit und Mysterium. Das Bild der Griechen von Ägypten* (Munich 2000)
Aufmesser, Max, *Etymologische und wortgeschichtliche Erläuterungen zu De Materia Medica des Pedanius Dioscurides Anazarbeus* (Altertumswissenschaftliche Texte und Studien 34; Hildesheim 2000)
Bagnall, Roger S., *Egypt in Late Antiquity* (Princeton 1993)
——, *Reading Papyri, Writing Ancient History* (London 1995)
Bal, Mieke, *Narratology. Introduction to the Theory of Narrative* (2nd ed.; Toronto 1997)
Bell, H.I., A.D. Nock and H. Thompson, *Magical texts from a Bilingual Papyrus in the British Museum* (London 1933)
Bergman, Jan, *Ich bin Isis. Studien zum Memphitischen Hintergrund der griechischen Isisaretalogien* (Acta Universitatis Upsaliensis—Historia Religionum 3; Uppsala 1968)
Betrò, M.C., 'Erbari nell'antico Egitto' *EVO* 11 (1988) 71–110
Betz, Hans Dieter (ed.), 'The Formation of Authoritative Tradition in the Greek Magical Papyri', in: Ben F. Meyer and E.P. Sanders (eds.), *Jewish and Christian Self-Definition. Volume Three: Self-Definition in the Graeco-Roman World* (London 1982) 161–170
——, *The Greek Magical Papyri in Translation. Including the Demotic spells* (Chicago 1986)

———, 'Magic and Mystery in the Greek Magical Papyri', in: Christopher A. Faraone and Dirk Obbink (eds.), *Magika Hiera. Ancient Greek Magic and Religion* (Oxford 1991) 244–259
———, 'Jewish Magic in the Greek Magical Papyri (PGM VII.260–271)', in: Peter Schäfer and Hans G. Kippenberg (eds.), *Envisioning Magic. A Princeton Seminar and Symposium* (Studies in the History of Religions 75; Leiden 1997) 45–63
Bierbrier, M.J., *Who was Who in Egyptology* (3rd ed.; London 1995)
Blackman, A.M., and H.W. Fairman, 'The consecration of an Egyptian temple according to the use of Edfu' *JEA* 32 (1946) 75–91
Blasius, A., and B.U. Schipper (eds.), *Apokalyptik und Ägypten. Eine kritische Analyse der relevanten Texte aus dem griechisch-römischen Ägypten* (OLA 107; Leuven 2002)
Bommas, Martin, *Die Mythisierung der Zeit* (GÖF IV.37; Wiesbaden 1999)
Bonner, C., *Studies in Magical Amulets chiefly Graeco-Egyptian* (Ann Arbor 1950)
Borghouts, J.F., 'Magical Texts', in: *Textes et Langages de l'Égypte Pharaonique* 3 Vol. (BibEt. 63: Cairo 1972–1974) vol. 3, 7–19
———, 'The Evil Eye of Apopis' *JEA* 59 (1973) 114–150
———, *Ancient Magical texts* (Nisaba 9; Leiden 1978)
Brashear, William M., 'The Greek Magical Papyri: An Introduction and Survey; Annotated Bibliography (1928–1994)', in: *ANRW* II 18. 5 (1995) 3380–684
———, *Magica Varia* (Papyrologica Bruxellensia 25; Brussels 1991)
Bresciani, Edda, Sergio Pernigotti, Maria C. Betro, *Ostraka demotici da Narmutti* (Pisa 1983)
Bresciani, E., and R. Pintaudi, 'Textes démotico-grecs et greco-démotiques des ostraca de Medinet Madi: un problème de bilinguisme', in: S.P. Vleeming (ed.), *Aspects of Demotic Lexicography* (Studia Demotica 1; Leuven 1987) 123–126
Burkard, Günter, 'Der formale Aufbau altägyptischer Literaturwerke: Zur Problematik der Erschliessung seiner Grundstrukturen' *SAK* 10 (1983), 79–118
Burkert, W., *Homo Necans. The Anthropology of Ancient Greek Sacrificial Ritual and Myth* (Berkeley 1983)
Burstein, S.M., *Graeco-Africana. Studies in the history of Greek relations with Egypt and Nubia* (New Rochelle 1995)
Cenival, Françoise de, *Le mythe de l'oeil du soleil* (Demotische Studien 9; Sommerhausen 1988)
Clarysse, Willy, 'Greeks and Egyptians in the Ptolemaic Army and Administration' *Aegyptus* 65 (1985) 57–66
———, 'Greek Loan-Words in Demotic', in: S.P. Vleeming (ed.), *Aspects of Demotic Lexicography* (Studia Demotica 1; Leuven 1987) 9–33
———, 'Ptolemaeïsch Egypte. Een maatschappij met twee gezichten' *Handelingen van de Koninklijke Zuidnederlandse Maatschappij voor Taal- en Letterkunde en Geschiedenis* 45 (1991) 21–38
Copenhaver, Brian P., *Hermetica. The Greek 'Corpus Hermeticum' and the Latin 'Asclepius' in a new English translation, with notes and introduction* (Cambridge 1992)
Crum: W.E. Crum, A Coptic Dictionary (Oxford 1939)

Cruz-Uribe, Eugene, *Hibis Temple Project I; translations, Commentary, Discussions and Sign List* (San Antonio 1988)
———, 'Opening of the Mouth as Temple Ritual', in: E. Teeter and J.A. Larson (eds.), *Gold of Praise. Fs. E.F. Wente* (SAOC 58; Chicago 1999) 69–73
DDD: Karel van der Toorn, Bob Hecking and Pieter W. van der Horst (eds.), Dictionary of Deities and Demons in the Bible (2nd ed.; Leiden 1999)
Daniel, Robert, *Two Greek Magical Papyri in the National Museum of Antiquities in Leiden. A Photographic Edition of J 384 and J 395 (= PGM XII and XIII)* (Papyrologica Coloniensia 19; Cologne 1990)
Daumas, François, *Les Moyens d'expression du grec et de l'égyptien comparés dans les décrets de Canope et de Memphis* (ASAE Suppl. 16; Cairo 1952)
———, 'L'alchimie a-t-elle une origine égyptienne?', in: Günter Grimm, Heinz Heinen and Erich Winter (eds.), *Das römisch-byzantinische Ägypten* (Aegyptiaca Treverensia 2; Mainz 1983) 109–118
Dawson, Warren R., 'Studies in medical history: (a) The origin of the herbal, (b) Castor-oil in antiquity' *Aegyptus* 10 (1929) 47–72
———, 'Anastasi, Sallier, and Harris and their Papyri', *JEA* 35 (1949) 158–166
Deines, H. Von, and H. Grapow, *Wörterbuch der ägyptischen Drogennamen* (Grundriss der Medizin der alten Ägypter 6; Berlin 1959)
Deines, H. von, H. Grapow and W. Westendorf, *Ergänzungen. Drogenquanten, Sachgruppen, Nachträge, Bibliographie, Generalregister* (Grundriss der Medizin der alten Ägypter 9; Berlin 1973)
Delatte, A., and Ph. Derchain, *Les intailles magiques gréco-égyptiennes* (Paris 1964)
Delatte, A., *Herbarius. Recherches sur le cérémonial usité chez les anciens pour la cueillette des simples et des plantes magiques* (3rd ed.; Brussels 1961)
Depauw, Mark, *A Companion to Demotic Studies* (Papyrologica 28; Brussels 1997)
Derchain, Philippe, *Le papyrus Salt 825 (B.M. 10051). Rituel pour la conservation de la vie en Egypte* (Brussels 1965)
Derchain-Urtel, M.-T., *Priester im Tempel: die Rezeption der Theologie der Tempel von Edfu und Dendera in den Privatdokumenten aus ptolemäischer Zeit* (GOF IV/19: Wiesbaden 1989)
Dickey, M.W., 'The Learned Magician and the Collection and Transmission of Magical Lore', in: D.R. Jordan (eds.), *The World of Ancient Magic* (PNIA 4; Bergen 1999) 163–193
———, *Magic and Magicians in the Greco-Roman World* (London, New York 2001)
Dieleman, Jacco, 'Ein spätägyptisches magisches Handbuch: eine neue PDM oder PGM?', in: Friedhelm Hoffmann and Heinz-J. Thissen (eds.), *Res Severa Verum Gaudium. Fs Zauzich* (Studia Demotica VI; Leuven 2004) 121–128
———, 'Claiming the Stars: Egyptian Priests facing the Sky' *Aegyptiaca Helvetica* 17 (2003) 277–289
Dieleman, Jacco and Ian Moyer, 'Miniaturization and the Opening of the Mouth in a Greek Magical Text (*PGM* XII.270–350)' *JANER* 3 (2003), 47–72
Dieterich, Albrecht, *Papyrus magica musei Lugdunensis Batavi*, Jahrbücher für klassische Philologie, Suppl. 16, 749–830
———, *Abraxas. Studien zur Religionsgeschichte des späten Altertums* (Leipzig 1891)
———, *Eine Mithrasliturgie* (Leipzig 1903)
———, *Kleine Schriften* (Leipzig and Berlin 1911)

Doresse, Jean, 'Cryptographie copte et cryptographie grecque' *Bulletin de l'Institut d'Égypte* 33 (1952) 115–129
———, 'Cryptography' *The Coptic Encyclopedia* 8 (1991) 65a–69a
Dornseiff, Franz, *Das Alphabet in Mystik und Magie* (2nd ed.; Berlin 1925)
Drioton, E., 'Essai sur la cryptographie privée de la fin de la 18e dynastie' *Rev.d'Egyptologie* 1 (1933) 1–50
———, 'Recueil de cryptographie monumentale' *ASAE* 40 (1940) 305–427
Edwards, I.E.S., *Oracular Amuletic Decrees of the Late New Kingdom* (British Museum, Hieratic Papyri, Fourth Series; London 1960)
Emmel, Stephen, 'Religious Tradition, Textual Transmission, and the Nag Hammadi Codices', in: John D. Turner and Anne McGuire (eds.), *The Nag Hammadi Library after Fifty Years. Proceedings of the 1995 Society of Biblical Literature Commemoration* (Nag Hammadi and Manichaean Studies 44; Leiden 1997) 34–43
Eschweiler, Peter, *Bildzauber im Alten Ägypten. Die Verwendung von Bildern und Gegenständen in magischen Handlungen nach den Texten des Mittleren und Neuen Reiches* (OBO 137; Freiburg and Göttingen 1994)
Fagan, Brian M., *The Rape of the Nile. Tomb Robbers, Tourists and Archaeologists in Egypt* (New York 1975)
Fairman, H.W., 'A Scene of the Offering of Truth in the Temple of Edfu' *MDAIK* 16² (1958) [Fs. H. Junker] 86–92
Faraone, Christopher A., 'Binding and Burying the Forces of Evil: The Defensive Use of "Voodoo Dolls" in Ancient Greece' *Classical Antiquity* 10 (1991) 165–205
———, 'The Mystodokos and the Dark-Eyed Maidens: Multicultural Influences on a Late-Hellenistic Incantation', in: Marvin Meyer and Paul Mirecki (eds.), *Ancient Magic and Ritual Power* (Religions in the Graeco-Roman World 129; Leiden 1995) 297–333
———, *Ancient Greek Love Magic* (Cambridge 1999)
———, 'Handbooks and Anthologies: The Collection of Greek and Egyptian Incantations in Late Hellenistic Egypt' *AfR* 2 (2000) 195–214
———, 'The Ethnic Origins of a Roman-Era *Philtrokatadesmos* (PGM IV 296–434)', in: Marvin Meyer and Paul Mirecki (eds.), *Magic and Ritual in the Ancient World* (Religions in the Graeco-Roman World 141; Leiden 2002) 319–343
Festugière, A.-J., *La révélation d'Hermes Trismégiste I: l'astrologie et les sciences occultes* (2nd ed.; Paris 1950)
Field, Fredric W., *Linguistic Borrowing in Bilingual Contexts* (Studies in Language Companion Series 62; Amsterdam, Philadelphia 2002)
Foley, William A., *Anthropological Linguistics* (Oxford 1997)
Fowden, Garth, *The Egyptian Hermes. A Historical Approach to the Late Pagan Mind* (Cambridge 1986)
France, Peter, *The Rape of Egypt. How the Europeans Stripped Egypt of its Heritage* (London 1991)
Frankfurter, David, 'The Magic of Writing and the Writing of Magic. The Power of the Word in Egyptian and Greek Traditions' *Helios* 21 (1994) 189–221

———, 'Narrating Power: the Theory and Practice of the Magical Historiola in Ritual Spells', in: Marvin Meyer and Paul Mirecki (eds.), *Ancient Magic and Ritual Power* (Leiden 1995) 434–476
———, *Religion in Roman Egypt. Assimilation and Resistance* (Princeton 1998)
———, 'The Consequences of Hellenism in Late Antique Egypt: Religious Worlds and Actors' *ARG* 2 (2000) 162–194
Fraser, P.M., *Ptolemaic Alexandria* (Oxford 1972)
Gager, John G., *Moses in Greco-Roman Paganism* (SBL Monograph Series 16; Nashville 1972)
———, *Curse tablets and Binding Spells from the Ancient World* (New York and Oxford 1992)
Gallo, Paolo, *Ostraca demotici e ieratici dall'archivio bilingue di Narmouthis II* (Pisa 1997)
Gardiner, Alan H., 'The House of Life' *JEA* 24 (1938) 157–179
———, *Ancient Egyptian Onomastica* 3 Vols. (Oxford 1947)
Gomaà, Farouk, *Chaemwese. Sohn Ramses II. Und Hoherpriester von Memphis* (ÄgAbh 27; Wiesbaden 1973)
Gordon, Richard, 'Reporting the Marvellous: Private Divination in the Greek Magical Papyri', in: Peter Schäfer and Hans G. Kippenberg (eds.), *Envisioning Magic. A Princeton Seminar and Symposium* (Studies in the History of Religions 75; Leiden 1997) 65–92
Goyon, Jean-Claude, *Rituels funéraires de l'ancienne Égypte. Introduction, traduction et commentaire* Littératures anciennes du Proche Orient, 4 (Les Éditions du Cerf; Paris 1972)
———, *Le Papyrus d'Imouthès fils de Psintaês au Metropolitan Museum of Art de New York (Papyrus MMA 35.9.21)* (New York 1999)
GMPT: Hans Dieter Betz, *The Greek Magical Papyri in Translation. Including the Demotic spells* (Chicago 1986)
Graf, Fritz, 'Prayer in Magical and Religious Ritual', in: Christopher A. Faraone and D. Obbink eds., *Magika Hiera. Ancient Greek Magic and Religion* (New York/Oxford 1991) 188–213
———, *Magic in the Ancient World* (Revealing Antiquity 10; Cambridge, Mass. 1997)
Grapow, H., *Von den medizinischen Texten. Art, Inhalt, Sprache und Stil der medizinischen Einzeltexte sowie Überlieferung, Bestand und Analyse der medizinischen Papyri* (Grundriss der Medizin der alten Ägypter 2, Berlin 1955)
Greener, Leslie, *The Discovery of Egypt* (New York 1966)
Griffith, F.Ll. and H. Thompson, *The Demotic Magical papyrus of London and Leiden*, 3 vols. (London 1904–1909)
Griffith, F.Ll., 'The Old Coptic Magical Texts of Paris' *ZÄS* 38 (1900) 86–93
———, 'The Date of the Old Coptic Texts and their Relation to Christian Coptic' *ZÄS* 39 (1901) 78–82
———, *Catalogue of the Demotic Graffiti of the Dodecaschoenus* Vol. 1 (Oxford 1937)
Griffiths, J. Gwyn, *Plutarch's De Iside et Osiride* (Cardiff 1970)
———, *Apuleius of Madaura. The Isis-Book (Metamorphoses, Book XI)* (EPRO 39; Leiden 1975)

Groff, William N., 'Étude sur la sorcellerie: ou, le rôle que la Bible a joué chez les sorciers' *MIE* 3 (1900) 337–415

Guglielmi, Waltraud, and Knut Buroh, 'Die Eingangssprüche des Täglichen Tempelrituals nach Papyrus Berlin 3055 (I,1-VI,3)', in: Jacobus van Dijk (ed.), *Essays on Ancient Egypt in Honour of Herman te Velde* (Egyptological Memoirs 1; Groningen 1997) 101–166

Haas, Chr., *Alexandria in Late Antiquity. Topography and Social Conflict* (Baltimore, London 1997)

Halbertsma, Ruurd Binnert, *Le Solitaire des Ruines. De archeologische reizen van Jean Emile Humbert (1771–1839) in dienst van het Koninkrijk der Nederlanden* (unpublished Phd thesis, Leiden 1995)

Halleux, Robert, *Les alchimistes grecs 1: Papyrus de Leyde, Papyrus de Stockholm* (Paris 1981)

Harrauer, Christine, *Meliouchos. Studien zur Entwicklung religiöser Vorstellungen in griechischen synkretistischen Zaubertexten* (Wiener Studien, Beiheft 11; Vienna 1987)

Heichelheim, F.M., 'On Medinet Habu Ostracon 4038' *JEA* 27 (1941) 161

Heinen, Heinz, 'L'Egypte dans l'historiographie moderne du monde hellénistique', in: L. Criscuolo and G. Geraci (eds.), *Egitto e storia antica dell' ellenismo all' età araba* (Bologna 1989) 105–135

Herbin, F.R., 'Les premières pages du Papyrus Salt 825' *BIFAO* 88 (1988) 95–112

Hess, J.-J., *Der gnostische Papyrus von London* (Freiburg 1892)

———, 'Bemerkungen zu einigen arabischen Wörtern des abessinischen Glossars (ZA XXI, 61ff)' *Zeitschrift für Assyriologie* 31 (1918) 26–32

Hoffmann, Friedhelm, *Ägypten: Kultur und Lebenswelt in griechisch-römischer Zeit. Eine Darstellung nach den demotischen Quellen* (Studienbücher Geschichte und Kultur der Alten Welt; Berlin 2000)

Hopfner, Theodor, *Griechisch-ägyptischer Offenbarungszauber* 2 vols. (Leipzig 1921–1924; 2nd ed. Amsterdam 1974–1990)

Hornung, Erik, *Der Eine und die Vielen. Ägyptische Gottesvorstellungen* (Darmstadt 1971)

———, *Das Buch der Anbetung des Re im Westen (Sonnenlitanei) nach den Versionen des Neuen Reiches* (AH 2–3; Genf 1975–1977)

———, *Die Nachtfahrt der Sonne. Eine altägyptische Beschreibung des Jenseits* (Düsseldorf and Zürich 1991)

———, *The Ancient Egyptian Books of the Afterlife* (Ithaca, London 1999)

Horst, P.W. van der, *Chaeremon: Egyptian Priest and Stoic Philosopher* (EPRO 101; 2nd ed.; Leiden 1987)

Iversen, Erik, *Egyptian and Hermetic Doctrine* (Opuscula Graecolatina 27; Copenhagen 1984)

———, *The Myth of Egypt and its Hieroglyphs in European Tradition* (2nd ed.; Princeton 1993)

Jasnow, R. and K.-Th. Zauzich, 'A Book of Thoth?', in: C.J. Eyre ed., *Proceedings of the Seventh International Congress of Egyptologists. Cambridge, 3–9 September 1995* (OLA 82; Leuven 1998) 607–618

Jelínková-Reymond, E., *Les inscriptions de la statue guérisseuse de Djed-Her-le-Sauveur* (BdE 23; Cairo 1956)

Johnson, Janet H., 'The Demotic Magical Spells of Leiden I 384' *OMRO* 56 (1975) 29–64

———, *The Demotic Verbal System* (SAOC 38; Chicago 1976)

———, 'The Dialect of the Demotic Magical Papyrus of London and Leiden', in: *Studies in Honor of George R. Hughes* (SAOC 39; Chicago 1976) 105–132

———, 'Louvre E3229: A Demotic Magical Text' *Enchoria* 7 (1977) 55–102

———, 'Text Abbreviations Used by the Chicago Demotic Dictionary. Including all references cited as of June 20, 1988' *Enchoria* 21 (1994) 128–141

Jordan, David R., Hugo Montgomery, Einar Thomassen (eds.), *The World of Ancient Magic* (Papers from the Norwegian Institute at Athens 4; Bergen 1999)

Junker, Hermann, 'Auszug der Hathor-Tefnut aus Nubien' *AkPAW* (Berlin 1911)

———, *Das Götterdekret über das Abaton* (Vienna 1913)

———, *Die Onurislegende* (DAW Wien 59/1–2; Vienna 1917)

Kákosy, László, 'Nubien als mythisches Land im Altertum' in: Idem, *Selected Papers (1953–1976)* Studia Aegyptiaca 8 (Budapest 1981) 131–138

———, 'Probleme der Religion im römerzeitlichen Ägypten' *ANRW* II 18.5 (1995) 2894–3049

Klasens, A., 'An Amuletic Papyrus of the 25th Dynasty' *OMRO* 56 (1975) 20–28

Köcher, Franz, 'Ein Text medizinischen Inhalts aus dem neubabylonischen Grab 405', in: R.M. Boehmer, F.Pedde, B. Salje (eds.), *Uruk: die Gräber* (Deutsches Arch. Institut, Baghdad 1995) 203–217

Koenig, Yvan, 'La Nubie dans les textes magiques. "L'inquiétante étrangeté"' *RdE* 38 (1987) 105–110

———, *Magie et magiciens dans l'Égypte ancienne* (Paris 1994) 147–149

Kramer, Johannes, *Glossaria Bilinguia Altera (C. Gloss. Biling. II)* (AfP Beiheft 8; Leipzig, Munich 2001)

Kurth, Dieter, 'Die Lautwerte der Hieroglyphen in den Tempelinschriften der griechisch-römischen Zeit—zur Systematik ihrer Herleitungsprinzipien' *ASAE* 69 (1983) 287–309

———, *Treffpunkt der Götter. Inschriften aus dem Tempel des Horus von Edfu* (Zürich, Munich 1994)

LdÄ: Wolfgang Helck and Eberhard Otto (eds.), *Lexikon der Ägyptologie* 6 vols. (Wiesbaden 1976–1986)

Lagercrantz, Otto, *Papyrus Graecus Holmiensis (P. Holm.): Recepte für Silber, Steine und Purpur* (Arbeten utgifna med understöd af Vilhelm Ekmans Universitetsfond 13; Uppsala and Leipzig 1913)

Lange, H.O., and O. Neugebauer, *Papyrus Carlsberg No. 1, ein hieratisch-demotischer kosmologischer Text* (Copenhagen 1940)

Leemans, Conrad, *Papyrus égyptien à transcriptions grecques du Musée d'Antiquités des Pays-Bas à Leide (Description raisonnée I 383)* 2 Vols. (Leiden 1839)

———, *Papyrus égyptien démotique I. 384 du Musée d'Antiquités des Pays-Bas à Leide* (Leiden 1856)

Lenormant, François, *Catalogue d'une Collection d'Antiquités Egyptiennes par M. François Lenormant. Cette Collection Rassemblée par M.D. Anastasi Consul Générale de Suède a Alexandrie* (Paris 1857)

Lexa, François, *La magie dans l'Égypte antique de l'ancien empire jusqu'à l'époque copte* (Paris 1925)

LiDonnici, Lynn R., 'Beans, Fleawort, and the Blood of a Hamadryas Baboon: Recipe Ingredients in Greco-Roman Magical Materials', in: Paul Mirecki and Marvin Meyer (eds.), *Magic and Ritual in the Ancient World* (Religions in the Graeco-Roman World 141; Leiden 2002) 359–377

Loprieno, A. (ed.), *Ancient Egyptian Literature. History and Forms* (PdÄ 10; Leiden 1996)

LSJ: H.G. Liddell, R. Scott and H.S. Jones, *A Greek-English Lexicon* (Oxford 1996)

Manniche, Lise, *An Ancient Egyptian Herbal* (London 1989)

Marganne-Mélard, Marie-Hélène, 'La Médicine dans l'Égypte romaine: les sources et les méthodes' *ANRW* II 37.3 (1996) 2709–2740

McBride, Daniel R., 'The Development of Coptic: Late-Pagan Language of Synthesis in Egypt' *JSSEA* 19 (1989) 89–111

Meeks, Dimitri, 'Pureté et purification en Égypte', in: *Dictionnaire de la Bible*, Supplément 9 (Paris 1979) 430–452

Merkelbach, R., *Isis Regina—Zeus Sarapis. Die griechisch-ägyptische Religion nach den Quellen dargestellt* (Stuttgart and Leipzig 1995)

Merkelbach, Reinhold, and Maria Totti, *Abrasax. Ausgewählte Papyri religiösen und magischen Inhalts—Band 1: Gebete* (Papyrologica Coloniensia 17.1; Opladen 1990)

———, *Abrasax. Ausgewählte Papyri religiösen und magischen Inhalts. Band 2: Gebete (Fortsetzung)* (Papyrologica Coloniensia 17.2; Cologne 1991)

Meyer, M., and R. Smith (eds.), *Ancient Christian Magic. Coptic Texts of Ritual Power* (San Francisco 1994)

Meyer, Marvin and Paul Mirecki (eds.), *Ancient Magic and Ritual Power* (Religions in the Graeco-Roman World 129; Leiden 1995)

———, *Magic and Ritual in the Ancient World* (Religions in the Graeco-Roman World 141; Leiden 2002)

Möller, G., *Die beiden Totenpapyrus Rhind des Museums zu Edinburg* (Leipzig 1913)

Moers, Gerald, *Fingierte Welten in der ägyptischen Literatur des 2. Jahrtausends v. Chr. Grenzüberschreitung, Reisemotiv und Fiktionalität* (PdÄ 19; Leiden 2001)

Morenz, Ludwig D., *Beiträge zur Schriftlichkeitskultur im Mittleren Reich und in der 2. Zwischenzeit* (ÄAT 29; Wiesbaden 1996)

———, '(Magische) Sprache der geheimen Kunst' *SAK* 24 (1997) 191–201

Montet, P., 'Le fruit défendu' *Kêmi* 11 (1950)

Müller, Max, 'Einige griechisch-demotische Lehnwörter' *RecTrav* 8 (1886) 172–178

Muysken, Pieter, *Bilingual Speech. A Typology of Code-Mixing* (Cambridge 2000)

Nagel, Peter, 'Akhmimic' *The Coptic Encyclopedia* 8 (1991) 19a–27b

Nedelmann, Birgitta, 'Geheimhaltung, Verheimlichung, Geheimnis—Einige soziologische Vorüberlegungen', in: Hans G. Kippenberg and Guy G. Stroumsa, *Secrecy and Concealment. Studies in the History of Mediterranean and Near Eastern Religions* (Leiden 1995) 1–16

Neugebauer, O., and R.A. Parker, *Egyptian Astronomical Texts* 3 Vols. (London 1960–1969)

Nock, A.D. and A.J. Festugière, *Corpus Hermeticum* (Paris 1946–1954)

Noegel, Scott B. (ed.), *Prayer, Magic, and the Stars in the Ancient and Late Antique World* (Pennsylvania 2003)

Nunn, John F., *Ancient Egyptian Medicine* (London 1996)

Onasch, Chr., 'Kusch in der Sicht von Ägyptern und Griechen', in: E. Endesfelder eds., *Ägypten und Kusch. Fs. Hintze* (Berlin 1977) 331–336

Osing, Jürgen, *The Carlsberg papyri 2: Hieratische Papyri aus Tebtunis* 2 Vols. (CNI Publications 17; Copenhagen 1998)

Otto, E., *Die Biographischen Inschriften der ägyptischen Spätzeit. Ihre geistesgeschichtliche und literarische Bedeutung* (PdÄ 2; Leiden 1954)

——, *Das ägyptische Mundöffnungsritual* (ÄgAbh. 3; Wiesbaden 1960)

Otto, Walter, *Priester und Tempel im Hellenistischen Ägypten: ein Beitrag zur Kulturgeschichte des Hellenismus* 2 vols. (Leipzig and Berlin 1905–1908; reprint Rome 1971)

Parker, Richard A., 'A Late Demotic Gardening Agreement. Medinet Habu Ostracon 4038' *JEA* 26 (1940) 84–113

——, 'A Horoscopic Text in Triplicate', in: Heinz-J. Thissen and Karl-Th. Zauzich eds., *Grammata demotika. Fs. Lüddeckens* (Würzburg 1984) 141–143

Parkinson, Richard, *Cracking Codes. The Rosetta Stone and Decipherment* (Berkeley and Los Angeles 1999)

Piccione, Peter A., 'The Gaming Episode in the *Tale of Setne Khamwas* as Religious Metaphor', in: David. P. Silverman, *For his Ka. Fs. Klaus Baer* (SAOC 55; Chicago 1994) 197–204

PGM: *Papyri Graecae Magicae* 2 vols. (Leipzig 1928–1931) [2nd ed., ed. by Albert Henrichs; (Stuttgart 1973–1974)]

Pleyte, W., *Chapitres supplémentaires au Livre des Morts, 162 à 174* 3 Vols. (Leiden 1881)

Preisendanz, Karl, *Papyrusfunde und Papyrusforschung* (Leipzig 1933)

——, *Papyri Graecae Magicae* 2 vols. (2nd ed; (Stuttgart 1973–1974)

Quack, J.F., 'Das Pavianshaar und die Taten des Thoth (pBrooklyn 47.218.48+ 85 3,1–6)' *SAK* 23 (1996) 305–333

——, 'Ein ägyptisches Handbuch des Tempels und seine griechische Übersetzung' *ZPE* 119 (1997) 297–300

——, 'Kontinuität und Wandel in der spätägyptischen Magie' *SEL* 15 (1998) 77–94

——, 'Der historisch Abschnitt des Buches vom Tempel', in: Jan Assmann and Elke Blumenthal (eds.), *Literatur und Politik im pharaonischen und ptolemäischen Ägypten* (BdE 127; Cairo 1999) 267–278

Quaegebeur, Jan, 'De la préhistoire de l'écriture copte' *OLP* 13 (1982) 125–136

Quecke, Hans, 'Eine griechisch-ägyptische Wörterliste vermutlich des 3. Jh. v. Chr. (P. Heid. Inv.-Nr. G 414)' *ZPE* 116 (1997) 67–80

Raven, Maarten J., *Papyrus: van bies tot boekrol: met een bloemlezing uit de Leidse papyrusverzameling* (Zutphen 1982)
———, 'Wax in Egyptian Magic and Symbolism' *OMRO* 64 (1983) 7–47
———, 'Magic and Symbolic Aspects of Certain Materials in Ancient Egypt' *VA* 4 (1988) 237–242
Ray, John David C., 'How demotic is Demotic?' *EVO* 17 (1994) 251–265
Reintges, Chris, 'Code-Mixing Strategies in Coptic Egyptian' *LingAeg* 9 (2001) 193–237
Reuvens, C.J.C., *Lettres à M. Letronne sur les papyrus bilingues et grecs, et sur quelques autres monumens gréco-égyptiens du Musée d'Antiquités de l'Université de Leide* 2 Vols. (Leiden 1830)
Reymond, E.A.E., *From the Contents of the Libraries of the Souchos Temples in the Fayyum. Part I: A Medical Book from Crocodilopolis (P. Vindob. D. 6257)* (MPER 10; Vienna 1976)
Riddle, John M., *Dioscorides on Pharmacy and Medicine* (Austin 1985)
———, 'High Medicine and Low Medicine in the Roman Empire' *ANRW* II 37.1 (1993) 102–120
Ritner, Robert K., 'Implicit Models of Cross-Cultural Interaction: a Question of Noses, Soap, and Prejudice', in: Janet H. Johnson (ed.), *Life in a Multi-Cultural Society. Egypt from Cambyses and Beyond* (SAOC 51; Chicago 1992) 283–294
———, *The Mechanics of Ancient Egyptian Magical Practice* (SAOC 54; Chicago 1993)
———, 'Egyptian Magical Practice under the Roman Empire: the Demotic Spells and their Religious Context' *ANRW* II.18.5 (1995) 3333–3379
———, 'The Wives of Horus and the Philinna papyrus (PGM XX)', in: W. Clarysse, A. Schoors and H. Willems (eds.), *Egyptian Religion. The Last Thousand Years. Fs. Quaegebeur* 2 vols. (OLA 85; Leuven 1998) vol. 2, 1027–1041
———, 'Innovations and Adaptations in Ancient Egyptian Medicine' *JNES* 59 (2000) 107–117
Robinson, James M. (ed.), *The Nag Hammadi Library in English* (3rd ed.; Leiden 1988)
Romaine, Suzanne, *Bilingualism* (Oxford 1989)
Satzinger, Helmut, 'The Old Coptic Schmidt Papyrus' *JARCE* 12 (1975) 37–50
———, 'Die altkoptischen Texte als Zeugnisse der Beziehungen zwischen Ägypten und Griechen', in: Peter Nagel (ed.), *Graeco-Coptica. Griechen und Kopten im byzantinischen Ägypten* (halle 1984) 137–146
———, 'Old Coptic' *The Coptic Encyclopedia* 8 (1991) 169a–75b
———, 'An Old Coptic Text Reconsidered: PGM 94FF' *OLA* 61 (1994) 213–224
Sauneron, Serge, *Esna I—Quatre Campagnes à Esna* (IFAO; Cairo 1959)
———, 'Les conditions d'accès à la fonction sacerdotale à l'époque gréco-romaine' *BIFAO* 61 (1962) 55–57
———, *Esna VIII—L'Ecriture figurative dans les textes d'Esna* (IFAO; Cairo 1982)
———, *Un traité égyptien d'ophiologie. Papyrus du Brooklyn Museum nos. 47.218.48 et 85* (PIFAO, Bibliothèque Générale 11; Cairo 1989)

Scarborough, John, *Pharmacy's Ancient Heritage: Theophrastus, Nicander, and Dioscorides* (The distinguished lectures, College of Pharmacy, University of Kentucky 1984)

——, 'The Pharmacology of sacred Plants, Herbs, and Roots', in: C.A. Faraone and D. Obbink (eds.), *Magika Hiera. Ancient Greek Magic and Religion* (New York, Oxford 1991) 138–174

Schott, Siegfried, *Urkunden mythologischen Inhalts. Bücher und Sprüche gegen den Gott Seth* Urk. VI 2 Vols. (Leipzig 1929–1939)

——, 'Ein Amulet gegen den bösen Blick' *ZÄS* 67 (1931) 106–110

——, *Die Schrift der verborgenen Kammer in Königsgräbern* (NAWG 4; Göttingen 1958)

——, *Bücher und Bibliotheken im alten Ägypten* (Wiesbaden 1990)

Schubart, W., *Der Gnomon des Idios Logos* vol. 1 (BGU 5,1; Berlin 1919)

Sethe, K., *Amun und die Acht Urgötter von Hermopolis* (Berlin 1929)

Smelik, K.A.D., and E.A. Hemelrijk, '"Who know not what monsters demented Egypt worships?" Opinions on Egyptian animal worship in Antiquity as part of the ancient conception of Egypt' *ANRW* II 17.4 (1984) 1852–2000

Smith, Mark, 'A New Version of a well-known Egyptian Hymn' *Enchoria* 7 (1977) 115–149

——, *The Liturgy of Opening the Mouth for Breathing* (Oxford 1993)

——, 'O.Hess=O.Naville=O. BM 50601: an Elusive Text relocated', in: E. Teeter and J.A. Larson (eds.), *Gold of Praise. Fs. E. Wente* (SAOC 58; Chicago 1999) 397–404

Sorensen, J.P., 'Ancient Egyptian Religious Thought and the XVIth Hermetic Tractate', in: G. Englund ed., *The Religion of the Ancient Egyptians: Cognitive Structures and Popular Expressions* (Uppsala 1987) 41–57

Speyer, Wolfgang, 'Religiöse Pseudepigraphie und literarische Fälschung im Altertum' *JAC* 8/9 (1965/66) 88–125 [reprinted in: Norbert Brox (ed.), *Pseudepigraphie in der heidnischen und jüdisch-christlichen Antike* (Darmstadt 1977) 195–263]

——, *Die literarische Fälschung im heidnischen und christlichen Altertum. Ein Versuch ihrer Deutung* (Handbuch der Altertumswissenschaft I.2; Munich 1971)

Spiegelberg, Wilhelm, *Der ägyptische Mythus vom Sonnenauge (der Papyrus der Tierfabeln—'Kufi') nach dem leidener demotischen Papyrus I 384* (Straßburg 1917)

Staden, Heinrich von, *Herophilus: The Art of Medicine in Early Alexandria* (Cambridge, Mass. 1989)

Sternberg-El Hotabi, Heike, 'der Untergang der Hieroglyphenschrift. Schriftverfall und Schrifttod im Ägypten der griechisch-römischen Zeit' *CdE* 69 (1994) 218–245

Stricker, B.H., *De grote zeeslang* (Leiden 1953)

——, 'Het grafisch systeem van de Magische Papyrus Londen & Leiden' *OMRO* 31 (1950) 64–71; *OMRO* 36 (1955); *OMRO* 39 (1958) 80–103; *OMRO* 42 (1961) 25–52; *OMRO* 45 (1964) 25–55

——, 'Asinarii I–IV' *OMRO* 46 (1965) 52–75; 48 (1967) 23–43; (1971) 22–53; 56 (1975) 65–74

Swarney, Paul R., *The Ptolemaic and Roman Idios Logos* (ASP 8; Toronto 1970),

Tait, W.J., 'A Duplicate Version of the Demotic *Kyphi* Text' *AcOr* 36 (1974) 23–37
———, 'The Fable of Sight and Hearing in the Demotic *Kyphi* Text' *AcOr* 37 (1976) 27–44
———, 'Guidelines and Borders in Demotic Papyri', in: M.L. Bierbrier (ed.), *Papyrus: Structure and Usage* (British Museum Occasional Papers 60; London 1986)
———, 'P. Carlsberg 230: Eleven Fragments from a Demotic Herbal', in: P.J. Frandsen (ed.), *The Carlsberg Papyri 1: Demotic Texts from the Collection* (CNI Publications 15; Copenhagen 1991) 47–92
———, 'Demotic Literature and Egyptian Society', in: Janet H. Johnson (ed.), *Life in a Multi-Cultural Society: Egypt from Cambyses to Constantine and Beyond* (SAOC 51; Chicago 1992) 303–310
Thissen, Heinz-J., 'Ägyptologische Beiträge zu den griechischen magischen Papyri', in: U. Verhoeven and E. Graefe eds., *Religion und Philosophie in alten Ägypten. Fs. Derchain* (OLA 39; Leuven 1991) 293–302
———, 'Nubien in demotischen magischen Texten', in: Daniela Mendel and Ulrike Claudi (eds.), *Ägypten im afro-orientalischen Kontext: Aufsätze zur Archaeologie, Geschichte und Sprache eines unbegrenzten Raumes: Gedenkschrift Peter Behrens* (Cologne 1991) 369–376
———, *Der verkommene Harfenspieler. Eine altägyptische Invektive (P. Wien KM 3877)* (Demotische Studien 11; Sommerhausen 1992)
———, '".....αἰγυπτιάζων τῇ φωνῇ ....." Zum Umgang mit der ägyptischen Sprache in der griechisch-römischen Antike' *ZPE* 97 (1993) 239–252
———, *Des Niloten Horapollon Hieroglyphenbuch. Band I; Text und Übersetzung* (München 2001)
Thomason, Sarah Grey, and Terrence Kaufman, *Language Contact, Creolization, and Genetic Linguistics* (Berkeley 1988)
Totti, Maria, *Ausgewählte Texte der Isis- und Sarapis-Religion* (Subsidia Epigraphica 12; Hildesheim 1985)
Vanderlip, V.F., *The Four Greek Hymns of Isidorus and the Cult of Isis* (American Studies in Papyrology 12: Toronto 1972)
Vandier, Jacques, *Le Papyrus Jumilhac* (Paris 1961)
Velde, H. te, *Seth, God of Confusion: a study of his role in Egyptian mythology and religion* (Leiden 1967)
———, 'Seth', in: *Oxford Encyclopedia of Ancient Egypt*, 269a–271a
Verbrugge, Gerald P., and John M. Wickersham, *Berossos and Manetho. Native Traditions in Ancient Mesopotamia and Egypt* (Michigan 1996)
Vergote, J., 'Sur les mots composés en Egyptien et en Copte' *BIOR* 18 (1961) 208–214
Verhoeven, Ursula, *Das Saitische Totenbuch der Iahtesnacht. P. Colon.Aeg. 10207* 3 Vols. (Papyrologische Texte und Abhandlungen; Bonn 1993)
———, *Untersuchungen zur spāthieratischen Buchschrift* (OLA 99; Leuven 2001)
Vernus, Pascal, *Essai sur la conscience de l'histoire dans l'Egypte pharaonique* (Paris 1995)
Vittmann, Günter, 'Semitisches Sprachgut im Demotischen' *WZKM* 86 (1996) 435–447
Vos, R.L., *The Apis Embalming Ritual. P. Vindob. 3873* (OLA 50; Leuven 1993)

WB: A. Erman and H. Grapow, *Wörterbuch der aegyptischen Sprache* (Berlin 1926–1963)

Wellmann, Max, 'Die Pflanzennamen des Dioskurides' *Hermes* 33 (1898) 360–422

———, *Pedanii Dioscuridis Anazarbei De Materia Medica Libri Quinque* 3 Vols. (Berlin 1907–1914)

Westendorf, W., *Handbuch der altägyptischen Medizin* I (Handbuch der Orientalistik 1. Abt., Bd. 36; Leiden, Cologne, New York 1999)

Wildung, D., *Die Rolle ägyptischer Könige im Bewußtsein ihrer Nachwelt* (MÄS 17; Berlin 1969)

———, *Imhotep und Amenhotep. Gottwerdung im alten Ägypten* (MÄS 36; Munich 1977)

Young, Robert, *Colonial Desire: Hybridity in Theory, Culture and Race* (London 1995)

Yoyotte, J., 'Contribution à l'histoire du chapitre 162 du Livre des Morts' *RdE* 29 (1977) 194–202

Zandee, J., *Der Amunhymnus des Papyrus Leiden I 344, Verso I–III* (Rijksmuseum van Oudheden; Leuven 1992)

# INDEX OF PASSAGES

*Admonitions*
   6/6–7: 83

*Amduat*
   title, ll. 3–8: 233
   short version, 292f.: 234

Ammianus Marcellinus, *Res Gestae*
   29, 2.28: 65

Apuleius
*Metamorphoses*
   II.28: 241
   XI.4: 167–168
*Apologia*
   90: 263

BGU 5
   1210, 181–187: 209
   1210, 188: 210

*Book of the Dead*
   1: 154
   30B: 224, 263, 272, 283
   64: 224, 272
   137A: 224, 272, 276
   148: 224, 263, 272, 276
   164: 142
   167 *Suppl.*: 227–228

*Book of the Fayum*
   line 40: 49
   line 187: 50

Chaeremon
*On the Egyptian Priestly Life*
   see Porphyry

Cicero, *Pro C. Rabirio Postumo*
   12.35: 239

Clement of Alexandria, *Stromateis*
   V, chapter 4, §20.3: 7
   V, chapter 4, §20.4–21.3: 6
   V, chapter 7, §41.1–2: 7
   V, chapter 7, §41.2–42.3: 6

*Corpus Hermeticum*
   XVI 1–2: 3

*Decree concerning Abaton, Philae*
   ll. 1–11: 167

Ps. Demetrius
*On Style*, 71: 65

Diodorus of Sicily
   I, 27.3–6: 274
   II, 55.1–2: 65
   VI, 1.4–7: 274

Dioscorides, *On the Materials of Medicine*
   I.10: 202
   II.104: 308
   II.118: 201
   II.136: 202
   II.159: 115
   II.178: 202
   III.58: 200, 201
   III.73RV: 114
   III.84RV: 114
   III.102: 202
   III.128: 115
   III.139: 201
   III.140: 202
   IV.33: 201, 202
   IV.37: 202
   IV.144: 202
   IV.148: 202
   IV.170RV: 307

V.107: 115
V.119: 115

*Djedhor, the saviour*
biography, §14/161f.: 220

Edfu
V 334/1–6: 215
VI 349/4–6: 213

*Enigmatic Book of the Netherworld*: 83–85

Esna
III, n° 197/16: 214
III, n° 197/18: 214

*Gardening Agreement*
C, 5–7: 43

Heliodorus, *Aithiopika*
2, 27.3: 239
3, 16.4: 248

Herodotus, *The Histories*
II, 39: 133

Hymn to Amun, el Hibe
ll. 108–111: 160

Iamblichus, *On the Mysteries of Egypt*
VII, 4: 5
VII, 5: 6
VIII, 5: 277
X, 7: 277

Lucian, *Philopseudes*
29: 245
31: 245
33–34: 242
35: 244

Macrobius, *Saturnalia*
I 20, 17: 162

*Onkhsheshonqi*
see P. BM. 10.508 212

Origen, *Against Celsus*
I, 25: 5

P. Anastasi I
11/1: 224

P. Berlin 3038
§124 (=10/12): 196
§163a (=15/1–5): 283

P. Berlin 3055
4/3–6: 177

P.BM. 10.508
8/18: 212

P.BM. 10.588
7/1–5: 142

P. BM. 10.822
see Setne II

P. Brooklyn 47.218.48+85
see Snake Book

P. Cairo 30.646
see Setne I

P. Carlsberg 230
fragment 1/10: 197
fragment 4+5, x+2/13: 197
fragment 8/x+7: 196

PDM
xii.21–49: 41, 295
xii.62–75: 33, 136, 296
xii.135–146: 33, 103, 296
xii.147–164: 33, 103, 296
xiv.1–92: 122, 264, 297
xiv.12–17: 39
xiv.93–114: 16, 41, 103, 123, 262, 297
xiv.117–149: 100, 297
xiv.127–137: 39
xiv.150–231: 101, 297
xiv.153: 39
xiv.194–204: 39

# INDEX OF PASSAGES

xiv.295–306: 39
xiv.304–309: 93
xiv.384–388: 96
xiv.387–389: 94
xiv.451–458: 103, 127
xiv.489–499: 39
xiv.627–635: 14, 262
xiv.627–629: 14
xiv.670–674: 39, 262
xiv.675–694: 103, 130
xiv.739–749: 95
xiv.772–780: 94
xiv.805–840: 39, 101
xiv.805–816: 58
xiv.812–815: 93
xiv.889: 193, 197, 202
xiv.953–955: 196
xiv.1043–1045: 93
xiv.1070–1077: 99
xiv.1097–1101: 138
xiv.1172–1179: 39
xiv.1206–1218: 96
lxi.95–99: 142

P. Ebers
  § 106 (=25/15): 196
  § 160 (=33/11): 196, 201
  § 166 (=34/5): 196
  § 188b: 83
  § 206b: 83
  § 334 (=55/17): 197
  § 770 (=92/6): 197
  § 854: 83

PGM
  I.42–54: 258
  I.96–130: 269, 276
  I.130f.: 258, 269
  I.192–194: 258
  III.71*–79*: 135
  III.119: 169
  III.332: 193
  III.633–731: 11
  IV.1–25: 14
  IV.52–85: 11
  IV.88–153: 11
  IV.154–162: 258–259
  IV.254–256: 25
  IV.260–285: 135
  IV.286–295: 188
  IV.475–485: 15, 259
  IV.776: 259
  IV.790f.: 259
  IV.850–929: 260, 262, 268, 271, 274, 278
  IV.1002–1007: 66
  IV.1928–2144: 266, 269, 277
  IV.2152–2178: 276
  IV.2442–2446: 260
  IV.2446–2455: 260
  IV.2967–3006: 187
  IV.3007–3086: 264, 267, 280
  IV.3172–3208: 188
  V.24–30: 66
  V.83–90: 66
  V.372–375: 266
  V.383: 266
  V.472–475: 169
  VII.193–196: 98
  XII.107–121: 64, 230, 260, 263, 295
  XII.155–158: 70
  XII.182–189: 69
  XII.201–269: 33, 103, 146f., 152, 183
  XII.227–238: 154
  XII.238–244: 158
  XII.244–252: 163
  XII.252–263: 164
  XII.263–267: 165, 203
  XII.270–350: 79, 146, 170–171
  XII.316–322: 175, 257
  XII.323–333: 176
  XII.334–350: 179
  XII.365–375: 26, 136f., 146
  XII.376–396: 33
  XII.397–400: 35, 100
  XII.401–444: 145, 185f., 189, 191, 220, 242, 257, 271, 274, 280, 284
  XII.445–448: 136–137
  XII.449–452: 33, 137
  XII.453–465: 103, 136f.
  XII.466–468: 137

XII.474–479: 33, 103
XII.480–495: 33, 103
XIII.81–86: 170
XIII.138–139: 170
XIII.149–160: 170
XIII.316: 193
XIII.454–470: 170
XIII.593–598: 170
XIII.732–1056: 65, 66, 158
XIII.1065–1069: 193
XIVa.1–11: 36, 41, 103, 123
XIVb.12–15: 36, 103, 127
XIVc.16–27: 26, 36, 103, 130, 132
XXI.1–29: 158, 161, 182

P. Greenfield
  Sheet 66: 180

P. Heidelberg G414: 191

Philostratus, *The Life of Apollonius of Tyana*
  I.2: 247f.

P. Insinger
  5/7–10: 216

*Piye/Piankhi Stele*
  see Urk. I

P. Leiden I 344
  verso 5/10: 159

P. Leiden I 346
  1/1–4: 153
  1/7–9: 155

P. Leiden I 348
  11/9: 197

P. Leiden I 350
  4/1: 157
  4/17–21: 161

P. Leiden I 384 recto
  13/24–15/28: 31

P. Leiden I 384 verso
  I*/1–29: 41
  II/8–11: 137
  IV/2: 38
  IV/8–11: 137
  IV/15–19: 137
  4/1–5: 64
  12/17–13/30: 145
  fragment c, line 6: 32

Pliny the Elder, *Natural History*
  30.6.18: 189
  30.9: 267

P. London-Leiden
  1/1–3/35: 39, 52, 112, 122, 297, 308
  4/1–22: 16, 32, 36, 41, 123, 313
  4/23: 254
  5/1–32: 39, 100, 119, 276
  6/1–8/11: 39, 53, 55, 68, 76, 101, 295, 297
  9/1: 41
  9/15: 74
  9/20: 41
  10/22–35: 39, 41, 58, 93
  11/4–11: 54
  12/12: 276
  12/31: 276
  13/17–21: 96
  13/21–23: 94
  14/14–16: 67
  14/22–24: 114
  15/24–31: 36, 127f., 314
  16/1–4: 72
  16/23: 276
  17/1–7: 39, 68
  21/1–9: 14, 71
  21/33: 74
  22/1–5: 39, 298
  23/1–20: 130ff., 298, 314
  23/24–26: 57, 77
  23/31: 276
  24/5: 92, 306–307
  24/6–14: 89–90, 298
  24/17–19: 90, 114, 119, 308
  24/22–25: 117

24/29–39: 95
25/23–31: 32, 94
25/37: 52
27/1–32: 39, 58f., 67, 93, 101, 119, 304
27/35: 138
28/1–4: 73, 299
V1/1–3: 117
V1/4: 202
V2/1–6: 112, 117
V2/7–15: 117, 120
V3/5–7: 113
V3/12–13: 117
V3/17–18: 113
V4/8: 119
V4/10–15: 117
V5/1–3: 299
V9/2–6: 90
V13/6–9: 93
V14/1–7: 90, 115
V17/1–8: 99, 300
V20/1–7: 138, 300
V27/1–8: 39
V29/3: 92
V32/1–13: 96, 301
fragment 1, line 2: 42
fragment 6, line 1: 42
fragment 6, line 3: 42

Plotinus, *Enneads*
   V, 8, 6: 6

Porphyry
*On Abstinence*
   4.6: 251
   4.8: 251

P. Louvre 3229
   2/25: 38

Plutarch
*Moralia*
   678C: 6
*On Isis and Osiris*
   10, 354F: 6
   11, 355B: 6, 136
   28, 361F–362A: 8

32, 363F: 6
37, 365E: 189
51, 371E: 6
62, 376B: 189

P. Oxy 1380
   iv, 76–105: 166

P. Rhind I
   6d/3–4: 159
   6h/4: 159
   10d/6–12: 153
   10h/5–10: 153

P. Salt
   1/1–2: 82
   5/10–6/3: 82
   7/1: 82
   7/6: 82

P. Smith
   20/18: 196

P. Spiegelberg
   1/5–7: 159

P. Tebt. 291
   ll. 40–45: 210

P. Turin CG 54051 (dupl.. 1993)
   rt. 4/4: 197

P. Westcar
   7/1–6: 224
   8/20: 224
   8/25: 224

*Ritual of Opening the Mouth*
   Scene 71: 181
   scene 74A: 176

*Rosetta Decree*
   ll. 6–7: 206

Setne I
   3/12: 222
   3/21–22: 231

3/30–35: 233
3/40–4/3: 234
4/17–19: 231

Setne II
  6/1–2: 237
  6/35–7/1: 237

*Snake Book*
  §43a (=3/1–2): 198
  §46g (=3/15): 197
  §61a (=4/7): 197
  §65a (=4/12): 197
  §65b (=4/12): 197
  §70 (=4/18–19): 198

Strabo, *Geography*
  17.1: 208, 246, 252
  17.2, 1–5: 252

Urk.
  I 50/16–51/1: 212
  IV 1344/11–12: 141
  VI 2, 120–129: 83
  VI 7/13–18: 135

Uru-anna=*maštakal*: 193f., 198, 202

# INDEX OF SUBJECTS

Abammon, 5
Abrasax, 57, 77–78, 123, 125, 148, 149–151, 153, 155, 158, 163–164, 170, 313, 324
Agathokles, 64, 260, 263, 295
Alexandria, 35, 113, 150, 163, 189–190, 202, 209, 239, 243, 251–252, 266, 279, 292–294, 321–322, 327
alphabetic Demotic
    function of, 71
    transcribing Egyptian epithets, 72 ff.
alternation, as linguistic process, 106, 121 ff.
Amenhotep, son of Hapu, 141, 150, 159–160, 124, 128, 172, 229
Amun, 57, 77 f., 92 f.
    as cosmic god, 162
    daily ritual of, 177
    as dispenser of life, 159 f.
    hymns to, 49, 159 ff.
    of Meroe, 140 ff., 315
    ineffable name, 161
    -Re theology, 150, 157 f.
    as wind god, 159 f.
Anastasi, Giovanni, merchant, 12–14, 21, 25–27, 40, 224, 219, 224
Aphrodite, 153, 262, 271
Aphroditopolis, city, 271–272, 284
Apion, grammarian, 189, 250
Apollo, 132, 262–263
Apollobex, 263, 267, 275
Apollonius of Tyana, 247–248, 260, 267, 270
Apuleius of Madaura, 245
    Metamorphoses, 167 f., 240 f., 242 f., 252, 277
    Apologia, 247, 263, 278
aretalogies, of Isis, 165 ff., 274
Arkhah-Alkhah, 127, 129, 314

Asclepius, 1–2, 253, 318
Assmann, Jan, 165, 180
Astrampsouchos, 264, 268

Betz, Hans Dieter, 19, 256
bilingualism
    study of, 105 f.
    in magical handbooks, 110 ff.
    in Roman Egypt, 2 ff., 104 ff., 185 ff., 210
Book of the Dead, 33 f., 49, 98, 134, 142, 154, 174, 180, 215, 217–218, 224, 227–229, 232, 263, 272, 276
botany
    in pharaonic Egypt, 190, 194–195
    Egyptian plant names, 189, 199 f., 202
*bômos* (altar), 148
*bothros* (sacrificial pit), 148

carmina figurata, 66
Celsus, 5, 111, 183
Chaeremon, 6–8, 250 f., 253, 322
Chapitres supplémentaires, Book of the Dead, 142, 227 f., 325
Chaldaeans, Babylonian priests, 246, 269
*charaktêres*
    function of, 97
    in Demotic spells, 99–101
    in Greek spells, 98, 100
chthonic offering, 148
cipher
    alphabet, 87 ff., 302 f.
    function of, 91, 96
    rules of application, 92–96
    words in, 304–307
Clarysse, Willy, 106 f., 109, 119
Claudianus, 267

## INDEX OF SUBJECTS

Claudius, emperor, 8
Clement of Alexandria, 6f.
*Corpus Hermeticum*
   and Magical Papyri
      Treatise XVI, 1–3, 9, 110, 121, 143, 168, 183, 290, 318, 325
cryptography, 83–87
   function of, 85
   rules of
      in pharaonic Egypt, 84f.
      in Greco-Roman Egypt, 86f.

Dardanus, 267
Darius, Persian king, 265, 281
Deckname, secret names, 190, 194, 197
Decree concerning Abaton, 167
Demokritos, 33, 200, 264, 267, 278, 293, 296
Demotic
   mixing with hieratic, 48ff.
   title in, 147
   use of one-consonantal signs, *see* alphabetic Demotic
*Demotic Gardening Agreement*, 40, 43, 325
Derchain-Urtel, M.-Th., 217f.
Dieterich, Albrecht, 15, 17, 145
Dioscorides, Pedanius, 115, 190, 199ff.
Djed-Hor, from Athribis, 219f.
Djedi, 224–225, 231–232, 238
Documents of Breathing, 263
Dreck-Apotheke, 93, 192

Egyptian language
   powers attributed to, 3–7
Egyptian priesthood
   and Hermetica, 1ff.
   as exotic sages, 7, 239–244
   as ritual experts, 211f., 220
   professional hierarchy, 205–208, 220
   representation in literature, 222ff., 239ff.
   Roman policy towards, 208–211
   self-presentation, 211, 217f.
   translating texts into Greek, 274f.
   way of life, 213–218
Emmel, Stephen, 22f.
encrypted scripts, *see* cipher
Ephesia grammata, 70, 172

Faraone, Christopher A., 19f., 292
fictitious letters, 270
Frankfurter, David, 9, 96f., 254, 287

Galen, of Pergamum, 194, 199f.
glosses
   Greek, 15, 28, 35, 63, 78, 104, 112, 122, 125f., 130, 136f.
   hieratic, 57f., 60–62
   Old Coptic, 15, 27, 35, 38, 56f., 60, 71, 75, 79, 127
Gnomon of the Idios Logos, 208, 210
Greek
   as language of social upward mobility, 106
   translated into Demotic, 120, 126, 128, 259
   loanwords in Demotic texts, 110ff.
   *see also* loanwords
Griffith, F.Ll., 18, 45, 55, 73, 88, 91, 114, 117, 129, 139, 302, 304–309, 311

Hadrian's gate, Philae, *see* decree concerning Abaton
Harpist's Song, 37, 177
Harris Magical Papyrus, 37, 160
healing statues, 186–187, 219
Heliopolis, city, 54, 154, 224, 226, 232, 238, 260, 266, 271–273, 279
   cosmology of, 156
Herakleopolis, city, 266, 284
Hermes, 1–3, 7, 12, 14, 22, 111, 185, 190, 198–202, 250, 261–263, 266, 271–272, 274–275, 277, 279, 282, 320, 329
   Trismegistos, 1, 262, 271, 279
Hermopolis, city, 235, 271–272, 282, 289, 293, 327

Herodotus, 8, 109, 132–133, 167, 221, 250
Hibis, Amun temple of, 160, 162–163, 174, 319
hierarchies of borrowability, 108
hieratic
    functional specialisation, 48
    glossing, 57f., 60–62
    mixing with Demotic, 49ff.
hieroglyphs
    Greco-Roman ideas on, 6f.
    in Ptolemaic temples, 78, 86
high priest, Egyptian priestly title, 165, 168f., 203, 205f., 209–220, 225–227, 229, 234, 260, 266
Himerios, 263, 295
holy man, 241, 244, 246, 248, 267
Hordedef, 224–225, 227, 272f., 282
Horus, 132, 141f., 152, 154, 175, 197, 214–216, 243, 263, 279, 283, 305, 315
Horus-cippi, 98, 174, 186f.
House-of-Life, 55, 82, 194, 206f., 220, 228, 242, 271
Humbert, Jean Emile, agent, 13, 25
*Hyroglyphica*
    by Chaeremon, 6
    by Horapollo, 6f.

Iamblichus, 5f., 183, 246, 266, 277
Iao, 65, 69f., 75, 78f., 137, 148–150, 172, 253
Ieu, the painter, 267, 269, 280
Imhotep, 41, 56, 123, 126, 224, 228, 234, 262, 313, 329
ineffability, of the god's name, 161
insertion, as linguistic process, 49, 106, 110ff., 119, 289
instruction texts, 216, 218, 232, 238
Iser, Wolfgang, 254
Isis, goddess
    aretalogy, 274
    mother of Horus, 6, 8, 31, 41, 56, 92f., 136f., 141–143, 150–153, 157–159, 165–169, 189, 197, 215, 229, 240–244, 250–253, 260, 263, 266, 271, 274f., 279, 283, 317, 321, 324, 328

Jacob, 172, 268
Jewish religion
    in magical papyri, 1f., 20, 78, 97, 170, 172, 182, 268f., 278–280
    in *Corpus Hermeticum*, 1
Johnson, Janet H., 18f., 28, 32f., 40, 44

Khaemwaset, Egyptian prince, 227f.

language change
    in bilingual societies, 105
    in Roman Egypt, 104, 107
language attitude, 3, 103–106, 109f., 121, 143f., 290
Leemans, Conrad, 30, 36, 44f.
Lenormant, François, 14
lesônis, Egyptian priestly title, 207
litany, 179–181, 183, 290
loanwords
    classes of Greek loanwords in Demotic spells, 104, 110ff.
    Greek loanwords in Demotic texts, 108f.
    as linguistic borrowing, 105f.
Lucian, *Philopseudes*, 241–247, 260

Ma'at, 212ff.
Magi, Persian priests of the fire ritual, 166, 168f.
Manetho
    Egyptian priest, 17f., 250
    *Aegyptiaca*, 7f.
    *Against Herodotus*, 8, 250
Maskelli-Maskello formula, 79, 172
materials of medicine and magic, 110f., 116, 190, 199–203, 308
Memphis, city, 31f., 41, 206, 208, 225–231, 234–236, 241, 243f., 251f., 273f., 278, 283
Memphite Theology, 272
Mithras liturgy, 15, 259, 262
morning ritual, in Egyptian temple, 176

Moses, 268, 280, 289, 317
Muysken, Pieter, 106, 108, 121
mystification motif
   in *Demotic Magical Papyri*, 126, 261
   in *Greek Magical Papyri*, 261, 276
   in Egyptian texts of pharaonic date, 263 f.
*Myth of the Sun's Eye* (*Mythus*), 25 f., 29–32, 40, 275
   translation into Greek, 43

Nag Hammadi Library, 2, 22 f.
Names of the Nations, 149, 165, 168 f., 182 f., 203, 289
Naneferkaptah, 228–234, 238, 243
Narmuthis, bilingual ostraca from, 107 f., 168, 274
National Museum of Antiquities in Leiden, 13, 15, 21, 25–27, 29, 42, 45
Neo-Platonism, 1, 5 f., 150, 169, 246
Nephotes, Egyptian priest?, 258 f., 266, 269
Nephthys, 41, 152, 157, 262
Nero, emperor, 8
Nikokreon, king of Cyprus, 162
Nubia
   in historical reality, 140, 236
   in Egypt's imagination, 140 ff., 236 ff.
   magicians from, 141, 235
Nubian language, 37, 139–142, 315

Old-Coptic
   as language phase, 57
   as script, 27, 35, 56–58, 71 f., 76, 87
   glossing, 15, 27, 35, 38, 56 f., 60, 71, 75, 79, 127
Olympian offering, 148
On the Materials of Medicine, *see* Dioscorides
Opening the Mouth, ritual of, 49, 170, 172–175, 177, 180–183
Origen, 4 f., 183
Osiris, 6, 8, 34–35, 41, 50, 53–55, 127–129, 132, 136 f., 143, 152–155, 157, 166, 189, 197, 223, 235, 243, 252, 258, 262, 266, 278 f., 189, 298, 314
Ostanes, Persian magos, 200, 264, 267–270, 275, 277–278, 293
Ouphôr, 170 f. 173–175, 177–183, 187, 200, 257, 264, 287, 289 f.
Ourbikos, 173, 175, 183, 257, 264
Ouroboros snake, 148, 171, 182, 233
Oxyrhynchus, city, 165 f., 169, 264, 293

Pakhrates, Egyptian priest, 260
palindromes, in Demotic spells, 68 f., 79, 289
Pancrates, 241–245, 260
Papyri Graecae Magicae
   compilation, 16
   numbering system, 16 f.
   translation into English, 19
'Paradox of Translation', 1, 4, 182 f.
Paysakh, Egyptian priest, 265, 292
P. BM., 10.700, *see* P. London-Leiden
Philae, temple of, 31, 155, 166 f., 174, 252
Philinna, the Thessalian, 267
Pibechis, 75, 263 f., 267, 280
Pitys
   king, 266, 269, 277
   the Thessalian, 277 f.
P. Leiden I, 383, *see* P. London-Leiden
P. Leiden I, 384 verso
   date, 41
   dialect, 40
   discovery, 12 f., 25 f.
   drawings on, 34
   Egyptian and Greek hand, 34 f.
   physical description of, 29 ff.
   provenance, 40
Pleyte, Willem, 14, 26 f.
P. Londen-Leiden
   date, 41
   dialect, 40
   discovery, 12 f., 25 f.
   Egyptian hand, 37 f.

physical description of, 35 ff.
provenance, 40
Plotinus, 6
Plutarch of Chaeronea, 6, 8, 136, 159, 189, 252, 266, 279
P. Magical, *see* P. London-Leiden
pneuma, 178
Pnouthis, Egyptian priest?, 257 f., 266
Porphyry of Tyre, 4 f., 183, 250 f., 278
P. Oxyrhynchus, 1380 165
'Prayer of Thanksgiving', 2
Preisendanz, Karl, 12, 14–16, 42, 136, 163, 186, 257, 263
priestly decrees, trilingual, 204, 251
prophet, Egyptian priestly title, 132, 161, 171, 200–201, 203, 205–207, 210, 240, 242, 248–249, 251, 260, 275, 280, 293
pseudepigraphy, 261 f., 264, 266, 281, 285
Ptolemy I, king, 8
Ptolemy II, king, 53, 205
purity
    as a state of being, 207, 209, 211–215, 218 f., 286, 290
    in temple cult, 4, 211 ff.
Pythagoras, 200, 246–248, 264, 267, 278, 293
    Pythagoreanism, 64, 169, 245–247

Reuvens, C.J.C., 15, 17, 26 f., 29 f., 40
rhetorical-didactic literature, 216, 218, 222, 232
ring spell, 147, 170, 173, 178, 182 f., 186 f., 257
Ritner, Robert K., 17, 19–20, 110, 123, 135, 179, 188, 226, 232, 269
Romaine, Suzanne, 105, 109

Sabaoth, 79, 148–150, 165, 170, 172
Sarapis, god, 151, 163 f., 251 f.
    and Manetho, 8, 266
    oracular answer, 162, 262
    priests of, 162, 250, 253
secrecy
    in Egyptian ritual, 82 ff.

in Egyptian texts, 83 f., 276
as rhetorical strategy, 276
Seth, 18, 33 f., 128, 130 ff., 155, 157, 197
    donkey as symbol of, 34, 132–137
    invoked in magical spells, 132, 134 ff., 291, 315
Setne Khamwase, 226 f., 229, 233
seven Greek vowels, 64 f.
    in Greek spells, 65 f.
    in Demotic spells, 67, 69, 79, 289
Shabaka Stone, 273
Solomon, 260, 268, 279
stereotype appropriation, 9 f., 254, 287 f.
Stoicism, 8, 162, 164, 178, 246, 250 f.
succedaneum, 193

Tebtunis, place name, 210
    onomasticon of, 50, 72, 166, 205
    temple library of, 31, 195 f., 226
temple scribe, Egyptian priestly title, 145, 185, 187, 203, 205–207, 220, 249, 251, 256 ff., 269, 271, 282, 286
Theban Magical Library
    composition, 11, 14 f.
    discovery, 12
    history of research, 15 ff.
    stages of sale, 12 ff.
Theophrastus, 111, 199 f.
Thessalos of Tralles, 9, 111, 245, 253
Thessaly, region in Greece, 169, 240, 277
Thissen, Heinz J., 123, 125, 139, 179, 257, 313
Thompson, Herbert, 18, 37, 45, 55, 88, 91, 99, 114, 117, 127, 139, 302, 304–309, 311
Thoth, 30, 41, 75, 153 f., 166, 172, 176, 181, 201, 222–226, 229, 236, 238, 262 f., 265, 272 f.
tourism to Egypt, ancient, 250, 253
translation
    from Egyptian into Greek, 31, 271, 274 f.

## INDEX OF SUBJECTS

from Greek into Egyptian, 120, 126, 128, 259
as mystifying motif, 261, 274 f., *see also* Egyptian priesthood
Typhonsep, *see* Seth

Uru-anna= *maštakal*, 193 f., 198, 202

Vergote, Joseph, 173
verse points, 37, 53 f., 57, 77, 288
verum nomen, 64, 135, 167 f.
*voces magicae*, 28, 32 f., 52, 68 f., 72, 76, 80, 100, 110, 150, 169, 172, 178, 181, 189, 289 ff.
 etymology of, 70, 76 f., 121, 125, 150, 170, 279
 formula, 79, 135 f.
 function of, 69, 97
 transcription of, 35, 40, 42, 56 ff., 60 ff., 71, 73 f., 77, 128, 136 f., 141, 303

wind
 lord of, 159
 four, 158–160

Zminis of Tentyra, 264, 295
Zodiac, 111, 163, 171, 182, 253

# RELIGIONS IN THE GRAECO-ROMAN WORLD

119. Pietersma, A. *The Apocryphon of Jannes and Jambres the Magicians.* P. Chester Beatty XVI (with New Editions of Papyrus Vindobonensis Greek inv. 29456 + 29828 verso and British Library Cotton Tiberius B. v f. 87). Edited with Introduction, Translation and Commentary. With full facsimile of all three texts. 1994. ISBN 90 04 09938 7
120. Blok, J.H. *The Early Amazons.* Modern and Ancient Perspectives on a Persistent Myth. 1994. ISBN 90 04 10077 6
121. Meyboom, P.G.P. *The Nile Mosaic of Palestrina.* Early Evidence of Egyptian Religion in Italy. 1994. ISBN 90 04 10137 3
122. McKay, H.A. *Sabbath and Synagogue.* The Question of Sabbath Worship in Ancient Judaism. 1994. ISBN 90 04 10060 1
123. Thom, J.C. *The Pythagorean Golden Verses.* With Introduction and Commentary. 1994. ISBN 90 04 10105 5
124. Takács, S.A. *Isis and Sarapis in the Roman World.* 1994. ISBN 90 04 10121 7
125. Fauth, W. *Helios Megistos.* Zur synkretistischen Theologie der Spätantike. 1995. ISBN 90 04 10194 2
126. Rutgers, L.V. *The Jews in Late Ancient Rome.* Evidence of Cultural Interaction in the Roman Diaspora. 1995. ISBN 90 04 10269 8
127. Van Straten, F.T. *Hierà kalá.* Images of Animal Sacrifice in Archaic and Classical Greece. 1995. ISBN 90 04 10292 2
128. Dijkstra, K. *Life and Loyalty.* A Study in the Socio-Religious Culture of Syria and Mesopotamia in the Graeco-Roman Period Based on Epigraphical Evidence. 1995. ISBN 90 04 09996 4
129. Meyer, M. & P. Mirecki (eds.) *Ancient Magic and Ritual Power.* 1995. ISBN 90 04 10406 2
130. Smith, M. & S.J.D. Cohen (eds.) *Studies in the Cult of Yahweh.* 2 volumes. ISBN 90 04 10372 4 (set)
    Vol. 1: *Studies in Historical Method, Ancient Israel, Ancient Judaism.* 1996. ISBN 90 04 10477 1
    Vol. 2: *Studies in New Testament, Early Christianity, and Magic.* 1996. ISBN 90 04 10479 8
131. Lane, E.N. (ed.) *Cybele, Attis and Related Cults.* Essays in Memory of M.J. Vermaseren. 1996. ISBN 90 04 10196 9
132. Lukian von Samosata *Alexandros oder der Lügenprophet.* Eingeleitet, herausgegeben, übersetzt und erklärt von U. Victor. 1997. ISBN 90 04 10792 4
133. De Jong, A. *Traditions of the Magi.* Zoroastrianism in Greek and Latin Literature. 1997. ISBN 90 04 10844 0

134. Frankfurter, D. *Pilgrimage and Holy Space in Late Antique Egypt.* 1998. ISBN 90 04 11127 1
135. Ustinova, Y. *The Supreme Gods of the Bosporan Kingdom.* Celestial Aphrodite and the Most High God. 1998. ISBN 90 04 11231 6
136. Healey, John F. *The Religion of the Nabataeans.* A Conspectus. 2001. ISBN 90 04 10754 1
137. Drijvers, J.W. & J.W. Watt *Portraits of Spiritual Authority.* Religious Power in Early Christianity, Byzantium and the Christian Orient. 1999. ISBN 90 04 11459 9
138. Dirven, L. *The Palmyrenes of Dura-Europos.* A Study of Religious Interaction in Roman Syria. 1999. ISBN 90 04 11589 7
139. Rothaus, R.M. *Corinth: The First City of Greece.* An Urban History of Late Antique Cult and Religion. 2000. ISBN 90 04 10922 6
140. Bricault, L. (éd.) *De Memphis à Rome.* Actes du Ier Colloque international sur les études isiaques, Poitiers – Futuroscope, 8-10 avril 1999. 2000. ISBN 90 04 11736 9
141. Mirecki, P., & M. Meyer (eds.) *Magic and Ritual in the Ancient World.* 2001. ISBN 90 04 11676 1
142. Horstmanshoff, H.F.J., H.W. Singor, F.T. van Straten, & J.H.M. Strubbe (eds.) *Kykeon.* Studies in Honour of H.S. Versnel. 2002. ISBN 90 04 11983 3
143. Morand, A.-F. *Etudes sur les* Hymnes Orphiques. 2001. ISBN 90 04 12030 0
144. Versluys, M.J. *Aegyptiaca Romana. Nilotic Scenes and the Roman Views of Egypt.* 2002. ISBN 90 04 12440 3
145. Fishwick, D. *The Imperial Cult in the Latin West.* Studies in the Ruler Cult of the Western Provinces of the Roman Empire. *Volume III: Provincial Cult.* Part 1: Institution and Evolution. 2002. ISBN 90 04 12536 1
146. Fishwick, D. *The Imperial Cult in the Latin West.* Studies in the Ruler Cult of the Western Provinces of the Roman Empire. *Volume III: Provincial Cult.* Part 2: The Provincial Priesthood. 2002. ISBN 90 04 12539 6
147. Fishwick, D. *The Imperial Cult in the Latin West.* Studies in the Ruler Cult of the Western Provinces of the Roman Empire. *Volume III: Provincial Cult.* Part 3: The Provincial Centre; Provincial Cult. 2004. ISBN 90 04 12806 9
148. Fishwick, D. *The Imperial Cult in the Latin West.* Studies in the Ruler Cult of the Western Provinces of the Roman Empire. *Volume III: Provincial Cult.* Part 4: Abbreviated Titles; Bibliography; Indices. (in preparation) ISBN 90 04 12807 7
149. Lancellotti, M.G. *Attis* between Myth and History: King, Priest and God. 2002. ISBN 90 04 12851 4

150. Bonnechere, P. *Trophonios de Lébadée.* Cultes et mythes d'une cité béotienne au miroir de la mentalité antique. 2003. ISBN 90 04 13102 7
151. Bricault, L. (éd.) *Isis en Occident.* Actes du IIème Colloque international sur les études isiaques, Lyon III, 16-17 mai 2002. 2004. ISBN 90 04 13263 5
152. Lupu, E. *Greek Sacred Law.* A Collection of New Documents (NGSL). 2005. ISBN 90 04 13969 1
153. Dieleman, J. *Priests, Tongues, and Rites.* The London-Leiden Magical Manuscripts and Translation in Egyptian Ritual (100-300 CE). 2005. ISBN 90 04 14185 5
154. Prent, M. *Sanctuaries and Cults in Crete from the Late Minoan IIIC to the Archaic Period.* Continuity and Change. 2005. ISBN 90 04 14236 3

Papyrus Leiden I.384 verso

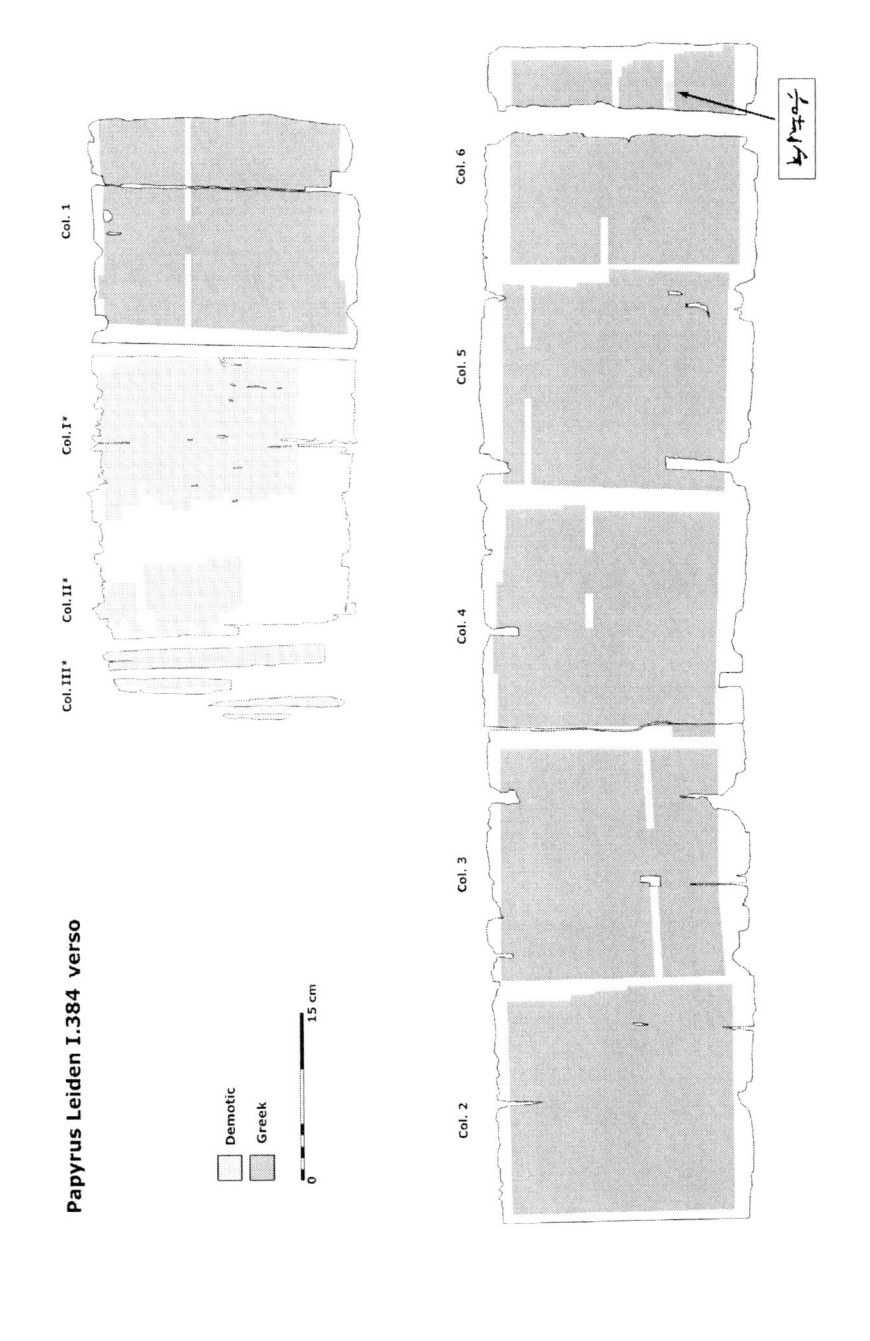

Demotic
Greek

0    15 cm

Col. 1
Col. I*
Col. II*
Col. III*

Col. 6
Col. 5
Col. 4
Col. 3
Col. 2

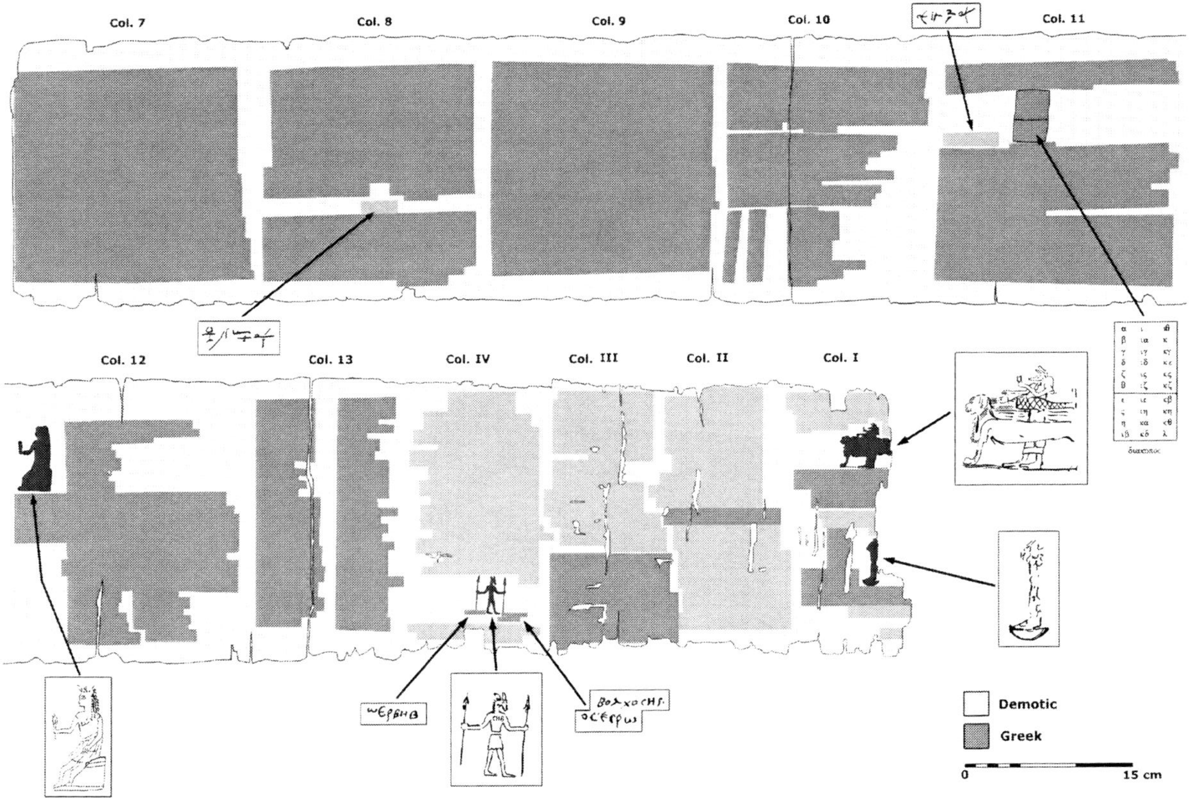
Col. 7
Col. 8
Col. 9
Col. 10
Col. 11
Col. 12
Col. 13
Col. IV
Col. III
Col. II
Col. I
Demotic
Greek
0
15 cm

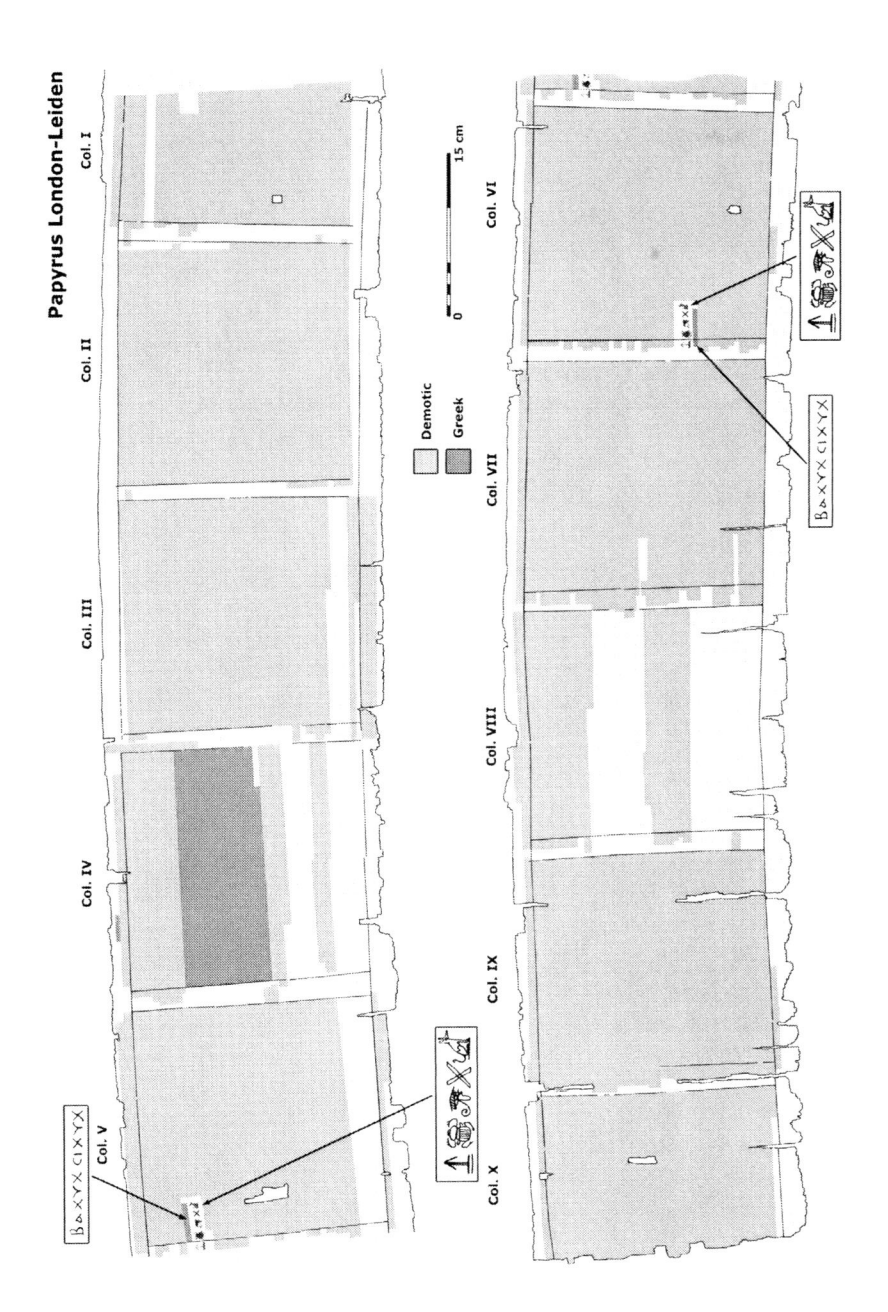

# Papyrus London-Leiden

ΛΕΗΙΟΥω

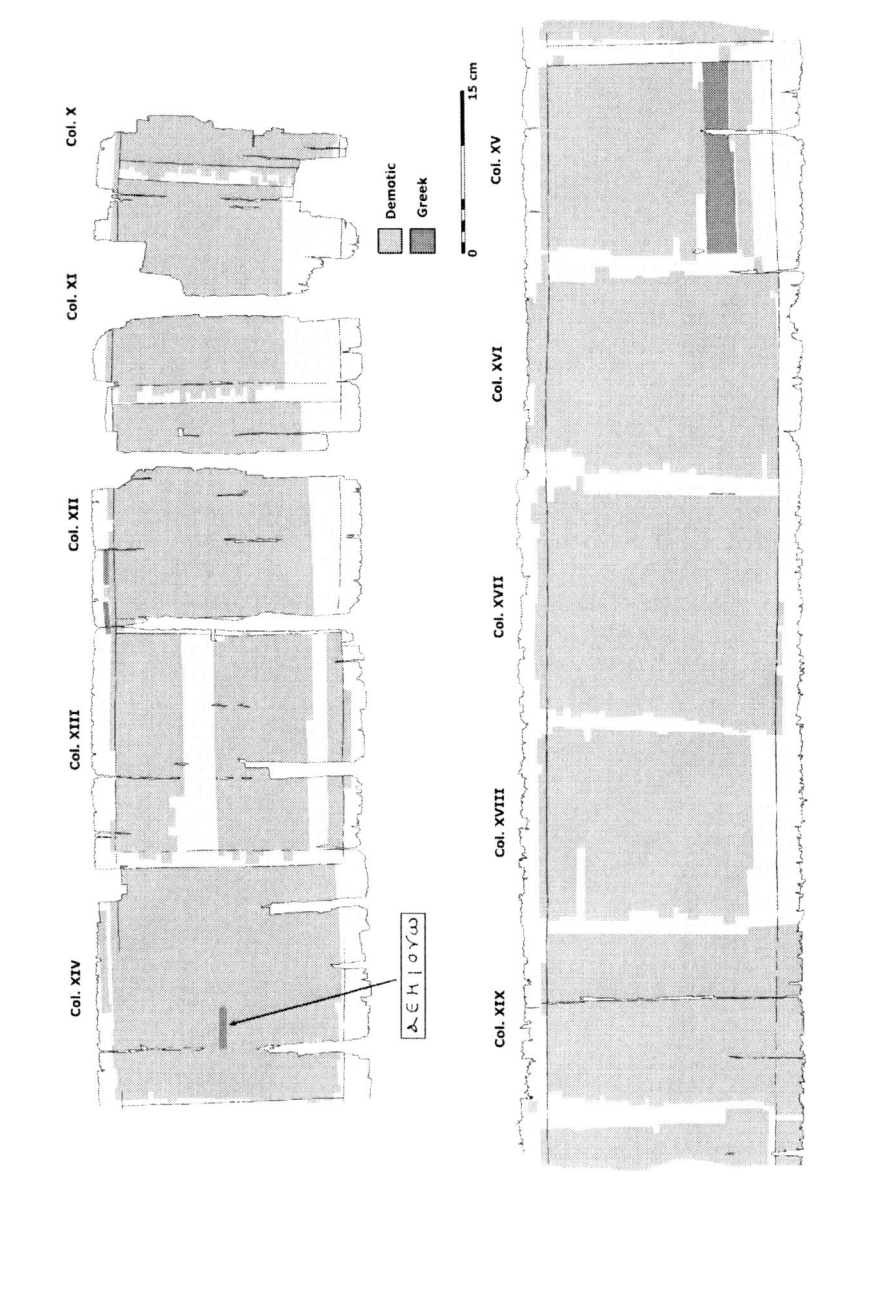

Col. XX  Col. XXI  Col. XXII  Col. XXIII  Col. XXIV

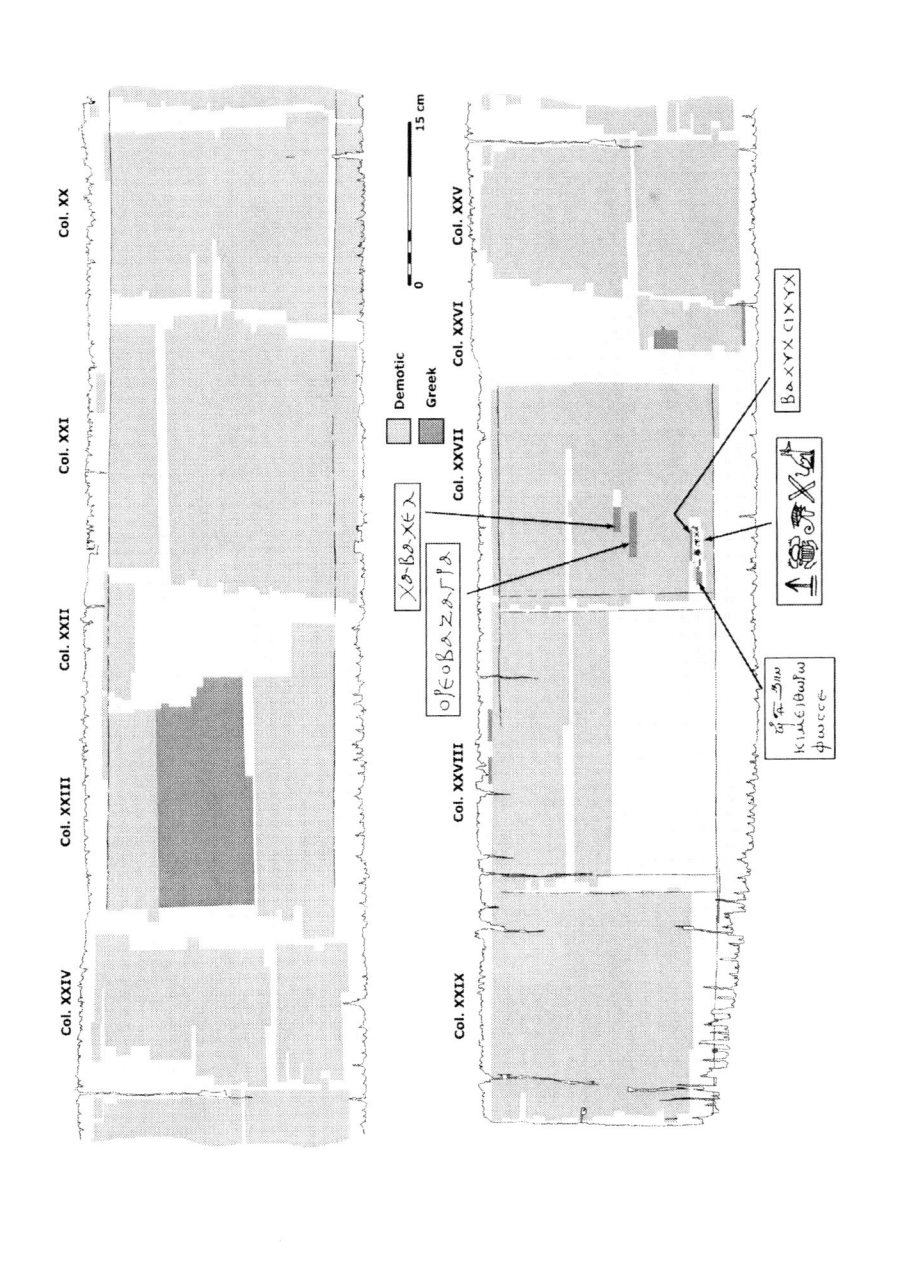

Col. XXV  Col. XXVI  Col. XXVII  Col. XXVIII  Col. XXIX

Demotic
Greek

0  15 cm

Χοβαχελ

ορεοβαζαγρα

Βαχυχ ςιχυχ

κιδειβυλ
φωσσε

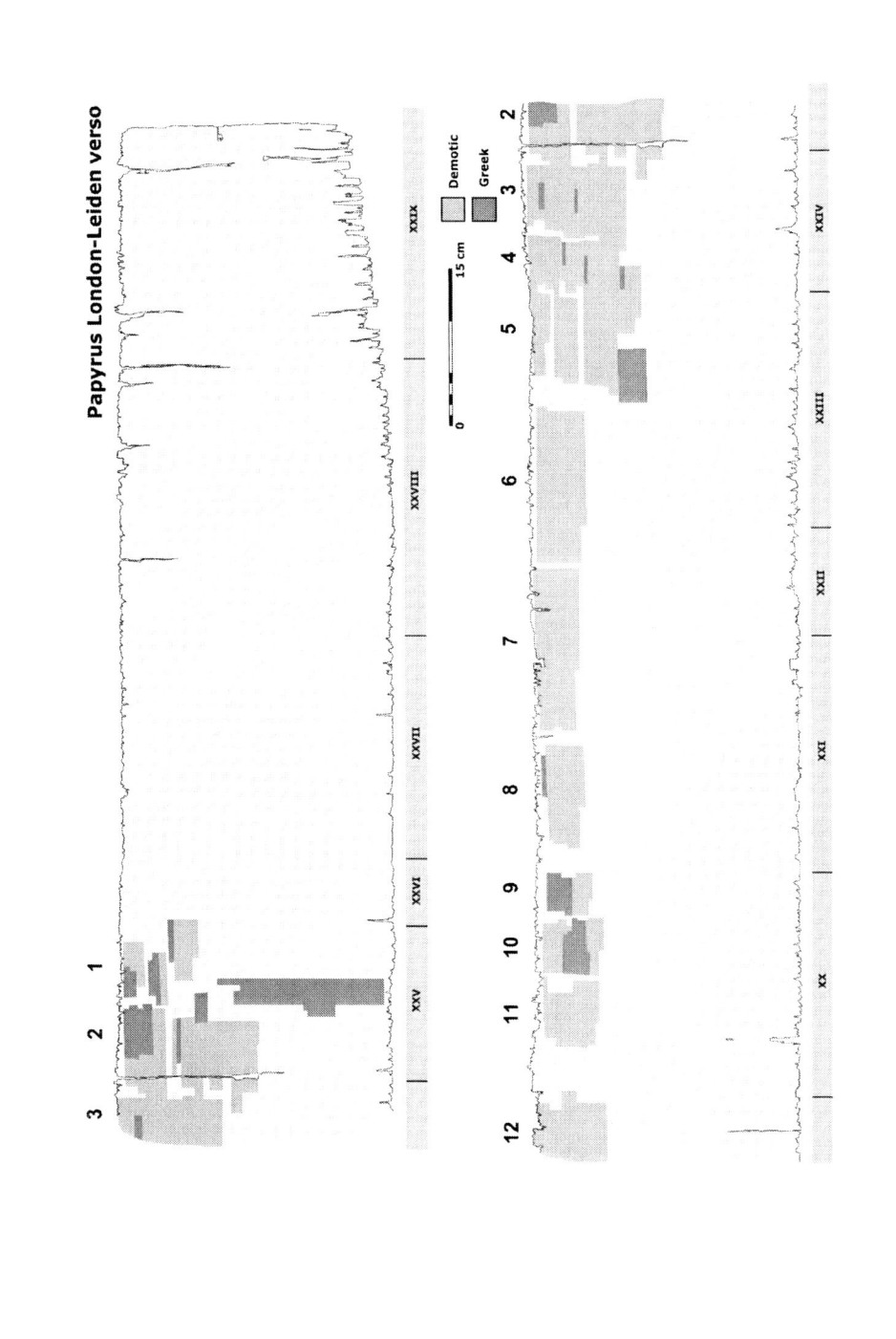

# Papyrus London-Leiden verso

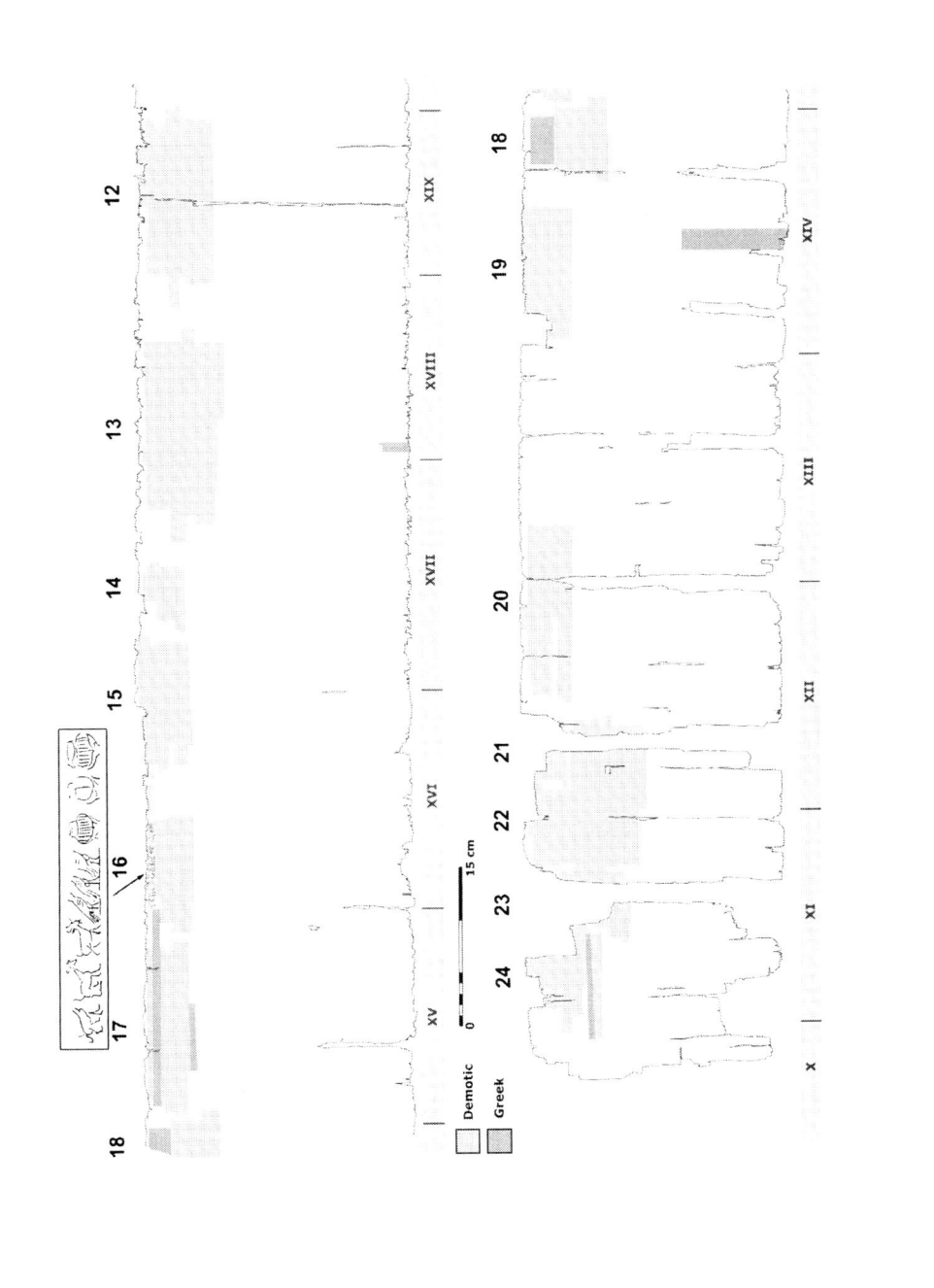

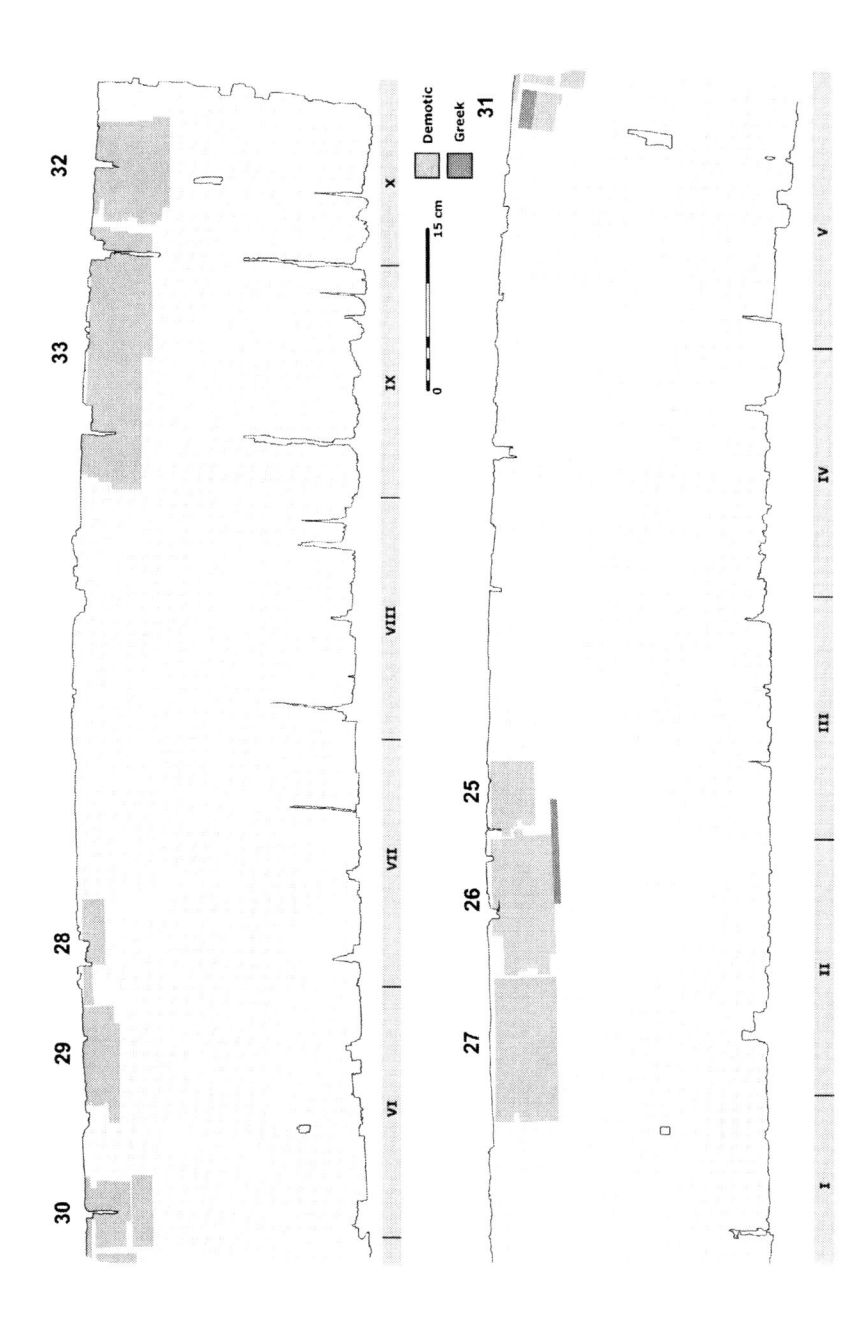